THE LAW
AND THE
PROPHETS

WITH A NEW POSTSCRIPT

THE LAW
AND THE
PROPHETS

A STUDY IN
OLD TESTAMENT CANON
FORMATION

STEPHEN B. CHAPMAN

B
BakerAcademic
a division of Baker Publishing Group
Grand Rapids, Michigan

Published by Baker Academic
a division of Baker Publishing Group
PO Box 6287, Grand Rapids, MI 49516–6287
www.bakeracademic.com

Baker Academic edition published 2020

Previously published in 2000 by Mohr Siebeck, Tübingen, Germany

Printed in the United States of America

Library of Congress Cataloging-in-Publication Data
Names: Chapman, Stephen B., 1962– author.
Title: The law and the prophets : a study in Old Testament canon formation / Stephen B. Chapman.
Description: Baker Academic edition. | Grand Rapids, Michigan : Baker Academic, a division of Baker Publishing Group, 2020. | Reprint. Originally published: Tübingen : Mohr Siebeck, c2000. | Includes bibliographical references and index.
Identifiers: LCCN 2020022059 | ISBN 9781540960481
Subjects: LCSH: Bible. Old Testament—Canon. | Bible. Old Testament—Criticism, Textual.
Classification: LCC BS1135 .C48 2020 | DDC 221.1/2—dc23
LC record available at https://lccn.loc.gov/2020022059

Hans W. Frei
1922 – 1988

†

In Memoriam
vox audita perit • litera scripta manet

Contents

Preface

Perhaps few subjects in the late twentieth century have received such attention as the political dimensions of language, resulting in a welcome public sensitivity to previously underrepresented views, but also in a new nominalism of terminological coinage and a rash of euphemism. The study of the Old Testament has been uniquely affected. How should we even refer to this collection of sacred literature, shared by at least three of the world's great religions — as the Old Testament, the Hebrew Bible, Jewish Scripture, Tanakh, or First Testament?[1] In the following study I have retained the traditional designations 'Old Testament' and 'the Law and the Prophets.' The current debate requires me to say a few words justifying my use of both expressions.[2]

1. My use of the term 'Old Testament' expresses my perspective as a Christian scholar in the service of the Church, but not narrowly. My desire is to hear in the words of the text God's Word to *ancient Israel* and thus a witness to Jesus Christ in its *pre*-Christian form.[3] By 'Old Testament' I therefore do not intend to 'christianize' the text or to deprecate other traditions and titles,[4] some of which I employ as ready synonyms, but rather to report honestly my own social location.

I have come to question whether the Enlightenment project of religiously 'neutral' investigation (i. e., the project usually underlying the term 'Hebrew Bible')[5] can successfully illuminate the character of a thoroughly religious literature or the particular forces that gave it birth.[6] Moreover, I am skeptical of Christian scholars who claim to put aside their identities in the course of such a

---

[1] For discussion, see the essays in BROOKS AND COLLINS, Bible? and ZENGER, Einleitung, 14-16. For the proposal First Testament, see J. A. SANDERS, Testament. SANDERS, however, did not coin this alternative expression. For the term's precursors and its further development, see ZENGER, Testament.

[2] Attention will be paid to the terms 'canon,' 'scripture' and 'authority' in the course of the essay.

[3] For this theological formulation, see CHILDS, OT Theology, 9.

[4] For these criticisms, see DAVIDSON, Testament? and SAWYER, Prejudices. SAWYER fulminates against the usage 'Old Testament,' but he does not approve of 'Hebrew Bible' either. He opts for 'Bible' as a general term and proposes 'the older parts of the Bible' as an appropriate scholarly reference, a circumlocution which in my judgment is much more awkward than 'Old Testament' and not really any different.

[5] E. g., ZENGER, Einleitung, 16.

[6] See the balanced remarks by CHILDS, NT Introduction, 38–39, on the possibility of a common descriptive task regardless of religious commitments, but only if such descriptions are willing to pay attention to 'the inner theological logic of the canon's witness,' and do not *presuppose* such a concern as out of bounds.

project. To reserve judgment as a test of one's presuppositions is good scholarship; to pretend to be something one is not may reflect 'self-delusion' or 'sleight of hand.'[7] (I would make the same point about the recent use of chronological designations like B. C. E. and C. E. for B. C. and A. D.)

In my judgment, U. S. universities should reconsider efforts to teach biblical literature somehow independently of its interpretive traditions (maintaining the pretense of neutrality implied by courses entitled 'Hebrew Bible') and instead offer courses like 'Torah,' 'Old Testament,' or 'Torah/Old Testament' in which the text as well as its interpretive echoes could be explored.[8] To gain a better understanding of religious literature, we are in need of study and dialogue among *particular* traditions of interpretation, not a 'neutrality' which actually *disrespects* difference[9] and, finally, simply does not exist.[10]

2. Critical scholarship on the Bible has popularized the view that 'law' is a misleading and inappropriate translation of the Hebrew term תורה. Explained as the legacy of the (mis-)translation of תורה by νόμος within the Septuagint (LXX),[11] the appellation 'law' has been rejected by many scholars in favor of 'instruction,'[12] 'story,'[13] or 'narrative.'[14] Use of 'law,' it has been maintained, only reflects and reinforces a Christian view of Judaism as a religion of legalism and obligation.[15]

However, recent linguistic work has discredited this matter of an LXX mistranslation.[16] It seems that the semantic range of LXX νόμος *does* include

---

[7] PROVAN, Canons, 23–24. Cf. R. W. L. MOBERLY, Testament, 162: "For the Christian theologian... the exclusive adoption of religiously neutral language is at best a dereliction of duty and at worst a deception (as much of self as others)."

[8] For a constructive teaching proposal, see KUGEL, Bible. I prefer the term 'Torah' for studies of scripture within the Jewish tradition precisely because the scope of the term *is* ambiguous. To restrict 'Torah' to the 'Hebrew Bible' is to 'emasculate' it, according to FRERICHS, Canon. Moreover, it is not clear to me that the biblical books were ever considered to form within Judaism the kind of discrete unity that they did in Christianity. See NEUSNER, Midrash, 1–22. 'Torah' thus points to the very different hermeneutical function of these books within Judaism, a difference which 'Hebrew Bible' and 'Tanakh' both obscure. Cf. idem, Judaism, 3. Similarly, it is not at all clear that 'Jewish Scripture' can be restricted *per definitionem* to 'biblical' books.

[9] See the forceful development of this point in TANNER, Respect, esp. 2.

[10] Thus LEVENSON, Bible, 84; 105. See also GOSHEN-GOTTSTEIN, Theology. Cf. C. R. SEITZ, Testament.

[11] DODD, Bible, 25: "No Greek would have chosen [νόμος] to express what he meant by religion."

[12] Ibid., 31–32.

[13] J. A. SANDERS, Torah, 3.

[14] ESKENAZI, Torah.

[15] SCHECHTER, Theology, 116–18; cf. STEGEMANN, Tora.

[16] WESTERHOLM, *Torah*.

the transcendent, religious sense of 'revelation' as well as that of 'obligation.'[17] Thus, Hellenistic Judaism cannot be blamed for simply equating תורה with legalism.[18] Moreover, where critical scholarship once stressed almost exclusively the history-like shape of תורה (*qua* Pentateuch), more recent approaches have emphasized the equal importance of the literature's 'rhetoric of command,'[19] the central position of Leviticus,[20] and the priestly stamp upon the final form of the whole.[21] Although I am not in agreement with their view, several scholars now promote the idea that the origin of the canonical Torah was its selection and use as a Persian-sanctioned legal code for post-exilic Israel,[22] which also suggests the appropriateness of 'law' as a title.[23] Finally, later traditions (Jewish as well as Christian) and critical scholarship have both used the term 'law' (νόμος) within the traditional expression 'the law and the prophets.'

I therefore employ the term 'the Law' as a synonym for the first portion of the canonical Old Testament. I understand this 'Law' to have been for Israel both story and norm, blessing and curse, gift and obligation.[24] By use of this term I do not intend to depict or imply the operation of a joyless legalism, but the exuberantly normative quality of the literature.[25]

I employ capital letters as consistently as possible in an effort to distinguish between traditions of law and prophecy ('law' and 'prophets') and written collections (the 'Law' and the 'Prophets').[26] I often use 'the Law,' 'the Pentateuch,' and 'the Torah' without intending any distinction at all; however, the elasticity of the Hebrew term תורה sometimes requires more care. In fact, part of my argument in this essay has to do with the way in which this terminological elasticity functioned even within the biblical period, and how the implications of

---

[17] SEGAL, Judaisms, 131–45; idem, Torah. Cf. the similar judgment in URBACH, Sages, 289.

[18] *Contra* DODD, Bible, 33. See further TALMON, Tora, esp. 142–45.

[19] FRYE, Code, 211. See also URBACH, Sages, 315–16 and the detailed examination of this question by MCBRIDE, Perspective. MCBRIDE discerns a 'prescriptive' sense to the usage of תורה, noting: "Torah is closer in meaning to decree than to edifying discourse, mandatory instruction than to insightful counsel; the differences in nuance are important" (48). After studying the semantic range of the word he concludes that Torah must be understood as 'both norm and story' (57).

[20] BLENKINSOPP, Pentateuch, 47; 52; 134–35.

[21] Ibid., 237–39.

[22] Ibid., 239–43.

[23] Cf. the point by WESTERHOLM (*Torah*, 326) that already in Ezr 7:12–26 Aramaic דת ('law,' 'decree') is used as a synonym for Hebrew תורה.

[24] See MCBRIDE, Perspective, 59; ZIMMERLI, Law.

[25] WESTERHOLM, *Torah*, 327: "...religious movements themselves need norms if they are to have coherence." Cf. TALMON, Tora, 147.

[26] On the need for more consistency on this point within biblical studies, see ORLINSKY, Terms.

this elasticity are frequently overlooked. Thus the semantic range of תורה some-times requires me to attempt to differentiate between 'Torah' when it means the first five books of the Bible (or Pentateuch) and when it is used in a different sense.

Throughout the essay I have sometimes taken the liberty of harmonizing various systems of transliteration, notation and spelling (including British spellings). I have attempted to cite English translations of scholarly works, when extant, in order to help a greater number of readers pursue further questions more easily. In making reference to endnotes in another work, I have usually given the page number on which the note is found in the text rather than the page number on which the note is given in full.

Unless indicated, biblical translations appear as rendered in the New Revised Standard Version (NRSV). When the numbering of verses varies between the Masoretic Text (MT) and the NRSV, the numbering is first given according to the MT, with the numbering of the NRSV in brackets following. German trans-lations are my own if a work's bibliographic listing contains no mention of an English version or translator.

An earlier version of the first portion of Chapter Three was previously pre-sented at the 1995 Annual Meeting of the Society of Biblical Literature under the title 'The Incomparability of Moses? Deut 34:10–12 and the Torah's Ca-nonical Shape.'

Acknowledgements

As I engaged in the research leading to this volume, I became acutely aware that I was learning just as much, if not more, from those scholars with whom I disagreed as from those scholars whose thoughts were similar to my own. I hope those scholars whom I criticize in this essay will accept my remarks in the spirit of open dialogue and debate in which they are made, together with my deep respect and genuine thanks.

The published form of this essay represents a revised version of my 1998 dissertation of the same title directed by Christopher R. Seitz at Yale University. The conclusion of the dissertation brought to a close many years of study at Yale, the length and richness of which have left me indebted to many for their contributions to my progress and to this work.

As an undergraduate I was privileged to have for my advisor Hans W. Frei, whose suggestion that I pursue doctoral work in the field of Old Testament has proved as clearly inevitable in hindsight as it seemed mysterious and improbable at the time. In memory of his uncanny perceptiveness, genuine wit and heartfelt compassion, this essay is dedicated to him. His life gives to us all an enduring example of open, unassuming, generous Christian scholarship.

If I owe the existence of this study to Prof. Frei, its shape reflects my incalculable debt to Brevard S. Childs, with whom I also began to study as an undergraduate. During my years at Yale he was my intellectual guide, mentor and friend. Yale taught me the importance of texts, but from Prof. Childs I learned to love books — to read eagerly and sympathetically, interrogating the self as much as the text. The diligence, scope and brilliance of his work will always challenge me to achieve my best.

Special thanks are also due to my advisor, Christopher R. Seitz, who helped me conceptualize this project when it was still in its earliest stages, gave me creative freedom along the way and provided encouragement when I needed it most, and to Robert R. Wilson, whose methodological precision and attention to detail always prompted me to clarify my ideas.

Over the years other teachers and colleagues contributed to my thinking about the Bible and canon: notably, Scott Bader-Saye, David M. Carr, Stephen L. Cook, Ellen F. Davis, Carol Engelhardt, Suzanne Estelle-Holmer, Rowan A. Greer, Richard B. Hays, Christine Helmer, Wolfgang Hüllstrung, Elizabeth Shanks and Mark S. Smith. I would also like to express my gratitude for the practical assistance of Roz Ferguson, Registrar for the Yale Department of Religious Studies, Susan Burdick, Circulation Desk Librarian at Yale Divinity School, and Susan's unfailingly helpful student employees.

Family and friends also contributed greatly to the writing of this book. My parents, Ian and Mary Jo Chapman, extended support and concern week by week. They provided me with an abiding sense of security and an appreciation for the sheer honor of pursuing a Ph. D. My friends, too, have been unflagging in their patience, solicitude and good-natured jibes. I wish especially to thank Linda DeLuca, Vivienne Girven, Elizabeth Mitchell, Andreas Nicolaou, Grace M. Pauls, Dale W. Peterson, James Starr, Joseph V. Tropiano, Audrey West and Andrea White.

While researching and writing the dissertation I served several American Baptist congregations in Connecticut as an ordained minister. I was also remembered and encouraged by my home church, Stepney Baptist Church of Monroe, Connecticut. For their pastoral care and ministerial expertise during this time I gladly acknowledge Larry Dobson, Lowell and Julie Fewster, William Harkness, David and Jennifer Johnson, and Linda Lea Snyder.

I wish especially to thank the people of the First Baptist Church in New Haven, Stafford Baptist Church, Asylum Avenue Baptist Church in Hartford and the American Baptist Churches of Connecticut for providing me with spiritual fellowship, financial assistance and opportunities to explore the role and function of the biblical canon within the local church. I recall with gratitude a Bible study on Joshua at First Baptist and another on 1 Samuel at Asylum Avenue, both of which gave me new insights into the way in which canonical shape helps faithful readers to discern the plain sense of Scripture.

Financial support is no less important to a project such as this than professional and personal assistance. The most critical phase of the writing was done with a year-long grant from the Whiting Foundation. Moreover, consistent financial aid by Yale University and Yale Divinity School over the past two decades provided a length and depth of critical engagement, which otherwise I simply could not have afforded.

Finally, I would like to acknowledge those who assisted in the publication of this volume. I thank Bernd Janowski and Hermann Spieckermann for the opportunity to publish this study in the Mohr Siebeck series *Forschungen zum Alten Testament*. Prof. Janowski not only warmly welcomed me into the activities of his *Lehrstuhl* during my stay in Tübingen, but generously contributed of his own resources towards the preparation of the *Druckvorlage*. In addition, Dietmar von Schütz greatly helped me in preparing the camera-ready manuscript. I am deeply grateful as well for the care and precision which Mohr Siebeck continues to devote so impressively to its craft and firmly committed to this particular venture.

Stephen B. Chapman   Tübingen   November 5, 1999

Chapter One

The Question of the Law and the Prophets

Introduction

In modern attempts to read the Law and the Prophets together, as well as in traditional readings, the Law or Torah (*qua* Pentateuch) has most often been understood to be the oldest portion of the Bible and at the root of the canonical process. The Law, it is claimed, has always been supremely authoritative and is hermeneutically privileged within the structure of the final form of the biblical text, or canon. The following verdict is typical:

"The impetus for the creation of Scripture begins with the law, and the authority of the Torah derived not from any concept of 'canon' but because, simply, it was the law and thus the supreme authority for the governing of the religious community in Judea."[1]

According to this view, the Prophets constitute a subsidiary and less authoritative addition to the Torah, which alone is scripture *par excellence*:

"The addition of the prophetic books is an intriguing process. We may assume that parts of this section, notably the Former Prophets, were already venerated because of a different reason — their *historical* reportage. Other prophetic collections were venerated because the prophets concerned had warned Israel of the catastrophe which had indeed befallen, and which had even now not been fully reversed. Their authority lay in their claim to be messages from God, proved as such by their fulfilment. But the promotion of this whole collection *alongside the Torah*, suggests that 'prophecy' had become established as a theological category and enshrined in a literary repository of reminders about the past history of Israel's disobedience to the Torah, and of divine promises about Israel's glorious future if — implicitly — it remained true to that Torah... Thus, Law-and-Prophets together constitute a mutually reinforcing system of law plus commentary — the commentary being the lessons of history and the moral exhortations, and promises, of the prophets."[2]

In other words, because the legal or nomistic aspect of the process of canon formation was generative and primary, the canon has assigned the Prophets the secondary, illustrative role of 'commentary' on the Law.[3]

---

[1] P. R. DAVIES, Collections, 372. Cf. ZENGER, Einleitung, 24.

[2] P. R. DAVIES, Collections, 372. His emphases.

[3] This perspective seems to be shared by some Jewish scholars, although for different reasons. Thus ARIEL, Foundations, 135, claims that "Only the Torah, the first five books, is re-

The thesis of this essay is that the standard theory of Old Testament canon formation has unravelled to the point where it can no longer account adequately for the complexity of the process it seeks to describe, if indeed it ever really could. Further, because this theory has served to buttress a nomistic depiction of early Judaism, the theory's demise necessitates a reopening of basic questions within the field: how then was the Old Testament canon formed? How was it read, understood and interpreted? And, more specifically, how are Law and Prophets related to each other literarily within the canon? Do any hermeneutical clues exist within the text to assist in answering these questions?

To seek for answers on these points means largely to investigate the biblical text itself. In this investigation I intend to pursue the kind of 'canonical approach' championed by B. S. Childs.[4] I shall endeavor to describe the shape of the final form of the biblical text and the way in which received traditions have been reoriented in order to function as an enduring theological witness. I employ historical-critical methodologies as a means of grounding and illuminating this process, but with the intention to avoid the danger of reductionism, which continues to be a major problem inherent to such methodologies.[5]

Of special concern will be an effort to discern the ways in which larger literary units within the canon were constructed and how the canon as an emergent collection of scripture exerted an influence upon its constituent parts.[6] I hope to show that the final form of the Old Testament canon contains a number of explicit indices and implicit allusions to guide its readers to a faithful construal of the whole.[7] In this way my essay may be considered an example of a 'canonical approach' as well as a reexamination of the history of the canon.

First, however, it will be helpful to review the previous study of these questions and the details of the standard theory of Old Testament canon formation.

---

garded as divine in origin. The Prophets and Writings are all attributed to human authors even though the texts themselves are regarded as part of a sacred canon." This view stems from rabbinic testimony, the traditional esteem for the Torah and a skiddishness over Christian use of the Prophets (cf. his 233–35). See also JACOBS, Bible.

[4] For an explanation of this approach, see CHILDS, OT Introduction, esp. 72–79, on the 'shaping' of scripture.

[5] Ibid.; cf. idem, Interpretation. See also HERION, Impact; MAYES, Sociology; MELUGIN, Problem; ROGERSON, Sociology.

[6] CHILDS, NT Introduction, 38; 52–53; idem, OT Theology, 6–15; esp. 12–13. Cf. SHEPPARD, Canonization; idem, Criticism.

[7] CHILDS, NT Introduction, 40.

The Rise of the Standard Theory

Recent interest in the development of the Old Testament canon has produced a vast number of detailed, but divergent studies.[1] In the remainder of this chapter I shall review and evaluate the major arguments of the last hundred years, with special attention to the formation of a 'majority view' and the persistence of critical 'minority.'

Such a review is necessarily selective. I shall attempt to trace the particular way in which theories about the canon have operated on the basis of certain assumptions concerning the relationship between the Law and the Prophets as two canonical subcollections, and the way in which those assumptions have largely dictated the shape of the theories. The debate over the 'closing' of the canon, which has most often occupied center stage in recent discussion, is included in this retrospective only to the extent that it pertains to the central question of the relation of first two parts of the canon to each other.

In the course of the review, I shall endeavor to highlight and analyze the basic assumptions and terms of previous studies, such as the nature of 'canon,' 'scripture' and 'authority.'

H. E. Ryle

The majority position with respect to the Old Testament canon ('standard theory') was established in the English-speaking world by the work of H. E. Ryle at the end of the nineteenth century.[2] The basic framework of Ryle's reconstruction is well-known. Admitting the paucity of external evidence for the process of canon formation, Ryle acknowledged the importance of internal evidence, averring "Scripture must tell its own tale."[3] Arguing that "...the triple division of the Hebrew Scriptures itself embodies an ancient tradition, that of a linear development in the formation of the Canon through three successive stages,"[4] Ryle reconstructed a three-stage history of Old Testament

---

[1] For general studies see the essays in BALDERMANN, Problem, esp. MILLER, Kanon; DOHMEN, Kanon; SCHNABEL, History. For additional literature, see REVENTLOW, Problems; 132–44 ('The Problem of Canon'); SNOEK, Bibliography.

[2] RYLE, Canon. For continental scholarship at this time, see BUDDE, Kanon; BUHL, Kanon; WILDEBOER, Entstehung. In his 'Preface,' RYLE states that he was able to consult WILDEBOER's reatment only after the main outline of his own work was completed. He also noted the results of BUHL's book, which had just appeared. Of greatest importance for Anglo-Saxon scholarship was the impressive agreement between RYLE's work and the latest findings of Old Testament literary criticism, as represented by DRIVER, Introduction. RYLE added cross-references to DRIVER's volume as he corrected the sheets of his own book for the printer.

[3] RYLE, Canon, 9.

[4] Ibid., 10.

canon formation corresponding to the three traditional subcollections of the MT known as 'Law,' 'Prophets' and 'Writings.'

According to Ryle, the books of scripture contained in the 'Law' were rendered canonical under Ezra sometime in the mid-fifth century B. C., prior to a schism between Jews and Samaritans in 432 B. C.[5] The books of the 'Prophets' achieved their canonicity by the end of the third century B. C., prior to the composition in approximately 180 B. C. of the extra-canonical book of Ecclesiasticus, or Ben Sira.[6] Sir 44–49 refer to events and figures featured in the prophetic corpus and mention the book of the twelve Minor Prophets as a unity. The 'Writings' were thought by Ryle to have received final approval and canonical standing by A. D. 100, perhaps at a rabbinical council held in Jamnia ca. A. D. 90.[7]

In his reconstruction Ryle employed an explicit conception of canon as nationally-observed, officially-authoritative and literarily-delimited. He maintained that by official admittance into the 'national' canon, certain writings were "separated from all other writings as the sacred and authoritative expression of the Word of God."[8] In short, Ryle conceived of the act of canonization as an *a posteriori* judgment on the part of official Israel, with 'Law,' 'Prophets' and 'Writings' each constituting *discrete* acts of canonization.

However, Ryle's reconstruction also depended upon an *absolute* distinction between "...the process of literary construction and the process of admission into the Canon..."[9] Thus, he suggested a three-phase process: 1) an 'elemental' phase, in which the 'literary antecedents' of the books of the Old Testament took their shape; 2) a 'medial' phase, in which these antecedents were compiled and edited according to their present form; and 3) a 'final' phase, in which the finished books were selected for "the position of honor and sanctity in the national Canon."[10] In this way, Ryle effectively restricted the process of canonization to a time after the literary formation of a book was *fully* complete.

Thus, Ryle negated by definition a possibility that he himself had raised hypothetically, namely:

"...were any books, that are now in the Old Testament, originally expressly composed for the purpose of forming, or of helping to complete, the Hebrew Canon? Or, was there, in every

---

[5] Ibid., 93.
[6] Ibid., 119; 123.
[7] Ibid., 183.
[8] Ibid., 17.
[9] Ibid.
[10] Ibid.

case, an interval of time, more or less considerable, which elapsed between composition and final acceptance in the Canon?"[11]

Ryle made it clear that he believed there to have been a significant 'interval of time' between the 'medial' and the 'final' phase in *every* case.

Ryle then applied his 'interval of time' assumption to the three divisions of the canon (within Jewish tradition), interpreting 'Law,' 'Prophets' and 'Writings' as *successive* acts of canonization. He consistently refused to allow the dates of any book's literary development to contradict his overarching three-stage reconstruction. Without arguing the point, Ryle simply asserted that it was also necessary to conceive of an 'interval of time' between each *stage* of canonization. Each book was understood to have become truly canonical only when its entire subcollection became canonical. At this point, however, Ryle consistently subverted his own argument by resorting to a kind of quasi-canonical status for books which did not appear to fit his theory.

Thus, in the case of Deuteronomy, which appeared to have preceded the Pentateuch in acquiring official status, Ryle argued that originally the book was not a 'canon,' but only a 'first instalment.'[12] However, his discussion of the effect of Deuteronomy upon other biblical books suggested a degree of influence greater than that suggested by a mere 'instalment.'[13] Ryle similarly undermined his own theory by acknowledging that the canonical Pentateuch had continued to undergo minor editorial changes, "so long as the great principles of the legislation were safeguarded."[14] The details of the canon's literary development at the very beginning were thus at odds with his explicit theory.

In the case of the Prophets, Ryle was forced to argue that the subcollection had been closed only by the end the third century B. C., even though much of the literature dated to an earlier period. Why then were the prophetic writings not granted canonical status earlier? Ryle appealed to the oral character of prophecy[15] and to a lack of popular and official support for the prophets' message.[16] In fact, he suggested that the prophets had only written down their oracles *because* of strong opposition: "The prophets wrote what they could not or might not utter."[17] However, here Ryle contradicted his earlier argument that Deuteronomy had not achieved full canonical status at first precisely because "the living voice of the prophet was still heard and took prece-

---

[11] Ibid.

[12] Ibid., 61–64.

[13] Ibid., 67. In an interesting literary way, RYLE argued that the additions to the book of Deuteronomy indicated the 'insufficiency' of its original status (68).

[14] Ibid., 84–86.

[15] Ibid., 110.

[16] Ibid., 39. He cited Am 2:12; 7:12–13; Mic 2:6.

[17] Ibid., 40.

dence in men's minds of any written oracle."[18] Ryle appeared to appeal to a book's authority only when it was convenient.

This weakness was especially obvious in his treatment of the book of Joshua, which he considered as having first formed part of a Hexateuch (Genesis–Joshua) — apparently without quite achieving canonical status — and then being separated into a kind of canonical limbo, where it had somehow waited until the closing of the 'second canon.' Ryle speculated that "the ground of the separation must have been, either that its narrative did not contain direct religious significance, or, as seems more probable, that the Book of the Law seemed to close more appropriately with the death of the great Lawgiver."[19] With this kind of formulation, Ryle again admitted more interaction between the process of literary development and the process of canon formation than his theoretical framework allowed.

With respect to the Writings, Ryle argued that by the time of Ben Sira certain of the books (e. g., Ezra, Nehemiah) had formed a kind of 'appendix' to the historical books in the prophetic collection.[20] "It is possible," he noted, "that other books may have occupied a similar position,"[21] yet he continued to insist on an *absolute* distinction between literary completion and canonical authority. At the same time, he held that the Writings had been canonized in two stages[22] and suggested that a quasi-canonical authority had adhered to this group before its boundaries were fully determined. Ryle argued that this 'third canon' was 'practically closed' by 105 B. C.[23]

What emerges from the details of Ryle's reconstruction, then, is real ambiguity in the relationship between canonical 'closure' and canonical 'authority.' This ambiguity, I contend, lies at the heart of the standard theory that Ryle advanced, and continues to bedevil investigations into the Old Testament canon. Ryle's great accomplishment, however, lay in his brilliant synthesis of the most recent historical-critical exegesis of the time and the traditional tripartite structure of the canon, a synthesis which continues to survive as the scholarly consensus and the standard presentation of introductory textbooks.[24] In fact, J. Barton has recently observed:

---

[18] Ibid., 67.

[19] Ibid., 107.

[20] Ibid., 124–25.

[21] Ibid., 121; cf. 131.

[22] Ibid., 140–47.

[23] Ibid., 184; 189.

[24] See B. W. ANDERSON, Understanding, 594–600; G. W. ANDERSON, Canonical; CARMODY, CARMODY, AND COHN, Exploring, 15–21; P. C. CRAIGIE, Old Testament, 12–17; CRENSHAW, Story, 438–41; FLANDERS, CRAPPS AND SMITH, People, 13–15; LASOR, HUBBARD AND BUSH, Survey, 19–21; SCHÜRER, History, II: 314–22; SMEND, Entstehung, 13–20; SOGGIN, Introduction, 13–18; WANKE, Entstehung; WEST, Introduction, 12–17; ZENGER,

"On the face of it there is agreement among scholars on only one matter concerning the canonization of the Hebrew Scriptures: that the present threefold division into Law (*tōrâh*), Prophets (*nbî'îm*)) and Writings (*ktûbîm*) provides a rough guide to the *relative* date at which these collections were regarded as 'canonical scripture.' The Law was already a fixed entity at the time when the later books of the Prophets were still being composed, and the Prophets were complete at the time when the last of the Writings were taking shape."[25]

Perhaps also because of its very flexibility, Ryle's proposal to date the Old Testament canon in stages corresponding to its literary divisions has remained persuasive to a majority of scholars despite his proposal's internal inconsistencies and the later invalidation of most of its crucial supporting arguments, a story to which we now turn.

Canon and Higher Criticism

Against the background of contemporary scholarship, Ryle's dating can seem somewhat conservative, so it is well to remember that his postponement of canonical status for the Pentateuch until the *post*-exilic period carried at that time the full polemical weight of 'higher criticism.' Over against the narrative account of the Old Testament itself, which to conservative ears still spoke historically of events hundreds, even thousands, of years prior to Ezra, Ryle subscribed to the new 'Wellhausen hypothesis': the present form of the Pentateuch dated from a time much later than the events it described, although a long chain of oral tradition could be posited to preserve some kind of a link between the events and their description.

Opposition to the three-stage view of the canon was at first exemplified by W. H. Green, who saw in the literary divisions of the text a conscious and simultaneous organization of older material according to its subject-matter.[1] However, the nature of Green's work was in reality more of a polemic against critical scholarship generally than a constructive argument for an alternate model of canon formation.

In fact, he declined to provide his own historical reconstruction of the development of the canon at all,[2] arguing only that all three divisions exhibited no real signs of having been formed at widely disparate times: "The [three-

---

Einleitung, 22-25. Only CRENSHAW varies the tripartite scheme slightly, dating the Former Prophets to the fourth century and the Latter Prophets to the second century B. C. Cf., however, the unusually reserved discussion in RENDTORFF, Introduction, 288–91. Evangelical scholarship has also been traditionally skeptical of the three-stage theory; see BRUCE, Canon, 36; HARRIS, Inspiration, 143; E. J. YOUNG, Authority, 89.

[25] BARTON, Significance, 68. His emphasis.

[1] W. H. GREEN, Introduction.

[2] Ibid., 111.

fold] classification is such as bears the marks of a single mind, and has been interfered with by no disturbing cause."[3] He held that the Law and the Prophets existed substantially in their present form before the Exile, reading 2 Kg 17:13 and similar passages as references to a pre-exilic scriptural canon,[4] and implied that the Writings had similarly ancient roots in liturgical practice.[5]

However, the defensive tone of Green's work illustrated the inability of conservative scholars to mount a persuasive historical alternative to the Wellhausen hypothesis. Ironically, Wellhausen's work was criticized by Green and others so polemically that the difference between Wellhausen's radical description of Israel's religious development and his much more traditional treatment of the Old Testament canon was effectively obscured.

J. Wellhausen

Despite what was suggested by the critical slogan *lex post prophetas*,[6] Wellhausen had not actually included the process of canonization within his critical reversal of Israel's history. When it came to the canon, he had simply amended the dates of the traditional view in which the law of Moses *preceded* the preaching of the prophets.

Thus, Wellhausen maintained that there was "no doubt that the law of Ezra was the whole of the Pentateuch,"[7] emphasizing that until that point in Israel's history the pentateuchal legislation seemed largely unknown. In spite of the fact that the *historical* prophets had preceded a written Pentateuch, any prophetic *writings* had never previously gained public, legal status. The Pentateuch thus formed the original canon of Judaism, ratified publicly by Ezra. As with Ryle, the book of Deuteronomy was interpreted as a precedent, but not an earlier 'canon.'

The prophetic corpus and the other books were added to the Pentateuch-canon only gradually and 'imperceptibly' gained public authority.

---

[3] Ibid., 92.

[4] Ibid., 97.

[5] Ibid., 100–01.

[6] According to MORGAN AND BARTON, Interpretation, 79, this phrase was more used about WELLHAUSEN than by him. They trace its beginnings to HENGSTENBERG's rejection of VATKE's late date for what would later be known as the 'Priestly source,' adding that at the end of the nineteenth century this phrase became 'a classic way of stating WELLHAUSEN's hypothesis.'

[7] WELLHAUSEN, Prolegomena, 408. He concedes later that 'alterations' may have been made to the Pentateuch after Ezra, but gives the impression that these must have been minor (409 n.1).

"The notion of the canon proceeds entirely from that of the written Torah; the prophets and the hagiographa are also called Torah by the Jews, though not Torah of Moses."[8]

For Wellhausen, the Torah was to be dated after the historical reality of prophecy, but before the prophetic writings and the other books. In his view, therefore, the Torah as a legally authoritative text still historically *preceded* the written Prophets, despite what the slogan *lex post prophetas* suggested.

Moreover, Wellhausen also employed his assumption that canonical 'authority' was synonymous with 'law' to characterize the post-exilic community as a legalistic religion, different in kind ('Judaism') from the previously unwritten, and therefore in his view vital, faith of Israel.[9] Left largely unaddressed by Wellhausen and the others who shared this view was the problem of how prophetic and wisdom texts were subsequently accepted into such a 'legalistic' canon.[10]

W. J. Beecher

There was a critical alternative. As early as 1896, W. J. Beecher objected to the emerging consensus on canon formation, asking searching questions about the strength of the evidence upon which it was based.[11] According to the consensus, Beecher argued, signs of a canonical Torah should be present within the Prophets from the period before they were promulgated as a 'second canon.' Similarly, 'the Law and the Prophets' should have left some trace of their canonical status as the Writings slowly took the form of a 'third canon.' Yet no clear evidence of such earlier 'canons' could be found in the supposedly later 'canons.'

Those who claimed that the Torah (or Pentateuch) was at one time regarded as the only authoritative scripture in Israel, he argued, relied anachronistically upon the rabbinic writings of later centuries, and even there the ter-

---

[8] Ibid., 409. Cf. his description on 2–3.

[9] Ibid., 410. In fact, WELLHAUSEN believed the very act of writing implied the end of a religious tradition's vitality. Thus his famous summary of the canonical process: "The water which in old times rose from a spring, the Epigoni stored up in cisterns" (410). Just as rhetorical, but slightly more revealing, is his comment that "...it is a thing which is likely to occur, that a body of traditional practice should only be written down when it is threatening to die out, and that a book should be, as it were, the ghost of a life which is closed" (405 n. 1). This assumption seems closely related to WELLHAUSEN's conclusion that the character of revelation remained oral in Israel until after the Exile. Work by ALT (Origins) and NOTH (Gesetze) severely weakened the latter view, showing the antiquity of legal writing throughout the ancient Near East. Scholars pursuing a variety of approaches have also strongly questioned the former by relating the act of writing to religious vitality rather than spiritual declension; e. g., J. A. SANDERS, Adaptable.

[10] One of the few to have grasped the fundamental nature of this problem was KÖNIG, Prophetenideal, esp. 17.

[11] BEECHER, Canon.

minology was ambiguous. The titles 'Torah,' 'Prophets' and 'Writings' were so elastic that it was best to view them as common designations for sacred scripture in general rather than particular canonical units.[12]

Distinguishing carefully between an 'aggregate' (or collection) and a 'canon,' Beecher rejected the idea that the only alternative to a theory of successive canons was "that Israel had properly no sacred writings till after the whole Old Testament was completed." Rather, he maintained, the "true alternative is that of a growing aggregate of recognized sacred writings."[13] While critical scholars might disagree about the exact dates of the prophetic writings, nevertheless "they would agree as to the fact that the writings were then in existence, and were believed to have divine prophetic authority; and that there was a certain public knowledge which recognized them as existing and authoritative."[14]

According to Beecher's model of canon formation, this 'aggregate' of writings began with the eighth-century *prophets* and then grew organically:

"As writings of this kind were regarded as possessing divine authority, they were called *torah*. As the revelation came through the prophets, they were called prophetic. They were spoken of as Writings to distinguish them from all oral *torot*. Thus we already have an aggregate of sacred scriptures known as the Law, the Prophets, and the Writings. From the time the aggregate was first recognized, it kept on growing, and at every step of growth, it was still the one body of Israel's sacred scriptures, consisting of the Law, the Prophets, and the Writings."[15]

The search for evidence of an official declaration of canonical authority in later centuries was therefore beside the point. At some point the collection simply stopped growing.

Beecher thus held, as Green did, that the precise form of the received three-fold canon was the product of much later reflection and organization:

"...the books whose contents fall within the lifetime of Moses came at length to be regarded as especially the Law. Some centuries later, doubtless after many fruitless attempts, the present line of demarcation between the Prophets and the Writings was settled upon. But through all, the original usage of the words persisted, to a certain extent, so that the whole aggregate has continued to be called, sometimes the Law, not seldom the Prophets, and constantly the Scriptures; that is to say, the Writings."[16]

---

[12] Ibid., 127.

[13] Ibid., 126.

[14] Ibid., 127. In fact, 'public knowledge' was usually denied the prophetic writings precisely to escape this difficulty within the standard theory, e. g., BUDDE, Schrifttum, 5.

[15] BEECHER, Canon, 127.

[16] Ibid., 128.

Many recognized that at a later point in time, the name of one section of the canon was used to refer to the whole (*pars pro toto*), but Beecher's assertion that this usage was 'original,' and his refusal to differentiate among terms at all, doomed his reconstruction to easy objection.[17] Beecher's work seems to have made little impact on the later course of research, yet the contours of his argument have turned out to be somewhat prophetic in light of current scholarship.

Far from echoing the usual conservative effort simply to supply the reconstruction of canon formation with earlier dates, Beecher instead went Wellhausen one better by putting forward an alternative reconstruction of the canon which began with the activity of the *prophets*, and thus built upon Wellhausen's own history of Israelite religion. The weak flank of what had already emerged as the standard model of canon formation was its contention that although the process leading to the prophetic writings began quite early, and affected the entire course of Israelite religion, the prophetic writings themselves remained unauthoritative until the period after the Exile. Beecher had perceived the fundamental contradiction between Wellhausen's reconstruction of the history of Israel and his reconstruction of the history of canon formation. Beecher therefore attempted to sketch a history of *canonization* in which the prophets came first, too.

As he did, Beecher developed an alternate conception of the nature of canonization itself. Rather than emphasizing the legal, restrictive aspect of the canon, he drew attention to the religious *authority* which writings in Israel must have had even prior to any official canonical designation.[18] Like other 'higher critics,' he thought that the date of such an 'official' act must have been relatively late in Israel's history, but he also acknowledged the paucity of the evidence. Moreover, he questioned whether this kind of formal canonization was as significant as many had seemed to imply. Critical study, he presciently maintained, was chiefly concerned with the writings of Israel as an aggregate, not a canon, anyway.[19]

---

[17] BUDDE, Canon, 657, called BEECHER's effort a 'total failure,' largely faulting his theory for being unable to account for the Samaritan schism (as then understood).

[18] W. H. GREEN, Introduction, 110, makes this point as well: "The canon does not derive its authority from the Church, whether Jewish or Christian; the office of the Church is merely that of a custodian and a witness. The collection of the canon is simply a bringing together into one volume those books whose sacred character has already secured general acknowledgement." In GREEN's hands, however, this view of canon functioned primarily to support his agenda of upholding mosaic authorship. BEECHER, on the other hand, argued insightfully that the critical idea of *lex post prophetas* should be applied more consistently.

[19] Cf. the remarks of CHILDS, OT Introduction, 79: "The usual critical method of biblical exegesis is, first, to seek to restore an original historical setting by stripping away those very elements which constitute the canonical shape. Little wonder that once the biblical text has been securely anchored in the historical past by 'decanonizing' it, the interpreter has diffi-

The alternative view of an organically-growing aggregate instead of a linear three-stage process will be repeated in various forms within the history of scholarship on this question and informs my own proposal for canon formation later in this essay.[20]

G. Hölscher

There was a curious seconding of Beecher's view by G. Hölscher.[21] It was curious in that Hölscher shared Beecher's scepticism of the consensus view and used his work, but nevertheless maintained the standard conception of 'canon' as a legal, restrictive norm. Where Beecher had sought to increase the awareness of the religious authority possessed by Israel's writings *prior* to formal canonization, Hölscher took the opposite position that only between the first century B. C. and the first century A. D. had Israel's writings become authoritative *at all*. These texts obtained authority *only* by virtue of formal canonization; prior to that stage, *tradition* rather than *texts* commanded respect and obedience within Israel: "Nicht das Buch als solches, sondern das in ihm enthaltene Gesetz war der Kanon der Gemeinde..."[22]

Hölscher designated tradition as the 'material canon,' to be distinguished from a 'formal canon' of texts. Thus, he restricted the religious authority of texts to those which had been rendered canonical in the formal sense. 'Scripture' and 'canon' were identical in his work; non-canonical texts *by definition* could not be considered authoritative scriptures. He did not consider the possibility of 'pre-canonical' scripture: "Der Kanon ist die bewußte Aussonderung einer bestimmten Anzahl 'heiliger' Schriften aus der größeren Menge des vorhandenen Schrifttums."[23] In Hölscher's view, the reason for eventual canonization lay in the threat posed to early Judaism by a growing body of apocryphal literature with highly apocalyptic tendencies. In response to this threat, Judaism developed a restrictive canon, becoming in the process, he maintained, the religion of the Talmud (*Talmudismus*).[24]

---

culty applying it to the modern religious context." CHILDS attributes this particular formulation of the problem to SHEPPARD.

[20] Many of the same criticisms are later found in ARNOLD, Observations, his 1922 Presidential Address before the Society of Biblical Literature in New Haven, CT. ARNOLD emphasized the prophetic character of canon formation and the form of Deuteronomy as a 'prophetic address.' He claimed that the earliest scripture of all must have been comprised of prophetic writings (16).

[21] HÖLSCHER, Kanonisch.

[22] Ibid., 17: "Not the book as such, but the law it contained was the community's canon..."

[23] Ibid., 25: "The canon is the conscious selection of a certain number of 'holy' writings out of the larger quantity of available written literature."

[24] Ibid., 77.

Like Wellhausen, Hölscher viewed the existence of a *literary* canon as implying the end of a religion's vitality.[25] He shared to some extent Beecher's idea of an organically-developing body of scripture within Israel, but by distinguishing so stringently between this development and the exercise of religious authority by a formal canon, he saw only religious routinization where Beecher had seen profound religious activity and conviction.[26] Despite its shortcomings, Hölscher's work brilliantly illuminated certain basic decisions for investigations into the Old Testament canon and prophetically expressed the direction which the scholary majority would increasingly take as it sought to make the standard theory more consistent.

Summary

The model of non-linear, organic canon formation, as voiced by both Beecher and Hölscher at the turn of the century, survived into later twentieth-century scholarship as the minority view. Lying dormant, but slowly to revive, was Beecher's challenge to the inconsistency of Wellhausen's claim of prophetic priority over the law.

Also to revive, but not until quite recently, however, was the fundamental question Beecher and Hölscher had raised in different ways about the meaning and significance of canonization. Did religious authority in Israel accrue to texts *prior* to canonization? Or were religious 'authority' and 'canon' fully identical terms? Because the whole question of written texts was mitigated at the turn of the century by form-critical methods stressing the orality of Israel's traditions, the question of the relationship between religious authority and canon slumbered.

The First Half of the Twentieth Century

Unusual opposition to the now standard theory of Old Testament canon[1] was found during the first half of the twentieth century in a book by M. L. Margolis, whose slight appearance still belies the weight of its argument.[2]

---

[25] Thus he wrote (Ibid.) of the "Gegensatz von Geist und Buchstabe, der hier wie so oft in der Geschichte der Religion zutage tritt."

[26] HÖLSCHER was aware of this difference with BEECHER. He noted (Ibid., 7 n.1) that he would consider BEECHER's work "noch wertvoller [zu] sein, wenn er deutlicher zwischen Sammlung und Kanonisation unterschiede."

[1] E. g., SELLIN, Einleitung.

[2] MARGOLIS, Scriptures.

M. L. Margolis

Margolis began his investigation of the canon, as Ryle did, from the internal evidence: "There is no other approach to antiquity except through tradition."[3] In this way, he attempted to trace the three-fold shape of the canon back to the three-dimensional character of revelation within Israel's earliest history.

Margolis impressively marshalled biblical material in support of his claim. His ultimate aim, however, lay in the defense of mosaic authorship and the reliability of biblical tradition in general, which resulted in conclusions similar to those of Green:

> "We have no reason to discredit this tradition. There was a Mosaic Torah which was code and constitution... Copies of that Torah were executed and kept in all the shrines, each a version or excerpt as conditions of time and place warranted, with such variations as all texts are subject to in the course of transmission and with other modification intended to keep pace with the development of the national life."[4]

This kind of description was as speculative a reconstruction as some of the more skeptical critics were guilty of, but it did take seriously aspects of the Bible's self-presentation often otherwise simply dismissed as mythic or fictive.

Thus, on the basis of the traditions reported in the text Margolis continued to maintain a reliable connection between the historical activity of Moses and the emergence of the Pentateuch: "Whether the Pentateuch as we have it *is* the Mosaic Torah may be a matter for debate. That it *has* the Mosaic Torah, which is neither in this strand nor in the other but 'dispersed in them all,' must be the conclusion of sound criticism."[5] Margolis may have aimed at bolstering a traditional understanding of the canon, but he did gather his evidence mostly from the biblical text itself, rather than from later post-biblical traditions.

Here again a critical voice dissented from the standard theory of canon formation by describing an *organic* process rather than a linear development:

> "Indeed the process of Scripture making will reveal itself not as one of consecutive addition of a second category after the first was well established and of a third when the second had been joined on to the first, but rather as one of consecutive enlargement within the three parts, all of which coexisted from the very beginning, and each of which, whatever its compass for the time being, remained identical in its character throughout the whole of the formative period."[6]

---

[3] Ibid., 52.
[4] Ibid., 114.
[5] Ibid., 119.
[6] Ibid., 53

It was ultimately the Holy Spirit, for Margolis, which ensured the constancy of Scripture's character. However, the further question of the relationship between the biblical text's 'character' and its 'compass' was to remain unresolved in his work.

While suggestive in its treatment of the three-fold nature of revelation within the biblical witnesses, the quasi-confessional argument of Margolis's book kept it an anomaly in the period, although it would increasingly give direction to a new generation of Jewish scholars seeking to reconcile traditional views with critical biblical scholarship.[7] Margolis's work also kept audible the continuing echo of objections to the standard theory.[8]

Mid-Century Views and New Findings

The three-stage model of canon formation, as expressed by Ryle and others, remained the regnant view of critical scholarship for the first half of the twentieth century, although the entire issue was pushed well into the background. Interest in the date and provenance of traditions anterior to the canonical form of the text held the focus of Old Testament study (i. e., form criticism, tradition criticism).[1]

By the middle of the century, however, it was becoming apparent that the question of the canon would have to be reopened in response to newer exegetical insights and methods. For example, form criticism maintained that it was methodologically incorrect to assume the date of Old Testament materials

---

[7] GREENSPOON, Margolis. See, however, the interesting criticism by ARNOLD in his address of the same year (Observations, 6) that MARGOLIS's view is actually no less 'untraditional' than that of his critics. For a Jewish study of this period supporting the standard theory, see ZEITLIN, Study.

[8] It is also interesting to compare MARGOLIS's views with those of E. J. YOUNG, Introduction. YOUNG also pursued the question of canonization within a confessional framework. Because the books of the Old Testament were 'immediately inspired of God,' they were 'recognized as such by his people from the time when they first appeared' (Introduction, 43). The manner in which YOUNG conceived of the nature of revelation thus led him to adopt the temporal priority of the mosaic Pentateuch, from which followed a weakened version of the standard theory. YOUNG also argued, for example, that even before the canonization of the Writings 'these books had [already] been in existence for some time' (42). However, the final result of YOUNG's work, unlike that of MARGOLIS, was basically the same progressive, tripartite scheme as the standard theory, just with earlier dates.

[1] Mid-century interest in cultic explanations for Israel's traditions also resulted in the effort to find a cultic background for the canon; see ÖSTBORN, Cult. However, ÖSTBORN's study did not result in a new model of canon formation, but in a speculative cultic background for the usual three-stage process.

based upon the date of their final form. But was this not precisely what the standard theory of the canon implied?[2]

In a later formulation of this problem, B. S. Childs writes:

"Even if one could identify the book which was discovered in 621 (2 Kg 22) with Deuteronomy, as most scholars do, it does not follow that one can infer that this event constituted the first stage of canonization of Deuteronomy nor that the laws of Moses were without authority up to that point in history. Many of the same assumptions can be questioned regarding the final stage of the Pentateuch's alleged canonization under Ezra resulting from the addition of the Priestly source according to the classic Wellhausen theory. To extrapolate a history of canonization from a highly complex and obscure literary process remains a very fragile and tentative enterprise."[3]

In effect, by emphasizing the traditions that had existed prior to the final form of the text, form criticism had subverted the significance of *formal* canonization by reopening questions about the authority of those traditions prior to the kind of public canonization to which Wellhausen and others had granted so much importance. Not surprisingly, it was at this point that serious questions began to be raised about the long-held assumption that the canon had been 'closed' by a rabbinic council in Jamnia ca. A. D. 90.[4]

Also important at this time were the demonstrations of P. Katz[5] and J. C. H. Lebram[6] (continuing the work of Hölscher) that the kind of alternative canonical orders and divisions of the Old Testament found in the LXX and other ancient sources were just as old as, if not older than, those of the MT. This called into question a three-stage development of the canon with some urgency. If the tripartite form of the MT was simply one order among several, in

---

[2] WELLHAUSEN, Prolegomena, 409, had already foreseen this objection and attempted to use the legal character of canon as his defense. The Pentateuch *as law* could not have been a long time in existence before becoming canonical (as the historical and prophetical books presumably were), due to the essential claim of law to public authority. Yet WELLHAUSEN maintained that Deuteronomy was legally authoritative for the period from Josiah to Ezra. What kind of *authority*, if any, he envisioned for the 'Yahwist' and 'Elohist' sources is difficult to know.

[3] CHILDS, OT Introduction, 53–54. Here it is evident that the roots of CHILD's work on the canon lay in his form-critical training and the application of that training to larger textual units, a process begun by CHILD's teacher, VON RAD in his landmark work on the Hexateuch (VON RAD, Problem). Often the difference between CHILDS's work and other form-critical approaches is not a difference in methodology *per se*, but the goal to which the methodology is applied: i. e., explicating the final form of the text, rather than excavating hypothetical oral traditions. Cf. RENDTORFF, Canon, esp. 48–50.

[4] This questioning has continued; see AUNE, Origins; LEWIS, Jabneh; G. MAIER, Abschluß; SCHÄFER, Synode; STEMBERGER, Jabne; VELTRI, Entwicklung.

[5] KATZ, Canon.

[6] LEBRAM, Aspekte.

what sense could it be said to be a reliable guide to the historical development of the text?

Similarly, the date of the so-called Samaritan 'schism' was subjected to serious question with the discovery of the Dead Sea scrolls. The separation between Jews and Samaritans had long been argued to provide evidence for the date of the canonization of the Pentateuch, as the Samaritans had famously restricted their scriptures to the Pentateuch alone. Ryle and others had maintained that such a restriction must mean that at the time of the break (432 B. C., according to Ryle) the Pentateuch represented the full canon of Judaism.

With work on the Dead Sea scrolls, however, it became clear that the separation between Jews and Samaritans had occurred gradually over centuries, perhaps culminating as late as the second century B. C., and thus having little bearing on the shape of Old Testament canon formation.[7] Rather than adopting what at the time was the whole of available scripture, the Samaritans instead appeared to have rejected portions of the canon which did not comport with their faith and practice, and to have kept only what did.[8]

The state of the question at the mid-point of the century is conveniently viewed in widely-used Old Testament introductions of the period. Generally speaking, they tended to narrow the gap between the respective dates of the Law and the Prophets as canonical collections, but continued to conceptualize the canonical process according to the three-stage theory.[9] I shall refer to R. H. Pfeiffer's work by way of example.

R. H. Pfeiffer

R. H. Pfeiffer also upheld the consensus view, along with its customary rationale.[10] Even before the work of M. Noth,[11] Pfeiffer relied on a conception

---

[7] For the second century date, see COGGINS, Samaritans; PURVIS, Pentateuch; idem, Samaritans. For a summary of the issues, cf. PORTON, Diversity, esp. 63. Even if the second century date is rejected, the fact of centuries of strife between these two communities resists any date which can be regarded as a firm alternative; see BECKWITH, Canon, 131; CHILDS, OT Introduction, 53.

[8] There is further evidence to suggest that the Samaritans' rejection of prophetic writings was based more on theological principles than ignorance; see PUMMER, State; idem Einführung. The objection of SUNDBERG, Church, that the Samaritans would have simply altered the Prophets (had they existed already in written form), does not convince. What the Samaritans apparently objected to was the *existence* of any prophet of God other than Moses. See MACDONALD, Samaritans, 204–11.

[9] An interesting exception was provided by JEPSEN, Kanon; which conceived of a more organic process and resisted the details of the three-stage theory. Although brief, the quality of his theological reflection also distinguished his treatment.

[10] PFEIFFER, Introduction, esp. 50–70; cf. idem, Canon.

[11] NOTH, History.

of a 'national history,' stretching from Genesis to 2 Kings.[12] This history was edited by the Deuteronomists, who inserted their own code (the book of Deuteronomy) into the work, constructing in the process an 'embryonic Pentateuch.' With the addition of the Priestly code during the fifth century, the Pentateuch took on its present form. Only in approximately 400 B. C., however, was the 'canonization' of the Pentateuch completed by being *separated from* the four historical books (1–2 Samuel, 1–2 Kings) 'with which they had formed a great historical corpus.'[13]

No attention was paid to the nature of the religious authority exercised by the pre-deuteronomic epic comprised of 'JE and the old sources.' Instead 'canonization' was firmly restricted: first, to the Deuteronomic 'embryonic Pentateuch' (JED) and then to its Priestly redaction (JEDP). Pfeiffer stated flatly: "There is no reason to doubt that as soon as the final edition of the Pentateuch was issued it was received as canonical. The Pentateuch is merely an enlarged edition of the book found in the Temple and is therefore in principle the prophecy of Moses."[14] The precise nature of concepts like 'issuance' or 'canonical' was left unexplored.

In this way, Pfeiffer held to the three-stage theory, dating the final stage of the 'collected edition of historical and prophetic books' to two centuries after the canonization of the Law.[15] In the case of both the Former and Latter Prophets, he believed that the 'numerous additions and changes' made during the period 500–200 B. C. proved that their literary form was not yet fixed. He also believed that the use of the Former Prophets by the Chronicler implied they were not yet canonical, and he dated the Chronicler to about 250 B. C. His *terminus ad quem* for the second portion of the canon was set according to the date of Ben Sira (ca. 180 B. C.), in which, he argued, the authority of prophetic material seemed to equal the Law (e. g., Sir 44–49).

Thus, Pfeiffer argued that a 'national history' had grown and developed somewhat organically before it was reworked and reorganized by the deuteronomists. However, he also maintained that the 'books' of the Former Prophets and 'books' of Amos, Hosea, Isaiah, Micah and other Latter Prophets had existed, in some cases, for *hundreds* of years prior to their canonization, even inspiring the deuteronomists.[16] He saw the roots of the 'notion of inspired scripture' in prophecy, yet he said of the book of Amos that while it was probably the very first collection of prophetic oracles, the 'concept of sacred scripture did not [yet] exist.'[17] Not for five-and-a-half centuries would the

---

[12] PFEIFFER, Introduction, 56–57.

[13] Ibid., 57.

[14] Ibid.

[15] See SUNDBERG's summary and critique (Church, 38 n. 27–28) of PFEIFFER's views.

[16] PFEIFFER, Introduction, 55.

[17] Ibid., 51.

book of Amos be 'officially canonized.' The improbability that an ancient book by a known prophet could have inspired the deuteronomists, yet would not have been considered 'sacred scripture,' does not seem to have occurred to Pfeiffer at all. He seemed to make the assumption of much historical-critical work on the prophets that Israel believed divine revelation to be exclusively oral until after the Exile.[18]

Following Wellhausen, Pfeiffer viewed the canonization of the Pentateuch as having been the major force in making 'sporadic divine revelation' through the prophets 'superfluous.' Beside an incipient Bible, prophecy became "either subservient to the written Law or, ceasing to be oral, a transcript of apocalyptic dreams."[19] Such a model begged the question of how the 'books' of the prophets ever began to take form *at all*, if they were fundamentally opposed to the nature of prophecy itself. The assumption of the priority of oral revelation, based quite loosely on comparative and anthropological evidence, rested uneasily with indications of the early presence of religious writing within Israel.[20]

In sum, Pfeiffer tried to account for the exegetical evidence at his disposal without adjusting the theory of canon formation which he had inherited. As a consequence, he was forced to combine what were really two different and contradictory descriptions of the process. Even then, it was clear that his effort to describe canon formation confirmed an ongoing problem instead of breaking any new ground. A fundamental reassessment of canonization was still needed.

Summary

In this way, the alternatives to the regnant tripartite theory of canon can be seen to have arisen not only from the erosion of the old monolith, but also by increasing recognition of a design flaw in Wellhausen's blueprint: what of the canonization of the prophetic corpus?[21] Was it really credible that the prophetic writings, portions of which were generally acknowledged to have been pre-exilic, were committed to memory, writing and revision for centuries, but only became 'authoritative' after the canonization of the Pentateuch in the fifth century B. C.? Or, if they *had* been authoritative in some sense, what was the relation between the kind of 'authority' they possessed and the 'legal' authority of the canon?

The standard theory of canon formation had never been able to account adequately for these questions, and as more exegetical work was done it grew

---

[18] Ibid.
[19] Ibid., 55.
[20] Ibid., 33.
[21] Cf. BARR, Scripture, 52–53.

increasingly difficult to make the facts fit the theory. Questions began to be raised anew about the adequacy of the linear three-stage model.[22]

The Rise of a Canonical Approach

In the second half of the twentieth century the topic of canon was revisited with new urgency in Anglo-Saxon Old Testament scholarship. Although the various causes of this development are difficult to isolate with precision, one reason for it lay in the debate about the nature of revelation within the Anglo-Saxon Biblical Theology movement of the 50s and 60s.[1] Interestingly, another reason had to do with the impact of German form-critical methodology on Ango-Saxon scholarship, as mediated by one particular Old Testament *Introduction*: O. Eißfeldt's *Einleitung* of 1956.[2]

Eißfeldt, who had studied with J. Wellhausen and H. Gunkel personally, had sought in his *Introduction* to bring together the contasting methodologies (source criticism and form criticism, respectively) of his two teachers.[3] In effect, however, his effort resulted in the first Old Testament *Introduction* to include a full treatment of form-critical methods and findings.[4]

At the same time, Eißfeldt's exploration of the pre-literary development of the biblical books led him to an analogous, but quite innovative, claim about the pre-literary development of the *canon*:

"Erst im 2. Jahrh. n. Chr. hat... die Bildung des alttestamentlichen Kanons ihren Abschluß gefunden. Aber ihre Vorgeschichte beginnt Jahrhunderte und Jahrtausende vorher. Ausgangspunkt ist der Glaube daran, daß bestimmte Äußerungen von Menschen tatsächlich Got-

---

[22] The standard model remained the consensus view, however, as expressed magisterially in VON CAMPENHAUSEN, Entstehung, esp. 6–10.

[1] Thus CHILDS proposed a renewed attention to the canon as a means of avoiding the same problems which had led to the Biblical Theology movement's demise. See the chapter, 'The Canon as the Context for Biblical Theology,' in CHILDS, Crisis, 99–107. CHILDS's early emphasis on the normativity of the *full* canon was shaped at least partly in response to the view of WRIGHT that a 'canon within a canon' was inevitable, and that therefore the 'truth' of the canon lay in its usage. See the section 'The Canon as a Theological Problem,' in WRIGHT's OT Theology, 166–85. An interesting article from this period which provides an overview of treatments of the canon by WRIGHT, BRIGHT, J. J. A. SANDERS and CHILDS can be found in MAYS, Discussions.

[2] EISSFELDT, Einleitung. The first edition of EISSFELDT's work appeared in 1934, but it was the second edition which received particular attention in English-speaking scholarship.

[3] SMEND, Eißfeldt, 326.

[4] RABENAU, Werk.

teswort darstellen und als solches besondere Autorität für sich in Anspruch nehmen können."[5]

This particular form-critical description of the Old Testament canon was cited explicitly by two of the leading figures in the new discussion about canon and canonization, P. R. Ackroyd[6] and J. A. Sanders.[7] In some ways, Eißfeldt himself seemed to have missed the force of his own insight, as Sanders pointed out.[8] The ensuing treatment of the process of canonization in Eißfeldt's *Introduction* followed the traditional lines of the standard theory.[9]

There is a certain historical irony to be found in locating the basic insight which fueled the Anglo-Saxon discussion of canon in a German Old Testament *Introduction*, where it was apparently for the most part disregarded by its German readers and even its author. However, it seems to have been the case.[10] Some of the force of this insight for Anglo-Saxon scholarship can probably be explained by a different reception of form-critical methodology, which developed broad appeal in Anglo-Saxon scholarship much later than within German scholarship and in a more concentrated way.[11] In any case, the

---

[5] EISSFELDT, Einleitung, 692. The crucial second sentence is identical to what already appeared in the first edition of his work (Einleitung, 615). Note that EISSFELDT's Introduction is subtitled as a 'Formation History' (*Entstehungsgeschichte*) of the Old Testament. That this approach is fully EISSFELDT's own is shown by the fact that GUNKEL himself believed, like WELLHAUSEN, that the canon arose only *after* the living tradition (which his method sought to describe) had died out: "...der Geist nimmt ab; die Gattungen sind verbraucht... Aber schon hat die Geschichte der Sammlung der Sammlungen begonnen: der Kanon entsteht." GUNKEL, Reden, 36; cited in KRAUS, Geschichte, 345.

[6] ACKROYD, Continuity, 13 n. 47. It was ACKROYD who went on to translate EISSFELDT's Introduction into English, suggesting a sustained engagement with EISSFELDT's ideas on ACKROYD's part.

[7] J. A. SANDERS, Adaptability, 534 n. 16.

[8] Ibid., 535. For further evaluation of EISSFELDT's theological understanding of the canon, see H.-J. ZOBEL, Eißfeldt, esp. 38.

[9] EISSFELDT, Einleitung, 698–704. In addition, EISSFELDT accepted (704) that the Law had always possessed superior authority in Israel's religious tradition and formed a 'canon within the canon' (*Kanon des Kanons*).

[10] Note, however, the similar statement of SMEND, Entstehung, 18 n. 23: "Jedes Prophetenwort enthält von vornherein einen Geltungsanspruch, der es auf Kanonizität hin angelegt sein läßt."

[11] Another irony may be that EISSFELDT's work was also a great inspiration to ALBRIGHT and therefore has influenced the 'Harvard School' of Old Testament scholarship, although for completely different reasons. ALBRIGHT was intrigued by EISSFELDT's archaeological work, especially EISSFELDT's investigation of the relationship between Israel and its Canaanite environment; see SMEND, Eißfeldt, 327. The irony of the situation is sharpened by the fact that EISSFELDT attributed his own interest in both the archaeology of early Israel and the pre-literary development of Israel's scriptural traditions to the influence of GUNKEL. See EISSFELDT, Jahrzehnte, esp. 4. Thus two major divergent directions in Anglo-Saxon scholar-

Eißfeldt connection illustrates that Anglo-Saxon scholarship on canon grew out of reflection upon a form-critical insight into the nature of religious tradition.[12]

P. R. Ackroyd

Against this background, the new Anglo-Saxon discussion about Old Testament canon and canon formation could be said to have begun with P. R. Ackroyd's 1961 inaugural lecture in the Samuel Davidson Chair of Old Testament Studies at King's College, London.[13]

Building on Eißfeldt's application of form-critical method to the history of the canon, Ackroyd used the term 'canon' to highlight an authoritative address or claim which must have been present even at pre-literary stages of the material in order for Israel's traditions to have been preserved. Thus 'canon' did not begin with Jamnia, or with the 'definition of a particular law as a standard':

> "[Canon] begins imperceptibly in the recognition of certain utterances of men as representing in reality the word of God, and in the acceptance as binding of such single utterances or groups of utterances... It is recognized that the requirements of God may be made precise in a particular form which continues to standardize the understanding and presentation of subsequent developments of belief."[14]

What was new in Ackroyd's description of canon formation was not so much his understanding of the way in which a 'canonical' authority attached to utterances that made a forceful claim upon individuals' consciousness, ensuring their preservation. Form criticism already assumed the preservation of oral traditions and their eventual commitment to written form. Instead, what was new was the insight that such 'canonical' traditions continued to *generate* and *standardize* subsequent understandings and beliefs within biblical tradition. Ackroyd termed this characteristic the 'canonical principle.'[15]

Although Ackroyd's lecture does not seem to have been widely remembered or cited, his description of canon formation as a generative and regulative *principle* was increasingly taken up, if sometimes only indirectly, by a variety of scholars in the second half of the twentieth century.[16] Ackroyd's

---

ship, and within U. S. Old Testament research especially, were both encouraged by EISSFELDT's work.

[12] This same form-critical insight is evident in a fascinating 1957 Heidelberg lecture by JEPSEN, Wissenschaft, esp. 28. Here JEPSEN was already proposing to use 'canon' as an organizing principle for the entire discipline, as pointed out by REVENTLOW, Problems, 137.

[13] Later published as ACKROYD, Continuity.

[14] Ibid., 13–14. Cf. idem, Making, 98-99.

[15] ACKROYD, Continuity, 15.

[16] BARR, Scripture, 7, refers to a 'principle of the *canon*' (his emphasis), but he cites Deut 4:2 as an example of it, surely a different conception. On the other hand, ACKROYD's insight

description of canon formation does seem, however, to have had a direct influence upon the work of R. E. Clements, as we shall see. However, already other voices were suggesting new possibilities.[17]

D. N. Freedman

Over the years, D. N. Freedman has developed an increasingly baroque theory of canon formation, but the essential lines of his reconstruction were drawn in a 1962 article in which he argued that the closing of the prophetic canon occurred much earlier than commonly thought.[18] Drawing on the theory of a 'Deuteronomistic History' advocated by M. Noth, Freedman's influential insight lay in perceiving the implications of an early collection of Former Prophets for the history of canonization.

Like Pfeiffer, Freedman hypothesized the sixth-century 'publication' of a 'Primary History' consisting of Genesis–2 Kings, from which the Pentateuch was later subdivided and a collection of Latter Prophets added.[19] Like Ryle and Wellhausen, he insisted on understanding canonization as the promulgation of 'public documents' by 'an official ecclesiastical group in the Jewish community.'[20] Freedman dated the closing of the canon quite early (by the end of the Exile!), based primarily upon the ostensive historical references he identified within the biblical text.[21] Here, however, his treatment elided the

---

seems to have influenced both JACOB, Principe; and KRAUS, Theologie, 335–47, esp. 345 on then-current continental canon scholarship: "Die Frage ist nur, ob unter diesen mit der Kritik hochgespielten Voraussetzungen *die Intention des Kanonprinzips und das Ereignis der Selbstdurchsetzung des kanonisch Umgrenzten in der Kirche* überhaupt noch in den Blick gelangen kann" (his emphasis).

[17] ACKROYD later adopted (Canon, esp. 214–19) a more customary reconstruction of canon formation, however, relying in part on SUNDBERG's formulation of the basic issues. He was then attracted to J. A. SANDERS's work (ACKROYD, Text), although here he also suggested the problematic notion of 'levels' of canonicity (Text, 233–34). One has the impression that ACKROYD was seeking a theoretical construct that would do justice to his exegetical instincts, but somehow never quite found it. In the end he seems to have largely accepted the standard theory (Making, 109).

[18] See the materials listed in the bibliography for FREEDMAN.

[19] FREEDMAN, Law, 251; 259. He dated the final form of the Latter Prophets to the end of the sixth or the beginning of the fifth century B. C.!

[20] Ibid.

[21] FREEDMAN, Canon, 131: "The bulk of the first two parts of the Bible (Instruction) and the Nebi'im (Prophets) was in existence by 587 B. C. The material was given its finished form in the half century after that date." Increasingly, however, FREEDMAN had to allow for some possibility of editorial changes and additions after 'canonization' in order to make his reconstruction work (e. g., his Law, 260–61), but he did his best to explain such possibilities away.

important methodological difference between a *terminus a quo* and a *terminus ante quem*.[22]

Still, Freedman reopened the question of the hermeneutical relationship between the Law and the Prophets in a provocative way by reemphasizing the role both played together as the 'central core' of scripture.[23] Thus Freedman suggested that the Writings were a subordinate collection dependent upon the 'central core.'[24] However, he also held that the Torah had been granted a 'special status' from the very beginning.[25]

The course of more recent scholarship has tended to confirm Freedman's notion of a more 'organic' canon, even as he has moved increasingly in the direction of an overly-complex numerical analysis to explain the canon's final form.[26] In some ways, Freedman's theories seem to revive those of Ryle (e. g., his description of a three-stage process of increasingly complete 'Bibles'). However, Freedman's numerical analysis is probably best viewed in the tradition of Green, as implying that the literary shape of the canon is the editorial product of a single 'rational mind.'

R. E. Clements

In 1965, R. E. Clements began to pursue similar 'canonical' questions regarding the Law and the Prophets.[27] As others had, Clements perceived that form-critical work since Wellhausen had illustrated the antiquity of law in Israel[28] and that the prophets could therefore no longer be said to be the originators of Israel's 'ethical monotheism.'[29] However, in Old Testament ac-

---

[22] I owe this lapidary formulation to PERSON, Zechariah, 43; 116–17.

[23] FREEDMAN, Law, 250.

[24] Ibid.

[25] Ibid., 252. Or at least from the time of Ezra; cf. FREEDMAN, Formation, 323. FREEDMAN now argues that Ezra's intention was to exalt the 'rule of law.' See his summary in outline form (Formation, 324–26) where he writes of a 'First Bible,' 'Second Bible' and 'Third Bible.' FREEDMAN has turned from a three-stage process of the canon's completion to three editions of largely the same text, with only minimal expansion over time.

[26] See FREEDMAN, Unity; idem, Symmetry.

[27] CLEMENTS, Covenant.

[28] It may be helpful to recall how slowly the full impact of this realization permeated the field. See ZIMMERLI, Gesetz, 252. Stemming from the work of ALT (Origins) and NOTH (Gesetze), the full impact of legal studies upon WELLHAUSEN's theory was felt in Ango-Saxon scholarship only with the work of MENDENHALL (Covenant; idem, Law) and the translations of the Old Testament theologies of EICHRODT (see his Theology, II:70–71) and VON RAD (see his Theology, I:190–91).

[29] Used approvingly in WELLHAUSEN, Israel; the language is generally attributed to DUHM, Theologie. By the time of CLEMENTS's book, 'ethical monotheism' had already been rejected as an interpretive category (see EICHRODT, Theology, I:351 n. 1 and VON RAD, Theology, II:298), but for other reasons — e. g., the unsuitability of understanding the phenomenon of prophecy as exclusively doctrinal, rational and anti-cultic. CLEMENTS, however, re-

counts of *covenant* Clements saw a 'canonical principle' at work, leading to the selection of certain traditions over others and the establishment of 'certain normative patterns.'[30]

For these reasons, Clements suggested:

"The picture that now presents itself to us of Israel's religious development is not that of a successive elaboration of the religious insights obtained by the great prophets of the eighth and seventh centuries, but of a series of traditions proceeding and developing side by side. Law, psalmography, Wisdom and prophecy all had their own distinctive place, and maintained their own particular traditions. Each of these traditions was able to work with a basis of inherited forms and ideas which Israel took over from Canaan, or brought with it into the land, whilst the controlling factor in the development of each of them was Israel's knowledge of its covenant relationship to Yahweh. At innumerable places the lines of tradition intersect. Law and prophecy proceeded together in Israel's life, and although the classical prophets could appeal to a tradition of law already in existence, they were not themselves without influence upon the recognition and development of the law. The same is true of the Wisdom schools and of the development of psalmography in the cult, which were not unaffected by the rise of the great prophets."[31]

Thus Clements formulated a new model for the relationship between law and prophets, in which both are contemporaneous and mutually-affecting.

It should be noted, however, that here Clements used the terms 'law' and 'prophets' to refer to religious *traditions* (i. e., 'law and prophecy') rather than to the specific canonical collections of *texts* (i. e., 'Law' and 'Prophets'). Adopting 'covenant' as a unifying framework,[32] he endeavored to illuminate the reciprocal development among various traditions which took place in history *prior* to the process of canonization. For example, he argued that it was the ability of certain prophecies to function as a distinctive witness to Israel's covenant which provided the 'primary consideration' for their retention as normative for new generations.[33]

---

jected the idea that 'ethical monotheism' provided an adequate category for prophecy on the basis that a covenantal 'ethical monotheism' had in fact preceded the prophets.

[30] CLEMENTS, Covenant, 8. CLEMENTS alluded in his introduction to an already-existing expression, namely the 'canonical principle,' but did not mention which scholar had coined the phrase. Presumably he had in mind ACKROYD (see discussion above). His reference to 'normative patterns' matches ACKROYD's language about 'standardization.'

[31] CLEMENTS, Covenant, 23–24.

[32] The adoption of 'covenant' as a unifying framework was not itself new. See esp. EICHRODT, Theology, I:36–37. Cf. WRIGHT, Biblical Theology, 50–55; idem, OT Theology, esp. 179, where WRIGHT placed an 'idea of canon' within the context of a reconstructed 'covenant renewal' ceremony. However, where EICHRODT used 'covenant' methodologically to provide a theoretical framework for a historically diverse biblical literature, WRIGHT and CLEMENTS (in this first book) viewed 'covenant' as a transhistorical constant within Israel's experience (e. g., CLEMENTS, Covenant, 119–20).

[33] CLEMENTS, Covenant, 128.

However, it was precisely the isolation of 'covenant' as a historical framework and theological criterion which left Clements's ideas vulnerable to the critical work of L. Perlitt only a few years later.[34] Perlitt argued that 'covenant' was strictly a post-exilic idea within Israel, deriving exclusively from deuteronomistic circles.[35] The strong reaction to his skeptical conclusions revealed how dependent the field had become upon the concept of covenant as a means to organize Old Testament traditions.

In retrospect Perlitt's work can be seen to have had a major effect on the direction of Old Testament scholarship. Since his book appeared in 1969, scholarship has increasingly emphasized the lateness of the biblical covenant tradition[36] (post-exilic dates are in general now very much the norm, even for what were once thought to be the earliest sources),[37] and stressed the importance of deuteronomism for the final shape of the canon.[38] Although certainly not everyone accepted the details of Perlitt's thesis, his view largely carried the day. After his work, the burden of proof no longer lay upon those who questioned the centrality of covenant in pre-exilic Israel, but upon those who would maintain it.

The weight of this burden compelled Clements to salvage what he could of his earlier book. Adopting a more redaction-critical approach, he neatly 'modified' his effort to find the unity of pre-exilic prophecy in an historically-reconstructed covenant tradition.[39] He still viewed covenant as the center of biblical prophecy, but now he conceded that this unity emerged slowly *out of* the deuteronomistic 'movement' instead of *vice versa*. He concluded:

"Thus we cannot reconstruct a consistent covenant theology as a distinctive and coherent tradition underlying the preaching of the prophets, but we can see that the traditions which the prophets inherited and used had a place in the emergence of a distinctive covenant ideology in Israel."[40]

Having made this crucial methodological reversal, Clements explicitly and fully endorsed Perlitt's conclusions and proceeded to examine with great skill the deuteronomistic shaping of prophetic traditions.[41]

---

[34] Idem, Tradition, 41.

[35] PERLITT, Bundestheologie.

[36] Cf. BALTZER, Formulary; KUTSCH, Verheissung; MCCARTHY, OT Covenant.

[37] E. g., for post-exilic datings for the Yahwist, see H.–H. SCHMID, Jahwist; KAISER, Introduction; VAN SETERS, Prologue; THOMPSON, History.

[38] On the danger of a resultant 'pan-Deuteronomism,' see ZIMMERLI, Religion, esp. 380; COGGINS, Deuteronomistic? LOHFINK, Bewegung?

[39] CLEMENTS, Tradition, 22; cf. 87–92. Note the slight, but telling, change in the title.

[40] Ibid., 23.

[41] Ibid., 41; 57. CLEMENTS does demur, as others have since, that PERLITT "appears too rigid in asserting an almost exclusively Deuteronomic interpretation of covenant in Israel,"

In his revised treatment, Clements illustrated persuasively that a *unified* understanding of prophets and prophecy had emerged at least by the time of the deuteronomistic movement (ca. sixth century B. C.).[42] In addition, Clements cited work done by scholars on the deuteronomistic redaction of certain prophetic books (esp. Amos, Hosea, Jeremiah) to make the case that the notion of covenant in the prophetic books, which Perlitt had shown to be secondary, nevertheless represented a conscious and coherent theological shaping of the material at a later date in the history of its transmission.[43]

Clements even surmised that the curious silence about the prophets within the Deuteronomistic History was more likely due to a desire on the part of those responsible for the History not to duplicate material readily found elsewhere than to any ignorance about the prophets on the part of the History's author(s).[44] The concerns of the Deuteronomistic History were so similar to those of the Latter Prophets that it would be 'surprising' if the deuteronomistic historian(s) had not had access to them. The redactional evidence of a close connection between the deuteronomistic movement and certain of the prophets (above all Jeremiah) suggested that "the silence of the Deuteronomic [sic] History about the great prophets can... be better explained as a consequence of their preaching having been regarded as the subject of a related literary collection, which was independently available..."[45] Thus, Clements posited that written collections of the Former and Latter Prophets — in some form — had existed together very early on.

In his search for the way in which Israelite tradition had molded the image of the prophet, Clements encountered the process of canonization. In fact, he discovered that tradition and canon were two different aspects of the same historical, literary and theological development. Deuteronomy and the Deuteronomistic History related the prophetic message to the Torah of Moses. This complementarity represented "the earliest state to which we can penetrate back to obtain any kind of external witness to the religious interests which led to the preservation of the prophetic literature."[46]

The close connection between Deuteronomy and the Deuteronomistic History argued for the view that the Deuteronomistic History also shared in the authority of the Torah early on. As passages such as 2 Kg 17:13 indicated, the message of the Latter Prophets was believed by the deuteronomists to possess the same authority as the law of Moses. Clements summarized:

(Ibid., 44 n. 9). Cf. BARR, Notes; CHILDS, Biblical Theology, 136; NICHOLSON, People; idem, Covenant.

[42] CLEMENTS, Tradition, 52.

[43] Ibid., 45–46.

[44] Ibid., 47.

[45] Ibid., 48.

[46] Ibid., 52.

"Thus, in principle, both the Former Prophets and a significant part of the Latter Prophets were considered to share in the authority which belonged to the law of Moses. This no doubt fell short of the very far-reaching authority which the idea of an Old Testament canon was ultimately to imply, but it none the less represents a very significant step towards it. What is striking is that it witnesses to a conception of 'the Law and the Prophets' which set them side by side as sharing together in this special 'canonical,' or 'proto-canonical,' authority. Instead of indicating a growth of the Old Testament canon which began with the Law and added the Prophets to this as a later, secondary stage, it suggests rather a very early joining together of 'the Law and the Prophets,' each of which subsequently underwent a good deal of expansion and further editorial development. The question of the priority of the Law or the Prophets, therefore, which is of quite considerable importance for an overall theological evaluation of the Old Testament, is set in a fresh light."[47]

In this way, Clements provided a critically-reconstructed model of canonization which broke decisively with the three-fold pattern of the standard theory.

Once again the notion of a more organic aggregate of scriptures had been introduced, but this time with a special emphasis on the integral unity of Law and Prophets, based upon their literary coordination within the biblical canon. Clements retained only a faint trace of the priority of the Law by continuing to privilege the book of Deuteronomy. However, his major breakthrough was to show that an authoritative *conception* of 'Law and Prophets' pre-dated the final form of both canonical subcollections and of the canon as a whole.

A brief comparison with two representatives of the older model may sharpen some points of difference. On the one hand, Ryle differed from Clements in that he considered the date of the latest redactions of the Former and Latter Prophets primarily to suggest the *terminus a quo* for the recognition of their canonicity.[48] This methodological assumption was often made, but completely missed the kind of 'proto-canonical' authority Clements so ably illuminated. For Clements, the *beginning* of the canonical impulse was not to be found at the level of the final redaction.[49] Instead, the 'canonical principle' which guided the process of redaction was to be understood as a demonstration of the religious authority which a text already possessed.[50]

---

[47] Ibid., 55.

[48] RYLE, Canon, 118. Other considerations for RYLE included a great esteem for increasingly rare prophecy in the post-exilic period (Canon, 111–12), the different recensions of Samuel and Jeremiah in the LXX (117), and the insufficiency of the post-exilic Torah alone to witness to the richness of Israel's faith as remembered from pre-exilic times (104–05).

[49] RYLE was not unaware of the problem his model introduced: if canonization was understood as an official designation by an official body within Israel, what guarantee of public acceptance would newly canonical literature have had? RYLE theorized in the case of the Prophets that their use in synagogue worship, while not preceding the period of their admission into the canon, nevertheless 'facilitated their reception as Scripture' (Canon, 126–27). CLEMENTS resolved this same problem by seeing the authority of scripture as preceding its canonization, rather than *vice versa*.

[50] Cf. CLEMENTS, People, 90–91.

It should also be noted that Ryle viewed the writings which eventually became the Former Prophets as only a few of the 'historical memoirs' that had once existed. In his view, those books which we now know as the Former Prophets were later 'selected' for their superior description. Ryle, however, rejected the view that prior to the Exile the testimony of the Latter Prophets had existed in sufficient literary form to "obtain any hold over the religious thought of the nation..."[51] Clearly Clements was advocating an earlier date for the literary development and influence of the prophetic writings, but the more significant difference from Ryle's reconstruction was Clements's insight into the theological interdependence of traditions and the literary coordination of Law and Prophets within the canon.

On the other hand, K. Budde had also thought that the Former and Latter Prophets were already known as literary collections to the scribes in the time of Ezra (fifth century B. C.).[52] However, Budde maintained that neither of these collections had shared in the canonical authority of the Law which Ezra promulgated. Of course, this left Budde in the difficult position of having to explain why these writings were *not* canonized along with the Torah in Ezra's day, only achieving that status for the first time several centuries later.

Budde attempted to resolve the problem by arguing that the concept of the canon had only gradually expanded to include 'historical interest' as well as legal obligation.[53] Such an explanation assumed not only that the Prophets were essentially time-conditioned, in contrast to what Budde termed the 'eternal validity' *(ewige Geltung)* of the Law, but also that 'canonization' was originally and primarily about legal obligation.[54] Rather than a narrow understanding of civil law, Clements's view of canon reflected a broader vision in which authoritative traditions were shaped, coordinated and passed on within a community of faith.

In sum, by synthesizing the results of a wide body of exegetical studies and pursuing a concept of 'proto-canonical' authority through the redaction history of the prophetic corpus, Clements succeeded in suggesting the broad outline of a new critical model of canon formation. Although he relied heavily on a historical reconstruction in which deuteronomism loomed large as a unified literary movement, more recent scholarship has largely upheld the importance of deuteronomism in the shaping of Israel's canonical traditions, even as it has raised questions about the social reality of this reconstructed 'movement.'[55]

---

[51] RYLE, Canon, 110.

[52] BUDDE, Kanon, 34–35.

[53] Ibid., 38.

[54] Ibid., 36. WELLHAUSEN's view of canonization was of course similar; see discussion above.

[55] KNIGHT, Deuteronomy, esp. 69–72.

In my judgment, the problems advanced against some of the components of this reconstruction (i. e., Noth's particular conception of the Deuteronomistic History) have not weakened the overall force of Clements's alternative proposal. Rather than the standard canonical theory, in which the Prophets only much later found a place next to a long-completed Pentateuch, Clements persuasively argued for an early integrated collection of 'Law and Prophets' (i. e., Deuteronomy and the Deuteronomistic History), which had then been gradually expanded by the ongoing addition of traditional materials and the continued redaction of both subcollections.

In his understanding of Israel's 'proto-canonical' writings as religiously authoritative, Clements' work also bore striking similarity to Beecher's notion of an organic 'aggregate' of texts. Although Clements still perceived canon formation as moving in stages (first Deuteronomy and the Former Prophets, then the Pentateuch and the Latter Prophets), both Beecher and Clements sought to understand and explain what they took to be a religiously authoritative body of texts *prior* to any official act of canonization. Clements, of course, was able to draw upon more recent exegetical scholarship, epecially with regard to deuteronomism and the Deuteronomistic History, in order to pursue his investigations.[56]

J. C. H. Lebram

Another work questioning the now-traditional three-fold model of Old Testament canon formation appeared in 1968. In a brilliant article, J. C. H. Lebram, a student of Hölscher, called renewed attention to the fact that the model of successive linear canonization was premised upon the idea that the main force behind canon formation was 'nomistic.'[57]

Working from the biblical references in the book of Ben Sira and the alternative order of the biblical books within the LXX, Lebram claimed that the 'nomistic' construal of biblical texts and authority had in fact been *secondary* to an original prophetic impulse.[58] This prophetic impulse had sought to structure Israel's sacred writings according to the prophetic books themselves. Thus, the triple format of past – present – future generally found in the prophetic books (i. e., Israel's sins of the past, the sins of foreign nations in the present, hope in God for the future) eventually became the shape of the canon

---

[56] Over the years CLEMENTS has not significantly changed his historical reconstruction of the canon, but he now accepts that its three-fold structure corresponds to three successive levels of authority, with the Prophets and Writings subordinated to the Torah. See his OT Theology, 15–19; 120–26.

[57] LEBRAM, Kanonbildung.

[58] Ibid., 184.

as a whole, as preserved in the LXX (i. e., the Pentateuch and historical books = the past; the Writings = the present; the Prophets = the future).[59]

Building on the work of Hölscher and Katz, Lebram argued for the priority of the LXX order and viewed the triple division of the MT as a secondary development caused by increased esteem for the Torah within later Judaism. Like Hölscher, Lebram saw this Torah piety as the beginning of rabbinic Judaism (*Rabbinismus*). Lebram, however, viewed the eventual shape of the MT (as determined at Jamnia, he believed) as a compromise. He considered the *arrangement* of the books in the MT to have followed a nomistic principle (*Nomismus*), but the *selection* of the individual writings to have been made according to historical-prophetic considerations.[60]

Lebram's formulation is problematic in the light of more recent scholarship. His assumptions about the priority of the order of the LXX and the legalistic effects of Hellenism on Israel lack convincing evidence. Of greater usefulness, however, is his view that authoritative prophetic writings *preceded* the canonical authority of the Law, and exercised an influence on the process of canon formation by providing an overarching pattern for the whole. Certainly the prophetic character of the biblical books was later felt to be an indication of their holiness.[61] Although Lebram's temporal pattern of past – present – future is really too general to be of great use, it is to his credit to have noticed the central inconsistency of the standard theory and to have considered head-on the impact of authoritative prophetic writings on Israel's traditions.

By stating the view, however, that a triple 'prophetic' pattern to Israel's scriptures had existed from the very beginning of the canonical process, Lebram raised unanswered questions about the date by which authoritative prophetic *books* would have had to exist in order to provide early enough such a pattern. Moreover, Lebram's Hellenistic date for the subordination of prophecy to law flew in the face of external witnesses to the canon from this period, such as Josephus.[62] If such a nomistic shift were to have occurred, it must have occurred somewhat later.

A. C. Sundberg, Jr.

Other problems in canonization were explored at this time by A. C. Sundberg. Sundberg's primary concern lay in judging the evidence for the hypothesis of a wider Alexandrian canon, which previous scholarship had supposed was rejected by Judaism, but later adopted by the early Christian church.[63]

---

[59] Ibid., 178. LEBRAM credits EISSFELDT for this insight into the character of the LXX.

[60] LEBRAM, Kanonbildung, 189.

[61] JOSEPHUS, Against Apion, I:37-43.

[62] See GERBER, Schriften, esp. 98 n. 36.

[63] SUNDBERG, Church; cf. idem, Christian Canon.

Sundberg framed the issue as "how the canon of the Jewish Bible and the Christian Old Testament came to differ,"[64] conceiving of a largely-open canon at the time that Christianity emerged. In other words, rather than an 'almost-closed' canon of Law, Prophets and Writings existing at the turn of the millenium, Sundberg advanced the theory that there were 'closed collections' of Law and Prophets, as well as a "wide religious literature without definite bounds," all of which "circulated throughout Judaism as holy scripture before Jamnia..."[65] It was from this body of religious literature that Christians later *selected* their Old Testament, and *after* that selection that Judaism canonized its own scriptures (ca. A. D. 90), an official act only much later performed by Christianity itself (end of the fourth century).[66]

Similar to Hölscher, Sundberg proceeded with the conception of an aggregate collection, but a narrow view of canonization. He attempted to differentiate strictly between a 'closed collection' and a formal canon, although he nowhere offered straightforward definitions of the difference. He somewhat polemically rejected the notion of a *de facto* canon, seeing the rabbinic discussions at Jamnia as leading to the actual conferral of religious authority upon approved texts, rather than the acknowledgment of a religious authority certain texts already possessed.[67]

It is difficult to see the reasoning behind Sundberg's rejection of a *de facto* canon in the pre-Jamnia period in light of his approval of the idea of 'closed collections' of Law and Prophets. He could contrast a 'closed collection' with a 'legally fixed' canon, implying that the difference between a *de facto* canon and a 'closed collection' would not turn on legal status. In what sense for him were the collections of Law and Prophets 'closed'? Why were they preserved? What kind of 'authority' existed for sacred writings prior to their 'legal' enforcement?

Sundberg appeared to suggest that because *other* religious writings continued to circulate, the 'closed collections' of Law and Prophets could not yet be understood as canonical.[68] In this view, it was the *exclusive* aspect of a canon which the collections of Law and Prophets lacked. To Sundberg's way of thinking it was insufficient for the Law and the Prophets simply to have been considered 'complete.' Properly understood, he maintained, canonical status dictated that no other writings could be read as religiously authoritative *at all*.

---

[64] SUNDBERG, Church, 79.

[65] Ibid., 103. SUNDBERG is sometimes misquoted (e. g., BARR, Scripture, 57) to the effect that there existed before Jamnia *only* a 'wide religious literature without definite bounds,' but he clearly considered the Law and the Prophets already to have formed closed literary collections. Cf. SUNDBERG, Christian Canon, 146.

[66] SUNDBERG, Church, 157–58.

[67] Ibid., 107.

[68] Ibid., 82.

Since there were in fact other writings, Sundberg believed that this proved the concept of canon to have been a later development.

In putting the issue this way, Sundberg had really only restricted the definition of canon to its narrowest sense and then reconstructed its history based upon his anachronistic definition of the term. It was increasingly clear that exclusivity was not the sole, or even the most telling, feature of scriptural canons, and certainly provided too slender a basis for definition or historical reconstruction.[69] Sundberg revealed his own discomfort with such a narrow view by occasionally subverting his own distinction, writing at least in one instance of the Law and the Prophets as previously (but only partially) 'canonized collections'![70]

For all his skepticism regarding the canonical status of the collections of Law and Prophets, Sundberg largely accepted the consensus view of a linear three-stage process.[71] In fact, he simply assumed the subordination of the Prophets to the Law, stating:

> "The Law possessed such a place of unique authority in Palestine that Prophets and Writings were subordinated to the place of commentary on the Law. This subordination, however, did not destroy the distinction between the collections of Prophets and Writings, which, as we have seen, represent successive periods of canonization."[72]

In accepting this subordination, Sundberg came very close to appropriating and extending to Palestine Eißfeldt's view that *only* the Law was canonical in Alexandria, with the Prophets and the Writings belonging to a wide literature possessing "no clearly fixed bounds."[73] Sundberg attempted to consign the Prophets and the Writings to distinct periods of canonization, but all the criticisms that *he* made against Eißfeldt's position *also* told against his own. Chief among those criticisms was the evidence of Ben Sira, which not only provided a warrant to differentiate between the Prophets and the Writings, but also clearly treated the Prophets as no less authoritative than the Law: it was thus "...hardly possible to escape the conclusion that the Prophets had attained canonical status by the time [the] translation of Sirach was made."[74]

In sum, the major impact of Sundberg's work on the discussion about the Old Testament canon was to reopen in a more forceful way the question of the authority of the *Hebrew* canon for early Christianity. His major contribution,

---

[69] I. e., in light of the foregoing scholarly discussion. For a later summary of comparative evidence against an exclusively 'exclusivist' position, see SHEPPARD, Canon.

[70] SUNDBERG, Church, 107–08 (my emphasis).

[71] Ibid., 37. SUNDBERG presents and slightly adjusts PFEIFFER's conclusions in his notes.

[72] Ibid., 73. He cites DRIVER for this view.

[73] See SUNDBERG's description (Church, 44) of EISSFELDT's position.

[74] SUNDBERG, Church, 46–47.

however, was to demolish the old hypothesis of an Alexandrian 'canon'[75] and to raise probing, if ill-defined, questions as to the significance of *exclusivity* for canon and canonization.

Like Hölscher, Sundberg also kept alive the critical alternative of an aggregate collection of scripture prior to a late act of canonization, but by retaining historical priority for the Law, he differentiated himself from Hölscher and accomodated his own views to the standard theory. The result of his treatment was still a view in which the literary divisions of the canonical text marked 'successive periods of canonization.' However, Sundberg also pushed the dates for these periods of canonization closer to the Christian era, thus radicalizing the historical and theological issues regarding the relationship between the Jewish canon and the Christian Church.[76]

T. N. Swanson

The 1970 dissertation of T. N. Swanson[77] marked the first attempt to examine comprehensively the question of the canonization of the entire Old Testament which also took into account the more recent historical conclusions of twentieth-century biblical study.

Swanson impressively marshaled internal and external evidence for the history of canonization, but was hampered from the outset by a problematic distinction between 'canon' and 'scripture.'[78] 'Scripture' was defined by Swanson, rather unremarkably, as "a writing regarded as possessing divine authority."[79] He did not pursue further the meaning of this 'divine authority,' however, asserting only that this 'scripture' would have been differentiated at some point in time from other 'Jewish religious writings' based upon the attribution of such authority.[80] According to Swanson, 'canon' refers in contrast to "a closed collection of these Scriptures."[81] Thus, like Sundberg, he restricted the meaning of 'canon' to exclusivity.

---

[75] Not that such objections were new. DE WETTE had already raised major difficulties with the theory; see his Introduction, II:45–48.

[76] Cf. SUNDBERG, Protestant Canon; idem, Christian Canon; idem, Bible Canon.

[77] SWANSON, Closing. Unfortunately, this important dissertation was never published.

[78] This distinction is attributed by SWANSON to STAERK, Kanonbegriff, 105-12, but its substance can probably already be found in HÖLSCHER, Kanonisch. Overlooked by SWANSON and by others since, however, is that even though STAERK viewed a *Kanonbegriff* as a late development in Israel's history, he also believed a *Schriftbegriff* to have been correspondingly early. Thus, he placed a *Schriftbegriff* in Israel well before the second century B. C. (Kanonbegriff, 111) and envisioned an *exilic* 'book of edification' (*Erbauungsbuch*) consisting of Genesis–2 Kings, from which the Pentateuch was later separated (115-16).

[79] SWANSON, Closing, 5.

[80] Of course, such differentiation already implies a degree of delimitation. On this point, PROVAN, Canons, 10.

[81] SWANSON, Closing, 5.

At the same time, however, Swanson registered doubt as to whether it was appropriate to speak of a 'canon' of Jewish scripture at all, noting that the rabbis never used such a term and that the role of oral law within Judaism made the 'Protestant Christian sense' of canon as sole norm (*sola scriptura*) a foreign imposition.[82] Swanson further suggested that the situation within early Judaism was much more like that of Roman Catholicism, in which both Scripture *and* tradition are considered authoritative:

"The Holy Scriptures were not the sole authority in rabbinic Judaism. The oral law was of equal authority; thus the Scriptures were that part of the revealed tradition which had been written down."[83]

Here Swanson clearly assumed the rabbinic situation and extended it back into the biblical period. In addition to the general difficulties involved in dating rabbinic sources, this move created serious problems for Swanson's own argument. For example, if the oral law was always equal in authority to scripture, as Swanson claimed, why were the Pharisees considered so controversial on this point? Mk 7:1–23 made it clear that the oral law could still be critiqued on the basis of scripture in the first century A. D.

Furthermore, as much as he protested against an anachronistic 'Protestant Christian' approach, Swanson exhibited that very prejudice[84] with his notion that 'canon' is to be understood exclusively as meaning 'dogmatic' and 'closed':

"Scripture is the basis of 'canon,' inasmuch as 'canon' is Holy Scripture under dogmatic fixing. 'Canonization' is the process whereby limits are set, in which a decision is made as to what books among those popularly considered to be Holy Scripture are indeed Holy Scripture, through which the collection of Holy Scripture is defined and closed, making it impossible for any other books to come to be considered Holy Scripture."[85]

These definitions are later Christian ones; by adopting such a narrow view of canon and canonization it should be no surprise that Swanson found little firm evidence for the object of his study. It is to be noted, however, that in his reconstruction Swanson did concede, unlike Sundberg, that formal canonization *confirmed* as well as elevated the status of books 'popularly considered to be Holy Scripture.'

---

[82] Ibid., 5 n. 1.

[83] Ibid.

[84] Thus, DULLES has noted (Authority, 19) that to the best of his knowledge 'the canon never has been defined in an exclusive sense' (i. e., within Catholic tradition). Cf. FISHBANE's observation in the same volume (Exegesis, 95) that from a Jewish perspective the Torah 're-quired interpretation *for the sake of* its ongoing vitality and authority' (my emphasis).

[85] SWANSON, Closing, 6.

As skeptical as both Sundberg and Swanson were about the precise boundaries of the Old Testament canon, each continued to affirm the temporal precedence of the Pentateuch as the primary 'stage' in the formation of the literature, while considering the Prophets and Writings to be two further discrete 'stages' — just with later dates than in the standard theory. The major difference was Swanson's insistence that the Prophets had attained 'scriptural' status by the last third of the second century B. C., but remained open as a 'canonical' collection into the Christian era, when it was 'fixed' along with the Writings (in his view, sometime prior to A. D. 50).[86] However, this conclusion in particular depended upon his extremely narrow and anachronistic understanding of canonization.

J. A. Sanders

In his 1972 book, *Torah and Canon*,[87] J. A. Sanders issued a programmatic call for 'canonical criticism.'[88] At the same time, he presented an attractive, popular synthesis, incorporating the results of new trends in scholarly work and teasing out their implications for descriptions of canonization.

Sanders maintained that the character of Torah was essentially that of a 'story' or 'narrative,' rather than that of a law code.[89] This 'story' originally included much of the material in the Former Prophets[90] until Deuteronomy "displaced Joshua and its conquest narrative as the climax of the canonical period of authority."[91] This displacement, for Sanders, represented a *conscious* decision on the part of the exilic community that "...true authority lay with the mosaic period only... every fulfillment of national promise, whether the conquest, the confederation, or the monarchy... was relegated to a status below that of the patriarchal promise and the mosaic exodus and wanderings."[92] Thus Sanders, in contrast to Sundberg and Swanson, put forward much earlier dates for the phenomenon of 'canonization,' but like them he, too, maintained the historical and theological priority of the Torah and subordinated the rest of the canon to it in principle.

At the earliest level, Sanders postulated the existence of a sacred history of Torah and Former ('early') Prophets as well as an early collection of Latter

---

[86] Ibid., 378–98.

[87] J. A. SANDERS, Torah.

[88] Ibid., xvii. SANDERS viewed this methodology as the successor of Old Testament tradition criticism. In 'canonical criticism,' however, the main question had to do not only with the nature of Israel's traditions, but with the 'function' or 'authority' they exhibited in particular contexts.

[89] Ibid., 4–5.

[90] Ibid., 6. Possibly through the end of the account of Solomon in 1 Kg 11.

[91] Ibid., 44.

[92] Ibid., 45.

('name') Prophets. With regard to finding a date for the division between the Torah and 'early' Prophets, and then for the increasing 'acceptance' of the 'name' Prophets, Sanders stressed the effect of the Exile experience. In his view, the impulse for canonization was closely related to the destruction of the Temple and the resultant crisis within the community over its religious identity. Thus, although "nearly everything in both the Law and the early Prophets dated from before the Exile experience" and the 'name' Prophets contained "much from the Second Temple Period," the overall shape of both was forged in the "sixth century B. C. experience of Israel's quest for identity in the midst of radical discontinuity."[93] With this kind of formulation it may be seen that Sanders possessed a much broader understanding of canonization, but worked with a highly self-referential concept of scripture. He saw the formation of the canon primarily as the means by which Israel had described its *own* identity. He was to address less adequately, however, the way in which Israel had also heard in its scripture a *challenge* to its identity.[94]

After seeming to move beyond the consensus view, Sanders appeared largely to adopt it in the details of his position. He concluded that the 'book of the law of Moses' brought by Ezra from Babylon (Neh 8) was the Torah "as we ourselves know it today."[95] In the decision to canonize this Torah, the already extant 'early' Prophets (esp. the book of Joshua) were consciously *excluded*, canonically subordinating them to the authority of the Torah. In Sanders's reconstruction, the Pentateuch of Ezra remains the 'Torah *par excellence*,'[96] and a 'canon within the canon.'[97]

With respect to the 'name' Prophets, Sanders argued that even though they did not cite specific laws from the Torah as warrants for their message of judgment, they consistently and almost exclusively referred to Israel's 'story.' For the prophetic books, that story "bore, even in its early oral forms, an authority approaching the force of 'canon.'"[98] He went on to clarify what he meant by 'canon':

"By canon we mean here not a story or tradition, which had been stabilized and set for all time; that is only a secondary and late characteristic of canon. Rather, we mean the seat or reference of authority."[99]

The reference of authority for the prophets, Sanders maintained, was Israel's *Heilsgeschichte*.[100]

---

[93] Ibid., 7.
[94] This is also the criticism of CHILDS, OT Introduction, 56–57.
[95] SANDERS, Torah, 51.
[96] Ibid., 53.
[97] Ibid., 52.
[98] Ibid., 56.
[99] Ibid.

Sanders also asserted, however, that the prophets had relied upon the authority of their own *experience* in being called to prophesy. In the dialectic between these two 'authorities,' he explained, was the warrant for the prophetic message. All told, the prophetic collection together with the Torah formed the community's response to the 'identity crisis' of the sixth century. Here, Sanders also contrasted the stability of the literary complex Genesis–2 Kings (at the end of the sixth century) with "dynamic character of a nascent collection of prophets."[101]

In other words, despite his stimulating literary observations showing that the Law, the Former Prophets and the Latter Prophets had originated for the most part at roughly the same time in Israel's history and were deeply interrelated, Sanders nevertheless held to approximately the same standard view of canonization as in the three-stage theory. Although the Torah and the Former Prophets might have begun as a single overarching complex, the canonization of the Torah alone by Ezra and the post-exilic community had divorced the Law from the Prophets. It was against the horizon of the 'canon' of the Law that a 'canon' of Prophets had formed. In Sanders's view, therefore, the subordinate status of the prophetic books had always been recognized, even as they were being made canonical together with the Writings 'sometime early in the second century' (B. C.).[102]

In evaluating Sanders's early work, two contributions appear central. First, he faced directly the problem of the status of prophetic writings prior to Ezra. Like others before him, however, his solution was to picture their loss of authority in Ezra's time, followed by the retrieval of their authority two hundred and fifty years later. What was interesting about Sanders's reconstruction was his idea that this development had to do with the detachment of the conquest from the canonical 'story' in order to point the whole collection forward to a future fulfillment. However, this conception of 'fulfillment' was itself basically a 'prophetic' conception. Was it likely that the Prophets would have lost authority at precisely the same time the Torah was 'eschatologized'?

Second, Sanders advanced a more nuanced view of canon which was less concerned with exclusion and more *dynamic* than a term like 'authoritative scripture' would suggest. In Sanders's version, this dynamism was integrally related to the search for communal identity:

---

[100] Ibid., 76. To make his point, SANDERS adduced what he terms the 'most salient' passages: Am 2:9–11; 3:1–2; Hos 2:16–17 [14–15]; 9–10; 11:1–4; 12:9–13; 13:4–5; Mic 6:4–5; Isa 1:21–27; 5:1–7; 43:1–2; 52:11–12; 54:9–10; Jer 2:2–3; 7:21–26; 31:2–3, 31–34; Ezek 20. He allowed that the tradition referred to in First Isaiah was davidic in character rather than mosaic (Ibid., 85), but otherwise claimed the mosaic story was the 'seat of authority' for the prophets.

[101] Ibid., 91.

[102] Ibid., 94. He cited the witness of Ben Sira for this conclusion; the books of Isaiah, Jeremiah, Ezekiel and The Twelve are alluded to in Sir 48:22–49:12.

"A canon begins to *take shape* first and foremost because a question of identity or authority has arisen, and a canon begins to *become unchangeable* or invariable somewhat later, after the question of identity has for the most part been settled."[103]

The description of canonization as 'identity formation' was inevitably reductive, but the generative, literature-forming impulse which Sanders located at the heart of canonization added to the discussion a crucial aspect which had been lost whenever the canon was debated purely on the basis of 'authority' or 'exclusion,' or when an absolute distinction between 'canon' and 'scripture' was advocated.

Sanders emphasized just this aspect of the canon in his companion article to *Torah and Canon*, entitled 'Adaptable for Life: The Nature and Function of Canon.'[104] Explaining how his approach emphasized canon as *function* rather than *closure*,[105] Sanders perceptively illuminated the generative dimension of the canonical process.

"There was no set creed, like Deut 26:5–9, that was expandable. But there was a story existing in many forms from early days... The nature of such an identifying story demanded that it be told in the words and phrases and sense-terms of the generation and local community reciting it. Adaptability, therefore, is not just a characteristic; it is a compulsive part of the very nature of the canonical story."[106]

Even though Sanders had previously stressed the 'adaptability' of the canonical 'story,' he now expressed the way in which the story itself *compelled* rereading and adaptation. Further, he drew attention to the fact that the traditional understanding of the text's ability to give 'life' was directly related to the persistent *claim* of the text upon each new generation of faith.[107] This description greatly illuminated the nature of 'authority' within the canonical process.

Sanders attempted to address the social and religious dimensions of canonization by developing an elaborate theory of the hermeneutical circle at work between communal experience and scriptural norm.[108] In this way, Sanders's model of 'canon' was explicitly to affirm the capacity of scripture within Israel to contradict other norms (i. e., experience)[109] and to question or

---

[103] Ibid., 91. The emphases are his.

[104] SANDERS, Adaptable.

[105] Idem, Torah, ix. Cf. his Story, 61; Canon, esp. 847.

[106] Idem, Story, 19.

[107] Ibid., 20; 30 n. 82. Cf. Ezek 33:10, 15; Sir 45:5; Jn 5:39; Rom 7:10; Gal 3:21; Aboth 2:8; 6:7.

[108] Idem, Community.

[109] SANDERS maintained, however, a primary role for the 'authority' of experience in his schema, which made his rhetoric of 'compulsion' seem at odds with his explicit formulations.

prohibit behavior as well as to generate and form identity. However, Sanders's rhetoric often stood in tension with his model. He tended to stress much more strongly the experiential side of the dialectic (i. e. 'adaptability' and 'survival') as the hallmark of the way in which the canon had functioned. The question raised by this ambiguity was central: if scripture was obedient to the needs of the community, what was to be made of Israel's self-understanding that it was obedient to scripture?[110]

S. Z. Leiman

In 1976 S. Z. Leiman attempted to correct the standard theory of canon from the perspective of later rabbinic evidence.[111] Leiman's methodology was skewed from the outset, however, not only by the difficult historical problems surrounding the use of rabbinic sources, but also by his decision only to consider references to scripture in matters of religious practice or doctrine as evidence of a book's canonical status.[112] This decision led him to make a problematic distinction between *two* further categories of 'canonical' literature: the 'inspired' and the 'uninspired.'[113]

At the same time, however, Leiman largely stayed within the general framework of the three-stage theory.[114] He emphasized the early appearance of 'canonical laws' within Israel and argued that canonization began as a legal process.[115] At first, these laws comprised Israel's 'inspired' writings; only after the Exile did they exist as canonical 'books.'[116]

Leiman further argued that there were no canonical prophetic books in the pre-exilic period because, he maintained, there were no cross references in any of them to another prophetic book.[117] On the other hand, there were references to prophetic books in the Writings (e. g., Isaiah in 2 Chr 32:32; Jer 25:12 in Dan 9:2).[118] This circumstance led Leiman to consider Dan 7–12 (second century B. C.) as the *terminus ad quem* for the closing of the prophetic canon.[119] In a move reminiscent of Freedman, Leiman based his location of an exilic *terminus a quo* for the prophetic corpus upon a examination

---

Cf. his Hermeneutics, 406: "Most biblical texts must be read, not by looking in them for models for morality, but by looking in them for mirrors of identity."

[110] In my judgment, SANDERS's attempts to ground his hermeneutical circle in a theory of 'pluralistic monotheism' have not succeeded in resolving this problem; cf. his Community.

[111] LEIMAN, Canonization.

[112] Ibid., 14–16; 127–28.

[113] Ibid., 14–15.

[114] Ibid., 16–17.

[115] Ibid., 21–24.

[116] Ibid., 25.

[117] Ibid.

[118] Ibid.

[119] Ibid., 26.

of its ostensive historical references.[120] Leiman eventually selected a date of approximately 500–450 B. C. for the collection, due primarily to its non-inclusion of Chronicles and Ezra–Nehemiah (dated quite early).[121]

Thus, Leiman arrived at a collection of Law in time the time of Ezra (Neh 8–13),[122] but a collection of Prophets existing centuries earlier than in the standard theory. The closing of the Writings he also dated much earlier, to 164 B. C. (based upon the reference in 2 Mac 2:14–15 to the literary activity of Judas Maccabeus).[123] However, Leiman did postulate that some of the Writings were likely to have been included originally among the Prophets, indicated by the survival of the expression 'the Law and the Prophets' as a designation for the entire canon (e. g., Acts 28:23; 2 Mac 15:9).[124]

With these questions and reassessments, Leiman outlined the trajectory of a counter-argument to the standard theory that others would continue to refine after him. He provided an important function in the discussion by radicalizing the question of the date of the prophetic corpus and made it impossible for anyone to work on the canon without addressing the witness of later Jewish sources. Further, he revitalized the possibility that the Church had in fact inherited a 'limited' canon from Judaism.[125] Once again, the standard theory had been found to be 'unacceptable.'[126]

J. Blenkinsopp

In 1977 J. Blenkinsopp published an innovative approach to mounting questions about the prophetic canon.[127] Blenkinsopp basically held to the standard theory, but mounted a persuasive case for the early existence of a corpus of Joshua–2 Kings, together with a deuteronomistic edition of sixth-century prophetic books, probably including the books of Isaiah, Jeremiah, Hosea, Amos, Micah, Nahum, Habakkuk and Zephaniah.

Blenkinsopp's major contribution, however, was to make explicit the implications of the standard theory for the relative authority of the Law and Prophets as canonical subcollections, arguing that in the creation of the Pentateuch the Prophets had not only been subordinated, but that this relationship had been inscribed paradigmatically in the final 'coda' to the Pentateuch in Deut 34:10–12. Blenkinsopp also argued, however, that with the inclusion of the prophetic books into the canon, the notice in Mal 3:22–24 [4:4–6] had been

---

[120] Ibid., 27.

[121] Ibid., 29.

[122] Ibid., 26.

[123] Ibid., 30.

[124] Ibid., 59 n. 287.

[125] Ibid., 135 n. 670.

[126] Ibid., 125. Cf. idem, Reflections.

[127] BLENKINSOPP, Canon.

added to readjust the hermeneutical balance of the entire canon in the direction of a more dialectical relation between Law and Prophets.

I shall examine Blenkinsopp's analysis of these two passages quite closely in Chapter Three of this essay, but a few general conclusions regarding his overall treatment are in order as part of this historical overview.

What was truly fresh about Blenkinsopp's work was his understanding of the *way* in which the biblical literature was 'canon-conscious'; namely, by providing hermeneutical *guidelines* for its own interpretation. These hermeneutical guidelines were to be found above all in the editorial conclusions to the subcollections of Law and Prophets. Blenkinsopp not only based his work upon the biblical text itself (rather than on later extra-biblical witnesses), but he made a persuasive case that these two texts (Deut 34:10–12; Mal 3:22–24 [4:4–6]) must play an important role in any reconstruction of canon formation.

As I shall illustrate later, however, a major stumbling block in his treatment was his reliance on the 'bipolar' sociological theory of O. Plöger, which led Blenkinsopp to argue for the fundamental *incompatibility* of traditions of law and prophecy within the canonical process, despite his appreciation for the antiquity and 'canon-consciousness' of the prophetic writings. In this way, his speculative sociological reconstruction finally functioned as another prop for the standard theory of canon formation.[128]

J. Conrad

In a brief article, J. Conrad argued in 1979 against the notion that the Law had ever been the sole 'canonical' or 'canon-like' (*kanonartig*) scripture of Israel, or even that the main force in the process of canon formation was legal in nature.[129] Like Lebram, he also called into question the antiquity of the understanding that the authority of the Law was greater than that of the Prophets or the Writings.

Rejecting evidence of pentateuchal priority from the LXX and the Samaritan 'schism' as inconclusive, Conrad noted how Ben Sira placed the Law and the Prophets on equal footing.[130] Exploring internal Old Testament evidence for canonization, he observed that recent biblical study was increasingly suggesting the Pentateuch had actually functioned as part of a fuller collection, either with the book of Joshua (e. g., G. Fohrer) or with the entire Deuter-

---

[128] Central to this reconstruction was thus the subordination of the Prophets; cf. CRÜSEMANN, Vaterland.

[129] CONRAD, Frage.

[130] Ibid., 12–13.

onomistic History (e. g., M. Noth).[131] In either case, Conrad found it very unlikely that the Pentateuch could have been separated from these other writings, set apart as Israel's only canonical scripture, but then *recombined* with them by the end of the third century B. C. (e. g., Ben Sira). Far more likely, according to him, was that the Pentateuch had *always* been part of a larger whole together with the Former Prophets.

Concluding that "Die Entstehung des Kanons ist nicht die geradlinige Folge einer Vergesetzlichung der Religion Israels,"[132] Conrad rejected the view that this pre-canonical 'canon-like' scripture of Israel functioned primarily as a legal code. To be sure, there were fundamentally 'legal' elements within the canon, but it was the *theological* dimension which had received the greater stress within the whole, he argued. Seen as a scriptural unity:

"...es geht doch nicht einseitig um den fordernden und ordnenden Gott, sondern vor allem um den, der Israel erwählt und mit großer Geduld and Treue durch die Geschichte geführt hat und weiterführen will, auch wenn das nicht ausschließt, daß er streng fordert und entsprechend straft. Es geht um den Gott, dem man sich anvertrauen und auf den man hoffen kann, der unter seinem Volk auch aus selbstverschuldeten Katastrophen einen Ausweg schafft."[133]

Although the circumstances of the post-exilic age would encourage a greater emphasis upon the need for legal regimentation within Israel's communal life, the message of its canon continued to stress God's grace as well as his law throughout the course of its earlier history.

For Conrad, like Sanders, this meant that the impulse behind canon formation was historical and theological (*geschichtstheologisch*) rather than legal. Drawing upon Lebram's work, Conrad maintained that the legal conception of Torah was a secondary development within the history of Judaism. In the face of a threatening syncretistic Hellenism, Judaism had found it necessary to create a legal core out of its tradition, forming a canon within the canon, the present Pentateuch.[134] Originally, however, Israel's scripture had arisen from a desire to understand and transmit a theology of history, which was still recoverable in the present form of the canon. Thus, Conrad concluded, the linear

---

[131] Ibid., 14; cf. n. 18. CONRAD believed that the Latter Prophets also had a 'canon-like' significance' (*kanonartige Bedeutung*) by about the same time as the Former Prophets, but he did not address this possibility in any detail.

[132] Ibid., 15: "The formation of the canon ist not the direct consequence of a nomisticization of the religion of Israel."

[133] Ibid.: "...it is however not one-sidedly about the demanding and organizing God, but rather above all about him, who chose and led Israel with great patience and faithfulness and wants to lead further, even if that does not exclude that he strictly demands and correspondingly punishes. It is about the God to whom one can entrust one's self and in whom one can hope, who among his people finds a way out of even their self-made catastrophes."

[134] Ibid., 16.

three-stage theory of canon formation represented an 'improper simplification' (*unzulässige Vereinfachung*).[135]

Despite his brief format, Conrad neatly summarized a central problem within the field, offered a counter-proposal and pointed to the important theological issues that hung in the balance. He showed how the field had begun to formulate new exegetical positions on individual books and collections within the Old Testament without addressing the implications of these positions for the history of canon formation. A contradiction had continued to widen between the results of historical scholarship of the literature and the standard theory of the canon. Because it was so brief, Conrad's own reconstruction of the history of the canon remained sketchy. However, his critique deepened dissatisfaction with the standard theory and increased the pressure to formulate a comprehensive alternative.

B. S. Childs

Considerable reluctance to assume the priority of the Law over the Prophets was apparent in B. S. Childs's 1979 *Introduction to the Old Testament as Scripture*.[136] Stating that the standard theory of canon formation had undergone 'serious erosion,' Childs called attention to the fundamental need within the field to reflect more thoroughly upon the hermeneutical significance of the biblical canon.[137] Drawing examples from the recent history of scholarship, he argued persuasively that while scholars such as Hölscher, Sundberg and Swanson had mistakenly divorced the literary growth of the Bible from the process of its canonization, scholars such as Freedman and Leiman had inappropriately fused the two.[138]

On the one hand, Childs maintained, assuming 'canon' to be a purely late, dogmatic notion had the effect of either dismissing the religious authority of biblical texts prior to their canonization altogether (e. g., Hölscher), or conceiving of their religious authority as merely inspirational rather than normative (e. g., 'scripture' rather than 'canon' in Sundberg, Swanson). On the other hand, however, to make little distinction between religious authority and canonization had led either to the ignoring of important features in the historical growth of the literature (e. g., Freedman, Leiman) or to a reinterpretion of the

---

[135] Ibid., 16.

[136] CHILDS, OT Introduction. The main roots of CHILDS's approach were twofold. On the one hand, he cited K. Barth as a major influence; see CHILDS, Barth. Cf. SCALISE, Hermeneutics. On the other hand, CHILDS shared a form-critical insight into the formation of the canon with ACKROYD, CLEMENTS and J. A. SANDERS. See CHILDS's Response, esp. 52: "In one sense, I have simply extended the insights of the form critical method which called for an exact description of the material's literary genre."

[137] CHILDS, OT Introduction, 53.

[138] Ibid., 54–55.

religious authority of the texts in terms of a speculative hermeneutical process (e. g., Sanders). Either way, Childs noted, "much of the present confusion over the problem of the canon turns on the failure to reach an agreement regarding the terminology."[139]

Having surveyed what he judged to be unsatisfactory directions, Childs then proceeded to chart his own course. Noting that the term 'canon' possessed both a historical and a theological dimension, he argued for a thoroughly dialectical approach to the problem. Like Sanders, he saw a long, complex process of growth preceding canonization. Much more than Sanders, however, Childs emphasized the *other* direction of the hermeneutical circle to which Ackroyd had initially given expression: not only did Israel 'shape' the biblical text through a historical and theological process of selecting, collecting and ordering the literature, but *the text authoritatively shaped Israel*, giving the *community* "its form and content in obedience to the divine imperative."[140]

The full recognition of this aspect of canon formation led Childs to make a crucial claim regarding the integrity of the 'canonical process':

"The formation of the canon was not a late extrinsic validation of a corpus of writings, but involved a series of decisions deeply affecting the shape of the books. Although it is possible to distinguish different phases within the canonical process — the term canonization would then be reserved for the final fixing of the limits of scripture — the earlier decisions were not qualitatively different from the later."[141]

Here Childs admitted that the term 'canonization' might in fact be properly reserved for the final stage of the process in which scripture became fixed and delimited, as Sundberg and Swanson had argued. He maintained, however, that this final stage could not be viewed as an isolated and extrinsic procedure, but was intrinsically connected to the earlier stages of the literature's growth. Prior to canonization there was a long history of interaction between Israel and its God which continued to be reflected in the literary form of the biblical books. The 'theocentric dimension' of this process guaranteed for Childs that earlier 'decisions' in the editing of the books were not 'qualitatively' different from decisions of canonization, i. e., they were just as normative for Israel's faith.

By insisting on this 'theocentric dimension' Childs sought to make clear his difference from Sanders:

---

[139] Ibid., 51.

[140] Ibid., 58–59.

[141] Ibid., 59. Although CHILDS does not himself call attention to EISSFELDT's influential formulation (see discussion above), note the similarity between the two at this point. Even if there was no direct influence in this case, it is again evident that both formulations essentially rely upon the same form-critical understanding of the nature of religious tradition.

"Israel did not testify to its own self understanding, but by means of a canon bore witness to the divine source of its life. The clearest evidence for this position is found in the consistent manner in which the identity of the canonical editors has been consciously obscured, and the only signs of an ongoing history are found in the multilayered text of scripture itself. The shape of the canon directs the reader's attention to the sacred writings rather than to their editors."[142]

Thus, Childs argued the seemingly contradictory point that the canonical process was 'conscious,' yet largely anonymous. In his view, it was the *theocentric* focus of the literature and its tradents that lay behind these two claims and joined them together.

In other words, he argued, to characterize the development of the canon as an existential search for identity and to 'psychologize' its tradents (e. g., Sanders) would ultimately serve only to diminish the theological character of Israel's scriptures and obscure the quality of 'coercion' that was characteristic of them from the very beginning. In this way, the theocentric focus of the tradents themselves had resulted in the futility of reconstructing the social-historical dynamics of the canonical process: the object of interpretation was the *text* that the tradents had transmitted as an abiding witness, and not the reconstructed historical processes behind their intentions.

For Childs, the reinterpretation of Israel's scripture as an adaptation to the changing needs of the community was the hallmark of later *commentary* (e. g., the *targumim*), rather than of the Bible itself.[143] The biblical dynamic was different in kind. Thus, his support for the theocentric interpretation of biblical texts over against anthropocentric readings did *not* proceed from dogmatic grounds (e. g., any methodological recourse to revelation or salvation-history), but rather from the *historical* premise that Israel itself possessed a theocentric perspective as it developed its canon.[144]

Childs freely admitted the existence of intertextuality and reinterpretation within the canon. Unlike Sanders, however, he did not see this reinterpretation as arising primarily from the needs of the community and the exigencies of its situation,[145] although he did not ignore this direction of the hermeneutical cir-

---

[142] Ibid.

[143] Ibid.

[144] This premise confirms CHILDS's connection to VON RAD. Cf. the comments of VON RAD (OT Theology, I:105–06) as to the necessity of constructing an Old Testament theology on the basis of 'Israel's own explicit assertions.' (For an account of the controversy which followed this formulation, see REVENTLOW, Problems, 65–71.) By illuminating the irreversible extent to which Israel's 'own assertions' have shaped every aspect of Old Testament literature, CHILDS effectively extended VON RAD's theological claim to function as a general hermeneutical principle. For CHILDS, the Old Testament is capable of many kinds of readings, but ultimately misread if not read as 'scripture.'

[145] CHILDS, OT Introduction, 79.

cle either.[146] Especially during the final stages of the formation of the biblical canon a 'skilful use of literary techniques, word-plays, and proto-midrashic exegesis'[147] emerged, coming to full flower in the rabbinic period. Following a suggestion of I. L. Seeligmann,[148] however, Childs held that even here the developing canon *itself* was the major factor in this process of reinterpretation. Such reinterpretation arose *primarily* from a 'consciousness of canon' (*Kanonbewußtsein*), rather than from a need to contemporize or make the biblical text 'relevant.'[149]

This late midrashic development, Childs maintained, thus illustrated in a secondary and derivative way the primary dynamic at work in the canonical process. That primary dynamic was always to transmit "the divine word in such a form as to lay authoritative claim upon the successive generations."[150] With this formulation, Childs made a historical case for the 'pre-canonical' consciousness of canonical 'authority.' In his view, any critical reading of the biblical text which ignored this kind of 'canon-consciousness' would therefore result in an inadequate interpretation of the biblical text on *historical* as well as theological grounds.[151]

Childs differentiated in his own work between the history of the Old Testament literature and the history of canon formation. Arguing that critics in the Wellhausen tradition had sought to correlate the two processes too closely,[152] Childs expressed skepticism about the possibility of neatly defining the two processes with respect to each other. The two were distinct in character, he maintained, and could not simply be fused. Thus, to a much greater extent than many of his predecessors, Childs acknowledged and warned against the historical speculation all too often involved in the historical reconstruction of the development of the canon. Of utmost concern to him was the fact that such speculation frequently dismissed from the outset precisely that theocentric dimension of canon formation which he held to be of primary importance.

---

[146] Which is precisely the reason why Childs, to the confusion of his more literary-minded readers (e. g., PROVAN, Canons, 26–30), spends so much time in his books rehearsing and debating historical-critical arguments.

[147] CHILDS, OT Introduction, 60.

[148] SEELIGMANN, Voraussetzungen.

[149] Cf. CHILDS, Analysis, 363.

[150] Idem, OT Introduction, 60.

[151] Thus CHILDS's insistence on the correctness of interpreting the Old Testament theologically is ultimately historically-grounded and not dogmatically-based, as some of his critics have alleged.

[152] E. g., the identification of Josiah's 'lawbook' (2 Kg 22–23) with a form of the book of Deuteronomy and the interpretation of the promulgation of that book as the beginning of the canonical process.

Despite the risk involved, however, Childs also attempted to describe the historical formation of the canon. In a way reminiscent of Margolis, he credited the tradition of mosaic authorship (Deut 31:24–26) as being the originating tradition for the canon, although noting that the scope of the law ascribed to Moses could not be fixed with any precision. Rather than viewing Josiah's discovery of the 'book of the law' (2 Kg 22–23) as the beginning of the canonical process, and thereby discrediting other traditions that figured earlier in the literature, Childs saw this episode as a further step in a process already previously begun, a confirmation of the 'already existing authority of the Mosaic law.'[153]

Evidence for the continued development of the canon was then provided by the redactional framework surrounding the Former Prophets, Childs claimed. He noted that in the book of Joshua "the leadership of the nation is not conceived of as an extension of Moses' office, but is pictured as dependent upon the divine law revealed to Moses and preserved in book form (cf. Jos 1:8; 4:10, etc.)."[154] It was the importance granted to the written word in these pre-canonical traditions which Childs took as an indication of the ongoing authority of Israel's developing biblical literature.

Observing that the laws recorded in Neh 8:13–18 reflected the Priestly code, Childs agreed that the Pentateuch probably took its final shape at about the time of Ezra. He also noted, however, that the literary history at this point is not fully clear; nor is the precise form of the 'Torah' to which the account refers. As for the Prophets, Childs was unpersuaded by arguments for an exilic 'canon' (e. g., Freedman, Leiman), but did not offer an alternative canonical *terminus a quo* for the prophetic collection. As others had done, he located a *terminus ante quem* for the Prophets at the time of Ben Sira (ca. 180 B. C.).

Childs went on, however, to note aspects of 'canon-consciousness' in *pre-exilic* prophetic preaching:

> "In both Isa. 8.16 and Jer. 36.1ff. one sees the transition from the spoken prophetic word to a written form with authority. Later, there is reference in Zech. 1.4ff. to the 'former prophets' whose writings appear to have a form and authoritative status. The exegesis within the Bible itself in the post-exilic period begins to cite earlier oracles *verbatim* as an authoritative text which it seeks to interpret (cf. Isa. 65, 25, which echoes Isa. 1.6ff.[sic]). Finally, Dan 9.2 offers evidence of some sort of fixed collection of prophetic writings."[155]

Here Childs had detected a move from oral to written word lodged deep within the prophetic traditions. As to the precise way in which this had occurred in Israel's history, Childs refused to speculate. He judged Lebram's view to be unpersuasive and Clements's work as most probably correct. In

---

[153] Ibid., 63.

[154] Ibid.

[155] Ibid., 65. The citations for the book of Isaiah should read Isa 65:25 and 11:6ff.

other words, although he did not view as likely the possibility that authoritative prophetic writings had preceded the canonical authority of the Law, he could conceive of the way in which the authority of Moses, especially if he was understood to have been a prophet (as in the deuteronomistic protrayal), might have been extended to developing prophetic books.

It was the signs of mutual influence between the two developing collections of Law and Prophets which suggested to Childs that Clements had been right:

"...the canonical process should not be conceived of as a closed section of Law to which the Prophets were joined only secondarily. At an early date the two collections, Law and Prophets, were joined and both experienced expansion. By the first century B. C. both sections of the canon were regarded as normative scripture..."[156]

To say any more than this, from Childs's perspective, was to engage in too much speculation. The biblical or extra-biblical sources necessary to reconstruct more of the history of canon formation were simply absent. For this reason, Childs proceeded to chart the way in which the interpretation of the biblical texts *themselves* could provide an account of the inner dynamic of canon formation. This was accomplished by studying the literary structure of the final form of each book, with an eye toward the editorial history implied by its received form. He called this kind of interpretation a 'canonical approach' to the biblical text.[157]

In the course of his discussion of individual texts, however, Childs offered a few further remarks concerning the relationship between Law and Prophets as canonical subcollections. First, he agreed with Sanders[158] that, despite indications that the early pentateuchal material told Israel's story from 'creation to conquest,' the final form of the Pentateuch was to be read as a theological decision by the post-exilic community to exclude the possession of the land from what was to be constitutive for its faith.[159] In other words, the significance of the land lay in its promise, not its past. Childs also cited R. Rendtorff[160] to the effect that there was evidence of a 'canon-conscious' editing of the entire Pentateuch after the point at which the last literary sources were combined. Childs took Rendtorff's evidence to indicate that the various parts

---

[156] Ibid.

[157] Ibid., 82.

[158] J. A. SANDERS, Torah.

[159] CHILDS, OT Introduction, 131.

[160] RENDTORFF, Problem. CHILDS gives RENDTORFF's example of the redacted promise formula 'the land which he swore to Abraham, Isaac and Jacob' (Gen 22:16; 23:6; 24:7; 50:24; also in Ex), which presumes the entirety of the pentateuchal story it serves to link.

of the Pentateuch were cross-referenced in the final stages of editing according to "the promises of the past or to an anticipation of the future."[161]

With respect to the Former Prophets, Childs emphasized the key role of the
book of Joshua as the literary link between Law and Prophets. As Noth had
perceived, Childs saw Joshua as dependent upon the laws of Deuteronomy,
but for Childs Joshua was not to be considered as simply a deuteronomistic
extension. The book frequently referred to Deuteronomy as 'the book of the
Torah.'[162] In Childs's view, the figure of Joshua was depicted as executing
mosaic law rather than as holding mosaic office. In this way the book of
Joshua functioned literarily to connect the later prophetic books with Deuteronomy even as it reappraised hermeneutically the significance of the Pentateuch as a whole.[163]

Furthermore, Childs thought that the Former Prophets had been structured
generally to accord with the covenant stipulations of Deut 28. Again influenced by Noth, Childs observed:

> "Not only is the correspondence between the prophecy and fulfilment continually made
> clear, but at crucial points in the history long 'Deuteronomic' speeches are inserted, which
> interpret theologically the course of Israel's history in the light of the Book of the Law (Deut
> 27–28; Josh. 1:2ff.; 22.1ff.; Judg. 2.6ff.; I Sam. 12; I Kings 8; II Kings 17 and 24)."[164]

Childs viewed this phenomenon as an attempt to coordinate evolving scriptural collections of Law and Prophets at a relatively early period in the history
of canon formation. However, Childs also saw the diversity of materials contained in the Former Prophets as an argument against Noth's conception of a
single 'author' who exercised an unofficial role and viewpoint in the shaping
of the final collection. Whatever theological concerns were at work within
this process, they clearly did *not* enforce a reduction of the variety of traditions and genres included in the final form of the literature.

Rather than expressing the compiler's own *personal* theology of history (as
in Noth's treatment), Childs reckoned with the 'canonical' force of the previ-
ously-existing traditions:

> "A far more plausible explanation would be to assume that the material which the final
> redactor gathered and shaped had already exerted such an 'official' force on the community
> by its use that he was unable or unwilling to attempt a change. Far from being the idiosyn-
> cratic opinion of one author, the shaping of the Former Prophets reflects a long process within
> the community of Israel which incorporated the witness of many earlier generations and thus

---

[161] CHILDS, OT Introduction, 132.
[162] E. g., Jos 1:8; 4:10; 8:3, 32, 35; etc.
[163] CHILDS, OT Introduction, 232–34.
[164] Ibid., 234.

acknowledged the authority which previous stages of the literature had already exerted through use."[165]

Here Childs succeeded in formulating additional reasons for the unity of Law and Prophets which Clements had proposed. In the case of *both* the Law and the Former Prophets, the religious authority of these growing collections of texts had existed from early on and was still recognizable in the ways each had shaped the other. The authority of each collection had forged connections between them and shaped them towards each other. At the level of final redaction, the Law had been eschatologized, even as the Former Prophets were shaped nomistically.

Examining the Latter Prophets, Childs decided against granting any great significance to the order of the books. Largely on the basis of the variant orders within the manuscript tradition, but also on the basis of the shaping of the individual prophetic books, he concluded that "the major effect of the canonical process lay... in producing a new entity of a prophetic collection which functioned within the canon as a unified block over against the Torah."[166] Although Childs acknowledged that a concern for chronology, catchword connections, or even mechanical factors appeared to have played a role in this process, in his view the historical forces involved in the collecting and ordering of the prophetic books remained obscure.[167]

Childs adduced the book of Jeremiah as the best example of the way in which individual prophetic books had been 'shaped' against the horizon of the Law. The deuteronomistic shaping of the book presented Jeremiah as standing within a series of prophets (e. g., Jer 25:4) who preached repentance and obedience to the Torah (i. e., Deuteronomy). The deuteronomistically-influenced form of the early chapters (Jer 1–25) and the final chapter (Jer 52) indicated how the prophet was viewed in later tradition:

"In light of the ensuing events of history, culminating particularly in the destruction of Jerusalem in 587, Jeremiah was understood as the prime example of the messenger of God — a picture shared and decisively formed by the scriptural tradition of Deuteronomy — who forecast the divine judgment."[168]

This reshaping of the prophet's original message according to *scripture*, Childs argued, should not be interpreted as a corruption or a distortion, but rather an 'authentic' interpretation of Jeremiah's ministry and significance. The new interpretation operated largely at the level of the prose tradition within the book, with the result that both continuity and discontinuity could be

---

[165] Ibid., 236.
[166] Ibid., 310.
[167] Ibid., 308–09.
[168] Ibid., 346.

registered in the comparison between poetry ('A material') and prose sections ('C material'), and between Jeremiah's original historical profile and the tradition's reshaping of him.

However, the continuity was clearly greater than the discontinuity for Childs. If deuteronomistic tradition had to a great extent 'absorbed' the original profile of the prophet, he asserted, it was also the case that "both Jeremiah's message and his office were immediately understood by his audience in terms congruent with the Dtr. intrepretation of the C prose." For this reason, he argued, the biographical prose of the book ('B material') was also "fully in accord with the Dtr. portrayal" and not "built on the early poetic material."[169] For Childs, then, the deuteronomistic Jeremiah reflected faithfully the effort on the part of subsequent tradition to hear the enduring address of God in the prophet's legacy.

In effect, Childs maintained that the deuteronomistic shaping of Jeremiah functioned largely to establish a close relation between the Law and the Prophets within the book. Instead of providing details about Josiah's reform, the biblical tradition:

"...placed Jeremiah within the tradition of preachers of the law and provided the later community with a prophetic interpretation of how the law properly functioned within the divine economy. To take this interpretation seriously rules out both an alleged conflict between the law and the prophets, and also a legalistic subordination of the latter into a minor role."[170]

In Childs's analysis, continuity thus ultimately prevailed over discontinuity. His assertion, however, that the deuteronomistic interpretation of the prophet Jeremiah was 'authentic' (i. e., not qualitatively different from the prophet's original historical profile) seemed to rely on an understanding of the general character of the 'canonical process' which in turn had to be inferred from the literary layers of the book. The reasoning was unavoidably circular. Of course, Childs might still be correct, and if he was, it was difficult not to grant the reasonableness of his conclusions. Jeremiah certainly provided additional evidence of the coherent deuteronomistic unity of Law and Prophets which Clements had set out.

Of central importance, however, was Childs's insight regarding the nature of this hermeneutical unity. To see prophetic traditions as being framed by legal traditions within the canon did not indicate that the Prophets were subordinated to the Law and relegated to the status of commentary, because the framing was dialectical. Within the present shape of the canon, the Law and the Prophets comprised equal and complementary voices within a single divine economy.

---

169 Ibid., 350.
170 Ibid., 353.

Writing more recently, Childs has emphasized the antiquity of law in Israel, criticizing those (e. g., Perlitt) who view the covenantal tradition as a deuteronomistic conception.[171] In spite of his earlier approval of Clements's revision of the history of canon formation, in his *Biblical Theology* Childs flatly equates the traditional view and the history of canonization: "The 'law of Moses' was first received as authoritative and only secondarily was the prophetic corpus canonized."[172] Later in the same volume, Childs conveys his judgment that not only would it be "inconceivable... to reverse the canonical order," but also that "the prophets can only be understood by assuming the authority of Israel's ancient covenantal law which they used as a warrant for their message of divine judgment (Am 2:6–16; Hos 4:1–3; Micah 6:1ff.)."[173]

At the same time, Childs makes haste to add that within the final form of the canon the subcollection of the Prophets possesses its own 'canonical integrity' and, *contra* Blenkinsopp, "is not in principle subordinated to the Torah."[174] However, Childs grounds this conclusion in the vitality of the prophetic collection's contents and the freedom of its overall presentation, rather than in any explicit textual warrant for a dialectical relationship between the two subcollections.

In my judgment, Childs has argued persuasively for the antiquity of legal traditions and their importance for prophecy. However, his most recent argument for the historical priority of the Torah is made on tradition-historical rather than canonical grounds. Certainly the influence of prophetic traditions is present just as strongly in the Torah as *vice versa*.[175] Uncharacteristically absent on Childs's part is the effort to gauge how later tradition has reflected upon the two subcollections and their mutual claims to authority. Otherwise, it is difficult to see how the Prophets can be successfully defended against the claim that they have been subordinated in principle, especially if despite the freedom of their presentation they are interpreted as merely drawing out the implications of the Law.[176]

Recent Proposals

The years following the publication of Childs's landmark *Introduction* have seen a remarkable interest in his particular proposals and in canonical issues

---

[171] CHILDS, Biblical Theology, 134–36.

[172] Ibid., 136–37.

[173] Ibid., 174.

[174] Ibid., 175.

[175] Ibid., 169–70.

[176] Ibid., 175.

generally.[1] In the following chapters of this essay I shall engage various proposals by those who have taken up since then the challenge of investigating canon formation and 'canonical' ways of interpreting the biblical text. It will prove helpful now, however, to summarize briefly the work of several of these scholars, focusing on the role of the standard three-stage theory in their reconstructions and the fundamental question of the relation between the Law and the Prophets.

J. Barr

Since at least as early as in 1973 J. Barr has urged for a clearer distinction between notions of canon as authority and as exclusion.[2] Conceding that there is 'no fixed point' within Israel's history at which a decision had been made to record 'all existing valued religious tradition' or to confer scriptural authority upon 'such written documents,'[3] Barr nevertheless argues for a restriction of the term 'canon' to the 'marking of the exact boundary of scripture.'[4] His rationale for this restriction is closely related to his theological position that the authority of the Bible is extrinsic, i. e., 'not from its own character and nature, but from the events which it relates.'[5]

In Barr's view, 'canon' therefore refers to a late, extrinisic codification of material according to "the principle that there is a holy scripture already recognized but with some degree of fuzziness at the edges thereto."[6] This kind of definition means critically that the dispute over 'marginal writings' becomes the single-most important indication of the canonical process at work.[7]

Barr continues to hold to the standard three-stage theory, however, prompting the question of how this theory can function without three 'fixed points' of official decision. This (unacknowledged) inconsistency leads Barr to argue further that, properly speaking, the Torah and the Prophets have never really been *canonized* at all![8] However, Barr does believe that a 'principle of the *canon*' was established in the deuteronomistic movement[9] that

---

[1] For a sampling of recent criticism regarding CHILDS and his approach, see BRETT, Crisis? KRAUTER, Programm; NOBLE, Approach; OEMING Text.

[2] BARR, Bible.

[3] Ibid., 116.

[4] Ibid., 155.

[5] Ibid., 24–25. BARR goes on to include within his understanding of biblical authority the faith of those who responded to those events as well as the 'saving content' of the events themselves. The relationship between the event and the response of faith is, however, precisely at issue. See CHILDS, Response, 57: "...there is no direct access to the fullness of that extrinsic reality on which the faith was grounded apart from Israel's own testimony."

[6] Ibid., 155.

[7] Ibid.

[8] Idem, Scripture, 51–52.

[9] Ibid., 7. His emphasis.

guided the formation of two scriptural collections: the 'story' that later became Genesis–2 Kings and the 'set of books named after prophets' (later the
Latter Prophets).[10]

On the basis of this reconstruction, Barr allows for the theoretical likelihood that the 'recognition' of the prophetic corpus might have been earlier
than the 'recognition' of the Torah. Since he maintains, however, that the Torah has always been regarded as supremely authoritative, he concludes that
prophetic scripture, although already religiously authoritative, "continued to
have that recognition, but necessarily in a position less dominant than the Torah."[11] Here Barr concedes that such a reconstruction entails a much earlier
date than usual for a scriptural collection of Prophets and notes the irony of
this fact in relation to Wellhausen's hypothesis.[12]

Barr goes on to discuss the possibility that the tripartite canon had originally been bipartite, with the initial inclusion among the Prophets of books
now found in the Writings.[13] According to Barr, the basic conception behind
the canon's bipartite shape was that "any non-Torah book that was holy
scripture was a 'Prophet' (e. g., 2 Mac 15:9)."[14] The Writings are said to have
been only gradually accorded a separate subdivision within the canon, but
Barr is not specific about just how or when this was done.[15]

Barr rejects Sundberg's thesis of the Torah plus 'a wide religious literature
without definite bounds' in this period, suggesting instead that Torah and
Prophets be conceived as "something more like a backbone, securely established, for the Torah and most, if not all, of the Prophets, plus the Psalms, and
beyond that a placing of other books at greater or lesser proximity..."[16] Addi-
tionally, Barr questions with characteristic ferocity unexamined assumptions
regarding the significance of canonical order, a monolithic view of ancient
Judaism and a conciliar view of canonization (e. g., Jamnia).[17]

Barr strongly criticizes Child's work, charging him with being inconsistent
in his terminology and attributing too much intentionality to the 'final form'
of the canon.[18] In Barr's view, 'no hermeneutical guidance' is given by the

---

[10] Ibid., 52.

[11] Ibid., 52–53.

[12] Ibid., 53.

[13] Ibid., 54.

[14] Ibid., 55.

[15] Ibid., 56.

[16] Ibid., 57; cf. 61. BARR appears to have misunderstood SUNDBERG on this point; see
discussion of SUNDBERG above.

[17] Ibid., 57–58.

[18] Ibid., 75–104; esp. 95: "...the canonical text... is not a faithful index of the religious
changes which affected its own development, and conversely the religion of any particular
time is not exactly reflected in scripture."

received form of the text.[19] Yet, Barr continues to affirm a 'principle of canon' back to 'the time of David and Solomon'(!): "...a sort of core of central and agreed tradition, a body of writings already recognized and revered" in the 'pre-canonical' period. Decisive appears to be Barr's methodological presupposition of discontinuity between such a 'pre-canon' and the received form of the canon.[20]

One effect of Barr's criticism has been to give a particular polemical thrust to the counter-argument against Childs's work for other scholars examining Old Testament canon formation, especially in Britain.[21] Also, his understanding of canon as 'delimitation' and 'exclusion' has helped to shift scholarly attention to issues regarding the closing of the canon and contributed to the way in which scholarship on the 'pre-canonical' intertextuality of the Bible has been kept separate from reconstructions of canon formation. This result seems unfortunate in light of Barr's own references to a 'canonical principle' and a 'core canon' which existed well *before* the canon was 'closed.'

J. Barton

J. Barton has followed very much in Barr's footsteps, operating with the same 'exclusive' understanding of canon.[22] In particular, Barton's work represents an impressive working out of the proposal made by Barr that all 'non-Torah' books were regarded as 'Prophets' prior to the closing of the canon.[23] Beginning with ancient extra-biblical sources, Barton works within the outlines of the kind of canonical process that Barr describes, applying a wide range of textual witnesses in support of Barr's theory.

Barton argues that the evidence of the extra-biblical sources (e. g., Ben Sira, Philo, Josephus, Baba Bathra 14b–15a) regarding the closure of the canon is fundamentally 'ambivalent.'[24] In his view, this 'ambivalence' indicates that the collections of Prophets and Writings remained open into the first century A. D., resulting eventually in what actually should be viewed as the two different canons of Judaism and Christianity.[25] Here Barton is even more insistent than Barr as to the way in which the attribution of significant order, harmonization or intertextuality of books is a function of their canonical,

---

[19] Ibid., 67; 98.

[20] Ibid., 83–84.

[21] Ibid., 130–71 ('Appendix II'); cf. idem, Introduction.

[22] BARTON, Oracles, 56: "...to speak of a 'canon' is to say that *at most* this particular group of books has authoritative status — or... *only these books*."

[23] BARTON acknowledges his debt to BARR in Oracles, 'Preface'; 44. Cf. the remarks of BARR, Scripture, 95–98. See also, however, BARTON, Prophets? 16, where BARTON states that much of his work in this article predated BARR's book.

[24] Ibid., 44–95.

[25] Cf. his Significance.

rather than scriptural, standing.[26] The absence of such features thus denotes the absence of canonization, according to Barton.

At the same time, however, Barton offers a closely argued defense of the theory that Israel's scripture possessed a bipartite structure prior to its later, more well-known tripartite form.[27] He even perceives a late canonical conception of 'Moses and the Prophets' as 'two ages in sacred history.'[28] Following Barr, however, he continues to grant the Torah 'pride of place,'[29] and suggests that the authors of Chronicles and Ezra–Nehemiah sought to impose another conception onto the canon by extending Israel's sacred history into the Persian period.[30] Although Barton at first suggested that the rationale for the eventual subdivision of the Writings from the Prophets was a consequence of the early synagogue liturgy,[31] he has more recently pronounced it 'mysterious.'[32]

Although Barton's thesis maintains that only the Law was 'closed' (and *therefore* canonical) in the first century A. D., it is often overlooked that he largely confirms the existence and *authoritative status* of most, if not all, of the books of the Prophets and Writings at a very early date.[33] In addition, Barton has raised important questions about how 'prophets' and 'the Prophets' were understood in antiquity. Although he is able to illuminate impressively that a variety of such understandings were available at the turn of the millenium, his use of such late witnesses makes for the ever-present danger of an anachronistic view of 'prophets' and 'Prophets' within the Old Testament itself. Writing more recently, Barton shows increased appreciation for more 'inclusive' definitions of 'canon,' and the difference such definitions make for reconstructions of canon formation.[34]

---

[26] Asserted most clearly in BARTON, Oracles, 72. BARTON does appear to allow for 'reinterpretation' within authoritative scripture (78).

[27] BARTON, Oracles, 44.

[28] Ibid., 78.

[29] For a strong statement of this position, see BARTON, Oracles, 171–72.

[30] Idem, Significance, 79.

[31] Idem, Oracles, 75–82.

[32] Idem, Significance, 81.

[33] Idem, Oracles, 91–92. Cf. BARTON, Writings, 112 n. 10. BARTON seems now to admit his earlier judgment that only the Torah was canonical at the turn of the millenium remains valid only to the extent an 'exclusive' understanding of canon is employed. However, he continues to insist that books other than those now included within the canon were considered *just as* authoritative in this period.

[34] BARTON, Oracles, 1–14. In this recent study of New Testament canonization, BARTON shows brilliantly how "the progressively later dating of 'canonization' from Zahn through Harnack to SUNDBERG is generated by an ever-narrowing definition for the term 'canon.'" See BARTON, Writings, 11–12; cf. idem, Significance.

R. T. Beckwith

Mounting a confessionally-driven response to the notion of an 'open canon' at the time of Jesus, R. T. Beckwith amasses an enormous amount of evidence in order to make the case for a closed tripartite canon already by the Maccabean period.[35]

Like Barton, Beckwith begins his treatment with extra-biblical witnesses to the canon, giving special weight to those of the New Testament.[36] Like Leiman, he modifies the standard theory by accepting the early existence of prophetic scripture, but argues further that the prophetic corpus was probably not venerated until after the canonization of the Pentateuch.[37] Although Beckwith does not consider seriously the possibility of the chronological priority of the Prophets over the Pentateuch, he allows that perhaps an open collection of prophetic books once 'stood alongside it.'[38]

In this way, Beckwith gradually comes to question the basic principle of Ryle's three-stage theory:

"Could it be that the earlier (often shorter) books which formed the original nuclei of certain canonical books were already, in their original shape, recognized as canonical, and then simply remained canonical as they were elaborated, completed and located in one of the three ultimate sections of the canon?"[39]

Beckwith believes such an understanding of the canon further implies that the three sections of the canon are not accidental, but the product of some kind of rationale.[40] Like Barr and Barton, he too argues that an original 'single collection of non-mosaic Scriptures' was later subdivided in order to form subcollections of Prophets and Writings.[41]

Unlike Barr, however, Beckwith follows Leiman's suggestion that this subdivision marked the closure of the canon as a whole, and attributes this accomplishment to Judas Maccabeus in 164 B. C. (cf. 2 Mac 2:14–15).[42] Beck-

---

[35] BECKWITH, Canon, 1–15; esp. 11, where he describes his effort as a defense of the Old Testament canon based upon 'its endorsement by Jesus and the apostles...' Cf. idem, Formation, which is basically a condensation of the argument in his book, absent the confessional underpinnings.

[36] BECKWITH, Canon, 7–9; 11–13. In this way, the two are perhaps more similar than different, although they themselves have only seen sharp contrast. For BECKWITH on BARTON, see BECKWITH, Theory. For BARTON on BECKWITH, see BARTON, Writings, 112 n. 10.

[37] BECKWITH, Canon, 127–38.

[38] Ibid., 132. The literary continuity between the Pentateuch and Joshua–Judges plays a major role in this conclusion.

[39] Ibid., 133. Cf. 65–68.

[40] Ibid., 137–38. Here the influence of GREEN is also apparent.

[41] Ibid., 138–80; esp. 139; 142–43; 149.

[42] Ibid., 152. As BECKWITH realizes (164), his second century dating makes the interpretation of Ben Sira crucial.

with also makes the important methodological point that, in light of the increasing sectarianism within Second Temple Judaism, the later the canon is dated the more difficult it is to explain the impressive agreement about its shape.[43] He does maintain, however, that the Law was always considered the most important part of the canon.[44]

In many ways, Beckwith's work enjoys the advantages and disadvantages of Green's almost a century before. On the one hand, he gives a persuasive account of many features in the process of Old Testament canon formation ignored or deemphasized in the standard theory. On the other hand, it is difficult to escape the sense that if the canon was arranged by a single 'rational mind' the 'rationale of the threefold structure' ought to be more perspicuous.[45] As with Green's work, one obtains the impression of 'special pleading' from Beckwith's analysis, driven by his desire to present the historical Jesus as the recipient of a closed canon of scripture.[46]

Still, in his concluding assessment Beckwith succeeds perhaps best of all in formulating the alternative conception of canonization which has been developing gradually within scholarship on this issue: "The Law was never the whole of the canon, and the other two sections were formed not so much by canonizing fresh material as by subdividing material already canonical."[47] Certainly no one else has examined this conception in relation to the extrabiblical witnesses as closely as Beckwith. If such an alternative model is to be accepted, however, the testimony of the *internal* biblical witnesses to it must be further clarified. In particular, a serious problem arises from Beckwith's use of late extra-biblical witnesses to argue that the Torah was always considered to be pre-eminent, when his own work suggests the early existence and authority of non-Torah scripture.

N. K. Gottwald

Working from an explicitly sociological perspective, N. K. Gottwald concludes in his 1985 *Introduction* that "despite the division between the two collections [of Law and Prophets], it is nonetheless evident that these two sets of traditions interacted intimately within the institutional life of Israel over approximately eight centuries from ca. 1050 to 250" (B. C.).[48] Nevertheless,

---

[43] Ibid., 152–53. An important related point is that the earliest witnesses to the canon do not assert the canonicity of scriptural books, but rather make assertions with regard to something *else* on the basis of scripture's acknowledged authority (76–77).

[44] Ibid., 143.

[45] Ibid., 154–66.

[46] Ibid., 165–66. And thus providing an unimpeachable warrant for a 'high view' of scripture.

[47] Ibid., 165.

[48] GOTTWALD, Introduction, 458.

Gottwald holds to the standard three-stage theory with only a few, albeit highly interesting, modifications.[49]

Gottwald sees the development by ca. 450 B. C. of two narrative complexes: Genesis–Numbers and Deuteronomy–2 Kings.[50] He argues that Deuteronomy was added to Genesis–Numbers to 'elevate the Law' by the formation of a Pentateuch.[51] Because the 'content and tone' of the remaining collection (Joshua–2 Kings) was 'blatantly political and military' it was not included in the community's 'written foundation,'[52] although these books continued to be read and used 'in various contexts of public life or private reading.'[53]

Eventually, the Deuteronomistic History would be joined together with the other prophetic books to form a 'logical supplement' to the Law, driven by a fundamental change in political circumstances:

"The decision to give the Deuteronomistic History the recognition it had missed in the fifth century as part of the Law was probably facilitated by a change in the political climate after the collapse of the Persian Empire. Apparently the Ptolemaic Hellenistic rulers of Palestine, who inherited the Jewish community of Palestine within their realm, were not as sensitive to ancient Jewish national independence as the Persians had been. Likewise, the temptations to Jews to misread Joshua–Kings as a stimulus to rebellion may by this time not have seemed a live danger to the Jewish leaders who did the collecting and accorded authority to the prophetic writings."[54]

Here Gottwald identifies a major problem with the standard theory of canon formation (i. e., why the Deuteronomistic History had not been canonized together with the Pentateuch) and attempts to resolve it through the attribution of a certain intentionality on the part of the tradents — in this case, however, on the reductive basis of a highly speculative reconstruction of the political context of post-exilic Israel.

Gottwald goes on to endorse the view that the final form of 'the Law and the Prophets' represents a 'consensus canon' reflecting a compromise among rival priestly factions.[55] The nature of this 'compromise' is sometimes curiously contorted, however. For example, the book of Deuteronomy is not viewed by Gottwald as having gained authority on its own merits, but as the result of a cynical move made by its *opponents*, the aaronid priesthood, to 'coopt' the book's levitical supporters. Ironically, the presence of subversive

---

[49] Ibid., 102–14. See esp. his Chart 3 on 104–05.
[50] Ibid., 106.
[51] Ibid.
[52] Ibid.
[53] Ibid., 107.
[54] Ibid.
[55] Ibid., 460–69. His emphasis.

prophetic themes in the book then allowed over time for an extension of the authority of deuteronomic law and the 'unintentional' expansion of the canon by the prophetic writings.[56]

Gottwald conjectures, following Blenkinsopp and Clements, that a collection of prophetic writings had been edited by the deuteronomists and accompanied the Deuteronomistic History since the early exilic period.[57] This collection could have included versions of Isaiah, Jeremiah, Hosea, Amos, Micah, Nahum, Habakkuk and Zephaniah, he maintains.[58] Again Gottwald identifies the supporters of this prophetic material as levitical 'protesters' and its opponents as aaronid 'establishmentarians.'[59] However, with the rise of the Torah's authority, references in the Prophets to תורה could then be read (mistakenly!) as references to the 'officially recognized' Torah.[60] The result was 'interreadings' or a 'canon-consciousness' in which the two collections were read in the light of the other.[61]

Using Blenkinsopp's work as a starting point, Gottwald grants the status of Deut 34:10–12 and Mal 3:22–24 [4:4–6] as canonical 'conclusions', but he argues that Deut 18:15–22 subverts the language of Moses' uniqueness found in Deut 34:10–12.[62] Gottwald opines further that with the placement of Law and Prophets together, deuteronomistic allusions of 'prophets yet to come' communicate a "signal to readers that the collection of Prophets was 'prophetically' foreseen by Moses the Lawgiver."[63] Similarly, the ending of the Prophets (Mal 3:22–24 [4:4–6]) remains open-ended for Gottwald: "...the final words of the Latter Prophets tell us that, although the *collection* is closed, the *work* of the prophets in the world is not finished." [64]

In sum, although Gottwald suggests some very interesting ways in which Law and Prophets might have been read and understood *intertextually* in the post-exilic period, he displays the thinnest possible notion of human agency in his reconstruction of the forces leading to the rise of those collections.[65] He

---

[56] Ibid., 462–64.

[57] Ibid., 464–65. Like CLEMENTS, GOTTWALD postulates that the 'non-mention' of the Latter Prophets within the Deuteronomistic History indicates both collections were intended to be read together.

[58] Ibid., 465.

[59] Ibid., 467.

[60] Ibid., 467–68.

[61] Ibid., 468.

[62] Ibid., 468–69.

[63] Ibid., 469.

[64] Ibid. His emphases.

[65] Ibid., 110–14; esp. 110: "The struggle to determine which of the Israelite/Jewish writings were authoritative, and in what way they were authoritative, was a struggle for power among contending groups in the community." In Gottwald's reconstruction of this struggle, 'class privilege' plays a very large role — thus, his explanation of the 'canon' as a major way

supports the three-stage theory, but never offers a compelling explanation of the status of the material in prophetic corpus prior to the date of its presumed 'official' recognition, ca. 200 B. C. Ironically, even though Gottwald is critical of previous accounts of canon formation for invoking uncritically the "public religious usage of the biblical writings," his presupposition of "a struggle for power among contending groups in the community" proves itself to be no less speculative.[66]

O. H. Steck

Writing in 1991, O. H. Steck discusses the need for greater attention to the place of the Prophets in the canonical process and subjects the entire prophetic corpus to a massive redactional analysis.[67] Like Blenkinsopp (and in contrast to Barton and Beckwith), Steck begins with the latest layers of the corpus itself, as he determines them, and attempts to reconstruct its literary development.[68] At the same time, however, Steck also assumes a sociological reconstruction of post-exilic Israel in which 'theocratic' and 'eschatological' worldviews compete for political dominance.[69]

Thus, Steck interprets the canonization of the Torah as a 'compromise' (*Kompromiß*) between these two worldviews.[70] He holds that it was interpolation of the Priestly source between Deuteronomy and the Deuteronomistic History which divided the Prophets from the Law.[71] In this way, deuteronomistic traditions were taken up and reinterpreted by the 'ruling Temple circles' (*herrschenden Tempelkreisen*), making out of the 'diverse streams' (*divergenten Strömmungen*) in post-exilic Israel a 'single unifying tradition' (*verbindende Einheitsüberlieferung*).[72]

From within this scriptural unity, however, the Law was then elevated in authority (again by Temple circles) by becoming the imperial law under Persian overlordship.[73] Steck dates this canon of Law and (Former) Prophets to 350 B. C.[74] Much like Gottwald, he argues that this canon was perceived as *anti-prophetic* and *anti-eschatological* by the theocratic circles who reworked

---

in which 'Jewish elites' attempted to gain support for their interests from 'non-elites.' For his defense of this kind of reconstruction, see GOTTWALD, Matrix.

[66] GOTTWALD, Introduction, 110.
[67] STECK, Abschluß; cf. idem, Kanon.
[68] STECK, Abschluß, 12.
[69] Ibid., 15–16.
[70] Ibid., 16.
[71] Ibid., 18.
[72] Ibid.
[73] Ibid., 19–21.
[74] Ibid., 21.

it, but that enough of its prophetic qualities remained to allow for its later interpretation in quite a different direction.

Steck then assumes that the Latter Prophets must have taken shape *after* this initial canon was formed, which means that he narrows his investigation of the prophetic corpus to the fourth through the early second centuries B. C.[75] In contrast to a book-by-book analysis, however, he begins his investigation of the Latter Prophets with a strong assertion as to the existence of 'literary layers' (*literarische Schichten*), i. e., 'horizontal' editorial layers across the entire corpus which, in his view, can therefore be organized to provide a relative chronology.[76] By harmonizing this redactional chronology with the history of the period, he argues that an 'absolute' chronology can be produced.

In Steck's reconstruction, the last pre-canonical 'layer' of the prophetic corpus (third century B. C.) can be identified by two series of 'continuations' (*Fortschreibungen*), now comprising the 'beginning' and 'end' of the corpus (i. e., the beginning of the book of Isaiah and the conclusions to the book of Malachi).[77] Thus, he expands on Blenkinsopp's insight that certain editorial changes reveal a synthetic, interpretive quality, especially at beginnings and endings.[78] From this vantage point, however, Steck then reconstructs eight extremely complex redactional 'layers' shared by Isaiah and the book of The Twelve,[79] followed by an effort to correlate these 'layers' with historical dates.[80]

The most serious methodological problem in Steck's treatment is not simply his astonishing confidence that he can date theological *motifs* so exactly, but his reductionist understanding of how theological motifs form and function. For example, his assumption that the presence of a theological conception of the world rule of God *must* reflect the downfall of the Persian Empire and the rise of Alexander[81] is suspect on historical grounds alone (why could the same conception not have emerged after the fall of the Assyrian or Babylonian Empires?).[82] Similarly suspect is the further methodological assump-

---

[75] Ibid.

[76] Ibid., 22–23.

[77] Ibid., 23–24.

[78] Ibid., 24 n. 29.

[79] Ibid., 63–72, esp. the summary, 70–72.

[80] See his 'Zusammenfassung' (STECK, Abschluß, 105–06). Here he charts seven precise stages shared between the book of Isaiah and the book of The Twelve between 332 and 220 B. C. For the eighth and final layer, see STECK, Abschluß, 127–36.

[81] STECK, Abschluß, 23.

[82] STECK assumes that up to this point in time Israel had only been *able* to conceive of God as opposing single enemies, not possessing world dominion. Cf. STECK's assertion (Abschluß, 79) that the 'shepherds' in Zech 10:3 'must' refer to the Diadochene dynasty, a connection which he then uses to date an entire 'layer' to between 320 and 315 B. C. Here the is-

tion that any other motif *related* to such a conception (in the judgment of the modern interpreter!) must then form a common redactional layer.[83] Most troubling of all, however, is the implication that theological conceptions are secondary derivations from political and economic forces (after all, why *exactly* could such a theological conception not emerge at *any* time?).

Steck concludes by dating the *main* growth of the prophetic corpus quite late (240–220 B. C.),[84] but agrees that Ben Sira provides the first external witness to its closure, which makes for a suspiciously short span of time in between.[85] He further considers the final redaction of the Psalms to be concurrent with the final redaction of the Prophets.[86] Steck stresses the eschatological, anti-Hellenistic and anti-theocratic cast of the final form of the Prophets[87] and supports those who postulate that the collection might have originally included some of the Writings.[88]

These conclusions can largely be seen as redactional refinements and modifications of the standard theory of canon formation which, in this case, ultimately collapses under the weight of its own complexity. Above all, the existence of such 'macroredactional' layers within the prophetic corpus is very much open to question. Steck's late dating for main development of the Prophets also appears difficult to maintain, given full consideration of the external witnesses (e. g., Ben Sira, Qumran, the LXX).[89] Moreover, Steck's reconstruction requires the positing of separate, opposing 'circles' responsible for the formation of the prophetic corpus and for the books of Chronicles and Ezra–Nehemiah, and all in the third century, B. C. Was it likely that such groups existed at the same time? For that matter, were Chronicles and Ezra–Nehemiah really so theocratic and anti-eschatological?

On the other hand, Steck concludes that Torah, Prophets and Psalms existed as a 'fixed, literarily authoritative frame of reference' (*fixe, literarisch-autoritative Orientierungsgröße*) by the beginning of the second century B. C., although these scriptures were variously understood and not yet com-

---

sue is not only whether such a reference is *ostensive* in character, but whether this kind of (reconstructed) ostensive referent has *determined* the usage of the reference within the text.

[83] Another serious problem relates to the existence of these editorial 'layers' *between* books. Such an exegetical theory is crucially dependent upon a particular view of scribal activity which no one has yet managed to demonstrate persuasively; namely, how would this kind of editing and rewriting between *scrolls* actually work?

[84] STECK, Abschluß, 119–20. He dates his eighth and final layer to between 220 and 200 B. C. (Abschluß, 150).

[85] Abschluß, 136–44.

[86] Ibid., 157–66; esp. 161.

[87] Ibid., 166–70.

[88] Ibid., 163. On the canonization of the Writings, see STECK, Kanon, 244.

[89] For additional criticism, see HENGEL, Schriftauslegung, esp. 15–16 n. 57.

pletely 'closed.'[90] To this extent, he expresses suggestively, there was indeed a 'theological unity of subject matter' (*theologischer Sachzusammenhang*) inherited by the early Church.[91]

E. E. Ellis

E. E. Ellis's 1991 examination of Old Testament canon formation is grounded in his judgment that the standard theory has 'failed.'[92] Ellis is especially critical of earlier treatments of external witnesses like Josephus and Ben Sira; he also considers the Dead Sea scrolls to have called into serious question the late dating that has become customary for certain biblical books.[93] In particular, Ellis argues that since all the books of the canon except Esther were discovered at Qumran, a more appropriate *terminus ante quem* for the canon is provided by the separation of the Qumran community from mainstream Judaism (ca. 152 B. C.).[94]

Ellis also argues, however, that the tripartite division of scripture was only one pattern in antiquity and not a 'fixed or necessary conception.'[95] He elects to leave 'open' traditional questions about the 'origin and meaning' of this tripartite division, noting that the fourfold LXX division is also probably pre-Christian and, moreover, that a twofold division remains a possibility.[96] Therefore, he suggests, the tripartite division probably emerged gradually (among others), perhaps as a result of lectionary practice in early synagogue worship, and only eventually became 'the prevailing usage in first century Judaism.'[97] A phenomenon connected with this usage, he theorizes, might have been the exclusion of certain books from public reading by their reassignment from the Prophets to the Writings (e. g., Ruth, Lamentations, Daniel).[98]

In addition, Ellis makes the crucial point that, if certain groups (e. g., the Qumran community, Christianity) later expanded their scriptures, it was not a

---

[90] STECK, Abschluß, 177. STECK seems to have altered his position slightly on this point. Cf. his earlier formulation (Kanon, 237): "Ich bin der Meinung, daß in dieser Zeit [2nd half of the 3rd cent. B. C.] der nachmals zweite, *Nebiim* genannte Teil des hebräischen Kanons als nunmehr unveränderliche Schriftensammlung nach dem Vorbild der Tora geschlossen wurde."

[91] STECK, Abschluß, 178.

[92] ELLIS, Canon, 37; cf. 125. See also idem, OT Canon, an article which appeared slightly earlier (1988).

[93] Ibid., 38–40; 125–26.

[94] Ibid., 40–42. ELLIS includes (41) Ecclesiastes and Daniel in this dating scheme.

[95] Ibid., 44–45. He considers the LXX four-fold pattern to be probably pre-Christian. As ELLIS also notes (45), later masoretic Bibles often employ a different four-fold division: Pentateuch, Megillot, Prophets and Hagiographa.

[96] ELLIS, Canon, 44.

[97] Ibid., 45. He means the first century A. D.

[98] Ibid., 45–46.

decision reached by any undefined 'openness' regarding the canon but by the recognition of the "prophetic inspiration and normative authority of their own books."[99] In his view, the early Church did not differ from the rest of Judaism in the canon that it received, but instead continued a hermeneutical process basic to the formation of the canon itself.[100]

Although his appeal to liturgical usage lacks persuasive supporting evidence, Ellis adds an important aspect to the discussion by his reminder that other canonical patterns existed within early Judaism. Although not central to the present study, his most important contribution lies in making a strong case against the position that the Old Testament canon had remained 'open' into the Christian era.[101]

J. W. Miller

An unusual, if somewhat speculative, contribution has been made to the discussion by J. W. Miller's 1994 study of canon formation.[102] He locates the origins of canon almost completely within a complex rivalry of 'priestly houses' in post-exilic Israel.[103]

Miller also views the process of canon formation as beginning with Deuteronomy and the Deuteronomistic History, with the later formation of a Pentateuch caused by the reassignment of Deuteronomy.[104] He explains the dynamics of this process differently, however, in arguing that the Deuteronomistic History was a collection made by levitical priests, which pre-dated the 'aaronite' priestly material found in the Pentateuch. He reconstructs an intense dispute between these two groups, which was only exacerbated further by a collection of written prophecies (the Latter Prophets), also sponsored by the levites.[105] On this view, the canon of 'Law and Prophets' later took shape as a compromise between these two priestly houses.[106]

---

[99] Ibid., 50.

[100] This emphasis on a hermeneutical process reveals the influence of GESE; cf. GESE, Erwägungen; idem, View, esp. 11, 30. GESE's proposal of a single hermeneutical process connecting the Old and New Testaments remains a major theological proposal within the field and has been frequently contrasted to CHILDS's way of relating the two Testaments (see SCHNABEL, Entwürfe), but GESE's view of the *history* of canon formation remains largely that of the standard theory (see GESE, Erwägungen, 13–14).

[101] On this, see ELLIS, Canon, esp. 3–36.

[102] J. W. MILLER, Origins.

[103] Ibid., 17–66.

[104] MILLER, Origins, 33.

[105] Ibid., 67–88. In MILLER's view, only the book of Haggai represents a Zadokite view.

[106] Ibid., 90. Cf. GOTTWALD, Introduction, 460–69.

Circularity is clearly a problem in Miller's sociological reconstruction,[107] and his focus on priestly groups leaves the impression that the prophets were more or less only spokesmen for priestly views. Moreover, his orientation is skewed by an over-reliance on the narrative of Ezra–Nehemiah and the surprising amount of credence that he gives to the report of Nehemiah's library (2 Mac 2:13) and the legend of a Great Assembly.[108] Miller himself had difficulty placing the tetrateuchal priestly narratives and legislation against the background of Ezra–Nehemiah (esp. Num 17:1–11; 18:5).[109]

However, Miller also finds ample indications that already by the time of Ezra there existed an authoritative corpus of prophecy.[110] The result is largely a confirmation of the dates already suggested by Beckwith, with a *terminus a quo* for the canon of Law and Prophets set at about 400 B. C.[111] Miller also follows Beckwith quite explicitly in his view that the Jerusalem Temple was the respository for 'master copies' of the scriptures.[112] Thus, Miller posits a 'closed' canon of Law and Prophets in the Maccabean period, understood as a single 'story' which culminated in Ezra–Nehemiah.

Miller also makes his own contribution, however, by suggesting that a growing collection of Latter Prophets (Jeremiah, Ezekiel, Isaiah and The Twelve) was added to Deuteronomy and the Deuteronomistic History *prior* to addition of Exodus–Numbers, which was shaped as an introduction to the existing collection. In his view, Genesis was added even later as a kind of 'prologue' to the whole.[113] Miller adduces as evidence of this sequence: first, the superscriptions of the four major prophetic scrolls, which coordinate them with the Deuteronomistic History; second, the 'correlation of significant place names' (e. g., Zion, Samaria, Anathoth, Shechem) between the Latter Prophets and the History; and third, the sharing of blocks of narrative between the two collections (2 Kg 18:13, 17–20:19 in Isa 36–39; 2 Kg 24:18–25:30 in Jer 52).[114]

Less successful is his supporting argument that a literary *inclusio* formed by Mal 3:22–24 [4:4–6] and Deut 5:1–5 indicates the extent of the pretetrateuchal canon.[115] Also problematic for Miller is the question of why the transition from Numbers to Deuteronomy would not have been made less

---

[107] Ibid., 71. E. g., MILLER argues that Hosea must have been a levite because the levites criticized the northern shrines and the book of Hosea does, too.

[108] Ibid., 92–106; 128 n. 4; esp. 103.

[109] Ibid., 188–89; 122.

[110] Ibid., 107.

[111] Ibid., 107. Here MILLER relies on evidence from the genealogies in Chronicles.

[112] Ibid., 128 n. 4

[113] Ibid., 111.

[114] Ibid., 114–16.

[115] Ibid., 116.

abruptly, and his claim that references to the Latter Prophets can be discerned in Genesis.[116] Most troubling of all, however, is his reductionistic description of canon formation as a political compromise among rival priestly factions.[117]

L. M. McDonald

The most recent major treatment of Old Testament canon formation is by L. M. McDonald, and is remarkable for his effort to repristinate the three-stage linear theory of the nineteenth century.[118] Declaring Ryle's theory 'more reasonable than some recent scholars have proposed,' McDonald goes on to argue Ryle's only 'unreasonable proposal' was that his date for the closing of the Writings, and thus for the canon as a whole, is much too *early*.[119] In a way directly opposite to that of Beckwith, McDonald's primary interest lies in making the case that Christianity did *not* receive from Judaism a completed canon.[120] To this end, he distinguishes as sharply as possible canon as 'authority' from canon as 'exclusion' and differentiates three phases (similar to those of Ryle) in the process of the canon's development.[121]

McDonald does not object to the view that the Former Prophets had circulated together with the 'books of Moses' since the late sixth or early fifth century, but has no explanation for their lack of canonical status other than his own narrow definition of canon.[122] In discussing the view of Leiman that the

---

[116] Ibid., 122–24. Here, of course, MILLER follows VAN SETERS, Prologue. The 'references' seem to be restricted to general religious themes (i. e., sin and judgment, Israel's origins, the problem of foreign nations). A similar problem exists with the relationship between the end of Genesis and the beginning of Exodus. MILLER asserts that Ex 1:1–7 originally served as the introduction to the Law and the Prophets. This, however, is a difficult claim: if Genesis was added later, why then is the literary transition between Genesis and Exodus not more smooth?

[117] MILLER does exhibit some concern with the 'theology' of these rival levite and Zadokite groups. Also, his treatment of the addition of the Writings displays a more theologically-sensitive handling of the literature. Particularly interesting is his observation that the place of Ruth within the canon is extremely difficult to explain if the Torah was hermeneutically *privileged* in post-exilic Israel, for Ruth celebrates precisely the kind of foreign marriage that the Torah condemned (cf. Deut 23:3–6). MILLER suggests, however, that Ruth's witness was not crudely 'subversive,' but rather represented an internal broadening of tradition.

[118] MCDONALD, Formation; cf. idem, Testament.

[119] MCDONALD, Formation, 29–30.

[120] Ibid., 25–26; 120; 127–29.

[121] Ibid., 130 n. 113. MCDONALD keeps the dates for the collections of Law and Prophets at ca. 400 B. C. and 200 B. C., respectively (Formation, 29; 32).

[122] MCDONALD, Formation, 31. He finds the view that there was a collection of Latter Prophets by this time 'less likely,' but offers no reasons other than a reference to the view of SANDERS that the experience of Exile provided the motivation for the crystallization of the prophetic corpus.

prophetic corpus was largely formed by 500–450 B. C., McDonald offers only Neh 8–9 as evidence of a Torah-only canon in this period.[123] By delaying the fixity and the uniformity of the Old Testament canon for as long as possible, McDonald is able to argue that its final form was designed by the same rabbis who edited the Mishnah (A. D. 200–400)![124] Resuscitating the theory of G. F. Moore that the narrower Jewish canon (as opposed to the wider Alexandrian canon, as Moore conceived it) was the result of anti-Christian and anti-New Testament sentiment,[125] McDonald then questions the *appropriateness* of a 'Jewish' canon for the Christian Church.[126]

At key points in this argument McDonald relies on dated arguments without apparent regard for important counter-arguments, or more recent scholarship within the field. Certainly despite his rhetoric of canon and canon formation, he seems to display little grasp of the complex exegetical issues involved or the insights of those we have been tracing in this chapter. Most disturbing of all is McDonald's argument against the "current Protestant canon" because it "appears to have been fixed by the Jews."[127] McDonald contrasts this narrow 'Jewish canon' with the wider 'canon of Jesus,' and in doing so forgets the *thoroughly Jewish* origins of both the Old Testament *and* Jesus!

The most charitable thing one can say about this kind of contrast is that McDonald's motivation appears to be anti-fundamentalist rather than anti-Jewish: by arguing for the Church's non-inheritance of a canon of scripture from Judaism, he hopes to encourage the use of a more diverse canon with a reduced level of authority (i. e., without doctrinal claims of infallibility or inerrancy).[128] In my judgment, however, the result is disastrous on both historical and theological grounds.[129]

---

[123] McDONALD, Formation, 34.

[124] Ibid., 92.

[125] Ibid., 126. Cf. G. F. MOORE, Definition.

[126] McDONALD, Formation, 127–33.

[127] Ibid., 132.

[128] Ibid., 250–57.

[129] Like BARTON (People? 83), McDONALD asserts that the 'true canon of faith for the church [is] our Lord Jesus Christ' and that recognition of this fact will free the church from 'inappropriate loyalties' (Formation, 257). However, McDONALD does not reckon at all with how we are to encounter and know Jesus Christ *apart* from the biblical text. On this problem, see BEST, Scripture. It is also helpful to compare McDONALD's superficial formulation ('Christ' = 'canon') with CHILDS's differentiated discussion of Jesus Christ as 'the one scope of scripture' (Biblical Theology, 725). CHILDS is concerned to define the relationship between biblical authority and christology — a relationship which *must* exist from the perspective of the church — but McDONALD ham-fistedly attempts simply to play christology off against the Bible. For further theological discussion see McGRATH, Reclaiming, 65-68.

Conclusions

With McDonald's study, we conclude our overview of the past century's efforts to understand the process of Old Testament canon formation, especially the relationship between the Law and the Prophets. McDonald's attempt to repristinate Ryle cannot hope to patch over the gaps that are now clear in the standard theory. At the same time, it may well be that McDonald has captured the prevailing attitude within the field at the century's end.[1]

Within recent treatments, one gains the sense that the bolder efforts to reenvision the history of canon formation characteristic of the mid-century have been moderated, whatever their earlier direction (e. g., Ackroyd, Barton, Childs, Clements). The persistent minority view which we have attempted to trace continues to attract its sponsors (e. g., Beckwith, Freedman, Leiman), but their view of an early canon of Law and Prophets suffers from a failure to give a compelling account of canonical 'authority.' In this view, what is the *difference* between the process of literary development and the process of canon formation?[2] On the other hand, scholars who understand canon as properly about 'exclusion' continue to fall short in offering a persuasive description of the 'pre-canonical' status of Israel's scriptures, especially the prophetic writings (e. g., Barr, Barton, McDonald). In this view, what is the *connection* between the process of literary development and the process of canon formation?

Before launching a new effort to reconceive the history of canon formation, now that we have deconstructed the standard theory, we must first delve even deeper into what is meant by 'canon.' As has been made repeatedly clear, a central historical problem for the standard theory of Old Testament canon formation has been the nagging question about the status of the prophetic writings prior to their canonization. In my judgment, however, the main reason for the intractability of this problem lies not simply with the paucity of the historical evidence, but with the assumptions of those doing research in this area about the nature of scriptural canons: how they come to exist and how they work.

---

[1] See also D. M. CARR, Canonization; TALMON, Schrifttum. CARR's approach is much more methodologically sophisticated than McDONALD's, but their historical conclusions are similar. I wish to thank Prof. CARR for graciously sending me a copy of his article prior to its publication. I shall examine his work more closely in Chapter Six.

[2] Here the recent work of BARRERA, Bible, esp. 156–67, seems to move in a promising direction, both acknowledging scripture's early authority and seeking to preserve the lengthy process of its textual development (151). He continues, however, to invest the Torah with temporal and hermeneutical priority (157–58) without addressing the status of the already extant prophetic writings (159–60).

Chapter Two

'Density within History'
Canon as a Theological Grammar

Introduction

The goal of my own investigation is thus to reassess the history of Old Testament canon formation in light of what history teaches us has been a central weakness: the relationship between the canonical subcollections of Law and Prophets.

Against the standard theory outlined in the last chapter, in which the Prophets are later in date and secondary in authority, I shall follow the lead of the critical minority, which has persistently suggested an originally collateral relation between the two subcollections and an equal level of authority. As we have seen, members of this minority first dissented from the standard view by arguing for a more organic pattern of growth at the pre-literary level (emphasizing the presence of legal traditions *behind* the Prophets or the prophetic traditions *behind* the Law), but have more recently shifted the focus towards the various ways in which both subcollections were edited jointly at the redactional level.

Following their cue, I shall argue that the final form of the canonical text preserves more hermeneutical intentionality than has usually been recognized. I intend to illustrate that there exists a variety of editorial changes, connections and conclusions within both subcollections that has as its origin and goal a reading of the whole text, in which Law and Prophets have a coordinated but dialectical relationship. I shall maintain that the final form of the canon fully preserves the freedom and authority of each subcollection with respect to the other. At the same time, however, I shall contend that a view of the *whole* — a 'theology' of 'Law and Prophets' — has *preceded* their final form and, in fact, given this form its shape.

My investigation at this point does not concern itself directly with the theological authority of this wholistic understanding for modern Judaism and Christianity.[1] It would be inappropriate to move too quickly from ancient religious formulations to contemporary statements of faith. Yet it is also true that the tradition of historical scholarship has inveighed too heavily against

---

[1] For the theological implications of my historical work, see Chapter Six.

the existence of 'theology' *in* the biblical text.[2] I am convinced that any theological framework that spans whole books or collections within the Old Testament, helping to provide the canon with its literary shape, must have significant implications for present theological work and demands our thoughtful consideration.

The nature of my investigation might well suggest that the most productive methodology to use would be a form of 'ideological criticism,' i. e., a description of the ideological presuppositions that have been employed in order to unite a wide variety of traditions and literary materials into a 'holy' writing or 'scripture.' In fact, in the course of my treatment I hope to make clear that: 1) there *was* a conceptual framework that expressed the rationale for the received shape of Israel's scripture; and 2) this framework found its most explicit expression in the post-exilic period, as particular formulations and conceptions were valorized within the biblical literature, sometimes even sacrificing literary and historical detail for the sake of advancing the formation of a unified whole.

Ideology and Historical Criticism

Putting the issue in this way brings my argument seemingly close to the position in the field exemplified by P. R. Davies. In his *In Search of "Ancient Israel"* Davies concludes that the biblical literature represents "...the fruits of a process of ideological expression which has its roots in the society of Persian period Yehud/Judah..."[1] Davies further determines that although the *content* of some of the biblical literature is no doubt more ancient "...the *ideological structure* of the biblical literature can only be explained in the last analysis as a product of the Persian period..."[2] Setting aside the matter of his dating for a moment, what Davies has helpfully perceived is the way in which the tradents of biblical traditions have creatively and deliberately shaped the biblical lit-

---

[2] SMEND, Theologie. The anti-theological disposition within the field played an important role historically in freeing critical study from dogmatic constraints, but also resulted in a misleading over-emphasis. According to SMEND, the denial of theology *in* the text depended upon the narrow view, especially in German scholarship, of the theologian as systematician and upon the dismissal of 'late' material in favor of what was 'original.' Although theological-style formulations have always been recognized in biblical texts and were generally viewed as increasingly present the later a particular text was dated, the significance of these formulations continues to be over-looked or flatly rejected. In SMEND's view, however, the theological formulations already present in the text are more a matter of connections, interpretations and summations than of abstract ideas or concepts.

[1] P. R. DAVIES, Search, 92; cf. 19. DAVIES goes on to caution that this view is that of a social elite and therefore remains partial.

[2] Search, 94. His emphasis.

erature so that it functions in particular ways in the future for their community of faith.

In my judgment, however, Davies's main achievement, contrary to his purpose, is to illustrate in the clearest possible way why such a methodology cannot hope to illuminate the inner logic of the Old Testament's witness or the unique features of the biblical canon. Davies's work is thus instructive to the present study as a foil: in my judgment, he exhibits quite clearly the inconsistent assumptions of his own methodology and illustrates the need to conceive of the task in a fundamentally different manner. By using Davies as an example in this chapter, I intend to show why the application of the concept 'ideology' to the biblical text fails by prejudicing the very matters it claims to analyze more neutrally.[3]

After discussing Davies's arguments in greater detail, I shall describe the same phenomenon that he terms 'ideological imperialism' as instead the formation of a *theological witness*. The issue turns on much more than semantics, and goes to the heart of critical biblical study. With the assistance of literary critic and philosopher C. Altieri, I shall argue that the cipher 'canon' illuminates the contours of the biblical text and the profile of Old Testament canon formation far more distinctly and informatively than the cipher 'ideology.'[4]

P. R. Davies

Davies pursues his search for the historical 'Israel' by drawing attention to ways in which he believes biblical scholars have been insufficiently critical in their efforts to reconstruct biblical 'history,' primarily because of their (often unacknowledged) faith commitments.[5] Much of his book thus presents a sharp critique of 'theological' readings of the biblical text, which, he argues, offer contemporary homiletics in the guise of serious historical investigation. Although he asserts his belief that this 'theological paradigm' will never be fully replaced, he celebrates a present 'climate' in which "a non-theological

---

[3] The term 'ideology' is variously used. For a detailed typology see GEUSS, Idea. I am indebted to S. C. Bader-Saye for this helpful reference. For a broader typology, but one within the field, see GOTTWALD, Ideology. Cf. CLINES, Parties, 9–25; PIPPIN, Ideology. While some definitions of 'ideology' might be broad enough to escape the pitfalls of DAVIES's treatment of the biblical material, such definitions (e. g., a 'pattern of ideas') quickly become so broad that they really provide no interpretive help at all. For some recent criticism along these lines and continuing questions about the value of 'ideology' as an explanatory category, see: BURKE, History, 91–96; RAILTON, Ideology.

[4] The application of the term 'cipher' to canon and canon formation is made by CHILDS, Biblical Theology, 70–71; 721; cf. idem, Reclaiming, 5. For an earlier use of 'cipher' with reference to ideology, see GOTTWALD, Tribes, 65.

[5] DAVIES, Search, 97; cf. 46.

paradigm is beginning to claim a place alongside the long-dominant theological one..."[6]

Davies rejects as methodologically-flawed all historical treatments that confirm the existence of an Iron Age 'Israel' and an Iron-Age Israelite 'faith.' Because the biblical literature, he avers, consciously and consistently idealizes and retrojects from its Persian period vantage point, the possibility of anything in the pre-exilic period resembling the biblical 'Israel' is so remote as to constitute improper scholarship.

Davies is then more specific in his criticism of the 'theological paradigm,' revealing that he is especially dissatisfied with treatments that reconstruct 'Israel's faith' by recourse to a hypothetical process of canon formation:

"The authorship of the biblical literature has often been presented in biblical scholarship as a corporate entity; it is said to enshrine the 'faith of Israel,' nourished and developed by 'the community,' its ultimate form lovingly and tellingly shaped by a 'canonical process.' However eloquent or theologically useful this view may be, it emerges in the light of historical or sociological reflection, or even plain common sense, as fantastical..."

He further asserts that the biblical literature was not even, in its intention, *religious*:

"...whatever the name given to the authors of the biblical literature, they are a small and elite class, and their creation, 'Israel,' a reflection of their class consciousness (to use a Marxian term). Whatever actual religion (if any) the biblical literature reflects, it is not the religion of people outside this class; and it remains to be demonstrated that the members of the class itself *had* a religion which the biblical literature could be taken to represent."[7]

Here Davies not only disputes the appropriateness of certain theological concepts within biblical scholarship, he himself substitutes for terms like 'faith' and 'community' the words 'religion' and 'class' as sociologically more precise and historically more accurate. In introducing a notion like 'class consciousness,' Davies means to suggest that social-material forces were historically more significant than 'religious' motives in the production of the biblical literature.[8]

---

[6] Ibid., 15. DAVIES goes on to assert that this paradigm will, however, 'never be replaced.' As other examples of the 'non-theological paradigm,' he cites (n. 3): GOTTWALD, Tribes; GARBINI, History; and ODEN, Bible. Note DAVIES's naive assumption that 'theological' readings of the biblical text constitute a single, unified paradigm!

[7] DAVIES, Search, 18–19. His emphasis. Cf. Search, 97 for his curious argument that biblical literature cannot reflect an actual religion because it is ideologically diverse and contradictory. Surely most religions are in fact ideologically diverse and even self-contradictory! Could it be instead that the biblical literature was relatively unconcerned to provide exactly the kind of seamlessly-consistent ideology Davies assumes to be essential?

[8] Regardless of which definition of ideology is adopted at the outset of an investigation, this view is often strongly implied even where not stated directly. Credit is due to GOTTWALD

The 'Marxian' (i. e., Marxist) view of religion as a secondary, derivative feature of human experience finds further expression in Davies's strange conclusion that it is inadmissable to construe pre-exilic 'Israel' as a 'religious' society at all. Rather, Davies asserts, biblical literature reflects a 'typical eastern Mediterranean culture' in which concepts such as 'secularity' and 'the non-religious' are meaningless. However, instead of arguing that this premise illustrates the way in which *everything* in such societies is religious, Davies concludes that 'religion' is therefore too broad a category helpfully to describe the origins of biblical literature *at all*:

"Given the world-view of societies in which social life, health, weather, and historical disaster involved the gods, and thus in which 'non-religious' was a virtually empty category, it is not necesary [sic] to assume that the biblical literature was originally written in the service of a particular cult or for the purposes of devotional study or liturgical recitation, and certainly not necessarily regulative or authoritative for the belief and conduct of a religious community or tradition."[9]

In this manner, Davies basically restricts the concept of religion to a dubiously narrow range and then rejects its applicability. With such sleight of hand, Davies admits the pervasive religious character of the social world that gave rise to the biblical writings, but then refuses to credit those writings with the religious character of the world in which they took shape.

In Davies's reconstruction:

"...the biblical literature almost certainly must have emerged as a political-cultural product of the Jerusalem 'establishment'... based in the temple there, though perhaps also in the court of the governor. By a series of processes... this literature became definitive of a traditional culture among certain classes, and in particular came to be adopted by groups wishing to adopt a 'Judaean' lifestyle."[10]

In his view, then, political and cultural factors *determined* the tradition which produced the biblical literature. I note his Marxist use of the terms 'product,' 'establishment' and 'classes.' Here again 'religion' becomes an additional quality which accrues to the texts secondarily and derivatively, their primary

---

for expressing this premise within the field so frankly. See GOTTWALD, Ideology, 143–47; cf. the chapter 'Socioeconomic Demythologization of Israelite Yahwism' in his Tribes, 692–99; cf. 65–66. However, even GOTTWALD claims at the outset of his book (Tribes, 66) that his use of the term ideology does not involve 'any particular view about the genetic or causal relationship between the religious ideas and the social relations of Israel.' Nevertheless, by the end of the same book he attempts to describe (692) how 'all of the primary aspects of the religion of Israel' can be demythologized into 'functions and expressions of socio-economic and communal-cultural existence...'

[9] DAVIES, Search, 19–20. DAVIES's logic here — quite contrary to his intention — would seem to imply that 'religious writings' are *essentially* authoritative and 'canonical.'

[10] Ibid., 20.

sense being political and cultural – and this in spite of the fact that Davies considers 'secularity' to be a 'meaningless concept' within ancient Near Eastern cultures!

Davies seems aware of the inconsistency in his argument at this point:

> "Although inevitably such literature [i. e., the 'traditional' literature of the Jerusalem 'establishment'] will have been concerned with the role of the deity or deities, cult practice, cosmogony, prophetic records and wisdom sayings, that does not immediately place it in the category of 'scripture.' But in many cases, the lifestyle sought was a religious one, or became more and more religiously defined, and the literature that was to become the Bible began to assume among such groups the functions of what we call 'scripture'... a political decision to institute this literature as a national archive explains the fixation of a standard text and establishes a set number of books that can subsequently be 'canonized.'"[11]

Here Davies not only appears to contradict his earlier statement that it is unnecessary "to assume the biblical literature was originally written in the service of a particular cult or for the purposes of devotional study or liturgical recitation,"[12] but he uses terms like 'religious' and 'political' in unclear and confusing ways.

Davies would seem to be arguing that although the early biblical literature was about certain ostensibly 'religious' things (i. e., deities and cult practices, etc.) and was preserved and treasured for ostensibly 'religious' reasons (i. e., the cultivation of a religious lifestyle), the unacknowledged, *real* forces at work were secular and 'political.' Criticizing a theological view in which "Israel's 'faith' shapes the 'formation' of its 'tradition,'"[13] Davies adopts what he conceives to be the opposite position, i. e., an 'ideological' view in which the 'traditions' of the *powerful* shape the 'formation' of 'Israel' and its 'faith.'

Here the problems begin to multiply. Because Davies wants to date the biblical literature very late as support for his program of 'no Iron Age Israel,' relegating only the most fragmentary sources to the pre-exilic period, he is forced to emphasize the great speed at which various 'recensions' of a literary work *could have* been produced. Against the standard view of a lengthy process of oral transmission and a corporate shaping of the literature, Davies instead suggests that individual scholars could have introduced the ideological biases commonly assigned to different levels of redaction as quickly as each time a text was copied. In this way he shortens the usual timeline *considerably*:

> "Certainly the literature was not commissioned and then made to order! But I do think it entirely feasible that the task of constructing a history of the society in which the cult, laws

---

[11] Ibid., 20–21.

[12] Ibid., 19–20. Cf. 94 where DAVIES describes the content of the earliest biblical literature as 'domestic and social customs, cultic and legal practices.'

[13] Ibid., 97.

and ethos of the ruling caste would be authorized was undertaken deliberately and conscientiously by the scribes serving the ruling caste, partly at their behest, partly from self-interest, and no doubt partly for creative enjoyment. I do not see why the task needs to have taken more than two or three generations."[14]

It is extremely difficult to make sense of this formulation in light of Davies's previous assertion that "the production of literature in Yehud (or any other ancient society) is not a matter of personal initiative nor of the automatic inscribing of whatever oral material is in circulation and in danger of being lost."[15] Here the interpretive issue is not simply that of dating various texts, but also the character of the scribal transmission of the text. To what extent may this process be described as deliberate and *self-interested*? To what extent did it maintain a liberal or conservative stance *vis à vis* inherited traditions? Was it more creative or automatic?

Despite his inconsistency on this point, Davies's rhetoric continues to aggrandize a typically Marxist view:

"These scribes write what their paymasters tell them to, or allow them to, which means generally that they write to safeguard or increase the power and prestige of the monarch or the temple. Their scribal duties cover a wide range of activities, among them the keeping of commercial records (control over the economy), archiving (control and possession of the past, control of the literature class), or history writing (control and possession of the past; matching the claims of neighboring powers), didactic writing (maintenance of social values among the élite), predictive writing (control over the future)."[16]

Here again it is difficult to square this formulation with Davies's earlier remarks about the scribes' 'self-interest' and 'creative enjoyment.' How is it exactly that these scribes produced a literature containing a *variety* of ideological stances in a relatively brief period of time if they only did what their paymasters told them? And what are we to make of the *anti*-monarchic, *anti*-cultic texts in the Old Testament?

Davies tries to make allowances:

"These scribes not only work for the governing institution; they are also part of it, by being a rather privileged élite. That does not prevent them from criticizing their own régime. There are texts in the Bible that contain quite trenchant denunciation. But this is always expressed in the words of an earlier prophet, so that no direct criticism of the current authorities is explicit."[17]

Is it true that such criticism is *always* archaized and indirect? Would such criticism really have been overlooked by the ideologically-astute paymasters

---

[14] Ibid., 120.

[15] Ibid., 106.

[16] Ibid., 107.

[17] Ibid.

Davies describes? What sense does it make to treat the Bible as a single, unified *ideology* if it contains such divergent points of view?[18]

Such questions become even more pressing as Davies makes clear his view that the main achievement of the ideologically-driven process of biblical formation was to create a *fictive* past: "The ideological triumph of the biblical story is to convince that what is new is actually old."[19] But how could this possibly work? Why would a community be willing to accept a fictive version of its past as true and divinely authorized, especially within two or three generations? Davies makes various assertions at this point: that "…there was no 'national tradition' to begin with…,"[20] that the biblical literature was at first restricted to an elite class,[21] and that the biblical literature was not 'used for religious purposes' prior to the early Hellenistic period.[22]

Davies conceives of three broad stages in the formation of the literature: 1) the creation of the historical material (Genesis–2 Kings; and Chronicles, Ezra, Nehemiah); 2) the adoption of historical and quasi-legal literature as a cultural (and only later 'religious') norm, but only for certain groups; and 3) the official establishment of a 'set of writings' as a 'national archive.'[23] I note that it is the *legal* impulse in this sequence which seemingly initiates and characterizes the earliest step in canon formation. This legal understanding of scripture seems related to Davies's acceptance of the traditions found in the book of Ezra–Nehemiah at more or less face value.[24]

Davies argues that: 1) no extra-biblical evidence calls the Ezra–Nehemiah traditions into question; and 2) subsequent events in 'Judaean history and religion' make developments such as those related in Ezra and Nehemiah 'antecedently necessary.'[25] But is this not precisely the kind of logic that Davies criticizes in the work of scholars who accept the veracity of certain pre-exilic traditions and the existence of an Iron Age 'Israel'?

---

[18] I note again DAVIES's statement (Search, 97) that the Bible is 'ideologically diverse and even self-contradictory.' He makes this assertion in an argument against a unified 'theological' reading of the Bible, but is it not equally damaging to the kind of unified 'ideological' reading on which his reconstruction depends? For an 'ideological' critique of 'ideological' readings, see further FOWL, Texts. FOWL would locate ideologies only in the interpreters of texts, not in the texts themselves.

[19] Ibid., 120.

[20] Ibid., 132.

[21] Ibid., 114–15.

[22] Ibid., 144–45.

[23] Ibid., 114. In DAVIES's reconstruction, the Psalms also began to be added to the collection in this second stage.

[24] Ibid., 78–87.

In any case, Davies has no sooner restricted the scope of the earliest biblical literature to the historical books than he is forced to make exceptions. Thus: "...the prophetic books of the Bible may well have a basis in collections of archived materials remaining from the Iron Age."[26] According to Davies, 'parts' of Ezekiel and Jeremiah can be dated to between 596–86 B. C.[27] Nevertheless, Davies continues to emphasize that the (received forms of the?) Deuteronomistic History, Chronicles, Ezra, Nehemiah, Ezekiel, Jeremiah, most of Isaiah, Haggai, Zechariah, Jonah, Esther, Daniel, Ecclesiastes, Lamentations, Malachi and the (final?) 'recension' of the Pentateuch all "post-date the Iron Age," and that there is "no *necessity* to assign *any* part of the formation of *any* biblical book to the period. [sic] of the historical kingdoms of Judah and Israel."[28] The consistency of all these statements is as questionable as the methodology which generates them.[29]

If some of the prophetic books do have a basis in Iron Age materials, how can Davies defend his description of canonization as the imposition of a legal 'norm'? The real rationale for his reconstruction would appear to be his own view of scripture as inherently oppressive and legalistic.[30] Thus the process of canon formation becomes, for Davies, "...an act of ideological imperialism by which a ruling caste appropriates the native peasant customs and, depriving them of all that is meaningful to the peasant, turns them into celebrations of their [sic] own dominant ideology: their acquisition of the law, their deliverance from Egypt, their wandering in the wilderness."[31] In his later discussion of the Hellenistic 'threat,' to which he partly credits the use of the biblical literature for *religious* purposes, Davies characterizes the response of 'Israel' to this threat as "the kind of nationalistic fundamentalism with which our own century is familiar, even to the extent of adopting values that are only *thought* to have been traditional."[32]

Davies himself cannot conceive of any *truly* religious dimension to the elements of Judean religion described in the texts for this period:

---

[25] Ibid., 86. DAVIES comes to this conclusion despite his own worry that too many reconstructions of post-exilic Judah use the books of Ezra and Nehemiah uncritically and his protestation (80 n. 6) that these accounts are not to be 'taken as *prima facie* reliable'!

[26] Ibid., 111.

[27] Ibid., 100 n. 9.

[28] Ibid., 99. His emphases.

[29] E. g., what is the nature of this 'necessity'?

[30] Descriptions of post-exilic Judaism as oppressive and legalistic represent a persistent, tragic tendency within critical biblical scholarship. See RENDTORFF, Image; NICKELSBURG, WITH KRAFT, Introduction, esp. 10–11.

[31] Ibid., 115.

[32] Ibid., 147. His emphasis.

"The establishment of a temple and priesthood, a sacrificial system, a caste system... and an ideology of holiness to support it, were not separable as 'religious' characteristics from other means of political control. To characterize, let alone glorify, these mechanisms as products of religious zeal would be bordering on the ludicrous."[33]

Why? Once again arguing from the interrelationship of religion and politics within ancient societies, Davies excludes rather than includes the role of religion (as such) from his reconstruction. Are not Davies's personal sympathies here masquerading as historical science?

In a culminating anachronism, Davies imagines a 'temple school' consisting of five 'colleges' (law, liturgy, wisdom, historiography, politics) in which the scribes pursued their "paymasters' project" of rewriting the past.[34] His reasoning is neatly circular: "Since college [sic] always strive for respectability and antiquity, it is not impossible that they believed themselves to have been founded centuries ago."[35] Davies pictures these 'colleges' as distinct but contemporaneous, producing literature exhibiting a broad range of consensus, but also varying degrees of internal difference and tension.

"Rather than envisage large-scale conceptions at the outset, we might better imagine a process of editing in which the various scrolls were shelved in what was decided was a chronological sequence. In the process of copying, the gaps between the scrolls would then be filled. In this stage, which might be called large-scale editing, we might see the incorporation of Deuteronomy in its present place, the wedging of Judges between Joshua and Saul, and the distribution of the legal material into the historiographical narrative."[36]

Thus, in the first stage of the process, as Davies conceives it, the end result was the formation of the large-scale narratives (Genesis–2 Kings; and Chronicles, Ezra, Nehemiah).

In his description of the second, more 'legal' phase, however, Davies now questions his own sequence:

"But while the creation of legal 'traditions' is undoubtedly an important part of the overall scribal activity in the Second Temple, the view that biblical law forms the foundation for both the rest of the biblical literature and the development of Judean culture ('Judaism') needs reassessing. The evidence of the Mishnah itself suggests rather differently; its structure and content both imply that there was no established place for the biblical laws in the conduct of

---

[33] Ibid., 117.

[34] Ibid., 120–23. I use the term 'rewriting' rather than 'writing' to make the point *contra* DAVIES that the textualization of traditions as he describes it could not have begun with a blank slate, but would have in effect involved a rewriting of experience and memory, if not also of earlier texts. At the very least, I would argue that this aspect of the scribes' task would have *somewhat* circumscribed their ability to innovate.

[35] Ibid., 121. I should note that DAVIES calls his description of these five 'colleges' an heuristic 'exercise in imagination' and claims not to intend it as a formal hypothesis.

Judaean society, as opposed to the practices of certain groups who in any case concentrated on purity laws and not civil behavior."[37]

At this point in Davies's reconstruction the textualization of legal traditions and their incorporation into large-scale narratives looks less like a reflection of 'legalism' and more like the provision of an *ideal* of jurisprudence. If he is correct about the Mishnah's goal being to provide a legal framework lacking in the biblical text, then it would seem difficult for him to argue that a legal understanding or impulse lies at the origin of the canon's formation.

Also moderating Davies's earlier emphasis upon the ascendancy of legalism in the Persian period is his attention to the phenomenon of prophetic texts and their eventual inclusion in the Judean 'national archive.' Davies acknowledges almost begrudgingly the presence of 'genuine social criticism' and 'real anger, real morality, real passion' in the prophetic literature.[38] He wants to restrict these texts as much as possible to the post-exilic period, but cannot date some of them much later than the fifth century B. C. This conclusion creates two problems for Davies: 1) how is such 'genuine' social criticism to be reconciled with the establishmentarian agenda of the scribes and their paymasters? and 2) if the prophetic books were being written and edited at the very same time as the historical narratives and legal materials, how can one understand the interrelationship between the subcollections of Law and Prophets, especially their differences and their lack of more significant cross-referencing?

Responding to the first problem Davies again reverses himself: "Simply because scribes work for the government does not mean they admire or approve of it."[39] This assertion may well help in explaining the presence of social criticism in the prophetic books, but the inconsistency between this formulation and his earlier statements does nothing to increase the persuasiveness of his overall argument. Actually, however, here Davies only *appears* to acknowledge greater intellectual freedom for the Judean scribes than he had previously, because now he proceeds to subordinate their social criticism to the establishment by the very fact of its *acceptance*: "...the fate of the best critics of an establishment is to be included posthumously within it, since their criticism is more damaging outside it."[40] But is this to be understood as 'fate' or someone's 'intention'? Davies resorts to casting a blanket of suspicion.

His response to the second problem is more satisfactory than the first, although it also remains difficult to know how to combine it with his earlier as-

---

[36] Ibid., 132.
[37] Ibid., 127.
[38] Ibid., 124.
[39] Ibid.
[40] Ibid., 133.

sertions. Here he points out that there are in fact a number of cross-references contained within the literature, although he minimizes their importance. Thus Mic 3:12 is cited in Jer 26:18. References to Jeremiah are also found in Ezr 1:1; 2 Chr 35–36; and Dan 9. Micah and Isaiah 'overlap a little.' The Latter Prophets are frequently dated according to the scheme of 2 Kings.[41] Several chapters are shared between the Latter Prophets and 2 Kings.[42] Rather than a process in which scripture is imposed as a legal norm (as his theory dictates), Davies actually proceeds to sketch a broadly dialectical framework of 'scrolls of tora' and 'scrolls of prophecy,' which complement each other even as they remain in tension.[43]

Then Davies describes the final, third stage of the literature: "...by some-time in the third century we have a substantial national archive, though how it became fixed or 'official' we cannot yet say, housed within the scribal schools, presumably within the temple complex."[44] Several factors, he insists, led to the establishment of this archive: 1) the encroachment of Hellenistic culture; 2) increased scribal education; 3) the rise of personal piety; 4) greater religious legalism; 5) the effects of manticism; and 6) certain physical and literary factors governing the maximum length of scrolls and narratives.[45] The Greek threat seems to play the largest role in his reconstruction, connecting the veneration of the biblical text and the preservation of a national archive under the Hasmoneans.[46]

Davies concludes that between 200 B. C. and A. D. 70 the contents of the 'national archive' in Jerusalem were considered 'scriptural' only by *some* of the many groups active at the time.[47] Giving a surprising degree of credence to the tradition of Nehemiah's library in 2 Mac 2:13, Davies implies that there existed a kind of 'official list' (= 'canon'?) of Jewish scriptures by the end of the second century B. C.[48] Such a Hasmonean Temple library marks for him the end of the literature's growth and the beginning of the process of the text's standardization.[49] Capping Davies's argument for a Hasmonean date is his claim that the Masoretic chronology in the biblical text has been calculated to

---

[41] Ibid., 124.

[42] Isa 36–39 = 2 Kg 18:13–20:19; Jer 52 = 2 Kg 24:18–25:30.

[43] Search, 128. Here DAVIES cites BLENKINSOPP, Canon, with the difference that he doubts BLENKINSOPP's theory of the Prophets as a later corrective to the Law. DAVIES sees instead an 'ongoing tension between different ideologies.'

[44] Search, 133. I note that here DAVIES's 'exercise of imagination' regarding 'scribal schools' seems to have been granted the status of a fact.

[45] Ibid., 144–54.

[46] Ibid., 146–47.

[47] Ibid., 153–54.

[48] Ibid., 157–61.

[49] Ibid., 160.

culminate in the rededication of the Jerusalem Temple by the Maccabees in 164 B. C.[50]

This last claim is far too easily asserted. While it does seem that the Masoretic chronology relies upon a 4,000-year era that culminates in the Hasmonean period, it is not at all clear when this scheme was imposed upon the biblical text.[51] Nor is this system of dating consistent throughout the books of the Old Testament and other Jewish writings of the period.[52] In sum, the Masoretic chronology gives every indication of being a later, albeit significant, modification of the biblical text and cannot serve as a proper *terminus ad quem* for canonization. Along these lines it should be remembered that the tradition of Nehemiah's library, generally regarded quite dubiously, also derives from a post-biblical text (103–02 B. C.?).[53]

In other words, Davies's date of the end of the second century B. C. for a *de facto* canon of scripture could easily overshoot the mark. No biblical evidence *necessitates* such a date (to argue from 'necessity' as Davies does). The crucial point for the present discussion, however, is to note how Davies's Marxist understanding of religion as a secondary, derivative phenomenon compels him to delay the religious veneration of the biblical text as late as he can in order to make his point. Is there any compelling reason why the kind of 'national archive' which he describes could not have been assembled any earlier?

Davies himself points to a different construal of the evidence in his exploration of the terms 'law' and 'prophets.' In the context of his argument, this exploration is adduced as further evidence for the postponement of the formation of a religious 'scripture.' Noting that there does not exist in Hebrew, Aramaic or Greek a term for 'scripture' as distinct from 'literature,' Davies argues instead for the priority of the term 'the law and the prophets.'[54] He follows J. Barr and J. Barton in understanding 'Prophets' as 'non-Torah materials,'[55] which also means that he agrees with those same scholars that the di-

---

[50] Ibid. DAVIES cites for this claim THOMPSON, Historicity, 15 and HUGHES, Secrets, esp. 234–35. The original theory, cited in HUGHES, seems to have been proposed by MURTONEN, Chronology.

[51] A point made by THOMPSON himself (Historicity, 15)! The Masoretic dating scheme appears close to what was probably the earlier Priestly chronology, but it seems to me that when it comes to chronology 'close' fails to constitute a sufficient criterion. For other problems, see HUGHES, Secrets, 233–35.

[52] HUGHES, Secrets, 235. It is telling that even the advocates of this view cannot quite agree on the exact manner of mathematical calculation. Cf. Secrets, 234 n. 1.

[53] GOLDSTEIN, 2 Maccabees, 157–67, esp. 166; cf. 186–87.

[54] DAVIES, Search, 134–44. On 'scripture' as a modern category he cites BARR, Scripture, 50.

[55] DAVIES, Search, 137. Cf. BARR, Scripture, 55.

vision between 'Prophets' and 'Writings' reflects a later rearrangement of bipartite scripture into tripartite scripture.

Davies's rejection of the term 'scripture' on linguistic grounds cannot help but appear somewhat disingenuous after his use of such thoroughly anachronistic terms such as 'class,' 'class consciousness,' 'establishment,' 'lifestyle,' and 'ideology.' Would he claim to find these terms in Hebrew, Aramaic or Greek? He writes: "'Scripture' can only exist as a *notion* only [sic] where there has evolved *a religious system which permits 'scripture' to have a function*."[56] But does this assertion really address the issue at hand? Could not a religious system allow 'scripture' to function without necessarily defining that function *explicitly*? Is this not precisely what *Davies* understands to have happened in the 'third stage' of the biblical literature's formation, i. e., the extension of official 'religious' status to writings already popularly venerated (by some groups)? To compare terms, was 'class consciousness' a 'notion' in ancient Israel? Would Davies argue it was any less functional or real?

Still, Davies makes an important point that the primary sources (biblical and extra-biblical) employ variations on 'the law and the prophets' in reference to the biblical writings. What did they understand such expressions to mean? Davies argues for two bodies of literature extant in the first centuries B. C. and A. D., generally referred to as 'Law' or 'Moses' and 'Prophets,' although these literary collections appear not to have been clearly defined or their precise boundaries consistently maintained.

Thus, Davies helpfully insists that the clearest evidence of anything like 'scripture' at Qumran is not indicated by 'citation formulas', but in references to 'Moses' and 'the prophets.'[57] These biblical cadences provide strong evidence of an authoritative scripture in bipartite form.[58] Also noteworthy is Davies's observation that although Philo refers overwhelmingly to the 'Law,'[59] he also presents Moses as a *prophet* and frequently gives statements from the 'Law' the prophetic title χρησμὸς ('oracle' or 'logion').[60] According to Davies, where 4 Ezra equates 'the Law' with 'the twenty-four books' (4 Ezr 14:45), Josephus exhibits an understanding of 'prophets' as a 'universal cate-

---

[56] DAVIES, Search, 145. His emphases.

[57] Ibid., 138: As DAVIES notes, the phrase 'by the hand of Moses and all his servants the prophets' occurs in 1QS 1:3; cf. 1QS 8:15–16; CD 5:21–6:1. 'Law of Moses' occurs in 1QS 5:8; 8:22; CD 15:2; 9:12; etc. The expression 'books of the prophets' is found in CD 7:17.

[58] Search, 138. DAVIES observes that these terms appear to refer to writings which 'were regarded as authoritative in some way,' with or without a 'defined list of contents.' It seems to me that this fact alone should push back his dating of 'scripture' to an earlier period.

[59] Half of PHILO's few non-Pentateuchal references are from the Psalms and Proverbs, DAVIES reports (Search, 137), citing AMIR, Authority.

[60] DAVIES, Search, 137.

gory' for all the biblical writings (Against Apion, I:37–43; but counting twenty-two books).[61]

Davies notes the way in which Jn 10:43 cites Ps 82 as 'law,' Rom 3:19 cites an assortment of Psalms and one prophetic text (Isa 59:7–8) as 'law,' and 1 Cor 14:21 cites Isa 28:11–12 as 'law.'[62] For Davies, this expansion of semantic range is a "late first-century C. E. phenomenon which points to the development of a notion of a self-contained and cohesive body of religiously authoritative writing."[63] Yet there are also similarities to *earlier* biblical instances of these expressions. Davies is too dismissive of biblical references to 'the law of Moses'[64] and to 'the books' (of the Prophets/of Scripture).[65] His argument also does not take sufficient account of the Prologue to Ben Sira ('the law and the prophets and / the others that followed them – / the other books of our fathers,' ca. 132 B. C.) and the way in which Sir 44–49 relates scriptural material about Israel's prophets (ca. 180 B. C.).[66]

In sum, Davies's conclusion that 'Law' or 'Moses' and 'Prophets' were recognized references for Israel's authoritative writings makes good sense, although it appears to subvert his other proposals. In my view, such writings constituted *religious scripture* and were considered 'self-contained and cohesive' much earlier than Davies is willing to concede, even if the boundaries of this 'canon' continued for a time to be somewhat porous.[67]

In addition to his important insight about what in effect are scriptural *titles*, Davies's chief methodological contribution has been to highlight the importance of the concept of *self-interest* to reconstructions of canon formation, especially those in which the approach is similar to Davies's 'ideological' study.[68] As we shall see, language of 'power' and 'control' typically assumes the *determinative* quality of self-interest, whether such self-interest is understood to be conscious, unconscious, or both.

---

[61] Ibid., 143.

[62] Ibid., 135.

[63] Ibid., 143.

[64] See Jos 8:31, 32; 23:6; 1 Kg 2:3; 2 Kg 14:6; 23:25; 2 Chr 23:18; 30:16; Ezr 3:2; 7:6; Neh 8:1; Dan 9:11, 13; Lk 2:22; 24:44; Jn 7:23; Acts 13:39; 15:5; 28:23; 1 Cor 9:9; Heb 10:28; cf. Tob 1:8; 7:13; Bar 2:2; Sus 1:3, 62; 1 Esd 8:3; 9:39; Sir 24:23; 2 Mac 7:30. See also 'all the law of Moses' in Deut 4:8; Jos 1:7; 2 Kg 17:13; 21:8; 23:25; 2 Chr 33:8 and 'the book of Moses' in Jos 8:31; 23:6; 2 Kg 14:6; Neh 8:1; cf. Tob 6:13.

[65] See Dan 9:2.

[66] DAVIES now asserts that Deuteronomy maintained its unique status as תורה until into the third century B. C., but also claims to see in Sir 38:34–39:3 a possible reference to other genres of ancient writings. See his recent work, Scribes, 94; 109.

[67] The later histories of Judaism and Christianity show that it is quite possible to debate the relative merits of certain books within the canon while still investing the canon as a whole with religious authority.

[68] E. g., GOTTWALD, Ideology, 140–43.

However, the main reason for this careful exposition and critique of Davies's views has been to reveal the way in which the 'ideological' approach is far less neutral than it often pretends to be.[69] As I hope to make clear in this essay, Davies's use of 'ideology,' most likely because of his antipathy for theological readings of the biblical text and his Marxist presuppositions about the nature of religion, consistently obscures the character of the process of biblical canon formation.[70] It certainly leads him to make selective and inconsistent use of the available data, as we have already seen.[71]

Without rejecting altogether Davies's criticism of naively theological readings of the biblical text (in my view, historical criticism has represented a definite advance in our ability to read the biblical text closely), I am convinced that an approach such as the one he employs will lead only to a methodological dead-end when it comes to the particular task of describing the canonical formation of the biblical literature. Is there an alternative?

A 'Canonical' Approach?

As will already be clear from our review of twentieth-century scholarship on Old Testament canon formation (Chapter 1), the task of defining such terms as 'scripture' and 'canon' has only rarely been pursued directly or comprehensively.

Most often, a vague attribution of 'authority' was said to distinguish 'scripture' or 'canon' from ordinary writings. Some argued that 'scripture' should be defined as writings possessing 'authority,' but not yet officially delimited in scope (i. e., 'canon').[1] The nature of 'authority' in this reconstruction was never persuasively described; neither was a distinction between 'authoritative scripture' and 'canon' consistently or convincingly maintained.

As B. S. Childs has observed, the semantic possibility of an 'open canon' provides *a priori* semantic evidence against a narrow identification of 'canon' with exclusivity.[2] I. Provan has similarly noted that the concept of 'scripture'

---

[69] A criticism which could serve as a warning for historical approaches generally; see CHILDS, Interpretation; HERION, Impact.

[70] As BARR recently noted (Review, 556): "...a bizarre phenomenon of today is that, in a time when Marxism, after decades of oppressive totalitarian power, has become a complete political and economic failure in its own territory, it continues to have life among *Christian* social-theological interpreters (who, as it happens, are personally well established within the capitalistic system and drawing good salaries from it!)." His emphasis.

[71] In addition, I simply note here my disagreement with DAVIES's rejection of the pre-exilic existence of 'Israel.'

[1] Above all, SUNDBERG, Church, and SWANSON, Closing.

[2] CHILDS, OT Introduction, 58.

must also imply *some* degree of limitation.[3] A great part of the difficulty, however, lies in understanding what *interpretive* value such concepts offer for descriptions of the historical context of ancient Israel.

Childs's 1979 judgment still holds: "...much of the present confusion over the problem of the canon turns on the failure to reach an agreement regarding the terminology."[4] The confusion, however, also goes beyond the matter of semantics. An equal measure of the difficulty in defining these terms in relation to the Old Testament derives from a wider contemporary debate over the nature of 'scriptures' and 'canons.'[5] The key point is to adopt a method which will illuminate the particular features of biblical canon formation, but avoid presuppositions which may unintentionally subvert that goal. As we have seen, the unexamined assumptions of the historical methods used by biblical scholars in previous treatments have often prejudiced the results of their ostensibly-neutral investigations.

In an effort to discuss these presuppositions from a fresh perspective, I shall now review a few noteworthy *literary* efforts to grapple with the phenomenon of canons and canonicity. In my judgment, an interdisciplinary approach at this particular point not only helps to understand the nature of the conceptual standstill in biblical studies, but offers new opportunities for a solution.

H. Bloom

In a recent book, H. Bloom offers the unexpected view that what makes for canonicity is a quality of 'strangeness.'[6] In Bloom's words, "When you read a canonical work for a first time you encounter a stranger, an uncanny startlement rather than a fulfillment of expectations." He continues lapidarily: "They [canonical works] make you feel strange at home." Such strangeness repre-

---

[3] PROVAN, Canons, 10.

[4] CHILDS, OT Introduction, 51.

[5] In addition to reconstructions of Old Testament canon formation *per se*, the categories of 'canon,' 'scripture' and 'authority' have been subjected lately to increased examination and theological debate. See P. J. ACHTEMEIER, Inspiration; BARR, Scripture; BARTON, People; DUNN, Word; GNUSE, Authority; W. A. GRAHAM, Word; GREENSPAHN, Scripture; HOFFMAN, Inspiration; LIGHTSTONE, Society; SHEPPARD, Future; W. C. SMITH, Scripture? SUNDBERG, Bible Canon. For recent discussion, see also the essays in the Journal of Religion 76.2 (1996) from a conference at the University of Chicago on 'The Bible and Christian Theology.'

[6] BLOOM, Canon, 3. The following quotations are all from this page. For another account of texts possessing the 'power of strangeness' see RORTY, Philosophy, 360. Cf. also TRACY, Imagination, 107–08, on the 'classic' as a "disclosure of reality... which surprises, provokes, shocks and eventually transforms us; an experience that upsets conventional opinions and expands the sense of the possible; indeed a realized experience of that which is essential, that which endures."

sents "...a mode of originality that either cannot be assimilated" (his example of this mode is Dante) "or so assimilates us that we cease to see it as strange" (here his examples are Shakespeare and the Bible).

In my judgment, Bloom's reader-response description of a 'canonical' text's psychological impact immediately suggests an alternative way to construe the meaning of a text's 'authority.' Might it not be possible, even preferable, to explore the authority of the biblical canon as a measure of its ability to convey *imaginative* power upon its hearers and readers? And what is the relationship between that kind of imaginative 'power' and the traditional concept of canon as a regulative 'norm'?

N. Frye

Perhaps no modern literary scholar has described the imaginative power of the Bible as suggestively as N. Frye.[7] Frye considered the Bible a 'gigantic myth,'[8] which he described as possessing 'two parallel aspects,' namely: "as a story it is poetic and is recreated in literature; as a story with a specific social function, it is a program of action for a specific society."[9] By using the term 'myth,' Frye was attempting to make a descriptive, rather than a normative, judgment. It was not, in other words, a comment about the Bible's claim to truth. In fact, Frye chose the term 'myth' precisely in an effort to escape what he saw as a common false distinction between 'history' and 'story': namely, that the first was 'fact' and the second 'fiction.'[10]

As an example of the first aspect of myth, Frye cited Gibbon's *Decline and Fall of the Roman Empire*. Intended as 'history,' still "the phrase 'decline and fall' in the title indicates the narrative principle on which Gibbon selected and arranged his material: that is his *mythos*, and without such a *mythos* the book could have had no shape."[11] This description reveals that by this kind of 'myth' Frye meant something like 'story,' 'narrative' or 'plot.'[12]

However, since a conception of myth as 'narrative' was so broad as to be less than fully descriptive of the biblical material, Frye also introduced a second class of myths which possessed a more restricted context, those that possess a "specialization in social function... they are the stories that tell a society what is important for it to know, whether about its gods, its history, its

---

[7] FRYE, Code. What is essentially volume two of this work appeared later as FRYE, Words.

[8] FRYE, Code, 224.

[9] Ibid., 49. Cf. 47.

[10] Ibid., 32.

[11] Ibid.

[12] Ibid., 31–33.

laws, or its class structure."[13] Because such myths are central to the 'maintenance functions' of a society, Frye argued,[14] they become 'sacred' and are eventually considered 'revelation.'[15] He did not describe in detail the process of this sacralization. What is crucial for the present discussion, however, is to note that Frye explained the origin of a *canon* in relation to the educative aspect of certain myths rather than to the story-like shape of myths in general. It was the *social* function of these myths which created and defined a 'canon.'

Specifically, Frye argued that 'secondary' myths like the Bible had two indicative qualities: 1) the sense of a 'canon' (by which he meant an interconnected group of myths or a 'mythology'); and 2) a relation to a specific society (even though myths can be shared between societies, they tend to reflect one specific culture, he argued).[16] In this way 'canon' could express for Frye the interconnectedness of a society's myths and the cultural unity between those myths and the society in which they functioned. However, Frye also understood 'canon' more narrowly in light of its social origins. Thus canons not only *described* a society's central 'maintenance functions,' they were themselves *derived* from the society's need to maintain itself. The 'authority' of a canon emerged from its ability to sustain a culture's identity, its social function, rather than from the 'visionary force of its structure.'[17]

In contrast, it was precisely the visionary structure of *myths* that Frye celebrated. He argued that although canons derived from social needs and cultural forces, the myths which comprised them represented a 'form of imaginative and creative thinking' and were consequently considered 'autonomous' and irreducible.[18] Here Frye displayed a strong aversion for what he saw as the tendency within biblical studies to seek historicist meanings behind the biblical text and and attempt to demythologize the irreducible.[19] However, Frye himself 'demythologized' *canon* as a domesticated form of myth.

Interestingly, Frye blurred his distinction between myth and canon in discussing a quality he named 'resonance,' or "the way in which a particular

---

[13] Ibid., 33. On this basis, Frye also distinguished between 'myths' and 'folktales,' the latter of which existed in his view primarily for the purpose of entertainment, not education.

[14] This view of myth is probably indebted on some level to the work of sociologist B. Malinowski. For discussion of Malinowski's ideas, their contribution and their problems, see BURKE, Theory, 101–09. As BURKE quite cogently points out, "social stability need not imply consensus. It may depend on prudence or inertia rather than a shared ideology" (109). Another problem with views that emphasize ideology or a common myth, he writes, is the neglect of individual motives.

[15] FRYE, Code, 33.

[16] Ibid., 33–34.

[17] Ibid., 33.

[18] Ibid., 35.

[19] Ibid., xvii–xix. Cf. FRYE's comments (Ibid., 35) on FRAZER, Folk-lore.

statement in a particular context requires a universal significance."[20] It was this notion of 'resonance' that Frye used in order to describe the irreducibility of myths in general and, specifically, the metaphorical intertextuality of the Bible. To be sure, biblical literature had an 'original context,' but it also possessed a 'power of expanding away from that context.'[21]

In this way the Bible as a 'gigantic myth'[22] embraced "an immense variety of material, and the unifying forces that hold it together cannot be the rigid forces of doctrinal consistency or logic, which would soon collapse under cultural stress, but the more flexible ones of imaginative unity, which is founded on metaphor."[23] The relationship — and tension! — between Frye's notion of the Bible as a resonant, imaginative *unity* and the biblical canon as a secondary, derivative construct was left unaddressed.

Moreover, Frye could also describe the Bible as a 'violently partisan book,' saying that "as with any other form of propaganda, what is true is what the writer thinks ought to be true..."[24] Perhaps even more revealingly, Frye wrote that at the *literal* level of meaning, the organizing principle of the Bible was the 'Feuerbach principle,' namely "that man creates his gods in his own image."[25] Thus, by reading the Bible on different 'levels' Frye sought to reconcile the immanence and the transcendence of the biblical text, in his terms, its status as canon and myth (respectively!). However, the relationship between such 'levels' of interpretation was also not made clear. Did the metaphorical power of the text ever transcend the 'maintenance functions' of the canon? Or was the metaphorical level of the text to be interpreted as a subtler form of 'propaganda'? Or could it be said that metaphor also performed a critical social function?

Frye made certain statements that seemed to imply there was also a crucial social role for *ideals*. For example, in discussing the commandment 'Thou shalt not kill' he wrote:

"It is less important as a law than as a vision of an ideal world in which people do not, perhaps even cannot, kill. Similarly, many of Jesus' exhortations are evocations of a world very different from the one we live in, so that we may find them unpractical or exaggerated as

---

[20] Ibid., 217.

[21] Ibid., 218.

[22] FRYE did not use the word 'canon' in this context, but he must have meant something like it; note the similarity of this formulation to the 'story' quality of myth which he discussed earlier (Code, 33–34).

[23] FRYE, Code, 218.

[24] Ibid., 40.

[25] Ibid., 228.

guides to practice. They are not guides to practice directly, however, but parts of a vision of an 'innocent world,' and it is that vision which is the guide to practice."[26]

By this formulation, Frye did not necessarily mean to suggest that 'ideals' and 'vision' were part of the maintenance needs of the societies which gave rise to the biblical canon, but rather that we as readers are able to move beyond the propagandistic, literal 'level' of the text by hearing it on a metaphorical 'level.'

Of course, a post-modern retort to this kind of reading lies close at hand. By claiming that canons *derive* from social maintenance functions, Frye opened up the possibility that whatever metaphorical resonance might exist in individual myths was effectively controlled within the limiting framework of the canon. Thus, G. Bruns has argued:

"A text... is canonical, not in virtue of being final and correct and part of an official library, but because it becomes binding upon a group of people... The distinction between canonical and noncanonical is thus not just a distinction between authentic and inauthentic texts — that is, it is not reducible to the usual oppositions between the inspired and the mundane, the true and the apocryphal, the sacred and the profane, and so on. On the contrary, it is a distinction between texts that are forceful in a given situation and those which are not. From a hermeneutical standpoint, in which the relation of a text to a situation is always of primary interest, the theme of canonization is *power*."[27]

Although Frye had maintained that the reach of myth exceeded the grasp of 'power,' by defining canons as *derived* from social functions he invited just the kind of argument which Bruns mounts.[28] And if canons are derivative, why not myths, too? Why not view *all* literature as someone else's 'propaganda'? Frye's treatment cannot defend against this critique on its own terms; still, by differentiating between visionary power and political power, Frye had raised a critical point.

The view of canon espoused by Bruns is actually not that different from that of Wellhausen. For both, it is the *nomistic* aspect of canon which dominated and dictated the origin and growth of the Old Testament canon. For Wellhausen, it was the prophets who shaped and formed Israelite religion, but it was the post-exilic priesthood that shaped and closed the canon. Bruns is

---

[26] Ibid., 219–20. The allusion is to W. Blake's poem, Auguries of Innocence.

[27] BRUNS, Canon. His emphasis. BRUNS finds easy support for his argument by reporting the views of various biblical scholars. For more on his views, see BRUNS, Hermeneutics. For recent agreement with BRUNS, see PARKER, Speech.

[28] BRUNS himself does not refer to FRYE, but this interpretation of FRYE's work is offered exuberantly by JAMESON, Unconsciousness, 68–74. He praises FRYE (69) for drawing the "basic, essentially social, interpretive consequences from the nature of religion as collective representation." One wonders, incidentally, just how far JAMESON would go to defend the *essentiality* of social consequences.

simply more explicit about the coercive authority such legal status implies. Perhaps Frye might have argued that even though brute power may lie *behind* the construction of canons, the present form of the biblical canon cannot be said to have been structured exclusively by the 'rigid forces of doctrinal consistency or logic.' Ultimately, however, such an argument would seem to hang on Frye's ability to establish various levels of meaning for interpretation.

To the contrary, Bruns's interpretation has the advantage of being blunt and visceral: 'canons' are expressions of the competition for power among groups within society and are imposed by the victors. Bruns does not even begin to struggle with any hermeneutical 'ditch' between what canons meant and what they mean:[29] the 'literal' level of the text, which describes for him the struggle for power, remains the primary meaning of the canon. Bruns comes to the same conclusions as many contemporary biblical scholars: the biblical canon illustrates the opposition of prophetic word and written Torah;[30] canonization resulted from a priestly appropriation of prophetic authority 'by means of the superior forces of writing and textuality';[31] the final form of the Hebrew Scriptures represents a political compromise.[32]

Something about these conclusions seems suggestive, just as Frye's basic connection between canon and social maintenance smacks of common sense. There are, however, crucial details missing in both formulations. What *kind* of knowledge does a society need to dispense or even seek in order to maintain itself? What is the relationship between that kind of knowledge and a 'canon'? What *is* social 'power' and is it reducible to 'self-interest'? Bloom's isolation of 'strangeness' as the *primary* feature of canons should serve as *prima facie* evidence to remind us that the identification of 'canon' with self-serving propaganda may be far less self-evident than it is often assumed to be.

As R. von Hallberg summarizes in his introduction to a rich selection of literary essays on this problem: "The question raised by the tension between these different perspectives on canon formation [he is referring to the perspectives in the volume] is not whether canons serve political functions but rather how fully their political functions account for their origins and limit their utility."[33] As both Frye and Bruns insist, there *is* a political function to canons and canon formation. Is that political function, however, to be understood as the sole, primary or overriding feature of canon formation? And

---

[29] For this classic formulation of the hermeneutical problem, see STENDAHL, Biblical Theology.

[30] BRUNS, Canon, 69.

[31] Ibid., 77. Cf. PARKER, Speech.

[32] BRUNS, Canon, 81.

[33] HALLBERG, Introduction.

again, what kind of political function is being referred to? By a 'political' function should we understand only 'power politics' and brute self-interest?[34]

Canons, Power and Self-Interest

A customary way to defend against charges of self-interest in the transmission of the biblical literature has been to defend the integrity of the scribal tradition.[1] In my judgment, however, any such blanket descriptions of reliable scribes[2] or providential guidance[3] will evoke quite justified charges of special pleading.

I take it as axiomatic that self-interest functioned together with a desire for faithfulness on the part of the biblical literature's tradents. However, I am further convinced that if the critical question is expressed simply as a matter of how self-interested the tradents were, the true nature of the problem and its solution will remain obscured. A much more productive approach is to consider *how* the tradents were 'self-interested,' rather than simply *how much*.

---

[34] As McGowan has noted (Postmodernism, 242–43), even the recognition that "commitment to social identity [is] an important (although not exclusive) motive for agents is necessarily to question the explanatory power of interest." He concludes that 'interest' is "an almost completely worthless tool in predicting political or social behavior" and that the usual usage of the term acts as a "red herring, highlighting one particular type of motive without considering the range of other motives."

[1] One of the best formulations of this position was made by B. J. Roberts (Suggestion, 167) with reference to the later scribal work of the rabbis: "It is significant that what the Rabbis did, both in their glosses and in their interpretation, was to add to the text merely that which was evoked by it. The prestige of the text was not thereby impaired, but actually enhanced... They never claimed for themselves the right to challenge Scripture or even to interfere with it except for elucidation." Such a view helpfully describes a possible rationale for such editors, but cannot defend against a charge of self-deception or 'false consciousness.' That defense must be made upon other grounds, in my view upon a fuller understanding of human agency. For a nuanced approach which tries to set out a typology of scribal work from the 'tendentious' to the 'revealed,' but still within a basic assumption of self-interest, see Fishbane, Interpretation, 536–42. A comparable typology is employed by Clements, OT Prophecy, 217–229 ('The Prophet and His Editors'). Clements describes three roles for prophetic editors: preservationists, creative originators and interpreters. Weber's theory of 'routinization' occupies the central position in Clements's reconstruction of the sociological processes at work.

[2] E. g., as in Vasholz, Canon.

[3] E. g., Margolis, Scriptures. Ryle also made this claim; see his Canon, 1.

C. Altieri

In a brilliant essay, philosopher and literary critic C. Altieri has probed the relation between self-interest and canon formation.[4] Altieri's argument is subtle and suggestive. Employing the philosophical categories of C. Taylor,[5] Altieri confronts the assertion that the self-interest of individuals and social groups limits the function of a literary canon to the confirmation of accepted dogmas.

Taylor has drawn an important distinction in moral philosophy between 'preferences,' which he defines as involving direct personal satisfaction, and 'strong evaluations,' by which he means second-order choices between and among meanings.[6] According to Taylor, second-order choices (unlike 'preferences') are contrastive, centering on meanings rather than objects. For example, if a person decides to be courageous, that person necessarily binds him- or herself to particular acts and attitudes over a lengthy period of time. These particular acts and attitudes may not be congruent with a person's usual preferences. However, in the decision to be courageous a person must adopt a consistent pattern of behavior which necessitates the performance and non-performance of certain acts and attitudes over time. If a person has decided to be courageous, then that person cannot do cowardly things. Thus, a second level of 'self-interest' may exist, requiring the *restriction* of personal preferences, not on the basis of some universal norm, but because certain preferences will conflict with the 'strong evaluations' chosen by the human agent.

Altieri does *not* deny that canons are ultimately constituted by the self-interest (more broadly understood) of the individuals and social groups responsible for canon formation. With help from Taylor's categories, however, Altieri in turn suggests that canons are constituted by the 'strong evaluations' of canonical tradents, which means that canons involve not only the projection of 'strong evaluations,' but also provide a *forum* for the debate between 'strong evaluations' and 'preferences.' In this way, canons invite, even compel, a contrasting of personal and communal alternatives.[7]

---

[4] ALTIERI, Idea. A revised, somewhat more cautious version of this essay also appears as the second chapter of ALTIERI, Canons.

[5] TAYLOR, Agency? idem, Sources; idem, Papers 1; idem, Papers 2. For a collection of assessments of TAYLOR's significance by fellow philosophers, see TULLY, Philosophy.

[6] ALTIERI, Idea, 44. For TAYLOR's description of 'strong evaluations,' see his Agency? cf. idem, Animals, esp. 65–68. He credits the basic distinction to FRANKFURT, Freedom. For a critique of TAYLOR's explanation of it, see FLANAGAN, Identity. It should be noted that in TAYLOR's printed response to the collection of essays about his work (TULLY, Pluralism, 213–57) he regrets his choice of the word 'evaluation,' which he now feels is too reflected and deliberate. What he meant, he says, was simply the *sense* of an agent that "some desires, goals, aspirations are qualitatively higher than others" (Pluralism, 249).

[7] I think it might have been helpful for ALTIERI to reflect further on the social dimensions of self-evaluations. To what extent are certain self-limitations prompted or modelled by oth-

For Altieri, the function of a canon is therefore not to preserve the past by projecting (or retrojecting) simple dogmas, but rather to form a kind of "permanent theater, helping us shape and judge personal and social values... our self-interest in the present consists primarily in establishing ways of employing that theater to gain distance from our ideological commitments."[8] Thus, in his view canons *subvert* ideals just as much as they enshrine them.

This subversive quality of canons and canon formation also means that a canon's 'ideals' are never reducible to one single historical or ideological context:

"If we imagine thinkers and artists over a long period of time criticizing the existing social order, producing alternative models and seeking judgment from within these alternatives, we see clearly how the very concept of imaginative ideals requires a dialogue between empirical conditions and underlying principles... We use alternatives the past provides in order to shape possible selves in the present. But once that is accepted, it is imperative that we produce a view of history complex enough to handle the ways agents base their actions on a range of contexts, each creating possible ideals and imaginary judges. In turn, that density within history affords grounds for basing arguments about the public good upon the models and what the past suggests is possible or desirable."[9]

Such 'density within history' suggests a very different model of 'self-interest' for reconstructions of canon formation.

In a sense, what Altieri has been able to do (with Taylor's help) is to overcome the distinction Frye observed between the Bible as myth and the Bible as canon, between the visionary quality of a myth and the importance of a canon for social maintenance. In Altieri's formulation, visionary ideals are *also* included within the 'social maintainence' needs of a society, for societies are never truly static, but rather always in the process of recreating themselves. Thus, the social importance of a canon of literature lies in its provision of a public 'theater' in which personal and communal alternatives can be re-

---

ers? TAYLOR's language of 'evaluations' suggests perhaps a more autonomous self than ALTIERI might really wish to maintain. The notion of self-identity presumed here seems more akin to the 'postliberal view' described by McGOWAN (Postmodernism, 243–44) in which self-identity is formed through some kind of 'constitutive action,' such as 'belonging to a community or engaging in its practices.'

[8] ALTIERI, Idea, 44. He credits T. S. Eliot for the notion of a 'permanent theater.' Altieri modifies the expression to 'enduring theater' in his Canons, 24.

[9] ALTIERI, Idea, 54. In my judgment, CHILDS approximates this position in the conclusion to his Biblical Theology (724), where he writes that "[canon] does not restrict the witness to one single propositional formulation... [but sketches] the range of authoritative writings [and] establishes parameters of the apostolic witness within which area there is freedom and flexibility." The important contribution of ALTIERI is to make a case for *why* canons do not result in such a restriction and to identify the inclusion of a multiplicity of witnesses as canon formation's primary *goal*.

hearsed and debate over goals and ends will be aired.[10] For this reason, the *range of ideals* contained within a canon is suggestively termed by Altieri a cultural 'grammar.'[11]

In concluding, Altieri argues that canons: 1) institutionalize an ongoing cultural process of idealization; 2) establish a source of social authority by providing a cultural 'grammar'; and 3) set the 'projective dimensions' for contemporary writing by new authors and critics.[12]

I believe Altieri's conception proves especially congenial to an interpretation of the biblical canon, although Altieri himself does not address this application of his work. In emphasizing the way in which the dialectical resources of a literary canon serve to distance a reader from the "empirical self... [and] undergo in imagination protean changes of identity and sympathy,"[13] Altieri's description recalls certain qualities Christian tradition ascribes to Holy Scripture:[14] in the apprehension of something 'other' outside the empirical self,[15] in the establishment of ideals which consistently subvert the existing social order,[16] and in the provision of a critical benchmark for future creative reflection and writing.[17] In my judgment, however, Altieri's subtle analysis of literary canons also serves as a helpful reminder of crucial aspects of the Old Testament canon which are routinely overlooked or even summarily rejected by biblical scholars.[18]

Of course there are also differences between literary canons and Holy Scripture. The tradition of the western literary canon, of which Altieri writes in support, has maintained fairly fluid boundaries reflecting humanistic ideals, while Christian tradition has largely stood by a 'closed' canon expressing the

---

[10] Cf. TRACY, Imagination, 102–03.

[11] ALTIERI, Idea, 46; 51–52.

[12] Ibid., 52–54.

[13] Ibid., 47.

[14] Cf. the conclusions similar to ALTIERI's in W. C. SMITH, Scripture?, 232–33. For an interesting theological work that conceives of scripture as a kind of 'theater,' although without using the expression *per se*, see PATRICK, Rendering, xvii–xix; 1–3. Cf. also the treatment of the religious 'classic' by TRACY, Imagination, 193–229.

[15] OTTO, Holy.

[16] TRACY, Imagination, 236–37; cf. SCHNEIDAU, Discontent.

[17] E. g., the various processes of redaction visible within the biblical material itself, but even more the later interpretive works of Qumran, Judaism and the early Church.

[18] For criticism of ALTIERI, much of it surprisingly complimentary, see READINGS, Canon, esp. 151–52 on ALTIERI: "...the most subtly argued defence of the canon as concept." READINGS himself, however, argues the extreme point that all representation is unjust, which leads him to reject any kind of canon, even ALTIERI's, that does not allow for a *total* 'heterogeneity of descriptions' (READINGS, Canon, 152). Obviously, such a position makes it impossible to have any kind of *identity*, other than an identity of pure 'heterogeneity.' And what would that be?

'Word of God.'[19] Also, Altieri wants the literary canon to provide for ethical reflection, but not directly to dictate or prescribe specific acts.[20] Specific prescription is clearly part — but not all! — of the traditional function of the biblical canon.

Thus, there are limitations to the usefulness of Altieri's notion of canon as a cultural 'grammar.' However, the most important contribution of Altieri to the present discussion is a methodological one. If we are to grant the truth of his notion that self-interest is much more *complex* than it is almost always assumed to be, and that the process of Old Testament canon formation might well turn on 'strong evaluations' rather than 'personal preferences,' then how are we to credit these features sufficiently in a reconstruction of canon formation? And how do we avoid the mistake of presuming their absence by making opposing assumptions?[21]

In the hope of arriving at such a methodological framework within which to pursue my investigation, I should now like to sketch a view, based on Altieri's work, of the Old Testament canon as a *theological* 'grammar.'

Canon as a Theological 'Grammar'

My appropriation of Altieri's ideas in this regard has less to do with the way in which communities of faith might presently understand and employ their canons of scripture, and more to do with the historical question of canon formation. Although I think contemporary communities of faith might have much to learn from Altieri's understanding of canon as a 'grammar,'[1] my ap-

---

[19] ALTIERI insists on viewing literary canons as 'open,' as yet another way of avoiding a charge of prescriptive ideology. Cf. READINGS, Canon, 151.

[20] ALTIERI, Idea, 55. Interestingly, ALTIERI's effort to avoid prescription in favor of 'negative ideals' is considered a failure by READINGS (Canon, 152) because in his view ALTIERI manages to retain a notion of canon as regulative. READINGS's criticism indicates that it is possible, and probably inevitable, to combine the 'negative' and 'positive' force of canonical ideals.

[21] Cf. THISELTON, Interpreting, ix: "Postmodernism... tells part of the story about the human self, but not the whole story. It takes account of imposed role performances within society with a greater degree of realism than the partly illusory optimism of modernity. But an adequate account of the self cannot stop with its situatedness in some instantaneous moment within processes of shifting flux. Selfhood discovers its identity and personhood within a larger purposive narrative which allows room for agency, responsibility and hope."

[1] For some intriguing suggestions, see the similar treatment of church doctrine as a 'grammar' by LINDBECK, Doctrine. In my use of the term 'grammar' I do not wish to eliminate the possibility of truth claims that refer to realities outside the system. I am sure that LINDBECK does not want to do so either, but his work is not completely clear on this point. See CHILDS, Biblical Theology, 21–22; idem, NT Introduction, 541–46 ('Excursus III');

propriation of Altieri's construal of canonical dynamics is for the purpose of making the *historical* claim that individuals and cultures within the process of biblical canon formation had a fundamental 'interest' in ideals that unsettled or even disconfirmed regnant ideologies, rather than in only those that reinforced the conventions and structures of brute power.[2]

It is precisely this insight which is so lacking in much of biblical scholarship on canon.[3] Whether it is imagined that 'ideals' only cloak assertions of power,[4] or that Israel was simply too 'primitive' to have possessed an interest in such 'ideals,' the history of canon formation is routinely reduced to the competition and compromises of political power groups. These power groups, in turn, are reconstructed from the very contrastive features of the canon that, I shall argue instead, were preserved or even designed by the canon's tradents to promote reflection within a common *range* of alternatives, rather than simply to record their disagreements or impasses.

The worst feature of this trend in biblical interpretation is the smug conviction of some that any description of canon formation which suggests a

---

PROVAN, Canons, 24–25. I note further that on at least one occasion, CHILDS similarly explained his approach as the description of a 'language game.' See CHILDS, Response, 52.

[2] Another possibility might be to argue that the relationship between confirmatory and disconfirmatory self-interest is dialectical or 'bi-polar.' See BRUEGGEMANN, Essays, 4–5. In BRUEGGEMANN's description, however, it seems that he can only impute a single view to a single social group at a time, so that the individual texts of the canon are said to represent *either* social legitimation *or* critique. Cf. the criticism of BRUEGGEMANN by GOTTWALD, Integrating. Judged by its treatment of human agency, BRUEGGEMANN's 'bi-polar' theology is therefore still reductive, a problem unresolved by his attention to the 'margins' of Israelite society. He quite unflatteringly describes the canonical process as 'hegemonic.' Cf. BRUEGGEMANN, Pluralism, esp. 457. In his recent Theology, BRUEGGEMANN has attempted to make a virtue out of his atomistic methodology, by asserting that in the Old Testament Israel's various testimonies have "no concern for a larger sketch of Yahweh... It is rather the work of those who hear the witnesses... to construe or imagine a comprehensive characterization..." (Theology, 267). The thesis of the present essay is precisely opposite; namely, that it was the effort to articulate a unified testimony to the God of Israel which generated the canonical process and gave the canonical literature its shape.

[3] A point made forcefully by KECK, Rethinking, 5: "...in our legitimate and relentless quest for historical origins, antecedents, parallels, and influences to explain each writing and its alleged sources, we may have forfeited... a fully historical understanding of the New Testament as a whole, namely, as canon... the New Testament as canon, like its constituent pieces before they were canonized, not only expresses the faith and ethos of early Christianity but also addresses them in order to correct them. To overlook this is to fail to understand the New Testament historically... the same is true of much of the Old Testament as well." Cf. also the argument by COHEN that the 'multivalency' of the canon was already understood in antiquity (COHEN, Maccabees, 193).

[4] Thus, e. g., KNIGHT, Deuteronomy, 73, describes the editors of the Deuteronomistic History as "guided by an agenda so pronounced, self-serving, and even tendentious that it colors much of the narrative itself."

force at work other than naked power is naive or 'idealistic.'[5] Arguing against this conviction in detail will occupy much of the rest of this book. For the moment, however, I simply observe that a major objection to this 'ideological' interpretation of canon formation is identical to the problem that has bedeviled the standard theory of Old Testament canon formation: the place of the Prophets within the canon.[6] How could Israel have been too 'primitive' or 'ideological' to allow for internal cultural alternatives and critique, given the way in which early on the prophets' delegitimation of certain 'ideological' features was granted canonical authority?[7]

However, even if the negative point be granted that canons are not simple ideological constructs (in the sense of self-confirming 'self-interest'), what positive contribution would the notion of canon as a *theological* 'grammar' make to historical reconstructions of biblical canon formation? Altieri describes three qualities of a 'grammatical' approach to literary canons and canonicity which, I believe, have important applications for the study of Old Testament canon formation.[8]

First, a canonical work exhibits 'forceful self-subsumption,' by which Altieri means that a work presents itself as an 'entity' and seeks to subsume the circumstances of its making to the ideals of which it enjoins consideration. Second, such a work needs to 'articulate shared values in a past culture that influence the present.' Finally, in order to judge between and among canons, critics have an "obligation to describe... the value of technical innovations or the wisdom and ethical significance" of a canon's overall content. Each of these qualities, I contend, can illuminate crucial but overlooked features in the process of Old Testament canon formation.

'Self-Subsumption' and the Old Testament Canon

Let us first consider the applicability to our task of Altieri's first quality of canons, 'forceful self-subsumption.' With 'self-subsumption,' Altieri again draws upon Taylor's revisionary approach to the philosophy of the self.

---

[5] Thus, GOTTWALD, Tribes, 592–607. Against this assumption I cite further NAGEL, Altruism. NAGEL argues that some reasons 'transcend' time conditionality (Altruism, 33–46). His examples are revenge and retribution: "...they may not be good reasons, but their form becomes intelligible if we give up the assumption that a reason must always be the product of circumstances existing at the time of action" (46 n. 1). This kind of 'transcendence' (58) is not grounded in a 'super-sensible realm' which is perceived in a Platonic sense 'when our practical intuitions are correct,' but rather in a 'metaphysics of the person,' which supports "the objective validity of prudential constraints by interpreting them as the practical expression of an awareness that persists over time."

[6] Despite his very different perspective, BERLINERBLAU agrees at this point quite precisely (Remarks, 164–66).

[7] See CHILDS, Reading, 372; NICHOLSON, Religion, 25.

[8] ALTIERI, Idea, 57. The following three points are all found on this page.

Critical historicism, Altieri maintains, generally considers only two aspects to self-interest: "the desire for power over others, and the pursuit of self-representations that satisfy narcissistic demands."[9] Two other claims, however, seem to Altieri to be equally plausible; namely, "that some people can understand their empirical interests to a degree sufficient to allow them considerable control over their actions, and that a basic motive for such control is to subsume one's actions under a meaning the self can take responsibility for."[10] In just the same way, Altieri believes, a canonical work integrates the concerns of readers and establishes compelling moral categories for them.[11]

I take it that canonical works are able to evidence this kind of 'forceful self-subsumption' because authors, and in the biblical case various tradents, sought to express the ideals and contrastive alternatives necessary to distance themselves from the mere calculation of means and create for themselves an opportunity for the consideration of ends.[12] In other words, authors or tradents *themselves* engaged in the process of making 'strong evaluations' in the production of their canon.[13]

Altieri draws the following hermeneutical conclusion from this understanding of the *historical* process of canon formation:

> "...the crucial enabling step is to insist on reading authors as I think most of them intended to be read: as agents constructing a version of experience with a claim to influence the ways generations of readers would view themselves and their world. This activity does entail partly reading against historical specificity, so as to highlight those qualities of the work that transcend the conditions of the work's genesis. Highlighting transcendent qualities does not mean ignoring history, nor does it require denying the historical commitments of a given writer. We need the specificity of the work, need it to maintain an otherness with something different to say to us."[14]

His remarks immediately suggest, and I believe support, the well-known observation of B. S. Childs that the biblical redactors have 'hidden their footsteps':

---

[9] ALTIERI, Canons, 28.

[10] Ibid. The similarity of ALTIERI's language to the title of TAYLOR's essay, 'Responsibility for the Self,' makes the dependence obvious. ALTIERI fully acknowledges TAYLOR's influence.

[11] ALTIERI, Canons, 41.

[12] On the attribution of this sort of purposiveness to the text's 'authorial presence,' and the difference between that kind of formulation and the positing of a determinate authorial 'intention,' see ALTIERI, Act; cf. idem, Canons, 12–14.

[13] It is worth pointing out that this process of second-order decision-making is conceived on the basis of TAYLOR's work as a human activity, and thus does not require being relegating for this reason alone to a class of intellectuals or specialists. *Contra* BERLINERBLAU, Remarks, 156–57.

[14] ALTIERI, Canons, 45.

"...basic to the canonical process is that those responsible for the actual editing of the text did their best to obscure their own identity... When critical exegesis is made to rest on the recovery of these very sociological distinctions which have been obscured, it runs directly in the face of the canon's intention... However, the one concern which is expressly mentioned is that a tradition from the past be transmitted in such a way that its authoritative claims be laid upon all successive generations of Israel."[15]

Common to both Childs's and Altieri's formulations is the idea of 'self-subsumption': without subordinating their immediate needs and concerns ('preferences') to the contemplation of second-order considerations ('strong evaluations'), the tradents of the biblical material could not have hoped to produce literature which would lay a persuasive claim upon future generations of hearers and readers.[16] And yet precisely this hope drives the process of canon formation.[17]

Childs is dismissive of efforts to 'psychologize' the tradents of the biblical material,[18] and on the interpretive danger of such efforts I agree. I am convinced, however, that a plausible *alternative* must be offered to the narrow psychology of self-interest assumed by much historical criticism, if we are to escape the reductionist reconstructions of biblical canon formation that glibly equate the interest of any tradent exclusively with political control and self-advantage.[19] Certainly an alternative is necessary to make persuasive the role of the 'theocentric dimension' which Childs claims is central to the process of canon formation, but nowhere defends psychologically or sociologically.[20]

I believe that Altieri's application of Taylor's philosophical categories provides such an alternative. Because of the 'self-subsumption' involved in

---

[15] Childs, OT Introduction, 78.

[16] Cf. Miller, Faith. He distinguishes faith from ideology on the basis of self-interest (Faith, 467), but does not explore the canonical implications of such a distinction. The difficulty with Miller's approach lies in his argument that 'faith' is different in kind from self-interest. In contrast, I have sought to distinguish between different kinds of 'self-interest.'

[17] Childs cites (OT Introduction, 78) as examples of this hope Deut 31:9–13; Ex 12:14, 26–28.

[18] Childs, OT Introduction, 62.

[19] Cf. Thiselton, Interpreting, x: "We need a hermeneutic of selfhood." For recent sociological criticism of facile generalizations about 'power' in Old Testament studies, see Berlinerblau, Remarks, 158–60. My objection to Berlinerblau's treatment of the issue is that he does not explore deeply enough the nature of the 'consensual power' to which he contrasts 'coercive power.'

[20] Thus Childs is criticized by Perdue (Collapse, 189) precisely for failing to account for the role of self-interest in the process of canon formation. Cf. J. J. Collins, Theology? 5–7 See also the criticism of Childs by Watson (Text, 43–44) on the charge of being 'idealist.' Childs himself seems increasingly concerned with this problem, see Childs, Analysis, 363; and idem, Reading, 372, where he explicitly identifies self-interest as a crucial methodological issue within the field. See also the discussion of 'ideology' in relation to Childs's approach in Brett, Crisis? 149–56.

Israel's canonical process, the 'transcendent qualities' of the text provide a surer basis as to the communicative intentions of the individual works in the canon and the canon as a whole. Rather than merely expressive of a political program or even the *status quo*, these transcendent qualities had and continue to have as their purpose a continued engagement with God.[21] On the basis of this hermeneutical fulcrum, I intend to reweigh the evidence concerning Old Testament canon formation in an effort to identify and amplify the ways in which the biblical tradents not only subordinated their own interests and contexts, but actively worked to construct formulations and frameworks which would communicate a *range* of theological *ideals* to future generations.

I shall argue in this regard that the most important theological framework set in place by the tradents for future interpretation of the canon is found in the construct 'the Law and the Prophets,' as it eventually came to be expressed. I shall show that variations of this construct appear in a number of terms and descriptions which appear from the earliest stages of the biblical 'canon' to which we have access.

Among other consequences, this means that the idea that the 'Prophets' were always subordinated to the 'Law' within the canonical development of the Old Testament is quite incorrect and results from a retrojection of later rabbinic evidence into the biblical period, aided and abetted by the standard 'nomistic' theory of Old Testament canon formation. 'Law' and 'Prophets' should instead be read as distinct but complementary theological witnesses, which were influenced by each other and mutually-coordinated from the beginning. In my judgment, 'the Law' was never the sole 'Bible' of Israel, nor were 'the Prophets' formally subordinated to 'the Law' within Judaism until well *after* the biblical period (i. e., the period of the Jerusalem Talmud).

Against my suggestion of a model of 'self-subsumption' and conscious 'theologizing,' it may be argued that the formation of the biblical canon was accomplished by groups rather than individuals, and that in the ancient period such groups were more likely to have been at the mercy of their contexts and 'needs' than able to subordinate them in the interests of 'theology.'[22] Some,

---

[21] BUSS similarly argues (Hosea, 89) against understanding religious canons generally as the result of 'self-assertion,' noting that a 'receptive relation' between human being and text is for them constitutive: "In the Hebrew Scriptures — including Hosea — receptivity is symbolized by the linguistic form of God speaking to human beings. This has ethical implications, for ethics involves an openness to the other." Interestingly, BUSS also argues (89–90) that this kind of receptivity characterizes the form and function of many Eastern religious canons (e. g., in Hinduism, Buddhism, Taoism). For further discussion of the importance of scriptural receptivity for diverse religious traditions, see LEVERING, Scripture.

[22] See, however, the judgment of MAYES (Sociology, 58–59), that sociological theory in general has been moving in the direction of giving greater attention to human agency and social psychology.

like P. R. Davies, will argue that use of 'theology' in this way is simply ana-chronistic.[23]

It is my conviction, however, that appeals to the primitivism or pre-theological worldview of Israelite society and religion founder in the pro-found theological depths of the biblical literature itself. Can anyone really doubt that those responsible for the Primeval History (Gen 1–11) or the Suc-cession Narrative (2 Sam 9–20; 1 Kg 1–2) possessed great theological in-sights?[24] Is it not also plausible that they sought to express those insights in a form persuasive to future generations, critically subordinating their own con-texts and agenda for the sake of that hope? Is it not at least possible that those today who view religious motives and theological concepts as a smokescreen for the 'real' fires of material and psychological forces are themselves only feeling the heat of late twentieth-century capitalism?[25]

A more important theological objection is raised by those who warn that a model of 'conscious theologizing' runs the risk of forcing unity where there really is none, and that the unity of the biblical literature lies not in itself but in the revelation it reports[26] or the reality to which it bears witness.[27] There is certainly no indication that "the ordering of the oral and written material into a canonical form always involved an intentional decision."[28] We dare not flatten or harmonize in our effort to find an inner logic behind the oppositions evident in the text.

For precisely this reason, it is crucial to move beyond what may be recov-erable in the way of motives and view the text as it now exists.[29] As I hope to illuminate, the tradents of the biblical literature provided hermeneutical

---

[23] See the various expressions of this viewpoint, along with the appropriate references, in SMEND, Theologie, 11–13.

[24] The ability to illuminate these theological insights is still the great strength of VON RAD's work, making it irreplaceable in spite of various problems. See his OT Theology, I:136–65; 308–18.

[25] Cf. THISELTON, Interpreting, 12: "The postmodern self perceives itself as having lost control as active agent, and as having been transformed into a passive victim of competing groups. Everyone seems to be at the mercy of someone else's vested interests for power. Mass advertizing has contributed much to the collapse of confidence in claims to truth, along with power-seeking in party-politics. People suspect that here 'truth' disguises only the desire for success and domination."

[26] BARR, Scripture, 100–02.

[27] CHILDS, NT Introduction, 43 [here about the New Testament; his view on the Old Tes-tament is similar]: "These writings were preserved, not because of interesting historical, re-ligious, or sociological data, but solely for their theological role in speaking of God's re-demption in Jesus Christ." Cf. idem, Biblical Theology, 18–20.

[28] CHILDS, OT Introduction, 78–79. Cf. BARR, Scripture, 95; CLEMENTS, OT Theology, 10.

[29] CHILDS, NT Introduction, 38.

guides to aid in a right construal of their work.[30] However, what is most important to understand about the tradents' motives, where they play a role, is that they consistently reflect 'self-interest' in the form of 'self-subsumption' rather than in the form of 'preferences.'[31]

The Articulation of Shared Values

This leads us to the way in which Altieri's second quality of canons illuminates study of the biblical canon: the articulation of shared values from the past. This articulation of values, however, does not prevent the canon from functioning as a theater, in which values are to be examined and debated in the present. In my judgment, the Old Testament articulates the values of Israel's past precisely in its ordering of biblical literature according to the construct 'Law and Prophets.'

As I shall argue, the conception of the prophets as 'proclaimers of the Law' and the related notion of a succession of mosaic prophets both lie at some distance from the history of prophecy as it can be reconstructed for the biblical period. Such ideas, however, are not to be interpreted as pious overlay or simple fiction. With these formulations, later tradents have communicated those values of their past culture which they believed were of greatest significance for the future. For example, even though the pre-exilic prophets largely did *not* base their oracles upon legal precedents or norms,[32] the correlation of their oracles to the Law within the canon by later tradents is no corruption of their message.[33] In preserving the prophets' words, the tradents of the canon preserved the enduring theological character of prophecy, emphasizing certain historical aspects and deemphasizing others. A theological judgment was thus rendered which preserved that character even as it was reoriented.

I shall argue that the writings of Prophets became canonical together with the Law (at approximately the same time) because the two evolving collections were conceived from the beginning as a dialectical construct in which the present reality of their tradents could be profoundly reviewed and adjudi-

---

[30] Ibid., 40. *Contra* BARR, Scripture, 67; 95.

[31] RAILTON notes (Ideology, 392) that those who pursue an ideological approach have yet to formulate a convincing *psychological* explanation for their theory: "Where is the structure of ideological explanations of beliefs and values? Is there a credible theory of the social psychological mechanisms by which social interests or symbolic needs shape individuals' beliefs and values in unacknowledged ways that are presupposed when ideologies are claimed to have a functional role?" In addition, RAILTON forcefully questions (392–93) whether the normative aspect of ideological criticism seems to presuppose the very kind of objective interests that 'attention to the social character of knowledge and valuation renders suspect.'

[32] KOCH, Prophets, II:1: "The prophets of the Assyrian period never appeal to any divine commandment as the basis of their arguments in their criticism of the social conditions of their day." Cf. CHILDS, OT Introduction, 353–54 (on Jeremiah).

[33] CLEMENTS, OT Theology, 63–65. Cf. P. D. MILLER, World, 107.

cated, which, as I have argued, is the central purpose of a canon. I shall further attempt to show that the biblical tradents were aware of both substantial similarities and differences between the subcollections of 'Law' and 'Prophets,' and sought to express the relation between the two by means of a salvation-historical framework in which the activity of God on behalf of Israel was viewed in two related but discrete major phases. The purpose of this framework was thus never simply to report the particulars of its implied 'history,' but to mount a witness to the fullness of God from the fullness of Israel's cumulative experience.

A Critical Benchmark

Finally, let us consider how 'critical obligation' — Altieri's third quality of canons — can be used to break new ground.

It has long been observed that the later layers of canonical writing depend on earlier material quite intentionally.[34] Increasing attention has been directed toward the phenomenon of written prophetic activity (*Fortschreibung, Schriftprophetie*) and the frequency of scriptural citations in later Psalms and other books in the Writings.[35] I. L. Seeligmann pointed out a variety of these features in his study of midrashic exegesis, employing the term 'canon-consciousness' (*Kanonbewußtsein*) to refer to the way in which certain citations and allusions to scripture observed, and even played with, its canonical status.[36]

I suggest that Seeligmann's insight can be expanded along the lines Altieri has suggested. Canons are 'entities' and, as such, additions to a given canon exhibit an 'obligation' to interpret themselves in light of the whole even when they stand in tension with the received tradition (e. g., J. Joyce's *Ulysses*). This is especially true in the case of the biblical canon, which has always been more of a 'entity' than the sundry classics of the Western literary tradition. I shall argue in the next few chapters that the reuse and reapplication of previous writings within biblical tradition argues for an implicit understanding of canonicity; also, that the editors of the biblical canon have intentionally inserted specific indications or reshaped existing literary junctures in order to interpret the various parts of the biblical canon in light of the whole. Furthermore, I maintain that this editing involved the application of hermeneutical guides which are *themselves* derived from the content of the biblical traditions and texts, and thus are incorrectly understood as foreign impositions of ideology or propaganda.

---

[34] SMEND, Theologie, 112–13.

[35] Ibid., 114.

[36] SEELIGMANN, Voraussetzungen; see also the magisterial treatment of these features in FISHBANE, Interpretation; and the overview by PORTON, Midrash.

I note in this regard my opposite conclusion from that of H. E. Ryle, who argued that none of the books of the Old Testament was "originally expressly composed for the purpose of forming, or of helping to complete the Hebrew Canon."[37] I shall argue that certain passages of biblical literature voice explicit concerns to amplify, reorient or further construct the biblical canon by calling attention to other portions of the canon and by weaving a rich web of references and intertextual possibilities (e. g., Deut 34:10–12; Mal 3:22–24 [4:4–6]).

It is not my contention that such canonical 'guides' are all the product of one group of tradents, or represent a single layer of redaction; rather, I will argue that the force of an emergent canon exerted itself on different tradents at different times, but in strikingly similar ways. Instances of this phenomenon can thus be conceived of as 'canon-conscious redactions.'[38] What various tradents of the biblical tradition increasingly felt was precisely the pressure to express the significance of the literature's overall content, as Altieri suggests. I hope to show that the conception which seemed to them to describe the most central elements of the canon was again that of 'Law and Prophets.' This conception allowed wide flexibility in the selection and incorporation of literary works into Israel's 'theological grammar' at the same time that it expressed the enduring theological logic of Israel's historical experience.[39]

'Canon' versus 'Scripture'

I believe Altieri's brilliant description of canons and canon formation represents a sophisticated working out of the basic literary feature of canons that H. Bloom noted at the beginning of this chapter: their *strangeness*. An ideological interpretation of canons and canon formation (e. g., P. R. Davies) must stress their confirmatory aspect in order to be consistent. We would rightly expect propaganda to seem somehow familiar and comfortable.[1]

Altieri reminds us that canons form and endure not by presenting the truisms of their current day, but by compelling readers to reach *beyond* them.

---

[37] RYLE, Canon, 17.

[38] The term is borrowed from SHEPPARD (Canon, 67–68), who describes the phenomenon as editing in which "assumptions about the normativeness... of the traditions and of their being read together in a specific collection... coincide."

[39] In this way, the proposal to understand the canon as a 'theological grammar' shares a basic similarity to CHILDS's description of the canon as a "hermeneutical guide by which to interpret this complex prehistory of the literature." See CHILDS, OT Introduction, 157.

[1] GUNN stresses (David, 23) that clarity is important for political propaganda to function; the very presence of nuance and subtlety works against an 'ideological' reading. I owe this reference to D. M. Carr.

Readers rely on a canon's presentation of the past even as they extend its vision into the future, subordinating their 'preferences' for the sake of 'strong evaluations.' This aspect of canons — the psychology of their generative and regulative power — has certainly not appeared at the forefront of the discussion of canon within biblical studies, although we noted the same aspect in the work of P. R. Ackroyd and others who have emphasized a 'canonical' approach to the Old Testament. A remaining problem has to do with the confusing relationship between 'canon' and 'scripture' within biblical studies. Could Altieri's description of 'canon' also help us to differentiate between the two?

Noting the confusion over basic terminology, G. T. Sheppard has helpfully set out a typology of the meanings of 'canon.' Taking a broadly comparative view, Sheppard explores world religions to conclude that sometimes 'canon' refers to the *authority* of a text or a collection of texts, while sometimes it refers to the *delimitation* of text(s). These two options Sheppard terms, respectively, canon 1 and canon 2.[2] As we have seen, the history of biblical scholarship in this area has indeed turned on which of these two senses of the word has received priority.

Missing from Sheppard's typology, however, is the *generative* feature of canons suggested by our review of historical and literary scholarship. In an interesting convergence, both J. A. Sanders and B. S. Childs relate 'canon' to 'life.'[3] The difference in their formulations of this convergence is that Sanders locates this 'life' within the function and use of the canon itself whereas Childs sees the canon as a witness to a divine source of life beyond it.[4]

Childs's concern is that the canon not be reduced to 'inspirational' literature at the loss of its normative function.[5] In my judgment, however, Altieri's exploration of canonical ideals as fundamentally *self-incriminating* indicates that this difference between Childs and Sanders may not be insuperable. The ability of the canon to transmit and generate 'life' depends upon *both* its

---

[2] SHEPPARD, Canon, 64–66. His typology is not to be confused with BARR's effort (Scripture, 75–80) at an analytic typology of CHILDS's use of 'canon' (BARR refers to 'canon 1,' 'canon 2' and 'canon 3') or with the comparativist typology of 'vectored ('Canon I') or 'vectoring' ('Canon II') texts advanced in FOLKERT, Canons.

[3] J. A. SANDERS, Story, 20; CHILDS, OT Introduction, 59. Cf. FRYE's use of 'resonance' (Code, 217). See also ACKROYD, Vitality.

[4] CHILDS, Biblical Theology, 724: "...the text itself is not the generative force of truth. Rather, through the Spirit the reality to which the text points, namely to Jesus Christ, is made active in constantly fresh forms of application." Cf. HERMS, Bibel, 151 n. 131: "Der Kanon bezeugt *nicht sich selbst* als den Identitätsgrund, *sondern Gottes synthetisches Handeln als Schöpfer, Versöhner und Vollender*. Und genau als dieses von sich selbst wegweisende Glaubenszeugnis fungiert es als Identitätszentrum der Glaubensgemeinschaft" (his emphases).

[5] CHILDS, OT Theology, 59.

imaginative *and* its normative functions. In any case, the 'life-giving' feature of the canon is completely obscured when the discussion frames the question in terms of *either* authority *or* limitation.

As we have seen, however, some continue to argue that use of the term 'canon' should refer only to a late extrinsic decision to fix the boundaries of scripture. Yet it is worth noting that this view is hard pressed to defend such an understanding in the ancient period.[6] In a recent article L. M. McDonald begins by arguing that many treatments of the biblical canon are flawed because they claim 'canon 2' status (i. e., fixity and delimitation) for 'canon 1' writings (i. e., authoritative scripture).[7] However, toward the end of his article McDonald all-too-revealingly proclaims: "There was never a time when the Church as a whole concluded that these writings and no others could help the Church carry out its mission in the world and inform it in its worship and instruction."[8] So why, one wonders, insist on a definition of 'canon' as a phenomenon which does not seem ever to have existed?[9]

With this narrow ('canon 2') understanding of the biblical canon in place, then 'authoritative scripture' or some similar formulation is used to refer to writings possessing status within the community, but not formally delimited ('canon 1'). As I have noted before, it is difficult to know how such 'authoritative scripture' could have been *completely* unlimited.[10] The reinforcement of 'scripture' with the adjective 'authoritative' is particularly troubling, as it implies that *mere* 'scripture' lacks a normative dimension. Although nothing in principle would prevent 'scripture' from referring to a norm, that is *not* how the term is usually used in biblical studies. Childs is therefore justified to worry about the implication that 'scripture' denotes 'inspirational literature' at the expense of its normative claim.

However, the real deficiency in using 'scripture' instead of 'canon' becomes evident when we recall the quality of 'life' identified with 'canon' previously. What this quality reflects is the characteristic process by which the scriptures of Israel were transmitted. 'Canon' in this sense refers to that aspect of the process of transmission which involved the selection and ordering of a *collection* of Israel's scriptures in order to construct a *range* of enduring witnesses. 'Life' emerges from the *muliplicity* of voices contained within the

---

[6] I think it is telling that BARR (Scripture, 49 n. 1) makes his case semantically, rather than on the basis of the Old Testament canon itself.

[7] McDONALD, Integrity, 102. He employs SHEPPARD's distinction.

[8] Ibid., 131–32.

[9] The answer, of course, is that here Protestant liberal theology is masquerading as historical investigation. Beginning from similar assumptions, both BARR (Scripture, 51–52) and BARTON (Oracles, 63) are also unable to affirm that the writings of the Old Testament were *ever* 'canonized.' At least BARR displays the consistency to reject the language of 'canon' altogether.

[10] PROVAN, Canons, 10.

canon, for only in the *chorus* of these voices are we able to learn to hear a voice other than our own.[11]

At the same time, the canon cannot contain an infinite plurality of perspectives; without limitation there can also be no 'chorus' and therefore no 'life.' However, the notion of limitation as such is secondary to the more primary sense of 'canon' as a *range* of scriptural witnesses, ordered in such a way that it invites and compels the continual examination of the self and the reexamination of the scriptures. It is precisely for this reason that both the exact ordering of a canon and the absolute fixation of its text are unnecessary for a 'canon' to function as such. Difference within the canon is *necessary* if readers are to entertain other 'possible selves.' On the other hand, *relative* stability within the canon is crucial if readers are to be willing to open themselves up to the possibilities of recreation.[12]

In my judgment, it is this *intertextual* sense that necessitates the retention of the term 'canon,' even for periods preceding the delimitation of the Old Testament. As Childs has written recently, the terms 'canon' and 'scripture' are 'very closely related, indeed often identical.'[13] In his view, however, the term 'canon' continues to be useful in bringing out a 'special nuance' of the process of transmission, namely, "the living and active tradents who... selected, formed and ordered the Scriptures toward the goal of engendering faith and instructing every successive generation in righteousness."[14] In other words, because the goal of the canonical process was to transmit a framework for interpretation (or 'grammar') along with the sacred writings themselves, the received form of the text contains literary features which act as hermeneutical guides for present-day readers.

In Childs's words: "...the editors shaped the biblical material throughout the various levels of transmission by means of signs, signals and structural features so that the reader could be guided in construing Scripture canonically, that is, kerygmatically."[15] With this understanding of 'canon' as a liter-

---

[11] For a penetrating discussion about why critical biblical scholarship finds it difficult in practice to recognize the multivalence of the biblical canon, and her own constructive proposal, see NEWSOM, Bakhtin.

[12] 'Adaptability' and 'stability' are used by SANDERS (Story, 11–39) to refer to something like what I am attempting to describe, but SANDERS writes of adaptability as 'primary' (19) and stresses 'pluralism' (20) so much that the only 'stable' element becomes a vague 'monotheizing tradition' (30). In my view, the relationship between the two poles is far more dialectical.

[13] CHILDS, Reclaiming, 9.

[14] Ibid.

[15] Ibid., 10.

ary and conceptual *framework* for scriptures,[16] or 'theological grammar,' I now propose to seek for such structural features within the biblical text. Their presence will not only confirm the intertextual understanding of 'canon' advanced here, but will also suggest a new way to conceive of the history of canon formation.

I venture to suggest, moreover, that although the terms 'scripture' and 'canon' can often be used synonymously, 'scripture' refers primarily to the *inspired* status of a writing or a collection of writings ('holy scripture'), and not to the possibility of the interrelationship or intertextuality of such writings. It is this unifying, intertextualizing process of growth to which 'canon' so helpfully refers and 'scripture' does not imply.[17] For this reason, I shall reserve the term 'scripture' for *discrete* holy writings or collections of holy writings in which the individual writings do not appear to have been edited and shaped towards each other.

Because there is no clear evidence for the influence of written traditions of Law and Prophets upon each other prior to the period of the deuteronomists, and much evidence for such written influence within deuteronomic circles and later deuteronomistic tradents, I shall generally refer to writings before that time as 'scripture' and only with the advent of deuteronomism as 'canon.'

---

[16] SHEPPARD refers (Future, 29) to the Old Testament canon in this sense as a 'common intertext of scripture,' the result of a process in which "editors in the late stages of the formation of biblical books registered their assumptions that these books belong together."

[17] Cf. SÆBØ, "Zusammen-Denken."

Chapter Three

No Prophet Like Moses?
Canonical Conclusions as Hermeneutical Guides

Introduction

As we have seen, investigations of Old Testament canon formation have usually begun with evidence for the 'legal' codification of Israel's pentateuchal traditions in the early post-exilic period. In the pursuit of such investigations, later layers of editorial work in the biblical text, especially in prophetic texts, were often disregarded and even deprecated.[1] During the course of the twentieth century, however, exegetical investigations of the editorial shaping of larger units of biblical material have grown in number and significance.[2]

Recent critical work especially has recognized that the trajectory of editorial work on a given text logically leads to questions about its final form within the canon, and that therefore redaction criticism in particular has not finished its work until it can account for the full transmission history of a text.[3] Textual critical work has also perceived the importance of understanding more fully the relationship between the stabilization of the biblical text and its canonical status.[4] It thus seems increasingly clear from a variety of perspectives that a *continuum* of textual shaping exists with respect to the biblical text; at issue, however, is the character and quality of that shaping, and the extent to which various methodologies do justice to it.[5]

---

[1] KRATZ, Redaktion, 16.

[2] COATS AND LONG, Preface, xi.

[3] RENDTORFF, Canon, 48–49.

[4] TOV, Criticism, 188; ULRICH, Process.

[5] See CHILDS, OT Introduction, 74–75, for a comparison of his 'canonical approach' with other methodologies. Cf. the remarks of RENDTORFF regarding new trends in Old Testament exegesis (Canon, 25–27). CHILDS's view of the difference between his approach and redaction criticism is subtle, but especially important; see also his Analysis. In CHILDS's judgment, redaction criticism is usually characterized by an 'etiological concern,' the point of which is to illustrate how theological traditions were continually threatened with contradiction or irrelevance and thus had to be brought into 'conformity with the present historical reality' (Analysis, 363). In this model, it is the *experience* of the community which holds ultimate authority. By contrast, CHILDS wishes to illustrate in his canonical approach the way in which the community felt it necessary to conform its experience to its *received traditions*. The diffi-

Following the suggestion of J. Blenkinsopp,[6] I propose to begin my search for *internal evidence* of Old Testament canon formation with a study of two late redactional conclusions: Deut 34:10–12 and Mal 3:22–24 [4:4–6]. In this way I hope to avoid the ever-present danger of reconstructing hypothetical earlier stages (which may never have existed!) of a long, complex process and then discounting the later redactional stages (which the text provides!) in favor of the hypothesis.

I shall argue instead that the completion of the biblical process of canon formation achieved ultimate expression in these two self-conscious 'endings.' Whether or not these endings represent the very latest layer(s) of the material is not essential to my argument, only that they represent the mature theological reflection of Israel's ancient traditions, summarizing those traditions in terms that illuminate their significance within the canon and convey their significance to future readers. In short, I shall make the case that these endings provide evidence of precisely the kind of theological 'grammar' for Israel's scriptures discussed in the last chapter.

While external factors must eventually be brought to bear in this search as a check to initial conclusions, in my view it is a mistake to privilege a hypothetical reconstruction based upon the sociology of Persian period Israel (e. g., Blenkinsopp) or upon later extra-biblical sources (e. g., Barton, Beckwith, Leiman). Instead, one should begin with the later editorial layers of the books in the 'Law and the Prophets' *themselves* (e. g., Steck). However, in contrast to an approach that would reconstruct a trajectory of text layers relying on the 'thin' view of human agency that I have criticized (*contra* Steck), I shall attempt to base my initial conclusions upon later passages which in my judgment refer self-consciously to the emergent biblical canon (*pace* Blenkinsopp).

As I shall argue, in Deut 34:10–12 and Mal 3:22–24 [4:4–6] the biblical canon possesses two 'canon-conscious' endings. They conclude the two constitutive portions of the biblical canon in the pre-Christian, pre-rabbinic era, and therefore indicate the way in which 'Law' and 'Prophets' were construed together in antiquity as a scriptural 'intertext' or 'canon.'[7] That the results of this study are difficult to fit within the usual historical treatments of the Per-

---

culty of redaction critics to incorporate his point suggests that the methodology is far less 'neutral' than it would claim.

[6] BLENKINSOPP, Canon.

[7] I am refraining at present from any investigation of a 'canon-conscious' conclusion for the collection of the Writings, but I hope to take up this subject in a future study. In the present essay I shall reserve judgment on the question of when the Writings became a discrete, fixed, coequal collection within the MT tradition. As I shall discuss in Chapter Five, STEINS has recently made the interesting proposal (STEINS, Chronik) that the books of Chronicles have been designed to function as a canonical conclusion for the collection of the Writings and (thus) for the entire canon. In my view, this suggestion merits further investigation.

sian period suggests a needed modification of some of the standard assumptions regarding the period rather than the continued dismissal of these texts.

Deuteronomy 34:10–12

Ever since the pivotal work of J. Wellhausen, the consensus view of Deut 34 has held that the final form of the chapter derives principally from the conflation of the book of Deuteronomy with the priestly redaction of the Tetrateuch in order to form a new five-book Torah.[1] In the work of M. Noth, this view was given its classic expression: Deut 34:1a, 7–9 represented the conclusion of the Priestly source which had been moved from the end of Numbers to its new position at the conclusion of the Torah.[2] Since the account of Moses' death now appeared so far from its original context in Num 27:12–23, Num 27:12–14 was also repeated in Deut 32:48–52.[3] Noth considered Deut 34:1b–6 to be the original deuteronomic account of Moses' death; Deut 34:10–12 was a later, deuteronomistic appendix.[4]

L. Perlitt has mounted a strong challenge to this now traditional assignment of Deut 34:1a, 7–9 to the Priestly source.[5] Perlitt argues that Deut 32:48–52, Deut 34:1a, 7–9 and Num 27:15–23 are all products of a deuteronomistic rather than a priestly milieu.[6] Close examination of the language of these texts reveals vocabulary and style not easily attributable to recognized priestly passages, he insists. The differences between Num 27:12–14 (P) and Deut 32:48–52 (Dtr) are especially telling. According to Perlitt, a much better explanation than the majority view is to see all of Deut 34 as the product of post-exilic redactors who were influenced by *both* priestly and deuteronomis-

---

[1] For the history of scholarship with respect to this particular issue, see PERLITT, Priesterschrift? 65–67.

[2] According to NOTH, this did not happen all at once or by the same person. See NOTH, Traditions, 16: "In the case of Deut 34, however, we deal no longer with the Pentateuchal redactor and his work, but rather with another redactor who connected the end of the completed Pentateuchal narrative with the beginning part of the great Deuteronomistic History."

[3] NOTH, Traditions, 19 n. 61.

[4] Ibid., 16.

[5] PERLITT, Priesterschrift? General support for PERLITT's views can be found in STOELLGER, Deuteronomium 34. STOELLGER attributes Num 27:15–23 to a priestly redactor, but interprets Deut 34 as a deuteronomistic critique of priestly theology and posits a series of redactional stages reflecting internal changes within the deuteronomistic school as leading to the final form of the chapter. Thus he shares with PERLITT the rejection of the view that Deut 34:1a, 7–9 is priestly material.

[6] PERLITT, Priesterschrift? 72–73.

tic streams of traditions.[7] Still, it is the 'theological energy of the deuterono-mists' that wins out in the final form of this 'bilingual' Torah.[8] As he puts it, even if Deut 34:7–9 were from a Priestly hand, it would still only 'come in between' two deuteronomistic passages (Deut 34:1b–6, 10–12), which are therefore hermeneutically controlling.[9]

As his conclusion implies, Perlitt is quite explicit in his view that deuter-onomism was a lengthy literary tradition, reflected in many layers of deuter-onomistic texts within the Old Testament.[10] Unlike other treatments of Deut 34, however, his includes careful consideration of Deut 34:10–12 in its analy-sis of the full chapter.[11] Of significance to the present study is his description of the redactional logic of these later additions to Deuteronomy. Perlitt dem-onstrates in his analysis that deuteronomism in the late period not only re-flected disparate streams of traditions, but was interested in *unifying* aspects of those traditions within the framework of an emerging Torah.[12]

Proponents of both critical reconstructions of Deut 34 agree that Deut 34:10–12 derive from one of the latest hands to work on the Torah. Although the precise identification of that particular redactor has always varied within the treatments of different scholars,[13] the deuteronomistic idioms of these verses are now not seriously questioned.[14] During the early twentieth century the prevailing view had held Deut 34:10 to be the deuteronomic conclusion to the original book and Deut 34:11–12 a later, deuteronomistic expansion.[15] It was Noth, however, who differentiated Deut 34:10 from the original core of

---

[7] Ibid., 88 (summary) Here PERLITT describes "...die Tätigkeit schriftgelehrter Redakto-ren, denen das dtr wie das priesterschriftliche Erzählungswerk längst zur Disposition stand. Die sprachlichen Merkmale der beiden Schulen beginnen in dieser Spätphase der Arbeit am entstehenden Pentateuch sich zu vermischen, aber die theologische und literarische Energie des Deuteronomismus ist unvermindert und weder durch P noch durch einen Rp abgelöst."

[8] Ibid., 87–88.

[9] Ibid., 77.

[10] Ibid., 72; 76; 87–88.

[11] That PERLITT considers these verses at all sets him apart from the majority of other scholars. His appraisal, however, is not particularly illuminating (Priesterschrift? 77): "...der Anschluß an V. 10 ist syntaktisch schauderhaft, die Sprache verwässert deuteronomistisch und der Rückverweis auf die Wundertaten in Ägypten hier ohne Sinn und Zusammenhang — ein trauriges Ende des Buches, aber keinesfalls ein priesterschriftliches."

[12] Ibid., 72–73. Perlitt uses (Priesterschrift? 88) the expression 'theologisch konsensfähig' to describe this aspect of the text.

[13] See the convenient chart of various critical positions held at the turn of the century in BERTHOLET, Deuteronomium, 112.

[14] Current criticism instead turns on whether these verses are properly 'deuteronomistic' or 'post-deuteronomistic' (i. e., reflecting a stylistic mix of influences common to the late post-exilic period). For recent treatments, see MARTÍNEZ, Deuteronomy 34; TIGAY, Signifi-cance.

[15] E. g., DRIVER, Deuteronomy, 425.

the book, preferring to see it as a redactional 'supplement' based upon Ex 33:11 and Deut 18:15.[16] His view became the standard one.[17] By and large, however, scholars trained to isolate what is 'original' have dismissed Deut 34:10–12 as so 'late' as to be of no critical importance.[18]

A Conclusion to the Torah

Adumbrating the general reappraisal of such verdicts, in 1977 J. Blenkinsopp gave detailed attention to Deut 34:10–12. Like Noth, he argued that since Jos 1:1 follows 'more naturally' after Deut 34:6 or 9, Deut 34:10–12 was likely added after the combination of Deuteronomy with the priestly Tetrateuch in order to provide a conclusion to the Torah as a newly-constructed whole.[19] In explaining the force of this conclusion, Blenkinsopp maintained that its verdict regarding Moses' incomparability functioned together with a cultic description of Joshua as Moses' official successor (Deut 34:7–9) to mandate supreme authority for the Torah over against prophetic traditions.[20]

Central to Blenkinsopp's interpretation is his argument that Deut 34:10–12 serves a crucial role as the 'last paragraph in the Pentateuch,' a 'coda' designed to make explicit questions of interpretation and authority raised by post-exilic social conflict and the process of canonization.[21] He grounds his view exegetically in the verbal tense of Deut 34:10a: "Never since has there arisen a prophet in Israel like Moses."[22] According to Blenkinsopp, despite any seeming ambiguity the grammatical construction עוד ...לא with the past tense cannot be understood as a reference to the future ('not yet') but must refer to the past ('never since'), as it does in biblical Hebrew in every other case.[23] Therefore, these final verses express an "all-inclusive retrospective evaluation of the period from the death of Moses to the time of the writing."[24]

---

[16] NOTH, Traditions, 129 n. 365.

[17] PREUSS, Deuteronomium, 61; 164.

[18] G. A. SMITH, Deuteronomy, 380, termed vv. 11–12 'irrelevant.' Many others have shared his opinion, but more circumspectly.

[19] BLENKINSOPP, Canon, 85–86.

[20] Ibid., 83–84.

[21] Ibid., 85–86.

[22] MT: ולא־קם נביא עוד בירשראל כמשה The NRSV seems to have adopted the same reading here, as the RSV previously translated: "There has not arisen a prophet since in Israel like Moses..."

[23] BLENKINSOPP, Canon, 86. He cites (n. 14) 2 Chr 13:20 as an example: "Jeroboam never again recovered his power during the lifetime of Abijah." He also cites Ex 2:3; Jos 2:11; 5:1, 12; Jud 2:14; 1 Sam 1:18; 2 Sam 3:11; 14:10; 1 Kg 10:5, 10; 2 Kg 2:12; 1 Chr 19:19; 2 Chr 9:4; Jer 44:22; Ezek 33:22.

[24] BLENKINSOPP, Canon, 86. He compares (n. 15) Deut 34:10–12 to 2 Kg 23:25, the statement of Josiah's incomparability. For an evaluation of this comparison, see below.

This conclusion to the Torah thus offers readers a summarizing construal of Moses's role and significance in light of the entirety of Israel's traditions.

However, Blenkinsopp also understands the reference to Moses' incomparability as a verdict on two competing claims to religious authority within early Judaism: the priestly and the prophetic, or (respectively) the theocratic and the eschatological.[25] The denial of parity between Moses and the prophets thus entails for Blenkinsopp the denial of the religious authority of eschatological prophecy by a post-exilic priestly theocracy, whose *interests* the Torah guarded and promoted.

Blenkinsopp grants that there has been pervasive prophetic influence on the final shape of the Torah, but claims that the move toward a Torah-canon (i. e., an authoritative Pentateuch) was intended to subordinate the rival authority claims created by 'free prophecy.' In fact, the achievement of canonical status for the Torah was largely responsible, in Blenkinsopp's view, for a post-exilic *eclipse* of prophecy.[26] He concedes that an authoritative edition of prophetic sayings (and with it a vigorous eschatological movement) eventually gained strength in spite of priestly efforts to the contrary, but according to him the last paragraph of Deuteronomy denies any parity between 'Law' and 'Prophets.'

Writing more recently Blenkinsopp's judgment is unchanged:

> "...the Pentateuch as a whole is rounded off with a statement which, in effect, denies parity between the mode of revelation proper to Moses ('face to face,' cf. Ex 33:11; 34:29–35; Num 12:6–8) and claims staked by prophets throughout the history... This final statement is meant to recall the promise of a 'prophet like Moses' in Deut 18:15–18, probably as a warning against interpreting it in such a way as to put prophetic mediation on the same level as that of Moses. It represents a resolution of conflicting claims to authority in the religious sphere by defining a certain epoch as normative and, at the same time, relativizing the problematic and ambiguous phenomenon of prophecy."[27]

Not only does Blenkinsopp assert here that the Pentateuch claims for itself a higher 'mode of revelation' than the phenomenon of prophecy, but also that by defining the mosaic epoch as normative the activity of the prophets is relegated to a secondary and subordinate dispensation of God.[28]

---

[25] The language can be traced to PLÖGER, Theocracy. BLENKINSOPP acknowledges fully (Canon, 114 and *passim*) his dependence. For criticism of PLÖGER on historical and exegetical grounds, see ALBERTZ, History, II:438–40; and SCHMITT, Geschichtsverständnis, 152-55.

[26] BLENKINSOPP, Canon, 94.

[27] Idem, Pentateuch, 232.

[28] Cf. idem, Canon, 86. BLENKINSOPP agrees that "the Law and the Prophets really form only one corpus since the prophets' essential task is to continue the work of Moses. Correspondingly, there is one epoch of revelation from Moses to the death of the last prophet or, alternatively, to Ezra," *but* only "according to the view which [later] became official" (Canon, 125 n. 1). In other words, what was viewed at the close of the Torah as two unequal periods

Later in his 1977 treatment, Blenkinsopp does argue that a kind of resolution to the tension between theocracy and eschatology can be found in the last three verses to the book of Malachi (Mal 3:22–24 [4:4–6]), which refer to both Moses and Elijah. This 'ending,' he argues, concludes the prophetic collection within the canon. Only there, he maintains, is the dialectical unity of institution and charisma, which the conclusion to the Torah sought to efface, acknowledged and reinstated.[29] For Blenkinsopp this conclusion to the prophetic corpus moves to restore the equal authority of Israel's eschatological traditions, thus flatly contradicting the conclusion to the Torah and enshrining the authority of both traditions within the final shape of the canon. However, at the level of its *witness* the conclusion to the Torah *remains* anti-prophetic for Blenkinsopp. It reports an ancient establishmentarian effort to forestall subversive competition and criticism, a literary epitaph — not to Moses — but to an anti-prophetic *ideology.*[30]

In my judgment, Blenkinsopp's primary achievement has been to make a strong case for understanding Deut 34:10–12 and Mal 3:22–24 [4:4–6] as a 'canonical indices' for interpretation. In his treatment of Deut 34:10–12 these verses convincingly emerge as a conclusion to the Torah as a whole, a conclusion which clearly reflects a post-exilic effort to situate the developing scriptural traditions of Law and Prophets with respect to each other within a broader theological construct. Rather than beginning with the effort to isolate 'original' traditions of law and prophecy in order to reconstruct the nature of their later interrelation, Blenkinsopp uses these late representations of law and prophecy within the final form of the canon as themselves an 'important datum in the religious history of Israel.'[31] However, in Blenkinsopp's treatment these representations are read primarily for the social 'reality' presumed to lie *behind* them, not for their theological witness. His reconstructed social context is derived from the social theories of post-exilic Israel advanced by O. Plöger, and then grounded in circular fashion by its conformity with Plöger's description.

I agree with Blenkinsopp that Deut 34:10–12 was intended to function as a canonical 'index' or guide for interpretation of the Torah, but I believe that careful exegetical investigation indicates a different interpretion of the message this guide was designed to convey. If there is a denial of parity in the

---

('Moses' and 'post-Moses') was only eventually transformed into two equally-normative periods of God's revelation to Israel. I maintain, in contrast, that by the close of the Torah, *both* periods of revelation were already considered normative.

[29] BLENKINSOPP, Canon, 120–21.

[30] Cf. the judgment of CRÜSEMANN, Perserzeit, 216: "Der Pentateuch in seiner Endfassung ist unprophetisch und uneschatologisch, ansatzweise sogar antiprophetisch und antieschatologisch. BLENKINSOPP hat das zuletzt überzeugend gezeigt."

[31] BLENKINSOPP, Canon, 93.

text, there is also an affirmation of common cause. Rather than referring obliquely to social conflict within the post-exilic period, I believe this conclusion to the Torah sets forth an explicitly *theological* interpretation of Israel's traditions, in which both 'Law' and 'Prophets' — as developing collections of *scripture* — function as joint witnesses to the one will of Israel's one God; in short, as a 'theological grammar.'

An Incomparability Formula

Appraisal of Blenkinsopp's treatment necessarily begins with Deut 34:10a and the central interpretive issue of the incomparability formula. In a study of incomparability formulas in the books of Kings,[32] G. Knoppers has observed that the usual exegetical understanding of incomparability has been one of *absolute* uniqueness, which has given rise to confusion and to a multiplication of redactional theories attempting to account for the resulting perception of 'contradiction.'

After all, 2 Kg 18:5 tells of King Hezekiah that "there was no one like him among all the kings of Judah after him, or among those who were before him." But 2 Kg 23:25 says of King Josiah: "Before him there was no king like him, who turned to the LORD with all his heart, with all his soul, and with all his might, according to all the law [תורה] of Moses; nor did any like him arise after him." And God's words to King Solomon seem similarly unequivocal (1 Kg 3:12): "Indeed I give you a wise and discerning mind; no one like you has been before you and no one like you shall arise after you."[33]

However, rather than understanding these references to incomparability as assertions of absolute uniqueness (and thus the kind of contradiction which might suggest distinct redactional layers), Knoppers proposes instead to read them as referring to *exceptional* traits or features within each king's reign. Thus, Solomon is not incomparable in every respect, Knoppers argues, but in his *wisdom* he is unsurpassed. Hezekiah's incomparability rests in his unique *trust* in God. Josiah's *reform* sets him apart from all other kings. In each case, Knoppers contends, the deuteronomistic editor of the books of Kings uses incomparability formulas to highlight 'the exceptional accomplishments of major figures within his history.'[34]

I agree with Knoppers that the function of incomparability formulas is to elevate particular *qualities* rather than to assert absolute uniqueness. I would also venture to express what I believe to be a related feature of such formulas. If it is true that incomparability formulas serve to highlight the exceptional accomplishments of an individual rather than to assert absolute uniqueness, it is because the formulas work by distinguishing that individual *within* a par-

---

[32] KNOPPERS, Incomparability.

[33] Cf. 2 Chr 1:11–12; Neh 13:26.

[34] KNOPPERS, Incomparability, 414.

ticular class or category for the purpose of comparison. In other words, incomparability formulas do not claim that an individual is *sui generis*, but *primus inter pares*. They make a comparison within a given category in order to assert the exceptional qualities of a particular, *pre-eminent* individual.[35]

This is not to say, however that the distinction involved in incomparability formulas is strictly quantitative rather than qualitative. Although there exists a broad range of incomparability rhetoric in the Old Testament which expresses itself in a variety of idioms,[36] D. N. Freedman has related the essential function of these idioms to certain uses of the superlative in biblical Hebrew (e. g., 'king of kings,' 'lord of lords'). Grammatically, he describes *both* a quantitative and a qualitative aspect to the distinction involved: "Such comparisons affirm that there is a valid basis for comparison but equally insist that the basis or degree of the comparison is nullified by the character and quality of the gulf between the attributes of the persons compared."[37] In my view, the emphasis on the gulf — to the exclusion of the implicit comparison it makes, even as it explicitly appears to negate it — has led to confusion and misinterpretation.

Following Knoppers and Freedman, then, I propose that the sense of such biblical incomparability formulas is better understood as *pre-eminence* than as uniqueness.[38] The distinction involved is more than strictly quantitative, but less than absolutely qualitative. While the degree of comparison may be so great as to challenge the limits of the comparison itself, the comparison only functions *within* the category it challenges. In other words, the 'apple unlike any other apple' is still an apple rather than an orange. Perhaps in English we would use the expression 'quite like' to catch the nuance involved: 'There has not arisen since in Israel a prophet quite like Moses.' Here the aspect of pre-eminence within a given category is expressed without the literalistic implication of absolute difference.[39]

---

[35] Cf. DRIVER (Deuteronomy, 228) on Deut 18:16–18: "It is not that the promised prophet is to be *equal* with him [i. e., Moses]: he is to be like him, [shown] in the *fact* of being Jehovah's representative with the people, but not necessarily in being His representative in the same *degree* in which Moses was..." (His emphases.)

[36] LABUSCHAGNE, Incomparability, 14 and *passim*.

[37] FREEDMAN, "Who?" 328.

[38] *Contra* the implication of LABUSCHAGNE's conclusion (Incomparability, 123) that "The proclamation of Yahweh's incomparability is just another way of proclaiming his uniqueness." He neglects to consider the difference between monotheism and monolatry. Cf. FREEDMAN on Ex 15:11 ("Who?" 328).

[39] BLENKINSOPP blurs the significance of this distinction. Although he pits Moses against the prophets in his treatment of Deut 34:10–12, he also calls Moses 'the prophet *par excellence*' (Canon, 41) and claims: "Deuteronomy... is presented as a prophetic book since its author was a prophet" (Canon, 81). Cf. his statements that "The intent [of Deut 34:11–12] was clearly to expand the words of praise for Moses as the *prophet* without equal" (Canon,

How might this view of pre-eminence be applied to Moses and Deut 34:10–12? Rather than woodenly reading Deut 34:10a as an assertion of a simple dichotomy between Moses and the prophets, on this interpretation of the incomparability formula we would instead proceed to attempt to locate that attribute or feature of Moses which is being singled out as exceptional. Three possibilities are suggested by the text, each of which, I shall argue, highlights a different but related feature of Moses' life and significance. I contend that in these features, Moses is depicted as pre-eminent in stature, but also fully *within* the general category of prophets and prophetic activity.[40]

Moses as Covenant Mediator

The pre-eminence of Moses is first defined by Deut 34:10b: "...whom the LORD knew face to face." As is well-known, similar phrases are used of Moses strategically throughout the Pentateuch.[41] Sometimes forgotten, however, is that an almost identical expression is used by Moses of God's speech to the people at Sinai in Deut 5:4–5a: "The LORD spoke with you face to face (פנים בפנים) at the mountain, out of the fire. (At that time I was standing between the LORD and you to declare to you the words [MT: דבר] of the LORD..." In its context, the phrase 'face to face' thus forms part of the introduction to the Decalogue (Deut 5:6–21). After seeing God's glory and hearing his voice out of the midst of the fire, the people are fearful and beg Moses to mediate God's word to them from then on (Deut 5:27). In this way 'face to face' within the deuteronomistic tradition refers to Moses, not simply as someone with whom God had intimate knowledge,[42] but in his role as covenant mediator (cf. Deut 28:69 [29:1]).

To be sure, the similar phrase 'mouth to mouth' in Num 12:6–8 (NRSV: 'face to face') suggests that Moses received divine revelation in a manner different from and superior to that of other prophets. The precise sense of this tetrateuchal passage, however, depends upon its wider context within the

---

88) and "We may take it, then, that Deut 34:10 affirms a *quantitative* difference between the epoch of Moses and that of the prophets" (89; my emphases). BLENKINSOPP, however, then goes on to speak of a more *qualitative* difference between Moses and the prophets, based upon the privileged mode of communication between God and Moses expressed in the Hebrew idiom 'face to face' (Deut 34:10). For discussion of this formula, see below.

[40] ZIMMERLI, "Prophet," 202.

[41] Ex 33:11 פנים אל־פנים; Num 12:8 פה אל־פה; Num 14:14 עין בעין.

[42] BLENKINSOPP (Canon, 89) on Ex 33:11: "Such a way of speaking would seem to indicate simply the easy and unstinted familiarity existing between friends." In my view, this interpretation arises from a much too romanticized notion of the Hebrew term 'friend' (רע). I would also maintain, despite BLENKINSOPP's protestations, that any view which privileges Moses' superior intercourse with God must offer more of an explanation for the apparent notice to the contrary in Ex 33:20 (!) than simply dismissing it as part of a 'late midrash' (Canon, 92).

complex of prophetic (!) stories in Num 11–12.[43] At the very least, Num 12:6–8 stands in stark contrast to Num 11:26–30, suggesting that the exegetical issue in these chapters is actually more complicated than a simple straightforward subordination of prophecy. The tension between the two passages must be adjudicated within the book of Numbers; whatever its resolution, it cannot be viewed as indicating a hermeneutical principle for the entire Torah. Furthermore, it must be reemphasized that the precise expression 'face to face' does *not* in fact appear in the Hebrew text of *either* Num 12:8 *or* Num 14:14, although in certain translations these differences are blurred (e. g., the NRSV reads 'face to face' for both).

The argument being made here is that the phrase 'face to face' has a distinct resonance within the book of Deuteronomy which has shaped its usage in Deut 34:10b. It is methodologically problematic to reconstruct a cultic meaning of 'face to face' on the basis of other texts (such as the use of פנים in the Psalms), as Blenkinsopp does, and then import that sense into Deut 34:10–12! Moreover, the use of the expression within Deuteronomy becomes more significant because of the prevalence of other deuteronomistic expressions within Deut 34:10–12.

In Deuteronomy, the phrase 'face to face' refers to Moses' role as covenant mediator.[44] Moreover, in Deuteronomy the role of covenant mediator is, in turn, closely related to the role of 'suffering intercessor' as well (Deut 1:37; 4:21; 9:6–29).[45] The point to be made is that while Moses is depicted in deuteronomistic traditions as mediator and intercessor *par excellence*,[46] neither of these roles belongs exclusively to him — only the extent to which he initiated and unified these roles remains unsurpassed. The prophets are also routinely characterized as mediators of the covenant[47] and as suffering intercessors.[48] Both kinds of prophetic portraits are carefully and explicitly drawn.

---

[43] It is also far from clear that Num 12 revolves around the issue of priestly authority. WILSON, Prophecy, 155–56, considers the passage a reference to *prophetic* conflict, *contra* CROSS (Myth, 203–04). At the very least, it seems that at stake in the passage is not *whether* Moses is a prophet, but what kind of a prophet he is.

[44] Moses' role as covenant mediator is, however, not restricted to Deuteronomy (cf. Ex 19:19; 24:3–8; 34:29–30).

[45] CLEMENTS, Deuteronomy, 36–37. Interestingly, Moses appears as mediator and intercessor in Ex 33, where the expression 'face to face' is also used (Ex 33:11).

[46] See P. D. MILLER, "Moses," 251–54. He cites in this context Deut 9:7–29; 10:10–11; Jer 15:1 and Ps 90. He further makes (253) the very important point that Moses' punishment of not being able to enter the land results from the sin of the *people* (Deut 1:34–37). For my present purpose I am interested only in the question of the depiction rather than the historical reality, although the two are obviously to be related in some way. For an historical evaluation of Moses as intercessor, see AURELIUS, Fürbitter.

[47] E. g., 1 Kg 17:13; Jer 7:25–26; 11:10; 25:4; Dan 9:10–12; Hos 4:1–6; Zech 1:6; 7:12; Mal 3:7; 3:22 [4:4]. This is true quite independently of the question as to whether there was ever an historical office of covenant mediator involving the cultic recitation of the law within

Since Deut 34:10–12 is to be dated well into the post-exilic period, it is reasonable to suppose that such prophetic portraits have influenced and been influenced by the deuteronomistic presentation of the figure of Moses. In my judgment, the figure of Moses in the book of Deuteronomy also exhibits the greatest possible influence from, and compatibility with, prophetic traditions.[49] The similarity of language between Deuteronomy and certain passages within the prophetic books has long been noted.[50] Furthermore, within the final form of the biblical text the prophets have been firmly set within a typological relationship to Moses.[51] Even within the Pentateuch, the figure of Moses provides the prototype for a succession of prophets who will continue to mediate God's word and intercede with him on Israel's behalf (Deut 18:15, 18).[52]

Although Blenkinsopp believes the common vocabulary in Deut 18:15, 18 and Deut 34:10–12 indicates a clear reference by the latter to the former, to maintain his anti-prophetic line of interpretation he is first forced to argue that the editor responsible for Deut 34:10 did not intend simply to negate the promise of a succession in Deut 18. Then he must argue that Deut 34 offers a negative judgment with respect to the possibility of *equality* with Moses that does not also contradict the apparently positive judgment as to the prophets' *similarity* to Moses in Deut 18.[53]

---

ancient Israel. For an attempt to prove such an office, see KRAUS, Verkündigung; idem, Worship. More recent scholarship is rightly quite skeptical of such a possibility; see WILSON, Prophecy, 157–58.

[48] E. g., 1 Kg 19:10; 2 Kg 17:13–14; Am 2:12; 7:2–6; Jer 7:25–26; 9:1; 11:18–23; 15:1; 20:7–18, 36–45; 29:19; 44:4; Ezek 3:22–27; Dan 9:6; Jon 4:3, 8; cf. Mt 13:34; Mk 9:13. Cf. P. D. MILLER, "Moses," 251–52 on Am 7:1–6. Again, this characterization obtains independently of whether the prophets ever functioned historically in an intercessory mode. For a brief description of the historical debate and more examples drawn from the prophetic corpus, see RHODES, Prophets. Cf. CHILDS, OT Theology, 127.

[49] This has been disputed recently in BARSTAD, Understanding. BARSTAD observes, in much the fashion of BLENKINSOPP, that Moses is characterized as the supreme *prophet* (Understanding, 248: "For the Deuteronomists, Moses is *the* prophet, with a capital 'P.'"), but for *the purpose of* subordinating all prophecy to the Law. BARSTAD further maintains that only Joshua is characterized as a successor to Moses in deuteronomistic traditions. See the rejoinders to his paper printed in the same volume by JEPPESEN, Deuteronomy? and esp. TENGSTRÖM, Moses.

[50] E. g., DRIVER, Deuteronomy, xlvii.

[51] LOHFINK, Distribution, 351.

[52] See Deut 18:15, 18. A 'succession' is indicated above all by the use of the imperfect verb. See WILSON, Prophecy, 162 n. 52; cf. BENKINSOPP, Canon, 44 n. 68. *Contra* BARSTAD, Understanding, 247.

[53] BLENKINSOPP, Canon, 86. The distinction between 'similarity' and 'equality' is that of DRIVER (Deuteronomy, 425).

In my view, a serious question thus arises regarding the significance of the 'parity' Blenkinsopp seeks to deny between Moses and the prophets in Deut 34:10. In light of his concession that the prophets continue to be understood as fundamentally *similar* in character and activity to Moses, might not Deut 34:10–12 actually serve to *elevate* the prophets by virtue of their close association with Moses rather than to subordinate them? After all, no other group (e. g., kings, priests, judges) appears to receive the high privilege of such a 'subordination' in this conclusion!

Moses as a Prophet

The second aspect of Moses' pre-eminence noted in Deut 34:10–12 occurs in Deut 34:11: "He was unequaled for all the signs and the wonders which the LORD sent him to do in the land of Egypt, against Pharaoh and all his servants and his entire land…"[54]

The syntax of the verse is plainly problematic. Beginning with -לכל, the Hebrew text seems to use a form of the *lamed* of specification ('with respect to') to modify the main clause in Deut 34:10a.[55] This usage is somewhat confusing, coming as it does after the relative clause introduced by אשר in Deut 34:10b, leading both the RSV and the NRSV to interpolate repetitions of the main clause.[56] Gesenius notes that on occasion (in late biblical Hebrew) a substantive introduced by *lamed* serves the same purpose as the *casus pendens* in beginning a new clause.[57]

However, the greater problem in reading Deut 34:11–12 together with Deut 34:10 has to do with the repetition of the information found in Deut 34:10a as another relative clause introduced by אשר in Deut 34:12b. The repetition suggests that Deut 34:11–12 was most likely a secondary addition to Deut 34:10, intended to expand upon the basic theme of Moses' pre-eminence. It is significant in this regard that Deut 34:11–12 does not understand Moses' 'face to face' knowledge with God cultically, but rather in *prophetic* terms.[58]

---

[54] The Targum and some Greek codices omit ולכל־עבדיו but this minor problem does not affect the following treatment.

[55] For the *lamed* of specification, see KAUTZSCH AND COWLEY (EDS.), Gesenius, par. 119-u; WALTKE AND O'CONNOR (EDS.), Introduction, 206–07.

[56] RSV: 'none like him…'; NRSV: 'He was unequaled…'

[57] Although good examples seem rare, something similar appears to be at work in Num 18:8, 1 Chr 7:1; 24:20–21; 2 Chr 7:21; and Eccl 9:2. For these and other possibilities, mostly doubtful, see KAUTZSCH AND COWLEY (EDS.), Gesenius, par. 143-e.

[58] Even if Deut 34:11–12 is considered secondary, it is difficult to see how its tradents would have simply contradicted the plain sense of Deut 34:10, as Blenkinsopp seems to suggest (Canon, 87).

Thus, Deut 34:11 accentuates Moses' role in the Exodus, reminding readers of Egypt and of Pharaoh.[59] Pre-eminently among all the leaders in Israel's history, Moses acted decisively, publicly and militarily to secure freedom for his people. Thus, his personal pre-eminence follows naturally from the pre-eminent place of the Exodus event within Israel's traditions.[60]

In their canonical context, these aspects of Moses' legacy have sometimes been understood to function most closely within a typological relationship to the figure of Joshua. As B. S. Childs has described, Joshua is depicted as emulating Moses by "crossing the sea (Jos 3), meeting the commander of the army of God (Jos 5) and raising his staff as a sign against God's enemy (Jos 8:18)."[61] The prophets, however, are also portrayed as public servants of God,[62] sharing with Moses his ability to confront worldly rulers with God's word[63] and delivering a divine word to foreign nations, including Egypt.[64] The prophetic portrait of Jeremiah, in particular, shares strong similarities with these aspects of Moses' legacy.[65]

In contrast, Blenkinsopp finds Deut 34:11–12 'anti-climactic,' and the 'idea of prophecy' introduced by these verses 'different and distracting'[66] — in his view a sure sign of a different source at work.[67] I would note that in making this statement Blenkinsopp appears to admit these verses are in fact a description of *prophecy*. In my view, they are not 'distracting,' although probably secondary to Deut 34:10; nor are the activities described restricted by the tradition to Moses alone. A typology is established in these verses which functions with regard to the *prophets* rather than any other individual or group, extending Moses' authority to them at the same time that it serves to set him apart.

---

[59] CRAIGIE, Deuteronomy, 406. Cvc. Deut 11:1–4 and 29:1–2 [29:2–3].

[60] CHILDS, Biblical Theology, 130–31.

[61] Idem, OT Introduction, 245. Cf. BLENKINSOPP, Canon, 48.

[62] E. g., Isa 45:14–24; 48:16; Jer 7; Ezek 12; Am 1:1–2:3; 3:7.

[63] E.g., Gen 20; Ex 4; 7–11; 2 Sam 12; 1 Kg 21; Isa 7; Jer 19; Am 7. I see no basis here for VON RAD's claim that Moses represents a 'special type' of prophet, namely the 'prophet of action [and] dramatic miracles' (Theology, I:293). Are not other prophets *also* prophets of 'action' (Am 7) and 'dramatic miracles' (1 Kg 18)?

[64] E. g. Isa 19; 30–31; Jer 43–44; Ezek 29–32; esp. Am 3:9 and Zech 14:18–19.

[65] See CLEMENTS, Jeremiah; and C. R. SEITZ, Moses. On the similarities between Moses and other major prophetic figures, see McKeating, EZEKIEL; and O'Kane, ISAIAH.

[66] BLENKINSOPP, Canon, 87.

[67] BERTHOLET, Deuteronomium, 113, makes a similar judgment based on the contrast between 'Gottschauen' and 'Wunderthaten.' In my view, the text works to smooth any possible contrast between these two categories rather than to sharpen it.

Dual Agency

The last aspect of Moses' pre-eminence to be mentioned appears in relation to the deuteronomistic phrases that pepper Deut 34:11–12. 'Signs and wonders,' 'a mighty hand,' 'great and terrible deeds,' 'all Israel' — each one is a stock phrase recurring frequently throughout the book of Deuteronomy.[68] In fact, as S. R. Driver observed, Deut 34:11–12 could have been almost completely constructed by piecing together a number of phrases from the rest of the book.[69]

Blenkinsopp observes that these cliches tend to appear in the sermonic portions of Deuteronomy, suggesting that perhaps the editor of Deut 34:11–12 is 'drawing upon familiar language from the cult.'[70] In support of this theory he cites Ps 105:26–27 and Ps 135:9, but concedes that these phrases are invariably reserved for God, except in Deut 13 and Deut 34. This creates what he terms a 'rather unfortunate' connection between the description of a *false* prophet in Deut 13:2–3 [13:1–2] (he will give a 'sign' or 'wonder') and the description of Moses in Deut 34:11 (he does 'signs and wonders'). Blenkinsopp is at pains to assert that the continuing force of Deut 34:10 overrides even the slightest hint in Deut 34:11–12 that Moses is somehow being associated with false prophecy.[71]

In my judgment, the significance of these deuteronomic phrases does not lie in the possibility of their cultic origin, but in the way they relate to the prophetic corpus. Here, as with other phrases in Deut 34:10–12, we see that it is the prophets who most closely resemble the mosaic portrait. Thus, the prophets are characterized as doers of 'signs and wonders,' or as 'signs and wonders' *themselves*.[72] The prophets report God's 'mighty hand' upon them as characteristic of their prophetic experience.[73]

---

[68] For a list of deuteronomistic vocabulary see WEINFELD, Deuteronomy, 320–70 ('Appendix A'); DRIVER, Deuteronomy, lxxvii–ix. I am not persuaded by CRAIGIE (Deuteronomy, 406) that in Deut 34:12 specific events after the Exodus are referred to. The language is far too general.

[69] DRIVER, Deuteronomy, 425. Specifically, he suggested Deut 4:34; 6:22; 7:19; 11:3; 26:8; 29:1b [2b].

[70] BLENKINSOPP, Canon, 88.

[71] Ibid., 89. This relationship with Deut 13:1–2 [2–3] actually represents a very strong challenge to BLENKINSOPP's assertion that in Deut 34:10–12 prophecy is being subordinated to mosaic tradition. If the tradents intended to make a distinction between Moses and the prophets, why then would Moses be characterized by the same terms used in a description of *false* prophecy? In my view, this terminology was used by the deuteronomists to describe prophecy in general. Thus false prophecy is indicated in deuteronomistic tradition not by the performance of a 'sign' or a 'wonder' *per se*, but rather by the use of such a performance in inciting the people to serve 'other gods' (Deut 13:2 [3]).

[72] האות והמפתים For such a characterization generally, see 1 Kg 13; 2 Kg 4–5; Isa 8; 20; Jer 13; Ezek 4; 12; 24; Joel 3:3 [2:30]; Zech 3:8. The plural form of the expression 'signs and

Even more significantly, expressions usually reserved for God are applied in Deut 34 to Moses, but in a syntactically ambiguous way. Might this not indicate *purposeful* reflection on the ambiguous notion of agency which lies at the heart of the biblical portrayal of prophecy?[74] The very form of messenger speech that the prophets employ creates or reflects this same ambiguity.[75] In prophecy, who speaks — God or the prophet? As even the story of Moses' call (Ex 3–4) indicates, the line between the agency of God and the agency of the prophet can rarely be precisely drawn. In my view, it is therefore entirely possible that here in the conclusion to the Torah the tradition has *meaningfully* preserved a theological conviction by means of an ambiguous grammatical construction, especially if the critical alternative consists of supposing that an unthinking and unskilled redactor has simply heaped on barely grammatical phrases of fulsome praise. I would argue that to pull apart the biblical construal in either direction — toward the agency of Moses or the agency of God — ignores the fulcrum of the biblical balancing act that is in fact at the heart of the passage.

D. T. Olson has recently offered a slightly different interpretation, writing that Deut 34:10–12 affirms "Moses' crucial role as the human agent of divine activity."[76] Olson maintains that in these verses "technical terms applied consistently in Deuteronomy to *Yahweh* alone... are attributed to Moses."[77] In this way "Moses and Yahweh are virtually identified in functional terms."[78] The judgment of A. D. H. Mayes is similar: "The power and activities of Moses are here exalted to the level of those of Yahweh himself."[79] In the view of Olson and Mayes, Deut 34:11–12 attributes 'signs and wonders' *directly* to Moses, although within the wider context of the book the reader

---

wonders' appears within the prophetic corpus only in Isa 8:18 and Jer 32:20–21; the singular form appears in Isa 20:3. Cf. Ex 7:3; Deut 4:34; 6:22; 7:19; 13:2 [1], 3 [2]; 26:8, 46; 29:2 [3].

[73] היד החזקה Cf. Isa 8:11; without the adjective, also Jer 1:9; 15:17; Ezek 1:3; 3:14; 37:1; 40:1. Cf. 1 Kg 18:46; 2 Kg 3:15. This list does not begin to ennumerate the occasions on which the prophets speak of the 'hand of God' in general (e. g., Isa 5:25) — only its relation to their prophetic role. Cf. J. J. M. ROBERTS, Hand; FISHBANE, Interpretation, 539. It is interesting that this expression is also used for the judges, providing a verbal link between the two groups within the Deuteronomistic History. For other similarities between judges and prophets, see BLENKINSOPP, Canon, 48 n. 82.

[74] I. e., the characteristic first person form of address (e. g., Ex 6:6–9). See SEELIGMANN, Heldentum.

[75] See ROST, Gesetz, 35; Cf. E. J. YOUNG, Servants, 175: "Oftentimes the personality of the prophet even recedes completely into the background, and the speaker appears to be God Himself."

[76] OLSON, Deuteronomy, 170.

[77] Ibid., 169. His emphasis.

[78] Ibid., 170.

[79] MAYES, Deuteronomy, 414.

learns to balance this praise of Moses with the more consistent and thorough-going praise of God (with the same words and phrases).

In my view, however, Deut 34:11–12 operates with same the understanding of *dual agency* that underlies biblical accounts of prophets and prophecy. The broader context of these verses within the book of Deuteronomy functions to ensure that the point is not lost, but even within these verses themselves the 'signs and wonders' of Moses are understood *by definition* to be the 'signs and wonders' of God. To say anything less would have been considered blasphemy within deuteronomistic tradition.[80]

Of course, there is sometimes a similar notion of double agency to be seen in descriptions of other offices and roles within the Bible (e. g., judges, priests, kings), but in my judgment only in the case of the prophets is there consistently the same fundamental ambiguity regarding human and divine agency. This ambiguity is more profound (and thus allowed the widest latitude) in the case of Moses than in the case of any other single biblical figure (in Ex 14:31 the people 'believe' in God *and* 'his servant Moses'!),[81] but among the various biblical traditions the profile most similar to Moses in this regard is clearly that of the prophet (Jehoshaphat asks the people to 'believe' in God *and* 'his prophets' in 2 Chr 20:20b).[82]

Summary

Rather than driving a wedge between Law and Prophets, Deut 34:10–12 construes the significance of Moses in such a way as to connect his work theologically with the work of the prophets who follow him.[83] This construal is no simple accident of history; historically it is unlikely the prophets continued Moses' role in any office or official succession.[84] Nevertheless, the work of the prophets stands behind the image of Moses in the Torah itself[85] and the

---

[80] E. g., Deut 13:4–6; 32:39; 1 Sam 2:1–10. *Contra* COATS, Motifs, 38: "Deut 34:11–12 moves the content of this motif from the relationship Moses enjoys with God to the mighty acts Moses did in the sight of all Israel, not God, but Moses." In contrast, my position is not narrowly theocentric; it is simply to adopt a both/and solution to the usual either/or. TIGAY, Significance, 137 points out the formal differences between Deut 34:10–12 and the death reports of a great leaders within biblical narrative.

[81] Cf. Acts 6:11.

[82] WILDBERGER, "Glauben."

[83] For other arguments supporting this conclusion, see O'BRIEN, Reassessment, 66; SCHMITT, Geschichtswerk.

[84] WILSON, Prophecy, 165.

[85] E. g., Ex 7–11; 24; 33; Num 12; Deut 18; 34. For evidence of prophetic influence on the final shape of the Pentateuch, see ALBERTZ, History, I:477–78. However, his larger theory of canon formation appears to operate with the narrow view of self-interest that I have already criticized. For an analysis of Ex 7–11 as prophetically-influenced, see SCHMITT, Plagenerzählung. Prophetic traditions have also been located behind Ex 3–4, although this is dis-

traditions in the prophetic corpus have been shaped along the lines of the mosaic portrait.[86]

That is not to say that some mosaic and prophetic traditions do not stand in tension with one another within the final form of the canon. For example, the tradition of Moses as a military commander[87] seems less important for prophetic traditions outside of the Former Prophets;[88] the stance of some prophets with regard to the cult[89] introduces a critique unexpressed in the Moses traditions;[90] and the prophetic inversion of Israel's salvation history[91] seems unimaginable within the framework of the Pentateuch. In spite of these constraints, however, this conclusion to the Torah understands Moses' significance in such a way that he and the prophets are seen to designate *twin* dispensations within a *single* economy of God.[92]

Although the language of this double appendix refers to Moses and the prophets as traditional personages, both the probable late date of these verses and the fact that 'Moses' and 'prophets' appear together at such a critical juncture within the canon suggest that a self-conscious reference to *scriptural* traditions is also intended.[93]

In the post-exilic period the figure of Moses was increasingly subordinated to the book of Moses, the emergent Torah.[94] However, as we have seen, the

---

puted. For an example of such an attempt, see H. H. SCHMID, Jahwist; for criticism, see TENGSTRÖM, Moses, 261 n. 9, and the other literature he cites.

[86]For a fuller description of this shaping and an historical reconstruction of its development, see CLEMENTS, Tradition, 41–42.

[87] E. g., Ex 17; Deut 1–3. Here, however, the judgment of NOTH (Traditions, 177) regarding Ex 17:8–16 and the function of Joshua within the Pentateuch applies: "...the adoption of Joshua into the unfolding Pentateuchal narrative is probably explained most simply in this particular case by the fact that elsewhere the tradition did not regard Moses as a military commander in time of war. Therefore Joshua, the later military leader of the occupation, was summoned to appear in one of the very few narratives dealing with military actions found in the preserved Pentateuchal narrative."

[88] Of course, the 'oracles against the nations' within the Latter Prophets might argue for a tradition-historical connection, but the later redactional shaping of the corpus itself does not seem to have emphasized this aspect of the prophetic *persona*.

[89] E. g., Isa 1; Am 5:21–26.

[90] E. g., Ps 99:6, but cf. Ezek 20.

[91] E. g., Am 9:7–10; Ezek 20.

[92] TIGAY, Significance, 138, argues, moreover, that the interpretation of Deut 34:10–12 as a subordination of prophecy involves a historical anachronism because it retrojects the medieval doctrine of Moses' incomparability. See his citations, 138 n. 4.

[93] See the similar judgment of PERLITT (Mose, 592) that in these verses "liegt eine Theologie vor, die 'das Gesetz *und* die Propheten' bereits in komplementärem Bezug sieht und Mose zum Deutewort für sie beide macht" (his emphasis).

[94] E. g., Ezr 3; Neh 13; 2 Chr 25. Cf. FEILCHENFELDT, Entpersönlichung; H. SCHMID, Mose, 110; cf. idem, Gestalt.

conclusion to this Torah also sets Moses in relation to the Prophets. The Torah, as the living legacy of Moses, has come to be described as both the authority and the criterion of the prophetic word,[95] while at the same time the prophets are seen as the authoritative heirs and interpreters of the mosaic tradition. Thus, the same dialectical relationship between Moses and the prophets summarized in Deut 34:10–12 is illustrated by the twin shaping of biblical traditions generally within the canon.

In other words, the scripturalization of the figure of Moses does not supersede but goes hand in hand with the characterization of Moses and the prophets in each other's image. In my view, this strongly suggests that the editors responsible for Deut 34:10–12 were aware of some form of prophetic scripture in addition to the Torah, and therefore sought to express in these verses a theological framework which would undergird and illuminate the meaning and the authority of both more fully.[96]

C. Dohmen and M. Oeming have reached conclusions similar to Blenkinsopp's, but by following Perlitt's analysis of Deut 34 rather than Noth's.[97] They have interpreted the chapter not as a competition of sources, but as a purposeful deuteronomistic conclusion.[98] In their view, Deut 34 represents a careful attempt to mediate the views of two groups of texts: Num 20; 27; Deut 32 and Deut 3; 31.[99] Deut 34 contains elements of both groups, they argue, demonstrating that the compiler of Deut 34:1–9 was a "später Systematiker, der alles auf eine Linie zu bringen versucht."[100] Given the prominence of Moses' characterization as a *writer* as well as a speaker within the book of Deuteronomy (e. g., Deut 31:24), they maintain that Deut 34:1–9 revolves around the death of Moses specifically in his capacity as 'mediator of revelation' (*Offenbarungsmittler*).[101]

For Dohmen and Oeming, Deut 34:10–12 thus completes the Pentateuch precisely by authorizing a completed and fixed Torah as the new locus of revelation. Revelation now exists in a book. As an 'addition' (*Fortschreibung*) to the entire Torah, Deut 34:10–12 represents the birth of the idea of the

---

[95] E. g., 2 Kg 17; Zech 7; Mal 3:22 [4:4].

[96] See TENGSTRÖM, Moses, 258: "From the very beginning of their activity the Deuteronomists must have been familiar with substantial and already to a large extent *written* traditions about prophets, and on the historical level they testify to the general importance of prophecy in Israel during the kingdom."

[97] DOHMEN AND OEMING, Kanon?

[98] Ibid., 58–68.

[99] Ibid., 61. For the critical background supporting these groupings, they cite the work of ROSE, Pentateuque, 134–40.

[100] DOHMEN AND OEMING, Kanon, 61: a "later systematician, who sought to bring everything into line."

[101] Ibid., 65.

biblical canon.[102] In their view, however, by reference to Moses' incomparability Deut 34 also relates the status of the two canonical collections of Torah and Prophets by giving full precedence to Moses and his Torah.[103]

In my judgment, Dohmen and Oeming rightly perceive the 'canon-consciousness' of Deut 34 and appreciate the struggle of this unknown 'theologian' to perceive the unity of Israel's traditions. However, even though they reckon with the scripturalization of mosaic traditions, like Blenkinsopp they fail to perceive the true force of the incomparability formula. I believe they have rendered an important service by illustrating the way in which Deut 34:1–9 describes the scripturalization of revelation through its account of Moses' death, but I disagree with their assertion that here revelation is equated with the Torah *alone*. In my view, that kind of interpretation may be precisely what Deut 34:10–12 was intended to *prevent*.

I contend that Deut 34:10–12 is best understood as a theological 'grammar,' that is, a description of the mature religious faith of post-exilic Israel, which reinterpreted what in some cases were no doubt historically separate and independent traditions, and placed them within an expanding textual description of God's manifold work in history.[104] The social tensions between institution and charisma or theocracy and eschatology which Blenkinsopp locates in the post-exilic period were perhaps to some degree a feature of the historical situation, yet the biblical tradition has left these tensions obscure and refrains from investing them with any independent theological significance. Instead, the tradition has moved in the opposite direction, finding unity for institution *and* charisma, theocracy *and* eschatology, in Israel's common witness to God.

---

[102] Ibid., 67.

[103] Ibid., 68.

[104] CHILDS, Biblical Theology, 71, has drawn attention to the way in which canonical shaping operated hermeneutically 'much like a *regula fidei*.' In his view, however, this 'rule of faith' was more of a "negative criterion which set certain parameters within which the material functioned, but largely left to exegesis the positive role of interpretation within the larger construal." For a historical description of the way in which a 'rule of faith' led to the formation of the New Testament canon, see KUGEL AND GREER, Interpretation, 109–10, and F. M. YOUNG, Creeds, 12–13: "...creeds belonged originally to a different context... not 'Articles of Belief' or a system of doctrine, but rather 'confessions' summarizing the Christian story, or affirmations of the three 'characters' in the story [i. e., the Trinity]. They tell who God is and what he has done. They invite the convert to make that story and that affirmation his or her own... To this extent they are natural successors to the summary passages of proclamation and acclamation of God and his saving action found in the Jewish scriptures." In this sense, 'rule of faith' would be quite close to what I am describing as a theological 'grammar' within the formation of the biblical material itself. According to YOUNG, only later did such creeds become 'tests of orthodoxy' (Creeds, 13). However, her distinction between descriptive and prescriptive creeds is anachronistic. For an highly illuminating study, and a critique of YOUNG on this point, see BLOWERS, *Regula Fidei*, esp. 223–24.

On a literary level, this 'grammar' functions as a crucial hermeneutical guide for the interpretation of the canonical text.[105] As the conclusion to the Torah, Deut 34:10–12 indicates that within Israel's common witness, Moses attained pre-eminent status as God's *prophetic* servant. However, as a transition to the prophetic corpus Deut 34:10–12 also makes clear that Moses was succeeded by faithful prophets who — more than anyone else — *continued* his work of mediating and interceding with God on Israel's behalf.[106]

Malachi 3:22–24 [4:4–6]

As in the case of Deut 34:10–12, the conclusion to the present form of the book of Malachi has often been considered to be a late redactional appendix,[1] or more often two later appendices.[2] This is true whether the additions of Mal 3:22–24 [4:4–6] are viewed as discrete redactional pieces,[3] or as part of larger redactional layers within the book.[4] As opposed to the general treatment of Deut 34:10–12, however, scholars have seemed more willing to consider the appendices in Malachi as forming an intentional conclusion to the book of The Twelve,[5] or even to the prophetic corpus as a whole.[6] In fact, a number of recent studies has propounded in various ways the idea that a wider canoni-

---

[105] DEMPSTER, "Fact," 51-56, has also followed and expanded upon BLENKINSOPP by arguing for Deut 34 and several other passages as canonical 'boundaries' (Jos 1:1–9; Mal 3:22–24 [4:4–6]; Ruth 4:18–22; Ps 1–2; 2 Chr 36:22–23), but claims to locate a Temple theme in this material. Such a theme, however, is completely lacking in Deut 34. In my view, DEMPSTER's effort does not persuasively indicate the particular significance of a Temple theme at his 'boundaries,' only the importance of this topic within the literature generally.

[106] P. D. MILLER, "Moses," 248.

[1] PETERSEN, Zechariah, 227–28.

[2] See the overview in NOGALSKI, Processes, 185–86. Some scholars disagree with the consensus: e. g., BALDWIN, Haggai, 251; GLAZIER-MACDONALD, Malachi, 245–46; VERHOEF, Haggai, 338.

[3] ELLIGER, Propheten, II:205–06; R. A. MASON, Haggai, 159; RUDOLPH, Haggai, 291. See also AMSLER, LACOCQUE AND VUILLEUMIER, Aggée, 23; COGGINS, Haggai, 79; MARTI, Dodekapropheton, 478; R. L. SMITH, Micah, 341.

[4] NOGALSKI, Processes, 246; BOSSHARD, Beobachtungen; idem, AND KRATZ, Maleachi; STECK, Abschluß, 34; idem, Kanon. BOSSHARD, KRATZ and STECK view Mal 3:22–24 [4:4–6] as part of a third layer of redaction within the book, including Mal 1:1, 14a and 2:10–12.

[5] Already in DUHM, Anmerkungen, 95; Cf. AMSLER, LACOCQUE AND VUILLEUMIER, Aggée, 254; COGGINS, Haggai, 84–85; CRAIGIE, Prophets, II:247; DEISSLER, Propheten, III:337; ELLIGER, Propheten, II:205–06; HILL, Malachi, 364; R. A. MASON, Haggai, 159; ROBINSON AND HORST, Propheten, 275. See also R. L. SMITH, Micah, 340.

[6] Already in WILDEBOER, Entstehung, 123. The suggestion was revived in a new form by RUDOLPH (Haggai, 290–93). I discuss RUDOLPH's proposal in detail below.

cal horizon was a major force in the shaping of the final form of the book of The Twelve.[7]

In Blenkinsopp's view, the last two 'paragraphs' of Malachi are "intended to serve as the conclusion to the entire prophetic collection, perhaps even to both Law and Prophets combined."[8] This assessment derives more, however, from his thorough-going acceptance of O. Plöger's 'bipolar model' of post-exilic society[9] than from the text itself. For Blenkinsopp, the crucial factor is the eschatological cast of the second appendix (Mal 3:23–24 [4:5–6]), as indicated by its language about Elijah (drawing on the reference to a 'messenger' in Mal 3:1), the 'day of the LORD' and 'family reconciliation.'

Comparing this last theme of 'reconciliation' to Sir 48:10, where similar language is paralleled by mention of the restored tribes of Jacob, Blenkinsopp moves by a kind of 'transitive' exegetical property to Isa 49:5–6 (where restoring the tribes is paralleled by the motif of the 'servant of the LORD,' but without the language of reconciliation). He then argues that the impulse toward the 'reintegration' of 'charismatic Israel' is fundamentally sectarian and "clearly... counter to the increasing propensity of the religious leadership to limit itself to the temple-community around Jerusalem, dictated largely but not exclusively by the need to oppose Samaritan claims."[10]

Even if Blenkinsopp is correct, and the mention in Mal 3:24 [4:6] of 'turning the hearts of fathers to their children' is an apocalyptic motif,[11] nothing in the text suggests a conflict between priest and prophet, except the references he has imported from Sir 48:10 and Isa 49:5–6 (as he interprets them)! To the contrary, the appendices to Malachi present such a complementarity of theocratic and eschatological impulses that even Blenkinsopp agrees that the disparity between the two (in his view, paradigmatically stated in Deut 34:10–12!) is here superseded. However, this means for Blenkinsopp that the 'tension' between theocratic and eschatological worldviews is 'restored,' rather than eliminated. What the conclusion to the Torah had attempted to exclude, in his view, the conclusion to the Prophets reintroduces as a productive counterpoint.[12]

---

[7] BOSSHARD AND KRATZ, Maleachi, 46; HILL, Malachi, 365; NOGALSKI, Processes, 210–11; 278–79; PETERSEN, Zechariah, 34; STECK, Abschluß, 127–28.

[8] BLENKINSOPP, Canon, 121.

[9] PLÖGER, Theocracy. The term 'bipolar model' comes from the concise summary and criticism of PLÖGER's views in ALBERTZ, History, II:238–39.

[10] BLENKINSOPP, Canon, 122.

[11] See below; I doubt the motif is originally apocalyptic, although like many others it may have been later used in this way. In its treatment of Elijah, Sir 48:10 is simply quoting Mal 3:23–24 [4:5–6] (note the formula, 'it is written'). BLENKINSOPP does not otherwise adduce a single biblical example of the motif in an apocalyptic context.

[12] BLENKINSOPP, Canon, 123.

In my view, the conclusion to the book of Malachi instead reveals the same basic perspective as the conclusion to the book of Deuteronomy: that Law and Prophets constitute a complementary unity. B. S. Childs makes exactly this point regarding Malachi:

> "...the final appeal to the normative role of the Mosaic law serves not to restrict, nor soften the prophet's proclamation, but rather to reaffirm the ground of Israel's existence testified to in the entire Old Testament. The canonical form of Malachi bears witness to Israel's conviction that the law and the prophets were not in opposition to each other, but constituted an essential unity within the divine purpose."[13]

In other words, whether or not the Malachi appendices are the product of the same hand or the same group of tradents, they functioned jointly in the late post-exilic period to portray eschatological prophecy and law as *complementary* dispensations within a single economy of Israel's God.

Here the historical datum of the final form of the text calls into sharpest question the sociological assumptions of Plöger and Blenkinsopp. Where in their assessments of post-exilic society are there tradents who could have possessed the unified view of Law and Prophets that these appendices set forth?

Appendices to Malachi Alone?

It should be noted that although I agree with Childs's view of the 'essential unity' of Law and Prophets reflected in Malachi's conclusion, I disagree with him as to the *scope* of this patently canon-conscious redaction. For Childs, the appendices function as a conclusion to the book of Malachi *alone*.[14] He rejects the attempt of W. Rudolph to see Mal 3:22 [4:4] as a conclusion to the entire prophetic corpus,[15] preferring to find the force of the appendices directed toward message of the book of Malachi itself. In my view, this does not prevent the appendices from also having a wider horizon within the prophetic corpus.

The strength of Childs's treatment lies in showing the close relationship between the appendices and the book. This is often overlooked in the move to wider canonical dimensions. Childs holds that these appendices represent

---

[13] CHILDS, OT Introduction, 497.

[14] Ibid., 495. Agreeing with CHILDS on this point are ELLIGER, Propheten, II:205–06; MITCHELL, SMITH AND BEWER, Haggai, 81–82; VAN DER WOUDE, Haggai, 158.

[15] CHILDS's reasons for this rejection are never fully clear. He seems to imply, negatively, that the evidence of a connection is too scanty and, positively, that the emphasis of the first appendix lies properly in the themes of the book rather than of the whole corpus. Against his negative judgment, I would remember that RUDOLPH saw a connection with Jos 1.2 as well as with Jos 1.7 — resonances which I take to be convincing, but by themselves not necessarily indicative of RUDOLPH's conclusion. Against CHILDS's positive argument, I would only question why the 'critical perspective' of the law is not as trenchant with respect to the prophets in general as to Malachi in particular?

editorial references to mosaic law and prophecy which provided a theological context for Malachi's own message and enabled it to be heard by future generations without antinomianism or complacency (respectively).[16] In light of Childs's arguments, there seems little doubt that the appendices were as carefully constructed to conclude the book of Malachi as they were to provide any broader sense of closure.

Appendices to the Prophetic Corpus?

Childs does not address, however, the *differences* between Mal 3:22–24 [4:4–6] and the rest of the book. In contrast to the dialogue form which constitutes most of Malachi, Mal 3:22–24 [4:4–6] takes the form of two admonitions.[17] 'Remember,' 'the law of my servant Moses,' 'statutes and ordinances,' 'Horeb' and 'all Israel' are familiar deuteronomistic expressions.[18] In fact, the linguistic similarities between Deuteronomy and Malachi have long been recognized.[19]

In the book of Malachi proper, the expression 'the coming day' is used of the *eschaton*,[20] but in Mal 3:23 [4:5] it is 'the great and terrible day of the LORD.'[21] The book of Malachi speaks of the תורה,[22] but not the תורת משה as in Mal 3:22 [4:4].[23] In contrast to the frequent use of the formulas אמר יהוה[24] and יהוה צבאות[25] within the book, both are lacking in the appendices. While the book always uses the short form of the first person pronoun,[26] Mal 3:23 [4:5] uses the long form.[27] Finally, Mal 3:22 [4:4] uses the familiar deuteronomistic expression כל ישראל, which is otherwise absent from the book.[28]

---

[16] CHILDS, OT Introduction, 495–96. He is particularly illuminating as he explores the intertextual relationships between the book of Malachi and the Elijah stories in 1 Kg 17–21, which, he argues, also serve to connect Mal 3:23–24 [4:5–6] with the rest of the book.

[17] R. L. SMITH, Micah, 342.

[18] MARTI, Dodekapropheton, 478.

[19] E. g., 'covenant of Levi' in Mal 2:4, 8. On the issue generally, see COGGINS, Haggai, 75–77; ELLIGER, Propheten, II:205; MITCHELL, SMITH AND BEWER, Haggai, 8; 81; SELLIN, Zwölfprophetenbuch, II:617. Cf. BLENKINSOPP, History, 242.

[20] Mal 3:2, 17, 19 [4:1], 21 [4:3].

[21] As also in Joel 3:4b [2:31b]; cf. Joel 2:11. See MITCHELL, SMITH AND BEWER, Haggai, 85. Cf. MARTI, Dodekapropheton, 478.

[22] Mal 2:8, 9.

[23] MITCHELL, SMITH AND BEWER, Haggai, 85.

[24] Ibid.

[25] MARTI, Dodekapropheton, 478.

[26] E. g., Mal 3:21 [4:3].

[27] MITCHELL, SMITH AND BEWER, Haggai, 85.

[28] The phrase 'all Israel' occurs just this once in the Latter Prophets, in two disputed passages in Genesis–Numbers (Ex 18:25; Num 16:34), never in the Psalms and very frequently throughout Deuteronomy and the Deuteronomistic History. See PERLITT, Deuteronomium, 9–10.

In addition, there is persuasive evidence that the appendices allude to textual units beyond the book of Malachi. Rudolph gave this proposal its current scholarly form, arguing that Mal 3:22–24 [4:4–6] "hat nichts mit dem Maleachibuch zu tun, sondern ist die Fermate zum ganzen Prophetenkanon, die an dessen Anfang in Jos. 1,2.7 erinnert."[29] In Rudolph's view, it was also no accident that Mal 3:22 [4:4] referred to Moses as 'servant of the LORD,' just as Deut 34:1–9 did.[30] He maintained that the appendices to Malachi had picked up the language that marked the critical transition from Pentateuch to Prophets in Deut 34.

'Servant' language is also used at the beginning of the Prophets (Jos 1:2, 7), with Jos 1:7 speaking of the 'Torah' that God had commanded 'his servant Moses' (משה עבדי) — a construction very similar to Mal 3:22 [4:4].[31] For Rudolph, this linguistic correspondence represented an literary *inclusio*, illustrating that Mal 3:22 [4:4] was "eine Zutat nicht zu Maleachi, auch nicht zum Zwölfprophetenbuch, sondern zum ganzen Prophetenkanon."[32] Then, however, Rudolph went on to say that this literary relationship reinforced the notion that the Prophets were understood as commentary on the Law.

Rudolph believed that the author of the appendices (who therefore also completed the book of Malachi) displayed numerous instances of using deuteronomistic language, but that since he most likely had the whole Pentateuch before him anyway the issue of a specific deuteronomic milieu was largely moot.[33] Rudolph also noted the similarity of language ('the great and terrible day of the LORD') between Mal 3:23b [4:5b] and Joel 3:4b [2:31b], speculating that Joel 3:1–5 [2:28–32] might have provided the background to Mal 3:1.[34] He took the *zayin* majuscule in the Hebrew text at Mal 3:22 [4:4] to provide further evidence of a 'special section' (*Sonderabschnitt*).[35] Since Sir 48:10 quotes Mal 3:24 [4:6] (with a citation formula), Rudolph concluded that 190 B. C. provided a firm *terminus ante quem* for the final form of Malachi

---

[29] RUDOLPH, Haggai, 250: "[it] does not have anything to do with the book of Malachi, but is rather the 'fermata' to the entire prophetic canon, which recalls its beginning in Jos 1:2, 7."

[30] Ibid., 291.

[31] The phrase in Jos 1:7 reads: רק חזק ואמץ מאד לשמר לעשות ככל-התורה אשר צוך משה עבדי. In Mal 3:22 [4:4]: זכרו תורת משה עבדי אשר צויתי אותו.

[32] RUDOLPH, Haggai, 291: "not a supplement to Malachi, or to the book of the Twelve Prophets, but rather to the entire prophetic canon."

[33] Ibid., 291 n. 2.

[34] The phrase in Mal 3:23b [4:5b] and Joel 3:4b [2:31b] is identical: לפני בוא יום יהוה הגדול והנורא.

[35] Unfortunately, the masoretic marking is somewhat mysterious. It appears in the Hebrew text also at Gen 1:1; Isa 40:1; Prov 1:1; Song 1:1; Eccl 1:1 and 1 Chr 1:1. Judging from this list, the marking would seem usually to indicate the beginning of a section rather than a conclusion.

and the book of The Twelve (and thus presumably for the prophetic corpus more or less as a whole).

In my view, Rudolph was largely successful in revealing the intertextual resonances of the appendices in Malachi within the wider prophetic corpus. In fact, increasing attention to his theory in recent treatments demonstrates that the results of an older literary-critical approach can still be illuminating for a new generation of scholars attempting to explore larger literary structures within the Old Testament. J. Nogalski, for example, has accepted Rudolph's insight and extended it further.[36]

In Nogalski's reconstruction, the final three blocks of material within the book of The Twelve (Zech 9–11; 12–14 and Malachi):

> "...all form a significant reflection to the beginning of larger sections of the prophetic corpus, working outward from the smallest to the largest. Zech 9–11 discusses the reconstitution of the monarchy, and concludes with references related to the beginning of Hosea. Zech 12–14 concludes with a chapter that unites the themes of the first book of the latter prophets, by combining the perspectives of Isa 2 and 66. Mal 3:22 deliberately takes up the beginning of the former prophets by playing off Jos 1:2, 7."[37]

Nogalski holds, moreover, that Malachi possessed an original integrity as a book and functioned from the beginning as the final book in the collection of The Twelve.[38] In his view, Zech 9–11 was first inserted into the collection, interrupting what had been a direct literary connection between Zech 1–8 and Malachi. Then Zech 12:1–13:2(–6) was added, followed by Zech 14:1–21 (displacing Zech 13:7–9), with Mal 3:22 [4:4] appearing as part of this last redactional layer.[39]

A Variety of Orders in the Prophets

Without examining every aspect of Nogalski's reconstruction, it is nevertheless necessary to level the same critique against his conclusions as against

---

[36] NOGALSKI, Processes, 204–06.

[37] Ibid., 245. NOGALSKI gives credit for the basic conceptual framework of this reconstruction to J. J. Owens (personal letter).

[38] Contra KRATZ AND BOSSHARD (Maleachi) and STECK (Abschluß), who argue that the book of Malachi originally formed a continuation of Zech 7–8 and only eventually achieved literary indendence as a result of later redactional developments. See also NOGALSKI, Processes, 245, n. 98.

[39] NOGALSKI, Processes, 245–46. NOGALSKI believes that the superscriptions in Zech 9:1 and 12:1 were added at this time, too, contra BOSSHARD AND KRATZ (Maleachi, 45–46) and STECK (Abschluß, 128–29), who believe Mal 1:1 belongs to the latest layer of redaction. NOGALSKI thinks the superscriptions in Zech 9:1 and 12:1 imitate Mal 1:1, rather than vice versa. See his Processes, 246, n. 99. Presumably Mal 3:23–24 [4:5–6] would then represent an even later addition. In NOGALSKI's view the book of Jonah was most likely added concurrent with Zech 12:2–13:6, but perhaps later still (Processes, 272–73 n. 79).

Rudolph's: namely, that the wide variety in the order of the prophetic books in later lists and manuscripts casts serious doubt upon the kind of architectonic intertextual relationships that Rudolph and Nogalski envision.[40] While it is true that according to extant Jewish lists and manuscripts the book of The Twelve always seems to have occupied the final position in the prophetic corpus (and the book of Joshua the initial position),[41] these lists and manuscripts date from the medieval period.[42] Also, a far greater variety of orders exists in Greek lists and manuscripts.[43] With the work of G. Hölscher, P. Katz and J. C. H. Lebram it is not possible simply to assume the priority of the Hebrew order against the LXX.[44]

The variety of orders occurring in Greek lists and manuscripts is all the more significant because of the initial position and uniform order of the Pentateuch in every case. In addition, in *almost* every case the book of Joshua follows directly after the Pentateuch. The book of The Twelve, however, most often occupies a position at the *beginning* of the four books later referred to as the 'Latter Prophets,' rather than at the end.[45] In fact, with the apparent minimal regard for any fixed order of biblical books at Qumran, and the knowledge that the codex form did not begin to replace scrolls for the writing of scripture until ca. A. D. 100,[46] serious question has been raised as to whether or not there existed a fixed order to the Prophets or the Writings until *after* the time that the biblical collection was closed.[47]

---

[40] For further information about the variation in orders, see BECKWITH, Canon, 449–68 ('Appendix B'); RYLE, Canon, 292–94 ('Excursus C'); SUNDBERG, Church, 75–77; SWETE, Introduction, 200–02 ('Excursus C').

[41] CHILDS, OT Introduction, 309. CHILDS refers only to Jewish text traditions when he implies the book of The Twelve is always last.

[42] GINSBURG, Introduction. JOSEPHUS, Against Apion, I:37–43, might be taken to provide an exception, but is not a list *per se*; Qumran also provides information as to the early period, but not a list of books.

[43] For a convenient printing of many of these lists, see MCDONALD, Formation, 268–73 ('Appendix I.B–I.C').

[44] HÖLSCHER, Kanonisch, 25–28; KATZ, Canon; LEBRAM, Aspekte.

[45] *Contra* HOUSE, Unity, 63–64, who neglects consideration of Greek lists and manuscripts. Cf. RUDOLPH (Haggai, 299), who argued that this position at the beginning of the Latter Prophets in the Greek manuscript tradition was a secondary development — largely on the basis of Mal 3:22–24 [4:4–6], which he argued (in circular fashion) proved Malachi must have originally occupied the final position.

[46] ELLIS, Canon, 35 n. 112. He notes that no codices were found at Qumran or Pompeii and cites additional literature on the subject.

[47] See SWANSON, Closing, 321–22; BARTON, Oracles, 82–83. Note, however, BECKWITH, Canon, 245–47. BECKWITH maintains that a fixed order to the books was possible, perhaps even necessary, precisely because there was no codex form to provide it.

Such difficulties have led Childs to conclude:

"...the order of the prophetic books within the collection of the Latter Prophets assumed no great canonical significance and thus differed from the attitude shown to the order within the Pentateuch. The major effect of the canonical process lay in the shaping of the individual prophetic books, and in producing a new entity of a prophetic collection which functioned within the canon as a unified block over against the Torah."[48]

Given the lack of firm evidence for any fixed order within the prophetic corpus until the post-biblical period,[49] Childs considers it highly questionable to assert that intertextual allusions within the prophetic collection reflect intentional efforts to structure the canon.

In the case of the twelve Minor Prophets, however, ample evidence does exist that from a very early period that they were combined literarily into a single work. Sir 49:10 (ca. 180 B. C.) refers to all twelve as a *literary collection* in its overview of biblical history and literature: "May the bones of the Twelve Prophets send forth new life from where they lie, for they comforted the people of Jacob and delivered them with confident hope." As Nogalski notes, the enumeration of biblical books given in 4 Ezr 14:45 (24) and Josephus, Against Apion, I:37–43 (22), as well as the list of biblical books found in the Talmud (Baba Bathra 14b), all appear to count The Twelve as one book.[50]

The evidence from Qumran provides further support for this notion, since several of the fragments from the Minor Prophets contain text from more than one book, and perhaps always in the masoretic order (a complete copy of the entire book of The Twelve has not been found).[51] One scroll (4QXII^a) appears to indicate that the book of Jonah may have followed the book of Malachi within the collection, but this possibility involves a supposition. A single fragment appears to indicate that the end of Malachi was followed by some additional writing, but not what this writing was (i. e., the material from Jonah is located on a different fragment). There is thus nothing to contradict the possibility that Malachi might have been followed by a text *other* than Jonah.

---

[48] CHILDS, OT Introduction, 310.

[49] Ibid., 666. Acts 7:42 refers to 'the book of the prophets,' 4Q397 to 'the book[s of the pr]ophets' or 'the book of the prophets,' and the Prologue to Ben Sira (ca. 132 B. C.) to 'the prophets,' but not to any fixed order. Even in JOSEPHUS, Against Apion, I:37–43 (ca. A. D. 95), the prophetic books are numbered (13), but not ordered. Numbering does not necessarily imply a fixed order. On the other hand, Sir 44–49 suggests something other than a strictly salvation-historical progression, since the 'minor prophets' do not appear where they would 'in history,' but as a concluding written volume (Sir 49:10). For further discussion, see below.

[50] NOGALSKI, Precursors, 2–3.

[51] Ibid., 2 n. 5.

This scroll apparently includes Mal 3:22–24 [4:4–6] and has been dated to the mid-second century B. C.[52]

The LXX also witnesses to the early unity of The Twelve, even though one Greek textual tradition (there are several) changes the order of the first six books (i. e., Hosea, Amos, Micah, Joel, Obadiah, Jonah).[53] The Babylonian Talmud (Baba Bathra 13b) even makes an exception for The Twelve when it comes to the spacing between biblical books: fewer lines (3) than the normal practice (4) are required of scribes when separating each of the books within the book of The Twelve.[54]

Canon-Conscious Appendices

Against the background of the unity of The Twelve, the significance of the allusions in Mal 3:22–24 [4:4–6] comes into clearer focus. It is possible to affirm Rudolph's observation that Mal 3:22 [4:4] draws upon the language of Jos 1:2, 7 without drawing the further conclusion that Mal 3:22 [4:4] was *originally intended* to provide a conclusion to the entire prophetic corpus. Certainly Mal 3:23–24 [4:5–6] draws upon Joel 3:1–5 [2:28–32] as much as Mal 3:22 [4:4] draws on Jos 1:2, 7.[55] Several scholars have also argued for substantial similarities between the book of Malachi and the Elijah narratives in 1 Kg 17–21.[56] In sum, Mal 3:22–24 [4:4–6] seems to exhibit its 'canon-consciousness' primarily in its allusion to and reuse of written prophetic narratives and oracles, or 'scribal prophecy' (*Schriftprophetie*).[57]

---

[52] For discussion of this scroll, see JONES, Formation, 6–7.

[53] SWETE, Introduction, 201–03. In the LXX, the order of the appendices is reversed, with Mal 3:23–24 [4:5–6] coming *before* Mal 3:22 [4:4]. Jones has recently argued (Formation, 118–25) that this order reflects that of its Hebrew *Vorlage*, although he still views Mal 3:23–24 [4:5–6] as the later addition (inserted between Mal 3:21 [4:3] and Mal 3:22 [4:4]). In my view, a more compelling explanation is to be found in the frequent reversal of prophetic oracles in ancient lectionary practice so as to avoid ending on a note of judgment. See MITCHELL, SMITH AND BEWER, Haggai, 83; on the general practice, see PATTE, Hermeneutic, 40. Furthermore, the more 'difficult' reading here (and thus the more probably original) is found in the order of the present MT.

[54] NOGALSKI, Precursors, 3.

[55] MITCHELL, SMITH AND BEWER, Haggai, 341: "The passage in Joel may be later than Malachi's time, but not necessarily later than this appendix." Not only does Mal 3:23b [4:5b] quote Joel 3:4b [2:31b] (cf. Joel 2:11), but the reference in Mal 3:24 [4:6] to turning 'the hearts of fathers to their sons and the hearts of sons to their fathers' echoes Joel's language about children and the outpouring of God's spirit on 'the day of the LORD' (Joel 3:1–5 [2:28–32]). See PETERSEN, Prophecy, 44.

[56] CHILDS, OT Introduction, 495–96; ELLIGER, Propheten, II:205; GLAZIER-MAC-DONALD, Malachi, 257; RUDOLPH, Haggai, 292; SELLIN, Zwölfprophetenbuch, 617.

[57] For some helpful explorations of the phenomenon of *Schriftprophetie*, see BERGLER, Joel; FISHBANE, Interpretation, esp. 458–99; PETERSEN, Prophecy; UTZSCHNEIDER, Künder? See also NOGALSKI, Precursors, 16.

Further Deuteronomistic Background

However, there is another fundamental source of tradition for the second appendix (Mal 3:23–24 [4:5–6]) which has not yet received enough attention. As several scholars have noted, the book of Malachi generally displays a preponderance of deuteronomistic characteristics.[58] However, the second appendix relies on these same characteristic deuteronomistic terms and ideas to make its admonition about expecting Elijah. Here, the verb 'send' (שלח) embodies the same 'charismatic' conception of the *prophetic* calling found throughout deuteronomistic literature and in Deut 34:11.

Moreover, the enigmatic reference in Mal 3:24 [4:6] to the way in which Elijah will (lit.) 'turn the heart of fathers to [their] sons and the heart of sons to their fathers' approximates the recognized deuteronomic expression 'to turn the heart.'[59] The only difference is that Mal 3:24 [4:6] uses the preposition על in contrast to the more usual preposition אל, which may in this case indicate a transitive sense for the verb,[60] or simply the flexibility of late biblical Hebrew.[61]

The presence of the deuteronomistic idiom is sometimes obscured by translation. Thus, in Deut 4:39, the Israelites are commanded by Moses to (lit.) 'know today and turn your heart to [the fact that] the LORD is God in the heaven above and on the earth beneath.'[62] Most significant perhaps is Deut 30:1–2, in which the expression 'turn your heart'[63] is followed by the importance of faithful 'sons' (Deut 30:2).

The citation in Deut 30:1 reveals the link between the idiom of 'turning the heart' and the central deuteronomistic conception of repentance ('returning,' שוב).[64] In deuteronomistic understanding, an aspect of internal observance (expressed by לבב) forms the necessary precondition for living an obedient

---

[58] AMSLER, LACOCQUE AND VUILLEUMIER, Aggée, 253; BLENKINSOPP, History, 242; COGGINS, Haggai, 76; DEISSLER, Propheten, III:337; R. A. MASON, Haggai, 159; ORELLI, Propheten, 235; PETERSEN, Zechariah, 228. There is a persistent scholarly minority that points to the presence of priestly influence on the book of Malachi; see MEYERS, Language; J. M. O'BRIEN, Priest, esp. 113–14. As PETERSEN points out (Zechariah, 32–33), however, the alleged examples of influence do not appear to indicate the influence of specifically *tetrateuchal* priestly material.

[59] Deut 4:39; 30:1; 1 Kg 8:47 = 2 Chr 6:37. Cf. Isa 44:19; 46:18; Lam 3:21. See WEINFELD, Deuteronomy, 357 (#10). The NRSV tends to translate 'take it to heart'; the RSV usually employs the expression 'lay it to heart.'

[60] I. e., with the meaning 'to turn someone's heart,' rather than the more usual relexive sense of this idiom.

[61] Cf. Isa 46:8; also Deut 30:1 in some Samaritan mss.

[62] The MT reads in part וידעת היום והשבת אל־לבבך. The NRSV translates, 'So acknowledge today and take to heart...'

[63] Cf. NRSV: 'call to mind.'

[64] On this conception, see WOLFF, Kerygma, 90–92.

life.[65] According to Deut 30:1, this internal observance arises from the existential comparison between later events ('when all these things come upon you') and the word of God as revealed in the book of Deuteronomy itself ('the blessing and the curse, which I have set before you, and you take *them* to heart among all the nations where the LORD your God has driven you' [my emphasis])[66]. Thus, in deuteronomistic understanding repentance ultimately arises from the study of *scripture*.

While the Hebrew verb used for renewed obedience ('returning') is almost always the same (שׁוב), the verb used to indicate the internal observance varies. In Deut 30:1, it is the *Hiph'il* form of the same verb (שׁוב, as in Mal 3:24 [4:6]) that is paired with the call to 'return' (שׁוב) in Deut 30:2. However, in 1 Sam 7:3 the *Hiph'il* form of the verb כון is paralleled with שׁוב.[67] In 2 Sam 19:15 [14], the *Hiph'il* form of the verb נטה is used in combination with לבב and שׁוב.[68] In Deut 29:17 [18] and Deut 30:17, the *Qal* form of the verb פנה is used to denote the internal movement of the heart on which outward obedience is contingent.[69]

Moreover, a constellation of further motifs also suggests a deuteronomistic tradition-historical background for Mal 3:23–24 [4:5–6], with shared references to the way in which God will 'blot out the names' of the unfaithful,[70] the devastation which the land will suffer on their account[71] and to future generations of the faithful.[72] In sum, Mal 3:23–24 [4:5–6] summons Israel *prophetically* to repentance. Social decay is but a symptom of a greater illness. The fundamental issue at hand is Israel's 'vertical' reconciliation with God, rather than any specific 'horizontal' social situation.[73]

'Horizontal' interpretations of the situation reflected in Mal 3:24 [4:6] (e. g., a Hellenistic 'crisis within the family')[74] are not very convincing.[75] Nor

---

[65] Ibid., 98–99. In the Deuteronomistic History sometimes the precondition is less 'psychological' and more a 'human deed,' according to WOLFF. Cf. 1 Sam 7:3.

[66] NRSV: 'and you call them to mind.'

[67] והכינו לבבכם אל-יהוה. Cf. Job 11:13; Ps 78:8. This expression seems to be functionally similar to the various forms of the chronistic idiom הכן לבבו לדרוש את יהוה/התורה: e. g., 1 Chr 29:18; 2 Chr 12:14; 19:3; 20:33; 30:19; Ezr 7:10.

[68] Without שׁוב but with similar meaning, cf. Jos 24:23; 1 Kg 8:58; Ps 119:36; 141:4; Prov 2:2; 21:1. The heart can turn away from God as well: e. g., 1 Kg 11:2, 3, 4; Isa 44:20. The usage in the *Qal* is sometimes similar: Jud 9:3; 1 Sam 14:7; 1 Kg 11:9; Ps 119:112.

[69] Note the parallel occurrence of שׁוב in Deut 30:10.

[70] Cvc. Deut 29:19 [20] and Mal 3:16–17.

[71] Cvc. Deut 29:20–22 [21–23] and Mal 3:24 [4:6].

[72] Cvc. Deut 4:40; 29:21 [22], 28 [29]; 30:2, 6, 19 and Mal 3:24 [4:6].

[73] Thus, E. ACHTEMEIER, Nahum, 197. This is also how the gospel of Luke seems to understand these verses (cf. Lk 1:16–17)!

[74] First suggested by TORREY, Malachi, 7; cf. RUDOLPH, Haggai, 292–94; MITCHELL, SMITH AND BEWER, Haggai, 83.

does Blenkinsopp's proposal of an apocalyptic motif carry conviction, as we have seen. While a third proposal is suggestive, namely, that this language of the 'heart' has its origins in wisdom traditions,[76] wisdom motifs do not otherwise appear to be prominent. Thus, the likeliest possibility, based on the linguistic parallels with the book of Deuteronomy which have been noted, is that the language of 'father' and 'sons' in Mal 3:24 [4:6] is also essentially deuteronomistic and covenantal,[77] turning on the worship of God rather than 'other gods.'[78]

Thus, within the context of the deuteronomistic stream of tradition the references to Elijah in Malachi (esp. Mal 3:23 [4:5]) serve to underscore the worship of God alone[79] rather than to valorize apocalyptic views. This particular theme is also a key feature of the Elijah acount in 1 Kg 17–21; for example, in 1 Kg 18:37–38 Elijah asks God to 'turn the heart' of the people back;[80] in 1 Kg 18:39 the people make confession to God in opposition to the prophets of Baal. The reference in Mal 3:24 [4:6] to the 'ban' or 'curse' (חרם) is thus to be expected as also part of the same constellation of covenantal motifs (cf. Deut 7:26).[81]

As in the case of Elijah, in the deuteronomistic conception of prophets and prophecy the admonition of 'return' is central.[82] Among the Latter Prophets, שוב appears quite prominently, particularly in the books of Jeremiah and Hosea.[83] Variations on the theme provide a major rhetorical structuring device in at least two different passages (Jer 3–4 and Am 4). Deuteronomistic and deuteronomistic-style redactions consistently characterize the pre-exilic prophets as 'servants of God' who preached precisely this kind of repentance.[84]

---

[75] GLAZIER-MACDONALD, Malachi, 245–46.

[76] WEINFELD, Deuteronomy, 304.

[77] VERHOEF, Haggai, 342. Cf. DEISSLER, Propheten, 338. Cvc. further Deut 5:9–10 with Mal 3:7.

[78] E. ACHTEMEIER, Malachi, 197. Cf. Deut 4:39; 29:15–18 [16–19], 24–27 [25–28]; 30:17.

[79] See R. A. MASON, Haggai, 160.

[80] Here the *Hiph'il* of סבב is used with the particle את; cf. Ezr 6:22.

[81] Cf. further Neh 10:30 [29]; Dan 9:11. MEYERS AND MEYERS point out (Haggai, 283) that a different word for 'curse' (עלה) can be synonymous with covenant or part of a hendiadys ('a curse and an oath') because a written document can be equated with its sanctions, according to ancient understanding. They cite CROSS AND SALEY, Incantations, esp. 45 n. 16.

[82] WOLFF sees (Kerygma, 95–97) the centrality of this idea as belonging to a later, second stage of Deuteronomy's redaction by someone trying to 'graft' deuteronomistic and jeremianic traditions onto the older material, 'framing' the core of the book by the addition of Deut 4 and 30.

[83] E. g., Isa 6:10; 9:12 [13]; 10:21–22; 31:6; Jer 3–4; 18:11; 25:4–5; 35:15; 36:3, 6; Ezek 13:22; 14:6; 18; 33:11; Hos 3:5; 5:4; 6:1; 7:10, 16; 11:5; 12:7 [6]; 14:2–3 [1–2]; Joel 2:12–13; Am 4; Zech 1:3–4; 9:12; 10:9.

[84] E. g., 2 Kg 17:13; Jer 25:4–5; Zech 1:4; Neh 9:26.

Moreover, in the Latter Prophets the violation of covenant also *results* in social disintegration.[85] This prophetic background is likely to have been widely understood: R. A. Mason notes that the LXX adds 'and the heart of a man to his neighbor' after Mal 3:24 [4:6], a phrase quite similar to Isa 3:5 (cf. Jer 19:9).[86] Could the translators of the LXX have been reading Malachi here in light of the book of Isaiah? At the very least, the closeness of this language emphasizes the way in which *covenant* and *prophecy*, rather than apocalyptic, provide the tradition-historical context for Mal 3:23–24 [4:5–6], just as *covenant* and *law* frame the background of Mal 3:22 [4:4].

In sum, the appendices in Mal 3:22–24 [4:4–6] thoroughly partake of deuteronomistic expressions and concepts, ultimately depending on this association for their own comprehensibility.[87] The historical distance between the probable date of these appendices (late 5th–4th B. C.?)[88] and that of the 'deuteronomistic movement' (650–500 B. C.)[89] may raise the question of precisely what is meant by 'deuteronomism,'[90] but it is nonetheless clear and significant that these appendices depend more heavily on deuteronomistic traditions than any others. This dependence illuminates the way in which these appendices *initially* functioned as examples of canon-conscious redaction: closing Malachi as a discrete book against the backdrop of an emergent deuteronomistic canon.

Appendices to Malachi and The Twelve

However, the full canon-consciousness of the Malachi appendices is not exhausted by their use of deuteronomistic traditions or the general phenomenon of *Schriftprophetie*. It also seems likely that from very early on Mal 3:22–24 [4:4–6] began to function as the conclusion to the book of The Twelve.

As D. L. Petersen has observed, "[The appendix] would not work well at the end of Zechariah. The epilogue presupposes a collection of latter prophets with Malachi at the end and with a collection of tora and former prophets preceding."[91] The foregoing analysis concurs with Petersen that this 'epilogue' presupposes the existence of such collections primarily by citation and allu-

---

[85] E. g., Isa 3:3–4; Jer 9:1–5; Mic 7:1–7.

[86] R. A. MASON, Haggai, 160–61.

[87] This is so much the case that one wonders whether Elijah is really meant to provide the specific referent of the language (*pace* CHILDS) or simply a particular instantiation of the prophetic ideal. In my judgment, the emphasis seems to be on the prophetic role generally rather than on the specific figure of Elijah.

[88] NOGALSKI, Processes, 186–87.

[89] WEINFELD, Deuteronomy, 1.

[90] LOHFINK, Bewegung?

[91] PETERSEN, Zechariah, 34.

sion.[92] However, Mal 3:22 [4:4] and Mal 3:23–24 [4:5–6] also draw upon the tradition-historical background of the Law and the Prophets, as it was understood within deuteronomistic tradition. The appendices regard these traditions authoritatively.

Thus, both appendices are canon-conscious not only by allusion and citation, but also by the various ways in which they rely upon the interpretive horizon of a deuteronomistic, covenantal 'grammar.' In these ways, 'Law' and 'Prophets' are not only presupposed, but also described, personified and enjoined. In their reception and representation of these scriptural traditions, the appendices to Malachi express the same deuteronomistic 'grammar' as in Deut 34:10–12.

In my view, the appendices in Mal 3:22–24 [4:4–6] were originally designed to close the book of Malachi alone, but exercised such literary force by the power of their canon-conscious allusions that they retained their status as a conclusion (at the same time broadening their scope) during the formation of the book of The Twelve and the prophetic corpus. *Contra* Rudolph, I would argue that the two appendices give every indication of being integrally related to the themes and message of the book.[93] *Contra* Childs, however, I would also argue that the function of the appendices to close the book of Malachi does not exclude the possibility of their also being used to conclude the book of The Twelve.[94]

The differences in form and language between the appendices and the book indicate the redactional status of the appendices. Their author(s) drew upon a variety of biblical traditions and books in their effort to conclude the book of Malachi. While the redaction history of the book of The Twelve is speculative at best, it seems likely that the concluding force of Mal 3:22–24 [4:4–6] is at least partly responsible for the placement of Malachi (the body of which probably dates from the end of the fifth century B. C.)[95] at the end of the collection. P. C. Craigie has described a similar possibility:

"It is possible [that the appendices] reflect an editorial addition from the hand of the editor of the Book of the Twelve. But the verses also combine law and prophecy in a manner typical of Malachi and they may well be authentic. Thus it may be that the Book of Malachi was placed at the end of the collection of the Twelve Prophets because its concluding words summarize so aptly not only its own substance, but also the message of the prophets as a whole."[96]

---

[92] Ibid., 232.
[93] E. g., Mal 3:1, 7. See CHILDS, OT Introduction, 495.
[94] Cf. HILL, Malachi, 364.
[95] Idem, Book.
[96] CRAIGIE, Prophets, II:247–48.

Because the redactional nature of the appendices seems undeniable,[97] however, I cannot agree with Craigie that the appendices could be original to Malachi.

In my view, rather, the writer of the appendices was not the author of the book, but someone who stood firmly in the same general deuteronomistic stream of tradition. This writer may or may not have been an editor of the book of The Twelve. In any case, it was indeed their trenchancy of theme and their vitality of expression that reserved a place for these verses at the end of The Twelve. The appendices probably also shaped the redaction history of The Twelve by compelling the addition of Zech 9–11 and then Zech 12–14 *between* the books of Zechariah and Malachi rather than after the Malachi appendices.[98]

It should therefore be of no surprise to find Mal 3:22–24 [4:4–6] at the conclusion of the entire prophetic collection as it now exists within the Hebrew canon.[99] Even though the evidence suggests that Mal 3:22–24 [4:4–6] was not originally designed as a conclusion to the entire prophetic corpus (the order was not yet fixed), its presence at the end of the book of The Twelve was no doubt felt to provide a firm sense of closure during the formation of the prophetic corpus, perhaps even influencing the eventual positioning of the book of The Twelve at the end of the Latter Prophets (at least in Jewish manuscripts and lists).[100] In this way, the theme of repentance in these verses continued to be heard as the heart of the prophetic message and as providing

---

[97] PETERSEN, Malachi, 228 n. 109, adds to the reasons already discussed above that Mal 3:22–24 [4:4–6] seems to desire to clarify Mal 3:1 — according to him, the 'best evidence' that Mal 3:22–24 [4:4–6] is secondary.

[98] The disagreement between the position of NOGALSKI and the position of BOSSHARD, KRATZ and STECK would seem to have important consequences for this question. If BOSSHARD, KRATZ and STECK are correct, and Malachi did not possess an original integrity as a book, but was separated at the last redactional phase in order to round out the book of The Twelve, then Mal 3:22–24 [4:4–6] was almost certainly added at the same time. More likely, in my view, is NOGALSKI's judgment that an earlier form of Malachi had already obtained final position in The Twelve, its concluding force helping to dictate the addition of Zech 9–11 and 12–14 at the end of Zechariah rather than after the 'end' of The Twelve (Mal 3:22–24 [4:4–6]).

[99] Even if Jonah did follow Malachi in 4QXII*, it is also true that both the LXX and MT orders have retained Malachi at the end of The Twelve. JONES himself cannot exclude the possibility (Formation, 130) that 4QXII* represents "an anomalous or erroneous exception in the transmission history of the Book of the Twelve."

[100] PETERSEN notes (Zechariah, 223 n. 129) that none of the other three books in the Latter Prophets has an epilogue. He makes an exception for Hos 14:10 [9] and Hab 3:19b (which in his view is really a simple dedication), leaving the intriguing possibility that the only two epilogues in the prophetic corpus are at the conclusion of the first (Hos 14:2–9 [1–8]) and last books in The Twelve.

the theological basis for a conceptual unity of Law and Prophets (cf. Lk 1:16–17!).[101]

The difference between the conclusion to the book of Malachi and the additions to the book of Zechariah (Zech 9–11 and Zech 12–14) proves instructive. According to Nogalski, the end of the prophetic collection has been successively shaped to provide a series of expanding canonical *inclusios*: Zech 11 matching Hos 1 (for The Twelve), Zech 14 matching Isa 2 and 66 (for the Latter Prophets), and Mal 3:22–24 [4:4–6] matching Jos 1:2, 7 (for the Prophets).

Although I think this design is far better organized than the literature it is supposed to explain, some of these relationships do bear further exegetical consideration. It may well be that as the book of The Twelve was extended by its tradents, new material was shaped according to an increasingly broader canonical horizon. However, in the final form of the present canon these relationships are largely submerged beneath the flow of the text and do not function in any substantive way — with the exception of Mal 3:22–24 [4:4–6] which is *explicitly* canon-conscious. Precisely by providing an explicit witness to the mutual *dependence* and essential *interrelation* of the Law and the Prophets, Mal 3:22–24 [4:4–6] achieved its summary position within the prophetic literature.[102]

Summary

Who were the tradents responsible for Deut 34:10–12 and Mal 3:22–24 [4:4–6]? According to Blenkinsopp, the circle of tradition behind Deut 34:10–12 was theocratic and priestly, whereas Mal 3:22–24 [4:4–6] stemmed from a prophetic and eschatological milieu. Our investigation, however, has demonstrated the deuteronomistic language and ideas of *both* sets of conclusions. Both are concerned to coordinate 'the Law' and 'the Prophets' as related *scriptural* traditions; both pursue their task of coordination primarily with deuteronomistic language and ideas.

However, there do exist differences between the two sets of appendices. Deut 34:10–12 functions primarily to describe Moses as a prophet, and thus

---

[101] The question of the relationship between the appendices to Malachi and the appendices to Deuteronomy must remain open. Is one intended to be a response or a restatement of the other? For the present discussion I would simply note that it is just as likely for the Malachi appendices to have pre-dated the Deuteronomy appendices as *vice versa*. I do not see great enough similarity to support the idea that both sets derive from the same redactor(s), although I think it is likely that the first set, whichever it was, has influenced the other.

[102] PETERSEN, Zechariah, 232. *Contra* DEISSLER, Propheten, 337, who understands Mal 3:22–24 [4:4–6] to reflect the Torah 'canon within a canon' of later Judaism.

complete the book of Deuteronomy and the Torah. Nowhere are portions of scripture explicitly referred to and the general tradition-historical context is provided by the Exodus event. Still, the hermeneutical effect of this kind of conclusion on the shape of the Torah cannot be gainsaid, especially coming directly after the account of Moses' death and Joshua's succession (Deut 34:1–9).

Whatever the extent of the possible priestly influence *behind* this account,[1] in the final form of the text such influence is subordinated to a prophetic interpretation of Moses' life and work in which a more 'charismatic' view predominates.[2] Central among those qualities of Moses which the author extols is that he 'did' (עשׂה, Deut 34:11, 12) what God 'sent' (שׁלח, Deut 34:11) him to do. Thus, the Torah ends with prophecy as well as law, and by virtue of this ending compels a reading of the whole in which both law and prophecy have a fundamental place.[3]

On the other hand, Mal 3:22–24 [4:4–6] is more explicit about its effort to coordinate *scriptural* traditions.[4] Coming at the end of the book of The Twelve, and eventually at the end of the entire prophetic corpus, Mal 3:22 [4:4] reminds its readers of the essential relation between the Prophets and the Law. Mal 3:23–24 [4:5–6] sets out the fundamental importance of worshipping the one true God, whose presence brings blessing to the faithful, but a curse to those who refuse to repent and acknowledge him.

At the same time, however, it would be too simple to reduce the relationship of Law and Prophets sketched by these verses to the following: Mal 3:22 [4:4] = Moses = Law and Mal 3:23–24 [4:5–6] = Elijah = Prophets.[5] While

---

[1] BLENKINSOPP, Canon, 82–83.

[2] *Contra* BLENKINSOPP, Canon, 84. The language belongs, of course, to WEBER, e. g., his Theory, 363–73.

[3] Cf. M. A. O'BRIEN, Reassessment, 66; SCHMITT, Redaktion; idem, Geschichtswerk..

[4] *Contra* VAN DER WOUDE, Haggai, 158.

[5] PETERSEN, Zechariah, 229, makes this error (opposite and yet formally similar to BLENKINSOPP's on Deut 34:10–12) when he observes that Moses' role is effectively deemphasized in the pairing of Law and Prophets: "This author is interested in Moses, not as paradigmatic prophet (Deut 18; 34:10–12) but as Torah recipient." This conclusion, however, introduces a problem for PETERSEN: how is Moses the prophet *par excellence* in Deut 18, but in Mal 3:23-24 [4:5–6] Elijah is *"the* prophet." His explanation? — that "...in the Persian period... Moses was increasingly associated with a distinct and nonprophetic body of literature, namely the torah or pentateuch." In my view, the alleged contradiction is better explained by literary than by historical factors: at the end of the story of Moses in Deuteronomy the *persona* of Moses had to embrace both law and prophecy; by the end of the prophetic corpus more characters are available from the emerging biblical story. The double dispensation of Israel's God expressed in the prophetic characterization of Moses in Deut 34:10–12 may now be personified as two characters. This does not neccessarily make Moses any less 'prophetic' or signify that a 'prophet like Moses' is no longer expected. In Mal 3:23–24 [4:5–6] the way

Mal 3:22 [4:4] refers to 'law,' it commends this law within the deuteronomistic framework of 'remembrance,'[6] thus *already* presuming the deuteronomistic understanding of the law as *prophetic*. Moreover, the verb צוה and the
noun עבד are used with reference to Moses, expressions rooted in deuteronomistic usage and prophetic associations.[7] Similarly, while Mal 3:23–24
[4:5–6] clearly revolves around the nature of the prophetic word, it also 'proclaims the *law*' according to deuteronomistic understanding. In this way, both
appendices reflect a *unified* conception of legal and prophetic traditions,
rather than each appendix representing one discrete tradition.

Moreover, the appendices to Malachi are styled as direct divine discourse,
as opposed to the third person narration of Deut 34. To be sure, their setting at
the end of the book of Malachi and the prophetic corpus places them within
the context of prophetic 'messenger speech.' The 'prophet' speaks in these
verses along with the voice of God. However, it is still *God* — as a character
in prophetic discourse — who here describes himself and his activity as
uniquely reflected in this complementarity of Law and Prophets.

In sum, both the appendices to Deuteronomy and the appendices to Malachi — within their respective books and within the larger canon — function
explicitly to combine Law and Prophets within a single 'story' about God.[8]
The true God, the God of Israel, is the God who has given the Law *and* the
Prophets to his people. Together, the Law and the Prophets represent the two
'chapters' of *his* story — two dispensations within a single economy of God.[9]
For the deuteronomists, Israel's theological 'grammar' at its most basic was

---

in which Elijah is presented fully accords with Deuteronomy's description of the 'prophet like
Moses.' Cf. GLAZIER-MACDONALD, Malachi, 267.

[6] See CHILDS, Memory, 50–52. Cf. SELLIN, Zwölfprophetenbuch, 617.

[7] SELLIN, Zwölfprophetenbuch, 617. Cf. K. ZOBEL, Prophetie, 201–02. The other association with עבד is with the monarchy, but the deuteronomistic context in this case strongly
suggests a prophetic resonance.

[8] Cf. RENDTORFF, Kanon, 64–71; esp. 71.

[9] Later this theological construct was historicized to provide an account of canon formation; see JOSEPHUS, Against Apion, I:37–43 (this trans. from BECKWITH, Canon, 118–19):
"Of these, five are the books of Moses, comprising the laws and the traditional history from
the birth of man down to Moses' death. This period falls only a little short of 3,000 years.
From the death of Moses down to Artaxerxes who followed Xerxes as king of Persia, the
prophets after Moses wrote the events of their own times in thirteen books... From Artaxerxes down to our own time, the complete history has been written, but has not been deemed
worthy of like trust with the earlier records, because of the failure of the exact succession of
the prophets." While the concern with chronology and authorship represents a further development of the tradition, the general division into the two periods of Moses and the prophets
continues to reflect the deuteronomistic theological conception which, according to the present argument, has framed the canonical literature.

this: the God of Israel is the God of the Law and the Prophets.[10] It was this deuteronomistic 'theological grammar' which thus provided the origin, norm and goal of Old Testament canon formation.

---

[10] Cf. HILL, Malachi, 390 (on Mal 3:22–24 [4:4–6]): "Together they composed a type of credo certifying the 'canonized' scriptures of the Law and the Prophets as the source of authority and the witness of the divine presence for the restoration community."

Chapter Four

The Law and...

Introduction

In the last chapter I showed how appendices have come to conclude the Pentateuch (Deut 34:10–12) and the prophetic corpus (Mal 3:22–24 [4:4–6]), coordinating pentateuchal and prophetic traditions within a common 'theological grammar.' In both cases, these canon-conscious appendices employ the language and style of the deuteronomistic tradition, although they themselves are likely to date a few centuries later than what is usually considered to be the heyday of that tradition in the seventh and sixth centuries (650–500 B. C.).[1] For this reason it could be argued that the 'grammar' expressed by both of these appendices was not, properly speaking, a tenet of deuteronomism *per se*, but rather a feature of late post-exilic Judaism in deuteronomistic garb.

The purpose of this chapter is to show that the 'theological grammar' expressed by these canon-conscious appendices is not a late artificial addition, but has its roots deep in the fertile soil of the earlier deuteronomic movement. Methodologically, it was necessary to begin this study with the concluding layers of the Old Testament — identified literarily as well as historically — in order to describe the final arc of the trajectory of the deuteronomistic tradition of prophecy and canon. After identifying the 'theological grammar' of 'Law and Prophets' that our exploration presented, we can now attempt to trace this tradition back through the history of the shaping and editing of the biblical texts. In this chapter I hope to show not only that the 'grammar' of 'Law and Prophets' was of considerable lineage within Israel's theology, but also that it functioned almost creedally within the process of literary formation to give a particular shape to the emergent biblical canon.[2]

---

[1] WEINFELD, Deuteronomy, 1. For arguments that 'deuteronomism' continued into the post-exilic period, see PERLITT, Priesterschrift? and PERSON, Zechariah.

[2] I. e., like a 'rule of faith.' HENN has noted (Faith, 203): "...the propensity of faith to find expression in short summaries or creeds... whether or not the precise word 'creed' is the best or most appropriate word to describe the phenomenon, both Testaments contain short summaries which attempt to concisely express a number of the most essential truths of faith." However, HENN does not consider whether the formulation 'the Law and the Prophets' itself functions as something like a 'creed.' On this general issue and something of its previous history within Old Testament scholarship, see MARTIN-ARCHARD, Theologies.

Historically the process of *scripture* in Israel began with the preservation of tradition and the commitment of tradition to written form. However, the origin of Israel's *canon* (when defined as a conceptual and literary framework for those scriptures) is to be found in the insight that 'the Law and the Prophets' comprise an indissoluble unity of tradition and faith.

Deuteronomy 31–34

Traditionally, the origin of written scripture within Israel was said to lie with Moses. In the so-called 'pre-critical' period of biblical scholarship, Jewish and Christian scholars alike maintained that Moses had written the Torah, based on the certain hints of authorship within pentateuchal texts.[1]

The dates advanced by historical-critical scholars for pentateuchal sources increasingly made such an idea quite unlikely,[2] although a few scholars continued to claim on occasion that certain portions of the Pentateuch were authored by Moses[3] and a number argued for a 'mosaic basis' to various Old Testament traditions.[4] The ability of the mosaic claim to survive its apparent historical disconfirmation points, I believe, to certain literary features of the text for which it retains explanatory power. B. S. Childs has made the important point that the biblical text itself *depicts* Moses as its ultimate source, indicating the continued importance of the figure of Moses for understandings of the canon's received shape.[5]

Deut 31–34 has often been viewed as one of the most important collections of texts in which Moses is characterized as author and *lawgiver*.[6] Little noticed, however, is the fact that in Deut 31–34 the traditions of Moses as lawgiver and prophet blend together, relating the beginning of written tradition precisely to this *union* of two roles and traditions. There is no question that the biblical narrative associates Moses with the general phenomenon of writing, and specifically with written law, but as we have seen Moses is also portrayed within deuteronomistic tradition as a *prophet* and the originator of a prophetic line of succession (Deut 18; 34). In my view, this presentation also implicitly relates the deuteronomistic rationale for a scriptural unity of Law and Prophets.

---

[1] E. g., Ex 24:1–11; 34; Deut 31:24–26. Cf. Baba Bathra 14b.

[2] On this shift, see BLENKINSOPP, Pentateuch, 1–5.

[3] Recently, in CRAIGIE, Deuteronomy; VASHOLZ, Canon.

[4] E. g., MARGOLIS, Scriptures, 119; RYLE, Canon, 31–33. Even DE WETTE supposed there might have existed with Moses a 'feeble commencement' of Hebrew literature. See his Introduction, I:24.

[5] CHILDS, OT Introduction, 62–63. Cf. GESE, View, 21.

[6] E. g., idem, OT Theology, 110–11; cf. PERLITT, Bundestheologie, 117.

The analysis of the concluding chapters of the book of Deuteronomy has resisted a clear consensus of scholarly opinion. The main legal core to the book is generally recognized to constitute Deut 12–26:15, with Deut 27–34 comprised of quite disparate additional materials.[7] Thus, Deut 27 begins by speaking of Moses in third person narration and reflects 'the law of Deuteronomy as an existing entity' (Deut 27:3).[8] Deut 27 also introduces the subject of blessing and curse (in second person address), which continues in an expanded format in Deut 28.

Deut 29–30 are sometimes referred to as Moses' 'Third Address' to Israel within the book,[9] but the boundaries of such an 'address' are disputed. Deut 31–34 resume third person narration and are frequently said to provide a series of appendices to the book, but here again there are clearly multiple literary layers. Much, if not most, of the material in Deut 27–34 is usually assigned to a secondary stage of deuteronomic redaction, or referred to as 'deuteronomistic.'[10] Typical in this regard is the work of A. D. H. Mayes, who also notes the close relationship between Deut 29–30 and Deut 4.[11]

Although the two main themes generally discussed in standard treatments of these concluding chapters are covenant and Joshua as Moses' successor, I shall argue that the 'conclusion' to the book of Deuteronomy, however narrowly or broadly construed, turns on the relationship between traditions of law and prophecy. I shall also maintain that in these chapters law and prophecy are framed in canon-conscious terms, with the intention of providing a 'theological grammar' for future generations. Although the investigation could just as easily begin at an earlier point in the book, I shall commence in Deut 30, where prophetic themes and idioms appear to intensify. In my view, these themes and idioms reach a climax in Deut 32, 'the Song of Moses.'

Deuteronomy 30–31

Deut 30 has itself been considered to be a series of post-exilic additions (Deut 30:1–10, 11–14, 15–20), in which the judgment of Exile is no longer seen as

---

[7] CLEMENTS, Deuteronomy, 7; 23–24; 33–34; cf. PREUSS, Deuteronomium, 144–46.

[8] MAYES, Deuteronomy, 341.

[9] Ibid., 358.

[10] Even if some of this material (e. g., in Deut 27) is ancient, it seems to have been added secondarily to the central legal core of the book. See CLEMENTS, Deuteronomy, 44–46.

[11] MAYES, Deuteronomy, 358–59. For the specifics of his redactional analysis, see also 41–43. Ever since the work of NOTH, Deut 1–3 have usually been thought to comprise part of the first stage of additions to an original deuteronomic core, in effect, as the introduction to the Deuteronomistic History. MAYES's treatment attempts to trace two consistent stages throughout the History, based on an initial distinction between Deut 1–3 and 4. For a view in which there are three main stages of deuteronomistic redaction, each of which is represented in Deut 4 and 29–30, see KNAPP, Deuteronomium, 128–30.

final and the return from Exile is reflected.[12] Here obedience to the 'commandments and decrees that are written in this book of the law' (Deut 30:10) is set forth as Israel's highest calling and its source of greatest blessing (Deut 30:9, 16). However, the tenor of the entire chapter is determined by its conformity to *prophetic* style. Unlike the preceding chapters, in the view of G. von Rad, Deut 30 "can no longer be called an exhortation; it contains no admonition, but, with regard to Israel's future, simple affirmative propositions, that is, it is clothed altogether in the style of prophetic predictions."[13]

As the speaker, Moses sets forth a choice between two ways (cf. Jer 21:8), either blessing or curse (Deut 30:1, 15, 19), using the formula הֵשִׁב אֶל־לֵב (Deut 30:1; cf. Deut 30:10).[14] Within the context of that choice comes the prophetic call for parents and children to 'return' (שׁוב). This call echoes the distinctive portrayal of prophetic preaching within the Deuteronomistic History[15] and in many passages in the prophetic books.[16] In fact, of all the instances of the verb שׁוב in a 'covenantal' context, the majority occur in the Prophets.[17] A narrower range of instances finds the verb also used specifically to mean the return from Exile, as it does in Deut 30.[18] These motifs prefigure the conclusion to the prophetic corpus in Mal 3:24 [4:6], which, as we have seen, probably draws on both the deuteronomistic construction הֵשִׁב אֶל־לֵב and the more general שׁוב motif.

Other phrases and themes recall prophetic preaching: the restoration of fortunes (Deut 30:3);[19] the gathering of the exiles back into the land (Deut

---

[12] Cf. Deut 4:25–31; 1 Kg 8:46–53. See PREUSS, Deuteronomium, 160–62.

[13] VON RAD, Deuteronomy, 183. For similarities and verbal correspondences between Deut 30 and the Latter Prophets, see VON RAD's treatment following (184–85).

[14] For this formula see also Deut 4:39; 1 Kg 8:47; 2 Chr 6:36; Isa 46:8; Lam 3:21; Mal 3:24 [4:6].

[15] E. g., 1 Sam 12:20–21; 2 Kg 17:7–23; cf. 2 Chr 24:19; 30:6–31; Neh 1:5–11.

[16] E. g., Isa 10:21–22; 19:22; 23:17; 35:10; 44:22; 51:11; 52:8; 55:7; Jer 3:1, 7, 10, 12, 14, 22; 4:1; 8:5; 21:8–10; 22:27; 24:7; 30:10; 31:8, 21; 44:14, 28; 46:27; 50:16; Ezek 7:13; 14:6; 16:55; 17:19; Hos 2:9 [7]; 3:5; 5:4; 6:1; 7:10; 8:13; 9:3; 11:5, 11; 12:6; 14:1–2; Joel 2:12–13; Am 4:6, 8–11; Ob 15; Jon 3:8–9; Mic 5:3; Zep 2:10; Hag 2:17; Zech 1:3–4; 8:3; 9:12; 10:9; Mal 3:7, 24 [4:6] Cf. Dan 11:9, 28–29. For my purpose here it is unnecessary to distinguish among prophetic passages which announce the impossibility of return, the conditionality of return, or the inevitability of return. I wish only to provide a basis for the conclusion that 'שׁוב pronouncements' constitute a central aspect of the prophetic portrayal within various (especially but not exclusively deuteronomistic) Israelite traditions. Such pronouncements are not even necessarily directed toward Israel (e. g., Isa 23:17; Jer 50:16; Ezek 7:13; 17:19)!

[17] HOLLADAY, SUBH. See also SOGGIN, שׁוב.

[18] E. g., in the *Qal*: Ezr 2:1; Neh 7:6; Isa 10:22; Jer 22:10; Zech 10:9–10; in the *Hiph'il*: 1 Kg 8:34; Jer 12:15–16. Cf. HARRIS, ARCHER AND WALTKE (EDS.), TWOT, II:909.

[19] Cf. Jer 29:14; 33:26; Ezek 39:25; Am 9:14; Zeph 3:20.

30:4);[20] prosperity and increase (Deut 30:5);[21] and circumcision of the heart (Deut 30:6).[22] Even the setting out of the two ways (esp. Deut 30:15) has its closest parallel in the prophetic corpus,[23] being closely related to the prophetic pronouncement of the conditionality of the covenant.[24]

In sum, Deut 30 sets forth a compendium of prophetic preaching in which obedience to Law and Prophets *together*, as a 'theological grammar' for the community, is both summarized and demanded. To be sure, the 'either/or' set out in the chapter (esp. Deut 30:15) has parallels with wisdom literature as well,[25] and the rejection of cosmic wisdom is itself a familiar wisdom motif.[26] However, these wisdom elements do not determine the form of the chapter; no contrual of Moses as a sage is intended or accomplished.[27] Instead, even the wisdom elements of the chapter recall the use of wisdom by the prophets[28] more than they suggest a context of cultic instruction[29] or the teachings of the wise.[30]

Only within Deuteronomy and the prophetic corpus is the same *urgency* of decision proclaimed.[31] Within wisdom literature, the 'decision' is extended over time to apply to the entirety of a person's life. In the understand-

---

[20] Cf. Isa 43:5–7; Jer 31:30; 32:37; Ezek 36:24; 37:21. This promise appears to be cited in Neh 1:8–9, along with Deut 28:64.

[21] Cf. Jer 23:3; 30:3.

[22] Cf. Jer 31:31–34; 32:37–41; Ezek 11:19–20; 36:26–28. Also Ps 51:10!

[23] Cf. Jos 23:15; 24:15; Jer 18:8, 10; and esp. the parallel formula in Jer 21:8–10.

[24] Cf. Jos 24; Jer 7:1–15; 17:19–27.

[25] Cf. Prov 11:19; 14:27; Lam 3:37–39.

[26] Cf. Ps 139:6–10; Prov 30:1–4; Bar 3:29–31; Sir 11:4. See WEINFELD, Deuteronomy, 258–59.

[27] Ibid., 10–11. WEINFELD refers to the book of Deuteronomy as an example of a 'didactic valedictory oration' by a national leader (cf. Jos 23; 1 Sam 12; 2 Sam 22; 23:1–7). He notes (Deuteronomy, 15–16; 26), however, that these idealizing, programmatic addresses have close parallels to the deuteronomic 'prophetic orations' of the Deuteronomic History (cf. 1 Kg 11:31b–39; 14:7–11, 14–16; 21:20b–26) and the book of Jeremiah (e. g., Jer 19). He also finds (Deuteronomy, 32–33) parallels to liturgical (e. g., Deut 3:23–25; 6:20–25; 26:5–10; 1 Kg 8:15–16; 2 Kg 19:15–19; Jer 32:17–23) and military (e. g., Deut 7; 20:3–8; 31:1–6; Jos 1) orations. Although WEINFELD argues strongly for a wisdom background to the book of Deuteronomy generally, even he is unable to make much of an argument that Moses is depicted within the book as a sage.

[28] E. g., Am 3:3–8; Isa 28:23–29.

[29] E. g., Ps 1.

[30] E. g., Prov 1 and *passim.*

[31] E. g., 'this day' (היום) — Deut 30:15; Jos 24:15; 1 Sam 8:8; 12:2, 5; 1 Kg 8:61; Isa 10:32; Ezek 21:25, 29; 24:2; 39:8. Even where the familiar prophetic idiom 'on that day' (ביום ההוא) is used instead of the deuteronomistic idiom ('this day'), the insistence that God has a *particular* day of judgment stands in contrast to wisdom's emphasis on the abiding daily challenges of faith (cf. such wisdom constructions as 'day by day,' 'all day long,' etc.).

ing of the wise, there is no single all-important decision of faith, but a myriad of choices. Obedience is existential, but also cumulative. No single decision ultimately determines one's obedience to God; every decision contributes to the obedient (or disobedient) shape of one's life. Only within the prophetic traditions is there the same insistence on a contemporary *crisis* of faith as in Deut 30.[32]

Deuteronomy 31

The prophetic shaping of mosaic traditions is thus *continued* rather than initiated in Deut 31. Although likewise presenting a complex fabric of interwoven influences, Deut 31 has also clearly received its decisive shape from deuteronomistic tradition.[33] Following M. Noth, von Rad believed that the use of the narrative past tense[34] and the presence of divine direct discourse[35] differentiated Deut 31 from Deut 30, and indicated the continuation of the Deuteronomistic History, into which Deuteronomy had been absorbed.[36]

It is generally observed that the contents of Deut 31 all revolve around the centrality of obedience to the Torah as written scripture.[37] An older critical view assigned Deut 31:1–13 and 24–30 to one or more deuteronomistic redactional layers, and Deut 31:14–23 (as perhaps the original introduction to the pre-existent 'Song of Moses' in Deut 32) to earlier pentateuchal sources (JE).[38] More recent investigations stress that the chapter contains several layers of material, all of which share the impress of deuteronomistic shaping by their editorial arrangement in the chapter and placement within the horizon of the conclusion to the book (Deut 31–34).[39] However, to note the centrality of

---

[32] E. g., Jer 7:13, 'and now' (ועתה). To be sure, this kind of language in Jeremiah is itself probably due to deuteronomistic shaping — or does the influence run in the other direction? On this basic methodological problem, see HOLT, Chicken? My point here is simply that in the final form of the text it is only prophets who are characterized as speaking in this way.

[33] PREUSS, Deuteronomium, 162–63. See the discussion by LABUSCHAGNE, Song.

[34] Deut 31:1–2, 7, 9–10, 14–15, 16, 22–25, 30.

[35] Deut 31:14, 16–17.

[36] VON RAD, Deuteronomy, 188: "Thus the method of presentation has abandoned the fiction that Moses is speaking in the land of Moab. It is looking back from a later point of time on the events immediately before the death of Moses."

[37] PREUSS, Deuteronomium, 163. WEINFELD attempts to draw a distinction between the exclusively military orations in Deuteronomy and the military orations in Joshua, which he claims combine 'religio-Torah motifs with military motifs' (Deuteronomy, 49 n. 1). On this basis WEINFELD classifies Deut 31:1–6 as a 'military oration.' He does not comment on the 'religio-Torah motifs' of Deut 31:9–13!

[38] E. g., DRIVER, Deuteronomy, 336–37.

[39] WIEBE, Form.

Torah to the exclusion of the prophetic elements present is, in my judgment, to misconstrue the force of the chapter.[40]

To be sure, Deut 31:9–13 grants mosaic authority to the practice of levitical/priestly law, but even here it is the *proclamation* of 'this law' that is emphasized, the oral quality of the proclamation (Deut 31:10–13) balancing the scribal aspect of Moses' authority (Deut 31:9). Treatments which fail to view this passage within the context of the *entire* chapter simply do not reckon with the way in which the emphasis on priestly law has been balanced by an emphasis on prophetic witness.

Thus, in the final form of the chapter calls for obedience to 'this law'[41] are evenly matched by *parallel* calls for obedience to 'this song.'[42] As the text now stands, the reference to 'this song' is clearly parallel to the 'Song of Moses' in Deut 32, which is literarily framed by Deut 31:19–22, 30 and Deut 32:44–47. The apparent contradiction between the authority of 'the law' and the authority of 'the song' is difficult to explain simply as the result of textual corruption or an accident of flatfooted redaction. The parallel construction is too consistent and careful. As scholars have increasingly concluded, the final form of Deut 31 is most likely an intentional redactional construct of later deuteronomistic editors.[43] The wider implications of this redactional joining, however, have remained largely unexplored.

In my view, it is the canon-conscious aspects of this redaction which are most significant.[44] Here, at the conclusion to the book of Deuteronomy, both 'law' and 'song' combine (Deut 32:44–47) to form a *joint* 'witness' against the people of Israel in future generations. I note that the term 'witness' does not appear in Deut 31:9–13 when the reading of 'this law' is commanded, but emerges for the first time with the mention of 'the song' in Deut 31:16–22.[45]

---

[40] MCBRIDE, Polity, 68.

[41] Deut 31:9, 11, 12, 24, 46.

[42] Deut 31:19, 21, 22, 30, 44. The two — law and song — are so evenly matched that the reference in Deut 31:28 to 'these words' is finally not ambiguous at all, but comprehensively refers to both 'the words of this law' (Deut 31:24) *and* 'the words of this song' (Deut 31:30). *Contra* MAYES, Deuteronomy, 380.

[43] PREUSS, Deuteronomy, 164: "Das Mit- und Nebeneinander von Lied und Gesetz ist redaktionsgeschichtlich voller Absicht, und so mögen zwar V. 16–22 sehr sekundär aussehen und recht ungeschickt eingegeschoben sein..., aber dies ändert nichts über ihre beabsichtigte Rolle im Kontext... Wie das Gesetz (31,16) soll auch das Lied 'Zeuge gegen Israel' sein (V. 19), und beide werden so dem Aufweis der Untreue und des Abfalls Israels dienen." In support PREUSS cites FLOSS, Jahwe, 314–16; G. SEITZ, Studien, 254–56.

[44] VON RAD, Deuteronomy, 189, argued that in Deut 31:9–13 'we have the first beginnings of the canon,' but he had in mind the reconstructed custom of an authoritative recital of the deuteronomic law by levitical priests. Although in his commentary VON RAD noted on several occasions the presence of prophetic elements and traditions in Deut 30–34, he did not consider their canonical implications.

[45] The plural עדות ('testimonies') can be found in Deut 4:45; 6:17, 20.

The witness formula היה לעד/ עוד+ב-/כ- used in this chapter[46] probably originates within the general tradition of jurisprudence,[47] but is also often used to introduce a basic prophetic theme.[48]

Most illuminating, however, are the references in 2 Chr 24:19 and Neh 9:26, 29–30, 34: "Yet [God] sent prophets among them to bring them back (להשיבם אל־יהוה) to the LORD; they testified against them (ויעידו בם), but they would not listen" (2 Chr 24:19); "Nevertheless they were disobedient and rebelled against you and cast your law behind their backs and killed your prophets, who had warned them (אשר־העידו בם) in order to turn them back (להשיבם אליך) to you, and they committed great blasphemies" (Neh 9:26). In later tradition *repentance* and *witness* are thus consistently cited as the two most fundamental qualities of prophets and prophecy. A prophet can even be described as 'witness' personified.[49]

Although scholarly treatments always refer to Deut 32 as *Moses'* Song, a more literarily-sensitive exegetical approach would assign the song's authorship to *God* as a character within the narrative. That the Song is attributed by commentators to Moses reveals in fact the presence of the prophetic device of messenger speech. Although Moses' own 'voice' does emerge toward the end of the composition, the Song is delivered as a *prophecy* from God.[50] It is this prophecy, the narrative framework reports, which will provide a witness for Israel in the days to come.

Only secondarily is the concept of prophetic 'witness' extended from Deut 31:16–22 (the original introduction to the Song?) and applied to the Law as well.[51] The uncertainty as to the precise reference in Deut 31:28 ('these words'?) most likely results from the fact that in the final form of the chapter 'witness' applies to Law and Song *together*.[52] As a joint witness, they present a "standard of faith and action... from which, in the case assumed, Israel will have visibly declined."[53]

---

[46] Deut 31:19, 21, 26, 28 (cf. Deut 4:26a = 30:19a).

[47] E. g., Num 5:13.

[48] For this and similar expressions, see Jos 24:27–28; 1 Sam 8:9; 12:5; 2 Kg 15:15; Isa 19:20; 30:8; 43:10; Jer 11:7; 29:23; 42:5, 19; Am 3:13; Mic 1:2; also Ps 50:7. Interestingly, the formula also appears near the end of the prophetic corpus in Mal 3:5.

[49] E. g., 'Oded' (עדד) in 2 Chr 28:9 (MT); see also 2 Chr 15:1, 8; and even Isa 43:10, 12! On the linguistic issues and ancient Near Eastern parallels, see WILSON, Prophecy, 130–31.

[50] Cf. Deut 33:1, where this device is absent.

[51] See Deut 31:24–29. Cf. DRIVER, Deuteronomy, 343: "It is remarkable that the same phrase which is applied in v. 19 to the Song, is used here with reference to the Deuteronomic law."

[52] See Deut 31:1b = 30:19a = 4:26a. Cf. LABUSCHAGNE, Song, 88–89.

[53] DRIVER, Deuteronomy, 343.

The particularity and definite status of 'this law' have led scholars to interpret the reference as to the book of Deuteronomy itself.[54] The reference to the
Song is more mysterious. Why is there such a calculated effort to balance the
authority of the book of Deuteronomy with the authority of a single chapter
appended to its conclusion? Could the prophetic characterization of the
Song's origin and purpose be an indication that its presence within Deut
31–34 has to do with the coordination of deuteronomic legislation and prophetic traditions? Does the use of the term 'witness' provide evidence of the
rise of scripture within Israel and an early deuteronomistic 'grammar' of
faith?

Deuteronomy 32

The Song itself (Deut 32) has been the subject of intense historical debate.[55]
Dates for its origin range from the mosaic period to the Hellenistic age, but in
my view its incorporation into the book of Deuteronomy during the late exilic
or early post-exilic period is most likely.[56] Opinion varies regarding the pre-
deuteronomic status of the composition, but it would also seem likely that
there are several layers of material within the song, some of which may be
quite old[57] and some quite late.[58]

Of most importance to the present study is the prophetic character of the
Song and its present function within the book of Deuteronomy. In the search
for the pre-deuteronomic origins of the song, several critical scholars early on
suggested theories of prophetic authorship. Thus A. Dillmann and S. Oettli
both proposed Elijah as the Song's originator[59] and, later, G. E. Mendenhall
suggested Samuel.[60]

If current scholarship seems inclined to stress the exilic/post-exilic character of the present form of the Song, it is in large measure due to the striking
similarities between the Song and exilic/post-exilic prophecy.[61] Where earlier

---

[54] Ibid., 335 (on Deut 31:9).

[55] See the collection of articles reprinted in CHRISTENSEN, Song; also the overview in P.
SANDERS, Provenance.

[56] Deut 32:8–9 is often adduced, however, as evidence for an earlier date. For an overview of the entire issue, see PREUSS, Deuteronomium, 165–66.

[57] Ibid., 166. For an argument that Deut 32:8–9 is pre-deuteronomic, see J. J. M.
ROBERTS, Origin, 340 n. 71. Although Deut 32:8–9 certainly seems ancient, an early dating is
not at all a foregone conclusion. MAYES, Deuteronomy, 384–85, calls attention to the similar
'thought' in Deut 4:19–20 and claims that here the later 'doctrine' of Dan 10:13, 20–21; 12:1
is anticipated. The two positions remind one of the general debate over 'archaic' or 'archaiz-
ing' elements in Hebrew poetry. For the Song's 'archaic' features, see GRAY, Legacy, 36.

[58] See the chart in P. SANDERS, Provenance, 44.

[59] Cited in PREUSS, Deuteronomium, 166–67.

[60] MENDENHALL, *"Rib."*

[61] PREUSS, Deuteronomium, 167. See also SKEEHAN, Structure.

treatments tended to consider Deut 32 as an early example of prophetic exhortation later adapted by the deuteronomists,[62] contemporary scholars more often treat the Song as a collection of prophetic-style exhortations made in reflection and imitation of the pre-exilic and early exilic prophets.[63] In either case, the prophetic stamp of the material is clear.[64]

Although there have been treatments which have also located the origin of the Song in the sphere of wisdom literature,[65] most scholars have seen in the structure and the language of the Song characteristically prophetic traditions, adjusted to the tenor and idiom of deuteronomistic parenesis.[66] Although once very popular, arguments for a single prophetic genre for the Song (i. e., the ריב) have become increasingly difficult to sustain, and most likely simply reflect the more general prophetic features present in the composition.[67] More persuasive is the idea of a mixed genre in which an overarching theology of history is rehearsed and its consequences announced.[68] As H. D. Preuss has

---

[62] In which case, the Song could still have influenced later prophecy. Cf. WEINFELD, Deuteronomy, 361.

[63] PREUSS, Deuteronomium, 167.

[64] DRIVER, Deuteronomy, 345: "The Song shows great originality of form, being a presentation of prophetical thought in a poetical dress, on a scale which is without parallel in the Old Testament." See also his Deuteronomy, 346: "...the theological ideas, the argument, the point of view, often also the expressions, display constantly points of contact with the writings of the canonical prophets, from the 8th century B. C. and onwards."

[65] E. g., VON RAD, Deuteronomy, 196–97; BOSTON, Influence.

[66] MAYES, Deuteronomy, 380–81; PREUSS, Deuteronomium, 167.

[67] Many scholars have pointed to the importance of the ריב for understanding Deut 32; for a summary of opinions, see PREUSS, Deuteronomium, 167. The classic treatment of Deut 32 as a ריב was that of WRIGHT, Lawsuit. For a more recent example, see MAYES (Deuteronomy, 380–82), who compares the Song to Isa 1; Jer 2; Mic 6 and Ps 50. In his judgment, the Song contains the following elements: "1. an introduction in which witnesses are summoned (vv. 1–3); 2. an introductory statement of the case at issue (vv. 4–6); 3. a speech of prosecution, recalling the good actions of Yahweh (vv. 7–14); 4. the indictment in which Israel is accused of apostasy (vv. 15–18); 5. declaration of guilt and threat of total destruction (vv. 19–25)." Note, however, that MAYES admits this form does not quite match the genre description: "Here the form has been adapted and expanded to serve a purpose quite different from that for which it was first created" (Deuteronomy, 380–81). For recent critique of the ריב as a genre, see DANIELS, Genre? DE ROCHE, Reassessment.

[68] Although EISSFELDT's theory of formal similarity between Deut 32 and Ps 78 (EISSFELDT, Lied) — and therefore a tenth century date for Deut 32! — has foundered on the shoals of an increasingly later date for Ps 78 (see PREUSS, Deuteronomium, 166), the points of similarity EISSFELDT adduced still make a good case for the general structure of the Song as an historical review. Ps 78 is now also judged as exhibiting the imprint of deuteronomism; see KRAUS, Psalms, 123–24.

observed, this history is one of increasing disobedience, thus exhibiting a basic similarity with certain historical reviews in the Prophets.[69]

A full exegetical treatment of the Song is not possible within the context of the present study. Several choice examples will have to confirm its prophetic aspect. I propose that there are basically three levels of similarity between the Song and prophetic traditions, as the deuteronomists understood them. At the first level are the Song's broad similarities to prophetic understandings of Israel's history as one of *disobedience.*

1. A Prophetic Account of History

As Preuss has suggested, the historical review which structures the Song mirrors prophetic teaching in its emphasis on Israel's disobedience. Thus, at the beginning of the body of the Song an announcement of God's faithfulness is contrasted with the unfaithfulness of Israel (Deut 32:4–9), the wilderness period is characterized as a time of original obedience (Deut 32:10–14), but the entrance into the land is said to have led to apostasy (Deut 32:15–18).

The unique features of Deut 32:8 should not detract attention from the overall similarity to the same prophetic view of Israel's history. Von Rad observed that the use of the term 'found' (מצא) in Deut 32:10 to express Israel's election also occurs in Hos 9:10 and probably in Jer 31:2–3.[70] As he also noted, the conceptual distance between this particular construal of election and other more typical pentateuchal traditions (i. e., the patriarchs, the Exodus) should not be underestimated.[71]

Although the section of the Song that recounts the wilderness period (Deut 32:10–14) does not exhibit prominent deuteronomistic characteristics,[72] the following portion regarding Israel's unfaithfulness (Deut 32:15–18) contains several. These include 'abominations' (Deut 32:16b),[73] 'anger' (also Deut 32:16b),[74] 'unknown gods' (Deut 32:17a),[75] and the 'fatherhood' of God

---

[69] E. g., Jer 2–3; Ezek 16; 20; 23; Hos 13–14; Mic 6; cf. Ps 78. See PREUSS, Deuteronomium, 167; DRIVER, Deuteronomy, 347: "...a prophetic meditation on the lessons to be deduced from Israel's national history..."

[70] DRIVER included (Deuteronomy, 356) Ezek 16:3–6 within this context as well.

[71] VON RAD, Deuteronomy, 197. In support of this point, he cited BACH, Erwählung, 687.

[72] PREUSS, Deuteronomium, 168.

[73] See 'abomination/s' (תועבה/ת) in Deut 7:25–26; 13:15; 17:4; 18:9, 12; 20:18; 1 Kg 14:24; 2 Kg 16:3; 21:2, 11; 23:13; Isa 41:24; 44:19; Jer 7:10; 16:18; 32:35; 44:4, 22; Ezek 5:9, 11; 6:9, 11; 7:3 and *passim.*

[74] See forms of כעס ('anger') in Deut 4:25; 9:18; 31:29; Jud 2:12; 1 Kg 14:9 and *passim*; 2 Kg 17:11 and *passim*; Jer 7:18 and *passim*; Ezek 20:28.

[75] אלהים לא ידעום; cf. Hos 13:4. Also cf. אלהים אחרים in Deut 11:28; 13:3 [2], 7 [6], 14 [13]; 17:3; 18:20; 28:14, 36, 64; 29:25 [26]; 30:17; 31:18, 20; Jer 1:16 and *passim*; Hos 3:1.

(Deut 32:6, 15, 18).[76] Deut 32:19–25 announces the divine verdict of total destruction through the agency of another worldly power ('no people'/'foolish nation'). Deut 32:26–27 reports the reluctance of God to implement the full measure of his verdict, out of concern that Israel's enemies would assign themselves, not God, the responsibility for Israel's destruction.[77]

That the punishment characterized in these sections could refer to the fall of the northern kingdom, the fall of the southern kingdom, or both, follows from the limitlessness of its scope: no one shall escape (Deut 32:25).[78] Telling in this regard are also the mention of 'arrows' (Deut 32:23, 42),[79] 'the teeth of beasts' (Deut 32:24c),[80] and 'crawling things' (Deut 32:24d).[81] Because there is otherwise no attestation in biblical Hebrew for the verb (MT: אפאיהם) in Deut 32:26a, it is probably best to follow H. Grätz's suggestion and amend the text to אפיצם, the *Hiph'il* of פוץ.[82] In the *Hiph'il* פוץ is often used to refer to Exile.[83]

The theme of exile as divine judgment is so pervasive within the prophetic corpus that it scarcely requires further comment. More interesting is the appearance in Deut 32:26–27 of a kind of divine soliloquy, in which God reasons himself into mercy on Israel's behalf for the sake of his reputation among the nations.[84] Whether in the form of an internal dialogue or not, the prophets' radical characterization of God's own intentions and motivations reveals the same kind of radical messenger speech. This kind of 'double agency' functions within prophetic tradition as in no other, and is also used, I have argued, to characterize Moses in the conclusion to the Torah now found in Deut 34:10–12.

---

[76] See Deut 8:5; Hos 11:1–4; Isa 63:16; 64:7; Mal 2:7. For the preceding terms and additional items, see also WEINFELD, Deuteronomy, 364. WEINFELD believes that Deut 32 predates Deuteronomy and, together with Hosea and Ps 78, may provide a 'prototype' for the later deuteronomistic style.

[77] This conclusion then appears to be mocked in Deut 32:27b–30.

[78] DRIVER cited (Deuteronomy, 369) the following passages for their reminiscent language: 2 Kg 8:12; 2 Chr 36:17; Jer 9:20 [21]; 18:21; 51:22; Lam 1:20b; 2:21; Ezek 7:15; Hos 14:1 [13:16].

[79] חצים. Cf. esp. Isa 49:2; Jer 50; Ezek 5:16 and *passim*; Lam 3:12–13; Hab 3:11; Zech 9:4. Cf. Job 6:4; Ps 7:14 [13]; 18:15[14] and *passim*.

[80] שן-בהמח. Cf. Ezek 5:17; Hos 2:14 [12]. See also 2 Kg 17:25; Jer 9:11.

[81] זחלי עפר. Cf. זחלי ארץ in Mic 7:17.

[82] Following the LXX; see DRIVER, Deuteronomy, 369, n. on Deut 32:26. This may not necessarily alter English translation; the NRSV already reads 'scatter.'

[83] Deut 4:27; 28:64; 30:3; Neh 1:8; Isa 24:1; 41:16; Jer 9:15; 13:24; 18:17; 30:11; Ezek 11:16 and *passim*. Cf. Gen 11:8–9. In the *Qal*, see Ezek 34:5; Zech 13:7. In the *Niph'al*, see Jer 10:21; 40:15; Ezek 11:17; 20:34, 41; 28:25; 34:6. See 1 Kg 22:17 for another prophecy of 'scattering.'

[84] Deut 9:28; Isa 48:9–11; Ezek 20:21–22; 36:22–23; Hos 6:4; 11. Cf. Gen 6:5–7. See VON RAD, Deuteronomy, 198–99.

2. Prophetic Motifs and Idioms

As will have been obvious from the preceding discussion of the major themes in Deut 32, individual prophetic motifs and idioms are present in abundance. Although it was necessary to discuss some of these already in order to make the first point about the prophetic nature of the historical review appearing in the Song, similarity of idiom provides a second level for my analysis. In addition to the idioms already discussed, I would also call attention to two further parallels with prophetic material, one of content and one of form:

a) Prophetic *content* emerges strikingly in Deut 32:39–42, the climax of the Song, in which God announces and celebrates his power as a deity, and asserts something approximating monotheism ('there is no god beside me'). Although rooted in the First Commandment (Ex 20:3; Deut 5:7) this kind of explicit formulation is typically exilic/post-exilic and characteristically deuteronomistic.[85] However, the connection between a theoretical position of monolatry/monotheism and the new theological conception of God which such a position requires,[86] although adumbrated in the deuteronomistic formulation of blessing and curses (e. g., Deut 28), appears in its most explicit form within the prophetic corpus.[87] Thus, S. R. Driver compared the resultant portrait of Israel's God as a 'God of war' (Deut 32:40–42) to several late prophetic portraits.[88]

b) A *formal* parallel between the Song and prophecy can be seen in the way the Song continually shifts from third person description and indictment into second person accusations and pronouncements (e. g., Deut 32:5–6). In

---

[85] E. g., Deut 4:35; cf. Isa 40–55. See the similar 'monotheistic creeds' given in WEIN-FELD, Deuteronomy, 331. As within Deut 32 (vv. 16–17, 21, 31?), such statements of monotheism (monolatry?) exist throughout deuteronomistic literature side by side with references to other deities (cf. WEINFELD, Deuteronomy, 320–21). VON RAD noted (Deuteronomy, 198) that in the historical review at the beginning of the Song (Deut 32:15–18), Israel's history is "reduced in a striking manner to the one sin against the first commandment," revealing an "obvious dependence on a view of history already much subordinated to theology." Israel's sin against the First Commandment and God's reaffirmation of it thus form the overarching theme of the Song.

[86] I. e., broad enough to provide the basis for all causation.

[87] Cf. 1 Sam 2:1–10; 2 Kg 5:7; Isa 19:22; 30:26; 41:21–24; 43:11–13; 44:6–8, 24–28; 45:5–7; 57:15–16; Jer 1:10; 33:1–9; Hos 5:13–14; 6:1; 11:3; 13:4–5; Am 5:6–9. Cf. Ps 115:3–8. ZIMMERLI's distinction (ZIMMERLI, Wort) between the priestly formula of self-introduction and prophetic messenger speech (idem, Yahweh, 23) is tangential to the point being made here. Regardless of the *origin* of the 'I am' formula, within the final form of the books of Isaiah and Hosea it now serves to illustrate the relation between monotheism (monolatry) and universal causation, just as certain instances of prophetic messenger speech do. It is precisely this connection, of course, that proves so problematic within wisdom traditions (e. g., Job 5:18; 10:8; 12:13–14; 13:15 and *passim*).

[88] E. g., Isa 34:5–6; 49:26; 63:3–6; 66:26; Jer 12:12; 25:30–33; 46:10; 50:25–29. See DRIVER, Deuteronomy, 379.

fact, second person discourse dominates and structures the present form of the text.[89] Although the second person form is lacking in Deut 32:10–14c and Deut 32:19–37, an explanation is not difficult to find. It seems probable that Deut 32:10–14c represents pre-deuteronomistic material and thus pre-dates the prophetic shaping evidenced in the later framework of the Song. Deut 32:19–37 contains the internal thoughts of God,[90] the gloating of Israel's enemies[91] and the perspective of the prophetic singer ('Moses').[92] From each of these points of view second person address can be naturally absent, depending upon the desired rhetorical effect. More significant is that these other points of view are now surrounded and framed by deuteronomistic material which adopts a manner of discourse so thoroughly prophetic.[93] The future tense prediction in Deut 32:36 also suggests prophetic speech. Moreover, the mocking of idols in Deut 32:37–38 reminds one of passages such as 1 Kg 18:27 and Isa 44:9–20.

3. Prophetic Citations and Allusions

The third level of similarity between the Song and the prophetic corpus has to do with literal citations and more general allusions. Although the direction of influence is disputed, the very existence of such parallels is quite suggestive.[94] M. Weinfeld has listed a number of exact phrases shared between Deut 32 and the book of Jeremiah, arguing that these indicate the influence of the Song upon jeremianic tradition(s).[95] On the basis of the reasons given above for an exilic/post-exilic date for Deut 32,[96] it seems to me more likely that it is Deut 32 which has been influenced — by prophetic traditions generally and by jeremianic tradition(s) perhaps most of all.[97] Interestingly, prophetic tradi-

---

[89] Deut 32:1, 6–7, 14d–15, 17–18, 38b, 43.

[90] Deut 32:19–27, 34–35, 37b–38a.

[91] Deut 32:27b–30.

[92] Deut 32:36–37a. Songs and singers also have a traditional connection with prophets and prophecy. Thus, Miriam the 'prophetess' is also remembered as a singer (Ex 15), as is Deborah (Jud 5), and the levites in Chronicles 'prophesy' by singing (E. g., 1 Chr 25). Cf. Isa 30:29–31; Ezek 33:30–33.

[93] VON RAD, Deuteronomy, 198.

[94] For a more detailed list of literal parallels between Deut 32 and the prophetic corpus, see DRIVER, Deuteronomy, 348 and *passim*.

[95] The shared phrases are Deut 32:9 = Jer 10:16; Deut 32:21 = Jer 8:19; Deut 32:22 = Jer 15:4; 17:4; and Deut 32:37–38 = Jer 2:28. See WEINFELD, Deuteronomy, 361.

[96] In addition, see the discussion about dating in DRIVER (Deuteronomy, 345–47) and the remarks of VON RAD (Deuteronomy, 200) regarding the similarity between Deut 32 and the Latter Prophets.

[97] DRIVER doubted (Deuteronomy, 348) any direct influence: "…the fact that the resemblances with Dt. are so few and slight makes it doubtful whether they are really reminiscences on his part from it. It is at least equally probable that Jer. and Dt. 32 are only connected indirectly; and that the resemblances (such as they are) are to be accounted for by the fact that the

tion is not the only source for allusions in the Song,[98] also suggesting the general force of the increasing *scripturalization* of Israel's traditions upon the Song's shape.

Conclusions Regarding Deuteronomy 32

In the light of these similarities and parallels, the view that emerges of 'Moses' Song' in Deut 32 is that of a typically prophetic interpretation of God's activity in history. The present text is a pastiche of prophecy, skilfully constructed so as to comprise a unity, but composed of elements from various sources and traditions.[99] In the most explicit manner possible, Moses is depicted here as a *prophet*: speaking for God, predicting his judgment, revealing his grace.

Deuteronomy 33

Although Deut 33 is most likely an older poem than Deut 32,[100] and does not exhibit the same close connections with prophetic language and tradition(s), even Deut 33 seems to have been set within a prophetic context by the tradents of the book. The prophet Moses now speaks a song of judgment (Deut 32), followed by a song of blessing (cf. Num 22–24).[101] This alternation of judgment and blessing forms a covenantal pattern. Even though the device of messenger speech is not used in Deut 33, Moses is given the prophetic title 'man of God'[102] and praised as the instrument of God's law.[103]

Summary of Deuteronomy 31–34

As the conclusion to the book of Deuteronomy, the material in Deut 31–34 has been shaped according to prophetic as well as legal traditions. In the final form of the book, deuteronomistic 'prophecy' is enjoined no less than deuter-

---

two authors lived in the same intellectual atmosphere, so that the same current expressions and ideas came to the lips of each."

[98] I note the parallel between Deut 32:36 and Ps 135:14.

[99] See the similar judgment of CORNILL (Introduction, 123), that Deut 32 represents a 'compendium of the prophetic theology.'

[100] Deut 33 is possibly a collection of genuinely ancient tribal blessings, see PREUSS, Deuteronomium, 169–70. For an overview of historical and redactional issues, see TIGAY, Deuteronomy, 519–24 ('Excursus 33').

[101] P. D. MILLER, "Moses," 255.

[102] Deut 33:1. See also Jos 14:6; Ps 90. Cf. Jud 13:6–8; 1 Sam 2:27; 9:6–9; 1 Kg 12:22; 13; 17:24; 2 Kg 4–8. For discussion, see VON RAD, Deuteronomy, 204–06. Cf. WILSON, who notes (Prophecy, 140) that although 'prophet' and 'man of God' may have had different origins and characteristics, they are blended together in the present biblical text, sometimes even being used interchangeably (e. g., 1 Sam 3:20; 9:6–8).

onomistic 'law,' and the unity of both is depicted as the standard of Israel's belief and action.

Nowhere is this more explicit than in Deut 32:44–47. After the Song has been sung, Moses tells 'all Israel' to 'lay to heart all the words' which he has given them, that they may command them to their children (Deut 32:46). Here, just as earlier in the chapter, 'all the words of this song' (Deut 32:44) and 'all the words of this law' (Deut 32:46) are thoroughly equated. Ultimate authority ('it is your life,' Deut 32:47)[104] rests with *all* the words that Moses has given Israel 'this day.' The mention of these 'words' does not refer to *either* the Law or the Song, but to *both* — although either Law or Song can be used to refer to the whole *pars pro toto*. In these verses, such canon-conscious language refers ultimately to the book of Deuteronomy itself: the book's constituent features of law and prophecy are proclaimed as a deuteronomistic *sine qua non* for Israel's faith and practice.

Thus, the shape of Deut 31–34 illuminates the later development of deuteronomistic tradition. This later 'deuteronomism' must have existed prior to, or coterminous with, the formation of the Torah as a whole and evidently sought to coordinate tetrateuchal and prophetic traditions.[105] Deut 31–34 thus reflect an explicit awareness of a growing canonical tradition. If 'this law' refers to some form of the book of Deuteronomy, as is commonly assumed,[106] 'this song' likely refers to Deut 32 *per se*, but also to the entire book of Deuteronomy as representative of *prophetic* traditions. In this way, the book also serves to direct attention ahead of itself toward the prophetic corpus.[107]

Although the precise form of Law and Prophets as collections of *written* scripture at the time of these references is unclear, in these concluding chapters to Deuteronomy an essential relationship between the two traditions is described and proclaimed as normative.[108] Just as the Song is incomplete without the Law, the Law is incomplete without the Song. Thus, the Torah in its

---

[103] Deut 33:4, in third person!

[104] Recall the importance of the theme of 'life' for 'canon-consciousness' within later traditions, as discussed in Chapters One and Two (cf. Ezek 33:10, 15; Sir 45:5; Jn 5:39; Rom 7:10; Gal 3:21; Aboth 2:8; 6:7).

[105] Note how this material is interwoven with material from other tetrateuchal sources and traditions (e. g., cvc. Deut 32:48–52 with Num 27:12–14; Deut 32:36 with Ps 135:14).

[106] PREUSS, Deuteronomium, 195. Cf. MAYES, Deuteronomy, 116–17 on Deut 1:5. Could the term already have been used in a broader sense?

[107] See the judgment of PREUSS (Deuteronomium, 22) that, because of similarities between Deuteronomy and the Deuteronomistic History (e. g., Deut 4 and 1 Kg 8; Deut 17 and 1 Sam 8), Deuteronomy "eng mit den folgenden Büchern durch die dtr Redaktion verbunden ist und sein soll." In my view, the same kind of similarities also obtain, but even more strongly, between Deut 31–34 and the Latter Prophets. Cf. DRIVER, Deuteronomy, 347–48.

[108] Presumably the Deuteronomistic History existed prior to this point, since Deut 31–34 received their final shape after Deut 1–3; 31:1–8.

final literary stages was confessed to be *part* of a more comprehensive 'theological grammar' for Israel's faith, a conclusion which challenges the usual view that the Torah was once the sole 'Bible' of Israel.

As von Rad noted, the combined fullness of Law and Song as *plural* 'words of life' is contrastively paralleled in Deut 32:47 with a *singular* 'empty word' (לא־דבר רק), thus suggesting a conception of the *unity* of Israel's traditions as well as an awareness of their variety. As he put it, "There stands behind this sentence a long, mainly prophetic experience of the creative power of Yahweh's Word."[109] Hopefully the preceding analysis will have made it clear that the actualization of the Law depicted in Deut 31–34 is accomplished by the use of prophetic traditions, and that here Law and Prophets together are confessed to be the essential constituents of the *full* Word of God.

Joshua

If the preceding analysis of a deuteronomistic effort to coordinate traditions of law and prophecy in the conclusion to the book of Deuteronomy is correct, then similar shaping should be in evidence in the Deuteronomistic History (Joshua–2 Kings). In the remainder of this chapter and in the one following, I intend to seek for evidence of such shaping.

The book of Joshua provides a critical test case for my thesis. On the one hand, the impact of deuteronomistic tradition is clearly apparent upon the present shape of the book.[1] On the other hand, prophetic traditions do not seem to play a significant role in the book and Joshua himself is never referred to as a prophet.[2] In order to discover whether there has been a coordination of law and prophecy in Joshua similar to that in Deuteronomy, it will be necessary to look closely at arguments regarding the composition of the book and, in particular, the deuteronomistic material that is believed to connect it with Deuteronomy and the rest of the Deuteronomistic History.

These are complex exegetical questions and we should acknowledge at the outset that no clear consensus has emerged as to the book of Joshua's literary development.[3] Although in the following discussion I shall also offer a recon-

---

[109] VON RAD, Deuteronomy, 201. Cf. idem, Theology, II:80–82; 91–93.

[1] CHILDS, OT Introduction, 244–46. CHILDS makes the important point that this deuteronomistic editing was the most determinative redaction for the final form of the book *even though* it was not the last stage of the book's literary development. This example counters the frequent misperception that CHILDS arbitrarily valorizes only the final stage of each biblical book's redaction history.

[2] WILSON, Prophecy, 159.

[3] For the history of research, methodological issues and a full bibliography, see NOORT, Josua.

struction of the book's historical growth, the precise details of the various proposed stages will be less significant than what they cumulatively suggest about a complementary understanding of law and prophets for the tradents of the book.

A 'Deuteronomistic History'

It is first necessary to attend to the larger question of a 'Deuteronomistic History.' Ever since the work of M. Noth,[4] the theory of the substantial unity and wholesale deuteronomistic redaction of Joshua–2 Kings has provided a powerful working hypothesis for scholars. According to Noth's influential treatment, the traditional material in Joshua–2 Kings had been reworked and adapted according to 'a clearly defined and strongly emphasized theological interpretation of history.'[5] On linguistic and theological grounds, Noth assigned this reworking to a single deuteronomistic editor.[6]

Central to Noth's argument was his observation that certain 'speeches of anticipation and retrospection' punctuated the overarching narrative, representing the view of the editor of the material.[7] These speeches provided a systematic framework for the history, marking the conclusions of: 1) the period of conquest (Jos 23); 2) the period of the judges (1 Sam 12); 3) the period of the early monarchy (1 Kg 8:14–21); and 4) the period of the divided monarchy (2 Kg 17).[8] In this way, Noth maintained, the editor "planned the history of his people in Joshua–2 Kings in accordance with a unified plan and divided it according to its subject matter."[9]

This single editor largely restricted his activity to the provision of this chronological framework for the pre-existent written sources at his disposal, which he sought faithfully to transmit. Still, his combination and arrangement of the sources was so comprehensive and purposeful that Noth ultimately preferred to speak of a deuteronomistic 'author' rather than an 'editor.'[10] The accomplishment of this 'Deuteronomist' was a narrative of remarkable diversity, yet one which in its final form evidenced artful cohesion and purpose.[11]

---

[4] NOTH, Dtr History.

[5] NOTH, Dtr History, 4.

[6] Ibid.

[7] Ibid., 9.

[8] Ibid. NOTH believed (Dtr History, 42–44; 77) that the Deuteronomist's most 'original' work lay in his creation of a specific period of judges "based on an inference from existing traditional material."

[9] NOTH, Dtr History, 9.

[10] Ibid., 76–77.

[11] Ibid., 10. For NOTH, such cohesion was only to be found in the framework of the material. Some passages (e. g., the accounts of the conquest; the Succession Narrative) give signs of having been unified prior to the deuteronomistic framework, but only at the level of the

It should also be observed that this understanding of the Deuteronomistic History was considered by Noth to illustrate the general dynamic of biblical canon formation. He conceived of the Old Testament in its final form as comprised of *only* 'a few large compilations.'[12] In each of these compilations (i. e., the Pentateuch, the Deuteronomistic History, the work of the Chronicler), diverse traditional elements and historical accounts had been systematized by later frameworks, each representing the situations and concerns of its framers.

However, Noth also drew a distinction between the shaping of the Pentateuch, in which he saw theological concerns as having been primary, and the shaping of the Deuteronomistic History and the work of the Chronicler: "In the works of the Deuteronomist and the Chronicler we have compilations in the strict sense of historical traditions, each work with its own purpose and particular point of view."[13] For Noth, the Deuteronomistic History was of utmost significance precisely as the first collection of historical traditions within Old Testament literature, and closely paralleled the works of Hellenistic and Roman historians.[14] He dated the History to the middle of the sixth century B. C.[15]

Although it is difficult to accept Noth's judgment that the Pentateuch is more 'theological' in its orientation than the Deuteronomistic History or the work of the Chronicler (or, for that matter, that the works of the Deuteronomist and the Chronicler are somehow more 'historical' than the Pentateuch), his observation regarding the formation of ever larger complexes of tradition within the canonical process finds support from contemporary scholars who have pointed to a similar dynamic at work.[16]

In addition, Noth's conception of the framework to the Deuteronomistic History as designed primarily to *periodize* Israel's history supports the findings of the present investigation.[17] For Noth, too, deuteronomistic editing exhibits a concern to find the consistency in Israel's experience of God, periodizing history as a means of balancing the diversity of their tradition against the unity of their faith.

It is also important to remember that Noth placed the additions to Deuteronomy (Deut 31–34) later in time than the framework of the Deuteronomistic

---

framework was a quality of cohesiveness given to the disparate nature of the overarching narrative.

[12] NOTH, Dtr History, 1.

[13] Ibid.

[14] Ibid., 2; 11.

[15] Ibid., 12.

[16] E. g., CLEMENTS, Patterns; FREEDMAN, Law; RENDTORFF, Introduction, 124–28.

[17] For more on such periodization, see ALBERTZ, Intentionen.

History.[18] He reasoned that since these additions to Deuteronomy 'postulate a new future' for Israel, and similar additions in Joshua–2 Kings are conspicuously lacking, they must have been made *after* Deuteronomy had been separated from the Deuteronomistic History.[19] Deut 31–34 are therefore additions to the Torah as a whole. The rationale for these additions, according to Noth, lay in the singular role of the Torah as the canonical document of the postexilic community. As he put it, "...the Pentateuch could not tolerate the idea that the destruction of Jerusalem in 587 was the final end."[20] Similar revisions, he believed, were not to be found in the Deuteronomistic History because it had not yet achieved canonical status.

As already noted, I disagree with the assumption of a Torah-only canon in the post-exilic period, and shall endeavor to illustrate in the course of my investigation that there are additions to Joshua–2 Kings which hold out a 'new future' for Israel in just the same way that Deuteronomy does.[21] For that reason, the location of these additions to Joshua–2 Kings in the same period as the additions to Deuteronomy, and among the same circles of tradition, seems justified. Provisionally, then, exploration of the Deuteronomistic History stands to provide additional evidence for a theological 'grammar' of 'Law and Prophets' governing the process of canon formation in the post-exilic period.

A Deuteronomistic Edition of Joshua

Ever since the Noth's seminal work, the major passages within the book of Joshua exhibiting deuteronomistic shaping have generally been considered to be Jos 1;[22] Jos 8:30–35;[23] Jos 12;[24] and Jos 23.[25] As many scholars have done

---

[18] Deut 4:1–43 should probably be included as well; see NOTH, Dtr History, 33–34. NOTH, of course, believed that Deut 1–3 were designed to provide the introduction to the Deuteronomistic History as a whole (Dtr History, 13–15).

[19] NOTH, Dtr History, 98 n. 9. A certain tension in NOTH's argument exists here. Although he also found references to a 'new future' in Deut 27–30, NOTH maintained that these additions came to an end when Deuteronomy was incorporated into the Deuteronomistic History, and that Deuteronomy consisted essentially of Deut 4:44–30:20 for the Deuteronomist (Dtr History, 16–17). In my view, it is somewhat problematic to claim that Deut 27–30 were added to Deuteronomy *before* its incorporation into the Deuteronomistic History and that Deut 4; 31–34 were added to Deuteronomy *after* its separation from the Deuteronomistic History, given the great similarities between some of this material (esp. Deut 4 and 29–30). The similarities could be explained in terms of literary dependence, but such dependence seems less likely to me in this case than the existence of a common source.

[20] NOTH, Dtr History, 98.

[21] Here I am following, and hopefully amplifying, the lines initially charted by WOLFF, Kerygma.

[22] Cf. Deut 1:7; 3:12–13a, 18–20; 31:7–8.

[23] Cf. Deut 27:2–8; 31:10–13.

[24] Cf. Deut 3:8, 12, 13a.

since, Noth also identified a number of secondary additions, which he believed a later 'author' had added to the basically deuteronomistic composition: Jos 1:7–9;[26] Jos 13–22;[27] and Jos 24:29–33.[28]

The most important shift in the interpretation of Joshua since Noth has been the increasing tendency to view Jos 13–22 as a part of the Deuteronomistic History, rather than as a later priestly supplement. The main reason for this shift derives from a deeper appreciation of the two-fold nature of Joshua's ordained task, according to the view represented in the Deuteronomistic History: he is commissioned to *divide* as well as conquer.[29] As N. Lohfink has persuasively argued, this two-fold commission supports the claim of an integral relationship between Jos 1–12 and Jos 13–22.[30]

The other main argument for viewing an earlier form of Jos 13–22 as an integral portion of the deuteronomistic edition of Joshua has to do with the persistent theme of the Transjordanian tribes.[31] Rather than a later priestly composition, Jos 13–22 appears to contain older source material which was added to the book of Joshua by those responsible for the Deuteronomistic History, to which several priestly-style additions were then subsequently made (esp. Jos 22:7–34).[32] The similarity of some of this material to Num 32–34 is particularly striking.

---

[25] Cf. Deut 4:25–28; see, NOTH, Dtr History, 36–38. The passages from Deuteronomy given here and above are those cited by NOTH to support his argument. Jos 24:1–28 represents a special case. NOTH believed (Dtr History, 8 n. 14) that this unit was an originally independent tradition which had been revised and inserted by the 'Deuteronomist.'

[26] NOTH, Dtr History, 36 n. 4. NOTH changed his mind about this in his second edition; see SMEND, Gesetz, 396 n. 12.

[27] NOTH, Dtr History, 40. NOTH argued this half of the book away from his original Deuteronomist by claiming that the beginning and end of this section 'inappropriately' repeated material found in other verses, and therefore must be secondary. Thus Jos 13:1a was said to be a copy of Jos 23:1b and Jos 21:43–22:6 was said to 'presume' both Jos 11:23 and Jos 23:9b, 14b. However, NOTH also claimed that Jos 13–22 included ancient lists of tribal boundaries and more recent lists of royal administrative districts, which were later revised in priestly fashion. Cf. NOTH, Josua. NOTH located (Dtr History, 41) late priestly additions interspersed among older materials in Jos 18:1–11; 19:1, 10, 17, 24, 32, 40; and 20.

[28] = Jud 2:7–9. See NOTH, Dtr History, 8 n. 15.

[29] Cf. Deut 1:38; 3:21; 31:3, 7, 23.

[30] LOHFINK, Darstellung. Cf. the summary by MAYES, Story, 45. MAYES argues that the same two-fold commission existed in an original combination of Deut 31:23 and Jos 1:6, now separated in the final form of the text by subsequent additions to the book of Deuteronomy. MAYES further suggests (Story, 47) that a parallel introduction to the resulting two sections of Joshua can still be glimpsed in Jos 1:1–2 and Jos 13:1.

[31] See Deut 3:12–17; 4:41–43; 29:8; Jos 1:12–18; 4:12; 12:1–6; 13:8–13, 15–31; 22:1–34. Cf. 2 Kg 10:32–33 and, on the basis of Qumran manuscripts, the NRSV's reconstructed text of 1 Sam 10:27.

[32] See SOGGIN, Joshua, 215, for evidence of priestly redaction and influence on Jos 22. Despite the presence of substantial priestly features, SOGGIN believes the original placement

Thus the bulk of Jos 1–12 (also containing older pre-deuteronomistic material) and Jos 13–22 was probably arranged within a deuteronomistic framework which placed the conquest and the tribal allotments into two sequential periods and included all twelve tribes. As this overview might suggest, the material found at the divisions within the framework was structured by those responsible for the Deuteronomistic History precisely to achieve this effect. Thus, there were probably also introductions to both parts of the book (still evident in Jos 1 and Jos 13), the second half of which reported on the Transjordanian tribes,[33] and conclusions to both parts (Jos 11:21–23 and Jos 21:43–45), also followed by mention of the Transjordanian tribes.[34]

A Second Deuteronomistic Edition of Joshua

A second significant shift in the interpretation of the book of Joshua since M. Noth lies in the increasing tendency of critics to identify and refine a later deuteronomistic layer of redaction within the book. Again, Lohfink's work receives pride of place. In his analysis of Joshua's two-fold commission, Lohfink isolates a three-part literary form which he believes can be traced back to an 'installation ceremony' within ancient Israel. He divides the form into: 1) a formula of encouragement, 'be strong and of good courage' (Jos 1:6a); 2) a description of a task, introduced by 'for you' (Jos 1:6b); and 3) a formula of support, 'the LORD your God will be with you' (Jos 1:9b).[35]

Lohfink's analysis of this literary form becomes crucial for interpretation because it offers an explanation for the way in which Jos 1:7–9a appears to interrupt its present context.[36] Building on Lohfink's work, R. Smend has detected another layer of deuteronomistic redaction in Joshua and the beginning of Judges.[37] Smend finds evidence for this redaction beginning with Jos 1:7–9a, a unit which thus breaks the pattern of Lohfink's form by separating Jos 1:6 from Jos 1:9b. According to Smend, this secondary redaction emphasizes the role of law rather than the movement of history, and conceives of the

---

of the chapter is to be attributed to the 'Deuteronomist' because of the significance given to a single sanctuary, as also found in Deut 12. In my judgment, Jos 22:7–34 appears to be a later addition to Jos 22:1–6. Note the repetition of Jos 22:6 in Jos 22:7.

[33] Jos 1:12–18; 13:8–13, 15–31.

[34] Jos 12:1–6; 22:1–6. For a similar explanation of the rationale to the deuteronomistic editing of the book, see MAYES, *Story*, 55. Although MAYES mentions the Transjordanian tribes, he does not indicate the way in which they always appear in the second half of the book's introductions and conclusions. I defend this interpretation of Jos 21:43–45 below.

[35] LOHFINK, *Theology*, 241–43.

[36] This is the case even though I question whether LOHFINK's form can be tied to a specific installation ceremony. As he himself notes (*Theology*, 241–42), this kind of language is typical and widespread in battle contexts, in which there is no 'office' at issue. Cf. Deut 20:3–4; 31:6; Jos 10:25.

[37] SMEND, *Gesetz.*

conquest as partial instead of total. He traces this 'nomistic' layer further, assigning to it Jos 1:7–9a; 13:1b–6; 23 and Jud 1:1–2:5, 17, 20–21, 23.[38]

A. D. H. Mayes, in turn, has confirmed Smend's textual observations,[39] illustrating that the language of Jos 1:7–9a also exhibits strong links to secondary deuteronomistic material within the book of Deuteronomy.[40] As Smend and others have done, Mayes draws a sharp contrast between the depiction of total conquest at home in the first deuteronomistic framework to Joshua (Noth's 'Deuteronomistic History')[41] and the recurring mention of 'nations remaining in the land' within the secondary deuteronomistic material.[42] According to these scholars, the later deuteronomistic material serves to make Israel's occupation of the land conditional upon its continued obedience to mosaic law.

The Problem of Joshua 23–24

Jos 23–24 represent a persistent problem in scholarship on the book of Joshua. Some scholars have supported Noth's attribution of Jos 23 to the main framework of the Deuteronomistic History, perhaps with the later addition of Jos 23:4, 7, 12.[43]

It seems unlikely, however, that simply positing the secondary status of these three verses can satisfactorily resolve the difficulties. The antecedent for the third person plural pronoun in Jos 23:5 makes more sense as the nations remaining in the land (Jos 23:4) than as the already defeated nations of Jos 23:1–3. Similarly, Jos 23:6 fits the context established by Jos 23:5, 7. As Mayes has argued, the notice 'to this day' in Jos 23:9b serves to harmonize the theological emphasis of the secondary material with the rest of the book.[44] The phrase 'these nations' in Jos 23:13 refers to the 'nations left among you' in Jos 23:12, and thus introduces the prediction of catastrophe (Jos 23:13b) which occupies Jos 23:15b–16. In sum, Jos 23 gives the appearance of a tightly constructed summary which construes theologically the material of the

---

[38] LOHFINK, Theology, 244, had already pointed to similarities between Jos 1:2–9 and Jos 13:1–7.

[39] With the exception of Jos 24:1–28 (on this, see MAYES, Story, 46 n. 12; 49–51; and the discussion below).

[40] MAYES, Story, 47 n. 15. Thus, 'according to all the law' (כְּכָל-הַתּוֹרָה, Jos 1:7 MT) figures in Deut 4:8; 29:30; 30:10; 31:26. Use of the verbs 'keep' (שׁמר) and 'do' (עשׂה) in relation to the law occurs also frequently, see Deut 4:6; 5:1, 32; 6:3, 25; 7:11–12; 8:1 and *passim*. As noted above, there are strong similarities between Deut 4 and Deut 29–30. For an argument that seeks to square the passages given here with the reconstruction of a similar second deuteronomistic layer within the book of Deuteronomy, see MAYES, Story, 22–24.

[41] Jos 1:2–6; 11:21–23; 21:43–45.

[42] Jos 13:1b; 23:4–8, 12–13. See MAYES, Story, 47–48.

[43] Thus, NELSON, Redaction, 21.

[44] MAYES, Story, 48.

book along lines congenial to other passages attributed to a second deuteronomistic layer.[45]

By itself, the motif of the remaining nations is inconclusive. As B. S. Childs points out, the idea of a more gradual conquest may well have equally venerable roots in tradition.[46] There could even be a hint of such a tradition in the primary deuteronomistic framework to the book (Jos 11:22b).[47] The whole of the evidence, however, indicates that the present form of Jos 23 should probably be viewed as *secondary* deuteronomistic material (*pace* Smend, *contra* Noth), which redirects the main emphasis of the book without diachronically or synchronically contradicting what preceded it.

Jos 24 has been a longtime crux within the field.[48] Its similarities to Jos 23 suggest that one of the chapters has influenced the form and the content of the other; however, the direction of influence is strongly debated.[49] On the other hand, the differences between the two chapters seem to preclude attributing them to the same redaction.[50] Therefore, if Jos 23 is assigned to a secondary deuteronomistic strand within the book, the options for Jos 24 are essentially three: either 1) Jos 24 functioned as the original conclusion to the first deuteronomistic edition of the book, which Jos 23 displaced without replacing;[51] or 2) Jos 24 represents older pre-deuteronomistic material which has been inserted by those responsible for the secondary deuteronomistic material (perhaps edited after Jos 23 as a model);[52] or 3) Jos 24 reflects a third layer of deuteronomistic material in the history of the book's development, again perhaps modelled on Jos 23.[53]

---

[45] Cvc. Jos 23:6 with Jos 1:7–8; and Jos 23:4, 7, 12 with Jos 13:1b.

[46] Cf. 'little by little' (מעט מעט) in Ex 23:30; Deut 7:22. See CHILDS, OT Introduction, 248–49.

[47] Unless, of course, this half-verse was a later addition.

[48] NELSON gives (Redaction, 94–96) a usefully concise overview of the main theories regarding the origin and placement of Jos 24:1–28. For a full history of scholarship, see KOOPMANS, Joshua, 1–95.

[49] Both chapters report public addresses given by Joshua; both addresses include references to Israel's salvation history; both display covenant/treaty features.

[50] Esp. since Jos 23 is cast in the form of a *valedictory* address (cf. Jos 23:1b, 2b, 14), an aspect conspicuously absent in Jos 24 and in Jud 2:6. Moreover, 'covenant' denotes a past reality in Jos 23:16, but a present challenge in Jos 24:25. The totality of the conquest depicted in Jos 24:18 is also somewhat jarring after references to an uncompleted conquest in Jos 23.

[51] SMEND, Gesetz, 503–05. Jos 24 may or may not have existed in a pre-deuteronomistic form according to this view.

[52] NELSON, Redaction, 96–98.

[53] MAYES, Story, 49–51. This option also does not preclude the possibility of a pre-deuteronomistic form for the material.

The Relation of Joshua to Judges

The position of Jos 24 at the end of Joshua and the difficulties attached to the introduction to the book of Judges suggest that the problem of Jos 24 cannot be viewed in isolation. Jud 2:11–3:6 has long been interpreted as the original deuteronomistic introduction to the book of Judges.[54] Here again, however, Smend and others have argued for the presence of a secondary deuteronomistic layer, on the basis of certain vocabulary shared with secondary passages in Joshua and the repeated theme of the nations remaining in the land.[55]

That a kernel of Jud 2:11–3:6 functioned as part of the original deuteronomistic introduction to the book seems to be illustrated by three factors: 1) Jud 2:11a ('and the people of Israel did what was evil in the sight of the LORD') shares a formal relationship with Jud 3:7, 12; 4:1; 6:1; 10:6; 13:1, which provides an indication as to how material within the book was structured in an earlier edition;[56] 2) mention of the 'enemies round about' in Jud 2:14 picks up the language of the summary statement in Jos 21:44,[57] rather than the language of the 'nations remaining' in Jos 23;[58] and 3) as Smend points out, the basic text of Jud 2:11–3:6 construes Israel's cyclical apostasy as resulting from the death of those judges to whom Israel had apparently listened,[59] even though Jud 2:17 negates the effect of the judges and makes the cause of Israel's unrest her disobedience to the commandments of God.[60] Thus, *secondary* material within Jud 2:11–3:6 can probably be identified by its similarity to the secondary material identified within the book of Joshua.[61]

---

[54] AULD, Joshua, 140; WEINFELD, Judges, 388 n. 1. WEINFELD further believes that Jud 2:7 (part of the the Deuteronomistic History) is contradicted by Jos 24:23, because it mentions the presence of foreign gods in Joshua's day.

[55] SMEND, Gesetz, 504–06; MAYES, Story, 67–69.

[56] For the roots of this expression in deuteronomistic tradition, see Deut 4:25; 9:18; 17:2; 31:29. The expression is conspicuous in the book of Joshua by its absence. For a description of the literary framework to the book of Judges and the other formal motifs used in combination with this expression, see MAYES, Story, 61–63. It is debated whether this framework derives from the Deuteronomistic History (thus NOTH) or from a pre-deuteronomistic collection (thus RICHTER, Bearbeitung, 63–67). If the basic framework to the book was pre-deuteronomistic, then those responsible for the primary deuteronomistic layer must have modelled their work very closely upon it (e. g., Jud 3:7–11; 10:6–16).

[57] SMEND, Gesetz, 504.

[58] In the primary deuteronomistic layer it is *external* enemies (e. g., Jos 21:44) rather than internal enemies to whom Israel falls prey. See MAYES, Story, 77. In this reconstruction, Jos 23:1 would have to be an exception, a secondary verse probably formed to introduce the chapter by combining Jos 13:1a and Jos 21:44.

[59] Jud 2:18–19; cf. the framework, e. g., Jud 2:11–12; 4:1; 10:5–6; 12:15–13:1.

[60] SMEND, Gesetz, 505.

[61] Ibid.; cf. MAYES, Story, 76–78. E. g., cvc. Jud 2:20–21 with Jos 23:5, 13, 16.

By contrast, *primary* deuteronomistic material is likely found in Jud 2:6–10, in which Joshua dismisses the people.[62] Jud 2:6–10 could therefore be understood as having originally followed Jos 22:1–6 within the Deuteronomistic History. Jud 2:6 repeats the dismissal of Jos 22:6, including the information that at this time the people took possession of the land (Jos 21:43).[63] The following verses in Jud 2:7–9 would fit the periodizing interests of the Deuteronomistic History.[64] The duplicate notice in Jos 24:29–31 is likely a secondary repetition designed to conclude the book of Joshua after its separation from the book of Judges.[65] Thus, Jud 2:7–9 reports the death of Joshua the 'servant of God,' matching the notice of Moses' death in Deut 34:5. Such an *inclusio* could have once demarcated the period of the conquest within the Deuteronomistic History. Jud 2:10, which is not duplicated in Jos 24, introduces the same cyclical notion of unfaithfulness as Jud 2:19 and sets the stage for the book of Judges.[66]

In sum, an earlier form of Jud 2:6–3:6 probably comprised the initial deuteronomistic introduction to the book of Judges, which was subsequently edited by the same secondary deuteronomistic editor(s) at work in Jos 1:7–9a; 13:1b–6; 23.

A Third Layer of Redaction?

The difficult transition between Jud 2:1–5 and Jud 2:6 suggests that Jud 2:1–5 does not belong to the primary level of the Deuteronomistic History, or perhaps even to the secondary level of 'nomistic' redaction that Smend and others have reconstructed. Against Smend, Mayes holds that Jud 1:1–2:5 is to be viewed as a late assortment of material which exhibits links to the appendices of the book of Judges (Jud 17–21) and connections with Jos 24.[67] Although

---

[62] The reports of his death now found in Jos 24:29–30 and Jud 1:1 represent later additions; note that Jud 2:7–9 parallels Jos 24:29–31, but in a different order.

[63] MAYES argues (Story, 60 n. 3) that Jud 2:6–10 originally followed Jos 24:1–28, but I would argue that Jos 24:28 is a secondary addition to Jos 24:1–27, modelled on Jos 22:6/Jud 2:6 in order to bring the chapter to an appropriate conclusion in light of its new setting within the book. NELSON maintains (Redaction, 43) that Jud 2:6 followed Jos 23:16, but he understands Jos 23:16 to be part of the primary Deuteronomistic History.

[64] NOTH, Dtr History, 102 n. 14; AULD, Joshua, 140.

[65] On this question, see NELSON, Redaction, 43 n. 2; JERICKE, Tod; and the literature they cite. JERICKE assigns Jud 2:6–9 to the Deuteronomistic History and Jos 24:28–31 to SMEND's nomistic editor. MAYES holds (Story, 60 n. 3) that the account in Jos 24:29–31 is prior because he believes Jud 2:6 follows Jos 24:28 and is therefore late.

[66] Cf. the similar introduction to the book of Exodus in Ex 1:6–8.

[67] MAYES, Story, 60; 79. Cf. WEINFELD, Judges. MAYES cites the references in these chapters to Bethel (Jud 2:1–5?; 20:18, 26; 21:2, 19), cultic activity and the ark of the covenant. He notes the same concern with covenant and ritual in Jos 24. The theme of 'weeping' (perhaps a play on another name for Bethel?) thus forms an *inclusio* between Jud 2:4 and Jud 20:23, 26; 21:2. It is interesting to consider whether this theme was intended to function as a

Mayes concedes the presence of a concern for law in Jud 2:1–5, I would argue that there does not exist the same specificity of legal language here as in other passages attributed to a 'nomistic' redaction.[68]

Furthermore, what Mayes describes as the characteristic subtlety of the nomistic editor is as absent from Jud 1:1–2:5 as it is from Jos 24:1–27.[69] If Jud 2:6–3:6 was reworked as comprehensively by the nomistic editor as Smend suggests, then why is the transition between Jud 2:5 and Jud 2:6 so abrupt?[70] The answer is that Jos 24:1–27 and Jud 1:1–2:5 probably derive from a common *tertiary* stage in the development of Joshua–Judges,[71] possibly along with Jos 22:7–34; 24:32–33; and Jud 17–21, all of which exhibit priestly-style concerns and share certain features.[72]

A fascinating and important feature of this material is its apparent familiarity with tetrateuchal tradition, strikingly absent in the primary layer of the Deuteronomistic History or in the secondary layer of 'nomistic' redaction. R. D. Nelson has shown quite convincingly how the scene in Jud 2:1–5 shares a close verbal relationship with Ex 23:20–33 and Ex 34:12–13.[73] The appearance of the 'angel of the LORD' (מלאך־יהוה) in Jud 2:1–5 thus fulfills God's promise of an angelic covenant-guardian and judge. Tetrateuchal echoes are also prominent in Jud 1.[74] Jos 22:7–34 makes reference to the sin of Peor (Jos 22:17, cf. Num 25).[75]

Significantly, the rehearsal of Israel's *Heilsgeschichte* in Jos 24 also draws heavily on tetrateuchal traditions (e. g., Terah, Nahor, Balak, Balaam), in contrast to the typically concise deuteronomistic adjuration to remember the con-

---

literary frame for the final redaction of the book. WEINFELD also argues that Jud 2:1–5 is late, but he fails to entertain the possibility of a third layer of redaction, although he does perceive a connection between Jud 1:1–2:5 and Jos 24:1–28.

[68] E. g., 'my command' in Jud 2:2 (NRSV) is not מצותי but קלי.

[69] MAYES, Story, 60.

[70] For objections that Jud 1 is a more 'historical' account of the conquest than is found in Joshua, and therefore unlikely to be a later addition, see the literature cited by MAYES, Story, 60 n. 6. Cf. AULD, Reconsideration.

[71] WEINFELD suggests (Judges, 398) that the purpose of Jud 1:1–2:5 was to aggrandize Judah's role and, at the same time, to criticize the northern tribes. Cf. AULD, Joshua, 133–35.

[72] Cvc. Jos 22:34 with Jos 24:22; Jos 24:24 with Jud 2:2; and Jos 22:13, 31–32 with Jos 24:33. See NOTH, Dtr History, 41, for late features in Jos 18–20. Cf.ROFÉ, Joshua, who argues by comparison with the LXX that Jos 20 is a deuteronomistic redaction of earlier priestly tradition. He dates the final form of the book of Joshua to the fourth century B. C. on text critical grounds.

[73] NELSON, Redaction, 45–46. NELSON assumes that the Exodus texts pre-date the text from Judges. I do not necessarily assume the same direction of influence.

[74] E. g., 'the Kenite, Moses' father-in-law' in Jud 1:16; 'Luz' in Jud 1:23, 26.

[75] See further the intertextual reference to the sin of Achan in Jos 22:20 (cf. Jos 7). See SOGGIN, Joshua, 215.

quest and the gift of the promised land.[76] There are verbal similarities to the Covenant Code (Ex 21–23) here as well.[77] Jos 24:32 relates to Gen 33:19; 50:25 and Ex 13:19.[78]

Nelson also makes a strong case for seeing the speech of the mysterious unnamed prophet in Jud 6:7–10 as part of the same stage of the book's redaction as Jud 2:1–5, since Jud 6:10 quotes Jud 2:2 and Jud 6:8–9 quotes 1 Sam 10:18.[79] Mention of 'the gods of the Amorites in whose land you dwell' also ties together Jud 6:10 and Jos 24:15.[80] The lack of a close formal correspondence between the material found in Jud 2:1–5; 6:7–10 and known oral genres further argues for the status of those units as late compositions based on literary motifs and exemplars, rather than as old oral material that has been subsequently revised.[81]

Joshua 8:30–35

A last addition to this tertiary group of texts is provided by Jos 8:30–35, which Noth had assigned to his 'Deuteronomist.' The passage is set apart by its emphasis on the law (Jos 8:31–32, 34–35) and the inclusion of foreigners within Israel (Jos 8:33, 35). Moreover, this latter theme displays an odd ambiguity in its use of the terms אזרח (= 'native born inhabitant') and גר (= 'foreigner'). The narrative first suggests (Jos 8:33) that the אזרח and the גר represent two groups *within* Israel, but then implies (Jos 8:35) in its ordering of the Israelites ('the men, the women, the children and the foreigners')[82] that the 'foreigners' represent someone *else*. Such an ambiguity could perhaps most easily have arisen in the post-exilic period, further suggesting that this text may have been a later addition.[83]

---

[76] It is true, as SOGGIN forcefully points out (Joshua, 227), that one might expect Moses and Sinai to figure in the historical recital if the text were to date from the post-exilic period, but the present argument is for Jos 24 as a post-exilic insertion and redaction, *not* as a post-exilic composition. Thus the presence of certain late features is methodologically more compelling than the absence of others.

[77] Cvc. Jos 24:11–12 with Ex 23:20–31. See SOGGIN, Joshua, 227. In this case and the next, SOGGIN assumes the chronological priority of the tetrateuchal material. I am not necessarily arguing for this direction of influence between the two texts, only for their common vocabulary and and motifs.

[78] SOGGIN, Joshua, 245.

[79] NELSON, Redaction, 48. Cf. AULD, Joshua, 161–63. AULD also notes the use of מלאך in the books of Haggai and Malachi.

[80] NELSON, Redaction, 49. Here NELSON is relying on the work of BEYERLIN, Traditionsbildung.

[81] NELSON, Redaction, 49.

[82] The MT lacks 'the men,' probably from haplography (והאנשים והנשים), but the word appears in the LXX. See BOLING AND WRIGHT, Joshua, 246.

[83] Although it clearly provides no evidence for any dating, it is interesting to note the aural resemblance between אזרח ('native born inhabitant') and עזרא, the post-exilic leader.

Noth assigned Jos 8:30–35 to his 'Deuteronomist,' in opposition to the view that the passage represented an older, pre-deuteronomistic tradition.[84] He saw that the purpose of the text was to report the fulfillment of Moses' instructions in Deut 27:2–8. In response to the objection that Deut 27:2–8 had in fact been derived from Jos 8:30–35, Noth observed that it was more likely that the straightforward summary statement in Jos 8:31aβ was an effort to clarify the complicated nature of Deut 27:5–7aα.[85] Also, he claimed that Jos 8:35b constituted a direct allusion to Deut 31:12. According to the rationale Noth attributed to the Deuteronomist, the hill-country of Ephraim was opened up to the Israelites for the first time with the conquest of Ai. Thus, Joshua is portrayed as complying with Moses' instructions in Deut 27:2–8 at the earliest possible opportunity (i. e., after the defeat at Ai had made possible an approach to Shechem).[86]

Against Noth's case, it can be observed that the literary history of Deut 27:2–8 is complicated, and gives every indication of containing secondary material.[87] Although he followed critical wisdom in adopting the more difficult reading as the more original, his argument was ultimately circular.[88] Finally, even Noth recognized that the inclusion of the 'ark of the covenant' in this passage went significantly beyond the deuteronomic injunction in Deut 27:2–8.[89] To be sure, Jos 8:30–35 registers a concern at some stage in deuteronomistic tradition to provide for the fulfillment of Deut 27:2–8, but the evidence is lacking which would *prevent* assigning this concern to a second or even third stage of deuteronomistic/post-deuteronomistic redaction.

In favor of such an attribution I can cite the following factors. First, the placement of Jos 8:30–35 *after* Jos 9:1–2 in the LXX may indicate the kind of textual instability caused by a late redaction.[90] Certainly Jos 9:1–2 originally followed Jos 8:28–29.[91] The presence of Jos 8:34–35 before Jos 5:2–7 in 4Q47-48 (4QJos^a) would seem to confirm such instability.[92] Second, the introductory phrases יהושע יבנה אז in Jos 8:30 and יהושע יקרא אז in Jos 22:1

---

[84] NOTH, Dtr History, 37 n. 10.

[85] Ibid., 38.

[86] Ibid., 52.

[87] NOTH worried about this, too (Dtr History, 38 n. 11).

[88] NOTH had already come to the conclusion that Deut 4:44–30:20 was in 'essentially the same form' when taken over by the Deuteronomist, based in part upon this same alleged relation between Deut 27:2–8 and Jos 8:30–35 (cf. NOTH, Dtr History, 16).

[89] NOTH, Dtr History, 95.

[90] TOV, Criticism, 332. See the entire section (Criticism, 327–32) for a helpful discussion of the relation between LXX Joshua and MT Joshua.

[91] SOGGIN, Joshua, 220–22.

[92] Here a redactor has moved the fulfillment of Deut 27:2–8 to its earliest possible point in the narrative, emphasizing Joshua's strict obedience to the letter of the law.

seem to relate the two altar-building stories to each other.[93] It could be argued that Jos 22:1, which Noth believed was a later addition to the deuteronomistic version of the book, has simply copied the phrase from Jos 8:30. It could also be the case, however, that Jos 8:30 and Jos 22:1 stem from a common redaction or that Jos 8:30 has borrowed its introductory phrase from Jos 22:1.

The Relation between Joshua 8:30–35 and 24:1–28

A. D. H. Mayes has mounted a persuasive case that Jos 8:30–35 and Jos 24:1–28 should be attributed to the same tertiary layer of deuteronomistic/post-deuteronomistic editing.[94] He describes four points of similarity between the two passages: 1) they both describe an event at Shechem; 2) both describe a ritual action in which all the tribes participate under Joshua's leadership; 3) both refer to a 'book of the law';[95] and 4) both passages disrupt the flow of the narrative into which they have been placed.

On the basis of these similarities, Mayes theorizes a late, third layer of redaction in which the themes of Shechem and covenant are highlighted. He relates the two passages in Joshua to similar passages in Deuteronomy (Deut 10:8–9; 11:29–30; 27:1–8, 11–26; 31:9–13, 24–29)[96] and Judges (Jud 1:1–2:5; 17–21).[97] All of these passages are associated with Shechem[98] and feature the levites.[99]

The purpose of this redaction, in Mayes' description, is somewhat obscure and does not appear to constitute a major reshaping of the deuteronomistic form of the books. He supposes the purpose of these 'very late' additions to have been the expansion of the theme of covenant and the attempt to reestab-

---

[93] BOLING AND WRIGHT, Joshua, 246; 508. The combination of אז + imperfect to introduce a unit is used only in these two places within the book. Was it used as a redactional formula of introduction? See RABINOWITZ, Device. He suggested that the formula was used to introduce an additional or supplementary account referring to a time prior to or concurrent with the main narrative.

[94] MAYES, Story, 51–52. The relationship between the two passages has long been noted. SOGGIN, Joshua, 241–44, actually inserted the text of Jos 8:30–35 between Jos 24:1–27 and Jos 24:28–33 (see his discussion, Joshua, 227–31). The final form of the text, however, has not insisted that both scenes at Shechem be understood as descriptions of the same event.

[95] MAYES attributes (Story, 51 n. 23) the difference between 'the book of the law of Moses' (Jos 8:31–35) and the 'book of the law of God' (Jos 24:26) to synchronic concerns rather than to diachronic factors.

[96] MAYES, Story, 51–52. Cf. Ibid., 37–38.

[97] Ibid., 60–61; 79–80. On prophetic echoes and allusions in Jud 17–21, see AULD, Joshua, 225–27. AULD agrees that these chapters are later than the deuteronomistic material (Joshua, 256).

[98] Explicitly in Deut 11:29–30; 27:1–8, 11–26; Jos 8:30–35; 24:1–28; implicitly (by the presence of the ark) in Deut 10:8–9; 31:9–13, 24–29.

[99] Explicitly in Deut 10:8–9; 27:11–26; 31:9–13, 24–29; Jos 8:30–35; implicitly (because of the connection with the law's blessing and curse) in Deut 11:29–30; 27:1–8; Jos 24:1–28.

lish the authority of Shechem as a major religious center.[100] He further postulates that the common features of these additions "suggest a time and place of origin in priestly circles from which the combination of deuteronomistic history and Tetrateuch ultimately derives."[101]

Redactional Summary of Joshua

Although this kind of redactional analysis must always remain tentative, the following redactional profile emerges from our investigation of the book of Joshua. Although there were clearly pre-deuteronomistic sources of some sophistication (still visible esp. in Jos 2–6; 13–19),[102] the most significant shaping of the material appears at the level of the *primary* deuteronomistic redaction (i. e., Noth's Deuteronomistic History). Congruent with expansions in the book of Deuteronomy, Joshua was placed within a theological history which emphasized its distinctiveness as the *fulfillment* of mosaic prophecy.

This deuteronomistic edition of the work sequentialized narratives of conquest and land division, constructing a two-fold period to illustrate the *fully* completed mosaic promise (still visible in Jos 1; 12–13; 21–22; cf. Jud 2:7–9).[103] This two-fold period of obedience would have reassured pre-exilic Israel that God's eternal promise of the land was certain[104] and served synchronically within the Deuteronomistic History to form a contrast with the fractious strife of the period of 'judges' which followed.

As Smend persuasively argues, the earlier deuteronomistic form of Joshua was skilfully edited in the exilic/post-exilic period in order to make explicit something which until then had only been *implicit* in the Deuteronomistic

---

[100] MAYES, Story, 57; 134–35. Cf. VON RAD, Studies, 41. The emphasis on Shechem is curiously out of place within the context of Deuteronomy, which insists on the central and exclusive status of the Temple in Jerusalem (although it is a question as to whether this was always the case within the tradition, e. g., Jer 7:12). The resulting contradiction thus supports the argument that this redaction reflects a later theological development.

[101] MAYES, Story, 135.

[102] On the problems of Jos 13–22, see CORTESE, Josua. However, his constructive efforts tracing the pentateuchal Priestly source into the book of Joshua are more than a little unpersuasive.

[103] This is so much the case that Joshua himself never receives the same complex characterization as other major figures in biblical narrative (e. g., Abraham, Moses, David). Simply put, Joshua never *sins*. He is that rarity in biblical narrative, a type — in this case a type of such perfect obedience that his own personality evaporates in the light of the theological point being made.

[104] Including the Transjordan; Jos 1:13–18; 12:6; 13:7. Here I opt for a pre-exilic date for the first version of the Deuteronomistic History. This is a debated point. In the present context I would only observe that the insistent inclusion of the Transjordanian tribes would seem to fit the pre-exilic period well. I suspect, however, that Reuben, Gad and Manasseh also take on a extended, almost metaphorical, character in the post-exilic period (eventually referring to those left in the land?).

History: that Israel's claim to the land and to national unity was conditional upon its adherence to mosaic law and ethnic separation (Jos 1:7–9a; 13:1b–6, 12b).[105] Although this *conditionality* is presented as an either/or, the consistent pattern in which the consequences of obedience (blessing) are followed by the consequences of disobedience (curse) suggests that the experience of exile underlies the apparent typology.

By also making explicit the presence of the peoples remaining in the land even in the period of the conquest (Jos 13:1b–6, 13), this *secondary* level of deuteronomistic redaction would have subverted all notions of nostalgia and triumphalism without sacrificing anything of the period's exemplary faithfulness and success. The Israel of Joshua could be perceived as standing under the same threat as the exilic community, as well as the same blessing (e. g., Jos 23:11–13).

Finally, as Mayes has theorized, Jos 8:30–35 and Jos 24:1–18 probably belong to a third layer of late deuteronomistic, probably post-deuteronomistic/priestly redaction within the book.[106] These texts feature ritual activity and Shechemite traditions. As we have seen, they also display an awareness of tetrateuchal traditions. They expand the themes of law and covenant found in the secondary 'nomistic' material into a theological construct able to embrace both the unconditionality *and* the conditionality of Israel's relationship with God, as expressed in prior phases of the formation of the book.

In other words, the major feature of this *tertiary* material appears to lie in its canon-conscious effort to situate the book of Joshua within larger biblical complexes, and in turn to inform those same complexes with the unique witness of the book of Joshua. The two literary complexes to which Joshua is related in these passages are, as we have seen, the Deuteronomistic History and the Tetrateuch. What has not yet been clear in our discussion is that this interrelation is achieved not primarily through citation or subtle cross-referencing, but by conformity with a 'theological grammar' of 'Law and Prophets.'

Prophecy in Joshua

A prophetic note is first struck even at the primary stage of redaction (Noth's Deuteronomistic History). The conquest is portrayed as a fulfillment of mosaic *prophecy* (Deut 27:2–8). The second stage of redaction (Smend's 'Dtr

---

[105] It is thus not a case of contradiction or correction, but of a different emphasis. Cf. MAYES, Story, 134.

[106] I would include Jos 22:7–34 and Jos 24:32–33 in this group as well. Moreover, I suspect that Jos 3–4; 5:13–15; 6 also contain redactional features from this stage of the book, but such a suspicion requires investigation beyond the scope of this study. Note that Jos 5:15 quotes Ex 3:5 and Jos 6:18–19 anticipates Jos 7:10–15. The final form of these chapters emphasizes the typological relationship between Moses and Joshua (Jos 3:7; 4:14; 6:27), cultic activity and holy war. Joshua's curse of Jericho also gives a prophetic impression (cf. Num 22–24).

N'), rather than focusing narrowly on mosaic law, affirms and reiterates the fullness of God's promise.[107] This divine promise is periodized, making it conditional upon following mosaic *law* (Jos 23:9b).[108] However, the future orientation of Joshua's speech in Jos 23 suggests the recognition of the authority of *prophecy* as well (Jos 23:5, 12–13, 15–16).

Prophetic language and themes become even more prominent in what has been identified as a third layer of deuteronomistic or post-deuteronomistic redaction.[109] Jos 8:30–35 provides the fulfillment for Deut 27:2–8. To be sure, the two accounts do not agree in their details,[110] but that only makes it difficult to argue that the point of Jos 8:30–35 has to do with the fulfillment of mosaic *law*. Of far greater importance is the way in which Joshua fulfills Moses' prophecy in Deut 27:2–8 by taking on the role of the mosaic prophet *himself*.[111]

A Prophet Like Moses

The curious appearance of בראשׁנה (RSV, NRSV: 'at the first') at the end of Jos 8:33 may also reflect this prophetic connection. Although the syntax of the verse is difficult, it seems unlikely that בראשׁנה functions together with the preceding infinitive (לברך, 'to bless'), especially since the present form of Deut 27–28 would seem to contradict such an understanding: there the curses (Deut 27:13–26) come *before* the blessings (Deut 28:1–14).[112] Thus, בראשׁנה is better understood as modifying the main verb (צוה, 'commanded'), which is how both the RSV and the NRSV translate the verse. But what is the exact sense?

It is helpful to note that while בראשׁנה may have a more general meaning,[113] it can also be used for a more specific temporal reference.[114] The term

---

[107] Jos 1:5a and Jos 23:9b function as an *inclusio* for the entire book at this second stage; note as well how Jos 23:6 recapitulates Jos 1:7.

[108] SMEND, Gesetz.

[109] There would also seem to be similarities between this material and the style and interests of Chronicles.

[110] AULD, Joshua, 59–60; BUTLER, Joshua, 92.

[111] Note the use in Deut 27:2a of והיה ביום. Against the view that Deut 27:2–8 was considered to be a prophecy, it might be objected that the language of Deut 27:1 (probably a later insertion) is legal in nature (e. g., כל־המצוה). However, such an objection overlooks the deuteronomistic understanding of the mosaic prophet (cf. Deut 18:18), who is to speak (דבר) all that God commands (צוה). If one assumes that Deut 18 had a place originally within the book, a unity of prophecy and law would be presupposed by deuteronomistic tradition from its beginning. For a different view of Deut 18, see LOHFINK, Distribution.

[112] See, however, Deut 27:11–12.

[113] E. g., 'previously,' 'formerly' in Gen 13:4; Jos 8:5–6; 2 Sam 20:18.

[114] E. g., 'first,' in Deut 13:10 [9]; 17:7; 1 Kg 20:9, 17.

can also be employed to give expression to an implicit *Heilsgeschichte.*[115] Thus, in Jer 7:12 בראשונה relates a past action by God to the present stance and activity of God on Israel's behalf. God made his name to dwell *first* at Shiloh and *now* at Jerusalem — the implicit periodization distinguishes, but also joins.

The question is whether a similar *heilsgeschichtlich* understanding informs Jos 8:30–35. The text is certainly concerned with Joshua's adherence to his mosaic role-model, but there is no suggestion here of a prophetic succession beyond than the figure of Joshua himself (e. g., as in Deut 18:15, 18). Joshua writes (כתב) and reads out (קרא) the law of Moses, but does not speak (דבר) in God's name as might be expected of a mosaic prophet.[116] Still, by this account of his faithfulness to Moses' commands Joshua is depicted as Moses' successor in a way that fully comports with the notion of mosaic prophecy.[117]

T. C. Butler's proposal that Jos 8:30–35 owes its placement to the rupture between Israel and God introduced by the sin of Achan in Jos 7–8 makes convincing sense.[118] The theological crisis of a broken covenant (Jos 7:11, 15) would have outweighed any geographical and chronological difficulties for the redactor(s).

The narrative in Jos 7–8 is actually an artful combination of two accounts, the seige of Ai (Jos 7:2–10; 8:1–29) and the sin of Achan (Jos 7:1, 12b–26), with a connecting passage relating the two stories to each other (Jos 7:11–12a).[119] An oracle of salvation in Jos 8:1 follows the prophetic lament of Jos 7:6–10; the prophetic indictment of Jos 7:12b–15 is to be distinguished from the later connecting passage by its sudden use of second person plural discourse.[120]

For the first time in the book, Joshua speaks God's word directly (Jos 7:13), not mediated through Moses or the law (cf. Jos 1:1, 13).[121] Only now does Joshua use the prophetic messenger formula, 'thus says the LORD, God of Israel' (כה אמר יהוה אלהי ישראל). Twice we are told that the covenant with God has been transgressed (Jos 7:11, 15). Just like the *prophet* Moses, Joshua intercedes with God on Israel's behalf (Jos 7:6–9).[122] Within this narrative

---

[115] E. g., 2 Sam 7:10; Jer 7:12.

[116] See, however, use of דבר as a noun in Jos 8:35.

[117] This is not to say that priestly and royal traditions have not also shaped this passage. See BUTLER, Joshua, 91–93.

[118] Ibid.

[119] Ibid., 80–81.

[120] Ibid., 81.

[121] See KRAUS, Worship, 111. Jos 3:9–13 is quite similar. However, even though in these verses Joshua claims to report the words of God, he does not use the convention of messenger speech, but speaks of God in third person. See also Jos 4:15-17. NELSON, Joshua, 21, also points to Jos 6:26.

[122] Cf. the tradition of Moses' covenantal *intercession*: e. g., Ex 32:11–14; Deut 9:25–29.

context, it is difficult not to attribute a prophetic quality to Joshua's actions when it comes to the report of the covenant's restoration (Jos 8:30–35).[123]

Such a quality is even more apparent in Jos 24. In Jos 24:2 another report of covenant making is begun with the prophetic formula of messenger speech (כה־אמר יהוה אלהי ישראל). The formula appears only at Jos 7:13 and Jos 24:2 within the entire book. Drawing upon various traditions, the recital of Israel's *Heilsgeschichte* (Jos 24:2b–13) moves toward the injunction (Jos 24:14) to 'fear' (ירא) and 'serve' (עבד) God alone.[124] 'Serving' God in particular receives great stress in this chapter.[125] As has been observed before, the hortatory aspect of the speech obscures the precise nature of the covenant being made.[126] However, it is precisely the same hortatory tone that also suggests a general similarity both to the book of Deuteronomy and to prophetic traditions.[127]

Thus, as in Deut 31, 'witnesses' (עדים) are appointed against the people in order to prevent them from serving other gods.[128] In Jos 24:22, however, it is the people's own affirmation which will serve to indict them in the future. The people promise to obey God's 'voice' (קול, Jos 24:24).[129] They 'choose' (בחר, Jos 24:15, 22) to serve God.[130] Although the ability of a people to 'choose' God is somewhat unusual within the Old Testament,[131] at least one very well-known prophetic parallel exists in 1 Kg 18:20.[132]

As D. J. McCarthy pointed out, Isa 43:8–13 offers another close parallel.[133] In this passage the language of monotheism is used in connection with the importance of Israel's witness to the nations. It is especially interesting that Isa 43:8 invokes the presence of 'the people who are blind, yet have eyes, who are deaf, yet have ears.' If the reference in this verse is to Israel, and not

---

[123] Cf. the tradition of Moses' role in covenant *restoration*: e. g., Ex 32:15–16; Deut 10:1–5.

[124] This theme is announced in Jos 24:2b and thus brackets the entire recital.

[125] Jos 24:2b, 14, 15, 16, 18, 19, 20, 21, 22, 24, 31.

[126] MCCARTHY, Treaty, 238: "[Jos 24] is not a document recording a covenant. It is an exchange during a popular assembly. Hence the opening and closing formulas. It is exhortation with the responses elicited."

[127] MCCARTHY wrote further (Treaty, 239–40) of Jos 24: "This is the prophetic world, the world of struggle with the local Baals, with the possibility of a choice in the gods to be served, as in 1 Kg 18, and ultimately the need for a change of heart as the true condition for the service of Yahweh."

[128] See also Deut 4:26; 30:19.

[129] Cf. Deut 4:12, 30, 33, 36; 30:2, 8, 10. See also Deut 5:4.

[130] Cf. Deut 30:19.

[131] Usually it is the other way around: e. g., Deut 4:37, but cf. Ex 32:26.

[132] Here, too, it is the 'voice' of God which is at issue, esp. in 1 Kg 18:24–29. Cf. Ex 33:26.

[133] MCCARTHY, Treaty, 239–40.

the nations (Isa 43:9), then, as McCarthy suggested, the language could describe a 'prophetic' view in which "Israel's inadequacies... make it antecedently impossible for it to fulfil its functions."[134]

This conception would then mirror that of Jos 24:19–24 ('you cannot serve the LORD').[135] A clear example of a prophetic tradition regarding the impossibility of faith may be found in Isa 6:9–10.[136] As McCarthy summarized, Jos 24:19 thus functions in its context as "a warning of a type familiar from prophecy used in place of a curse formula" (i. e., within a covenant formulary).[137] In light of our earlier treatment of Malachi, I also note the presence of similar covenantal features in Jos 24:19–20 and Mal 3:22–24 [4:4–6].[138]

The Final Form of Joshua

The most interesting thing about this review of prophetic aspects within the book of Joshua is that the highly prophetic elements found in Jos 7–8 and Jos 24 thus appear in what is probably the last redactional layer of the book. What kind of effect do they have on its final form?

It cannot be said that the portrait of the figure of Joshua within the book is an exclusively prophetic one. Nor does it seem that the prophetic elements in Jos 7–8 and Jos 24 serve to reorient prior traditions in such a way as to subordinate them to prophetic concerns. It must be admitted, however, that the last level of redaction greatly increases the role of prophecy within the book and reveals a heightened consciousness of an emerging canon.

The literary shaping moves in the direction of an all-inclusive statement of Israel's traditions, as expressed in the form of an ideal vision.[139] The book of Joshua portrays an Israel in which Moses' promises have *finally* been fulfilled — and just *before* its fall into disobedience and apostasy. Into this ideal vision have been retrojected all the central institutions of later post-exilic Israel, *not* in a calculated ideological effort to ground their authority in a 'false' history, but as a theological confession that God gave all these institutions to Israel for its 'good' (Jos 24:20).

---

[134] Ibid.: "[Isa 43:8–13] opens with a call to a deaf and blind Israel and summons her to witness to the fact that Yahweh is God and there is no other. The conception and the organization is the same as that of Jos 24:19–24, though much different in expression."

[135] SOGGIN has described (Joshua, 235) the material beginning in Jos 24:3 as expressing a prophetic insistence on the 'absence of all merit.' In comparison, he cites Deut 17:16; Isa 2:7–11; 30:16; 31:1; and Jer 51:21.

[136] MCCARTHY suggested (Treaty, 240) the presence of such a tradition in Am 3:1–2 as well. Cf. SOGGIN, Joshua, 239.

[137] MCCARTHY, Treaty, 240.

[138] Cf. Deut 5:9–10.

[139] BLEEK, Joshua. He points out the strong similarities to Neh 8 (i. e., one people, one Torah).

Covenantal and prophetic traditions are thus granted their place in the Deuteronomistic History synchronically prior to the time at which they likely became central elements of Israelite worship.[140] Similar to the way in which Abraham (Gen 20:7) and Miriam (Ex 15:20) are called 'prophets' in the Pentateuch,[141] Joshua speaks as a 'prophet' before the History has introduced them as such.[142] Then again, both the Pentateuch and the Deuteronomistic History never *synchronically* introduce prophets and prophecy at all, but everywhere presume their existence.[143]

Thus, certain prophetic elements were identified in earlier layers of the book of Joshua. For example, some commentators have seen Joshua's succession of Moses as parallel to the tradition of Elisha's succession of Elijah, especially with regard to the motifs of the transfer of spirit and the parting of the waters.[144] This suggests that a certain awareness of prophetic tradition exists already at the *first* level of deuteronomistic redaction of Joshua.[145] Commentators have also postulated that Jos 1:7–9 sounds a prophetic resonance when heard together with the language of certain prophetic call narratives.[146] This would amplify the ways in which an awareness of prophecy exists at the *second* level of deuteronomistic redaction of the book.

However, it is only at the *third* level of redaction that the figure of Joshua is cast explicitly into the role of a prophet, speaking for God directly (in first person) and summoning the people of Israel to make a covenant. While this portrait of Joshua is not exclusively prophetic (it also contains priestly, military and royal aspects), it does include prophetic elements in a way that grants them a central place in Israel's *Heilsgeschichte*. Joshua's portrait sets a pattern for the prophets who will arise from now on within the Deuteronomistic History. Like Joshua, the 'servant of Moses in *prophecy*' (Sir 46:1; my emphasis), the prophets of the Deuteronomistic History will summon Israel to remain faithful to its covenant with God, proclaim the law and announce God's judgment.[147]

---

[140] PERLITT, Bundestheologie, 239–47.

[141] ZIMMERLI, "Prophet."

[142] Is this the concern behind the 'diachronic' notice in 1 Sam 9:9?

[143] E. g., Gen 20; Jud 4:4; 1 Sam 2:27–29; 3:20.

[144] T. COLLINS, Mantle, 137; SCHÄFER-LICHTENBERGER, "Josua."

[145] Thus KRAUS argues (Worship, 111) that Jos 1:1, 13 already reflect a prophetic understanding.

[146] E. g., Jer 1:17–19; Ezek 2:6–7; 3:9. See AULD, Joshua, 9–10.

[147] In my opinion, the relationship between Joshua and Moses cannot be viewed as a subordination of prophecy to law. It is often forgotten that Joshua's fidelity to the mosaic model also consists of doing what Moses himself could *not* do: i. e., entering the land. In this connection I note that Joshua also gives instructions to Israel that are *absent* in his mosaic mandate (i. e., the book of Deuteronomy), e. g., the practice of circumcision (Jos 5). For a traditional Christian reading that emphasizes the way in which Joshua (as a 'type' for Christ) ex-

The book of Joshua concludes by referring in comprehensive fashion to 'all the work which the LORD did for Israel' (Jos 24:31). As von Rad noticed, the *singular* form of 'work' (מעשה) in this verse (cf. Jud 2:7) indicates the conclusion of an important 'epoch' within the Deuteronomistic History.[148] As we have seen, however, deuteronomistic tradition also uses this kind of periodization to make a theological statement about the *unity* of God's purpose. As diverse and multiple as the traditions within the book are, they are all nevertheless confessed to fit within the framework of God's way with Israel. For the book of Joshua, that framework not only means the essential unity between promise and fulfillment, but also between Law and Prophets.

To summarize: although there are prophetic elements in what seem to be *every* redactional layer to the book of Joshua, it is the last layer (Jos 7–8; 24) which shows most use of prophetic traditions. This layer is also the most 'canon-conscious' (e. g., its intertextual connections to tetrateuchal material). Where a secondary layer of redaction had been concerned to fulfill the promises of Deuteronomy and insist on continued obedience to the legal tradition, the tertiary layer relates a written Torah to covenant traditions through the use of prophetic motifs. Thus, it seems to have been the growing scriptural authority of a canon of Law and Prophets which exerted in the post-exilic period a theological force upon the book of Joshua, giving it an idealized orientation and a covenantal shape.

---

ceeded and surpassed the Law, see DEANE, Joshua, 212. Ironically, in this case DEANE's theological presuppositions yield a reading closer to certain aspects of the text than those of most 'presupposition-less' historical-critical exegesis.

[148] VON RAD, Theology, I:306.

Chapter Five

The Law and the Words

Introduction

Up to this point, I have argued that a theological 'grammar' of 'Law and Prophets' was responsible for shaping the two scriptural subcollections later bearing those names into a complementary, dialectical unity. I have also undertaken to illustrate various ways in which the end of the Pentateuch (Deut 31–34) and the beginning of the Former Prophets (Joshua) display such editorial shaping. I concluded that the prophetic characteristics and idioms featured were not so much the result of prophetic traditions *behind* the text, but more the consequence of the existence of a prophetic corpus in *front* of the text.[1]

In other words, the prophetic characteristics and idioms present in Deuteronomy and Joshua have less to do with the historical phenomenon of prophecy and more to do with the way in which that phenomenon has been construed theologically within the deuteronomistic tradition; namely, as the application of Torah after the manner of Moses, or as 'instruction' in the Law (Deut 5:1). Conversely, 'law' in this tradition is regarded as the message that prophets like Moses proclaim ('the word of the LORD,' Deut 5:5).[2]

In this chapter I shall explore the continued effect of this complementary shaping — the various ways in which certain portions of the prophetic corpus (esp. the Deuteronomistic History, Jeremiah, Zech 1–7) and later post-deuteronomistic writings (Chronicles, Ezra–Nehemiah, Daniel) have been edited to portray the dual authority of Law and Prophets. Here again my conclusion will be that the 'law' and 'prophets' which have shaped the later literature are not simply general historical traditions, but those traditions as they have been refracted through the emergent scriptural canon of the Law and the Prophets.

As we have already seen, the initial formulation of 'law and prophets' as a 'theological grammar' was a deuteronomistic achievement, which served to unify Israel's diverse literary traditions even as it gave enduring voice to their

---

[1] In this way, my approach differs from problematic efforts to make a case for the origination of the History within prophetic circles of tradition; for further discussion, see WILSON, *Prophets*.

[2] Following the MT of Deut 5:5. Even if one adopts the plural דברי, following the Samaritan Pentateuch and other ancient versions, the prophetic allusion remains unmistakable.

diversity. However, I shall also argue in this chapter that the 'grammar' of 'law and prophets' was retained and strengthened in the priestly-style chronistic writing that later took up and reworked deuteronomistic tradition. In this way, I hope to illustrate how the deuteronomistic 'grammar' of 'Law and Prophets' continued to function as a canonical framework for later biblical traditions.

The Deuteronomistic History Revisited

As with the book of Joshua, I shall base my treatment of the rest of the Deuteronomistic History on those sections designated by M. Noth as secondary, editorializing 'speeches' inserted into the narrative.[1] In addition to the material in Joshua discussed above, 1 Sam 12:1–24 and 1 Kg 8:12–51 were included by Noth among these speeches. He also considered as secondary certain prose passages detailing the fall of the northern kingdom (e. g., Jud 2:11–22 and 2 Kg 17:7–18, 20–23).[2] Others have suggested since Noth that the dynastic oracle to David (2 Sam 7:1–16, 18–29) and the account of the man of God from Judah (1 Kg 13) also appear to be secondary within their narrative contexts.[3]

Noth's influential thesis of the Deuteronomistic History as an integrated, exilic work by a single author has generally shifted to a view of the work as consisting of two or three stages.[4] F. M. Cross and his students have promoted a two-fold history of redaction, in which a propagandistic Deuteronomistic History ('Dtr 1') from the time of King Josiah, which levied judgment upon the north and promise to the south, has been overwritten in order to extend judgment to the south and to bring the history up to the date of the exilic period ('Dtr 2').[5] By contrast, R. Smend and his students have argued for a three-fold redactional history, in which an original Dtr History (Noth's 'Dtr')

---

[1] My argument does not depend on the precise identification of the author(s) of these speeches, and is only partially concerned with the extent to which they contain multiple levels of redaction. The main point is to explore the deuteronomistic theology they purposefully present.

[2] NOTH, Dtr History.

[3] For a concise summary of scholarship on the Deuteronomistic History since NOTH (with a helpful bibliography), see MCKENZIE, Use, 1–15. For a detailed reevaluation of NOTH's work, see M. A. O'BRIEN, Reassessment.

[4] The exception is provided by HOFFMANN, Reform.

[5] CROSS, Myth, 274–89; NELSON, Redaction. Cf. BIRCH, Rise; FRIEDMAN, Exile; MCCARTER, Samuel.

has been retouched, first by a 'prophetic' editor ('Dtr P') and then by a 'nomistic' one ('Dtr N').[6]

It will clearly not be possible within this chapter to advance a complete redactional explanation for the Deuteronomistic History in its final form. Instead, I would like to detail the notion of 'law and prophets' present in the secondary (or tertiary) material. It may then be possible to compare the results of our analysis with the reconstructions of these other scholars.

Of course, there has been much work done on the traditions and views of prophecy represented in the Deuteronomistic History. With a few exceptions, however, this work has tended much more to focus on recovering the historical reality of prophecy *behind* the text than elucidating the views of prophecy enshrined and promoted *before* the text, that is, those views which in effect function as a theological 'grammar' of prophecy for the deuteronomistic editors.[7]

The Book of Judges

Turning again to Jud 2:1–15; 6:7–10; 10:11–16, with their stereotypical deuteronomistic language,[8] we are reminded that this material exhibits strong links to tetrateuchal material,[9] evidence supporting a later, secondary provenance. Furthermore, each of the three insertions relates a prophetic oracle that issues forth judgment upon an implied 'all Israel' in response to its apostasy.

Significantly, however, these passages all refer to a prior *statement* on God's part which has now been violated by Israel. Thus Jud 2:1–2: "I *said*, 'I will never break my covenant with you...' But you have not obeyed my command. See what you have done!" Jud 6:8–10: "Thus *says* the LORD, the God of Israel: I led you up from Egypt... and I *said*, 'I am the LORD your God...'" But you have not given heed to my voice." Jud 10:11–13: And the LORD

---

[6] SMEND, Gesetz; idem, Entstehung, 110–25; DIETRICH, Prophetie; idem, David; VEIJOLA, Königtum; idem, Dynastie; WÜRTHWEIN, Könige.

[7] One of the great strengths of the study by WILSON (Prophecy) lies in his attention to the way later biblical accounts of prophecy may illuminate our understanding of the bearers of those traditions. WILSON very helpfully describes (Prophecy, 157–59) the deuteronomistic notion of a 'prophet like Moses' and illustrates why this understanding cannot be traced back to an historical 'office' of 'covenant mediator,' as KRAUS seeks to do. See KRAUS, Verkündigung; idem, Worship, esp. 102–112.

[8] On deuteronomistic language, see WEINFELD, Deuteronomy, 320–70 ('Appendix A'); DRIVER, Deuteronomy, lxxvii–ix. On the problems of such stereotypical language in general, see WILSON, Prophecy, 167–69. NELSON distinguishes (Redaction, 48) Jud 10:11–16 (= Dtr 1) from the other two passages (= Dtr 2), but still considers all three deuteronomistic.

[9] E. g., Jud 2:1, the promise to the fathers; Jud 6:7, deliverance from Egypt, the gift of the land and the rejection of the Amorites; Jud 10:11–16, deliverance from Egypt and the nations. See NELSON, Redaction, 43–53.

said..., "Did I not deliver you...? Yet you have abandoned me and worshipped other gods; therefore I will deliver you no more."[10]

In Jud 2:1–5 God's judgment is communicated by an angel (מלאך־יהוה), in Jud 6:7–10 an unnamed prophet (נביא) speaks and in Jud 10:11–16 God discourses directly. However, both the angel and the prophet use the first person messenger speech of prophecy to relate God's message. By citing a previous 'word' of God, these passages all reveal an understanding of prophecy as a response to the violation of a *known standard* of behavior.

It will not do simply to dismiss these 'citations' as general allusions to the *events* of the Pentateuch. Whether or not the 'word' of God in question is recorded as such somewhere else in scripture is not nearly as significant as the understanding of prophecy these oracles assume: the remembrance of God's *stated* will for Israel and the indictment of Israel for failing to live in accordance with it. Thus there already exists in these passages an implicit deuteronomistic understanding of 'law' and 'prophecy' as the two related and complementary *scriptural* foundations of Israel's faith.[11]

The Books of Samuel

The deuteronomistic characterization of the prophets as 'proclaimers of the law' becomes more pronounced within the books of Samuel. Thus the oracle of the anonymous 'man of God' (איש־אלהים) in 1 Sam 2:27–36 exhibits the same understanding of the unity of law and prophecy.[12] In this case, the immoral behavior of Eli's sons is held to be in violation of God's prior acts of general (1 Sam 2:27, Israel in Egypt) and particular election (1 Sam 2:28–30, 'your family').

Crucially, however, both of these events are treated as *statements* rather than mighty acts *per se*: 1 Sam 2:27, "Thus the LORD *has said*, 'I revealed myself to the house of your father...'"; 1 Sam 2:30, "Therefore the LORD God of Israel *declares*: 'I *promised* that your house...'; but now the LORD *de-*

---

[10] My emphases. In this last verse the emphasis seems to lie with God's prior *acts* rather than God's prior *words*, but a text-critical problem makes a precise determination difficult. One should observe, nevertheless, that here the prophet reminds his audience of God's mighty acts by means of *reported speech.*

[11] WILSON, Prophecy, 168–69 on Jud 6:7–10: "The final shape of the overall unit thus may indicate the editor's belief that in the time of the judges prophets helped to preserve Israel by pointing out the people's violations of the Deuteronomic law." In my view, here the deuteronomistic editor is not consciously historicizing ('in the time of the judges'), but simply describing prophets and prophecy as he understands them always to have functioned. I would also argue that 'Deuteronomic law' may well have included certain authoritative prophetic oracles.

[12] Ibid., 171: "...orthodox Deuteronomic theology... [they] suffer because they violate God's commands."

clares... (1 Sam 2:31) 'See, a time is coming...'"[13] Here the understanding of prophecy as an extension of, and a response to, a *previous* 'word' of God has turned the recitation of God's gracious deeds into the form of statements of obligation. Or, to put it another way, the existence of an emergent *scripture* has perhaps strengthened the tendency of the deuteronomists to think of God's self-revelation and the work of the prophets as primarily *verbal*.

This tendency provides a point of major contrast between prophets and judges in the Deuteronomistic History, for in no instance does any of the judges make reference to a previous statement by God (the three passages previously noted did not feature judges!). The significance of the contrast is heightened (it is, admittedly, an argument from silence) when one remembers that in many other ways the judges are said to display behaviors and functions quite similar to those of the prophets (e. g., irregular and charismatic succession, 'spirit possession,' war leadership and oracles).[14]

In fact, within the context of the Deuteronomistic History the rationale for the period of the judges may well be to illustrate by negative example Israel's need for the prophetic word.[15] The increasing lawlessness of the final chapters in Judges and the repeated refrain 'all the people did what was right in their own eyes' (בעיניו, Jud 17:6b; 21:25b) appear to be set in contrast to the lawfulness of the monarchy (Jud 17:6a; 21:25a: 'In those days there was no king in Israel...' Cf. Jud 18:1; 19:1).[16] Furthermore, the mention of 'eyes' is difficult not to connect with 1 Sam 1–3, given the many references in those chapters to blindness or sight.[17]

Thus the blindness of Eli serves as the culmination of Israel's spiritual blindness throughout the period of the judges, to which the revelation of God to Samuel provides a direct response and contradiction. In this context, 1 Sam 3:21 emphasizes *visual* revelation: "The LORD continued to *appear* (להראה) at Shiloh, for the LORD *revealed* himself (נגלה) to Samuel at Shiloh by the word of the LORD" (my emphases). In 1 Sam 1–3, then, a mosaic prophet

---

[13] My emphases.

[14] See WILSON, Prophecy, 166–69; GOTTWALD, Kingdoms, 50–51.

[15] WEINFELD, Conquest, 398, points out that in the final form of the book of Judges the problems of the period are blamed upon the sin of the north in not expelling the Canaanites — as the north was *told* to do (Jud 1:28; 2:1–5).

[16] I wonder in this context whether מלך in Jud 17:6; 18:1; 19:1; 21:25 is intended to refer to a *human* monarch at all. The belief is clear from the Gideon cycle (e. g., Jud 8:22–23), the Abimelech account (Jud 9) and the anti-monarchial Saul stories (e. g., 1 Sam 8:7; 10:17–19; 12:12) that only God should be sovereign in Israel. It therefore seems somewhat contradictory to introduce a positive concept of a human monarchy within Judges. Is it not perhaps possible that the absence of a 'king' here refers just as much to Israel's willful distance from its *divine* sovereign as merely the absence of a human ruler? See Isa 43:15.

[17] E. g., 1 Sam 1:18; 2:17, 29, 32–33; 3:1, 2, 21.

'sees' by the 'word,' as opposed to those increasingly blind judges (e. g., Samson!) for whom the word of God was 'rare.'[18]

Aspects of the deuteronomistic understanding of prophecy are also quite pronounced in the story of Saul's rise to the monarchy (esp. 1 Sam 7; 8; 10:17–27; 12).[19] Thus 1 Sam 7:3–17 displays the same pattern of prophetic deliverance discerned in Jud 6:7–10.[20] God's speech in response to Samuel's intercession in 1 Sam 8:7–9 continues the idea of prophecy as 'warning' (עד, 1 Sam 8:9) and deliverance of 'the words of the LORD' (1 Sam 8:10) that we encountered in the book of Deuteronomy. Motifs of the Exodus and serving 'other gods' (אלהים אחרים) also figure prominently in the passage, but most important is the understanding of prophecy as the repeated communication (העד תעיד, 1 Sam 8:9) of a *known standard* of behavior. In fact, it is precisely the inevitable royal violations of such a standard which form the basis of the extended critique of the monarchy in 1 Sam 8:10–18.

The same understanding functions in 1 Sam 10:17–27, in which Samuel speaks prophetically to the people at Mizpah. Here again, the event of the Exodus is cited in the form of a *statement* of God (1 Sam 10:18) that provides a prior standard (1 Sam 10:19, understood as behavior that acknowledges God's sovereignty). Then the speeches of 1 Sam 8:7–9 and 1 Sam 10:17–19 find their narrative completion in 1 Sam 10:25, in which Samuel writes the 'manner' (משפט, cf. 1 Sam 8:9) of kingship in a book and lays it up 'before the LORD.' In an explicit way, this notice relates the prophetic role not only to acknowledged verbal standards of behavior, but to *written texts*.

An implied standard also figures behind Samuel's defense of his office (1 Sam 12:1–5) and his recitation of Israel's salvation history (1 Sam 12:6–18). This is the first example of a major prophetic speech after Jos 23–24. As in Jos 24, the motif of 'witness' structures the whole. Here, however, explicit mention is made of God's spoken commandments[21] and the people's ethical obligation.[22] Israel's salvation history continues to provide an *implicit* standard (1 Sam 12:24), which is invoked to undermine the people's request for a king (i. e., other than God). However, the *specifics* of Samuel's own defense (i. e., he claims not to have stolen, defrauded, oppressed, or taken a bribe) and reference to 'the good and right way' (בדרך הטובה והישרה) refer to *explicit* standards, which are apparently sufficiently known as to be without need of further definition or enumeration.

---

[18] 1 Sam 3:1; cf. the deuteronomistic summary in Jud 2:10–11.

[19] For justification of these sections as 'deuteronomic,' see WILSON, Prophecy, 172–74. Cf. BIRCH, Rise.

[20] WILSON, Prophecy, 179.

[21] See קל and פי יהוה in 1 Sam 12:14–15; but cf. קל in Jos 24:24.

[22] See בדרך הטובה והישרה in 1 Sam 12:23.

The deuteronomistic conception of 'law and prophets' appears in a new formulation in 1 Sam 15. There, the scene of Saul's rejection, God's 'word' (דבר) is mentioned several times,[23] both as that which Samuel reports and that which Saul rejects. Decisive, however, is Saul's remark to Samuel in 1 Sam 15:24 that he has transgressed 'the commandment of the LORD and *your* [i. e., Samuel's] words.'[24] Not only is authority hereby granted to Samuel's prophetic pronouncements ('your words'), but their authority is firmly paired with the authority of God's commandments.[25] In my judgment, this dual conception of 'the commandment and the words' is not only typically deuteronomistic, but also proto-canonical in terms of its content, form and function: the law and the prophets.

The Books of Kings

Turning to the books of Kings, we find the same proto-canonical understanding of 'law and prophets.' 1 Kg 8, a chapter long thought to exhibit multiple layers of deuteronomistic redaction, uses the occasion of Solomon's dedicatory prayer at the newly-completed Temple to 'proclaim the law' to the people.[26] In spite of the fact that a critical consensus regarding redactional layers in this chapter has not emerged, the general deuteronomistic character of the material is not seriously disputed.[27] Whatever the precise editorial history, the present text depicts Solomon as calling upon mosaic tradition (1 Kg 8:9, 16, 21, 51, 53, 56), adjuring Israel to keep the covenant (1 Kg 8:21, 24) and to observe the law (1 Kg 8:56–61).[28]

As with figures in the passages from Judges and Samuel already discussed, Solomon also cites authoritative prophecy from the past,[29] but these 'citations' are never prefaced by any prophetic formula. Rather than a prophet himself, Solomon *repeats* the authoritative 'word' (1 Kg 8:26, 56, 59) delivered to God's servant David *through* (ביד) God's servant Moses (1 Kg 8:53, 56). Moreover, Solomon does not distinguish here between the direct speech of God to David and the prophetic oracle delivered by Nathan in 2 Sam 7 (cf. 1 Kg 8:18, 'the LORD said…').

---

[23] Pl. in 1 Sam 15:1; sg. in 1 Sam 15:10, 23, 26.

[24] את־פי־יהוה ואת־דבריך acc. to the MT; my emphasis. Many other mss exhibit the singular דברך. For a similar formulation of 'dual' authorities, cf. 1 Sam 12:14–15, 23.

[25] Cf. 1 Sam 3:21–4:1, with the pairing of 'the word of the LORD' and 'the word of Samuel.'

[26] See NELSON, Redaction, 69–71, for a discussion of exegetical issues and the history of interpretation. He argues for the assignation of 1 Kg 8:44–51 to his reconstructed 'second deuteronomist' and 8:52–53, 59–60 to a still later editor (following NOTH).

[27] See LEVENSON, Temple.

[28] To be sure, Solomon is also depicted as referring to David and to God's promise of a royal dynasty (1 Kg 8:15–20, 24–26, 66).

[29] 1 Kg 8:12–13, 15–16, 18–19, 25, 29; cf. the statement by God in 1 Kg 9:5.

Not only is God's word characterized prophetically as 'fulfilled' (מלא),[30] but all of the prophetic words of the past are viewed as constituting a collective unity. Thus in 1 Kg 8:56 we read that "not one word has failed of all [God's] good promise [sg.!], which he spoke through his servant Moses." Here most explicitly — but implicitly shot through the rest of the chapter by use of the term דבר (= NRSV 'promise') — is the sense that *all* of prophecy comprises a unified 'good word' communicated at various times and contexts by God's faithful servants.[31]

As in Deut 34:10–12 it is therefore the *prophet* Moses (1 Kg 8:53) who provides the model for communicating God's word of deliverance (1 Kg 8:51–53) and obedience (1 Kg 8:58). In keeping with deuteronomistic tradition, the stress here lies upon the stance of the *heart*[32] necessary for true obedience to God's 'commandments, statutes and ordinances.' Just as the deuteronomistic Moses and the prophets do (Mal 3:22–24 [4:4–6]), Solomon proclaims that obedience requires repentance. This basic deuteronomistic motif functions within a conceptual framework in which legal traditions and prophetic traditions have coequal authority.

1 Kings 17–19, the Elijah Stories

Although they are not deuteronomistic 'speeches,' the Elijah–Elisha sagas (1 Kg 17–2 Kg 13) dominate the final form of the books of Kings by virtue of their unusual length and central placement. Interestingly, traces of deuteronomistic editing are thought to be slight in these chapters. Rather, it seems likely that the narrative existed in substantial form prior to the work of the deuteronomists and was subsequently incorporated into the Deuteronomistic History with only modest modifications.[33] This suggests in turn that any indications in these stories of coordination between legal and prophetic traditions may well mark the early beginnings of such an impulse, especially if other typical deuteronomistic language and expressions are absent.[34]

There do exist some deuteronomistic *terms*. In 1 Kg 18:18 Elijah refers to the 'commandments of the LORD' (מצות יהוה) and in 1 Kg 19:10, 14 to God's 'covenant' (ברית). In 1 Kg 18:37 Elijah uses a deuteronomistic expression for 'turning' one's heart (ואתה הסבת את־לבם אחרנית), similar in conception to others previously analyzed in this study.[35] Taken together, these references

---

[30] 1 Kg 8:15, 24; cf. לא־נפל דבר אחד in 1 Kg 8:56.

[31] Cf. Deut 32:44–47; Jos 23:14–16.

[32] See 1 Kg 8:37, 38, 47, 48, 58; cf. 9:4.

[33] WILSON, Prophecy, 192–94.

[34] I. e., because the absence of other deuteronomistic features could indicate this coordination of traditions pre-dates the deuteronomistic editing of the narrative.

[35] Cf. Deut 4:39; 30:1, 10 and Mal 3:24 [4:6].

subtly shape the literary portrait of Elijah in the direction of a deuteronomistic prophet, but without major editorial expansion.

More significant, however, are the many ways in which the *figure* of Elijah is depicted as a prophet like Moses. It would be difficult to over-emphasize the number of parallels or the force of their combined literary effect.[36] Even Joshua pales as a claimant to Moses' role and authority when viewed in comparison to Elijah.

In large measure, Elijah's singular relation to Moses hangs upon his prophetic reenactment of the Sinai theophany (1 Kg 19).[37] Journeying miraculously for forty days and nights (cf. Ex 24:18; 34:28) to 'Horeb the mount of God' (1 Kg 19:8), Elijah is told to stand upon the mountain (cf. Ex 19:20) while God passes by (cf. Ex 33:19–23). A great wind rends the mountains and the rocks, followed by an earthquake (cf. Ex 19:18). But in direct contrast to God's speech to Moses in the 'thunder' (קוֹל, Ex 19:19), God responds to Elijah in silence (קוֹל דממה דקה, 1 Kg 19:12)[38] and then with an audible question (קוֹל, 1 Kg 19:13), which elicits from the prophet a complaint (1 Kg 19:14).

Then God responds again, this time with specific directions for the prophet (1 Kg 19:15–18). These directions conclude with reference to the 'seven thousand in Israel' whose 'knees have not bowed to Baal' (1 Kg 19:18), tying this passage to 1 Kg 18, as well as to Ex 32. The intertextual connection with the book of Exodus is strengthened by the similarity of Elijah's injunction in 1 Kg 18:21 ("If the LORD is God, follow him; but if Baal, then follow him.") to Moses' charge to the people in Ex 32:26 ("Who is on the LORD's side? Come to me!").[39]

The literary relationship of 1 Kg 19 to the Sinai narrative is thus impossible to ignore.[40] To be sure, contradictions and doublets within 1 Kg 19 suggest that 1 Kg 19:9b–12 are secondary.[41] This probably indicates a later deu-

---

[36] WILSON, Prophecy, 197–99 for a more detailed discussion and additional citations.

[37] Ibid., 198.

[38] = NRSV: 'a sound of sheer silence.'

[39] Cf. also Jos 24:15.

[40] This is true even if the direction of influence was historically opposite, and the Elijah story/tradition lies behind the present form of the Sinai theophany. The effect of the final form of the text is that Elijah *repeats*, and thus partakes in, Moses' great work. However, influence from the Elijah tradition upon the Sinai narrative would also help to undergird my earlier argument for seeing the mosaic portrait as prophetically-influenced, and thus provide supporting evidence for the early authority of prophetic stories.

[41] MONTGOMERY, Kings, 313. In 1 Kg 19:13 Elijah has not yet left the cave he was in (cf. 1 Kg 19:9a), although 1 Kg 19:11–12 appear to presume that he is on top of the mountain as God had directed. 1 Kg 19:13b–14 repeat 1 Kg 19:9b–10.

teronomistic intensification of the pattern already present in the source material (cf. Deut 4:33, 36; 5:22–27).[42]

Finally, there is the reference to Elisha in 1 Kg 19:16 as a prophet 'in your [i. e., Elijah's] place' (תַּחְתֶּיךָ). This formulation operates within the conceptual framework of a prophetic succession. In fact, the Elijah–Elisha relation occupies such a significant literary position within the books of Kings that it is difficult not to view their example as typifying prophetic succession for those who shaped the material.[43] This succession clearly has a mosaic connection; it cannot be accidental that Elisha's first prophetic act after picking up Elijah's mantle is to part the waters of the Jordan.[44]

In the final form of the text, however, the figure of Elijah is not subordinated to that of Moses at all.[45] The repetition of the Sinai theophany, that most central of all Moses' actions, invokes an equal authority for Elijah the *prophet*, even as it relates him intrinsically to the role of Moses the *lawgiver*:

> "The account of the theophany enhances Elijah's authority in two ways. First, by portraying him as a mosaic prophet, the text assigns Elijah a status which is superior to that of his prophetic contemporaries. As a prophet like Moses, Elijah's word always comes true (cf. 1 Kg 17:16, 24), and his actions are based on a unique relationship to Yahweh. Second, the theophany itself confers a new status on Elijah and by extension on all future mosaic prophets. Elijah's authority is the authority of Moses, and the prophet's word is a divine word, fully comparable to the Torah, the Law given to Moses at Horeb."[46]

Unlike Moses, Elijah does not receive written dictates from God (cf. Ex 34:27–28), yet the authority granted to the prophetic role in this episode is astonishingly weighty.

In fact, clearly visible within the present canon is a conception of *two* Sinai experiences, affirming the *two* primary media of God's revelation: law and prophecy. Elijah is rendered paradigmatic — the prophetic 'father' not only of a 'company of prophets,'[47] but of a particular prophetic mission (cf. Mal 3:23–24 [4:5–6]). The success of this mission is noted at the conclusion of the Elisha stories (2 Kg 9:36–37; 10:10). The essentiality of the prophetic role within Israel is assumed (2 Kg 5:8; 6:12). Furthermore, 2 Kg 2:19–25 would

---

[42] The pre-deuteronomistic version of this account was probably also set at Sinai, as indicated by the question God asks in 1 Kg 19:9b (= 1 Kg 19:13): 'What are you doing *here*, Elijah?' Even if the reference to Horeb in 1 Kg 19:8 is redactional, the word 'here' (פֹּה) implies the same location. Also, the identity of '*the* [!] cave' (הַמְּעָרָה) may have already been intended to match Ex 33:22–23, which tells of the 'cleft of the rock' (בְּנִקְרַת הַצּוּר) in which Moses hid. For more on this possibility, see WILSON (Prophecy, 198).

[43] SCHÄFER-LICHTENBERGER, "Joshua"; T. COLLINS, Mantle, 136–37

[44] See 2 Kg 2:13–14. Cf. Moses in Ex 14; Joshua in Jos 3.

[45] *Contra* T. COLLINS, Mantle, 133–34.

[46] WILSON, Prophecy, 199.

[47] Ibid., 140–41.

appear to reflect an understanding of prophecy as blessing (2 Kg 2:19–22) and curse (2 Kg 2:23–25),[48] an understanding closely connected to the deuter-onomistic idea of 'covenant.'

In sum, it is not evident in these chapters to what extent prophecy (or law!) has been conceived of as an emergent textual tradition,[49] but clearly an effort was made to portray the authority of prophecy as fully equal to that of the law. The effect has been intensified by the later redactional addition of 1 Kg 19:9b–13a, and is nowhere contradicted within the final form of the text: God spoke directly to Elijah at Sinai, too.

2 Kings 17:7–23 and 21:10–15

To pursue the move towards a more textualized understanding of law and prophecy, one need only turn to 2 Kg 17:7–23, the deuteronomists' great dis-course on the fall of the northern kingdom. Like other passages we have ex-amined, the bulk of this chapter represents another of the deuteronomistic compositions identified by Noth.[50] The redactional problems of this chapter are extremely complicated and no single reconstruction has gained wide ac-ceptance. My present purpose, however, is the more modest one of illustrating how this chapter contributes to the growth of a theological conception of 'law and prophets' within the Old Testament.

Credit goes to R. E. Clements for recognizing the full significance of 2 Kg 17:7–23 for later views of prophecy, especially that of prophecy as 'pro-claiming the law.'[51] As Clements has shown, here the deuteronomistic unity of law and prophets is made fully explicit and historicized. The prophets are treated as a collective initiative of God within history. Despite God's com-mand not to serve idols,[52] the people of Israel did 'wicked things' (דברים רעים) and 'provoked the LORD to anger' (2 Kg 17:11). However, in a second, patient dispensation, God 'warned' (ויעד)[53] Israel 'by (ביד) every prophet and every seer' (2 Kg 17:13).

On this understanding, every (true) prophet and seer within Israel's history performed essentially the same function. They continue to be heard as having spoken for God as if in one voice: "Turn from your evil ways and keep my

---

[48] T. COLLINS, Mantle, 138.

[49] Note the contrast to a passage like 2 Kg 14:6.

[50] For discussion, see NELSON, Redaction, 55–57. Whereas NOTH attributed 2 Kg 17:7–20 to the Deuteronomistic Historian and 2 Kg 17:21–23 to a secondary deuteronomistic editor, NELSON (Redaction, 63) assigns 2 Kg 17:7–20, 23b to a secondary editor and 2 Kg 17:21–23a to a later, third phase of redaction. On 2 Kg 17:24–26, see NELSON (Redaction, 63–65).

[51] CLEMENTS, Tradition.

[52] Formulated in 2 Kg 17:12 as a prior apodictic statement!

[53] Cf. prophecy as 'warning' in Deut 31; Jos 24; 1 Sam 8; 12.

commandments and my statutes in accordance with all the law that I commanded your ancestors and that I sent to you by my servants the prophets" (2 Kg 17:13). Not only do these words 'proclaim the law,' but here the prophets indirectly enjoin obedience to themselves ('all the law'// 'my servants the prophets').[54] Together the seers and prophets delivered God's 'warnings' (עדות, 2 Kg 17:15), warnings for Israel to keep its covenant with God.

Now, however, these warnings have received the same rejection as the law (2 Kg 17:15–16), which provokes God to even greater anger and results first in Israel's destruction and then Judah's (2 Kg 17:18–20). From the deuteronomistic perspective, not only has Israel's rejection of the law brought about the Exile, but its rejection of the prophets as well.

It is interesting in this context to note that in 2 Kg 17:34b–40, a passage perhaps from the same hand as 2 Kg 17:7–20,[55] the term תורה is used rather unimpressively as simply *one part* of the complete codification of God's will — "the statutes and the ordinances and the law (תורה) and the commandment" (2 Kg 17:34, 37) that *God* 'wrote' (!) for Israel. R. D. Nelson has suggested that this use of תורה entails a demotion of written law, as here it is only one term within a series.[56] In reality, however, each of these formulations (*contra* Nelson) is slightly different. Also, it is not at all clear that these formulations reflect a conscious effort to 'demote' mosaic Torah, they may simply acknowledge the diversity of Israel's religious inheritance.

2 Kg 21:10–15 provides another summary of the words of God's 'servants the prophets,' a pastiche of prophetic judgment statements delivered in response to Manasseh's reintroduction of the 'abominable practices of the nations' (2 Kg 21:2).[57] Against the background of 2 Kg 17, it is clear that the contrast in 2 Kg 21 is not simply between the practices of the nations and the practices that God desires for Israel, but between apostate practices without basis in Israel's authoritative tradition and the practices authorized and enjoined by Israel's mosaic tradition of 'Law and Prophets' (2 Kg 21:8, 10). The

---

[54] The phrase '[my] servants the prophets' could be an old expression, with its roots in the history of the northern kingdom: e. g., 2 Kg 9:7. See NELSON, Redaction, 58; GRAY, Kings, 541. Here, however, the expression appears to be used in a more inclusive sense (cf. 2 Kg 17:23). This is especially the case if, as WILSON has argued (Prophecy, 224 n. 132), the inclusion of 'every seer' (כל-חזה) was intended by the deuteronomists to make the role of Jerusalemite 'intermediaries' theologically parallel to that of the Ephraimite prophets in Israel's history.

[55] NELSON, Redaction, 65.

[56] Occurring also, NELSON notes (Redaction, 64–65) in Jos 22:5; Jer 44:10, 23 and Ex 24:12.

[57] See LONG, Kings, 249; MONTGOMERY, Kings, 520–21. LONG stresses the 'stylized' quality of the deuteronomistic language; MONTGOMERY helpfully provides parallels from the prophetic books for particular words and phrases.

written basis of this tradition is then reemphasized by the account of Josiah's discovery of 'the book of the law' in 2 Kg 22–23.[58]

Because 2 Kg 22–23 has been central to historical-critical efforts to date the *origin* of authoritative scripture within Israel,[59] it is often overlooked that such a view is entirely at odds with the narrative's self-understanding. Just what 'book' was found during the reign of Josiah is not clear; however, the Deuteronomistic History *presumes* the existence of a written law from the time of Moses (e. g., Deut 31–32; 1 Kg 2:3). Within the final form of the text, Josiah's discovery seems to be set against the fifty-five year reign of Manasseh, perhaps suggesting a belief that the document had been hidden in the Temple for safekeeping at the time of Manasseh's construction there of new altars (1 Kg 21:5).

There is some indication that the discovered book contained unknown laws of greater antiquity than the time of Hezekiah (2 Kg 23:22), but there also appears to be a familiarity with its existence (2 Kg 22:8, note the definite article), if not with the details of its contents. The synchronic assumption seems to be that although the book had existed from the time of Moses, its specifics had been ignored or disregarded (2 Kg 22:13) — thus the significance of the subsequent proclamation in which 'all the words' were read to 'all' (2 Kg 23:2).[60] Certainly there is no sense in the narrative of the kind of 'pious fraud' that historical scholarship since de Wette has frequently insinuated.[61]

Summary

Throughout the Deuteronomistic History both mosaic law and mosaic prophecy are viewed as already-recognized authorities. In the earliest layers of the work, prophecy is already regarded as just as authoritative as mosaic law (e.

---

[58] 2 Kg 22:8, 11; cf. 2 Kg 23:24; cf. also the 'book of the covenant' (ספר הברית) in 2 Kg 23:2–3, 21.

[59] It was DE WETTE who made the historical argument that the reason the contents of the lawbook were previously disregarded was because they were in fact unknown. Written on the authority of Moses, these previously unknown laws formed the basis for the deuteronomic reforms introduced in the time of Josiah. DE WETTE's reconstruction made it possible to date Deuteronomy with a new certainty and thus provided a starting point for historical reconstructions in Old Testament studies which has been used ever since. See ROGERSON, Founder. In my treatment I am not rejecting DE WETTE's argument completely, only attempting to illustrate the distance between historical reconstruction and the self-understanding of the narrative, a point now made generally within biblical studies with greater frequency and urgency than even a generation ago. I simply wish to make the case that the final form of the text stands at some distance to the view that there are no traces of a written law until this period in Israel's history.

[60] RYLE, Canon, 61–63.

[61] DE WETTE himself was more cautious than to make the claim of a 'pious fraud,' arguing only that the historical evidence was insufficient for a determination of the book's origin. See ROGERSON, Criticism, 31.

g., 1 Kg 17–19); later layers of the history increasingly refer both to the written character of the law and the collective character of the prophets.

It is this collective aspect, especially when paralleled with written mosaic law, which suggests an awareness of an emergent prophetic corpus of scripture. Increasingly the prophets are heard to speak with one voice,[62] perhaps because as written texts their 'words' can now be read and heard together. It seems unlikely that such a development would have occurred on the basis of exclusively oral traditions.

In fact, oral prophecy appears to be in the process of being replaced by a kind of textual prophecy in which the words of the prophets can be heard to prophesy without the agency of any particular prophet at all (2 Kg 17:13; 21:10; 24:2; cf. 24:13). The words the prophets 'speak' are now 'former' words which resonate, fulfilling themselves in a contemporary situation removed in time from the narrative setting of the texts in which they are preserved (e. g., 2 Kg 21:11–15). As in the case of Deut 32, the composite character of this new kind of prophetic oracle likely points to an emergent prophetic corpus.

Thus, although it could be argued that the prophetic words reported in this way are general allusions (i. e., not explicit citations of written texts) and could have been appropriated from oral tradition, in my judgment the depiction of these prophetic words as spoken with *one* voice by a *collection* of largely *anonymous* prophets suggests a form of written prophetic tradition parallel to the tradition of written law.[63]

In this way, a dialectic of law and prophecy exists within the Deuteronomistic History which cannot be restricted to one or more levels of redaction, *contra* Smend and his followers.[64] Furthermore, there is good reason to believe that the kinds of themes and motifs identified by Cross and his students may be more complementary than competitive.[65] Still, there do seem to be redactional motifs within the History, and even groups of similar material,

---

[62] 2 Kg 17:13; 21:10; 24:2; cf. 2 Kg 24:13.

[63] WILSON, Prophecy, 291: "The increase in prophetic anonymity also accounts for the late tendency to write prophetic oracles rather than deliver them orally. Anonymous prophecy cannot be oral..."

[64] For further criticism, MCKENZIE, Use, 1–15; WILSON, Prophets. As MCKENZIE points out, the prophecy-fulfillment scheme is far too general to ascribe to a particular level of redaction. This renders the status of 'Dtr P' especially problematic within the reconstructions of those scholars who follow SMEND's theory.

[65] For this criticism, see FRETHEIM, History, 26.

which appear to reflect a common perspective and shaping.[66] I hope I have given adequate reasons for my position that from the earliest deuteronomistic material in the History to the latest, a chief concern for the deuteronomistic editors was the *joint* authority of mosaic law and prophecy — both of which were in the process of becoming increasingly textualized as the History itself was being edited.

Jeremiah

With the prevalence of the view that associates the prophet Jeremiah (or the redaction of at least one edition of his book) with the deuteronomists,[1] it is to be expected that a theological construct as important as the one for which I have argued should occur here, too. As I shall argue, the book of Jeremiah does not fail to provide further evidence for the thesis.

In this case, much of the exegetical evidence necessary to support my claim has already been marshaled in a brief article by U. Rüterswörden.[2] Rüterswörden's starting point is the LXX substitution of ἐξηγητὴς for MT חזון in Prov 29:18, a particularly problematic translation because the Hebrew substantive 'vision' (חזון) is apparently replaced by a kind of occupation ('exegete'?).[3] Wishing to explore this curiosity further, Rüterswörden agrees that the LXX has understood the חזון of its Hebrew *Vorlage* as an Aramaic nominal form (חזן), which is otherwise attested and would thus be read as 'seer' on parallel with 1 Chr 29:29 (החצה).[4]

In making that connection, however, Rüterswörden also notes that the seer of 1 Chr 29:29 is not really a 'seer' at all, but a 'prophet who writes canonical portions' (*ein Kanonsteile schreibender Prophet*).[5] Next he adduces further evidence to show that the Greek ἐξηγητὴς carries prophetic overtones and associations, relating the Greek understanding of ἐξηγητὴς to later Jewish notions of the 'prophet' as an inspired interpreter of the Law. Then Rüterswör-

---

[66] The judgment of ALBERTZ (Intentionen, 40) seems appropriate in the light of current scholarship: "...der Text Dtn 1 – 2. Kön 25 [läßt] an vielen Stellen ein Wachstum erkennen; doch bezweifle ich, daß sich die Ergänzungen durchlaufenden Redaktionen zuordnen lassen. Angemessener ist es, mit einem fortlaufenden Diskussionsprozeß innerhalb der Trägergruppe zu rechnen."

[1] See HYATT, Edition; NICHOLSON, Preaching; THIEL, Jeremia 1–25; idem, Jeremia 26–45; WEINFELD, Deuteronomy; WEIPPERT, Prosareden; WILSON, Prophecy, 231–51.

[2] RÜTERSWÖRDEN, Exegeten.

[3] Ibid., 326.

[4] Ibid., 327.

[5] Ibid.

den asks about the inner-biblical developments that led to this later notion. How was it that 'prophet' later came to mean something like 'exegete'?

Here Rütersworden also notes that in the Hebrew text (Prov 29:18 MT) חזון is parallel to תורה. He considers, but then rejects, the view of G. Wildeboer that these references are canon-specific, referring to the first two subcollections of the Old Testament.[6] Following the standard three-stage theory of canon formation, such identifications would confirm the 'very late' date of this material, and describe a canon with the first two parts already closed and the third still open.[7]

Rütersworden, however, advances the view that instead of references to the *canon* these terms refer to an earlier view of *prophecy*; namely, that the prophetic 'office' involved in various ways the correlation of the contemporary social situation to the mosaic Torah.[8] Rütersworden then argues that prophecy increasingly came to be institutionalized within society, and traces the beginning of this development back to the deuteronomists (e. g., Deut 16–18).[9]

Identifying the earliest idea of prophecy in the book as that of mediation or intercession (e. g., Jer 6:14),[10] Rütersworden goes on to claim that this earlier idea was then reworked in several ways by the deuteronomists in order to highlight their own view of 'institutional' prophecy. Here Rütersworden points to the redactional heading 'concerning the prophets' (לנבאים) in Jer 23:9, which in his view illustrates the deuteronomistic view of prophecy as an institution.[11] In addition to adducing this kind of redactional material, Rütersworden argues that the deuteronomists also introduced new formulations into the main body of the text[12] (illustrating again the deuteronomistic tendency to view prophecy as an institution parallel to the monarchy and the priesthood), and repeated earlier sayings in the jeremianic tradition to make the same point.[13]

In my view, whether or not prophecy functioned historically as an *institution* parallel to the monarchy and the priesthood, these passages serve to indicate the later view of the prophets as a collective unity within Israel's history

---

[6] Ibid., 328. He cites WILDEBOER, Sprüche, 83: "Unter חזון und תורה versteht unser Sammler wohl die Bücher der Nebiim und der Thora. Er ist davon überzeugt, daß der Unterricht der Weisen darauf gegründet ist und damit übereinstimmt."

[7] RÜTERSWORDEN, Exegeten, 328.

[8] Ibid.

[9] Ibid., 330. It is interesting that RÜTERSWORDEN explicitly differentiates his position here from that of WEBER (cf. his Sociology, 46–59). In RÜTERSWORDEN's view institutionalization does not necessarily imply the absence of charisma.

[10] RÜTERSWORDEN, Exegeten, 331.

[11] Ibid., 332–33.

[12] E. g., Jer 2:8, 26; 4:9; 8:1; 13:13; 32:32; cf. Jer 1:18.

[13] E. g., Jer 8:10–12 from Jer 6:12–15, precipitated by the *Stichwort* תורה in Jer 8:8 and the reference to the 'wise.'

and connect the treatment of prophecy within the book of Jeremiah to the deuteronomistic tradition.

Even more important for my purposes are Rüterswörden's examples of the shaping of this 'institution' within the tradition. Here he notes the deuteronomistic notion of תורה as being 'in the mouth of the prophets.'[14] Thus Jer 1:9b recapitulates and fulfills Deut 18:18, the promise of a prophetic succession originating with Moses.[15] This promise functions polemically within the book, true prophets being understood as those who confront the people with the message of their total failure before the Law. This basic understanding of prophecy issues forth in two further related motifs: the 'words' of God as referring to a unified message *parallel* to the תורה, and references to God's 'servants the prophets' as that succession of mosaic prophets responsible for the proclamation of a *unified* message.

'The Law and the Words'

As an example of the first motif, Rüterswörden adduces Jer 6:19b: "...because they have not given heed to my words (דברי), and as for my teaching (ותורתי), they have rejected it." Here the parallelism of 'words' and Torah entails greater specificity than simply referring to divine speech in general. Rüterswörden takes דברים in this sense to refer to prophetic *teaching*, to which priestly teaching or תורה is parallel. He again rejects the notion that such terms refer to parts of the written canon, instead postulating a deuteronomistic conception of the prophetic word which is neither the 'oral Torah' or the written Torah, but 'something in-between.'[16] It is this same conception, he believes, that ultimately connects Prov 29:18 (MT) and Prov 29:18 (LXX).

In my view, however, the תורה and דברים of this formulation, although surely not identical to the first two parts of the MT, most likely refer to the emerging collections of scripture that later came to bear the names תורה and נביאים. The full oracle compares (Jer 6:16–17) God's 'words' and 'teaching' to 'ancient paths' (נתבות עולם) — tangible guides to conduct ('the good way') and reliable sources of fulfillment ('rest for your souls.'). The people are asked to 'see' (ראו) these paths,[17] to 'walk in them' (לכו-בה) and to 'heed' (הקשיבו) the sound of the sentinels who call attention to them. The very *tangibility* of these expressions could provide evidence for written texts as opposed to oral traditions.

---

[14] Jer 1:9; 9:12; 16:11; 26:4–6; 32:23; 44:10, 23.

[15] RÜTERSWÖRDEN, Exegeten, 329; cf. SEITZ, Moses. T. COLLINS has even argued (Mantle, 159) that ultimately *all* of the prophetic call narratives serve to "underline the parallel between the prophets of the books and the Moses who speaks in Deuteronomy."

[16] RÜTERSWÖRDEN, Exegeten, 336.

[17] Jer 6:16, according to the MT; a reconstruction דרכי מראש is also possible.

Rüterswörden cites Isa 1:10 as another text in which the prophetic 'word' is parallel to תורה.[18] On its face, the call to 'hear the word of the LORD' in Isa 1:10 would seem to contain little that would indicate a written text or its interpretation. The two passages contain more in common than the parallelism of 'word' and Torah, however. Thus, the reference to the unacceptability of sacrifices and burnt offerings in Jer 6:20 is paralleled in Isa 1:11.

In my judgment, Isa 1:10–11 most likely comprises a deuteronomistic addition to the book, expanding on the reference to Sodom and Gomorrah in Isa 1:9, but also with an eye towards Jer 6:16–19. It is interesting that the reference to Sodom and Gomorrah moves from a first person metaphor in Isa 1:9 ('we would have been like Sodom and become like Gomorrah') to a second person simile in Isa 1:10 ('you rulers of Sodom... you people of Gomorrah'). There exists in these words (*pace* Rüterswörden) a sense of the prophet as one who relocates the characters and events of Israel's *Heilsgeschichte* within contemporary events. However, there also subtle indications that prophetic traditions had already begun to be textualized and shared (in addition to Jer 6:20, cf. Jer 23:14).

This kind of intertextuality suggests a further question in light of the parallelism found in Jer 6:19b: could the term 'words' refer sometimes in the book of Jeremiah to something like prophetic scripture?

'My Servants the Prophets'

Rüterswörden highlights a second prophetic motif in his treatment of Jer 26:4–6: "Thus says the LORD: 'If you will not listen to me, to walk in my law (תורה) that I have set before you, and to heed the words (דברי) of my servants the prophets whom I send to you urgently...'" Just as in the books of Kings,[19] the language of the prophets as God's 'servants' implies their collective purpose, and the language of sending (שלח) implies the deuteronomistic notion of mosaic succession (cf. 2 Kg 17:13). Here, again, the 'words' of God's 'servants the prophets' are found parallel to God's Torah, *both* of which have been set before the people. In the context of Jer 26, הדברים seems to refer to this specific oracle,[20] but the oracle itself demands that the people obey both God's 'law' and his 'words.' There is thus a *twin* source of authority to which Jeremiah lays claim and upon which God's judgment is said to be founded. The textual nature of this authority would seem to be confirmed when later in the same chapter a century-old prophecy of Micah is cited as an authoritative precedent (Jer 26:18; cf. Mic 3:12).

---

[18] Ibid., 334.

[19] See 1 Kg 14:18; 15:29; 18:36; 2 Kg 9:7, 36; 10:10; 14:25; 17:13, 23; 21:10; 24:2.

[20] Jer 26:2, 7, 12, 15; cf. Jer 26:20.

It is possible that Jer 26:5 represents a later gloss,[21] but the understanding reflected in the final form of the text is neither a foreign intrusion into the chapter, nor a contradiction of the previous deuteronomistic handling of the material. Language of God's 'servants the prophets' runs throughout the book of Jeremiah[22] and could easily have been borrowed for Jer 26:5. The similarity of perspective shared with the books of Kings is amply illustrated by comparison of Jer 25:4–6 and 2 Kg 17:13. In both cases a succession of prophets is not only cited, but *quoted*, as if one single message could be distilled from the immense variety of prophetic actions and oracles throughout Israel's history (cf. Jer 35:15). The deuteronomistic provenance of this conception is clear, with parallel references to God's 'anger'[23] and 'other gods.'[24]

Although 2 Kg 17:13 refers to God's 'servants the prophets' in connection with God's 'law'(cf. 2 Kg 17:15–16) and the prediction of Israel's downfall, it does not refer to the message of God's 'servants the prophets' as 'words,' but rather as 'warnings' (עדות, 2 Kg 17:15). The designation of the prophets' collective message as דברים emerges only when we come to the book of Jeremiah.[25] Jer 44 prefers to speak of God's 'law and statutes' (בתורתי ובחקתי, Jer 44:10 MT), but even here there is reference to Jeremiah's 'word' (הדבר, Jer 44:1, 16), and 'the voice of the LORD' is cited parallel to God's 'law and statutes and decrees' in Jer 44:23.[26]

Thus the terms דבר and דברים display an important collective sense within the book of Jeremiah, which appears to indicate an awareness of a non-Torah collection of authoritative writings.

The 'Word' and the 'Words'

My argument is certainly not that every reference to God's 'word' or 'words' refers to an emergent scripture. 'Words' can refer to God's verbal communications to a particular prophet,[27] or even the oracles of 'false' prophets.[28] The true 'word' of God is not simply to be equated with the 'words' of the prophets[29] any more than with the תורה of the scribes.[30] Still, God's 'word' to the prophet Jeremiah, a true mosaic prophet, is faithfully expressed in Jeremiah's

---

[21] There are grammatical difficulties; see HOSSFELD AND MEYER, Prophet, 47.

[22] See Jer 7:25; 25:4; 29:19; 35:15; 44:4.

[23] See the use of כעס in Deut 32:19, 27; cf. 2 Kg 17:17; 23:26.

[24] אלהים אחרים in Deut 5:7; 6:14; 7:4; 8:19; 11:16, 28; 13:3 [2], 7 [6], 14 [13]; 17:3; 18:20; 28:14, 36, 64; 29:25 [26]; 30:17; 31:18, 20; cf. 2 Kg 17:7, 37.

[25] Jer 7:25–27; 25:4–8; 29:19; 35:13–15; 44:4–10; but see 1 Sam 15:24!

[26] Thus: ולא שמעתם בקול יהוה ובתורתו ובחקתיו ובעדותיו; cf. Deut 15:5; Jer 9:13!

[27] E. g., Jer 5:14; 18:18.

[28] E. g., Jer 23:16.

[29] E. g., Jer 5:13; 23:16–17, 23–32; 27:14–15, 16–18.

[30] Jer 8:8!

'words.'[31] These 'words' in turn come to be represented by the 'words' written "in this book which Jeremiah prophesied against the nations."[32] Jer 36:27 also illustrates a relationship *and* a distinction between God's 'word' and Jeremiah's 'words.'

Thus, a *trajectory* of references to God's 'word' exists with the final form of the book,[33] which realizes itself in the textualization of those 'words' *as a book.*[34] The clearest references to this textualization of the prophetic word are those that also appeal explicitly to *both* of the other motifs we have explored: God's 'servants the prophets' and God's Torah.[35] To this group may then be added those passages that pair 'law' and 'words' without mentioning God's 'servants the prophets.'[36] Within this category, a subgroup seems to exist of passages which mention 'law' and God's 'voice.'[37] Completing the list are those passages in which the expression 'words' appears to have a quasi-technical designation for a written prophetic legacy, but without an accompanying reference to 'law' or 'commandment.'[38] There is, it should be noted, at least one passage in which תורה alone is cited as an authority,[39] but also three passages in which the law is criticized.[40]

To these references may be added the view of L. Rost that within the jeremianic tradition (perhaps for the first time within Israelite thought) the word of God comes to be perceived as something 'objective' which encounters the prophet from outside himself.[41] Thus the 'word of the LORD' (דבר־יהוה) 'comes to' (היה + אל) the prophet,[42] who cannot speak on his own,[43] yet has divine words 'placed' in his mouth.[44] Even though these words are ingested by the prophet,[45] God's word cannot be captured and must ever be sought

---

[31] E. g., Jer 1:4, 9; 30:1–2; 45:1.

[32] Jer 25:13; note the 'speaker' here is God!

[33] Cf. SÆBØ, Canon, 294–96.

[34] Jer 1:1; 25:13; 30:2; 45:1; 51:60–64.

[35] Jer 26:4–5; 44:1–10; cf. without explicit reference to תורה, Jer 7:21–26 (but note Jer 7:9); Jer 29:19 (but note Jer 29:23); Jer 35:13–15 (but note Jer 35:14).

[36] Jer 6:19; 16:10–11.

[37] Jer 9:13; 11:1–5; 44:23. That 'voice' can be a synonym for 'words' in these semantic contexts is indicated by Jer 7:27–28.

[38] Jer 7:27; 25:4, 8, 13, 30; 26:12–13; 29:1, 19; 30:2; 35:13; 36 *passim* (esp. 36:27); 45:1; 51:60–64.

[39] Jer 31:33 [32]; however, the context is highly eschatological.

[40] Jer 2:8; 7:21–25, but without the word תורה; Jer 8:8.

[41] ROST, Gesetz, 29.

[42] Jer 1:2, 4, 11, 13; 2:1; 13:3, 8; 14:1; 16:1; 18:5; 24:4; 25:3; 28:12; 29:30; 43:8; 46:1; 47:1; 49:34. On this formula, see WILSON, Prophecy, 145.

[43] Jer 1:2; 23:31.

[44] Jer 1:9; presumably their origin lies in the divine council, cf. Jer 23:18.

[45] Jer 15:19; 20:7–9.

anew (Jer 37:17).[46] Jer 37:2 emerges as a fitting summary of the relation between God's words and words of the prophets: 'the words of the LORD' are
spoken by God 'through' (בְּיַד) Jeremiah.[47]

A trajectory of the textualization of Jeremiah's 'words' can thus be traced
from occasional letters (e. g., Jer 29; 51:60–64a) to the conscious effort to
construct a compendium of the prophet's teaching (e. g., Jer 30:2; 36; 45) and
even to the book of Jeremiah itself, although in different forms (Jer 25:13; Jer
51:64b; also LXX Jeremiah). Taken together, I believe this evidence points to
a textualized understanding of the 'law and the prophets,' as persistently-
twinned sources of authority within the deuteronomistic/jeremianic tradition.[48] Clearly such textual collections were significantly different from the
final form of the MT and the books that now comprise it; in view of the evidence, however, it seems very unlikely that these cited authorities of 'law'
and 'prophets' were exclusively oral.

A 'Prophet Like Moses'

Rüterswörden discusses a third prophetic motif in the book which also proves
to be useful for the present argument: the characterization of Jeremiah as a
prophet like Moses. Here the most interesting passages are Jer 11:1–5 and Jer
15:1.[49] In Jer 11:1–5, the prophet delivers an oracle enjoining the inhabitants
of Judah to adhere to the mosaic covenant. The covenant referred to is the Sinai covenant of the book of Exodus rather than the Moab covenant of the
book of Deuteronomy.[50] In Jer 15:1, Jeremiah is related to Moses and Samuel
specifically in his role as a prophetic intercessor.[51]

Rüterswörden mentions two other passages in a different context which, it
seems to me, also contribute in a significant way to the characterization of

---

[46] Cf. ROST, Gesetz, 29. He argued interestingly that with the objectification of God's דבר
arises a new suspicion of the prophets. Now that the 'word' is considered to be something
external, the issue of its reliability is more and more expressed as that of its faithful reception
and transmission. The less control prophets claim to have over the content of this 'word,' the
more suspicion attaches itself to them (e. g., Jer 23:28).

[47] Cf. the singular, Jer 27:18.

[48] This is especially true, if, as ROST argued (Gesetz, 13), the formula 'all these words'
(Ex 20:1) derives from the prophetic tradition of the 'word of God.' ROST also noted that
Deuteronomy has been styled as a *prophecy* of Moses within the framework of the book (Ge-
setz, 19). Thus, he proposed, a similar terminology was developed for the recep-
tion/transmission of *both* mosaic law and prophetic word (Gesetz, 38). Cf. LIEDKE,
Rechtssätze, 194–95.

[49] RÜTERSWÖRDEN, Exegeten, 335.

[50] Note, however, that even here (Jer 11:4) the people are commanded to 'listen' to God's
voice as well as to 'do' what God commands; cf. Jos 24:24.

[51] For other parallels and similarities between Jeremiah and Moses, see CLEMENTS,
Jeremiah; and C. R. SEITZ, Moses.

Jeremiah as a mosaic prophet: Jer 17:19–27 and Jer 34.[52] In Jer 17:22 the Decalogue is cited by the prophet quite explicitly.[53] A similar move is seen in Jer 34:14, where the prophet Jeremiah quotes Deut 15:1a, 12 (again, with explicit reference to the mosaic covenant). In these passages, Jeremiah appears to be as much a lawgiver and covenant mediator as Moses (cf. Jer 7:9). While preserving the contours of their *Heilsgeschichte*, the deuteronomistic editors of the book have identified Jeremiah as a covenant mediator like Moses, just as the deuteronomistic editors of Deuteronomy gave the figure and words of Moses a decisively prophetic cast.

Summary

Rüterswörden illustrates convincingly the essential parallelism of the prophetic 'word' and Torah throughout the book of Jeremiah and within deuteronomistic tradition. He consistently underestimates, however, the way in which these authorities represent, already for the book's deuteronomistic editors, emergent scriptural collections. Nevertheless, his treatment serves to illuminate how this parallelism began to function, developing into a canonical framework which would continue long afterwards to coordinate biblical traditions within a basically *heilsgeschichtlich* shape.

With respect to Rüterswörden's skeptical conclusions about canon formation, one must ask if, in light of all the available evidence, it seems plausible that by the time of LXX Proverbs a body of written scripture known as 'the Law and the Prophets' still did not exist. In my view, here Rüterswörden betrays signs of the same problem that bedeviled H. E. Ryle: he is unwilling to concede the existence of anything 'canonical' until texts have been alterably fixed for an 'interval of time.' On the other hand, perhaps Rüterswörden's description of an authoritative prophecy 'in-between' oral pronouncement and written text is finally not at odds with my understanding of an *emergent* body of scripture.

From my perspective, the evidence from the book of Jeremiah not only points to a textualized form of scripture known and acknowledged by the deuteronomists, but also to the way in which they worked to shape scriptural traditions within a 'grammar' that they designated by an overarching parallelism: 'the law and the words.'

---

[52] RÜTERSWÖRDEN, Exegeten, 334.

[53] Cf. Ex 20:8, 10; Deut 5:12, 14. This example does not confute the assertion that the pre-exilic prophets nowhere appealed to the law as the basis for their judgments (the passage is deuteronomistic), but it should provide a caution. For a statement of the assertion, see KOCH, Prophets, II:1. However, even if it is true that these prophets themselves did not appeal to the law, the editors of the books named after them clearly had no difficulty in providing legal precedents for their sayings.

Zechariah 1 and 7–8

First Zechariah (Zech 1–8) presents a continuation of the deuteronomistic conception of 'law and prophets,' but at the same time expands it in new directions. In fact, biblical scholarship has increasingly viewed the entire book of Zechariah as an example of the way in which various pre-exilic streams of tradition were joined in new combinations after the Exile.[1]

Of greatest interest to the present study is the framework to the reconstructed first edition of the book, now found in Zech 1:1–6; 7–8.[2] A persuasive argument has been made that this material is deuteronomistic in origin and outlook.[3] At the same time, however, an equally vigorous argument has been mounted to attribute the framework of the book of a chronistic 'milieu.'[4] In my view, *both* deuteronomistic and chronistic influences play a role; the material reflects the more fluid situation of post-exilic Israel in which the re-use of earlier and sometimes disparate traditions constituted a new *modus operandi* for traditional prophecy.[5]

In making this point I wish to avoid from the outset what appears to me to be a rather hopeless effort to attribute the book of Zechariah *either* to deuteronomistic (and thus, to certain eyes, 'prophetic') *or* chronistic (to certain eyes, 'priestly') tradents. An alleged dichotomy here between 'theocratic' and 'eschatological' parties simply will not work.[6] Thus:

> "We should probably be wise to admit that we have insufficient evidence to enable us to spell out the detailed structure of the [emergent Jewish] community. This is true in general; with specific reference to Haggai and Zechariah we need also to bear in mind... that their

---

[1] WILSON, Prophecy, 289 and the literature he cites in n. 66. Although the deuteronomistic stamp on the material is strong, other traditions are also present, *contra* PERSON, Zechariah. PERSON is apparently unaware of the important work of BEUKEN, Haggai, which persuasively demonstrates the material's links to 'chronistic' traditions. On the mixture of traditions in the post-exilic period generally, see PERLITT, Priesterschrift?

[2] This framework is shared with the book of Haggai; see R. A. MASON, Purpose; R. J. COGGINS, Haggai, 26–28; and esp. MEYERS AND MEYERS, Haggai, xli–xliii. The MEYERS argue persuasively that since Haggai and Zech 1–6 share only a common date formula, the preponderance of shared materials between Haggai and Zech 7–8 suggests that the two books were joined at the same time Zech 7–8 was added to Zech 1–6.

[3] PERSON, Zechariah; see also BLENKINSOPP, History, 235.

[4] BEUKEN, Haggai; R. J. COGGINS, Haggai, 27–29; R. A. MASON, Prophets, 148–50. BEUKEN and MASON helpfully compare Zech 1:3–6 to 2 Chr 30:6–9 and Zech 8:9–13 to 2 Chr 15:3–7.

[5] ZIMMERLI, Proclamation.

[6] *Contra* HANSON, Dawn. For various damaging critiques, see R. J. COGGINS, Haggai, 53–54; COOK, Prophecy, 140–42, 153–55; R. A. MASON, Prophets, 151; idem, Echoes?

words have been edited in such a way as to prevent a picture significantly different from that of their own time."[7]

It is just this editing which is so much at issue. Rather than merely glossing or 'updating' the legacy of the prophet, here the movement of the tradents has been towards the increased reliance upon earlier biblical traditions. In fact, a major feature of Zech 9–14 is often said to be its dependence on earlier prophetic traditions.[8] As we shall see, Zech 1–8 also exhibits this feature.

Prophecy in First Zechariah

As R. J. Coggins has correctly seen, the phenomenon of intertextuality inevitably subverts the historical referentiality of a biblical text.[9] For example, Coggins asks, does the supposed historical reference to Alexander the Great in Zech 9:1–8 remain convincing if we now understand the entire passage as an 'exegesis' of Ezek 28? On the other hand, the phenomenon of intertextuality should not be taken to suggest that prophecy no longer represents a vital tradition of its own. As other exegetes have pointed out:

"Zechariah's sermonic tone and midrashic tendencies may distinguish his work from that of older prophets, but his concern for truth and justice are the same as those of Israel's greatest prophetic figures."[10]

Proceeding from both of these points, I shall argue that the kind of intertextuality discerned in the book reflects a living tradition of prophecy, but one in which prophecy has been transformed from its pre-exilic, oral role into a new pre-occupation with interpreting and reinterpreting written texts.[11]

This process of reinterpretation would have served to express the fresh currency of earlier prophetic material in light of a new situation,[12] but at the same time could not have functioned if that earlier material were not considered to hold authority and power. Post-exilic prophecy such as we find reflected in the book of Zechariah, R. A. Mason reminds us, is increasingly derivative (which is not to say, he notes, that it is therefore lacking in originality

---

[7] R. J. COGGINS, Haggai, 57.

[8] Ibid., 64; cf. R. A. MASON, Haggai, 79; for a list, see MITCHELL, SMITH AND BEWER, Haggai, 237–38 This feature also points to the unlikelihood that Zech 13:1–6 is 'anti-prophetic,' an interpretation I shall address directly in Chapter Six. On this point, see R. A. MASON, Echoes? 234.

[9] R. J. COGGINS, Haggai, 65.

[10] MEYERS AND MEYERS, Haggai, 432.

[11] R. J. COGGINS, Haggai, 21.

[12] Ibid., 31–33.

or inventiveness) precisely *because* emergent prophetic collections were growing in authority.[13]

This is the view stated explicitly by the introduction to the book of Zechariah itself. In Zech 1:1–6, the prophet is directed to tell his contemporaries to 'return' (שׁובו) to God and not be like their fathers, to whom the 'former prophets' (הנביאים הראשנים) 'proclaimed' (קראו) in vain (Zech 1:4). Both their fathers and these prophets no longer live (Zech 1:5) because God's 'words and statutes' (דברי וחקי), which he commanded 'his servants the prophets' have 'overtaken' (השׂיגו) them, fulfilling God's threatened judgment. Zechariah's contemporaries are mindful of the history lesson and repent (Zech 1:6). There then follow, in Zech 1:7–6:15, the seven visions of the prophet.

This introduction provides a fascinating window into post-exilic views of prophecy and scripture. Here we have a new sense of a period of 'classical' prophecy (cf. Zech 7:7, 12). Whatever the precise sense of the qualification 'former,'[14] the parallels found in Zech 7 make it clear that the reference is to *pre-exilic* prophets,[15] as contrasted to the prophets of the Restoration (Zech 8:9–13) of which Zechariah himself is understood to be a part (Zech 1:1).[16]

'The Law and the Words'

The distinction 'former' serves to bind as well as to separate. Like the prophets before the Exile, Zechariah's word from God is also to 'return' (Zech 1:3). As is often the case in the Deuteronomistic History and in Chronicles, however, here too the Exile provides the incontrovertible example of the truth of God's message and God's messengers. The 'former prophets' now possess the greatest kind of prophetic authority: they were right (cf. Deut 18:22). The correctness of their message has outlasted their own mortality (Zech 1:5) because their words continue to be available as 'the words and statutes' of God (Zech 1:6). This expression is paralleled in Zech 7 by the formula 'the law and the words' (את-התורה ואת-הדברים), which God 'sent' (שׁלח) 'by his spirit' (ברוחו) 'by the hand of the former prophets' (Zech 7:12; cf. Zech 7:7). The phrases are striking in their construction and their specificity.

In their commentary, C. and E. Meyers have shown great sensitivity to the scriptural force of these formulas, suggesting that 'the word and the statutes'

---

[13] R. A. MASON, Prophets, 141–42. MASON sets this thesis directly against those who have argued that the living tradition of prophecy disappeared because it was considered to have failed (e. g., CARROL, Prophecy) or had lost its political position after the demise of the monarchy (e. g., CROSS, Myth, 223–29).

[14] I have argued in another context that a variation of this term is sometimes used in deuteronomistic literature to refer to an earlier *period* within Israel's *Heilsgeschichte* (cf. Jos 8:33; Jer 7:12); see Chapter Four.

[15] Zech 7:7, 12–14; cf. Zech 8:11, 'former days' (כימים הראשנים).

[16] *Contra* R. J. COGGINS, Haggai, 83, who argues that for Zechariah 'prophets' only existed in the past.

and 'the law and the words' refer to an emergent canon.[17] Clearly both 'torah/ statutes' and 'words' are presented as twin categories of divine revelation, transmitted (in *both* cases!) through prophetic agency. The pairing suggests a more specific reference than general teaching or instruction. The Meyers see especially in the phrase 'the torah and the words' a "connection to past usage and the invention of a new idiom which may well have a technical connotation."[18] Could 'the torah' here refer to the emergent Pentateuch and 'the words' to an early corpus of prophetic writings, as I have argued for the book of Jeremiah?[19]

'The words' (הדברים) would be a sensible title for a prophetic collection, since many of the prophetic books begin with, and group oracles together, with various 'word' formulas.[20] The resulting superscriptions possess a deuteronomistic flavor, and it has been argued that their uniformity gives a clue to a deuteronomistic collection of prophecy which formed the original nucleus of what later became the prophetic canon.[21] The roots of the literary formulas are likely to be found in an oral call to 'hear the word of the LORD'[22] and, even more fundamentally, in the twin notions of a God who 'speaks' and of a prophet who 'speaks for.' The formulas express the view that it is not the prophet himself who is heard, but the *words* of the prophet — the message of God. Thus the reified language of a 'word' that 'comes to' the prophet as if from outside him-/herself.[23] Failure to understand this very point called forth God's judgment (e. g., Jer 36:29).

---

[17] MEYERS AND MEYERS, Haggai, 402. As I came to the same conclusion independently, working from the Deuteronomistic History and the book of Jeremiah, I feel this conjunction of views provides additional confirmation of the thesis.

[18] Ibid.

[19] The MEYERS (Haggai, xliii; 278) follow FREEDMAN's theory (FREEDMAN, Law) of a Primary History (Genesis–2 Kings), suggesting that התורה in this case may reflect a situation before Deuteronomy was separated from the Deuteronomistic History.

[20] E. g., Jer 1:1–2 (pl.-sg.), 4, 11; 2:1 (narrative), etc.; Hos 1:1; Joel 1:1; Am 1:1 (pl.); Jon 1:1; Mic 1:1; Zeph 1:1; Hag 1:1 (narrative); Zech 1:1 (narrative); Mal 1:1; Ezek 1:3. The exceptions are provided by Isa 1:1 ('vision' = חזון; but note Isa 1:2, 10; 2:1 and similar passages); Ezek 1:1 ('vision' = מראות; but note the verse shows 'word/s' in some LXX and Syriac traditions; it is also interesting that Ezek 1:1–3 contains both kinds of terms, descriptive of sight and sound); Ob 1:1 ('vision' = חזון); Nah 1:1 ('oracle' = משא); Hab 1:1 ('the oracle' = המשא). On these exceptions as reflecting another tradition of prophetic 'intermediation,' perhaps as known in Judah and Jerusalem, see WILSON, Prophecy, 135–46; 253–63.

[21] TUCKER, Superscriptions. In addition to the arguments that TUCKER advances, note that although Dan 1:1 lacks the usual superscription (cf. Dan 7:1; 8:1), the formula appears in the reference to the book of Jeremiah in Dan 9:2!

[22] For discussion, see MEIER, Messenger, esp. 186-90.

[23] A further step is taken in the tradition when in Dan 9:10, 11, 14 the 'voice' (קול) of God is heard from 'the books' (Dan 9:2) which record the prophets' pronouncements of

These Zechariah passages recall similar passages in the book of Jeremiah, not only because of the use of 'word' as the category for prophetic speech, but also by reference to God's 'servants the prophets' (Zech 1:6). As we have previously noted, this phrase also appears in the Deuteronomistic History,[24] in Am 3:7 (usually taken as a deuteronomistic gloss) and the book of Jeremiah.[25]

Here, too, it might be argued that the expressions 'my words and statutes' and 'the law and the words' refer to oral traditions, or are simply later glosses within the book. However, the character of both expressions is so definite as to preclude the possibility of general traditions. Although it has been argued that these expressions reflect later understandings of scripture and canon,[26] I have already shown with reference to Deuteronomy, the Deuteronomistic History and the book of Jeremiah that the basic conception of a two-part history of Israel before God and a two-fold message from God to Israel existed from the very beginning of Israel's canonical impulse.

The same pairing exists in Deut 31–32, with references to 'the words of this song' and 'the words of this law,' or in Jos 1, in which 'the law that my servant Moses commanded you'[27] is paired with 'the word that Moses the servant of the LORD commanded you.'[28] Clearly there is no *a priori* reason to assume it was too early for there to have been behind these references in Zechariah an emergent body of written scripture comprised of two complementary collections.[29]

The Meyers persuasively argue on the basis of a large number of shared connections between Zech 7–8 and the book of Haggai (and the relative paucity of such connections in Zech 1–6) that Zech 7–8 were added to Zech 1–6 when the two books were joined together.[30] Based on the date of the refounding of the Temple (December 18, 520 B. C.), which both Haggai and Zechariah mention, and the date of the rededication of the Temple (516/15 B. C.), which neither book mentions, Haggai and Zechariah 1–8 probably com-

---

God's word according to the law of Moses (Dan 9:10, 11, 13). Cf. Bar 1:21; 2:10, 24, 28–29; 3:4.

[24] 2 Kg 9:7; 17:13, 23; 21:10; 24:2.

[25] Jer 7:25; 25:4; 26:5; 29:19; 35:15; 44:4.

[26] BEUKEN, Haggai, 97.

[27] Jos 1:7, with reference to the past.

[28] Jos 1:13, with reference to the future, including the quotation of a prediction.

[29] Glosses in Zech 1–8 are usually recognizable as first person intrusions into the third person narrative frame: e. g., Zech 7:4; 8:18; perhaps Zech 8:1 also. See MEYERS AND MEYERS, Haggai, 433.

[30] MEYERS AND MEYERS, Haggai, lxi; 405. In their view Zech 7:1 is an artful transposition of Hag 1:1. Note the repetition of the formula in Zech 1:7 and Zech 7:8. Thus Zech 1:1 introduces the book and the introductory section; Zech 1:7 introduces the visions and oracles in Zech 1:8–6:15; and Zech 7:1 introduces Zech 7–8 (Haggai, 398).

prise a single work dating to the period just before 516/15 B. C.[31] The significance of this reconstruction is to provide a date by which we can postulate an already established awareness of a bipartite scriptural heritage.[32]

Citations and Allusions

Other indications that the expressions in Zech 1:6; 7:7, 12 may refer to sacred *writings* can be found in the way in which First Zechariah repeatedly alludes to specific pentateuchal and prophetic traditions. Thus Zech 8:3 seems to refer to Isa 1:21 and Zech 8:8, 13 to Jos 1:6. Nor is it only prophetic hues which color the writer's conceptual palette. In Zech 7:9–10 and again in Zech 8:16–17 we find a summary of God's 'words,' each time set in the form of four imperative statements.[33] The first set appears to be a description of the preaching of the 'former prophets' (Zech 7:7),[34] while the second set recapitulates and reauthorizes the same law for the restoration community (cf. Zech 7:14).

These summaries are not *citations* of scripture as such, at least not in the modern sense. Are they references to oral traditions, or to written texts? The degree of correspondence between reference and referent is not so close as to answer the question in favor of written texts or so distant as to rule written texts out. Clearly the 'literalness' of the allusion/citation is an important, but finally insufficient criterion for a solution to such problems.

Broadening the question to consider Zech 9–14, it should be observed that particularly in these later chapters the *allusion* to scripture becomes more obvious, functioning in such a widespread manner that it arguably becomes the single most defining feature of these chapters.[35] Because this tendency emerges in later Zechariah tradition, it seems plausible that a preoccupation with scripture was likely not to have been foreign to earlier tradents of the work either (i. e., Haggai–Zech 8).[36]

As the Meyers note, moreover, the summaries in Zech 7:9–10 and Zech 8:16–17 are set into the mouths of prophets (pre-exilic and post-exilic), yet the style of the speeches themselves does not seem very prophetic. Rather, the style of address ('these are the things,' Zech 8:16) is reminiscent of Deuteron-

---

[31] Ibid., xliv–xlv.

[32] Ibid., 406.

[33] Ibid.

[34] Understanding Zech 7:8 as a gloss, *pace* R. J. COGGINS, Haggai, 28.

[35] Above all, see R. A. MASON, Haggai. Cf. idem, Relation; BRUCE, Zechariah; R. J. COGGINS, Haggai, 64; MITCHELL, SMITH AND BEWER, Haggai, 237–40.

[36] As R. J. COGGINS, Haggai, 58–59, notes in a slightly different context, it is unlikely that Zech 9–14 would have been completely different or opposed to the views found in Zech 1–8, since they have been joined together literarily into one book.

omy (cf. Deut 1:1).[37] Here would seem to be a new style of prophetic address, which 'proclaims the law' according to the deuteronomistic view of prophecy, but also consists of making "creative use of the evolving corpus of ancient Hebrew scripture."[38]

There are additional indications that written texts may be at issue. First, there is the use of 'proclaim' (קרא) in Zech 1:14, 17; 7:7, 13. The prophet is commanded by God or God's angel to 'proclaim' the divine will, just as by the 'former prophets' God 'proclaimed... the words' (Zech 7:7, הדברים). The Meyers note the use of this verb sometimes to mean reading from a scroll (cf. Jer 36:8, 10; Neh 8:3, 8; Hab 2:2). In this way Zech 1:14, 17 might better be translated 'read,' perhaps inviting the prophet to read particular passages of 'scripture' that speak to his situation. Or, again, Zech 7:7 would suggest that the former prophets had 'read' the words in Zech 7:9–10 to a stubborn, dis-obedient people.[39] The historical point to be made here is not that the pre-exilic prophets were 'readers' of prophecies,[40] but that they were *viewed* as 'readers' by post-exilic prophets *on analogy with* their own post-exilic under-standing of the prophetic role and practices.[41]

There is also the use of the idiom 'from the mouth of the prophets' in Zech 8:9 (מפי הנביאים). Again it is the Meyers who have recognized the textual con-notation of this language, citing its use in Jer 36:4, 6, 17, 18, 27, 32; 45:1 to mean 'dictation.'[42] In Zech 8, the reference seems to be to those post-exilic prophets who were present when the building of the Temple was begun (among whom would have been Haggai, presumably). Thus, the sense here could include personal audition as well as written dictation, suggesting that the author(s) of Zech 7–8 (and perhaps Zech 1:1–16) had actually heard the prophecies of those whom they now sought to record. This might also explain why the idiom is not used in reference to pre-exilic prophecy. It is to be noted, however, that in Zech 8:9 the reference to 'the words' (הדברים) serves to con-fer the same kind of authority upon the utterances of the post-exilic prophets that the sayings of the pre-exilic prophets already possessed.[43]

---

[37] MEYERS AND MEYERS, Haggai, 425–26.

[38] Ibid., 406–07.

[39] On the basis of the deuteronomistic parallel, 'these... words' would point forward to Zech 7:9–10, not backward to Zech 7:5–6.

[40] See, however, Jer 29; 36; 51:60–64! Cf. the chapter, "The Reading-out of 'Booked Re-alities' as a Means of their Effectuation," in RABINOWITZ, Witness, 61–65.

[41] I simply note in passing that Zech 7:13 remains problematic in several ways.

[42] MEYERS AND MEYERS, Haggai, 419–20.

[43] On this issue generally, see R. A. MASON, Prophets, 141.

Summary

By way of summation we return to the key terms of Zech 1:6 and Zech 7:7, 12. If it be accepted that these are references to post-exilic Israel's growing scriptural collection of 'Law and Prophets,' then it remains necessary to point out the standing of the subcollections 'Law' and 'Prophets' relative to each other. In the view presented in Zechariah, *both* God's 'words and statutes... overtook' (נשג, *Hiph.*) the pre-exilic generations (Zech 1:6), just as was promised in the course of God's blessings and curses in Deut 28:2, 15, 45 (also נשג, *Hiph*). The 'former prophets' preached the law (Zech 7:7–10), but the pre-exilic generations refused *both* 'the law and the words' that God had sent through 'his servants the prophets' (cf. 2 Kg 17:13, 23).

Thus, both Law and Prophets were divinely revealed and authorized. Both Law and Prophets were communicated through the prophets who came to Israel in the generations before the Exile. Both Law and Prophets were refused, resulting in Israel's destruction.[44] In other words, there is no trace here of a more authoritative Torah; Israel's disobedience to 'the words' was just as egregious and provocative in God's eyes as its disobedience to 'the law.'

Moreover, the similarity between the historical retrospectives in this book and those of Chronicles[45] suggests that with Zechariah we have moved beyond the deuteronomistic tradition of 'law and prophets' into a new post-exilic situation. In this context, the deuteronomistic contours of the 'law and prophets' tradition remain visible, but become porous, admitting of adaptation and expansion in new ways due to the influence of other traditions. For example, the central roles of the cult and the priesthood in both Haggai and Zechariah now combine with the old deuteronomistic tradition of prophecy in surprisingly easy ways (e. g., Zech 7:3; 8:9; cf. Jer 7!). If this material has its *Sitz im Leben* in Second Temple 'sermons' or 'addresses,' as Mason has argued, it might provide further support for such adaptation of traditions.[46]

For my purposes, I wish only to make the case that Zechariah shapes a received theological construct of 'law and prophets' in the direction of Chronicles and later post-biblical traditions.[47] Whether the similarities between the

---

[44] MEYERS AND MEYERS, Haggai, 407.

[45] E. g., cvc. Zech 1:3–6 with 2 Chr 30:6–9 and Zech 8:9–13 with 2 Chr 15:3–7. See further R. A. MASON, Prophets, 148–49.

[46] Idem, Echoes, 233.

[47] I am quite in agreement with those who view HANSON's sociological treatment of Haggai and Zech 1–8 as highly unsatisfactory. For HANSON's view that this material is exclusively 'theocratic,' see his Dawn, 247–50. For various criticisms, see R. J. COGGINS, Haggai, 37–38; 53–54; R. A. MASON, Prophets, 145; also 151 (on Haggai, Zechariah and Malachi together). For an important sociological argument that strikes a mortal blow at the 'deprivation theory' at the heart of HANSON's thesis, see COOK, Prophecy. In my view both priests and prophets played a substantial role in post-exilic Israelite society (e. g., Zech 7:3; cf. WILSON,

addresses in Zechariah and those in Chronicles have their setting in a specific Second Temple context, or in the general post-exilic milieu, they still exhibit the same important feature for my argument: they maintain and proclaim a tradition of 'law and prophets' just as the deuteronomists did. Noteworthy is the fact that while the references to these collections become more specific and the written nature of the material referred to becomes more sure, there is no apparent change or growth in the degree of authority which inheres to either genre. One never gains the sense that the authority of 'the law' or 'the words' depends upon the precise nature of their contents or the degree of their textual fixity. To the contrary, their combined authority and shape were understood to have been pre-ordained by history, tradition and divine will.

Chronicles

To understand the significance of the books of Chronicles for theories of canon formation, one need only acknowledge their probable Persian period date. As A. C. Sundberg had already noted in his discussion of R. H. Pfeiffer's work, a later date for the separation of the Samaritans from mainstream Judaism means that "the Chronicler's apparent use of a completed Pentateuch emerges as the primary factor in fixing a *terminus ad quem* for the canonization of the Pentateuch."[1] I further note that according to the view being developed in the present study, the books of Chronicles would have originated *after* the period in which 'the Law and the Prophets' emerged as a canonical framework for Israel's scriptures. At issue therefore is whether we perceive a heightened 'canon-consciousness' of a bipartite scripture within these books.

In the following treatment of Chronicles I shall rely largely on the conclusion of H. G. M. Williamson that Chronicles represent a 'substantial unity,' although there are a few passages of secondary expansion (e. g., 1 Chr 15–16; 23–27).[2] I shall not assume the common origin of both Chronicles and Ezra–Nehemiah, as was common in biblical scholarship until quite recently. I accept the work of various scholars that the differences in language, outlook and theology between Chronicles and Ezra–Nehemiah mitigate the persua-

---

Prophecy, 289) and therefore, in the absence of indications to the contrary, I think cooperation provides as likely a theoretical model as conflict. After all, cooperation does not exclude the possibility of real differences, despite the frequent assumption to the contrary. I confess simply not to understand those who maintain that 'establishmentarian' prophets are no longer able to be genuine prophets (for further criticism of this view, see MEYERS AND MEYERS, Haggai, xliii. A more supple sociological approach is provided by WILSON (e. g., see his summary in Prophecy, 297–308), who argues for 'central' as well as 'peripheral' prophets (or 'intermediaries') throughout Israel's history.

[1] SUNDBERG, Church, 38 n. 27.
[2] WILLIAMSON, Chronicles, 14.

siveness (and the interpretive usefulness) of such a theory.[3] At the same time, I do not rule out the possibility of a family resemblance between the two works, since they have been joined into one common narrative structure. In fact, I shall argue that one frequently-cited difference between the two, namely their respective views on prophets and prophecy, is not really a difference at all. I contend that all of these books bear witness to the existence of a 'canon' of Law and Prophets in this period.

Williamson has discussed the significant factors for dating Chronicles, setting the likeliest date for the books' formation at ca. 350 B. C.[4] First, the citation of LXX Chronicles by Eupolemos in the second century B. C. requires an earlier date for their literary formation.[5] The existence of Chronicles (already in Greek translation!) thus suggests a third century date or earlier.[6] Second, no Hellenistic influence is visible in Chronicles, suggesting a date prior to 333 B. C. As Williamson adroitly observes, Hellenistic dates for Chronicles in the past have depended on the unity of Chronicles with Ezra–Nehemiah; without that unity, the late dating for Chronicles becomes insupportable.[7]

Third, Williamson believes that 2 Chr 16:9a quotes Zech 4:10b, which would exclude a date earlier than 520 B. C.[8] The putative citation is brief and appears without a citation formula, which might call into question the weight he places upon this single example. Yet Williamson rightly credits the place of this citation within one of the many addresses in Chronicles which are replete with scriptural allusions and quotations: "...the citation is put on a level footing with citations from pre-exilic, canonical prophets; form-critically, it cannot be simply explained away as a reference to the saying of a contemporary."[9] The full impact of this example emerges when it is realized that here the words of a *post*-exilic prophet could appear in the mouth of a *pre*-exilic prophet because the word of God was understood to be timeless.[10]

Taken together, these factors indicate that the books of Chronicles likely took shape in the middle of the fourth century B. C. The kind of scriptural

---

[3] E. g., HOGLUND, Administration, 36–40; JAPHET, Authorship; WILLIAMSON, Chronicles, 5–11. See also KALIMI, Bibliography. Therefore when I refer to the 'Chronicler,' I do so loosely and without reference to Ezra–Nehemiah.

[4] WILLIAMSON, Chronicles, 15–17. The following three points are all found on these pages.

[5] See also TOV, Criticism, 137.

[6] As WILLIAMSON, Chronicles, 15, notes, Sir 47:8–10 (ca. 180 B. C.) also appears to know Chronicles in some form. Moreover, it is *later* material in Chronicles, generally speaking, to which Ben Sira appears to refer (e. g., 1 Chr 16; 23).

[7] WILLIAMSON, Chronicles, 16.

[8] Ibid., 15; see also VON RAD, Sermon, 269–70.

[9] WILLIAMSON, Chronicles, 15.

[10] R. A. MASON, Preaching, 54.

collection to which they testify will thus provide crucial evidence for the history of canon formation, especially of the prophetic corpus.

Prophecy in Chronicles

There are three main features of Chronicles that relate to prophets and prophecy: 1) a considerable number of stories about prophets and prophetic-type figures; 2) a series of prophetic addresses that punctuate the narrative; and 3) a group of citation formulas referring to prophetic literary works.

1. Stories about Prophets

The general importance of prophetic stories in Chronicles has long been noted, but recently received renewed attention.[11] The major literary issue in dispute has to do with the relationship between the prophetic stories in Chronicles and those in the Deuteronomistic History; the interpretive issue at stake turns on the function of these prophetic stories within the Chronicler's overall purpose. Specifically, is the purpose of these stories more akin to an 'exegesis' of the Deuteronomistic History or an independent effort at 'history'?

The fact that some prophets appearing in Chronicles never appear in the Deuteronomistic History and *vice versa* has led some scholars to argue that either the Chronicler was not constrained by the authority of scripture (i. e., the Deuteronomistic History was not yet canonical) or that a common source lies behind the Deuteronomistic History and Chronicles, and was used by the Chronicler when he did not follow the Deuteronomistic History.[12]

More persuasive, however, is the argument that either the Chronicler has created his 'non-synoptic' prophetic stories to serve his theological purpose, or that he has so shaped traditional material that it is now his view more than any other which is visible.[13] In any case, it is clear that a major purpose of these stories is to use the literary device of prophetic speech to advance a theological interpretation of Israel's post-exilic situation. Furthermore, these prophetic speeches consistently illustrate and enjoin the practice of textual interpretation.[14] Just as in the Deuteronomistic History, but more explicitly,

---

[11] BEGG, Ezekiel, 342–43; idem, Prophets; idem, Elisha; MICHEEL, Überlieferungen; VAN ROOY, Prophet; SCHNIEDEWIND, Prophets; idem, Word; SEELIGMANN, Auffassung; WILLI, Chronik.

[12] For the first view, see KALIMI, Historian? 79. For the second view, see RAINEY, Chronicler, 38. Complicating the picture, and all too often overlooked, is the probability that the version of the Deuteronomistic History used by the Chronicler (i. e., his *Vorlage*) was not the form of the Deuteronomistic History known to us, but a previous redaction, fragments of which may have been discovered at Qumran. See MCKENZIE, Use.

[13] SCHNIEDEWIND, Prophets, 214.

[14] See the criticism of this view in KALIMI, Historian? 77–81. KALIMI, however, works with an extremely narrow understanding of interpretation and canon (Historian? 79). He de-

the addresses in Chronicles lay claim to a canonical legacy and strive to express an abiding canonical message. The debate, then, between the historical and exegetical dimensions of the Chronicler's purpose frequently misses the point. As I shall illustrate, the Chronicler's effort is a theological endeavor in which both the historical and exegetical dimensions have a place.[15]

Before turning to the addresses themselves, however, I would like to examine generally the prophetic narratives and the figure of the prophet. In my view, the nature of the Deuteronomistic History's canonical authority for the Chronicler is actually indicated by some of the *differences* between the two accounts. Thus, the Chronicler sometimes *refers* to prophets and prophecies in the Deuteronomistic History which he himself nevertheless does not relate. For example, the prophecy of Ahijah is said to be fulfilled in 2 Chr 10:15, yet was never previously related in Chronicles (cf. 1 Kg 11:29–39). So, too, the prophets Samuel and Shemaiah are referred to by the Chronicler (respectively: 1 Chr 11:3; 2 Chr 12:5, 7–8), but otherwise go unmentioned.[16] This phenomenon appears to indicate that not only did the Chronicler himself rely upon the Deuteronomistic History, he expected his own work to amplify and not replace it. For this reason, the Chronicler's intention is better understood as the interpretation of Israel's history *as related in* the Deuteronomistic History than an interpretation of Israel's history in general. This will become clearer as we examine other prophetic features in Chronicles.

It follows that there are reasons other than a presumed lack of authority for the omission of several deuteronomistic prophets from Chronicles. For example, with the orientation of the Chronicler's history toward the southern kingdom and the resultant loss of northern narratives, a number of significant prophets in the Deuteronomistic History no longer possessed a narrative con-

---

fends the view that the Chronicler's primary purpose was not to interpret texts, but to write 'history.' This kind of either/or is misleading. The exegetical aspect of the Chronicler's work is clearly highly significant, even when seen in combination with other aspects of his rewritten history.

[15] This view has been developed most of all by ACKROYD, Exegete; and R. J. COGGINS, Chronicles, 5–6. KALIMI criticizes this view (Historian? 82 n. 44) by making a comparison with ancient Near Eastern inscriptions. These inscriptions (e. g., Mesha, Kurkh), he notes, use 'theological' language, but are never interpreted as 'theology' by scholars. He argues that the Chronicler's convictions might have converged with his historiography, but that 'sacred history' is still 'history.' However, the differences between these inscriptions and the books of Chronicles actually tell against KALIMI's position. First of all, the Chronicles are not inscriptions, but books in a religious canon of scripture. Second, in the inscriptions KALIMI cites there is no exegetical dimension present. Third, the focus in these inscriptions is clearly on the past, whereas the interest of the Chronicler is much more on the present. Fourth, the ascription of a theological purpose to the Chronicler need not imply his antipathy or disregard for 'history.'

[16] These examples are given by VAN ROOY, Prophet, 169–70.

text in which to appear.[17] Thus, a synchronic dimension likely plays a greater role than the diachronic dimension when it comes to the appearance of prophets within the work. This synchronic dimension becomes more apparent when it is realized that for almost every Judean king one and only one figure bears the title 'prophet.'[18]

In this way, the Chronicler likely reveals his continued belief in the mosaic succession of prophecy,[19] a belief he held so strongly that, if a particular 'prophet' for a given king's reign was unknown to him from the Deuteronomistic History, it was then necessary to introduce him.[20] Not only do the prophets in Chronicles primarily address kings, the prophets usually appear in the narrative after a royal failing and before the enactment of God's judgment.[21] This 'triggering' function of the prophetic role certainly increases its importance: without prophets the law appears almost impotent. H. V. van Rooy notes succinctly that in the narratives, "The fate of people and king often depended on their response to the prophetic word."[22]

Of course, the greatly increased role of the levites in Chronicles also bears attention. It has been argued that the Chronicler gradually replaces prophets with levites in order to claim prophetic authority for levitical personnel within the Second Temple.[23] In my view, the move by the Chronicler is exactly the reverse. The 'replacement' of the prophets by levites does not mean that prophets have outlived their usefulness, but that the levites require an infusion of prophetic authority.[24] Moreover, the levites are not the only ones to be painted in prophetic colors: kings appear as prophet-like figures, too.[25]

Once again, the overlooked dynamic here at work has to do with a process of textualization. Thus, we encounter general references to the prophets as a collectivity,[26] but also to the prophetic word as *part of* the abiding 'commandment of God.'[27] New in Chronicles, moreover, is a full-blown description of prophets as *authors*.[28]

---

[17] A point made by SCHNIEDEWIND, Prophets, 213–14; VAN ROOY, Prophet, 172–73.

[18] VAN ROOY, Prophet, 174; MICHEEL, Überlieferungen, 19.

[19] See Deut 18:15, 18; cf. 2 Chr 24:19; 36:15–16.

[20] BEGG, Prophets, 106–07.

[21] VAN ROOY, Prophet, 175.

[22] Ibid., 175–76.

[23] Ibid., 177. VAN ROOY cites 2 Chr 34:30 (cf. 2 Kg 23:3) as an example. Cf. WILSON, Prophecy, 293.

[24] VAN ROOY, Prophet, 179.

[25] Ibid., 172–73; 177–78; cf. BEGG, Prophets, 102–03.

[26] See 1 Chr 16:22 (= Ps 105:15); 2 Chr 20:20; 24:19; 36:16.

[27] See 2 Chr 29:25; 35:15.

[28] WILLI, Chronik, 234. See 1 Chr 29:29; 2 Chr 9:29; 12:15; 13:22; 20:34; 26:22; 32:32; 33:18–19.

The variety of terms for prophetic figures and roles has been subjected to detailed analysis by W. M. Schniedewind. He has sought not only to sharpen the profile of terms in Chronicles like 'prophet,' 'seer,' 'man of God' and 'servant of the LORD,' but also to argue that use of the term 'messenger' (מלאך, esp. 2 Chr 36:15–16) reflects a new understanding of prophets and prophecy in the post-exilic period.[29] Schniedewind concludes from his study that in Chronicles the role of the 'messenger' is to exhort the people through an interpretation of texts, while the role of a prophet is to address the king with an interpretation of events.[30]

Schniedewind wants to understand the 'messenger' as generally within the prophetic tradition, but also as a new role characterized by the charismatic non-prophetic figure within the narrative, who nevertheless assumes prophetic-type functions.[31] In Schniedewind's view, however, the differences between the two finally outweigh the similarities. He suggests that 2 Chr 36:15 actually refers to three *different* sources of revelation within Israel's history: תורה, prophets and 'messengers.'[32]

In my view, Schniedewind has helpfully explored the force of textualization upon post-exilic understandings of prophecy, but has pressed the distinction between 'messenger' and 'prophet' too hard. Just as the various terms in Chronicles used for prophecy seem somewhat interchangeable,[33] and various traditional formulas appear to be used in a rather impressionistic way,[34] so too the use of the term 'messenger' is better understood as a generalizing term for all of the speakers within the narrative who have sought to impart the knowledge and will of God.[35] Rather than intending to underwrite a new, discrete form of prophecy, the books of Chronicles instead reflect the understanding that *all* of Israel's leaders must exercise certain prophetic functions if they are to communicate God's will faithfully.[36]

As I hope to develop, the basic conception of authoritative, textual revelation employed by the Chronicler is still fundamentally dual: Moses and the Prophets. As tentative proof of this position, I would note that it is not only the 'messenger' figures who interpret texts within Chronicles, as Schniedewind's reconstruction would suggest. For example, 2 Chr 16:9a cites Zech 4:10, as has been already observed. It may well be that the primary purpose of

---

[29] SCHNIEDEWIND, Word, esp. 83–84.

[30] Ibid., 118; 122–24.

[31] Ibid., 83–84.

[32] Ibid., 84.

[33] E. g., ibid., 47–51. See also R. A. MASON, Preaching, 136.

[34] E. g., SCHNIEDEWIND, Word, 56–59.

[35] WILLIAMSON, Chronicles, 122; R. A. MASON, Preaching, 137.

[36] WILLIAMSON, Chronicles, 122; R. A. MASON, Preaching, 142. For an extension of this phenomenon into the post-biblical period, see also BARTON, Oracles.

this episode is to interpret the relationship between act and consequence, as Schniedewind claims,[37] but this citation illustrates that 'prophetic' figures also interpret scriptural texts within the narrative. Moreover, in my view the *concluding* use[38] of the root מלא in 2 Chr 36:21 and the root כלה in 2 Chr 36:22 (in reference to 'the word of the LORD spoken by [the mouth of] Jeremiah'!)[39] indicates the abiding priority of prophetically-discharged revelation, subsuming the language of 'messengers' within the prophetic tradition.

2. The Prophetic Addresses

The addresses in Chronicles have received several attentive treatments.[40] G. von Rad's pioneering study in particular has seldom been granted its true significance. Its real importance was not to be found in the isolation of a 'levitical sermon' genre,[41] but in his form-critical insights into the way prophetic *scripture* had patterned the speeches. Von Rad saw not only that the speeches revealed a tendency to cite texts, but also that a concerted effort had been made to conform the style of the speeches to traditions of prophetic proclamation.[42] However, von Rad noted on several occasions as well that the context of the original prophetic oracles appeared to have been ignored by the Chronicler in his reapplication of them,[43] leading him eventually to misinterpret the canonical implications of the phenomena he had observed.

In fact, the perceived imprecision of the Chronicler's reuse of prophetic oracles does not reveal an attitude of minimal authority, but the opposite. For the Chronicler, prophetic oracles from the past were written and sure (e. g., 2 Chr 36:21–22); they applied not only to one situation, but to *every* situation confronting the people of God because they represented God's abiding will. As in the case of the *pesharim* found at Qumran, it was precisely the unquestioned authority of these texts which created the possibility of their use beyond their 'historical' context.

For von Rad, as for others since, these speeches reflect the actual practice of levitical instruction during the Second Temple period,[44] which, if true, would certainly necessitate an earlier date for the canonization of prophetic

---

[37] Thus SCHNIEDEWIND, Word, 106–07

[38] R. A. MASON, Preaching, 122.

[39] Cf. Jer 36:12. The phrase מפי ירמיהו could refer to the reading or interpretation of a text; see the discussion of Zechariah above.

[40] Esp. VON RAD, Sermon; also R. A. MASON, Preaching; WILLI, Chronik.

[41] For a critique of VON RAD along these lines, see R. A. MASON, Echoes? MATTHIAS, Predigt.

[42] VON RAD, Sermon, 270; 274 n. 27.

[43] Ibid., 269–70. There were instances (Sermon, 272–73) where VON RAD felt the use of a particular quotation by the Chronicler was 'appropriate': e. g., 2 Chr 19:6–7; 20:15–17.

[44] Ibid., 271; R. A. MASON, Preaching.

scripture than is customary.[45] However, von Rad's full appreciation of this feature was obscured by his view of the post-exilic period as one of legalistic declension.[46]

This view of declension arose from his interpretation of the books of Chronicles not according to their theological witness, which was later to be the expressed intention of his *Old Testament Theology*,[47] but according to their reconstructed *Sitz im Leben*:

> "...[the] speeches are intended pre-eminently to support the prophetic claims of the Levites as conceived by the Chronicler... institutional and political interests predominate in them."[48]

In fact, here von Rad shares Wellhausen's view of the post-exilic dynamic, equating the move toward the quotation of earlier written sources with a "declension in religious vigor and spontaneity."[49]

Von Rad also appears to have worked with two inconsistent concepts of citation. On the one hand, he noted the Chronicler's *quotation* of prophetic sayings, a practice he proved repeatedly by comparing the 'sermons' in Chronicles to biblical prophetic texts.[50] On the other hand, however, he endeavored to distinguish between 'quotations' and 'allusions' (von Rad never revealed his criteria),[51] finally remarking that the lack of citation formulas indicated that the 'sermons' did *not* utilize quotations, not in "the strictest sense of the term."[52]

This inconsistency persisted into his conclusions regarding canonization. Arguing from the nature of the references as *quotations*, von Rad rejected a 'narrow legalism' in this period, claiming that in these speeches:

> "...the pre-exilic and the earlier post-exilic writings have received literary recognition, and, what is more important, they are deeply cherished. The quotations presuppose a lively interest in ancient writings and exemplify the keen desire to make their contents known to the people so far as is humanly possible."[53]

But then seemingly reversing himself, von Rad argued for the nature of the references as mere *allusions*, maintaining that a difference existed between

---

[45] I. e., were fourth century levitical instructors already quoting prophetic scripture?

[46] VON RAD, Sermon, 279 — at least in this early article (orig. 1934).

[47] Idem, Theology I:105–15.

[48] VON RAD, Sermon, 274.

[49] Ibid., 279.

[50] Ibid., 271, e. g.

[51] Ibid., 275, e. g.

[52] Ibid., 279.

[53] Ibid., 280. One wonders why this 'lively interest' is to be subordinated to the institutional and political interests of the levites in interpreting the final form of the text.

quotations of the Pentateuch, which employed citation formulas,[54] and 'quotations' of (allusions to?) prophetic texts, which did not. However, he was
also forced to admit that the distinction was not fully consistent, causing him
to go on to question the canonical status of the Pentateuch as well as the
Prophets in this period, which subverted his own earlier claims about the vitality and authority of these writings.[55]

This fundamental inconsistency does not detract from the brilliance of von
Rad's article, or its usefulness. It simply indicates the necessity of greater precision regarding the nature of the quotations/allusions in the prophetic addresses of Chronicles and the probable shape of the Chronicler's canon.

It must be openly acknowledged that the argument for the presence of actual quotations in the addresses rests more on the great preponderance of suggestive evidence rather than any few indisputable examples. One cannot work
through the volumes by T. Willi and R. A. Mason without being soundly im-
pressed by how central the reuse of literary traditions is to the Chronicler's
task. Of particular forcefulness are four features of the Chronicler's method:
a) the clustering of allusions from different prophetic books within the same
address;[56] b) the reuse of material from the Latter Prophets in the addresses,
especially as an expansion of the basic narrative of the Deuteronomistic History;[57] c) the sustained presence of wordplay in the addresses, suggesting the
kind of close attention to precise wording, as is typical of work with written
texts (as opposed to oral traditions);[58] and d) the absence or admixture of traditional prophetic oral conventions and genres.[59]

All of these features suggest that the Chronicler relied upon written texts
for the composition of his speeches. In the course of his history, the Chronicler employed techniques of *both* allusion and citation, without really distinguishing between the two. For this reason, the presence or absence of citation
formulas is not decisive. Whatever the precise technique employed, the
Chronicler's sources are better understood as written texts than oral traditions.

Thus, the speech of Azariah (2 Chr 15:2–7) draws on a variety of pentateuchal and prophetic sources, including Deut 4:29–31; Am 3:7; Hos 3:4 and
Zech 8:9–11.[60] The point to be made is that here the words of a prophetic fig-

---

[54] See 2 Chr 23:18; 25:4; 30:5, 18; 31:3; etc.

[55] VON RAD, Sermon, 279–80.

[56] R. A. MASON, Preaching, 48–49; 113; 137–39.

[57] Ibid., 36 (on 2 Chr 12).

[58] Ibid., 37; 82; 137–39.

[59] Ibid., 24–25. 64–68.

[60] FISHBANE, Interpretation, 388–92; idem, Garments, 14–16. [FISHBANE, Garments, 15,
mistakenly makes reference to Amos 3:17 (17 is the number of the footnote in FISHBANE's
earlier text). The error is continued in SCHNIEDEWIND, Word, 114.] For comparison with
Zech 8, see R. A. MASON, Preaching, 49–51.

ure are conformed by the Chronicler to the deuteronomistic pattern of pre-exilic prophecy now existing in *scripture*. It is for this reason that M. Fishbane has described this speech as a "new-old voice: a voice of the present hour, but also a voice which verbalizes older language for the sake of the re-appropriation of the tradition."[61] The purpose of such a 'exegetical anthology' is not only to authorize a contemporary interpretation of events, but to draw the reader/hearer into the scriptural world. "Here," Fishbane concludes, "all significant speech is scriptural or scripturally-oriented speech."[62]

No passage in Chronicles illustrates this premise more clearly than Jehaziel's prophecy in 2 Chr 20:15–17 and King Jehoshaphat's response in 2 Chr 20:18–21. Once again, the speech is found to consist of strong allusions to pentateuchal and prophetic scripture. Jehaziel, termed a levite in the narrative (2 Chr 20:14), begins his speech with the prophetic formula, כה־אמר יהוה (2 Chr 20:15). His oracle draws upon holy war tradition (Deut 20:2–4) and bears strong resemblances to both Ex 14:13 and 1 Sam 17:47.[63] In response, Jehoshaphat tells the inhabitants of Judah and Jerusalem to 'believe' (אמן, *Hiph.*) in God and in his prophets (2 Chr 20:20b).

Not only is the public call to *belief* in the prophets striking because of the rarity of this kind of language within biblical tradition for anyone other than God (otherwise only Moses; see Ex 14:31),[64] but also because the phrasing of this call to belief is clearly based upon the prophetic oracle in Isa 7:9b. In this way, the reference is clearly not only to the oracle of the prophet Jehaziel, but to the entire *prophetic heritage* of Israel. Thus, at one move this call to belief in the prophets proclaims that their message is essential to faith in God and locates that message within *scripture*.[65] Ancient prophecy can be reapplied, therefore, not because it lacks authority or historical specificity, but because the fullness of its truth is understood to be continually emerging in the unfolding of history.[66]

The textualization of prophecy is also seen in the appearance of a prophecy by Elijah in the form of a letter (2 Chr 21:12–15). The Chronicler's concen-

---

[61] FISHBANE, Garments, 16.

[62] Ibid.

[63] VON RAD, Sermon, 273. Isa 41:8–13 is also suggested by WILLIAMSON, Chronicles, 298.

[64] WILDBERGER, "Glauben," 380. There are a few instances of this expression being used in relation to other figures (e. g., 1 Sam 27:12; 2 Chr 32:15, without – ב following), but not as a confession for Israel.

[65] FISHBANE, Interpretation, 387. FISHBANE sees behind this citation of Isaiah a deepening of religious experience resulting from the knowledge and study of written prophecies in the post-exilic period (Garments, 71–73).

[66] FISHBANE, Interpretation, 437. Thus these type of allusions were not made *for the purpose of* authorizing the practice of exegesis (so SCHNIEDEWIND, Word, 118), but rather employed exegesis as a lens through which to understand the will of God.

tration on the southern kingdom most likely explains the lack of a more extended treatment of this prophet. Still, the letter form calls to mind the move toward prophecy as reading within the book of Jeremiah (cf. Jer 29; 51:60–64a). It is in the light of these and other considerations that C. T. Begg and others have concluded that Chronicles not only emphasizes the role of prophets and prophecy even more than the Deuteronomistic History, but that the prophets in Chronicles more closely resemble the classical prophets of the prophetic books than those of the Deuteronomistic History.[67]

3. Citation Formulas

As previously noted, within the narrative of Chronicles the prophets are cited as the *authors* of the Chronicler's sources.[68] Furthermore, the references to these sources indicate that they may have been influenced by the 'titles' of the prophetic books.[69] Thus, 2 Chr 32:32 refers to "the acts of Hezekiah, and his good deeds, [which] are written in the vision of the prophet Isaiah son of Amoz in the Book of the Kings of Judah and Israel." Here 'the vision of the prophet Isaiah son of Amoz' matches Isa 1:1, even as the reference to Hezekiah perhaps implies that 2 Kg 18–20 is understood as authored by the prophet Isaiah. In fact, the understanding seems to be that much, if not all, of the Deuteronomistic History is the result of prophetic authorship (cf. 1 Chr 29:29; 2 Chr 9:29), perhaps ultimately the conception behind the expression 'former prophets' for Joshua–2 Kings.[70]

The precise contents of the Chronicler's תורה have been hotly debated. It seems clear that the Chronicler knows both deuteronomic and priestly legislation.[71] At issue is the fact that other non-pentateuchal traditions also seem to have binding authority for him.[72] J. R. Shaver's conclusion that there was 'no canonical text' for the Chronicler[73] is based upon the narrow view of canon as fixed and delimited. Such a view is extremely hard to combine with the references to the authority of written law within Chronicles itself.[74] Much more likely is a view of canon in which Israel's scriptural heritage is so authoritative as to include even *more* than 'what is written.'[75]

---

[67] BEGG, Prophets, 106–07; cf. the similar judgment of WILLIAMSON, History, 34–35.

[68] WILLI, Chronik, 234. See 1 Chr 29:29; 2 Chr 9:29; 12:15; 13:22; 20:34; 26:22; 32:32; 33:19.

[69] SCHNIEDEWIND, Word, 42–43; 227.

[70] BLENKINSOPP, History, 22.

[71] KELLERMANN, Anmerkungen, 67–70 for a helpful chart; SHAVER, Torah, 87–88.

[72] SHAVER, Torah, 88–117.

[73] Ibid., 127. SHAVER also assumes the unity of Chronicles and Ezra–Nehemiah, which affects the results of his analysis.

[74] 1 Chr 16:40; 2 Chr 17:9; 23:18; 25:4; 30:16; 31:3; 34:1, 14–16, 18–19, 21, 24; 35:12, 26.

[75] WILLI, Thora.

In this way, prophetic scripture probably also formed part of תורה for the Chronicler. For example, Shaver notes that in 2 Chr 30:13–17 the penta-teuchal warrant for priestly and levitical participation in the passover rite is lacking, but could have come from Ezek 44:10–16.[76] Moreover, Chronicles displays the same conception of the prophets as the tradents of law as in the Deuteronomistic History: "...for the commandment (המצוה) was from the LORD through his *prophets*" (2 Chr 29:25; cf. 2 Chr 36:15–16).

At the same time, the 'word of God' also takes on an expanded role. Just as the prophets are viewed within the tradition of תורה, the תורה is also under-stood as a witness to the 'word of God' (e. g., 2 Chr 35:6). Schniedewind has argued that in Chronicles the 'word of God' is "no longer just the spoken word of the prophets but also the written word of the scribes."[77] In several in-stances where the term appears (independently of its use in Kings) the refer-ence is to legal/cultic tradition.[78] Schniedewind maintains convincingly that this expanded usage indicates the subsumption of "both prophetic oracles and the mosaic law under the broader category of the 'word of YHWH.'"[79]

Schniedewind's conclusion might be strengthened by consideration of the plural expression '*words* of the LORD,' which he overlooks. Thus, at the con-clusion of 1 Chronicles we read: "Now the acts of (דברי) King David, from first to last, are written in the records of (דברי) Samuel, and in the records of [דברי] the prophet Nathan, and in the records of (דברי) the seer Gad" (1 Chr 29:29). Although obscured in translation, the Hebrew text reveals the same conception of prophetic scripture as דברים that we encountered within the deuteronomistic tradition.

'Words' reside within true prophets (2 Chr 19:3) and, when pronounced, possess enduring expression (2 Chr 15:8; 18:12). The deeds of kings can also be termed דברים because they are thought to have been *recorded* by proph-ets.[80] For this reason, prophetic oracles and writings can both be known as 'words.'[81]

---

[76] SHAVER, Torah, 114. He also traces (Torah, 115–16) the warrant for 2 Chr 15:11–12 to both Ezek 45:21–24 and Num 28:16–25. The reference to the levitical distribution in 2 Chr 35:12 is another such crux.

[77] SCHNIEDEWIND, Word, 130.

[78] See 1 Chr 15:15; 2 Chr 19:11; 30:12; 34:21; 35:6.

[79] SCHNIEDEWIND, Word, 137.

[80] See 2 Chr 9:29; 12:15; 13:22; 20:34; 25:26; 26:22; 27:7; 28:26; 32:32; 33:18–19; 35:26–27; 36:8. Note that David is considered to be a prophet, too (2 Chr 29:30), presumably because he is understood to have authored the Psalms. Hezekiah also achieves prophetic status through the use of this formula (2 Chr 32:8), as does the Pharaoh Neco (2 Chr 35:22). An apparently new expression for prophetic writing also appears here (מדרש in 2 Chr 13:22; 24:27), but it is difficult to ascertain the precise sense of the term within Chronicles.

[81] Cf. 2 Chr 11:4; 26:22; 29:15; 36:16.

In the account of Hezekiah's reform, Hezekiah's reference to Jer 29:18 (2 Chr 29:8) is followed by an acknowledgment that his reform has been authorized by prophetic scripture ('the words of the LORD,' 2 Chr 29:15). In the same way, references to Josiah's lawbook as 'word/words' convey its prophetic quality (2 Chr 34:19, 21, 26–27, 30–31). This 'law' is heard as a neglected prophecy from the past (2 Chr 34:21). It is the *prophetess* Huldah who is asked to confirm the 'law,' and her own 'word' (2 Chr 36:28) adds to the authority and the meaning of the newly-discovered book.

Thus, the theme of Chronicles is the story of the rejected message of God's compassion, as announced through history by his *prophets* (2 Chr 24:18–20; 36:15–16).[82] Although threatened by disobedience, God's mercy ever exceeds his wrath. In this way the books of Chronicles reach their conclusion with the fulfillment of Jeremiah's prophecy (2 Chr 36:21–22) and the emergence of new hope. Even the Hebrew title of Chronicles (דברי הימים) might imply or reinforce this basically prophetic understanding of history.

Summary

There is certainly no sense in Chronicles of a subordination of prophecy to law, or of Prophets to Law. The books of Chronicles take up and expand the deuteronomistic conception in which the prophets serve as proclaimers of mosaic law and mosaic law is fundamentally prophetic.[83] Moreover, these books indicate an awareness of scripture beyond the Pentateuch and even beyond the Former Prophets.[84] The Chronicler works with a canon of scripture very much like the one we know, and he works within a conception of scripture which we can recognize as that of 'the Law and the Prophets.'[85]

G. Steins has recently interpreted the books of Chronicles as shaped by a 'canon-closing phenomenon' (*kanonisches Abschlußphänomen*).[86] In my judgment, Steins's approach shares with my own an interest in looking at how the Chronicler has sought to reinterpret and conclude the canonical tradition. Steins argues, as I have, that the Chronicler is consciously at work to construct a kind of 'narrative theology' (*Theologie in narrativer Form*).[87] The difference lies in how we understand the Chronicler's 'theology.'

For Steins, the Chronicler attempts to unite diverse traditions of the past *in order to* direct the focus of his community to the importance of the Temple and its cult. Here again, I observe a narrow view of human agency at work. In my view, the Chronicler's primary concern lies in coordinating the two emer-

---

[82] Note the absence of תורה in 2 Chr 36:15–16.
[83] KELLERMANN, Anmerkungen, 81–82.
[84] *Contra* SCHNIEDEWIND, Word, 227.
[85] WILLIAMSON, History, 31–35.
[86] STEINS, Chronik.
[87] Ibid., 490.

gent scriptural collections belonging to the community, not for a specific socio-political purpose (e. g., the Temple cult), but so that scripture may proclaim God's abiding will in a new age. The Chronicler may well have viewed the Temple as the fulfillment of sacred scripture, but he certainly did not believe that he himself had engineered this fulfillment! [88]

Ezra–Nehemiah

If the prominent role of prophets within Chronicles has often been acknowledged, in the book of Ezra–Nehemiah prophecy has usually appeared conspicuous only by its absence.[1] In fact, Ezra–Nehemiah has often been used as a *terminus post quem* for the canonization of the prophetic corpus. On this view, since mosaic law is referred to on several occasions (sometimes with a citation formula),[2] and prophetic scripture is comparably absent, the redaction of the book (400–300 B. C.?) must have occurred *after* the promulgation of the Law but *before* the canonization of the Prophets.[3] Some have argued, in fact, that the book reaches its climax in a covenant ceremony involving the reading of the Law by Ezra (Neh 8–10), which may well describe the original canonization of the Pentateuch alone as Israel's 'first Bible.'[4]

Prophecy in Ezra–Nehemiah

Contributing to the appearance of an absence of prophecy in the book has been the pervasive Christian interpretation of Israel's post-exilic period as a legalistic declension, with the reappearance of a truly 'prophetic' religion only

---

[88] There are also historical problems with STEINS's thesis, not the least of which concerns the fluctuating order of the Writings in Jewish manuscript traditions and lists. STEINS's argument seems to require that the books of Chronicles were originally in *final* position within the Writings. For evidence that Chronicles may have in fact originally been in *initial* position, see GINSBURG, Introduction, 2–3; and J. A. SANDERS, Canon, 840; 846. As SANDERS points out, Chronicles holds initial position within the Writings in both the Leningrad and Aleppo codices, as well as in the 'best' Tiberian and Spanish mss. On this and other problems with STEINS's thesis, see KOOREVAAR, Chronik.

[1] For the evidence that already in antiquity Ezra–Nehemiah constituted one 'book,' see BLENKINSOPP, Ezra, 38–39. For an expression of the view that prophecy is noticeably missing from the book, see ESKENAZI, Prose, 27. Interestingly, ESKENAZI also argues brilliantly for the disappearance of Ezra as a character within the book (Prose, 136–44), prompting my thought that perhaps the book has been structured with an eye toward highlighting themes of absence and ambiguity generally.

[2] See Ezr 6:18; 7:6, 10, 11, 14, 25–26; Neh 8:1–18; 9:3, 13–14, 29; 10:29–30 [28–29], 35 [34], 37 [36]; 13:1.

[3] E. g., RYLE, Canon, 89–90; MCDONALD, Formation, 28–32.

[4] J. A. SANDERS, Torah, 50–52.

at the time of Jesus and the Church.[5] However, if one rejects these sorts of prejudices and reads the book closely, several surprisingly *prophetic* features emerge.

1. A Surprising Beginning

Thus, the book begins in a surprising way, by indicating that what is to follow comes as the fulfillment of Jeremiah's prophetic message (Ezr 1:1). If a reference to a specific prophecy of Jeremiah is intended, then most commentators have suggested Jer 29:10–14, understood as a prediction of the end of the time of Exile (cf. 2 Chr 36:21).[6] This association is reinforced by the duplication of verses in Ezr 1:1–3 and 2 Chr 36:22–23. However, the actual language of these verses is more reminiscent of certain passages in Second Isaiah (e. g., Isa 41:2, 25; 44:28; 45:1, 13) than Jeremiah.[7] This phenomenon suggests a 'conflation' of two prophetic traditions,[8] the interpretive character of which indicates the likelihood that these traditions were by this time in written form.

T. C. Eskenazi has argued provocatively, however, that the reference in Ezr 1:1 is not narrowly focused upon the duration of the Exile, but rather intends to provide a literary warrant for reading the *entire book* prophetically, "inviting the reader to ponder what precisely will be completed."[9] She argues for reading the narrative about Nehemiah as a fulfillment of Jeremiah's prophecy, too, relating his work on the city wall to the sanctification of the city of Jerusalem promised in Jer 31:38–39 (cf. Zech 14).[10] In this way she also proposes a persuasive solution to the interpretive crux of why the newly-built city wall is garrisoned with temple singers and levites (Neh 7:1): the entire city is now considered holy (Neh 11:1, 18).[11]

The fulfillment motif has been extended by Williamson to cover certain details of the Second Temple. He notes that the plans for the new Temple conform to the first[12] and that continuity is explicitly claimed for temple vessels, personnel and practices.[13] He therefore sees these details as indications of a basic *heilsgeschichtlich* conception which frames the book.[14] Williamson,

---

[5] BLENKINSOPP, Ezra, 11–12; 35. See also RENDTORFF, Image.

[6] E. g., BLENKINSOPP, Ezra, 74; ESKENAZI, Prose, 44.

[7] WILLIAMSON, Ezra, 87. WILLIAMSON also cites Jer 51:1, 11; but the Isaiah passages are closer to Ezr 1:1, especially Isa 45:13. BLENKINSOPP, Ezra, 74, also notes a similarity to 1 Chr 5:26; 2 Chr 21:16; and Hag 1:14.

[8] BLENKINSOPP, Ezra, 74.

[9] ESKENAZI, Prose, 44.

[10] Ibid., 44; 85.

[11] Ibid.

[12] Ezr 6:3, as restored = 1 Kg 6:2.

[13] Ezr 1:7–8; 3:3–6, 10–11; 5:14–15; 6:5, 18–20; 8:35; Neh 8:13–18; 10:30–40 [29–39]; 12:24, 45–46; 13:10–14. See WILLIAMSON, Ezra, 82–84.

[14] WILLIAMSON, Ezra, 79–81.

however, attributes the motivation for this framing to a Samaritan 'threat,' which created a need for the 'propaganda' that the Jerusalem Temple alone was the legitimate successor to the Temple of Solomon.[15] In this way he recognizes the symbolic dimension of the literature, but employs only the narrow model of self-interest in explaining it.

Another possibility comes into view when one acknowledges the critical function of textualization for the formation and message of the book. No one has seen this more clearly than Eskenazi, who directly relates the composition strategy of the book to the book's understanding of revelation:

> "...God's messages, in Ezra–Nehemiah, are transcribed by divinely appointed human subjects (e. g., Cyrus, Moses) into writings which become the definitive forces in the unfolding reality... In the prophets the prophetic word is actualized. In Ezra–Nehemiah the written text comes to be fulfilled."[16]

Thus, the documentary organization of the book, which most critics have found merely confusing, may in fact represent a crucial part of the book's witness. This is not to say that the book represents a single layer of redaction, or functions on only one level of intentionality; nor is it to say that there were not accidental factors at work in the book's formation.[17] It is rather to say that in the formation of the book a commitment to written sources of revelation and an understanding of revelation as a process of textual interpretation have overridden concerns about chronological consistency.[18]

Moreover, Eskenazi makes a persuasive case that the inclusion of documents within the book reflects not only a respect for written texts, but a purposeful effort to preserve a *plurality* of views: "The use to which Ezra–Nehemiah puts its sources reveals an innovative and paradigmatic shift away from homogeneity to a harmony of diversity."[19] The difference between this conclusion and the typical view of Ezra–Nehemiah as legalistic propaganda could not be put more sharply.

2. *A Surprising Ending*

The book also ends in a surprising way, with an account of reforms that were needed in Jerusalem (Neh 13:4–31), even *after* the reading of the Law (Neh 8), a national observance of covenant (Neh 9–10) and the dedication of the city wall (Neh 12). In the end, the Temple is defiled regardless (Neh

---

[15] Ibid., 46.

[16] ESKENAZI, Prose, 41–42.

[17] CHILDS, OT Introduction, 630.

[18] Apparently this understanding of revelation has overridden linguistic consistency, too, since the final form of book includes an Aramaic portion as well as a Hebrew one.

[19] ESKENAZI, Prose, 184.

13:4–14); the sabbath is broken (Neh 13:5–22); Jews are marrying non-Jews (Neh 13:23–31). Why would legalistic propaganda end like *this*?

Again Eskenazi proves helpful, this time by drawing a comparison between Ezra–Nehemiah and 1 Esdras, an alternative ancient version of the book in Greek.[20] The origins of this version are disputed and its relation to MT Ezra–Nehemiah unclear.[21] It has sometimes been argued that 1 Esdras represents the earlier version of the material and Ezra–Nehemiah a later rearrangement.[22] Others have maintained that 1 Esdras already reflects the existence of a 'canonical' Ezra–Nehemiah, although 1 Esdras may also preserve some older readings.[23]

By contrasting the description of the Restoration in both books, Eskenazi is able to clarify the literary shape of each. In her view:

"1 Esdras strives for restoration as a return to a perceived golden age, the halcyon days of David. Its structure practically obliterates the disjunction between pre- and post-exilic reality. Ezra–Nehemiah, however, separates from much of the past. Instead, it envisions a restructuring of life which orients itself around the community, not the individual hero; the city, not merely the temple; the book, not only the cult."[24]

What is especially interesting about this description of 1 Esdras is that it sounds so much like customary interpretations of Ezra–Nehemiah!

In contrast, Eskenazi views Ezra–Nehemiah as explicitly anti-heroic. In a brilliant analogy, she compares 1 Esdras and its commemoration of the hero Zerubbabel to the Washington Monument in Washington, D. C., but Ezra–Nehemiah to the same city's Vietnam Memorial "with its countless names." She astutely observes: "The shape of the book and the prevalence of lists ensure that the reader is aware of the real actors."[25] From this perspective Neh 13 would actually end the book *well*, acknowledging the limitations of its 'hero' and the unfinished business of the prophetic promises with which the book began.

Rather than operating with a simple 'realized eschatology,' then, the book of Ezra–Nehemiah portrays *both* an 'ideal community'[26] based upon Law and Prophets *and* the distance between that ideal community and post-exilic Jerusalem. Both portrayals are retained unharmonized in the final form of the text; both portrayals are 'real.' The book never gives a sense of total completion or accomplishment. In other words, the successes of Ezra and Nehemiah do not

---

[20] Ibid., 155–74.
[21] On this problem generally, see BLENKINSOPP, Ezra, 70–72.
[22] E. g., TORREY, Ezra.
[23] BLENKINSOPP, Ezra, 71.
[24] ESKENAZI, Prose, 174.
[25] Ibid., 188.
[26] CLINES, Ezra, 234.

foreclose the possibility of future acts of God or the need for a dynamic obedience in the light of changing circumstances. In fact, the book implicitly points beyond itself to a 'future realization of the prophetic promises.'[27]

What kind of accomplishment does the book then narrate? Eskenazi makes the point that the final form of the text has made Nehemiah's reforms (Neh 13) appear to be the execution of the pledge made in Neh 10, whatever the precise historical sequence of events.[28] Such shaping contributes to a view which might arguably be called anti-apocalyptic,[29] but certainly not anti-prophetic:

> "The prophetic promises of a holy community are not cast into the future in bright technicolors or as cosmic drama. They are implemented daily, inch by inch, in the process of translating Torah into life, in the tenacity of diverse and numerous people working together, in ceremonies that sanctify city, people, and book."[30]

Here, I believe, Eskenazi captures the heart of the book's message. The form and the content of Ezra–Nehemiah witness to the establishment of a communal life based upon the ongoing interpretation of an authoritative but *plural* scripture. In this way, the book of Ezra–Nehemiah does not describe the origin of Israel's canon, but the origin of the canon's 'Israel.'

3. Prior Knowledge of the Law

The above interpretation is borne out by the fact that nowhere in Ezra–Nehemiah is the Law ever presented as anything new. To the contrary, prior knowledge of the Law is consistently assumed (e. g., Ezr 7:6, 25).[31] Even if the book's various terms for scripture reflect different stages in the development of the Pentateuch,[32] in the final form of the book all of the expressions are clearly understood to refer to a single canon of scripture.[33]

On the one hand, the Law referred to in the final form of the text is clearly conceived as a combination of deuteronomistic legislation and priestly material,[34] which suggests that at least *a* Pentateuch was largely formed by the pe-

---

[27] JOHNSON, Purpose, 75.

[28] ESKENAZI, Prose, 124–25.

[29] Note Neh 12:43, 44; 13:1.

[30] ESKENAZI, Prose, 192.

[31] BLENKINSOPP, Ezra, 152–53; ZENGER, Pentateuch, 12. As BLENKINSOPP observes, this impression is only further strengthened if Ezra–Nehemiah is read together with Chronicles, where an authoritative mosaic תורה is even more noticeably assumed.

[32] RENDTORFF, Esra.

[33] ESKENAZI, Prose, 75–76 n. 93.

[34] BLENKINSOPP, Ezra, 152–54; 315–17. E. g., Neh 10:32b [31b] combines the law of the seventh fallow year (Ex 23:10–11; Lev 25:1–7 = P) with the law of the seventh year release (Deut 15:1–18; cf. Ex 21:2–6). Similarly, BLENKINSOPP maintains, the instructions to gather

riod of the book's redaction (400–300 B. C.). On the other hand, however, there are a few curious passages in which a religious law is referred to, but no such regulation exists in the final form of the Pentateuch.[35] In these cases the reference may well be to a necessary extension or reinterpretation of written law.

This type of extra-canonical reference can exist even when a citation formula is employed. Thus Ezr 6:18 records the reestablishment of priestly divisions and levitical courses at the Temple 'as it is written in the book of Moses,' but no specific pentateuchal warrant exists for this practice (cf. 1 Chr 23–26). Here again the reasoning would seem to attribute to 'the book of Moses' itself legislation only implied by its explicit injunctions (cf. Neh 8:15). Thus the purpose of such references appears to be the extension of Torah-authority to cover new communal exigencies.

More important, perhaps, than the extension of such authority in these particular instances is the modelling of the way in which such extension is to be done.[36] Rather than suggesting that the Torah was not yet canonical, such extensions imply that תורה was in sufficiently determinate form to provide a warrant for a new practice or belief.[37] Torah-authority could ground new laws, but only if they were regarded as 'facilitating laws' for the purpose of following the תורה.[38] There could be no legislative creation *ex nihilo*. In other words, a central issue in the book is not the promulgation of new law, but the interpretation of the body of law that already exists.[39]

4. The Authority of Prophetic Scripture

The further point to be made is that in Ezra–Nehemiah a similar authority accrues to prophetic scripture. To be sure, there is no mention of a 'book' or 'books' of the Prophets, but there exists a wealth of other features which attest to the canonical force of prophetic scripture upon shape of Ezra–Nehemiah.

The beginning and ending of the book have already been discussed. It bears further mention that a prophetic *inclusio* embraces Ezr 1–6 (cvc. Ezr 1:1 and 6:14), a feature even more significant, if, as Williamson has suggested, Ezr 1–6 represent the latest level of redaction within the book.[40] In this mate-

---

wood for the wood offering (Neh 10:35 [34]) are not included within the pentateuchal legislation (Lev 6:8–13), but nevertheless 'logically necessary.'

[35] BLENKINSOPP, Ezra, 155.

[36] WILLIAMSON, Ezra, 94–97.

[37] It is likely, of course, that the Torah was not yet in final form. A further interpretive issue is whether the תורה in question refers to the Torah of the historical figures Ezra and Nehemiah or the Torah of the *book* of Ezra–Nehemiah.

[38] WILLIAMSON, Ezra, 94.

[39] BLENKINSOPP, Ezra, 189.

[40] Ibid., 44–46. For a different assessment, see ESKENAZI, Prose, 176.

rial the prophets Haggai and Zechariah are mentioned as true and authoritative messengers of God (Ezr 5:1–2; 6:14).[41] Moreover, the 'prophets of God' referred to in Ezr 5:2 may well extend to prophetic figures beyond Haggai and Zechariah.[42]

Even if these references are not expressly textual in their orientation, other features of the book are. K. Koch has broken with the prevailing view that the book of Ezra–Nehemiah is exclusively theocratic, pro-Persian and anti-eschatological.[43] Koch points to previously-overlooked features within the book that link its contents to prophecy. The central features that he discusses are the typological use of the Exodus tradition, as in Second Isaiah, and the use of the number twelve to symbolize the eschatological reunification of the twelve tribes.[44]

Koch held, however, that these motifs reflected Ezra's self-understanding rather than the theological understanding of the book's editors, a claim which did not seem to take the literary shaping of this material adequately into account. The latter position has now been iterated and developed by J. G. McConville.[45] In his treatment, ample evidence is given to support Koch's claims, but at the level of the book's redaction. It bears repeating that such features would have been added to the book, or developed from within it, in precisely the period customarily treated as anti-prophetic and anti-eschatological.[46]

5. Prophetic 'Words'

In light of the present study, it remains to be noted that the book of Ezra–Nehemiah contains many of the features indicative of a tradition of 'Law and Prophets' that we have already analyzed in other books. Thus Neh 1:1 bears the superscription דברי נחמיה בן־חכליה, 'the *words* of Nehemiah son of Hacaliah.'[47] Moreover, Nehemiah recalls (Neh 1:8) 'the word' (הדבר) that

---

[41] From these brief references, it is difficult to know if the historical figures or the biblical books are in mind. WILLIAMSON, Ezra, 44, thinks the books as well as the figures are meant.

[42] BLENKINSOPP, Ezra, 117.

[43] KOCH, Ezra.

[44] For further indications of the Exodus typology, see WILLIAMSON, Ezra, 84–86; of the number twelve (e. g., Ezr 2:2; 6:17; 7:27; 8:3–14, 24, 35), see BLENKINSOPP, Ezra, 160.

[45] McCONVILLE, Ezra.

[46] BLENKINSOPP, Ezra, 160, notes that these prophetic features within the book "might suggest an interpretation of Ezra's work significantly different from the one which has prevailed in modern scholarship."

[47] BLENKINSOPP, Ezra, 203, argues against viewing Nehemiah as a prophetic figure. In this context he notes that דברים are understood as 'deeds' rather than 'words' in 1 Chr 29:29; 2 Chr 9:29; 12:15; 13:22; 16:11; 20:34. In contrast, it should be remembered that this position is immediately weakened if the unity of Chronicles and Ezra–Nehemiah is rejected. Also, the passages from Chronicles which refer to דברים may have the semantic sense BLENKINSOPP

God commanded (צִוָּה) his 'servant Moses' (paraphrasing Deut 30:1–5). Nehemiah also acts like a prophet, performing prophetic sign-acts (Neh 5:13) and disputing with false prophets (Neh 6:1–14). Prophetic behavior is also attributed to Ezra (Ezr 9:1–10:1, 6; cf. Dan 10:2–3).[48]

The category 'word/words' is applied to Israel's scripture on several occasions, with particular reference to the book of Deuteronomy.[49] However, these citations seem to be understood prophetically (e. g., Ezr 9:4; Neh 1:8) as well as legally (e. g., Neh 8:13). If anything, it would seem that traditions of law and prophecy have now blended together, both understood as the *written* revelation of God.

Thus it should come as little surprise to find reference to the 'commandments' (מִצְוֹת) which God 'commanded' (צִוָּה) by his 'servants the prophets' (Ezr 9:10–11), paralleling the reference to God's 'servant Moses' in Neh 1:8. Tellingly, the reference to the prophets in Ezr 9:10–11 introduces the citation of various pentateuchal texts (Ezr 9:11–12).[50] Here the prophets are understood to have authored commandments, just as Moses is understood to have uttered prophecy.

Nowhere in the book does this conception figure as prominently as in Neh 9, itself largely a skilful pastiche of scriptural passsages from throughout the Law and the Prophets.[51] Not only does the content of the prayer rehearse the events of the Pentateuch and the Former Prophets (Neh 9:6–23; 24–31), but it explicitly cites *twin* authorities for Israel's faith (Neh 9:29–30): God 'warned' (וַתָּעַד) Israel to 'turn back' (לַהֲשִׁיבָם), to 'the law' (אֶל-תּוֹרָתֶךָ), but God's 'commandments' (מִצְוֹתֶיךָ) and 'ordinances' (מִשְׁפָּטֶיךָ) *and* his 'warnings' (עֵדְוֹתֶיךָ) went unheeded (Neh 9:34). Here the term 'warnings' clearly possesses a prophetic character, yet parallels the legal terms.

In my judgment, close study reveals that both תּוֹרָה and דָּבָר come to be used within Ezra–Nehemiah to express a revealed totality of 'Law and Prophets.' Both categories offer a crucial perspective from which to consider the unitary and enduring will of God, and at the same time complement each other's line of sight. The complementarity of these two perspectives makes it difficult to imagine that the Prophets were considered any less authoritative than the Law at the time of the book's redaction, and implies that a similar

---

indicates, but surely it is important that such דברים of various kings are said to have been recorded in various prophetic writings. Once again, this relation bears out the understanding that דברים are within the province of prophets.

[48] BLENKINSOPP, History, 250 n. 58.

[49] Thus Ezr 9:4 refers to Deut 7:1–4; Neh 1:8 to Deut 30:1–5; Neh 8:9, 12–13 to Deut 14:29; 26:12–13.

[50] E. g., Lev 18:24; Deut 7:1–4; 11:8–9; 23:4–7. See KELLERMANN, Anmerkungen, 81–82. Interestingly, Tob 4:12 also connects the prohibition against intermarriage with the legacy of the prophets.

[51] MYERS, Ezra, 169–70.

textual status had been reached by the two collections of writings, forming a bipartite scripture.

This also means, of course, that one cannot assume within Ezra–Nehemiah that תורה refers only to pentateuchal traditions. As in later traditions, תורה here can refer to the totality of life before God, including the formulation of new 'facilitating' laws. In fact, Torah now becomes a way of employing ancient scripture wisely (Ezr 7:25). A close reading of Ezra–Nehemiah illustrates that for the book's editors this scriptural way of wisdom included the Prophets as well as the Law (Neh 9:24–31).[52]

Daniel

With the book of Daniel we come to the diachronic conclusion of the canonical tradition of 'Law and Prophets' that we have been attempting to trace.

Likely to have reached its final form in the mid-second century B. C., the book of Daniel includes reference to 'the word of the LORD to the prophet Jeremiah' as found within 'the books' (ספרים, Dan 9:2), thus employing a new apellation for a canon of scripture ('the books') as well as a traditional designation for prophetic scripture ('the word of the LORD to the prophet Jeremiah,' cf. Jer 1:1–4 and *passim*).

As in Neh 9, however, here too God's 'servants the prophets' (Dan 9:6, 10) are understood to have been the instruments of God's 'law' (תורה). 'The law of Moses (תורת משה) the servant of God' (Dan 9:11) is paralleled with God's 'words' (דבריו, Dan 9:12).[1] Moreover, God's 'law' and 'voice' (קול יהוה) are also paralleled (Dan 9:11), as in the book of Jeremiah (e. g., Jer 44). In Dan 9:13 the written Torah of Moses (כאשר כתוב בתורת משה) is even treated as a prophecy!

In fact, the variation between the second and third person singular pronoun in Dan 9:11d may have resulted partly because the identification between

---

[52] It seems to me that much of the discussion of the status of the Law in Ezra–Nehemiah has been unduly influenced by the language of a 'book of the law' in Neh 8. In my view, whatever 'book' Ezra may actually have possessed has been expanded conceptually by later editors to refer to the whole of scripture. In this expansion the actual mechanics (how much would fit on a single scroll?) have been left unaddressed. NEUSNER, Structure, 49, has made a similar argument regarding references in the Mishnah to the Torah as a single 'book' or 'scroll.' Presumably this phenomenon was possible precisely because Ezra's law was not considered something 'new,' but part of a tradition of ancient scripture. See CHILDS, OT Introduction, 636. For an overview of different theories of the contents of Ezra's lawbook, see KLEIN, Ezra, 366–68.

[1] The parallelism remains if one follows the *Qere* in Dan 9:12 and reads the sg. ('his word'), but the existence of a traditional formula תורה ודברים would provide an additional argument for the *Ketiv*.

Moses, the Prophets and the revealed will of God had become so close. The MT reads, "So the curse and the oath written in the law of Moses, the servant of God, have been poured out upon us, because we have sinned *against him/it*" (כי חטאנו לו), although other manuscripts (and the NRSV) read 'against *you*.' Behind this simple confusion may lie the idea that to sin against God now means just as much to sin against the law of Moses, for Moses and the Prophets have come to represent the enduring, written revelation of God's will.

Although the latter portion of the book embraces an entire panoply of apocalyptic themes and motifs, including an eschatological 'book of truth,'[2] the abiding authority of *scripture* is never questioned, only its proper interpretation (Dan 9:20–27). Thus, the book of Daniel begins with a portrait of Daniel as an exemplary adherent and proponent of the law.[3] In the book's use of prophetic (e. g., Dan 9:20–27) as well as pentateuchal scripture (e. g., Dan 7:9–14), and the emphasis upon Daniel's status as an *interpreter* of God's will (rather than a new lawgiver or prophet), the canonical foundation of the book's shaping is clear and a crucial aspect of its message is preserved.[4] The Law and the Prophets, here explicitly understood to represent the *form* as well as the *content* of Israel's ancient covenant, are confessed to constitute the *conditio sine qua non* of faithfulness to God.

---

[2] Dan 10:21; cf. Dan 12:1, 4, 9.
[3] E. g., Dan 1:8–21; 6:4–5, 10–11, 22–23; 7:25.
[4] FISHBANE, Garments, 67–69.

Chapter Six

The Pre-Eminence of Torah?

Introduction

In the preceding study I have endeavored to show on the basis of evidence internal to the Old Testament that: 1) there existed a theological 'grammar' of 'Law and Prophets' which functioned authoritatively earlier than the scriptural collections later known by those titles achieved their final form; and 2) that this conclusion, in turn, casts doubt upon H. E. Ryle's 'interval of time' assumption, according to which the final form of a text or a canonical sub-collection always preceded any ascription of authority to it. Instead, I have argued that an authoritative theological construct shaped Israel's emerging canon, which in turn suggests a process of canon formation more organic and pluralistic than the usual nomistic model.

If the existence of this theological construct in the biblical literature is accepted, then I believe two further questions arise, to which I shall respond in this final chapter: 1) how do we account for the tradition, within confessional interpretation and modern scholarship, of the hermeneutical supremacy of the Torah (*qua* Pentateuch) over the Prophets and the Writings? and 2) how would the existence of such a construct of 'Law and Prophets' fit within the broader history of Old Testament canon formation, especially with regard to the evidence for that history external to the Old Testament?

Counter-Indications: Grounds for the Torah's Pre-Eminence

In order to provide answers to these questions I should now like to investigate the standard arguments for the Torah's pre-eminence and the linear tripartite model of Old Testament canon formation. After a brief review of the *internal* evidence for this model, I shall proceed to analyze the *external* evidence offered in support of it. Building upon my own exegetical work and the alternative process of canon formation they have suggested, I shall then propose a fresh way of construing the external evidence, which I believe will lend further support to my exegetical arguments. Thus, in my view these potential 'counter-indications' of my thesis will in fact be shown to strengthen my case and further illuminate the alternative reconstruction of canon formation which I have proposed.

Internal Evidence

Ever since Wellhausen, who always conveniently, if imprecisely, marks a watershed in the history of Old Testament scholarship,[1] a strange inconsistency has exercised profound influence on scholarly reconstructions of Old Testament canon formation. As others of his day, Wellhausen saw in Israelite prophecy the origin of the true genius of Israelite religion. However, his understanding of and extreme distaste for the role of authoritative written texts within religion generally led him to view the rise of written scripture in Israel's post-exilic period as the imposition of a dour legalism upon that genius, which consequentially languished until its revival by Jesus and his followers.[2]

Thus, Wellhausen's influential historical reconstruction of Israelite religion created a paradox: although the prophets preceded 'law' in Israelite religion (when both are viewed as historical phenomena), a written 'Law' still preceded a written 'Prophets' (when viewed as canonical subcollections). This is the model, constructed mostly on the basis of internal biblical evidence and certain implicit theories of religion, which Ryle and others supported and strengthened on the basis of external historical evidence. As we have seen, the result of this scholarly work was the explicit formulation of a linear three-stage process corresponding to the major canonical divisions of the MT.

Ryle's explicit statements have had more influence than his implicit arguments. His model defined what would become the standard view of the canonical process: that 'canonization' proper represented an official act of valorization which was only possible after a text had become literarily 'complete,' its text standardized, and an 'interval of time' passed for its authority to

---

[1] NICHOLSON, Pentateuch.

[2] It has often been alleged that WELLHAUSEN's characterization of Judaism as a legalistic religion stemmed from an anti-Semitic, or at least anti-Jewish prejudice. See BLENKINSOPP, Pentateuch, 12; SILBERMAN, Wellhausen. Without wishing to absolve WELLHAUSEN of this charge undeservedly, it does seem to me that his notion of scripture as *essentially* legalistic indicates a broader bias. I suspect his profound misunderstanding of scripture arose just as much from the other traditional 'threats' to German Protestant critical biblical scholarship in the nineteenth century: conservative Protestant ecclesiasticalism and Catholicism (cf. SILBERMAN, Wellhausen, 78–79). In fact, I am reminded of contemporary biblical scholars who, in their rush to disassociate themselves from the threat of 'fundamentalism,' wish to place all religious authority in the historical events *behind* the biblical text and none in the biblical text itself. (Cf. my treatment of BARR and McDONALD in Chapter One.) However, this move behind the text is one that these 'anti-fundamentalist' scholars actually *share* with fundamentalists, as H. W. FREI slyly portrayed in his historical study of hermeneutics (FREI, Eclipse). The central difficulty for both camps is the fact that the primary access to the events the Bible describes is through the biblical text itself.

become established through religious usage.[3] Implicit to Ryle's argument, however, was often a view of scripture very different from that of Wellhausen: that scriptural 'authority' began with the *use* of scripture within a concrete community of faith, only later receiving official acknowledgment of an authority they *already* possessed.[4]

Despite the force of Ryle's model, the inconsistency between what were really *two* different reconstructions of canon formation was noticed immediately and persistently by a variety of dissenting scholars. A fundamental question focused the conceptual difficulty: namely, if Wellhausen was correct that the material in the Former and Latter Prophets reflected so clearly an earlier stage in Israel's religion and the Pentateuch a later stage, why then was it the Pentateuch that had become 'canonical' first? Conversely, why did the prophetic writings become 'canonical' so late, especially if they had already existed in an earlier form?[5]

Usually, however, questions about the written development (*Verschriftung*) and canonization of the prophetic books were overlooked,[6] partly because of the pre-eminent role of pentateuchal scholarship within the field. Wellhausen's Yahwist and Elohist sources for the Pentateuch were dated to the time of the monarchy.[7] Although the influence of the phenomenon of proph-

---

[3] Here again we see the fear of a more conservative position shaping a critical scholar's reconstruction. RYLE's emphasis on functional authority fits the evidence for Old Testament canon formation better than more conciliar theories (e. g., those which have emphasized the role of Jamnia), but his insistence that usage must *precede* authority betrays an Anglican skiddishness over more conservative views of biblical 'inspiration.' RYLE wished to argue that the inspiration of the Bible transpired over the entire history of the transmission of the text (entrusted to the safekeeping of the apostolic Church), rather than in a process of divine 'dictation.' It is for this reason that he is at such pains to insist that no part of the Old Testament was written *in order to be scripture*. It is also for this reason that he frequently writes of the Holy Spirit 'overruling' the history of the canon: rather than a quaint relic of belief such statements are intended to counter conservative claims of *immediate* inspired authorship. See, e. g., RYLE, Canon, 1; idem, Study, esp. 89–93; 95–96.

[4] Thus KAISER, Introduction, 411: "It has frequently, and correctly, been emphasized that the formation of such a theoretical idea of a canon can only be understood if it has been preceded by a fairly lengthy period in which the books later regarded as canonical already enjoyed the sort of respect that is given to a canon."

[5] ARNOLD, Observations. WELLHAUSEN's own answer to this question was to construe the process of canonization as primarily legal. Thus he summarized (Prolegomena, 409): "...it is easy to understand that the Torah, though as a literary product later than the historical and prophetical books, is yet older than these writings, which have originally in their nature no legal character, but only acquired such a character in a sort of metaphorical way, through their association with the law itself."

[6] KRATZ, Redaktion, 16. He dates (Redaktion, 19–22) the beginning of *written* prophecy in Israel to the Assyrian period (second half of the eighth century B. C.).

[7] The Yahwist to the time of Solomon (late ninth century B. C.); the Elohist to the eighth century B. C. in the northern kingdom.

ecy on these sources, especially the Elohist, was often theorized, the sources still appeared largely to pre-date written prophetic traditions.[8] Factors regarding the independent dating of the Former Prophets were obscured at first by the effort to locate the same pentateuchal sources as continuing within them. The final form of the Pentateuch could be dated to a time (fifth century B. C.) several centuries earlier than the presumed final form of the Latter Prophets.[9]

Questions about the canonical relation between the Law and the Prophets as two canonical subcollections were also deflected by the massive influence in the early twentieth century of H. Gunkel and form-criticism. Form-critical approaches emphasized the orality of prophetic traditions to the exclusion of textual questions. The antiquity of legal traditions was reasserted by a trio of German scholars: A. Alt, M. Noth and G. von Rad. Taken together, they slowly effected a reappraisal of law and prophets as historical institutions which emphasized their ancient roots and their setting within abiding traditions.[10] In their work, the prophets no longer appeared to lie at the root of Israelite religion, but marked instead the reflorescence of an already noble vine.

Only with Noth's thesis of a deuteronomistic collection of Former Prophets (in terms of its impact, clearly one of the most influential shifts in Old Testament scholarship during the twentieth century) did the old question of the growth and authority of the written prophetic corpus regain currency and strength.[11]

If the collection Former Prophets could be attributed largely to deuteronomistic tradition within Israel, and if the final form of the collection was to be dated to the early post-exilic period, then at least *some form* of the Deuteronomistic History must have preceded or have been coterminous with the final form of the Pentateuch (if viewed as emerging in the period of the Restoration under Ezra). After all, had not Wellhausen dated the final form of the Pentateuch to the time of Ezra precisely in comparison to the Former Prophets which, in his view, consistently gave evidence for an earlier stage in Israel's religion?

Because it continued to be assumed that the prophetic writings became canonical only *after* they became a complete collection, exegetical investigations detailing the composite nature of the books of the Latter Prophets and

---

[8] I. e., the earliest written prophetic books: Amos; Hosea and First Isaiah. The shift toward this position may be seen by comparison with the pre-Wellhausen view. E. g., DE WETTE had attributed (Introduction I:25) the origin of Hebrew literature — including the Elohist source — to the 'prophetic schools' (*Prophetenschulen*) of Samuel.

[9] E. g., Hellenistic influence was alleged for late prophetic material such as Third Isaiah and Second Zechariah.

[10] ZIMMERLI, Gesetz, 252.

[11] On the abiding impact of NOTH's thesis, see MCKENZIE AND GRAHAM, History.

the late dating of certain books or sections (e. g., Third Isaiah, Second Zechariah, Joel, Jonah) were customarily held to provide *termini post quem* for the canonization of the entire prophetic corpus.[12] Increasingly, scholars were constrained to explain why early written prophetic texts were *not* considered authoritative in the period during which they presumably would have possessed the greatest force (i. e., the exilic and early post-exilic periods as Israel reflected upon the fulfillment of the prophetic message), and only gained authority in the period during which they presumably would have had the least acceptance (i. e., the Persian period of 'legalism' and priestly 'theocracy,' as it was frequently characterized).[13]

To put the issue more sharply, if the prophetic writings did not possess any authority until the second or even the first century B. C., how could they have gained any canonical status over against the Torah in the very period of its ascendancy?[14] Thus, K. Budde had already felt compelled to argue that although prophetic writings existed in Ezra's time they were not considered canonical due to the Torah's pre-eminent religious authority and because the prophets' words were viewed from the outset as 'time-conditioned.'[15] Budde explained their later canonization by arguing that the idea of canonicity had been extended from a strictly legal type of authority to one which also included 'historical interest.'[16]

However, the theological construct of 'law and prophets' that I have detailed in the biblical text argues against both an early notion of the Torah's religious pre-eminence over the Prophets and against Budde's assertion that the prophets' words were considered time-conditioned.[17] To the contrary, the prophetic word was viewed as standing forever true, even if capable of multiple fulfillments.[18] Despite scholarly assertions to the contrary, I have endeavored to show in my treatment of the relevant biblical material that no exegeti-

---

[12] The book of Daniel played an important role here, as it was often assumed that as a 'prophetic' book it would have been included in the prophetic 'canon' had it still been 'open.' Thus it was argued — circularly — that canonization must have proceeded by stages. In addition, the final form of Daniel was often dated to the Hellenistic period, which was usually interpreted to mean that the prophetic canon had become 'closed' only slightly before.

[13] HENGEL, "Schriftauslegung," 16, now characterizes this period as 'schöpferisch' in contradistinction to the Wellhausen tradition.

[14] This question is being radicalized in quite a different direction by those who now date the final form of the Torah to the Hellenistic period. See ROSE, Deuteronomist; H. H. SCHMID, Jahwist; VAN SETERS, Prologue; VORLÄNDER, Entstehung.

[15] BUDDE, Kanon, 36–37.

[16] Ibid., 38.

[17] Cf. KRATZ, Redaktion, 22.

[18] See Deut 31–32; Isa 2:1–4; 46:8–13; 55; Jer 44:29. In Jer 26:18 a century-old prophecy from Micah (Mic 3:12) is quoted authoritatively. In Dan 9:2 the book of Jeremiah (Jer 25:11–12; 29:10) is cited authoritatively.

cal warrant exists for the subordination of prophetic scripture to pentateuchal scripture on the part of the editors and scribes responsible for the Old Testament.

Those who maintain that prophecy was institutionalized and 'routinized' in the post-exilic period (a view of which I am unconvinced, but which is not at the center of my argument) unfairly extend this sociological theory of institutions to refer to the canonical subcollections of Law and Prophets (i. e., is it assumed that only 'free,' 'radical' prophets could appreciate and use prophetic writings? or that 'truly prophetic' groups would refuse the authority of Torah?). Although there does exist evidence for tensions and disagreements between various sociological groups at various points in Israel's history, the reductionism involved in many reconstructions of social conflict has often beggared belief.

Thus, M. Weber and O. Plöger argued (following Wellhausen) that the ascendancy of the Law, and the institutional theocracy that enforced it, banished prophecy into secret underground conventicles.[19] On this view why should the Prophets ever have gained general acceptance? Did the elevation of the Prophets, as T. K. Cheyne long ago suggested, become a kind of reaction to the 'spirit of Ezra'?[20] When? How? In the same way, it has been suggested that remarks in Jeremiah critical of the תורה of the priests reflect criticism of the move toward the canonization of the Law;[21] or, that contradictions between Ezekiel's 'law of the Temple' and the instructions for the building of the Temple in the Pentateuch indicate the subordination of prophetic teaching by a priestly group.[22]

These speculations, however, remain starkly reductionistic in their assumptions. The context for Jeremiah's criticism is far from clear (i. e., the nature of the historical moment and the identity of his addressees); he has abundant criticism for prophets, too. The purpose of Ezekiel's Temple Vision is also obscure, but is not the fact of its inclusion in the canon at least *some* indication of its ability to be read together with the Pentateuch in a complementary (or at least dialectical) way?[23]

Nevertheless, it continues to be alleged on the basis of the later books of the Old Testament that the prophetic writings did not receive the same atten-

---

[19] WEBER, Judaism, 380: "[Prophecy] vanished [from public eye] because the priestly political power in the Jewish congregation gained control over ecstatic prophecy in the same manner as did the bishopric and presbyterian authorities over pneumatic prophecy in the early Christian congregation." Cf. PLÖGER, Erbe. See also BUDDE, Schrifttum, 5.

[20] CHEYNE, Origin, 363, cited in RYLE (Canon, 118), although it is not clear whether RYLE was referring to this volume or to CHENEY's earlier lecture.

[21] E. g., Jer 2:8; 7:21–25.

[22] RYLE, Canon, 67.

[23] On this question, see LEVENSON, Theology.

tion or respect as the Torah.[24] This verdict tends to emerge especially from the work of scholars who tabulate the *quantity* of references and citations, especially those heavily relying on 'citation formulas' (in essence, a modern distinction). I have attempted to show that a different possibility arises when one takes the *quality* of those references and citations into account. For instance, if one recalls the persistent pairing of law and prophets (esp. in Chronicles, Ezra–Nehemiah), the number of Torah citations relative to the number of citations from the Prophets hardly seems decisive. There are other reasons that the Chronicler might have cited more from one than the other — synchronic[25] as well as diachronic.[26]

Similarly, a recent introduction to the Old Testament claims that Neh 9 and Pss 78, 105, 106, 135, 136 know only events in the Torah, suggesting that this means the canonization of the prophetic corpus had not yet occurred.[27] However, this is not the case. The passages in question *do* include references to events from prophetic books and even prophetic themes,[28] but even if they did not, the absence of this material would not necessarily imply any such thing. In my judgment, the passages I have discussed which pair Law and Prophets provide a major check against this line of interpretation: above all, 2 Chr 20:20b.[29] Apart from God himself, only the prophets share with Moses (Ex 14:31) the honor of being considered *objects* of 'belief' within Israel[30] – and this from the Chronicler![31]

---

[24] SWANSON, Closing, 45–47; 358.

[25] I. e., within the *synchronic* context of the Chronicler's narrative, the period of Moses lay in the past and could be cited in a summary way, but not the age of the prophets. It was thus necessary to work implicitly (e. g., 2 Chr 20:20b).

[26] For the Chronicler to devote more attention to Torah legislation might simply have had to do with particular issues important to the intention of the work, and not necessarily imply that the scope of the prophetic corpus was not yet fixed or canonical. E. g., just because the New Testament writings tend to quote more from Isaiah does not imply that their authors thought less of the other prophetic books.

[27] P. R. DAVIES, Collections, 372.

[28] The influence of the Deuteronomistic History is particularly evident. See esp. Neh 9:23–37 and Pss 78:55–72; 105:8–10, 15, 44–45; 106:34–46; 135:12, 15–18; 136:21–26.

[29] Again, I note the collective sense. The reference to Isa 7:9b proves that written prophecy is here in view.

[30] WILDBERGER, "Glauben."

[31] ALBERTZ, History, has formulated a new variation on the same old problem by arguing that the Deuteronomistic History was separated from the book of Deuteronomy at the time of the canonization of the Torah (II:472–73) because its emphasis on state and cult proved offensive to Israel's Persian overlords (II:547–48). The Deuteronomistic History was then re-integrated into authoritative scriptural tradition by the theocratic scribes responsible for Chronicles (II:553–54), who thought that: 1) the earlier decision about the canon needed revision; and 2) the prophetic writings should be given official status (II:547; 550–51). Here one speculation is generated to prove another.

In sum, there exists no persuasive *internal* biblical evidence to exclude the possibility in the post-exilic period of a canonical subcollection of 'Prophets' equal in authority to the 'Law.'[32]

External Evidence

It will not be possible in the rest of this chapter to discuss in detail all of the external witnesses to the history and shape of the Old Testament canon. My intention is anyway more modest: to challenge the customary view that the Law was always considered more authoritative within Israel.

There is no question about whether the Torah *eventually* became more authoritative than the Prophets or the Writings in the eyes of the rabbis. A whole host of practical instructions for the care and copying of religious scrolls reveals a preferential treatment for the Torah.[33] Also, later rabbis used explicitly hierarchical formulations to designate the different levels of authority inhering to each section of the canon.[34]

From the perspective of the standard theory of canon formation, with its insistence that the Law was canonized 'first' under Ezra in the mid-fifth century B. C., the usual move has been to assume that the Law was always considered more 'authoritative' within the canon — on historical grounds, theological grounds, or both. Once the three-stage linear theory is called into question, however, does the evidence for a 'more authoritative' Torah in the period *before* the rabbis remain as compelling?[35] Let us examine the arguments:

1. Persian Policy

The theory has been advanced that the canonization of the Torah in Ezra's time was due in large measure to a Persian policy of codifying local laws

---

[32] Cf. BARR, Scripture, 72: "...the canon as such does not specify the greater importance of the Torah." Nevertheless, BARR contends that its 'dominance' is generated extrinsically and that the canon 'testifies' to it.

[33] For a sampling of this material, see BECKWITH, Canon, 113–14.

[34] BECKWITH, Canon, 114, argues for a two-tiered conception, based on his analysis of the scribal rules for copying. LEIMAN, Canonization, 66 n. 294–95, maintains that the familiar three-tiered view of biblical authority is medieval, not talmudic.

[35] If we assume the Jerusalem Talmud was compiled beginning around the time of Jerome, in the fifth century A. D., it must be admitted that an argument for the earliest notions of canon based on information gleaned from the same period would hardly be considered overwhelming. Even if some traditions are earlier (i. e., the Mishnah dates from the third century A. D. and may contain even older, oral material; on this dating, see BAR-ILAN, Writing, 28), might not the rabbinic instructions be equally well understood as a later effort to *establish* a privileged postion for the Torah rather than the reflection of an already ancient tradition always and everywhere preserved? If everyone in the rabbinic period agreed that the Torah *qua* Pentateuch was supremely authoritative, why did the point have to be insisted upon with such vigor?

throughout the empire as a means of political administration and control.[36] Since the conferral of authority upon prophecy would have proved too ambiguous or too threatening to Israel's overlords (e. g., Neh 6:7), prophetic literature was, in effect, demoted by being left out of the original canon. This exclusive 'Torah perspective,' it is argued, can be illustrated by the material in the book of Ezra–Nehemiah.[37]

Against this theory I would maintain: a) that the Persian evidence, while intriguing, does not refer explicitly to Judah;[38] b) that even if the Persian evidence did include the terms of its Judahite policy, it would only tell us about the authority of Judahite 'law' for the *Persians* and not necessarily the Jews. Surely it is somewhat romantic to imagine that the Persians would have simply conceded to the precise terms of Jewish religious law — no less and no more; c) the biblical text itself nowhere suggests Persian policy has had any role in the formation of the canon; d) within the biblical literature, the really flattering remarks about Persian power are to be found in the Prophets, not the Law (e. g., Cyrus in Isa 45). Why then would these remarks have been 'demoted'? e) as we have seen in the previous chapter, Ezra–Nehemiah cannot be said to reflect the view that the Torah *qua* Pentateuch is exclusively authoritative.[39] Rather, Ezra–Nehemiah and Chronicles witness consistently to dual sources of religious authority within Israel and a twin corpus of scripture; and f) finally, one must ask why this Persian 'Torah' does not more exactly fit the post-exilic situation (e. g., why not mention Persia directly? — the Prophets do) and why this Israelite legal code is cast in the form of a narrative history.[40]

---

[36] In the absence of direct evidence, the point is made for the most part on the basis of an Egyptian parallel. See HOGLUND, Administration, 234–36; P. FREI, Zentralgewalt; idem, Reichsautorisation; BLENKINSOPP, Mission; idem, Pentateuch, 239–43. Note that HOGLUND takes the reference to 'the law of the king' in Ezra 7:26 in an exclusively secular sense (Adminstration, 230–31), an interpretation which even BLENKINSOPP, otherwise supportive of this theory, rejects (Mission, 418 n. 45).

[37] So CARR, Canonization, 31–32.

[38] LOHFINK, Bewegung? 369–70.

[39] CARR admits (Canonization, 32 n. 28) that Ezr 9:10–12 presents an apparent exception, but argues that since pentateuchal regulations follow this citation, it is, in effect, the exception that proves the rule. Against his interpretation, I have argued that this passage is not a solitary exception, but reflects the consistent pairing of Law and Prophets as authoritative scripture. The point here is that the prophets were considered *instruments* of Torah (Ezr 9:10–11) and the 'pentateuchal' passage following can therefore be quoted as a prophecy now fulfilled (Ezr 9:13), which in turn provides the 'commandment' with a new urgency and force (Ezr 9:14–15).

[40] See further, RÜTERSWÖRDEN, Reichsautorisation?

2. Prior Canonization

Similarly the argument is still made that, for whatever reason, if the Torah was 'canonized' in the fifth century B. C. then it must have preceded the corpus of 'Prophets,' which contains demonstrably later material and therefore must not only be a subsidiary canonical collection, but also of lesser authority.

There is a good case to be made that Ezra's lawbook was something like our Pentateuch, since there are strong indications that D and P material are both presupposed.[41] Yet even if it is assumed that this 'something-like-the-Pentateuch' emerged at about the time of Ezra, it is usually maintained that this corpus continued to evolve, although perhaps in relatively minor ways.[42] In other words, Ryle's old notion that the canonization of the Pentateuch implied the absolute fixity of the text cannot be adopted by those dating the Pentateuch to Ezra. As we have already noted, an increasing number of scholars would date the final form of the Pentateuch considerably later than the mid-fifth century B. C., which only weakens further the notion that the Torah preceded the Prophets. Even if a proto-Torah was somehow recognized at the time of Ezra, the evidence strongly suggests that this Torah continued to be shaped *after* such recognition.

All these points serve, as we have seen before, to place the proximate dates of canonization for the Law and the Prophets much closer together, which in turn only creates increased suspicion that these two processes were not separate at all, but closely linked.[43]

---

[41] GESE, Gestaltwerdung, 315 n. 21. According to GESE Neh 13:5 presupposes Deut 14:22 and Num 18:21–24 (P); Neh 10 relies on D and P in a variety of ways. See also Chapter Five above.

[42] BLENKINSOPP, Pentateuch, 240–41.

[43] E. g., GESE, Gestaltwerdung, 315, now dates the Torah to 398 B. C. under Ezra and the 'frame' of the prophetic corpus to the middle of the fourth century B. C. (Gestaltwerdung, 319)! GESE admits the presence of prophetic literature already by Ezra's time and argues that the Torah did not attempt to take the place of all inspired scripture in Israel, but was only supposed to represent the *Urzeit*, the authoritative mosaic period (Gestaltwerdung, 316). Nevertheless, because of later witnesses to the Torah's pre-eminence (e. g., the Sadducees, Samaritans, PHILO), GESE also maintains that the Torah comprised Israel's only 'canonical' literature. Without a trace of self-consciousness he remarks: "*Trotzdem* muß sich eine Erweiterung des Kanons um die Propheten im 3. Jh. weithin durchgesetzt haben" (Gestaltwerdung, 316, my emphasis). As I hope I have shown by now, this '*trotzdem*' is the Achilles' heel of the consensus view of Old Testament canon formation. Note, however, that with the Pentateuch dated to 398 (still undergoing slight changes) and the prophetic corpus dated to ca. 350 B. C. the two processes have narrowed considerably in GESE's reconstruction. But how can this reconstruction hope to explain the canonization of prophetic literature in Israel '*trotz*' the presumed pre-eminence of the Torah within fifty years or so, and then the *re*subordination of prophetic literature to the Torah almost immediately thereafter?

3. Text Criticism

In my judgment, it is now clear that the proto–masoretic text was not shaped in the first two centuries A. D., but in the last two centuries B. C.[44] Although the text was not completely standardized for several centuries, the Dead Sea scrolls have provided clear evidence that proto-Masoretic texts received an enormous amount of care in the process of transmission.[45]

It has sometimes been alleged that the textual tradition for the Pentateuch is 'markedly less fluid' than for other biblical books, also suggesting the Torah's pre-eminence.[46] However, E. Tov has denied the appropriateness of such a judgment. He writes that while the Torah "might be expected to have a special position from a textual point of view... The evidence does not, however, support such an assumption."[47]

Tov agrees that the orthography of the Torah in the Masoretic tradition is generally more conservative than the rest of biblical literature,[48] but notes that the number of variant readings preserved in that tradition is just as great as for other biblical books.[49] In fact, Tov concludes, the only possible point of distinction for the Torah's textual transmission is a slightly greater awareness of 'inconsistencies' between the narrated stories and a correspondingly slight inclination to smooth over potential contradictions (i. e., *more* extensive editorial 'intervention,' not less).[50]

In sum, the textual evidence does not support any distinction of sanctity between the Torah and the other biblical books.

---

[44] MULDER, Transmission, 98; cf. CROSS, Canon, 205-29. CROSS dates the pharisaic recension of the Hebrew text to the early first century A. D., but also sees significant activity in the first century B. C. which led up to that recension (216-17; 222). For this reason, I refer to the 'shaping' of the text in the last two centuries B. C. This dating may even be slightly conservative: TOV, History, 60, notes that proto-Masoretic texts are attested from the third century B. C.

[45] TOV, History, 57. TOV also notes that although the New Testament text was not standardized until the work of Erasmus in the sixteenth century, the text was nevertheless held to be canonical.

[46] CARR, Canonization, 35.

[47] TOV, Criticism, 196.

[48] It bears reminding that 'conservative' in this context only means 'exhibiting defective orthography,' on the theory that defective orthography represents an older writing practice. See TOV, Criticism, 229.

[49] This is also true, TOV argues, for the LXX, pre-Samaritan texts and the Samaritan Pentateuch. See his Criticism, 196.

[50] This point is made by TOV in his discussion of pre-Samaritan texts (Criticism, 85–86). See also his *caveat* that this kind of evidence is always skewed by the random method of its preservation and discovery (Criticism, 196).

4. The Samaritan Pentateuch

The so-called Samaritan 'schism,' while now widely held to have reached its critical stage at the beginning of the second century B. C., is still adduced as evidence of the Torah's early pre-eminence for at least *some* Jewish groups.[51] The point would seem to be that for the Samaritans anyway the Torah was pre-eminent, so we as historians should include this group[52] under the umbrella term 'Judaism' rather than dismissing them from consideration. For example, D. M. Carr considers the 'irreducible plurality' of Judaism in this period to indicate that a *variety* of 'scriptures' were in use.[53]

However, this line of argument merely begs a further question: in what way should the Samaritans be considered part of Second Temple Judaism? Perhaps the restriction of their canon to the Torah alone[54] indicates that a much different religious understanding prevailed among the Samaritans than that within Palestinian Judaism, with its wider canon (4Q397; Sir, Prol.)?[55] Should we, as historians, disregard the distinction that Jews and Samaritans made between themselves?[56] Should we disregard the way in which this distinction has shaped the attitudes toward the Samaritans exhibited in post-exilic biblical literature?[57] Even J. D. Purvis, who argues that it is appropriate to regard Samaritanism as 'a variety of Judaism,' admits that Samaritanism has to be described as 'an aberrant position within this complex.'[58]

It is finally important to heed Tov's reminder that pre-Samaritan texts and the Samaritan Pentateuch also exhibit 'extensive editorial intervention' in the Torah.[59]

---

[51] CARR, Canonization, 35. For literature on the Samaritans, see PURVIS, Samaritans.

[52] CARR would include 'the Alexandrians' and 'certain priestly and/or other establishment groups in Palestine' within this 'pre-eminent Torah' group.

[53] CARR, Canonization, 27; 63–64.

[54] Even this point is not so clear as commonly assumed, as noted by LIGHTSTONE, Prolegomenon, 137. The Samaritans apparently used a version of the book of Joshua; see CROWN, Chronicles; PURVIS, Pentateuch.

[55] See BARRERA, Bible, 211–17; 220–21.

[56] As BARRERA points out (Ibid., 211) Samaritans consider themselves to be the 'true Israel' and the 'Jews' to be schismatics. On this basis alone, I question the methodological fairness of classifying them under the rubric of 'Judaism.' I note, however, that BARRERA does not view them (215) as 'opposed' or 'separate' from Judaism in the period.

[57] For an example of an alternative approach, see the biting critique by NEUSNER (Structure, 3–7) of a position seemingly similar to CARR's held by COHEN, which NEUSNER disparages as 'nominalist.' Judaism cannot be described, NEUSNER argues, as the 'sum of all diversities' without the abrogation of the critical function of scholarship. In my judgment, however, NEUSNER overstates his case. For a more balanced approach to this question, see PURVIS, Samaritans.

[58] PURVIS, Samaritans, 92.

[59] TOV, History, 62.

5. The Septuagint

There is also an argument made from the LXX. If the usual interpretation of the Letter of Aristeas is followed, the Greek translation of Jewish scripture began with the Torah in third-century B. C. Egypt.[60] Moreover, Greek translations of the Prophets and the Writings use vocabulary from the LXX Pentateuch and even quote its characteristic Greek expressions.[61]

However, any translation is likely to start at the 'beginning' of a work, which is not at all the same thing as presuming a distinctive sanctity for the Pentateuch apart from its literary role. Even if a special sanctity did adhere to the LXX Pentateuch, it might well say more about the religious perspective at Alexandria than Jerusalem. Philo's favoring of the LXX Pentateuch is clear,[62] but this usage could easily result from factors other than a more restrictive canon.

The Prophets and the Writings were neither unknown nor uncanonical to Philo and others in the diaspora. Tov notes that Chronicles is quoted by Eupolemos in the middle of the second century B. C. and that Job is cited by Pseudo-Aristeas at the beginning of the first century B. C.[63] He goes on to note I. L. Seeligmann's view that LXX Isaiah reflects the historical context of 170–50 B. C.[64]

There exist no Greek lists of canonical scripture from this early period, and it is quite right to be skeptical about the existence of *an* LXX, a single 'Greek Bible.'[65] Moreover, the circumstances suggest that some individual Greek translations of the Prophets (e. g., Isaiah) occurred too long *after* the time of their literary compilation (in Hebrew) to date the process of canon formation within Palestinian Judaism.

The best solution is to consider the Alexandrian 'canon' in principle to have been no different from the Palestinian canon.[66] This position still receives its best support from the evidence of a Naḥal Ḥever scroll (8ḤevXIIgr)

---

[60] Idem, Criticism, 136. Tov notes that several papyrus and leather Greek fragments recovered from Qumran and Egypt date to the second century B. C., securing this date as a *terminus ante quem*.

[61] Ibid., 137. Tov dates the Greek translations of most of the Prophets and the Writings to the beginning of the second century B. C. based upon the notice in the Prologue to Ben Sira, which he understands to refer to the existence of the bulk of these books in Greek at that time.

[62] See section 13 below.

[63] Tov, Criticism, 137. Here Tov is citing SWETE, Introduction, 25–26.

[64] Tov, Criticism, 137; SEELIGMANN, Version, 76–94.

[65] CARR, Canonization, 59. See also ELLIS, Canon, 34; SUNDBERG, Church.

[66] As SUNDBERG, Church, has persuasively shown, there was no Alexandrian canon as such. However, the further conclusion which SUNDBERG draws from this finding, that the canon was only acknowledged *after* the split between Judaism and Christianity, is not a necessary corollary and in my judgment remains doubtful. For a better formulation, see BARRERA, Bible, 229–33.

discovered in 1952, which contains a *revision* of the book of The Twelve in Greek.[67] The scroll and the *kaige*-Theodotion revision of which it is part date to the late first century B. C. and represent an effort to produce a Greek translation more closely resembling the developing proto-Masoretic (Hebrew) text.[68] This continued tendency within a series of LXX revisions over centuries[69] also testifies to the controlling authority of the Hebrew text and canon.[70]

6. The Dead Sea Scrolls

Another allegation of Torah pre-eminence is frequently made on the basis of the distribution of the Dead Sea scrolls.[71] The further point is made that, given the wide variety of textual variants of biblical material and the existence of new 'sectarian' documents, it is impossible to view the biblical text as having yet been stabilized or canonized. However, this position misrepresents the evidence:[72]

a) The Biblical Fragments

The sheer variety of biblical manuscripts may well have existed for reasons only indirectly related to the Qumran community's understanding of a scriptural canon.[73] As Tov argues, a number of the Dead Sea scroll fragments apparently originated at other locales in Palestine.[74] The presence of such widespread textual variety may have much more to do with preservation than canonicity, and from this aspect may parallel *geniza* finds at ancient synagogues.

---

[67] BARTHÉLEMY, Devanciers; TOV, Scroll; idem, Scriptures, 224–25.

[68] TOV, Criticism, 143–45.

[69] Idem, Scriptures, 225; cf. CROSS, History. The disputed proto-Lucianic recension, dating to the first century B. C. (if it in fact existed), would have also worked to conform the Greek text to a Hebrew text, according to CROSS.

[70] This is not to claim that every revision of the LXX constitutes a revision according to a Hebrew *Vorlage* (the LXX was also worked on independently), only that continued revisions on the LXX were made in the direction of Hebrew sources and that this direction of influence was therefore controlling.

[71] I note, however, that the frequency of discovered texts does not support this conclusion. According to TOV, Criticism, 104 ('Table 19'), Qumran's 'favorite' texts were Deuteronomy, Isaiah and the Psalms, with both Genesis and Exodus as close seconds.

[72] For a recent comprehensive study of these issues, see VANDERKAM, Literature.

[73] *Contra* BROOKE, Scrolls, 63: "The overall theological outlook of the group to be linked with the Qumran site... might be measured by the number of manuscripts to have survived there of any particular work and by the references in any texts to other texts deemed as authoritative."

[74] TOV, Criticism, 102–03. He reaches this conclusion on the basis of the distinctive orthography, morphology and scribal practice of the Qumran scribes, which are not shared by all the recovered fragments.

Having made the negative point, it remains to note positively that fragments of every biblical book except Esther have been discovered at Qumran[75] and several fragments contain material from more than one book.[76] More significantly, Tov also argues persuasively that the 'great number' of proto-Masoretic texts found at Qumran (more than 40% of the total) 'probably reflects their authoritative status' in the period between the third century B. C. and the first century A. D., even though the general status of biblical texts seems to have been one of 'plurality and variety.'[77]

A comparison of proto-Masoretic fragments with other text types leads Tov to advance a distinction between 'vulgar' and 'non-vulgar' texts.[78] Tov argues that the conservative orthography, morphology and careful scribal practice routinely reflected in the proto-Masoretic texts supports their authoritative status, especially within 'temple circles' or, perhaps, a 'central stream in Judaism.'[79] By contrast, other 'vulgar' texts are much more idiosyncratic, even careless to the point of numerous erasures and corrections. Additions and alterations in these fragments indicate a derivative relation to other texts.[80]

Textual stabilization is not to be confused with canonization, but the two processes are clearly related. Although it is not clear at what point the proto-Masoretic texts achieved their 'preponderance' at Qumran, Tov argues that by

---

[75] Ibid., 103. As TOV notes, Esther's absence is as likely to be an accident of history as an indication of disagreement over the book's status: it is a short book (see his n. 75). By contrast TALMON, Schrifttum, 68, doubts the canonical status of Esther and Daniel at Qumran, but his reasons are not compelling. VANDERKAM, Literature, 382, notes the further absence of Nehemiah, based on his view that Ezra and Nehemiah originally formed two separate works.

[76] TOV, Criticism, 103–04 (esp. 'Table 19'). Three scrolls contain portions of two consecutive books of the Torah; one scroll from Wadi Murabba'at illustrates that the book of The Twelve was considered a single book (scroll). TOV also notes that some scrolls seem to have contained only a portion of what was later considered to be the final form of a biblical book, but there could have been many reasons for this.

[77] Ibid., 117; idem, Groups. CARR alleges (Canonization, 49 n. 74) on the basis of TOV's work that proto-Masoretic texts only begin to predominate in first century A. D. texts at Qumran, but this is far from clear. By contrast, TOV argues (Groups, 94) that the proto-Masoretic texts are of greater antiquity because they have resisted being copied in the 'Qumran practice' used for 'virtually all the Qumran sectarian writings.'

[78] TOV, Criticism, 192–94.

[79] Ibid., 194. See also his Criticism, 190. TOV notes that only with the proto-Masoretic texts is there evidence of careful revision, limiting variation in order to safeguard the text tradition. Thus: "...the earliest Qumran finds dating from the third pre-Christian century bear evidence... of a tradition of the exact copying of texts belonging to the Masoretic family..."

[80] Ibid., 193. TOV would include in this group those texts reflecting the 'Qumran practice' and the clearly secondary pre-Samaritan and Samaritan texts, which, while not careless, contain 'harmonizing additions... linguistic corrections... and contextual changes.' This does not mean, TOV notes, that these texts also do not sometimes contain 'ancient readings superior to all other texts.'

the first century A.D. the biblical text entered a new period of 'uniformity and stability.'[81] Thus, none of the *textual* evidence at Qumran contradicts the possibility of a biblical canon (of the type I have described), and several factors suggest the presence of an authoritative scriptural collection (e. g., portions of more than one biblical book on the same fragment or text; the growing preponderance of Masoretic texts; the 'vulgar' character of most, if not all, other text types).[82]

b) The Non-Biblical Texts

There also exist among the Dead Sea scrolls portions of books already known to us from the Apocrypha and the Pseudepigrapha, as well as previously unknown works presumably having their origin within the Qumran community. Both of these facts have been taken to mitigate the existence of a canon of scripture in this period. Sometimes a study of citations has been combined with these facts in an attempt to show by weight of textual references which books the Qumran community (as well as later rabbis and Christian writers) considered to be authoritative.[83]

However, the mere *existence* of these books at Qumran is no more significant than their existence anywhere else, and reference to them in the Qumran material does not necessarily indicate their canonical authority.[84] Similarly the production by the Qumran community of its own documents does not provide conclusive evidence that these documents were considered canonical,[85] nor does the use of such documents indicate an undifferentiated, equally-authoritative body of written material.[86]

---

[81] Ibid., 194–95. Tov rejects the view that this development reflects intentional textual displacement, arguing instead that it was the indirect consequence of political and socio-religious factors in the first century A. D. (i. e., the survival of certain groups within Judaism after the destruction of the Second Temple).

[82] J. Maier, Interpretation, 109–10, has argued that only the Torah represented the scriptural canon at Qumran, but he once again retrojects the three-fold (medieval) rabbinic understanding.

[83] E. g., Brooke, Scrolls, 63; Talmon, Schrifttum, 68–69; VanderKam, Literature, 389-402.

[84] See the balanced statement by J. J. Collins, Scrolls, 90: "It is uncertain whether there was a clear distinction at Qumran between the Kethubim and other authoritative writings." I note again that such a distinction only becomes crucial for a judgment with respect to the existence at this time of a 'canon' of scripture if one understands 'canon' as primarily about exclusivity.

[85] Tov, Criticism, 103 n. 76.

[86] One could draw a rough parallel with the New Testament canon and the writings of the Apostolic Fathers.

The most tantalizing document which has come to light recently is the so-called 'Halakhic Letter' or 4QMMT (also referred to as 4Q394–99).[87] Paleographical analysis in the official edition of the text dates the fragments comprising 4Q394–99 to the period 75 B. C. to A. D. 50.[88] Moreover, the likelihood exists that these fragments are copies of an older document.[89] A major difficulty for interpretation has to do with the fact that the vocabulary of the fragments seems to reflect later, mishnaic Hebrew, while their grammar is more similar to biblical Hebrew — a phenomenon which led the text's editors to postulate initially that the text was one of the earliest works composed at Qumran.[90]

Of this letter the following fragmentary texts have been found: "the book of Moses [and] the book[s of the pr]ophets and of Davi[d...] [the annals of] each generation. And in the book it is written [...]" (4Q397 14–17.10–11); and "remember the kings of Israe[l] and reflect on their deeds, how whoever of them was respecting [the... La]w was freed from afflictions, and those who so[u]ght the Law" (4Q398 11–13.6–7).[91] In the first reference, the phrase 'the book[s of the pr]ophets and of Davi[d...]' has been partially reconstructed in order to fill the right amount of space in the line.

Although the three- or four-part canonical formula in 4Q397 is important,[92] we also find in other writings from Qumran dual formulas similar to those denoting 'Law and Prophets' in the biblical books.[93] The Qumran community possessed the formal idea of a cumulative scripture, which operated with only an *indirect* relation to the stabilization of the text or the precise

---

[87] For a discussion of the basic issues, see CALLAWAY, 4QMMT. For the *editio princeps*, see QIMRON AND STRUGNELL, Cave 4. This edition has been criticized for presenting a composite text which implies too unified a reading of the six or more manuscripts actually found (see CALLAWAY, 4QMMT, 18–19).

[88] QIMRON AND STRUGNELL, Cave 4, 108; see discussion in CALLAWAY, 4QMMT, 28–29.

[89] QIMRON AND STRUGNELL, Cave 4, 109. This paleographical dating positively rules out the suggestion of McDONALD (Formation, 43) that the fragments may date from as late as A. D. 150.

[90] QIMRON AND STRUGNELL, Cave 4, 107–08; cf. QIMRON, Hebrew, 117, has suggested that MMT reflects the spoken language of Qumran, and that this language also survives in the Mishnah, but his view has been criticized for going beyond the available evidence (CALLAWAY, 4QMMT, 28).

[91] Translation and reconstructions from MARTÍNEZ AND TIGCHELAAR, Edition II:800–03.

[92] As VANDERKAM notes, (Literature, 387–88), the established status of these books is reinforced by the fact that here the Qumran sectarians are referring their *opponents* to writings which already constituted a shared authority for both groups.

[93] 'By the hand of Moses and all his servants the prophets' (1QS 1:3; cf. 1QS 8:15–16; CD 5:21–6:1); 'Law of Moses' (1QS 5:8; 8:22; CD 15:2; 9:12; etc.); 'books of the prophets' (CD 7:17). See P. R. DAVIES, Search, 138.

definition of the scriptural collection's contents.[94] It should be noted that the existence of such a canonical situation confirms some of the theoretical arguments of the current study and reveals the Qumran community to have shared a family relationship with other Jewish communities of the period, at least on this central issue.[95]

In sum, Qumran illustrates the way in which the *idea* of the canon preceded its final form(s).[96] Moreover, the idea of the canon at Qumran clearly extends beyond the Torah to embrace *at least* the prophetic writings.[97] The existence of an authoritative canonical framework occurring before the precise determination of its contents helps to explain how alternate canons emerged in antiquity.[98] What clearly did not happen was the attribution of sanctity or authority to a canon only after its contents were fixed.

7. Ben Sira

On its face, the book of Ben Sira would appear to offer an external witness to a tripartite biblical canon by the early second century B. C. (180 B. C.), but this has been debated.

The major points under dispute are these: a) that in the body of the book (Sir 44–49) Israel's salvation history is retold in a way that includes the major prophets and kings of the Deuteronomistic History; the book of The Twelve is cited as a unity (Sir 49:10) and Mal 3:24 [4:6] is quoted (Sir 48:10); and b) the present form of the book contains a prologue by the grandson of the author (ca. 132 B. C.) which explicitly refers to "the Law and the Prophets and the others that followed them/the other books of our ancestors," and "the Law itself, the Prophecies, and the rest of the books."

As has already been noted, the imprecision of the third category may suggest that the third canonical grouping was not yet exactly defined. If so, what may be interesting in this case is that the *category* was distinct even if its *title*

---

[94] VANDERKAM, Literature, 388.

[95] To argue that the Qumran scribes have simply used the language of Deuteronomy and the deuteronomistic tradition only begs the point. According to TOV (Criticism, 104 n. 77), the scribes relied heavily upon Isaiah and the Psalms, too. Why were expressions like 'Moses and the prophets' retained or revived? Presumably because the community believed these expressions denoted the authoritative witness of their past and the claim of that witness upon their present and future.

[96] See VANDERKAM, Literature, esp. 384, for his argument that 'canon' does not represent an 'anachronism' at Qumran.

[97] Ibid., 401. VANDERKAM proposes a 'core of books' as having existed at Qumran, or a "common tradition of works that all Jews would have accepted as definitive or authoritative." In his judgment, the 'Law' and 'the Prophets' as well as the Psalms probably already belonged to this collection.

[98] Thus, the 'Moses and the Prophets' conception is already found in 1QS, which dates to the second century B. C. according to DUMBROWSKI, Remarks, 31.

and *contents* were not (cf. 4Q397). Thus it has also been argued that these references provide evidence for the way in which a tripartite canon emerged; namely, from an essentially bipartite canon in which the first group was closed ('Law') and the second group ('Prophets') was still open, expanding beyond itself.[99]

Conversely, a tripartite formula may have more to do with the *ordering* of the books within the canon than with the canonicity of the books *per se*. Here in Ben Sira, the framework binding the canon together (i. e., the traditional theological construct of 'Law and Prophets') appears to be expanding in a new direction, perhaps to incorporate new literature or perhaps simply to re-classify certain books already known.

Several objections have been raised to this straightforward view, especially with regard to the canonical status of the Writings. Rather than discussing the Writings, however, I would like instead to take up those objections having to do with the pre-eminence of the Torah.

Two main arguments work in tandem to maintain a notion of Torah pre-eminence: a) the 'Prophets' referred to in the Prologue are not yet a closed, distinct subcollection possessing canonical status; and b) use of the term 'Law' as an umbrella term for the whole of scripture points to its superior hermeneutical status.

a) The Prophets as a Canonical Collection

In response to the first criticism, I would note that the particular definitions adopted go far in deciding the answer. If 'canon' is taken in its most narrow, exclusive sense — under the assumption that the contents of the prophetic collection had to be determined precisely (and therefore distinguished from the Writings) before true canonical authority could emerge — then perhaps it would be correct to say the Prophets are not yet fully canonical.[100]

---

[99] BARTON, *Oracles*, 47–48. He argues that only the Torah was canonical into the New Testament period, with 'prophets' referring to all non-Torah books. BARTON also understands the references in the Prologue to 'the rest of the books' to mean books outside of Scripture ('literature in general') and assumes that some of the books now found in the 'Writings' were once included in the category 'Prophets.' There are problems with BARTON's interpretation, however: 1) the Prologue explicitly coordinates all three categories chronologically, with the 'other books' *following* 'the Law and the Prophets.' Why would this have been true, or thought to have been true, of 'literature in general'? and 2) these 'other books' are granted the authority of 'the fathers' and characterized by 'learning and wisdom,' but in such a way that acceptance of 'these disciplines' would lead to a better life *under the law*. This distinguishes these books from the pseudepigraphical, eschatological works BARTON presumably has in mind.

[100] BARTON, *Oracles*, 48. Is there anything that would prevent us from using the same argument to allege the non-canonicity of the Law on the basis of Ben Sira alone?

If, however, 'canon' is taken to mean a 'theological grammar' only indirectly related to the definition and delimitation of a scriptural collection's contents, then arguments against the canonicity of the Prophets made on these grounds fall well short of conviction.[101] Although the prophets mentioned in Sir 44–49 do appear in roughly chronological, rather than 'biblical' order, the additional figures mentioned in Sir 49:14–16 suggest an operative distinction between biblical and extra-biblical figures.[102] The citation of The Twelve in Sir 49:10 points in the same direction.

In other words, I do not feel it is necessary to prove Ben Sira or his grandson possessed the same view of the contents of 'the Law and the Prophets' as we do, or even that their contents were defined and precisely fixed, in order to claim that they held canonical authority for them. The lack in the Prologue of a specific title for the third subcollection of scripture may indicate a somewhat lesser status due to the lack of definition, but only indirectly. It is the antiquity and profundity of the books that commend them, not their literary fixity. This kind of canonical authority is shown by the use of scripture within the body of the book, most notably by the reference to the book of The Twelve (Sir 49:10), which indicates that canonical, as well as chronological order can be determinative for the author.[103]

At the same time, there is an important argument to be made that the Prophets comprised a completed collection by the time of the quotation of Mal 3:24 [4:6] in reference to the prophet Elijah (Sir 48:10), especially if, as I have argued in a previous chapter, this appendix to the book of Malachi gradually came to serve as part of the conclusion to the entire prophetic corpus (Mal 3:22–24 [4:4–6]).

b) Use of the Term 'Torah'

In response to the argument that Ben Sira illustrates the pre-eminence of Torah by using תורה as an umbrella expression for the whole of scripture,[104] I would note that it is far from self-evident that this usage has to do with the Pentateuch's pre-eminent canonical status. Such usage might just as easily derive from the simple abbreviation of 'the Law and the Prophets' to 'the Law.'

---

[101] The contradiction is illustrated nicely by BARTON (Oracles, 49–51), who argues against the existence of a canon on the basis of conflicting canonical orders up through the fourth century A. D. Does BARTON really imagine that there was no canon at all, even functionally, up to this point? (he says as much; see Oracles, 57!). Does it not make more sense to adopt the view that canonical authority might precede, or operate somewhat independently from, the precise definition of a canon's contents? Does not the current Christian canon illustrate this very point, being unitary in its conception (only one canon is confessed by any particular communion), but manifold in its particular instantiations?

[102] BECKWITH, Formation, 46.

[103] *Contra* BARTON, Oracles, 89. See BEGG, Sirach; ORLINSKY, Terms.

[104] E. g., CARR, Canonization, 43.

As we have seen, it is anyway false to assume that 'the Law' refers in literature of this period to the Pentateuch alone. Even if the Pentateuch proper is here singled out, it might well be because of its role in relation to the 'learning and wisdom' which the Prologue advocates, or some other purpose on the part of the author.

In sum, the evidence leads back to the position argued in the current study, that the basic canonical conception of early Judaism was that of 'the Law and the Prophets,' in which both subcollections were judged to be equally authoritative in a profoundly interrelated and dialectical way, but not so exclusively that another category of ancient writings (or writings perceived as ancient) could not emerge. However, unlike the construct of 'Law and Prophets,' which *preceded* the final form of the literary subcollections to which it later referred, the category of 'Writings' could well be a 'back-formation' based upon an increasingly uncertain place of a number of texts within the traditional bipartite structure.

8. The Apocrypha and Pseudepigrapha

Detailed examination of this literature would offer numerous examples of citations and references to books from all three canonical subcollections: Law, Prophets and Writings.[105] However, the Torah's pre-eminence has sometimes been argued on the basis of books such as Tobit or 1–2 Maccabees, all of which can seem to reflect and advocate a Torah-based piety.

On this view, references to 'the Law' or 'the Law of Moses' are taken narrowly to mean to the Pentateuch alone, combined with the influence of another argument for the Torah's pre-eminence in the Hellenistic period, the so-called 'cessation of prophecy' (see section 9 below). 1 Maccabees in particular reports the absence of prophecy in the form of a dogmatic principle, integrally related to a particular trajectory of salvation history (1 Mac 4:46; 9:27; 14:41). If prophecy was no longer a living tradition, the argument goes, then it was naturally 'the Law' which possessed pre-eminent authority.

This argument suffers from a not uncommon failure to appreciate the force and function of the process of textualization. The 'former' prophets, it is true, are no longer alive, but they are only as dead as Moses (e. g., 2 Chr 24:9). Rather than indicating their subordination, the consignment of the prophets to the past serves to express their canonical authority within the larger framework of the *Heilsgeschichte*. Not only does the acknowledged absence of living prophets in this period fail to indicate a lack of respect for prophetic tradition (cf. Jn 8:52–53), but the dogma of prophecy's cessation is in fact a state-

---

[105] For a full discussion, see BECKWITH, Formation, 45–47; DIMANT, Use. DIMANT draws a helpful distinction between an 'expositional' use of biblical material (which uses formal markers) and a 'compositional' use (which does not use markers), as well as the possibility of a 'middle' or didactic style.

ment primarily about the high authority of the prophetic *texts*, in comparison with which all other oral prophecy was increasingly considered less compelling.

Thus, 1 Mac 2:49–68 makes it clear that 'the Law' (1 Mac 2:67) includes scriptural books now found in both the Prophets and the Writings. In 1 Mac 7:17 a scriptural psalm (Ps 79:2–3) is quoted as a prophecy finally fulfilled. In 2 Mac 15:9 Judas Maccabeus exhorts his troops from 'the law and the prophets,' and in 4 Mac 18:10–19 a mother encourages her children by recounting from 'the law and the prophets' (cf. 1 Mac 2:49–68). She includes events from Daniel, and cites by 'author' Isa 43:2; Ps 34:19; Prov 3:18; Ezek 37:2–3 and Deut 32:39 ('the song that Moses taught').[106]

The book of Tobit provides a particularly good example of the way in which the Prophets functioned together with the Law within extra-biblical literature. Because of its great emphasis upon the performance of righteous deeds (e. g., Tob 2:14), one frequently finds that interpreters treat the book as an encomium to the 'law of Moses.'[107] Moreover, in their eyes the literary prominence of certain ritual acts, such as levirate marriage, the giving of alms and the burial of the dead, casts doubt upon any similar 'prophetic' influence. This is especially significant, given that the book is most commonly dated to the second century B. C.,[108] thus occupying with Ben Sira a crucial position between the books of Chronicles (fouth century B. C.) and 1–2 Maccabees (first century B. C.?).[109]

Yet the recent commentary by C. A. Moore finds prophetic influence throughout the book, especially in references to the Exile (Tob 1:3–10; 3:1–5; 14:3–4) and the Return (Tob 13–14), and the mention by name of Amos (Tob 2:6) and Nahum (Tob 14:4, 8; in some mss. 'Jonah').[110] Moreover, 'the prophets of Israel' are cited as a collective, authoritative source in Tob 14:4–5. These prophets are thus credited with predicting the Return as well as the Exile. Moore's judgment is an appropriate one: "Clearly, the canonicity of the prophets was recognized by the Jews of the author's day."[111]

---

[106] A date for 4 Maccabees of approximately A. D. 40 appears to be gaining ground over against the more traditional second century A. D. dating. For discussion, see MACK AND MURPHY, Literature, 398.

[107] Mentioned several times in the book: see Tob 6:13; 7:11–13.

[108] C. A. MOORE, Tobit, 52. MOORE himself opts for a third century date (Tobit, 42) arguing that the absence of any reference to the strife of the Maccabean period (167–135 B. C.) commends an earlier period of origination.

[109] 1 Maccabees dates to approximately 100 B. C. The date of 2 Maccabees is more complicated; the better dates range from 124 B. C. – A. D. 70. See ATTRIDGE, Historiography, 317; 320–21.

[110] C. A. MOORE, Tobit, 21.

[111] Ibid., 290.

Additional cadences exist in the book which might be overlooked if it were not for their resonance within this study. Thus, in Tob 14:9 we read: "But keep the law and the commandments, and be merciful and just..." This is perhaps more than simple poetic parallelism, expressing as it does the essential duality of divine revelation within Israel. Moreover, I note that eschatological notes are struck freely here along with injunctions to follow the Law (e. g., Tob 13:16–18; 14:4–7).

Of great interest is the way in which endogamous marriage is grounded in tradition. At first Tobit enjoins his son Tobias not to marry within his extended family because 'we are the descendants of the prophets' (Tob 4:12). The ancestors named, however, are hardly figures usually thought of as prophetic (Noah, Abraham, Isaac and Jacob), leading to the surmise that in this period any authoritative figure from past (or, perhaps more properly, from scripture?) was considered to be a 'prophet.'[112] Thus, a 'prophetic' principle of endogamous marriage is not only grounded in the example of the patriarchs, it is united in the narrative to the custom of levirate marriage mandated in the 'Law of Moses.'[113] Rather than pitting 'Law' and 'Prophets' against each other, the book considers them to comprise a unity of faith and action, to be almost interchangeable authorities in what they require or preclude.[114]

Thus, in Tobit, as in Chronicles and Ezra–Nehemiah, there also exists a conception of the 'law of Moses' which extends beyond the Pentateuch proper, including the substance of the Prophets and at least some of the Writings, and probably certain aspects of oral teaching as well. The 'law of Moses' as used in the book of Tobit seems to refer most properly to a comprehensive view of "moral and ethical conduct, notably in such acts as almsgiving and burying the dead, neither of which is highlighted in the mosaic Law."[115] In fact, this broad view of moral conduct known as 'the Law' grounds its precepts upon the Prophets just as much as upon Moses (Tob 4:12; 14:4–5), its halakhic interpretations and developments being based upon a conception of the whole of scripture, and not just one part.[116]

---

[112] BARTON, Oracles, 54–55. This possibility does not necessarily lead to BARTON's further conclusion that the Prophets were therefore not yet canonical as such.

[113] See Tob 6:11–13, 16–18; 7:10–12; cf. Deut 25:5–10.

[114] At the very least, the view within Tobit that endogamous marriage is authorized by the *prophets* should provide a stern warning to those who relate such themes to 'anti-prophetic' ritualism or legalism, and to those who assume that 'legal' material must have come from the Pentateuch!

[115] MOORE, Tobit, 205. Cf. 2 Chr 24:9 and the 'tax levied by Moses.'

[116] GAMBERONI, "Gesetz," has pointed in this direction, but without the same conclusions about the state of the canon. It should be noted here that if תורה is understood as a comprehensive 'grammar' in this period (e. g., Ben Sira, Prol.), but actually represents an abbreviated form of 'the Law and the Prophets,' it would also unseat the argument (e. g., TALMON,

These few examples will have to suffice in the present context as evidence not only that the apocryphal and pseudepigraphical literature had a canonical corpus of prophetic writings available to them, but also that these prophetic writings had a non-negotiable place within early Jewish 'Torah' piety.

9. The Cessation of Prophecy

This theory rests upon a few frequently cited passages which, I shall argue, are usually misunderstood. This misunderstanding, in turn, reinforces the view that the rabbinic principle of the Torah's pre-eminent authority was always the basic Jewish conception, rather than an innovation. In my view, prophecy never really ceased at all,[117] although it often functioned in the late period as a more scribal form of activity.[118] Therefore, I would argue, the dogma of the pre-eminence of the Torah cannot be retrojected into this early period, but must be ranked as one of the greatest achievements of the rabbis for *Talmudic* Judaism. The biblical texts at issue are Neh 6:10–14; Ps 74:9; Zech 13:2–6; 1 Mac 4:44–46; 9:27 and 14:41.

The text in Nehemiah reports an incident, it is true, which does not reflect favorably on the institution of prophecy, portraying several of its practitioners as woefully meretricious. There is, however, no evidence within the book that these 'bad' prophets are meant to represent *all* prophets in the period (e. g., see Neh 9:32). To the contrary, Sanballat suborns the prophet Shemaiah (Neh 6:7) and uses the prophetess Noadiah and others (Neh 6:14) expressly to prevent Nehemiah and *other* 'good' prophets from rebuilding the wall around Jerusalem. Rather than a condemnation of the institution of prophecy *per se*, this exchange should be situated within the deuteronomistic tradition of a confrontation between 'true' and 'false' prophets (cf., 1 Kg 22; Jer 28; Am 7), perhaps combined with a tradition of Samaritan prophecy as particularly unreliable (cf. Jer 23:13).[119]

Similarly, the lack of prophecy referred to in Ps 74:9 appears episodic and does not provide any indication that the absence of prophecy to which it refers occurred on a permanent basis. To the contrary, the absence of prophecy in Ps

---

Schrifttum, 60) that usage of 'the Law' to refer to all of scripture illustrates its perceived superiority, *pars pro toto*.

[117] GREENSPAHN, Prophecy; THEN, "Propheten?"

[118] See SOMMER, Prophecy? SOMMER argues impressively for a decline of prophecy in the Second Temple period; but his strongest argument is for a *perception* of prophecy's decline in this period. This perception certainly existed, but was it consistent among various groups and over time? In fact, it seems that this perception intensified with later rabbis — why? SOMMER also describes a 'transformation of prophecy' (Prophecy? 36) during this period. It is not clear to me why a 'transformation' of prophecy should be interpreted as a decline.

[119] As GREENSPAHN notes (Prophecy, 40), even a tradition of false prophecy indicates the presence of prophetic activity.

74 is tied to the destruction of God's sanctuary and land by Israel's enemies, whose eventual defeat promises to restore the institutions only *presently* endangered (Ps 74:9). The 'cessation' of prophecy in this context is thus clearly temporary.[120] Moreover, the exilic 'cessation' of prophecy is evenly matched within the canon by a similar cessation of תורה (Lam 2:9), something usually overlooked by those making the case for Torah pre-eminence.

In Zech 13:2–6, the cessation of prophecy is characterized as permanent, but not yet accomplished. In this passage, the 'end' of prophecy is thoroughly eschatologized (Zech 13:2), reflecting the belief that at the time of Jerusalem's cataclysmic battle with the nations (Zech 12–14) and Jerusalem's eschatological purification (Zech 13:1) prophecy will no longer be necessary, perhaps because all Israel will have then received the prophetic gift (cf. Joel 3:1–2 [2:28–29]). In this way prophecy is also no different than the law, which will be internalized and democratized at the *eschaton* (Jer 31:31–34), no longer requiring official representation or admonition.

The passages in Maccabees do relate a more enduring, dogmatic judgment about prophecy. While this viewpoint might reflect a real lack of prophetic activity in the Hasmonean period, it certainly does not reflect a devaluation of prophetic revelation, whether as a 'living' tradition or as scripture. The canonical authority of the Prophets is clear (2 Mac 15:9; 4 Mac 18:10–19). In fact, the dogmatic position that prophecy has 'ceased' actually serves to consign prophecy to a single, unique era in Israel's *Heilsgeschichte* as a means of grounding and protecting its authority. 'Cessation' statements probably operate within the general conception of a succession of mosaic prophecy which is intermittent and therefore only currently absent.[121] Right alongside direct statements of cessation within this tradition (e. g., 1 Mac 9:27) exists the view that prophecy not only may but *will* revive, and that at its reappearance it will resume its precedence over the high priest (1 Mac 4:46; 14:41: note the qualification 'until'!).

Also, even if those responsible for the books of Maccabees believed that prophecy had ceased in the Hasmonean period, other (roughly coterminous) traditions clearly differed. Thus, Wisdom 7:27 insists: "...in *every generation* [wisdom] passes into holy souls and makes them friends of God, and prophets..."[122] Similarly, prophecy continues to play a major role in the works of Josephus.[123]

---

[120] Ibid. GREENSPAHN observes that an exilic date for Ps 74 would make this reference to the absence of prophecy roughly coterminous with Ezekiel!

[121] Ibid., 39–40.

[122] My emphasis. Cf. Sir 36:20–21. On the dating of the Wisdom of Solomon, see MACK AND MURPHY, Literature, 387. They suggest the first half of the first century A. D.

[123] For discussion, BLENKINSOPP, Prophecy; FELDMAN, Prophets; GREENSPAHN, Prophecy, 41; MICHEL, Prophetentum; SOMMER, Prophecy? 34–37.

In sum, although there may be indications of a transformation of prophecy in the post-exilic period, there is no persuasive evidence that this transformation resulted from or contributed to a dogmatic elevation of the Torah *qua* Pentateuch over the Prophets.[124]

10. The New Testament

The witness of the New Testament is so consistent in its references to 'the Law and the Prophets' that I am unaware of anyone who has argued that the early church privileged Pentateuch over Prophets.[125] In fact, sometimes the reverse point has been made: that in the case of early Christianity we are presented with a Jewish group which, *contrary* to mainstream 'Temple' practice, considered the Prophets to be on par with the Torah.[126]

At sharp variance with this reconstruction is the witness of the New Testament itself. At no point in Jesus' disputes with the Pharisees and Sadducees, despite a great number of references to 'the Law and the Prophets,' is there any explicit disagreement over the shape of the canon or its authority (e. g., Mt 16:1–4). To be sure, the very nature of these passages as disputes suggests a tendentiousness that betokens caution. However, if certain texts (especially prophetic texts) were believed by 'Temple Judaism' to be less authoritative, would it not be likely that such dubiety would have evoked a spirited defense from Jesus and the early church? The witnesses of the New Testament are silent on this point, contributing to the conclusion that it was not the canon itself which was disputed, but its interpretation. In other words, the New Testament shares a common body of scriptures with early Judaism.[127]

11. The Sadducees' Canon

It is partly for this same reason that arguments for a Torah-only canon among the Sadducees lack conviction. The evidence that the Sadducees did not accept the prophetic books has long rested upon meager references by Origen and Jerome,[128] the nature of which might just as well indicate a later confusion (second or third century A. D.) of the Sadducees with the Samaritans.[129]

---

[124] Cf. BARTON, Oracles, 111–16; see also ALEXANDER, "Prophecy," 431.

[125] In theory this point could be argued of a 'judaizing' faction within the early church, but I am not aware of any reconstruction of such a faction that includes a canonical privileging of Torah.

[126] CARR, Canonization, 38–39; 48–49. CARR includes the Qumran community and certain prophetic/apocalyptic 'opposition groups' in his list of strong supporters of the bipartite canon.

[127] BARRERA, Bible, 234.

[128] ORIGEN, Against Celsus, 1.49; JEROME, Commentary on Matthew, on 22:31.

[129] For references, LEMOYNE, Sadducéen, 142–44. Cf. SUNDBERG, Church, 77–78. The confusion may have arisen from the actual fusion of these two groups in this period.

Building on the work of J. Maier,[130] Carr has concluded that despite this possible confusion, and the complete absence of any confirmatory evidence in the writings of Josephus,[131] early Mishnaic regulations indicate that priestly circles including the Sadducees 'revered the Torah alone.'[132]

However, it is clear in Josephus' work that the issue of contention between the Pharisees and the Sadducees did not have to do with a different scriptural canon, but with the authority of oral law, which the Pharisees championed.[133] Thus, to argue that Josephus overlooked the disagreement between the two groups over the scriptural canon is also to argue that he created a controversy over the oral law where none existed, and that he retreated from his effort to present a unified Judaism in one instance, but not in the other. Surely it is more likely that Josephus simply meant what he said.

Moreover, the witness of the New Testament provides another conspicuous silence for this theory. The Sadducees and Pharisees are reported to have had differences,[134] yet there is never any indication that these differences were canonical. To the contrary, in a passage such as Mt 16:1–4, Jesus responds to the request of the Pharisees and Sadducees for a sign by referring to the 'sign of Jonah' without any indication that such a reference would have failed to satisfy the Sadducees.[135]

The dispute in Mt 22:23–33 is sometimes interpreted as evidence for the Sadducees' reliance solely upon the Torah.[136] This interpretation is based upon the Sadducees' refusal to accept a belief in the resurrection of the dead (cf. Acts 23:8), a belief said to be unsupportable by the Torah alone, and requiring the use of certain key prophetic texts.[137]

---

[130] J. MAIER, Auseinandersetzung.

[131] CARR, Canonization, 36 n. 39. CARR terms this absence 'conspicuous,' but explains it away as the consequence of JOSEPHUS' own goal of presenting a unified Judaism with a single canon. *Contra* CARR, it would seem a rather weak point for JOSEPHUS to make if it was so patently untrue.

[132] Ibid., 37–38. See my discussion of the Mishnaic evidence in section 2 above.

[133] JOSEPHUS, Antiquities, 18:16; cf. Antiquities 13:297. CARR admits this point (Canonization, 36 n. 39), which then provides another example of interpreting 'the law' too narrowly. Cf. the sound judgments of BECKWITH, Formation, 74; and BRUCE, Canon, 40–41.

[134] E. g., Mt 22:23 = Mk 12:18 = Lk 20:27.

[135] To be sure, the synoptic passage Mk 8:11–13 indicates that Matthew has probably added the Sadducees to the passage secondarily, but then Matthew has also apparently added the reference to 'the sign of Jonah.' It is strange that he would have added both if they were mutually contradictory, on the theory that the Sadducees rejected the Prophets.

[136] Cf. Mk 12:18–27; Lk 20:27–39.

[137] This is already highly questionable in light of the history of biblical interpretation: thus, passages from the Pentateuch have been used in support of resurrection in Jewish (e. g., Deut 32:39; cf. Pes. 68a; see also Sifre Deut 306!) as well as Christian tradition. I note again that here the Sadducees do not dispute Jesus' *sources*.

On this argument, Jesus formulates his response as a proof from pentateuchal tradition (Mt 22:32). However, Jesus does not criticize the Sadducees
for an ignorance of 'Moses' or the 'Law,' but their misunderstanding of 'the
scriptures [and] the power of God' (Mt 22:29). His reply possesses extraordinary force not because it is from pentateuchal tradition, and *therefore* supremely authoritative, but because it uses scripture to ground a belief in resurrection in God's own *self*, and thus makes resurrection an essential tenet of a
'scriptural' faith.

Mk 7:1–23 illustrates that even among the Pharisees 'the commandment of
God' was more authoritative than the oral law (i. e., 'the tradition of the elders').[138] This finding suggests, in turn, that a disagreement about scripture or
canon would have been regarded as fundamental and certainly meriting attention, yet not one clear indication of such a disagreement exists in the New
Testament.[139] To the contrary, the position of the Prophets is presented as not
only canonical, but well-established in the liturgy of the synagogue (e. g., Lk
4:14–30).

Since the encounter between Jesus and 'the Jews' in Jn 8:48–59 also turns
on the issue of the resurrection of the dead, the Sadducees are presumably in
mind, yet here 'the Jews' make explicit reference to Abraham *and* 'the prophets' as authoritative examples (Jn 8:52–53). In sum, it hardly seems appropriate to use the Sadducees as evidence of an alternate, Torah-only canon.[140]

12. Synagogue Lectionaries

Another argument bases itself upon the reading practices of the synagogue. It
is clear from later sources (as well as current Jewish practice) that since antiquity the sabbath reading of a pre-determined prophetic passage (הפטרה) has
followed a set reading from the Torah within a lectionary cycle.[141] These
readings from the Prophets do not appear to have been fixed originally in a
sequence, nor were they read completely through over the course of the cycle

---

[138] Note the citations from 'the commandment of God' are from the book of Isaiah as
well as the Decalogue!

[139] In this connection I cannot help but also mention Lk 1:5–23, the story of the angel
Gabriel's annuniciation to Zechariah the priest. Despite Zechariah's position as a part of the
'priestly establishment,' even his physical location in the Temple, Gabriel refers in his discourse to Elijah and to Mal 3:23–24 [4:5–6] without a demurral. Indeed Zechariah, despite
being an 'establishment' priest, also serves as a prophetic figure himself, becoming mute for a
time (Lk 1:20–22), performing a miraculous sign-act (Lk 1:59–64) and speaking prophecy
through the power of the Holy Spirit (Lk 1:67–69, esp. Lk 1:70). Is this not an additional indication that the frequently invoked opposition between priest and prophet obscures more
than it illuminates? Cf. Lk 2:36–38.

[140] Now see the additional arguments of BARRERA, Bible, 217-22, which lead him to a
quite similar conclusion (220).

[141] See BARTON, Oracles, 76, and the literature he cites.

(unlike the Torah).[142] Nevertheless a reading from the Prophets (in addition to a reading from the Torah) appears to have been *de rigeur* from quite early on.[143]

Moreover, the Writings never found their way into the lists of הפטרות; only later did the five מגלות and the Psalms come to find a place in the synagogue liturgy.[144] An earlier stage in this development seems to be reflected in the New Testament sources and in the differing lists of מגלות discovered in the Cairo Geniza.[145]

Thus, it is argued that the continuous reading of the Torah illustrates its special sanctity, especially since the episodic readings from the Prophets often appear to build upon the Torah readings, and not *vice versa*.[146] Supporting evidence is provided by M. Megillah 4:4, where the abbreviation of a הפטרה reading is allowed, but not a תורה reading, which must always be read word-for-word in its entirety.[147]

There are two major problems for this line of argument: first, aside from the New Testament we possess no reliable evidence of synagogue reading practice dating before the second century A. D.[148] Further, the evidence regarding the existence and distribution of the synagogue itself is extremely thin.[149] The origins of the synagogue in Israel can be traced confidently only to the events of the Hasmonean period and its characteristic architecture first appears in the first century B. C.[150] Such evidence as does exist indicates a

---

[142] BECKWITH, Canon, 144. He cites Lk 4:16–20 and M. Megillah 4:10. The Prophets are still not read in their entirety in the Jewish liturgy, although the sequence has been fixed since the rabbinic period.

[143] BARTON, Oracles, 76. Cf. M. Megillah 4:2; Acts 13:15. BARTON makes the point that the contents of the 'Prophets' do not yet appear to have been fixed, since the Psalms could be cited as part of 'the Law and the Prophets' (Acts 13:33–35). There is another possibility, however: the books later included in the Writings could have been considered part of the 'Law and Prophets' without undue worry over their precise classification; 'Law and Prophets' would simply have been used as an umbrella term for the totality of scripture. Note the trenchant observation of CHURGIN, Jonathan, 40, that if the Prophets had *not* been read, prophetic *targumim* would have been unnecessary.

[144] BARTON, Oracles, 76.

[145] On this point BARTON (Ibid.) cites PERROT, Lecture, 45–47.

[146] See PERROT, Reading, 157.

[147] BARTON, Oracles, 77.

[148] Ibid., 76.

[149] GUTMANN, Origins, 6 n.7 and the literature he cites. For further analysis of the current debate about synagogues and a critique of the traditional position, see MCKAY, Synagogues.

[150] LEVINE, Years, 10; idem, Nature; cf. GUTMANN, Synagogue, 1–6. LEVINE offers a full discussion of sources and archaeological sites. He notes the earlier existence of a least one diaspora synagogue at third century B. C. Elephantini, but argues that the synagogue in Israel appeared later with the expansion of the Jewish population and the Hellenistic emphasis upon the role of communal structures. LEVINE postulates the existence of open-air synagogue-type

rich diversity of structures, customs and names within early Jewish synagogue practice.[151]

The dating of all this evidence suggests that it is at least as likely that the emerging canon shaped the emerging synagogue, or that they shaped each other, as it is that the synagogue determined and 'closed' the canon.[152] This indicates, in turn, the further possibility that the heightened role of the Torah within the synagogue lectionary may well reflect a move to *raise* its authority rather than ensconcing a distinction always and everywhere held. [153] Thus C. Perrot has stated his judgment that it is 'open to doubt' whether the Torah reading cycle was originally a continuous one, given that our earliest evidence for this practice is mishnaic.[154]

Also, it should be remembered that Karaite Jews preserved an ancient form of the alternative, one-year Palestinian lectionary cycle well into the medieval period. The Karaites were criticized by talmudic rabbis for their view that the commandments found in all three divisions of the Bible should be observed, rather than only those found in the Torah (as interpreted by the Mishnah).[155] Karaitism has recently been described as getting its start "…at the very last moment before the Talmud became sufficiently well established… to prevent any further deviations."[156]

Also, a distinction must be maintained between canonical status and lectionary usage. As R. T. Beckwith trenchantly notes, the Writings have never been read in the liturgy (with the exception of the מגלות and the Psalms), but

---

services dating back to the time of the Exile or even to the end of the First Temple period. However, the earliest archaeological evidence for a synagogue in Israel is the Theodotus inscription from Jerusalem, dating to the *end* of the first century B. C. Only four synagogues have been found that may date before, but not much before, A. D. 70: Gamla, Masada, Herodium and Delos.

[151] LEVINE, Years, 13–14.

[152] E. g., there exists hardly any evidence, despite frequent claims to the contrary, that the shape of the Pentateuch has been influenced by liturgical practice, other than some very minor late editing; for discussion, see PORTER, Pentateuch.

[153] This could have been for literary as well as theological reasons, with the Torah providing a more manageable literary unit. Perhaps the Torah seemed more complete and 'closed' in this literary sense (cf. BECKWITH, Canon, 137); perhaps as containing the life and work of Moses it seemed more receptive of 'systematic' treatments than the Prophets.

[154] PERROT, Reading, 145. PERROT also sees some evidence for the possibility of an earlier *lectio continua* of the Prophets (Reading, 156). He cites Bar 1:14–21 for an example of the authoritative reading of the Prophets (including Daniel). He also notes (Reading, 152–53) that Qumran פשרים read the Prophets in continuous sequence. Cf. CHURGIN, Targum, 39–40.

[155] KAHLE, Geniza, 86–88. For beautiful Karaite descriptions of the three-fold nature of scripture, as found in the Ben Asher Codex of Prophets from the Cairo Geniza, see idem, Bibeltext, 69–72. It is highly interesting that praise for a tripartite scripture was at home at this time among the Karaites rather than in rabbinic circles.

[156] SCHNUR, Karaites, 156–57.

are canonical nonetheless.[157] There are numerous reasons why a canonical book might or might not be read in public worship which do not affect the terms of its canonicity.[158] Thus, different rules for reading the Torah, as opposed to the Prophets, could be entirely unrelated to putative differences in sanctity or canonical status.

In sum, the evidence from early Jewish lectionary practice is insufficient (at best) to make the case for a concession of special sanctity to the Torah (proper) in the pre-mishnaic period and (at worst) an anachronistic confusion of categories.

13. Philo

Carr notes in his recent study on canon two important features of Philo's use of scripture: first, that Philo clearly cites 'non-Torah texts as scripture' and, second, that he cites Torah texts 'approximately 40 times as often as [other biblical] texts.'[159] Carr deduces from these facts, together with the description of the LXX translation found in the Letter of Aristeas, that Alexandrian Judaism had "a propensity to focus on Torah alone, or *almost* exclusively on Torah."[160] Surely his conclusion thus elides a significant point: either Philo focused *exclusively* on the Torah or he did not — and Philo clearly did *not* focus on the Torah alone.[161] Not only did he cite other biblical books, but he cited them as *scripture*.

The real question, therefore, has to do with Philo's *conception* of non-pentateuchal books. To answer it, we would do well to observe a distinction between usage (or citation) and *canon*. J. Barton has perceived the problem that arises if this distinction is ignored: namely, that significantly more of Philo's non-Torah citations are from books later included in the Writings (esp. Psalms and Proverbs) than from books later found in the Prophets.[162] Should

---

[157] BECKWITH, Canon, 144.

[158] It might be added as well that the same distinction applies to non-canonical works which are nonetheless read liturgically (for example, the sectarian works at Qumran?). In contemporary Christian worship, all sorts of non-canonical texts are sometimes read. This does not alter the canon of Scripture directly, although one sadly acknowledges the force of the erosion.

[159] CARR, Canonization, 35. He refers here to KNOX, Note, 30.

[160] CARR, Canonization, 35 (my emphasis). CARR's study, while in some ways helpful, suffers from the lack of a clear distinction between a 'functional canon' and a 'formal canon.' E. g., Philo's functional canon was probably more or less the Pentateuch, but it is just as clear that he accepted the rest of the Hebrew scripture as fully authoritative.

[161] It may well be, however, that Alexandrian Judaism possessed an elevated regard for the Torah, or even a different *halakhic* tradition from that of Palestinian Judaism. See GOODENOUGH, Jurisprudence; cf. the discussion by HECHT, Issues.

[162] BARTON, Oracles, 43. He notes that Joshua and Ezekiel do not appear at all. Cf. P. R. DAVIES, Search, 137.

we conclude from this that the Prophets were not yet canonical, or not quite as canonical as certain of the Writings?

This seems doubtful, especially since Philo works within an overarching framework of scriptural authorship from two sources: Moses and the 'disciples of Moses.'[163] This bipartite conceptual framework corresponds to the 'theological grammar' of 'Law and Prophets' which we have traced in the present study.[164] Even if Philo's 'functional canon' *was* the Pentateuch, it is possible that such usage might simply reflect his Alexandrian context and there would *still* exist no firm basis on which to argue that the prophetic books were unknown to him or non-authoritative.[165]

It could be the case that the bipartite 'grammar' for scripture ('Law and Prophets') has become slightly altered in Philo's milieu ('Moses' and the 'disciples of Moses'), perhaps in order to include those books increasingly perceived as both non-pentateuchal *and* non-prophetic (i. e., the Writings).[166] There already existed in the first century B. C. to the first century A. D. a growing recognition of the distinctiveness of the books later called the Writings,[167] yet the theological conception for the whole of scripture continued to be that of 'the Law and the Prophets.' The developing unity of the Writings as a collection, and the interpretive power of wisdom as a theological construct, can also be seen in the increasing sapientialization of pentateuchal and prophetic traditions.[168] This would help explain how some of the books now found in the Writings could have had their place within Philo's bipartite canon of scripture without the overarching theological conception of scripture being greatly affected.

From this perspective, the *conception* of scripture remained essentially bipartite for Philo, with the Writings gradually gaining separate status as a ca-

---

[163] BARTON, Oracles, 49. Cf. CARR, Canonization, 39, who admits not only the presence of this feature, but also the tension in which it stands with his earlier conclusion of an Alexandrian focus *exclusively* on Torah.

[164] As BARTON points out (Oracles, 49), it is not only 'prophetic' figures who are referred to, since the Psalmist and Solomon are considered 'disciples of Moses' in just the same way as Zechariah. Another possibility, however, is that these 'non-prophetic' figures (from our perspective) were in fact considered prophetic at the time.

[165] This is especially the case given the likely dates for the LXX translations of prophetic books used at Alexandria. Cf. SWETE, Introduction.

[166] E. g., the Dead Sea scrolls also indicate that most of these books had already been in existence *in some form* for a long time. Note, moreover, the important point by BECKWITH (Formation, 83) that Philo 'never once quotes an uncanonical book' as scripture.

[167] Lk 24:44; Ben Sira, Prol.; PHILO, On the Contemplative Life, 3:25.

[168] SHEPPARD, Wisdom.

nonical subcollection.[169] There is no evidence that such a reconfiguration of the subcollections involved for him a diminution of status for the basic theological construct of 'Law and Prophets.'

14. Josephus

With Josephus we come to the first explicit effort to describe a canonical 'order' (Against Apion, I:37–43), made at the end of the first century A. D.[170] In his account of the sacred books, we are told of 'only' (!) twenty-two books, set within a *heilsgeschichtlich* frame: the five books of Moses, the prophetic history from Moses to Artaxerxes (in thirteen books), and four books of hymns and precepts. Moreover, Josephus characterizes the collection as an ancient, fixed text accepted by the entire Jewish people: for "long ages... now passed... no one has ventured either to add, or to remove, or to alter a syllable... it is an instinct with *every Jew*" (my emphasis).

Although some scholars have played up the possibility of Josephus' having a political agenda in this passage[171] and the differences between his description here and others from later periods,[172] it goes beyond the evidence to imagine that here Josephus speaks only as a spokesman for a 'pharisaical canon,'[173] especially as this is to read very much against the grain of what Josephus writes. He portrays the unity, not just of the Pharisees, but of all of Judaism.[174]

As I suggested previously regarding Josephus' general reliability, if his strong characterization of a unified canon was so at variance with the reality of the situation in Palestine, would he (or anyone else) have considered it a convincing *apologia*? Or, on the other hand, if Josephus had so little regard for truth as to misrepresent his religion, could he not easily have made an even stronger case? Why, for example, did he feel it necessary to mention that the "complete history... from Artaxerxes to our own time.... has been written... but... not been deemed worthy of equal credit with the earlier records..."? Certainly not only because he wished to confer supreme status on the twenty-two books (note: not just the Torah!), but also because it was no doubt true. Books outside of the twenty-two book canon were not 'deemed

---

[169] SWANSON, Closing, 371–78; BECKWITH, Formation, 57; ORLINSKY, Terms, 487–90. BECKWITH holds that the subdivision between the Prophets and the Writings was made in approximately 164 B. C. by Judas Maccabeus.

[170] The passage is given in BARTON (Oracles, 26) and many of the other books on the Old Testament canon. I quote from BARTON's text in the following.

[171] Ibid.; also CARR, Canonization, 51–53.

[172] Especially those which indicate a twenty-four book collection. See BARTON, Oracles, 26–28; 38–39; CARR, Canonization, 51–53.

[173] CARR, Canonization, 53. For important *differences* between JOSEPHUS and the Pharisees, see S. MASON, Josephus, 342–56, which CARR cites to his own disadvantage.

[174] ATTRIDGE, Historiography, 324.

worthy of equal credit,' perhaps more explicitly in pharisaic circles, but certainly outside pharisaic circles as well.

Here again we encounter the emergent tripartite canonical conception of 'Law and Prophets' and 'others.' Josephus, however, has taken the further step of merging Israel's *Heilsgeschichte* together with the history of its scriptural canon, an understanding perhaps shared by Philo — but only implicitly (i. e., 'Moses' and the 'disciples of Moses').[175] It should also be noted that Josephus includes the 'remaining four books' in his twenty-two book count, even though they seem to exist somewhat independently of the overarching *Heilsgeschichte*.[176]

Josephus explains his tripartite conception of the canon,[177] and perhaps even arranges it, so as to be "comprehensible... to Gentile readers,"[178] but it is difficult to imagine that the art of his description is intended to conceal a lack of canonicity.[179] Josephus' own strong statement of canonicity bases itself upon the syllabic text, not upon his grouping of the books. Whatever the precise nature of his canonical order, he gives a strong statement of canonicity from within the basic tradition of a bipartite scripture. He does not grant an explicitly higher status to the Torah as opposed to other portions of the canon, but to the twenty-two books of the canon as opposed to any other books.

15. Literary Position

There is one final argument for the supremely authoritative status of the Torah which is so apparent as to be often overlooked. This is the privileged position of the Torah at the *beginning* of the scriptural corpus.[180] The literary position of the Torah is naturally to be viewed in relation to its function as 'the beginning' of the story and the paradigmatic history of God's election of Israel. As we have seen, there has been a effort to create this paradigmatic 'dispensation' by the creation of a separation between Torah and Prophets, including the shaping of the material at the end of Deuteronomy and the beginning of Joshua, in order to effect and ensure this reading (Chapter Three above). Does

---

[175] BARTON, Oracles, 49.

[176] BARTON suppresses this point (Ibid., 37–38) when he argues that Josephus' criterion for scriptural status is prophetic authorship. Josephus nowhere states that the 'four remaining books' were written by prophets, and strongly implies ('remaining') that they lie *outside* the provenance of prophetic authorship.

[177] His conception seems bipartite again at the end of this section: 'the laws and the allied documents.'

[178] BARTON, Oracles, 48.

[179] S. MASON, WITH KRAFT, Canon, 232–33. MASON and KRAFT further note that a recognition of a viable canon at the time of JOSEPHUS "...removes the force from appeals to circumstantial evidence as proof that the Dead Sea Scrolls authors or Philo or Ben Sira had an open canon" (Canon, 234).

[180] TALMON, Schrifttum, 60; ZENGER, Pentateuch, 5–7.

this not involve a heightening of the authority of the Torah above that of the Prophets?[181]

Yet, as we have seen, the evidence indicates a shaping in *both* directions (e. g., Deut 32), resulting in the basic bipartite *heilsgeschichtlich* conception we have traced into the New Testament, Philo and Josephus. How else are we to understand the prophetic features of the Torah?[182] In my view the shaping appears remarkably even-handed, even as it acknowledges tensions and differences.[183]

This conclusion receives strong support from the theory of a Deuteronomistic History, or, more simply, the relative antiquity of the historical books. Whether a division was made within the larger historical work of Genesis–2 Kings (D. N. Freedman's 'Primary History') or a reordering of two antecedent historical works took place (Genesis–Numbers and Deuteronomy–2 Kings, *pace* R. E. Clements), the initial position of the mosaic Torah within the canon must be viewed as a literary accomplishment rather than an indication of its greater antiquity or authority. In brief, the Pentateuch begins the canon synchronically, but not did not begin the canon diachronically. From the perspective of this esssay, it seems likely that from the very beginning there existed one scriptural corpus grouped around the age of Moses and another collection of holy writings treating the age of the prophets.

It is therefore the resultant *literary* force of the Torah *qua* Pentateuch which lies behind the use of the term as a reference for all of scripture, *pars pro toto*. This literary effect continues to be powerful enough to influence those modern treatments (and not only conservative ones!) in which the Torah is presumed to be of greater antiquity simply because it comes 'before' the Prophets and treats the earliest period of the 'story.' Thus, it was the literary placement of Gen 1 which first led to early datings of the Priestly source (at that time 'G') and the same placement which made the later Graf-Wellhausen reversal so controversial.[184]

---

[181] Above all, BLENKINSOPP, Canon.

[182] For a description of a number of these prophetic features, see SCHMITT, Redaktion; cf. ALBERTZ, History, II:477–79, on the 'pre-priestly Pentateuch.' ALBERTZ notes these features, but claims that they were domesticated to placate the Persians: first, by their consignment to the past; second, by the elevation of Moses; and third, by the attachment of prophetic inspiration to the elders (Num 11). In my judgment, the shaping of the Pentateuch has been in the opposite direction, toward *increased* compatibility with the prophetic traditions rather than less.

[183] BARTON, Significance, 78, also interprets the canon of Moses and the Prophets (which he dates considerably later than I do) as a description of two ages in Israel's sacred history. He gives 'pride of place' to the Torah, however, followed by the Prophets. BARTON argues that this 'older' two-part conception has survived in JOSEPHUS, even though it was modified by the author(s) of Chronicles and Ezra–Nehemiah, who continued the sacred history into the Persian period (Significance, 79).

In sum, the literary placement of the Torah is hermeneutically significant and should continue to shape readings of the Old Testament, but the evidence suggests that its initial placement in the canon has to do with *story* rather than with *status*.

The Twin Authority of Law and Prophets

Now that I have reviewed the external evidence for the historical and theological *pre-eminence* of the Torah (*qua* Pentateuch) in the pre-rabbinic period and found it lacking, I wish to explore whether there exists any additional external evidence for the *complementarity* of 'Law' and 'Prophets' within the same period.

Christian Tradition

The evidence from Christian tradition is plain and for the most part undisputed. The most canon-conscious designation for the Old Testament in the New is the formula 'the Law and the Prophets' and certain variants of it.[1] Sometimes the expression 'the law'[2] or 'the law of Moses'[3] appears to be used to refer to (or especially to cite) the Pentateuch. Sometimes the reference is made simply by citing 'Moses.'[4]

Sometimes the expression 'the law' is used, but the scope of the reference is unclear. For example, in Mt 22:36 the question put to Jesus has to do with 'the law' and his answer consists of two citations of the Pentateuch, yet these citations are said to sum up both 'the law and the prophets.'[5] Similarly, in Mt 23:23 Jesus is said to have criticized hypocritical scribes and Pharisees who 'neglected the weightier matters of the law,' namely 'justice and mercy and faith.' These uses of 'law' appear to include the Pentateuch, but expand beyond it.[6] They certainly do not exclude prophetic scripture. Jesus' word to the

---

[184] For the details of this critical reversal, see ROGERSON, Criticism; more briefly, BLENKINSOPP, Pentateuch, 1–12.

[1] See Mt 5:17; 7:12; 11:13; 22:40; Lk 16:16; 24:44; Jn 1:45; Acts 13:15, 39–41; 24:14; 28:23; Rom 3:21. Cf. 'Moses and the prophets' in Lk 16:29, 31; Acts 26:22.

[2] See Mt 12:5; Lk 10:26; Jn 1:17; 7:19, 49, 51; 8:5, 17.

[3] See Lk 2:22–24, 39; Jn 7:23; Acts 15:5; 1 Cor 9:9; Heb 10:28

[4] See Lk 5:14; Jn 7:22; Acts 6:11, 13–14? 15:21; Rom 10:5, 19.

[5] See Mt 22:40; cvc. Lk 16:16 with Lk 16:17.

[6] See also Jn 12:34, in which the crowd listening to Jesus foretell his death (by citing Isa 52:13?) responds by saying they have learned of the eternal existence of the Christ in 'the law.' While this is certainly not impossible, given the varieties of interpretation practiced at the time, it does seem likelier that 'law' is used here to refer to certain passages in the Prophets or the Writings that would support such a doctrine more directly (Ps 89:36–37? Ps 110:4? Isa 9:6–7?).

scribes and Pharisees could not be more similar to the message of the prophets of old (cf. Mic 6:8; Zech 7:9–10).

In the same way, Lk 2:22–24 and Lk 2:39 provide references to 'the law' (of Moses), but also surround the highly prophetic material about Simon (Lk 2:25–38). Should the expression 'teachers of the law' be narrowly construed (= 'teachers of the Pentateuch')?[7] Clearly 'law' is used on occasion to refer to the Old Testament canon rather than the Pentateuch *per se*. In every example this possibility seems more likely than the notion that the New Testament writers intended to draw a contrast between a 'prophetic' Jesus and a Pentateuch-only Judaism. Lk 5:17–26 could perhaps be interpreted along such lines; Jesus is characterized in highly prophetic terms. However, the issue between Jesus and other Jewish leaders is never depicted as turning on the literary scope of the canon, but always on the canon's interpretation. In fact, it was only the *complete* canon which could explain to them why it was necessary for Jesus to die (cvc. Jn 19:7 and Acts 13:27).[8]

Further evidence of this conclusion is provided by citations of 'the law' which refer directly to non-pentateuchal passages of scripture. Thus in Jn 10:34 Jesus quotes Ps 82:6 as 'law'[9] and in 1 Cor 14:21 Paul quotes as part of 'the law' Isa 28:11–12![10] It is obviously a mistake simply to assume that a reference to 'the law' in this period (first century A. D.) refers narrowly to the Pentateuch, or, more to the point, to use references to 'the law' as evidence for the subordination of the rest of scripture (since both the Prophets and the Writings may already be included in the reference!). Sometimes 'the Law' is used in the sense of an overarching interpretation of the canon and clearly includes 'the Prophets' as well as the Pentateuch.[11]

Moreover, both the expressions 'the Law and the Prophets' (Jn 1:45) and 'the prophets' (Acts 3:18; 13:40–41) are used in 'intrafaith' contexts where a common canon is assumed. In Rom 10, Paul grounds his mission to the Gentiles quite explicitly in the exegesis first of 'Moses' and then of Isaiah (Rom 10:18–21). In the book of Acts, Paul virtually defines his ancestral faith for Felix as "believing everything laid down according to the law or written in the

---

[7] E. g., Lk 5:17; Acts 5:34; cf. Acts 22:3; 1 Tim 1:7.

[8] Jesus' death is paralleled by Stephen's in Acts 7. In response to the charge that he has spoken against 'the law' (Acts 6:13), Stephen not only recounts Israel's salvation history (Acts 7:2–52, citing Am 5:25–27 and Isa 66:1–2), but he concludes by charging his accusers: "You are the ones that received the law as ordained by angels, and yet you have not kept it." Once again, the issue is not the acceptance of the canon, but of its interpretation (cf. Acts 23:3).

[9] See also the citation of Psalms as 'law' in Jn 15:25. Cf. Jn 12:34.

[10] See also Paul's citation of Isa 8:14; 28:16 in Rom 9:33.

prophets" (Acts 24:14). Acts 13:15 tells of the sabbath reading of 'the Law and the Prophets' in synagogue. No difference in authority between the two collections is indicated, not even a difference in reading practice (although the account lacks specific details).

There does exist a small number of instances in which the divisions of the Old Testament canon are contrasted for a theological purpose. These contrastive interpretations of the canon tend to favor the Prophets over the Law. Thus, in Heb 7:28 'the word of the oath' (Ps 110:4 in Heb 7:21) is given additional hermeneutical weight because it 'came later than the law.' Because of their more recent origins and the clarity of their messianic witness, the Psalms and the Prophets (cf. Lk 24:44) are thereby regarded as more complete revelations of God's will.

This move is typical only of the writer of Hebrews, but it will become increasingly problematic within early Christianity.[12] In contrast to Paul, who could advocate laying claim to promises *prior* to the Law (Gal 3:17) the early Church will increasingly develop a model of historical and theological supercessionism in which the fullness of revelation is located in the Prophets *over against* the Law. Thus, in Heb 10:1 we read: '...the law has only a shadow of the good things to come and not the true form of these realities...' Increasingly at risk will be the ability of the Church to hear in the Pentateuch a direct and contemporaneous word of God.[13]

If I am correct in interpreting the formula 'the law and the words' as a reference to the subcollections of 'Law' and 'Prophets' within the Old Testament, then this usage might well be expected in the New Testament also.[14] Thus, it is not surprising to discover references such as Lk 3:4a, 'as it is written in the book of the *words* of the prophet Isaiah...' (my emphasis). Since the following citation (Lk 3:4b–6) is of Isa 40:3–5, the reference to 'the words' would presumably be to the title of the book. However, Isa 1:1 reads 'the vision of Isaiah' (also in the LXX), not 'the words.' Isa 2:1 reads 'the word of Isaiah' (sg.). Is it possible that here the title of a collection known as 'the words (of the prophets)' has been combined quite naturally with the title of a book within that collection (cvc. Dan 9:2 with Jer 1:1)?

---

[11] E. g., in Rom 3:21, where Paul also draws an explicit distinction between the Old Testament canon, which he accepts, and its traditional interpretation, which he rejects. Similarly, in 1 Tim 1:8 we find: "Now we know that the law is good, if one uses it legitimately."

[12] See SOULEN, God, 25–48, on the use of the Old Testament by Justin and Irenaeus in the latter half of the second century A. D.

[13] In this case the reference to 'the law' appears to mean the Pentateuch rather than the entire Old Testament. Not only do the contents of this law deal with sacrifices and offerings (Heb 10:8), but Ps 40:6–8 is cited as a 'prophetic' word against the theological importance of this 'law' (Heb 10:5–7). In fact, Christ is said to have now *abolished* it (ἀναιρεῖ, Heb 10:9).

[14] See Jm 1:22–25.

Similarly we find in Acts 7:42 a citation of Am 5:25–27 as from 'the book of the prophets' (the book of The Twelve?)[15], but in Acts 15:15 a citation of Am 9:11–12 is referred to as from 'the words of the prophets.' Also, in Acts 13:27 we have a reference to 'the words of the prophets' that are read in synagogue every Sabbath. 2 Pet 3:2 refers to 'the words spoken in the past by the holy prophets.' Various expressions in the Revelation to John may also have been shaped by this traditional usage.[16] As with the expression 'the law,' the whole Old Testament canon can also be termed 'the word' of God (e. g., Acts 13:44), just as 'the word of God' can be used to refer to a particular interpretation and actualization of the Old Testament canon greater than the sum of its parts (e. g., Acts 13:46).

Jewish Tradition

Now turning to Judaism, we must again pose the question of any evidence for the non-supremacy of the Law. In later rabbinic tradition, the tremendous respect accorded the Law makes its supremacy plain. However, when did such elevation of the Torah begin? It must be recalled that it is by no means obvious that when the rabbis refer to 'Torah' they mean the Pentateuch *per se*. As we have seen in Old Testament, New Testament and intertestamental literature, the expanded sense of the term 'Torah' was already well-established in the Hellenistic period.[17]

There also exist, however, a few highly interesting passages in rabbinic literature which illustrate the ability of the prophetic corpus to exercise an authority independent of, and sometimes even over against the Torah *qua* Pentateuch. It is to these passages that I now turn.

Thus, in S. Schechter's classic exposition of rabbinic theology the supremacy of Torah by the rabbis was asserted, but sometimes also curiously qualified.[18] Schechter argued that, in addition to certain explicit biblical warrants (e. g., Num 12:6–8; Deut 34:10), the rabbis held a view of the Torah's superiority over the Prophets mainly because they could not find anything in the Prophets which contradicted it.

No sooner had Schechter made this claim, however, than he had to acknowledge that the rabbis did indeed notice such contradictions, which he

---

[15] Cf. 4Q397, 'the book[s of the pr]ophets' or 'the book of the prophets.'

[16] E. g., Rev 1:3; 22:6–7, 10, 18–19.

[17] See the judgment of URBACH, Sages, 287: "It may be said that in the Hellenistic Period, before the Maccabean Revolt the word 'Torah' comprised the corpus of precepts, the teaching of the prophets, and the wisdom of the elders. But at the same time the term denotes particularly the Torah of Moses in all its parts and not just the sections treating of the commandments and ordinances."

[18] SCHECHTER, Aspects, 118.

then attempted to class as matters of 'detail, not principle.'[19] Nevertheless, the rabbis felt it necessary to attempt a reconciliation between the contradictions between the description of the Temple in Ezek 40–48 and descriptions in the Torah (Shabbat 13b; Menaḥot 45a). In another case, the contradiction between Isa 6:1 ('I saw the LORD...') and Ex 33:20 ('No man shall see me and live...') was acknowledged, but left unreconciled (Yebamot 49b).[20] In light of the significant debates over these issues, such differences seem to have involved more than mere 'details' for the rabbis. In fact, both subcollections of scripture appear to have functioned authoritatively in these examples — otherwise there would have been no hermeneutical problem to adjudicate.

Schechter then proceeded to describe a theological view of the complementarity of Law and Prophets similar to the one for which I have argued in this essay. He observed: "Of any real antagonism between Mosaism and 'Leviticalism' and Prophetism, which modern criticism asserts to have brought to light, the Rabbis were absolutely unconscious."[21] Even so, Schechter construed this complementarity in a somewhat one-sided way, with the Prophets as "only a complement to the Torah," but he also gave as an example the reading of Isa 58 ('one of the most prophetic pieces of prophetism') as the accompanying lesson for Lev 16 ('the most levitical piece in Leviticalism') on the Day of Atonement.[22] In my view, this example suggests a much more dialectical view of Law and Prophets than Schechter was willing to acknowledge in his explicit formulations.

On one occasion Schechter even observed that the rabbis generally accepted (Makkot 24a) Ezekiel's view of retribution (Ezek 18:20) over that of Moses (Ex 20:5), an instance of the rabbis accepting a 'direct prophetic improvement upon the words of the Torah'![23] It is thus significant, I would argue, not only that the word תורה extended beyond the Pentateuch in rabbinic understanding, but that both Prophets and Writings were also believed to be תורה in their own right. This view was based on scriptural warrants found in Dan 9:10 ('his תורה which he set before us by his servants the prophets') and Ps 78:1 ('Give ear, O my people, to my תורה').[24] Rather than a subordination of the Prophets and the Writings to the Pentateuch, I believe this language indicates the full canonical authority of both subcollections for the rabbis.

---

[19] Ibid.

[20] Ibid., n. 4.

[21] Ibid., 119.

[22] Ibid.

[23] Ibid., 187–88.

[24] Ibid., 122. Cf. URBACH, Sages, 287 nn. 7–8, for citations of verses from the Prophets and the Writings given in answer to the rabbinic question, 'Where in the Torah do we prove this from?'

More work needs to be done on the attitudes of the rabbis toward prophetic *scripture* (as opposed to studies of their beliefs about prophecy),[25] and the way in which the canon of Law and Prophets functioned authoritatively within their religious tradition. Of particular importance, given the results of my essay, is the question of when the elevation of the Torah to a superior hermeneutical position occurred within Judaism.

Schechter noted the 'special emphasis' of the Jerusalem Talmud upon the importance of the Torah, which he claimed was the "result of opposition to sectarian teaching [i. e., Christianity], demanding the abolition of the Law," on the grounds that the Messiah had now come.[26] This expectation of abolition, as Schechter noted, has roots deep within the prophetic writings of the Old Testament (e. g., Jer 31; Ezek 20). However, rather than seeing the interpretive elevation of the Torah as a creative response to a competing interpretation of the canon, Schechter viewed the Talmud's 'special emphasis' on Torah as the 'retention' of a view that had always existed.[27]

It is not the case therefore, as B. J. Roberts tried to argue, that the rabbis did not distinguish between sections of the canon, or that they did not *generally* regard Torah as more authoritative than the Prophets or the Writings.[28] Many examples to the contrary could be cited, and the expression קבלה ('tradition') for the Prophets and the Writings as distinct from the Torah seems to make the *eventual* elevation of the Torah beyond doubt.[29] At issue again, however, is how to trace the change in this understanding of the canon over time.

At the very least, some rabbinic passages appear to illustrate a much greater interpretive freedom in relating 'Law' and 'Prophets' to each other, as Roberts also argued.[30] Thus, Roberts provided an example from Mishnah Yadaim 4:4, which tells of a dispute between the rabbis Gamaliel and Joshua (ca. A. D. 10–80) over an Ammonite proselyte. In the exchange, Gamaliel cites a commandment from the Law (Deut 23:3) as a warrant for rejecting the Ammonite, but Joshua uses a promise from the Prophets (Isa 10:13) against

---

[25] See URBACH, Sages, 301–02. He notes additional occasions on which *prophecy* could 'temporarily suspend' rulings of Torah, even in the Talmudic period, arguing that prophecy was not allowed to originate new rulings. However, this question needs to be distinguished from the role and function of prophetic *scripture* within rabbinic thought.

[26] SCHECHTER, Aspects, 123–24 n. 5

[27] Ibid.

[28] B. J. ROBERTS, Suggestion, 171.

[29] BRONZNICK, Qabbalah. BRONZNICK cites one instance, however, where *qabbalah* refers to the Torah, but LEIMAN argues that the correct reference is to Ezek 34:25 (Canonization, 57 n. 278). For further discussion, see W. S. GREEN, Scriptures, 34–36.

[30] B. J. ROBERTS, Suggestion, 172.

the continuing validity of the deuteronomic commandment![31] Gamaliel then attempts to argue that prophetic scripture also supports his judgment by relegating the abrogation of the law to the *eschaton* (citing Jer 49:6). However, Joshua counters from the verbal tense of Jer 30:2 that the prophecy under discussion must *now* be fulfilled. The Ammonite is accepted!

This certainly appears to be a clear case in which the authority of the Torah is 'qualified.'[32] What Roberts neglects to consider is the likelihood of an early date for this story from the Mishnah.[33] It is now beyond question that prophetic scripture was also used for the derivation of *halakhah* at Qumran.[34] The Torah cannot simply be equated with halakhic law within early rabbinic Judaism;[35] *halakhot* were also found in non-Torah passages of scripture.[36]

In my judgment, all of these examples provide strong evidence for an earlier complementarity of Law and Prophets within Judaism, and a later elevation of the Law (*qua* Pentateuch) which began to function fully only at the time of the Jerusalem Talmud.[37]

---

[31] This account also neatly refutes BUDDE's theory that the prophetic corpus was considered 'time-conditioned' in contrast to the 'eternal validity' of the Law. For background, see Chapter 1.

[32] B. J. ROBERTS, Suggestion, 172, claims that this 'qualification' of Torah happens in 'many other places' within rabbinic literature, but unfortunately does not produce many other citations of it.

[33] It is also important to consider the judgment of SALDARINI (Reconstructions, 441) that "the teachings of the early Amoraim (third and fourth centuries C. E.) show that they did not accept the Mishnah as final and authoritative but argued against it and tried to assign anonymous laws to earlier authorities in an attempt to limit the greater authority assigned to anonymous teachings."

[34] QIMRON AND STRUGNELL, Cave 4, 133; SCHIFFMAN, Reclaiming, 248. Debated, however, is whether this practice should be considered 'sectarian' (thus SCHIFFMAN, Reclaiming, 277) or the general situation in early rabbinic Judaism.

[35] MÜLLER, Beobachtungen

[36] SAFRAI, Halakha, esp. 123–25; 135–36; 154–55.

[37] SALDARINI, Reconstructions, 438, also warns: "...evidence for rabbinic Judaism is derived from collections that date from 200 C. E. and later. Stories, anecdotes, *halakhah* and historical statements may also be suspected of anachronism and distortion by later experience and have become increasingly uncertain as sources for the reconstruction of *early* rabbinic Judaism. It is very likely that the antecedents of Mishnah, Midrash, the schools, and the rabbis were very different from their later mature progeny and that they underwent a complex development in varied social and historical settings and in response to important human and theological needs" (his emphasis). Obviously, the opposite position of total discontinuity between early Judaism and rabbinic Judaism is also unsatisfactory. However, full recognition of the 'astonishing' discontinuity between the two (NEUSNER, Studies, 105–07) serves as an important corrective to facile views of continuity. NEUSNER further notes that the Hebrew Bible appears to have exerted little influence on the formation of traditions about the Pharisees, and that even in the legal material there are 'few literary traits or forms in common' between the Bible and the Mishnah.

Reconstruction and Conclusions

Old Testament *scripture* began with the conviction that the preservation of certain words and deeds in writing would form an enduring indictment of self-interest (e. g., Deut 12:8) and a persuasive reminder of God's goodness and mercy for future generations (e. g., Deut 12:28). The Old Testament *canon* emerged in the effort within Israel to transmit its differing insights and experiences of God in such a way that their internal consistency could be explored and affirmed, but also so that their particularities would continue to stimulate, provoke and challenge (e. g., Deut 4:2; 13:1 [12:32]).

Thus, at the level of its *witness* the Old Testament is a statement of *ideals*, but *not* ideologies.[1] The distinction is crucial, but rarely observed. Israel's ideals have clearly been shaped and transmitted within specific historical situations and cultural contexts, but the peculiar effect of its religious understanding has been to indict the self (e. g., Deut 6:10–12; 9:4–5). This means that a viewpoint finding expression within the canon has been recognized by the community as an insight leading to self-discipline and the good of the other, and not merely as a propagandistic effort on the part of the politically powerful to restrict or condemn those with whom they disagree.

'Ideology' may be found within the Bible, however. Again on the level of the Old Testament's *witness*, 'ideology' is best understood as a kind of 'mythology' — those ideals which do *not* challenge or subvert the hegemony of the self.[2] Thus, the critical distinction is not whether a given ideal in the Bible supports the position of those in power, but whether or not an ideal applies to the powerful as well as the powerless, and challenges them no less and encourages them no more than anybody else (e. g., Deut 15:7–11; 16:18–20; 17:14–20).

Israel's earliest canon consisted of a variety of traditions, grouped broadly into two subcollections of mosaic and prophetic scripture, which represented not only Israel's perception of two major historical initiatives of God, but also her confession of two different means of apprehending (e. g., Job 33:14; Ps 62:12–13a [11–12]) God's unitary character and will (Deut 6:4). In this way, the formation of the Old Testament canon is best understood as the develop-

---

[1] Cf. P. D. MILLER, Faith. MILLER also differentiates the Old Testament's witness from 'ideology,' but his description of this witness as 'faith' is not, in my judgment, adequately defended against a charge of special pleading. I would argue that MILLER's account fails to show how 'faith' can overcome self-interest, an alternative which I have sought to make compelling through a more differentiated understanding of first-order and second-order interests. Now see the critique of MAYES, Ideology, 58–59; 73–74.

[2] SCHNEIDAU, Discontent, 9–11; cf. P. D. MILLER, Faith. In my judgment, the failure to perceive precisely this distinction lies at the root of the contradictions encountered in FRYE, Code, as discussed in Chapter Two.

ment of a literary and conceptual framework of written scriptures in which mercy and sacrifice, promise and fulfillment, grace and responsibility are all allowed to retain the integrity of their individual witness — not harmonized, but grounded firmly in the unitary nature of God.[3]

As W. Zimmerli noted in opposition to G. von Rad's isolation of various Old Testament traditions as 'theologies,' the tradents of the Old Testament fully recognized that the God of the Exodus (e. g., Hos 12:10 [9]; 13:4) was the same God as Isaiah's 'holy One of Israel' (e. g., Isa 10:17).[4] And yet these differences were also preserved as meaningful. By their inclusion in the canon, such differences are confessed to have their unity not in historical contingency or literary consistency, but in the constancy of God: "Vor ihm, dem Gott Israels, weiß man sich auch bei auseinanderlaufenden Traditionen als vor dem Einen stehen."[5]

It is precisely for this reason that the reconstruction of social groups behind such 'theologies,' which, it is argued, must have been opposed to each other because of the differences preserved in the text, tends to miscontrue the force and function of the canon. This is not to say that theological differences and oppositional social groups did not exist, but rather to affirm the role of the canon in preserving a plurality of traditions — not in order to flatten or harmonize them, but to function as an enduring *challenge* to the presuppositions, customs and traditions of the community which treasured it. Israel had no 'interest' in a canon which would only affirm its present beliefs and practices.

Thus, the widest possible latitude was exercised in the selection and redaction of materials, with great emphasis placed upon preserving written witnesses from the past, even if they were confusing or not fully understood. There was always the hope that a witness from the past would speak anew (e. g., Deut 31:19–21, 26–29). This 'prophetic' quality is so basic to the Old Testament canon that it has been called its 'canonical principle.'[6] Yet these scriptures of the past were also shaped and coordinated in countless ways so as to establish a framework for the entire collection and an interpretive range for its subsequent use.

The exegetical evidence points to the mid-sixth century B. C. as the time when the broad shape of such a canonical framework originated.[7] To borrow a term from J. J. Collins, one could speak of a 'core canon' emerging in this

---

[3] KRATZ, Redaktion, 23. Cf. HENN, Faith, 208, who points to the relation between a canon of scripture and the belief in the unity of God's Word.

[4] ZIMMERLI, Traditionsgeschichte, 24–25. Cf. idem, Rezension.

[5] ZIMMERLI, Traditionsgeschichte, 25: "Before him, the God of Israel, one knows one's self even [when faced] with diverging traditions to be standing before the One."

[6] ACKROYD, Continuity; CLEMENTS, Covenant; JACOB, Principe.

[7] CLEMENTS, Covenant; FREEDMAN, Law.

period under deuteronomistic auspices.[8] This core canon was likely comprised of a early version of Deuteronomy and the Deuteronomistic History (Joshua–2 Kings), which would continue to be reworked. Also at this time, an edition of prophetic oracles took shape,[9] expanding the witness of the canon to the responsibilities attending Israel's election by God.[10] An edition of tetrateuchal traditions (Genesis–Numbers) also dates from this time, or was made slightly later (fifth century B. C.) to fill out the profile of the Law as a witness to irrevocability of Israel's election.

The resultant scriptural collection would continue to be edited and enlarged by the addition of new material, but its essential character would be preserved in its bipartite structure of 'Law and Prophets.' This literary and conceptual framework exercised an authority upon the scriptures included within it which was greater than the sum of its parts. If 'canon' is defined as an *intertextual collection* of scriptures, then sixth century deuteronomism emerges as the dividing point between 'scripture' and 'canon' within Israel's religious history.

Prior to the coordination of 'the Law' and 'the Prophets,' evidence can be discovered for the existence of individual scriptures (e. g., Ex 22–24; Deut 12–26; or the pre-deuteronomistic form of books such as Joshua or Amos), but not for an overarching literary and conceptual framework in which various discrete scriptures are related to each other and understood. *Traditions* of law and prophecy exercised mutual influence upon each other prior to the formation of this deuteronomistic 'canon.' However, such pre-canonical influence was mostly *ad hoc* and does not for the most part give the appearance of having been mediated by written material. For example, certain pentateuchal figures were early on given prophetic characteristics (e. g., Abraham in Gen 20;

---

[8] J. J. COLLINS, Canon, 232. COLLINS holds to the standard three-stage theory, although he dates the Writings late. He uses the term 'core canon' as a way to refer to Torah and Prophets prior to A. D. 70, arguing that by the first century A. D. these collections were already authoritative, but not yet fully closed. Cf. the notion of a early scriptural 'backbone' of 'Law and Prophets' in BARR, Scripture, 57; 61. I prefer the term 'core canon' to the term 'core of books' (VANDERKAM, Literature, 401) because of the *intertextual* nature of 'canon' which I have described as central to its purpose.

[9] The likely possibilities according to GOTTWALD are: Hosea, Amos, Micah, Nahum, Habbakuk, Zephaniah, First Isaiah, Jeremiah. Of course, at this point in time these books would not have had the form they now exhibit. Cf. T. COLLINS, Mantle, 97, who follows STECK in positing a common redaction of Isaiah and The Twelve, but much earlier: first in Babylon (538 B. C.) and then in Palestine (515–500 B. C.), until the completion of the entire corpus in approximately 400 B. C. Ezekiel represents something of a problem for COLLINS; see his Mantle, 93–95.

[10] TUCKER, Superscriptions, 69; NOGALSKI, Precursors, 278–80. TUCKER identifies a deuteronomistic corpus of prophets in the mid-sixth century (Hosea, Amos, possibly Isaiah, Micah, Jeremiah, Zephaniah). NOGALSKI suggests that Hosea, Amos, Micah and Zephaniah circulated together as a 'Deuteronomistic corpus,' based largely (but not exclusively) upon their superscriptions.

Moses in Hos 12:13)[11] and certain prophets likened to Moses (e. g., Elijah in 1 Kg 19; Joshua in Jos 3–6) already before the deuteronomistic movement.

Beginning with the mid-sixth century, however, a theological framework for Israel's scriptures is established and remained indispensable to the understanding of the various texts within it, even as they continued the process of their literary development. Scriptural traditions now influenced each other increasingly as *written* authorities within a common literary 'intertext', allowing for a more sustained reflection upon the similarities *and* differences among texts, and therefore more subtle possibilities for editorial 'interreadings.'

This core canon is sometimes expressed by the deuteronomistic expression 'the law (of Moses) and the words (of the prophets)' and a number of similar *dual* expressions. As a way to coordinate literary traditions, the deuteronomistic tradents of the canon also formulated an ideal of prophetic succession, beginning with Moses (e. g., Deut 18; 2 Kg 17; Jer 1). At some point in the tradition, a more explicitly canon-conscious division was made between the books of Deuteronomy and Joshua, not in order to subordinate the Prophets to the Law, but to preserve the integrity of each collection even as they were further coordinated.[12] The theological framework itself also exhibited signs of development, functioning more explicitly in the later post-exilic period as a summary of Israel's confession, like a 'grammar' (Deut 34:10–12; Mal 3:22–24 [4:4–6]).

It appears that this framework or 'canon' of Law and Prophets was already functioning by the time of the redaction of the books of Ezra–Nehemiah (fifth century B. C.). The 'core canon' continued to be edited and enlarged, but always within the theological construct or 'grammar' of 'Law and Prophets.' The evidence points to the attainment of a relatively stable form for both canonical subcollections sometime in the fourth century (400–350 B. C., i. e., before Chronicles). It may be that the *text* of the Law stabilized slightly earlier than the text of the Prophets, but its canonical standing was attained *together with* the Prophets, and not apart.[13] In fact, the relative dates for literarily stable forms of both collections are likely to be much closer in time than has been usually thought.[14]

There is thus no getting 'behind' the deuteronomistic notions which were designed to bind the canon together (such as the prophets as 'proclaimers of the law'), if one reads the Old Testament at the level of its own witness.[15] It is

---

[11] For additional examples, see ZIMMERLI, "Prophet," 197–211.

[12] M. A. O'BRIEN, Reassessment, 66; SCHMITT, Geschichtswerk.

[13] HOUTMAN, Pentateuch, 441–46; SÆBØ, Canon, 305–06; SCHMITT, Geschichtswerk, 279.

[14] GESE, Gestaltwerdung.

[15] CLEMENTS, Tradition, 52; HERRMANN, Restauration, 156, 167; RENDTORFF, Canon, 55; 64–65.

important to probe such notions historically, of course, but then to disparage them as merely 'ideal' rather than 'historical' (i. e., 'real') simply misses the point. Such ideals represent historical expressions of the enduring significance of historical figures and events for the ongoing community of faith.[16] As such, they constitute explicit formulations of the implicit possibilities of history. Thus, the canon provides an *historical* witness that the traditions now found in the Law and the Prophets were never entirely unrelated or antithetical, even if it is not evident that these traditions were as explicitly coordinated and framed within history as they appeared to be for the deuteronomists, who gave witness to their inner theological logic through the formation of the canon.

Despite increasing diversity within Judaism, it was adherence to this 'grammar' of 'Law and Prophets' which more than anything else defined what it meant to be faithful tradents of the past witness (e. g., Qumran, Hellenistic Judaism, Christianity). The example of the Samaritans proves the point by grounding their severance from Jewish identity in their rejection of the indispensable 'grammar.'[17]

It should be acknowledged, however, that there also exists a remarkable discontinuity between this 'grammar' and later rabbinic practice, in which the interpretation of scripture was often produced by the juxtaposition and patterning of discrete biblical verses, and without regard for any *heilsgeschichtlich* patterning.[18] For this reason, J. Neusner has concluded that "the Mishnah's subordination of historical events contradicts the emphasis of a thousand years of Israelite thought."[19] Similarly, although Christianity was to retain in larger measure the *heilsgeschichtlich* conception of the Hebrew canon, in practice the Pentateuch was often subordinated to the Prophets, if not rejected outright. In this way, *both* interpretive traditions would keep the basic *formal* canonical construct of 'Law and Prophets,' but in their actual *usage* shift the interpretive balance in one direction or the other.[20]

The Place of the Writings?

Zimmerli observed in his study of 'the Law and the Prophets' that it was only "these two headings which have a particular theological signification, whilst

---

[16] HERRMANN, Restauration, 170.

[17] The point is not *our* judgment as to whether the Samaritans were part of Judaism or not, but the judgment of ancient Jews and Samaritans, and their reason(s) for it. As FISHBANE has noted (Exegesis, 95–96) it is highly significant that the divisions in ancient Judaism were *depicted* as primarily about the interpretation of scripture.

[18] W. S. GREEN, Scriptures, 42. However, for the argument that intertextuality played an important role in rabbinic interpretation, see GOLDBERG, View; SEELIGMANN, Voraussetzungen.

[19] NEUSNER, Structure 115; cf. idem, Mishnah. See, however, the criticism of NEUSNER's position in GOLDBERG, View, 162–63.

[20] ZIMMERLI, Gesetz, 17–18.

the subsequent fixing of the canon did not go beyond giving to its third part the colorless designation, the Writings."[21] He based this observation largely upon the use of 'Law and Prophets' as a formula for the Old Testament within the New Testament, and not upon the way in which the Old Testament *itself* pairs themes and motifs of law and prophecy. However, in the expression 'the Law and the Prophets' Zimmerli noted an 'almost-creedal' affirmation in which both terms denoted a 'single reality... the one will of God.'[22] He did not see that the Writings were of 'similar authority.'[23]

Zimmerli's position has been roundly criticized, but also caricatured in the process. He had no intention of dismissing the worth of the Writings[24] or the theological importance of wisdom traditions.[25] Zimmerli's point was simply that both Law and Prophets achieve a kind of 'theological signification' that the Writings, viewed as a canonical subcollection, do not. The present study bears Zimmerli out, extending his insight from the New Testament back into the Old.

Clearly Old Testament traditions have been 'sapientialized,' especially in later layers of the canon's growth and shaping.[26] But to what extent can one make the case that this sapientialization was 'canon-conscious'? What about examples of a *triple* formula similar to the double formulas of 'law and prophets' explored in the present essay? Are there passages which not only *reflect* (e. g., Jer 18:18; Ezek 7:26) but actually *enjoin* a tripled authority to match an emergent tripartite canon within Israel?

Ps 1–2 may provide an example of such a 'tripling,' with the presence of motifs and themes that can be grouped under the three rubrics of law, prophecy and wisdom.[27] Only in the case of the term תורה (Ps 1:2), however, does a motif or a theme receive an unmistakably *canon-conscious* designation. Traditions of prophecy and wisdom remain in the background, although they have also exerted a major influence on the final form of this 'twin' psalm, which now seems to function as an introduction to the Psalms as a collection. G. T. Sheppard has referred elsewhere to this kind of canonical shaping as the "thematizing of historically dissimilar traditions under the rubrics of 'Torah,' 'Prophets' and 'Wisdom.'"[28]

---

[21] ZIMMERLI, Law, 10.

[22] Ibid., 6; 14. Although ZIMMERLI rejected the idea that this formula had actually functioned as a 'creed,' it seems telling, in my view, that he considered this possibility at all.

[23] Ibid., 13.

[24] Cf. ZIMMERLI, Erwägungen, 49–51.

[25] See idem, Struktur.

[26] SHEPPARD, Wisdom.

[27] Ibid. 136–44; Idem, Future, 69; 73–74. See also BRUEGGEMANN, Psalms; MAYS, Place.

[28] SHEPPARD, Canonization, 21–22.

Yet the point to be made from the results of the present study is that this kind of thematization is much more explicitly *textual* in the case of 'the Law' and 'the Prophets' than in the case of 'the Writings.' This is especially the case if the formula 'the law and the words' (and its variants) refer to written collections of scripture, as I have argued. Only *after* the formation of the bipartite Old Testament canonical formula do we find instances of a formula referring to a triple framework of scripture (e. g., 4Q397; Sir, Prol.; Lk 24:44). In other words, if we examine the Old Testament canon at the level of 'canon-conscious redactions' as opposed to the level of 'thematizations,'[29] it is difficult to locate an awareness of a *collection* of Writings or its impact on the other biblical books and subcollections.

The lack of this awareness within the Old Testament *itself* could simply be an accident of history, with the Writings coalescing too late to affect the literary shape of the Law and the Prophets. I would argue, however, that the oldest materials in the Writings (e. g., Psalms, Proverbs) would have possessed the same 'pre-canonical' authority which has been shown for the emergent collections of Law and Prophet. In my judgment, this likelihood further suggests that the idea of compiling a later third collection *from scratch* cannot be sustained, and that the books of the Writings most likely occupied an earlier place within the 'Law and the Prophets' as they continued to develop over time.

Still at issue, however, is how to gauge hermeneutically the position of the Writings within the final form of the canon. Was the collection intended to function as a fully equal and authoritative 'third' of the canon, as the literary structure of the MT would imply?[30] Or are the Writings to be interpreted as a commentary on, and an application of, a 'more authoritative' Law and Prophets?

These questions must remain for further study, but hopefully they will have been sharpened by the results of this essay. In my view, the absence of any reference in Deut 34:10–12 and Mal 3:22–24 [4:4–6] to wisdom traditions or to the Writings as a canonical subcollection must be given substantial weight in exploring such questions, given the probable date and hermeneutical function of these canonical 'conclusions.'

Theological Implications for Jewish and Christian Traditions

If the Law and the Prophets grew literarily *together*, mutually-influencing each other, and the Law never comprised the sole 'Bible' of Israel, then it seems that Judaism and Christianity developed opposite emphases within the same dialectical framework of their common scriptures. Early Judaism read the Torah, often to the virtual exclusion of the Prophets; early Christianity

---

[29] The distinction is SHEPPARD's own (Ibid., 23).

[30] Thus WESTERMANN, Elements, 6.

read the Prophets, often disregarding the Law. Nonetheless, the same canon has continued to provide a remarkably similar range of personal and communal interpretive options within each religion, as well as binding both religions together as interpretive partners.[31]

Differences remain, of course. An altogether different hermeneutical relationship to the Old Testament was created for Christianity in its addition of a New Testament, resulting in a new Christian Bible, than was established for Judaism by its production of the Mishnah and Talmud.[32]

If the Law and the Prophets previously existed as a canonical complementarity within Judaism, then the full ascendancy of Torah must be credited to rabbinic tradition and to the Talmud. I am not competent to evaluate fully the legacy of this development for Judaism, especially in a post-Holocaust age, but I would venture to suggest that real danger lies in the subversion of the prophetic witness,[33] especially since this study makes clear just how integrally-related the Law and the Prophets were held to be within ancient Judaism.[34]

M. Greenberg has offered a searching critique of modern Judaism's use of scripture on two counts: 1) the need to reflect further on the implications of a modern Jewish state for its reading of scripture; and 2) the need to formulate more clearly the relation of its scripture to non-Jews.[35] In my judgment, closer attention especially to *prophetic* scripture would address these very issues and yield important theological insights into the danger of divorcing the blessings of election from the responsibilities of righteousness. I offer my hope that a renewed appreciation for the *full* shape of the biblical canon[36] might inspire

---

[31] On this point, see CLEMENTS, Patterns, 55.

[32] On this and related issues, see SAWYER, Prophecy, esp. 147–53, where he discusses the 'relatively low priority given to the Prophets in Judaism.' SAWYER also notes (Prophecy, 156), however, the complicating factor that modern Zionism has been heavily influenced by prophetic scripture.

[33] The subversion comes not from lack of familiarity, but lack of authority. E. g., a recent popular account by BLECH (Judaism, 300) distinguishes the supreme, infallible authority of the Torah from that of the Prophets, reasoning that Moses was a scribe who took dictation, but the prophets were 'mediators' in whose writings, he strongly implies, the possibility of error therefore exists.

[34] An important related question to pose is why the rabbis appear to have had comparatively little interest in the Former and Latter Prophets. On this question, see W. S. GREEN, Scriptures, 32. GREEN's view is that the rabbis' primary interest lay in explicating scripture which would perpetuate the 'levitical system' in the wake of the Temple's destruction in A. D. 70 and the loss of the Temple cult (Scriptures, 33–34). Thus the Law increasingly became the 'sacred center' which enabled the continuation of their piety.

[35] GREENBERG, Sharing, 459–60; idem, Use.

[36] This appreciation could well take the form of an emerging Jewish biblical theology. Thus, BRETTLER, History, 576 has sharply questioned the thesis of LEVENSON, Bible, 55 that

Judaism to recapture the integrity of the witness of the Prophets: that election is *for* the nations, not against them; that Israel was not chosen on the basis of merit, but of grace; that its presence in the land depends on the quality of its justice, especially for the stranger (e. g., Ezek 20; Am 9:7–8; Zech 7:9–10).[37]

In the case of Christianity, I would first observe that if the Torah was not pre-eminently authoritative in pre-talmudic Judaism, then early Christians did not initially dismiss the authority of the Torah simply by the status they conferred upon the Prophets,[38] but rather continued to share with Judaism the same literary and conceptual framework for their Old Testament scriptures. Thus, this 'shared canon' serves as an important reminder of just how deeply early Christianity was rooted in early Judaism. As we have seen, however, certain currents in Christianity came soon enough to emphasize the Prophets to the virtual exclusion of the Law (e. g., Heb 10), resulting in a perennial temptation toward antinomianism and anti-Jewish prejudice.[39] For this reason, I believe it to be crucial for Christianity to recover in the *full* shape of the Old Testament canon the integrity of the *Pentateuch* to speak to the Church as the direct and contemporary Word of God.

Greenberg has also perceptively challenged Christianity's use of scripture:

"...our world has not yet been redeemed by the returned Christ, and so we find ourselves more in the situation of the Old Testament community than the New. We must have institutions that regulate relations between men, and between groups of men. The Old Testament alone of the canonical books of Christianity contains specific rules and regulations aimed at fashioning a righteous society. Christian reluctance to accept the validity of the law may be countered by Jewish appreciation for the law... not motivated by a system of rewards and punishments; [but as a] response of gratitude both for God's announced intent to take him for his own, and for the salvation of God that he has experienced."[40]

In my judgment, this kind of appreciation for the Law is needed if the full grain of Old Testament righteousness is to be harvested by the Church for a

---

"it is hard to see how a biblical theology that did not respect the doctrine of the priority and normativity of the Pentateuch could be authentic to the Jewish tradition."

[37] I would also continue to argue that this renewed appreciation is ultimately not about greater familiarity with the prophetic scriptures, but about their *authority* for religious praxis. A related question for Judaism has to do with the *interreligious* consequences of deriving הלכה solely from pentateuchal legislation (as interpreted by the oral law given in the Mishnah). In my view this question has highly important implications for present interfaith dialogue between Jews and Christians.

[38] *Contra* BARR, Bible, 116–17; idem, Scripture, 62–63.

[39] On the pervasiveness of Christian supersessionism, see SOULEN, God.

[40] GREENBERG, Sharing, 460–61. In my view, however, the New Testament must also be said to contain 'specific rules and regulations' for a 'righteous society' (e. g., Mt 5–7; Rom 12–14; Heb 13).

new generation.[41] Too much of recent Christian theology has attempted to appropriate the social critique of the Prophets without sufficient attention to the building of a *holy community* in which God's will for humankind can begin to be realized (Ex 19–20:17; Lev 19; Deut 5; 30). Moreover, greater attention to the Law would further serve as a necessary reminder to the Church that, rather than replacing the Synagogue, the Church *shares with it* a place in God's holy community, necessarily divorcing every tendency toward anti-Semitism from Christian proclamation and life.

In the Law and the Prophets, Judaism and Christianity have not received 'Law plus commentary' or 'Prophets plus background,' but the fully mature witness of Israel to a dialectic that continues to be constitutive of the reality of God. Within this biblical dialectic of Moses and the prophets, election and righteousness, law and promise, grace and repentance, there exists the enduring witness that God is sovereign and just, unitary in character and purpose, but persistently twofold in human telling.

> Once God has spoken;
> twice have I heard this:
> that power belongs to God,
> and steadfast love belongs
> to you, O LORD.
>
> Psalm 62:12–13a [11–12a];
> cf. Job 33:14.

---

[41] See the thought-provoking efforts by CRÜSEMANN, Tora, 423–25; KAISER, Theologie; MARQUARDT, Reintegration; STEGEMANN, Tora; ZENGER, Pentateuch. For criticism and evaluation, see FREY, Tora; JANOWSKI, Weg, 89–90. My own fundamental reservation with the former treatments is that they exhibit the tendency simply to adopt a (rabbinic) view in which the Prophets and the Writings are fully subordinated to the Torah *qua* Pentateuch (KAISER, Theologie, 331, 349; ZENGER, Pentateuch, 5–7), or even propose that a Christian הלכה should now be derived in the same fashion as by the rabbis (MARQUARDT, Reintegration, 676). In my view, a Christian הלכה restricted to *pentateuchal* texts will not be able to find any warrant within the New Testament. Moreover, even an *unrestricted* use of הלכה as an approach to Christian life and practice will be hard pressed not to compromise the crucial Christian doctrine of justification by faith (as MARQUARDT's critique of this doctrine illustrates; this is not to say that all interpretations of the doctrine are beyond critique, μὴ γέ-νοιτο!). What I am advocating here is an appreciation and use of the Law (*qua* Pentateuch) as a direct and authoritative witness to Christian faith and practice which would at the same time *not* involve the subordination of the other Old Testament witnesses. For a recent effort, see CHILDS, Biblical Theology, 678–85; 704–12; idem, OT Theology, 51–57; 63–91.

Postscript

Twenty Years Later

Despite the well-known cliché that 'history is written by the victors,'[1] important histories are also written by the losers. As Perez Zagorin points out,

> "One thinks, for instance of Thucydides, himself an exile, the author of a history relating the defeat of Athens, his city; or of Tacitus, the greatest of Roman historians, whose *Annals* and *Histories* were not the work of a victor but of a man who lamented the irrecoverable loss of Roman republican liberty... A significant part of contemporary German historiography is the work of scholars of a defeated nation seeking to explain how the German people submitted to the Nazi regime and the crimes it committed. Many histories have exposed the discreditable methods by which power has been acquired and exercised, and many others have been written to vindicate lost causes, religious minorities, and oppressed peoples."[2]

This kind of insight and common sense should reframe any number of arguments in biblical studies about how the production of biblical texts only advanced the material interests of the powerful *or* how the generation of biblical texts was purely a form of compensation for the political losses of the powerless. The relationship between a text and a social situation is more subtle and varies more widely than most exegetical arguments recognize or allow.

Individuals and groups think *through* texts, through the process of texts' literary composition and through the developing traditions of their use. Deep within the logic of modern historical criticism of the Bible, and the liberal Protestant theological tradition that birthed it and sustains it, is the notion that biblical texts are social residue, cultural detritus — what was left over after the life they describe had gone. Friederich Schleiermacher set this default assumption at the outset of the nineteenth century by observing,

> "Every holy writing is merely a mausoleum of religion, a monument that a great spirit was there that no longer exists; for if it still lived and were active,

---

[1] On the history of this expression, see DOYLE, MIEDER, AND SHAPIRO, Dictionary of Modern Proverbs, 122.

[2] ZAGORIN, History, 13.

why would it attach such great importance to the dead letter that can only be a weak reproduction of it?"[3]

On a rhetorical level, his comment is easily recognized as a problematic example of a question assuming its own conclusion.

But on a deeper level, Schleiermacher's judgment also betrays a fundamental failure to grasp the true nature of scripture as a genre. The root problem with much of the historical work in biblical studies is not only that secure determinations of authorship and dating have proven much more difficult to make than was once thought, or that the links between those determinations and some derived notion of intention (whether authorial or social) are even less secure, but that the dynamics of scripture as a literary-theological phenomenon have been bypassed or misunderstood. There are few books of the Christian Bible which were probably written all at once by only one person. No book of the Old Testament likely has a single author or can be assigned to a single social context or agenda. 'Scripture' is not characteristically a one-time, single-author deposition but a socio-literary means of providing corporate religious testimony over time, a way of describing and enshrining an account of God's nature and activity in the past, present, and future so that such testimony continues to be readily and reliably available for an ongoing community of faith.[4] What scripture denotes is finally a particular relationship between text-making and texts on the one hand, and a distinct religious community on the other. The literary composition and use of scripture, at its core, is best understood not as a celebratory expression of political propaganda or as a compensatory product of social bereavement but as a lively and life-giving human search for the transcendent.[5]

A shift in focus from original author to extended tradition has in fact gained ground within biblical studies because of redaction-critical studies of the biblical books,[6] because of the compositional intertextuality evident within the biblical

---

[3] SCHLEIERMACHER, On Religion, 50. Cf. WELLHAUSEN, Prolegomena, 405 n. 1: "Yet it is a thing which is likely to occur, that a body of traditional practice should only be written down when it is threatening to die out, and that a book should be, as it were, the ghost of the life which is closed."

[4] Cf. DEINES, Term and Concept of Scripture: "The texts which later formed the *Tanakh* were not preserved primarily to report a past history or revelation, but to mediate this past revelation into a means of encountering God in the future" (278).

[5] See SMITH, Scripture?, 18–19. Smith characterizes the "activity" of scripture as a trilateral engagement among humans, the transcendent, and a text. He concludes his comparative religions investigation by submitting that scripture functions symbolically "as a channel for something beyond itself" (239).

[6] Even with heightened skepticism in many quarters about the accuracy of highly detailed redactional reconstructions, many of which disagree with each other, redaction criticism has underscored the composite nature of the Old Testament writings and pushed toward the assignment of multiple social settings for the contents of the biblical books, rather than just one. See further WILLIAMSON, Vindication of Redaction Criticism, 26–36.

texts,[7] because of the general shift toward later dates for Old Testament writings,[8] and because of the continued impact of textual studies of the Dead Sea Scrolls and related manuscript finds from the Judean desert.[9] The Persian period, which was often previously viewed as an uncreative era of narrow religious orthodoxy, is now thought to have been intellectually robust and conducive to literary activity because many of the Old Testament books appear to have been completed during that time.[10] Indeed, the pendulum has swung so far that some biblical scholars currently identify *only* ongoing literary activity in this period and polemicize against any claims for a recognized body of authoritative writings within post-exilic Yehud.[11] Between the Scylla of static originalism and the Charybdis of endless textual diversity lies not only Israel's scripture but the process of biblical canon formation.

Konrad Schmid's literary history of the Old Testament reflects these recent developments and locates exactly the right sweet spot between the two extremes:

> "Many Old Testament texts and writings possess both an oral and a written prehistory as well as a post-history even within the Old Testament itself, so that discussing them in the context of one literary-historical epoch and not another need not mean that the material and texts that are used and worked over at this point were conceived from scratch in this or that writing and were not altered thereafter. Rather, the Old Testament is in principle to be regarded as *traditional literature*."[12]

In other words, Old Testament texts remained "in motion" as streams of tradition even after they began to be committed to writing. They made use of older traditions and were themselves supplemented in turn. The frequently repeated platitude that the Bible is not a single book but an 'anthology' or 'library' falls short of providing an adequate description of the biblical writings, since books within a modern library do not typically possess the same kind of historically extended formation, are not composite to the same extent, and therefore lack the same degree of compositional sharing, overlap, or imbrication.[13] (For a visual depiction of imbrication, see Paula Gibson's cover design for this book.)

---

7 FISHBANE, Interpretation.

8 See further ACHENBACH, Pentateuch, 253–85.

9 See, e. g., BROOKE, Qumran Scrolls, 25–42.

10 See further GERSTENBERGER, Israel in the Persian Period.

11 E. g., BOCCACCINI, Biblical Literature, 41–51, proclaims, "The battle has started and we have solid canonical walls to tear down." Cf. REEVES, Problematizing the Bible, who asserts that "Labels like 'canonical' and 'non-canonical' are meaningless categories for Second Temple Judaism" (15), and KRAFT, Para-mania, who inveighs against the "tyranny of canonical assumptions" (10).

12 SCHMID, Old Testament, xiii (my emphasis).

13 I realize that some accounts of post-modern hermeneutics, following M. BAKHTIN and J. KRISTEVA, would identify every text as an intertext, "a mosaic of quotations" absorbing and transforming other texts. See KRISTEVA, Word, 66. However, the biblical process of

In further articulating this perspective, Schmid memorably describes the books of the Old Testament as "agglutinating interpretive literature."[14] He concludes on this basis that circulation of the Old Testament writings must have been fairly restricted in ancient times, since:

> "It is scarcely imaginable that a multilevel continuous process of writing bibli-
> cal books — and their different textual witnesses refute any attempts to dispute
> such a process — could have been carried out, simply from a technical standpoint,
> if numerous copies of the books had been in circulation."[15]

The key phrase here is 'multilevel continuous process.' With his additional insight about the limited distribution of books within such a process, Schmid's approach is admirable not only for his awareness of recent critical insights about the restricted range of literacy in the ancient world but also for his willingness to let the character of the literature guide the task of historical reconstruction rather than imposing on biblical literature a reconstruction based upon external criteria and considerations.

What Schmid terms the 'agglutinating' quality of Old Testament writings is, in my judgment, another way of describing one aspect of what Brevard Childs termed the 'canonical' dimension of the biblical literature. Childs was primarily interested in canon not as a list but as a 'process':

> "The lengthy process of the development of the literature leading up to the final
> stage of canonization involved a profoundly hermeneutical activity on the part of
> the tradents... The material was transmitted through its various oral, literary, and
> redactional stages by many different groups toward a theological end. Because
> the traditions were received as religiously authoritative, they were transmitted
> in such a way as to maintain a normative function for subsequent generations
> of believers within a community of faith. This process of rendering the material
> theologically involved countless different compositional techniques by means of
> which the tradition was actualized."[16]

The transmission of these normative traditions also generated new traditions and scriptural supplements.

---

compositional intertextuality was more direct and genetic in nature than is the case with books shelved in a modern library. The biblical books also exhibit more common ground with each other in terms of their shared content, being united as they are by a common focus on God, Israel, and the nations.

14 SCHMID, Old Testament, 34.
15 Ibid.
16 CHILDS, Biblical Theology, 70.

As emphasized by Christoph Dohmen (among others), some texts and/or text portions now found in the Bible even have their *origin* in the combination and juxtaposition of other (prior) texts:

> "New texts are not always produced in isolation and later edited and brought together. Rather, though the tradition permits an element of conservation to be seen, it is more often one of participation. Thus the foundations of 'canon' are laid down in terms of a canonical process. Recognition of a binding character of scripture, which points to the constitutive function of the subject that the text as such acknowledges, is articulated in the canonical process."[17]

This textually productive dynamic is especially evident in the phenomenon of scribal prophecy.[18] More fundamentally, the generation of new texts emerges from the activity of interpretation itself — "participation," as Dohmen styles it. Michael Fishbane has likewise described how ancient interpretation of the Bible represents "the religious duty to expound and extend, and so to *reactualize* the ancient word of God for the present hour."[19] Instead of viewing this kind of internal actualization within the developing texts — in the form of editorial alteration and supplementation — as an indication for the absence of textual normativity, as is sometimes done, these scholars understand instead that the type of textual change observable in the formation of the biblical literature is itself an expression and outgrowth of textual normativity.[20]

What these scholars have all perceived is a reciprocal relationship between the literary formation of the Old Testament writings and their religious use within a concrete faith community. It is crucial to see that this reciprocal relationship is posited in the first instance as a descriptive historical claim rather than a normative theological one. Childs would, of course, proceed to develop the theological implications of this historical claim, but at its base it constitutes a literary-historical appraisal of the biblical writings as a genre. 'Scripture,' Childs called it — traditional religious literature that was growing and in the process of being gathered into a literary collection or canon. This is precisely why Childs's 'canonical' proposal cannot be treated as a purely synchronic approach to biblical interpretation,[21] and

---

17 DOHMEN, Biblische Auslegung, as cited in JANOWSKI, Contrastive Unity of Scripture, 57.

18 See further DE JONG, Biblical Prophecy.

19 FISHBANE, Garments, 38 (his emphasis).

20 Cf. KRATZ, "Siehe, ich lege meine Worte,": "Die Auslegung innerhalb der prophetischen Bücher ist nicht weniger inspiriert als der ausgelegte Text, insofern sich die Interpretation, die in den Text eingeschrieben wird, aus der Inspiration des überlieferten Texts speist" (38).

21 *Contra* BARTON, Reading the Old Testament, 100–03. BARTON later admitted that he had not gotten CHILDS quite right. See BARTON, Canonical Approaches, 199–209. It is true, he concedes, that CHILDS did not consider the 'final form' of the biblical text to be a 'unified aesthetic object' (201). But BARTON still misleadingly characterizes CHILDS's approach as advocating 'close attention to the Bible as it stands' (199) and depicts it as a return to naïve 'precritical' exegesis (204–06).

why he spent so much time in his publications rehearsing historical-critical arguments about the diachronic formation of the biblical books.

Textual modifications certainly occurred for a variety of reasons, not all of which were explicitly theological, and some of which may have been pragmatic or even mechanical. Yet close study of the biblical literature reveals a process of literary formation and transmission with a steady long-term goal of assembling a compelling witness to the God of Israel,[22] a literary arena *of* and *for* collective theological reasoning,[23] a scriptural *corpus* able to offer ongoing religious guidance to contemporary and future believers.

Writing *The Law and the Prophets*

When I approached the task of writing this book, my doctoral dissertation at Yale, I did not set out to write about the history of Old Testament canon formation. What had instead gotten my attention was the basic problem of how the Pentateuch and the prophetic books related to each other. Initially I framed the issue in the customary historical-critical way: What legal traditions or laws had been known by the historical prophets, and how had the prophets reflected them, perhaps critiqued them, and ultimately transformed them?[24] I dutifully wrote out a first proposal and proceeded to rip it up without showing it to another soul. (I actually did print it out, read it, and rip it up.) I shared my second try at a proposal with my dissertation advisor, Christopher Seitz, who responded by saying, gnomically, "I think what you want to talk about is the canon." It took me some time to work that out, but I realized he was right and composed a third proposal that laid the groundwork for this book. Without Seitz's critical intervention, for which I am enduringly grateful, this book would not have been written.

The task of writing that third proposal sent me back into the stacks of the Yale library, since I also realized that I did not know nearly enough about the historical reconstructions of biblical canon formation on offer in current scholarship, not to mention how such reconstructions might bear on the question of the correlation and coordination of the developing scriptural traditions of law and prophecy. As I describe in the book, what I encountered in the secondary literature was a linear three-stage theory of canon formation, which had been formulated at the end of the nineteenth century and remained suspiciously unaltered throughout twentieth-century Old Testament scholarship.[25] According to this theory, the Pentateuch had

---

22 On this point, see further OEMING, Way of God.

23 On 'collective reasoning' within the emerging canon, see SÆBØ, "Unifying Reflections."

24 As in TUCKER, Law in Eighth-Century Prophets.

25 I characterize this lack of change as 'suspicious' because, given all of the twentieth century's critical iterations regarding the reconstructed origins and developmental trajectories of the various biblical books, one would be inclined to think that the history of the biblical canon had likewise been affected. In fact, what I attempt in large part to do throughout the book is to build on the findings of historical-critical scholarship, especially redaction-critical

been 'canonized' at the time of Ezra (ca. 444 B. C.), followed by the prophetic corpus in approximately 200 B. C., with the Writings — the third division of the Hebrew canon — being added at the end of the first century A. D., thereby 'closing' the canon as a whole. Not only did this theory thus treat the Pentateuch alone as Israel's original 'Bible,' it implied a historical development consisting of what were in effect three different successive 'Bibles,' and postponed the closure of the Old Testament canon until after the time of Jesus and the earliest New Testament writings. This latter point especially prompted subsequent scholarship to trace two different historical processes of biblical canon formation, one within Judaism and another in Christianity.[26]

Writing just before me (1996), John Barton insisted that although debate had arisen about many questions regarding Old Testament canon formation,

> "there is agreement among scholars on only one matter concerning the canonization of the Hebrew Scriptures: that the present threefold division into Law (*tōrâh*), Prophets (*nbî'îm*), and Writings (*ktûbîm*) provides a rough guide to the *relative* date at which these collections were regarded as 'canonical scripture.' The Law was already a fixed entity at the time when the later books of the Prophets were still being composed, and the Prophets were complete at the time when the last of the Writings were taking shape."[27]

My own research increasingly called this blanket assessment into question, and so I set out to deconstruct it and propose an alternative. Barton's 'rough guide' accurately conveyed the majority opinion at that stage in the discussion. However, on closer review, the history of Old Testament scholarship exhibited persistent minority voices that had raised a variety of perceptive objections to a sequential three-stage progression of the canon and ultimately to the very spot on which Barton had planted his flag — the link between the order of the canonical divisions and their relative dates.[28]

---

work, both to problematize the standard theory of biblical canon formation and to develop a more plausible alternative. I have therefore been puzzled to read on occasion that my work on the canon is somehow 'text immanent.' E. g., JONKER, Chronicler and the Prophets, 163–64 n. 46. Jonker nonetheless believes that my proposal is a viable one.

[26] E. g., McDONALD, Biblical Canon, 186–89.

[27] BARTON, Significance, 68 (his emphasis).

[28] This link was affirmed and made central in the work of numerous scholars at the end of the nineteenth century and the beginning of the twentieth, above all in the influential treatment of RYLE, Canon. It is sometimes forgotten that the theory was already something of a hedge from the start, given that the previous tendency in scholarship had been to relate the canonical divisions more directly to a progressive development within the history of Israelite religion. See, e. g., OEHLER, Canon of the Old Testament, 1:546: "The threefold division of the O.T. Canon is not accidental or arbitrary: it rather accords with the developing process of the O.T. religion." The linear three-stage reconstruction formulated by RYLE and others was intended to modify this approach in order to allow for the critical findings of

It turned out that individual building blocks of the theoretical superstructure had been crumbling for some time, and voices in addition to mine were concluding that the edifice itself could no longer stand. Roger Beckwith (1985) had been one of the first,[29] but the response to his work had regrettably reduced the debate to more or less a single question — When was the canon closed, early or late? — without taking up his critique of an approach to Old Testament canon formation that treated the order of the canon's divisions as indicative of discrete stages in the canon formation process. Similar conclusions about the inadequacy of the standard theory of canon formation had been voiced by E. Earle Ellis (1991), who wrote bluntly of 'the demise of the three-stage canonization theory,'[30] and Arie van der Kooij (1995), who determined that the theory 'niet langer houdbaar is.'[31]

My work in *The Law and the Prophets* (2000) drew on these insights, even as it attempted to strengthen them, partly by rooting them in a longer critical discussion and bringing in additional conversation partners from the history of scholarship.[32] I was intrigued to discover early outliers like J. Willis Beecher (1896), who preferred to speak of the Old Testament canon as a 'growing aggregate of recognized sacred writings' rather than consenting to the notion of canonical development in discrete stages.[33] Or Eduard König (1884), who perceptively called attention to the way in which the standard theory of canon formation followed Wellhausen in viewing the biblical prophets as the crucial eighth-century turning point in the history of Israelite religion but then postponed the Prophets as a completed canonical division of Old Testament scripture until much later.[34]

Was it really plausible that the prophetic writings had lacked any sort of scriptural authority until the second century B. C.? And if they did lack such authority, what had ensured their retention and transmission? Were they locked up in a chest somewhere? Was not the continuing process of their literary development actually a sign of their religious importance and recognition by the community? What was

---

modern biblical scholarship, including J. WELLHAUSEN's move to date prophetic faith prior to priestly religion (but without losing the notion of a progressive revelation in history). The result was to date the Pentateuch to the exilic period and the Prophets to an even later time in order to preserve their relative order in the canon, even though this move effectively reversed WELLHAUSEN's reversal. In other words, the roots of the three-stage theory lay in a framework in which the divisions of the canon were seen to reflect stages in the history of Israelite religion, but after RYLE they no longer clearly did so. The sequence of the tripartite canon was preserved, but its direct relation to the history of Israelite religion was lost. For a full treatment of scholarship on the Old Testament canon in the nineteenth century, see my Modernity's Canonical Crisis, 651–87.

29 BECKWITH, Canon; idem, Formation.

30 ELLIS, Canon, 37.

31 VAN DER KOOIJ, De canonvorming van de Hebreeuwse bijbel, 61; idem, Canonization of Ancient Books.

32 I regret that at that time I had overlooked VAN DER KOOIJ's 1995 essay.

33 BEECHER, Canon.

34 KÖNIG, Hauptprobleme.

the place of prophetic *scripture* within the history of Israelite religion? This basic question became central to my treatment. Indeed, my fundamental conclusion was that the developing collections of Pentateuch and Prophets had mutually influenced each other throughout the various stages of their formation and that they had stabilized more or less together, as expressed by the *theologoumenon* of 'the law and the words,' which had its roots in deuteronomic tradition.[35]

In the years after my dissertation was published, critiques of the standard three-stage theory picked up steam, although the theory appeared to maintain its grip on introductory textbooks and dictionary articles in the field. Nevertheless, Jack Lightstone also took a position (2002) against the standard canon theory.[36] And just over ten years after Barton's 'rough guide' assertion, Karel van der Toorn could announce the opposite conclusion (2007) with just as much critical confidence: "Today this theory of canonization is no longer in favor with the scholarly community... The history of the canonization of the Hebrew Bible has to be written anew."[37] Summarizing the discussion even more recently (2013), Timothy Lim concludes,

> "This study confirms the conclusions of previous scholars that the three-stage theory of the late nineteenth and early twentieth centuries cannot be maintained. Elegant in its simplicity of a stage-by-stage closing of the Pentateuch, the Prophets, and the Writings the theory tottered and finally collapsed when its rotting pillars were pulled apart."[38]

At issue then is not only how to construct a new history of biblical canon formation but how to understand the origin of the canonical divisions and what they represent.

In this endeavor, the nature and process of canonization will also need to be reconceived. In part because the Pentateuch or 'Law' has long been believed to be the oldest portion of Old Testament scripture, and in part because in the standard theory of canon formation it functioned for a time as Israel's sole 'Bible' before the

---

35 See further CHAPMAN, "Law and the Words"; idem, Second Temple Jewish Hermeneutics. For additional support, see WARHURST, Chronicler's Use of the Prophets: "Already in the Second Temple era the community shows signs of being a 'people of the Book' which is devoted not only to the principles of Torah but to the world view of the Prophets as well... The Chronicler's harmonization of material which later comprised the Former and Latter Prophets suggests that the two types of literature were already held in equally high regard by the time of the community of Chronicles and were capable of correlation" (180–81). Cf. GERSTENBERGER, Prophetie in den Chronikbüchern, who similarly describes Chronicles as providing indirect evidence for the beginnings of prophetic scripture.

36 LIGHTSTONE, Rabbis' Bible, 166: "Scholars wrongly presume that the tripartite Jewish canon (Torah, Prophets, and Hagiographa) developed in linear fashion, with each part being, for the most part irrevocably, 'closed' in succession. Such historical 'mono-linearity' is highly unlikely."

37 VAN DER TOORN, Scribal Culture, 235.

38 LIM, Formation, 178.

prophetic corpus was added to it, canonization itself has been understood primarily in a legal fashion.[39] The scene depicted in Nehemiah 8 has provided an imaginative framework and scriptural warrant for this conception.[40] Yet it is not at all clear that canonization occurred as an intentional act by a central deliberative body intent on establishing a nationally binding legal standard for communal behavior. Not only does such a process seem to require an institutional structure in Judaism that is not evident within the historical sources, but it appears to impose a Christian conciliar model of canonization on ancient Judaism.[41]

W. M. L. de Wette had perceived a more persuasive basic alternative prior to the rise of the standard theory, a theoretical road not taken in which "the whole of the Old Testament came gradually into existence, and as it were of itself, and, by force of custom or public use, acquired a sort of sanction."[42] Another way of putting the point is to say that the biblical canon was defined from the center rather than from the margins[43] — or even that the Old Testament canon was a reality before it became a problem. Part of the difficulty attached to the ongoing debate has been the persistent effort to modulate an organic process based on custom and use into a series of rational group decisions. It does not work. The idea that representative bodies 'make' and 'close' canons is extrinsic to the phenomenon itself.[44] Even the notion of canonical 'closure' is misleading. Given the available evidence for biblical canon formation, 'stabilization' is closer to the historical reality than any sort of formal closure.[45]

Speaking Past Each Other

For some time terminological and conceptual disputes have obscured the high degree of consensus about the scope of the biblical canon in the last two centuries B. C. Most scholars recognize the existence of an acknowledged core of authoritative

---

[39] Cf. the critique of this type of approach in CONRAD, Frage.

[40] The state of the Pentateuch at the time of Ezra no longer seems to have been so complete or purely a product of Persian imperial policy. See, e. g., BLENKINSOPP, Was the Pentateuch the Constitution; DE TROYER, When Did the Pentateuch Come into Existence?; SCHORCH, What Kind of Authority?

[41] For this criticism, see LIGHTSTONE, Formation of the Biblical Canon.

[42] DE WETTE, Introduction, 33.

[43] This formulation was suggested to me by Jan Dochhorn.

[44] Cf. SCHWARTZ, Bible, 121–22: "No record exists, however, of a particular time and place at which the biblical canon was established, and no single institution ever existed in Jewish history that would have had the power to establish the canon. Rather, the canonization of the Bible was a natural, gradual process, by which those writings popularly believed to be of great antiquity and divinely inspired were accorded sacred status."

[45] Even in the Christian tradition, canonical councils deliberated on whether books that already had a place in Christian practice, at least in some communities, should continue to be considered authoritative. They did not 'make' books canonical or impose them without any prior history or custom.

books, even as they concede the fuzziness or fluidity of the collection's boundaries.[46] As Lee McDonald has aptly summarized,

> "If by 'canon' we mean a collection of authoritative sacred texts that circulated in either Jewish or Christian communities and that were acknowledged as scripture, there is no question that Judaism and early Christianity had a canon of scriptures; but if we mean by it a fixed biblical collection to which nothing could be added or taken away, then there are problems."[47]

Fair enough — but if the first definitional possibility is perfectly acceptable, then why should the second be preferred, as McDonald systematically proceeds to do?[48]

This undefended preference is also on display in Timothy Lim's work. He opts at the outset, consequentially, to use 'canon' to mean a *list* of biblical books.[49] Yet he only selectively explores the strengths and weaknesses of other canonical definitions and criteria and fails to justify his own adequately.[50] Like many scholars, he employs the term 'authoritative scriptures' as a reference to scriptural collections prior to the first extant canon lists. But as Lim acknowledges, there was 'continued fluctuation' of such lists well into the Middle Ages (and actually even beyond),[51] so why is the existence of lists his defining criterion for a canon, especially if the lists do not all agree with each other and exhibit change over time? Is it perhaps a canon's "list-ability" (i.e., and not the specific contents of the list) that is its key feature? Elsewhere, for example in his treatment of Ben Sira, Lim implies that *closure* is the crucial factor and not strictly equivalent to the list criterion.[52] As much

---

46 E. g., BARTON, Writings, 23 ("core," "central books"); J. COLLINS, Canon, 232 ("core canon"); T. COLLINS, Mantle, 232 ("core canon"); LIM, Formation, 185 (" a core of prophetical books"); McDONALD, Forgotten Scriptures, 9 ("core books"); ULRICH, Dead Sea Scrolls, 60 ("central core"); VANDERKAM, Revealed Literature, 23 ("core canon"); ZEVIT, Second-Third Century Canonization, 150 ("implicit canon").

47 McDONALD, Forgotten Scriptures, 22.

48 McDONALD attempts to face up to this question in his essay What Do We Mean by Canon?, in which he concedes that "those who adopted earlier notions of canons or standards never suggested that they were closed or fixed categories" (11). In the end, however, he simply reinscribes his presumption that 'canon' is best reserved for "the final stages of canonization that take place in the fourth and fifth centuries [A. D.] when various books are identified as 'canon' and catalogues of sacred books appear."

49 LIM, Formation, 4.

50 E. g, LIM, Formation, 11–13, does discuss the use of citation as a marker of authority, but he basically passes over in silence the entire other side of the canon debate, in which canon is fundamentally understood as a matter of *authority*. For a classic expression of canon as 'function' rather than 'list,' see SANDERS, Adaptable. His most precise statement is found in idem, Canon, in: FREEDMAN.

51 LIM, Formation, 26.

52 E. g., LIM, Formation, 101: "That the grandson did not have a closed canon is further evidenced by the grammar of the Prologue in v. 3." If 'list' were the only factor at issue,

as Lim wants to avoid the 'teleological fallacy' of positing a canon too early,[53] he admits that "early collections of authoritative scripture do overlap to a large extent with the lists of books found later in Josephus, 2 Ezra, Mishnah Yadayim, and early church fathers, and Baba Bathra."[54] So why again is the existence of a list the most significant canonical criterion?

Lim further acknowledges, in a footnote, how studies by Joseph Blenkinsopp, Odil Hannes Steck, Stephen Dempster, and me have all determined that the canonical divisions of Law and Prophets began to form early in the Persian period, but he rejects this idea without argument, citing only Arie van der Kooij's criticism of identifying this Persian-era 'scriptural intertext' as 'canonical.'[55] Yet as Lim reports earlier in his book,[56] van der Kooij himself believes that an official and authoritative canon existed already in the second century B. C.,[57] a view at odds with Lim's own preference for a first century A. D. date. The difference in dating is merely definitional. Where van der Kooij sees the Prologue to Ben Sira as providing ample evidence for a biblical canon on other grounds, Lim insists that the Prologue does not contain a full list of authoritative books and provides insufficient evidence of closure, and that, therefore, a canon did not yet exist. Not only does van der Kooij's date rest on a broader understanding of canon as authority, he explicitly rejects the idea that canon was understood in antiquity as synonymous with list.[58] As for Lim, he agrees that beginning sometime in the second century B. C., various Jewish groups possessed collections of authoritative scriptures, but he wants to stress how these collections may have differed from each other, and how they likely included, in some cases, certain books that did not survive in the later rabbinic canon.[59]

Lim's insistence on these points reveals that his primary concern is not actually with canonical lists after all, but with canonical *scope* — the canon as a fixed and delimited collection of scripture. He simply uses canon lists as dispositive evidence for a delimited scope.[60] His reason for approaching the task in this fashion

---

there would be no need to discuss the Prologue at all, since it does not contain a fully specified list of biblical books.

[53] His use of this phrase comes from DAVIES, *Loose Canons*.

[54] LIM, *Formation*, 187. Cf. ALEXANDER, *Formation of the Biblical Canon*, "What the Rabbis were doing was defending a canon which they had received already more or less defined (save for a little fuzziness around the edges) from the pre-70 period" (65).

[55] LIM, *Formation*, 216 n. 14. He refers to VAN DER KOOIJ, *Canonization of Ancient Hebrew Books*. Note, however, that VAN DER KOOIJ appears to misunderstand my position as an argument for a final canonical redaction in the Persian period (28).

[56] LIM, *Formation*, 29.

[57] VAN DER KOOIJ, *Canonization of Ancient Books*, 22; *Canonization of Ancient Hebrew Books*, 31–33.

[58] VAN DER KOOIJ, *Canonization of Ancient Hebrew Books*, 29.

[59] LIM, *Formation*, 183–85.

[60] By contrast, in the more recent study of GALLAGHER AND MEADE, *Biblical Canon Lists*, xvii–xviii, two sensible notes of caution are struck with regard to lists as a criterion for canon: 1) canon lists "do not bear a direct relation" to the books that were used authoritatively; and

is to allow for the real possibility that other books — like Ben Sira, for instance — may once have been considered 'canonical' within certain strands of Judaism. Yet another definitional/methodological possibility is to decouple canonical scope from canonical authority from the beginning, to imagine historically that the canon always had varying scopes and orders at different times within different groups and communities — just as, incidentally, is still the case with the biblical canon today. In the end, one has to ask why fixity and closure should function as privileged critical markers for canonicity when *there has never been a single, fixed scope and order of the biblical canon right down to the present.* The fuzziness of the biblical canon's boundaries needs to be viewed as inherent to the kind of thing a canon is, rather than as a perpetual exception to it.[61]

As these examples indicate, the differences in how scholars position their arguments and express their views is less about the situation 'on the ground' in the ancient world and more about the markers they privilege for the attribution of canonical status, especially how significant they believe the phenomenon of fixity is. Also in dispute is how scholars conceive of the socio-historical process of canonization broadly, with some researchers reconstructing an evolutionary process in which occasional writings, which really began as 'secular' statements, gradually took on religious significance over time and were only later affirmed or even 'made' canonical by the Jewish community.[62] Proponents of this approach typically want to postpone 'theology' and 'theologizing' to the latter stages of the biblical texts' formation, sometimes openly claiming that later dogmatists harmonized and domesticated the earlier secular writings, which possessed greater vitality and daring. The sympathies at work in this type of reconstruction are plain.

But other researchers, myself included, have seen the 'agglutinating' character of Jewish scripture as an earlier indication of a growing 'canon consciousness' within the biblical literature. The critical slogan that 'no biblical text was written to be scripture' is accordingly in need of qualification and revision.[63] As scripture

---

2) "lists often (not always) date to a time when the major formative stages of the biblical canon had already taken place."

61 Cf. ALEXANDER, Textual Authority: "If what we have from the third century [A. D.] on is indeed a canon, then fuzziness in itself offers no good grounds for denying that what we have in late Second Temple Judaism is a canon as well" (44).

62 E. g., ULRICH, From Literature to Scripture. For a nineteenth-century example of such a view, well-established in historical-critical scholarship, see EWALD, Über die Heiligkeit der Bibel. This approach lies also behind the move to distinguish sharply between 'scripture' and 'canon.' See McDONALD, Forgotten Scriptures, 24: "The notion of scripture predates the notion of canon and the latter always assumes the former, but the reverse is not historically true." This statement is correct only if one defines 'scripture' and 'canon' in the way that McDONALD favors.

63 E. g., McDONALD, Wherein Lies Authority?, 205: "Some students of the Bible assume that the ancient writers were consciously aware of writing sacred Scripture, but almost without exception, this was not the case." McDONALD's argument for this claim is that the biblical text continued to sustain changes later in its process of transmission, and so it could

grew literarily, its various portions and segments influenced each other by affecting subsequent editorial work throughout the expanding corpus, and even generating new textual additions. The concern on 'our side of the aisle,' as they say in the U. S. Congress, has all along been to resist the preferential status of fixity as the defining feature of canonical status, as well as the artificial and misleading distinction now routinely made between 'scripture' and 'canon.'[64] What occurs repeatedly in the critical debate is that first a canonical criterion of no decisive interest to ancient Jews is selected as a litmus test for critical investigation (e. g., 'closure'), and then that criterion is used to demonstrate its own insignificance (viz., ancient Jews were not especially concerned about closure).[65]

There is a historical and theological concern at the heart of this debate, and it has to do with the way that scripture was *perceived* in ancient Israel. Were notions like 'scripture' and 'canon' only retrospective categories levied by the community after the literary collections such terms designate had been completed and reconceived? Or was there perhaps a sense of canonical authority operating already in the expansion, elaboration, and reinterpretation of these texts *prior* to their fixation? The phenomenon of scribal prophecy and the manuscript finds at Qumran both gesture in the latter direction.[66] The point is that ancient Jews considered these scriptural texts, the act of interpreting these texts, and even the process of producing new texts, as vehicles for the conveyance of God's word to the community.

From a theological perspective, it is therefore fitting to conclude that God spoke to Israel not only through historical events and human mediators but *through*

---

not yet have been considered sacred scripture. But textual change is not an adequate reason to deny the existence of scripture, let alone a reason to draw conclusions about the ancient writers' state of mind.

[64] On the distinction between 'scripture' and 'canon,' see my essay Canon Debate, esp. 277–79. In this regard, I would reiterate a point that I have made before. McDONALD's influential 'canon 1 — canon 2' schema, which he attributes to SHEPPARD, Canon, is based on a misreading of SHEPPARD and ignores exactly what SHEPPARD was attempting to demonstrate; namely, that 'canon 1' and 'canon 2' versions of canon are 'poles' rather than stages. For SHEPPARD, they cannot be reduced to a simple linear progression. McDONALD takes the view that 'canon 1' is an authoritative collection of scripture which is not yet fixed and delimited, that 'canon 2' is a fixed and delimited authoritative collection of scripture, and that 'canon 1' always precedes 'canon 2,' and 'canon 2' always presumes 'canon 1.' Yet SHEPPARD provides persuasive examples of how 'canon 2' type understandings cannot be restricted to late external decisions about a 'canon 1' corpus, because 'canon 2' understandings already appear in 'canon conscious' redactions *within* the biblical corpus. On this point, see further my Second Temple Jewish Hermeneutics, 282–84. McDONALD may continue to employ this distinction in the way he does, but he should acknowledge that he is using it differently from SHEPPARD and is actually sidestepping SHEPPARD's main point.

[65] ALEXANDER, Textual Authority, 68, also describes closure and textual stability as concepts "which were actually not all that important in late antiquity."

[66] E. g., WEISSENBERG AND UUSIMÄKI, Are There Sacred Texts in Qumran?, describe how "divine revelation takes a textualized form" at Qumran, and how revelation was understood to continue "through inspired interactions with texts" (41).

scripture.[67] Scripture was a means of revelation and not only a record of it. In its most extreme form, the critical opposition wants to eliminate scripture as a religious source of revelation within ancient Judaism, and one quickly gains the impression in the contemporary debate that those who adopt this historical perspective are waging a proxy war against some specter of biblicism or fundamentalism keeping them awake at night.[68] The rhetoric in the debate often invokes the danger of anachronism. But what runs the greater risk of anachronism — positing that ancient Jews took scripture too seriously? Or that ancient Jews had all the same hesitations and suspicions about authoritative scripture that modern, right-thinking people have today?

Reconstructing Canon Formation

Some readers of this book have been quick to conclude that I opt for an improbably early canon. This kind of response reflects the hegemony of the dating question in studies of canon formation, as if the most important critical determination to be made is whether the canon was early or late. I do locate the origins of the *concept* of canon in the deuteronomic tradition's synthesis of Moses and the prophets.[69] But because 'canon' has never been primarily about scope or fixity or lists for me, I also consider this emerging canon to be a work very much in progress. I neither exclude the likelihood of alternative canonical forms and formats in different streams of Judaism nor reject the possibility that certain books may have secured a place in one format or another at one time only to lose that place later on. My claim is rather that an *idea* and *emerging shape* of the canon is evident in the sources prior to an apparent concern about fixity or scope.

I believe my position is in line with what Dead Sea Scrolls specialists are increasingly concluding; namely, how textual variants at Qumran indicate that "authority resided in a book rather than in a particular textual form of that book."[70] Although scholarship on the Dead Sea Scrolls is sometimes held to illustrate the absence of any biblical canon, I understand this body of scholarship to provide my thesis with

---

67 MAIER, Biblical Hermeneutics, 81, thus refers to biblical revelation as 'enscripturated.'

68 E. g., McDONALD, Biblical Canon, 429, warns darkly of 'inappropriate loyalties.' He was more forthcoming in the previous edition, his Formation of the Christian Biblical Tradition, 257 n. 18, by deprecating "those Christians who continue to place the Bible first in their creeds instead of God."

69 For two similar proposals which appeared independently in the same year that my work was originally published, see RÖMER, L'école deutéronomiste, and VERMEYLEN, L'école deutéronomiste. Now also see RÖMER, Moses, and VERMEYLEN, Les écrivains deutéronomistes. E. NICHOLSON made a strong supporting case for a book of *torah* and a 'core collection' of prophetic books already by the time of Deut 18:9–22, which he viewed as exilic or early post-exilic. See his Deuteronomy 18:9–22. NICHOLSON described the deuteronomistic redactor responsible for Deut 18:9–22 as 'conjoining' Law and Prophets (159).

70 J. COLLINS, Uses of Torah, 51. Cf. ULRICH, Qumran and the Canon: "The book, not its specific textual form, is canonical" (59).

additional support. To my mind, the Dead Sea Scrolls demonstrate how a normative notion of scriptural authority preceded a fixation of the biblical text and a finalization of the scriptural collection's scope. (The later fixation of the text and the finalization of the collection's contents were significant developments but even then not absolute, since both continued to exhibit a degree of further change.) Perhaps 'open canon' will yet emerge as the best way to combine the concerns of both sides in the canon debate as a means of describing early scripture's acknowledged, normative core as well as its unfixed, nondelimited boundaries.[71] If so, it will need to be recognized even more clearly that this 'open' canon was not just an 'amorphous pool'[72] but possessed a distinctive profile, unity, and claim for its religious community.[73]

As soon as this book first appeared, reviewers predictably asked, What about the Writings? I do posit a basic 'grammar of Law and Prophets' as having been in place prior to a full-fledged tripartite scriptural framework. This part of my argument has subsequently been accepted and affirmed, in different ways, by a number of other scholars.[74] Although some researchers continue to work with the idea of a Pentateuch-Bible or a privileged Pentateuch in the Persian and Hellenistic periods, it

---

[71] On 'open canon' as perhaps an acceptable term, see ALLERT, High View of Scripture?, 107. Note, however, the appropriate qualification in SEITZ, Goodly Fellowship, 30: "It is meaningful to speak of an 'open canon,' if by that is meant the capacity of the Law and the Prophets to function as canon, no matter the precise number or order of the books in the third distinctive section." I myself have advocated for broader awareness and use of the *de facto* consensus term 'core canon.' See my Canon Debate, 289–90.

[72] For this expression, see BARTON, Oracles of God, 57. To be precise, BARTON employs this expression as a characterization for scripture outside the Pentateuch. Cf. the assertion by MROCZEK, Hidden Scriptures, that sacred writing in early Judaism "did not have a stable essence" because it lacked specific boundaries (395).

[73] Cf. CHILDS, OT Introduction, 77: "By shaping Israel's traditions into the form of a normative scripture the biblical idiom no longer functions for the community of faith as free-floating metaphor, but as the divine imperative and promise to a historically conditioned people of God whose legacy the Christian church confesses to share."

[74] See especially SEITZ, Goodly Fellowship, 26, where my idea of a Law and Prophets 'grammar' is employed and extended. Taking up the challenge of the third division, he insightfully articulates a perspective with which I would like to associate myself: "The Law and the Prophets are the fundamental grammar of the scriptures of Israel, and the third division defers to that and works alongside it in its own special way" (44). As he persuasively explains, "[The] Writings derive their logic, canonically, from being external to, independent of, but in loose association with, not one another, but the individual books or mature arrangements of the Law and the Prophets. Any association they have with one another within the Writings — and here the contrast with Law and Prophets is clear — is a much weaker form of relationship. This means the books can and do migrate in subsequent listings in the Christian church, even as within Judaism senses of internal association are achieved by establishing stable orderings of the Writings" (99–100). This all seems exactly right to me. See further his final chapter The Accomplishment of the Writings (105–25) and his Elder Testament, 174: "The Ketuvim serve the purpose of establishing the centrality of the core canon of the Law and the Prophets." I had gestured toward such a view in my article Canonical Approach to Old Testament Theology? More recently, ILAN, Term and Concept of TaNaKh, does not use the term 'grammar' but similarly concludes that "before the creation

has been gratifying to see how other researchers have begun to explore and stress the role of prophetic books of scripture in the Second Temple era.[75] I have also recently explored the triple citation convention evident in rabbinic writings (as well as in the New Testament), which corresponds to the tripartite shape of what eventually became the Jewish biblical canon.[76] Although the dating of these sources is very difficult, I can imagine how this kind of composite citation practice and the eventual expansion from a bipartite to a tripartite canon concept could be grounded in the liturgical practices and pedagogical customs of late Second Temple Judaism.[77]

For me, the most important word in the title of this book has always been the preposition 'in.' Rather than calling the book a study 'of' biblical canon formation, I hoped to signal my sense that there is an unavoidable constructive dimension to any exploration of the biblical canon. From the beginning of the project, I was interested not only in how the biblical canon was formed but in how, because of its distinctive manner of formation, its received literary shape continues to offer hermeneutical indices to guide its readers to a proper construal of its sense and meaning. My book is therefore a study *in* biblical canon formation. This constructive aspect will also be evident in the proposals that I offer about how the history of the Old Testament canon might influence contemporary biblical hermeneutics, especially (but not exclusively) for Christians who recognize Israel's Scripture as the first part of their two-part Bible. Lastly, this constructive element is present at an even more basic methodological level and intended to acknowledge a certain post-critical awareness of the historical endeavor as such. There is no study 'of' that is not also a study 'in.'

About the Book

I wish to thank Mohr Siebeck, which has given permission for this book to be published in a U. S. edition by Baker Academic. As part of the agreement, substantive revisions could not be made. Happily, I do not feel that such revisions are needed, although it is tempting to press the case anew based on subsequent scholarship, much of which I find congenial to my position. The main text therefore appears unaltered and the pagination is unchanged, although I have been able to correct a number of minor errors and typos. I have also appended an updated,

---

of the Hebrew Holy Scriptures, as we know them today, already the *Torah* and the *Nevi'im* were closely related one to the other, but not the *Ketuvim*" (229).

75 Here the work of E. BEN ZVI is of particular importance. For representative samples, see his Concept of Prophetic Books, and Remembering the Prophets. More recently, in his Prophetic Memories, BEN ZVI imagines a collection of fifteen (still forming) prophetic books in Persian Yehud. As will be evident throughout my own work, however, I disagree with BEN ZVI's assessment that "the main approach of Deuteronomy to prophets and prophecy may be characterized as one of social and ideological containment," a statement found in his Observations on Lines of Thought, 3.

76 CHAPMAN, "Threefold Cord."

77 On the Writings in general, now see MORGAN, Oxford Handbook.

full bibliography detailing scholarly publications relating to Old Testament canon formation since 2000, when this book was originally published in the Mohr Siebeck monograph series Forschungen zum Alten Testament. My hope is that this bibliographic supplement will provide an added benefit to scholars with an interest in canon formation. May their tribe increase!

I had originally prepared this book for publication while I was a postdoctoral student in Tübingen. Professor Bernd Janowski was a generous sponsor and host during my time there, providing me with office space and financial assistance for the task of formatting the manuscript. Even so, the circumstances were often daunting as I attempted to navigate computer systems and various administrative processes at a university overseas. I remain deeply grateful to Professor Janowski for his unhesitating support and friendship.

I am also grateful to Jim Kinney and Bryan Dyer at Baker Academic. Publishing a U. S. edition of this book was Jim's idea, and Bryan served as the project's editor. Working with both of them is always informative, helpful, and enjoyable. I especially appreciate Jim's longstanding interest in my scholarship and his personal encouragement.

Finally, this book is dedicated to Hans Frei, with whom I studied as an undergraduate at Yale. It is manifestly true that Brevard Childs provided me with much of my basic orientation to the field of biblical studies. When I think of myself as an Old Testament scholar, Bard is always my model and touchstone. But my encounter with Frei occurred at an earlier, in some ways more crucial, time in my education. He helped me begin to see how it might be possible to live and work as a Christian and a scholar and a pastor simultaneously, with intellectual generosity and cheerful confidence that God's good truth will, in the end, come to light. Above all, Frei led me to understand how biblical texts are not only sources but witnesses. Indeed, they are the words of life.

Stephen B. Chapman
April 12, 2020
Easter

Bibliography

Abreviations for the following entries are based upon SCHWERTNER, S. M., Internationales Abkürzungsverzeichnis für Theologie und Grenzgebiete (IATG), Berlin / New York: de Gruyter ²1992, as supplemented by idem, Abkürzungsverzeichnis der Theologischen Realenzyklopädie (TRE), Berlin / New York: de Gruyter ²1994.

ACHTEMEIER, E., Nahum – Malachi (Interp.), Atlanta: John Knox 1986
ACHTEMEIER, P. J., The Inspiration of Scripture. Problems and Proposals (BPCI), Philadelphia: Westminster 1980
ACKROYD, P. R., Continuity: a Contribution to the Study of the Old Testament Religious Tradition, Oxford: Blackwell 1962 = in: idem, Studies, 3–30
— The Vitality of the Word of God in the Old Testament: A Contribution to the Study of the Transmission and Exposition of Old Testament Material, ASTI 1 (1962) 7–23 = in: idem, Studies, 61–75
— The Open Canon, Colloquium. The Australian and New Zealand Theological Review 3 (1970) 279–91 = in: idem, Studies, 209–24
— The Old Testament in the Making, in: ACKROYD AND EVANS (EDS.), CHB I:67–112
— The Chronicler as Exegete, JSOT 2 (1977) 2–32 = idem, Age, 311–43
— Original Text and Canonical Text, USQR 32 (1977) 166–73 = in: idem, Studies, 225–34
— Studies in the Religious Tradition of the Old Testament, London: SCM Press 1987
— The Chronicler in His Age (JSOT.S 101) Sheffield: JSOT Press 1991
ACKROYD, P. R., AND C. F. EVANS, EDS., The Cambridge History of the Bible (CHB; 3 vols.), Cambridge / New York: Cambridge University Press 1963–70
ACKROYD, P. R., AND B. LINDARS, EDS., Words and Meanings (FS D. W. Thomas), Cambridge: Cambridge University Press 1968
AHRBECK, H., ET AL., EDS., Gottes ist der Orient (FS O. Eißfeldt) Berlin: Evangelische Verlagsanstalt 1959
ALBERTZ, R., Die Intentionen und die Träger des Deuteronomistischen Geschichtswerks, in: ALBERTZ, GOLKA AND KEGLER (EDS.), Schöpfung, 37–53
— A History of Israelite Religion in the Old Testament Period (OTL; 2 vols.), trans. J. Bowden; Louisville: Westminster John Knox 1994 = Religionschichte Israels in alttestamentlicher Zeit (GAT 8; 2 vols.) Göttingen: Vandenhoeck & Ruprecht 1992
ALBERTZ, R., F. W. GOLKA AND J. KEGLER, EDS., Schöpfung und Befreiung (FS C. Westermann), Stuttgart: Calwer 1989
ALEXANDER, P. S., "A Sixtieth Part of Prophecy": The Problem of Continuing Revelation in Judaism, in: J. DAVIES, HARVEY AND WATSON (EDS.), Words, 414–33
ALT, A., The Origins of Israelite Law (orig. 1934) in: idem, Essays, 79–132 = Die Ursprünge des israelitischen Rechts, in: idem, Schriften I:278–332 = in: idem, Grundfragen, 203–57
— Kleine Schriften zur Geschichte des Volkes Israel (3 vols.), Munich: C. H. Beck 1953–60
— Essays on Old Testament History and Religion (BiSe), trans. R. A. Wilson; Sheffield: JSOT Press 1989 = Grundfragen der Geschichte des Volkes Israel. Eine "Auswahl" aus den "Kleinen Schriften," ed. S. Hermann; Munich: C. H. Beck 1970

ALTIERI, C., Act and Quality. A Theory of Literary Meaning and Humanistic Understanding, Amherst, MA: University of Massachusetts Press 1981
— The Idea and Ideal of a Literary Canon, in: H ALLBERG (ED.), Canons, 41–64 = idem, Critical Inquiry 10 (1983–84) 37–60
— Canons and Consequences. Reflections on the Ethical Force of Imaginative Ideals, Evanston, IL: Northwestern University Press 1990
AMIR, Y., Authority and the Interpretation of Scripture in the Writings of Philo, in: MULDER (ED.), CRI 2.1, 421–53
AMSLER, S., A. LACOCQUE AND R. VUILLEUMIER, Aggée, Zacharie 1–8, Zacharie 9–14, Malachie (CAT 11C), Geneva: Labor et Fides ^{2}1988
ANDERSON, B. W., Understanding the Old Testament, Englewood Cliffs, NJ: Prentice–Hall ^{3}1975
ANDERSON, B. W., AND W. HARRELSON, EDS., Israel's Prophetic Heritage (FS J. Muilenburg), New York: Harper 1962
ANDERSON, G. W., Canonical and Non-Canonical, in: ACKROYD AND EVANS (EDS.), CHB I:113–59
— ED., Tradition and Interpretation. Essays for the Society for the Study of the Old Testament, Oxford: Clarendon 1979
ARIEL, D. S., What Do Jews Believe? The Spiritual Foundations of Judaism, New York: Schocken 1995
ARNOLD, W. R., Observations on the Origins of Holy Scripture, JBL 42 (1923) 1–21
ASSMANN, A., AND J. ASSMANN, EDS., Kanon und Zensur. Beiträge zur Archäologie der literarischen Kommunikation II, Munich: Wilhelm Fink 1987
ATTRIDGE, H. W., Jewish Historiography, in: KRAFT AND NICKELSBURG (EDS.), Judaism, 311–43
AULD, A. G., Judges 1 and History: A Reconsideration, VT 25 (1975) 261–85
— Joshua, Judges, and Ruth (Daily Study Bible), Philadelphia: Westminster 1984
— ED., Understanding Poets and Prophets (FS G. W. Anderson; JSOT.S 152), Sheffield: Sheffield Academic Press 1993
AUNE, D. E., On the Origins of the "Council" of Javneh Myth, JBL 110 (1991) 491–93
AURELIUS, E., Der Fürbitter Israels. Eine Studie zum Mosebild im Alten Testament (CB.OT 27) Stockholm: Almquist & Wiksell International 1988

BACH, R., Die Erwählung Israels in der Wüste, Diss., Bonn 1952
BALDERMANN, I., ET AL., EDS., Zum Problem des biblischen Kanons (JBTh 3) Neukirchen–Vluyn: Neukirchener 1988
— EDS., Biblische Hermeneutik (JBTh 12), Neukirchen–Vluyn: Neukirchener 1997
BALDWIN, J. G., Haggai, Zechariah, Malachi. An Introduction and Commentary (TOTC), Downers Grove, IL: Intervarsity 1972
BALTZER, K., Das Bundesformular. Sein Ursprung und seine Verwendung im Alten Testament (WMANT 4), Neukirchen–Vluyn: Neukirchener, 1960 = idem, The Covenant Formulary in the Old Testament, Jewish and Early Christian Writings, Oxford: Blackwell 1971
BAR-ILAN, M., Writing in Ancient Israel and Early Judaism: Part Two, Scribes and Books in the Late Second Commonwealth and Rabbinic Period, in: MULDER (ED.), CRI 2.1, 21–38
BARR, J., The Bible in the Modern World, New York: Harper & Row 1973
— Some Semantic Notes on the Covenant, in: DONNER, HANHART AND SMEND (EDS.), Beiträge, 23–38

— Childs' Introduction to the Old Testament as Scripture, JSOT 16 (1980) 12–23
— Holy Scripture. Canon, Authority and Criticism, Philadelphia: Westminster 1983
— Review of J. Levenson, The Hebrew Bible, the Old Testament and Historical Criticism, JThS 47 (1996) 555–60

BARRERA, J. T., The Jewish Bible and the Christian Bible. An Introduction to the History of the Bible, trans. W. G. E. Watson; Leiden / New York / Cologne: Brill; Grand Rapids: Eerdmans 1998

BARSTAD, H. M., The Understanding of the Prophets in Deuteronomy, SJOT 8 (1994) 236–251

BARTHÉLEMY, D., Les Devanciers d'Aquila. Première Publication intégrale du Texte des Fragments du Dodécaprophéton (VT.S 10), Leiden: Brill 1963

BARTON, J., "The Law and the Prophets." Who are the Prophets? in: VAN DER WOUDE (ED.), Prophets, 1–18

— Oracles of God. Perceptions of Ancient Prophecy in Israel after the Exile, London: Darton, Longman & Todd; New York / Oxford: Oxford University Press 1986.

— People of the Book? The Authority of the Bible in Christianity, Louisville: Westminster John Knox 1988

— The Significance of a Fixed Canon of the Hebrew Bible, in: SÆBØ (ED.), Bible, 67–83

— Holy Writings, Sacred Text. The Canon in Early Christianity, Louisville: Westminster John Knox 1997

BEATTIE, D. R. G., AND M. J. MCNAMARA, EDS., The Aramaic Bible. Targums in their Historical Context (JSOT.S 166), Sheffield: Sheffield Academic Press 1994

BEATTY, R. C., J. P. HYATT AND M. K. SPEARS, EDS., Vanderbilt Studies in the Humanities (VSH 1), Nashville: Vanderbilt University Press 1951

BECKWITH, R. T., The Old Testament Canon of the New Testament Church and its Background in Early Judaism, London: SPCK; Grand Rapids: Eerdmans 1985

— The Formation of the Hebrew Bible, in: MULDER (ED.), CRI 2.1, 39–86

— A Modern Theory of the Old Testament Canon, VT 41 (1991) 385–95

BEECHER, W. J., The Alleged Triple Canon of the Old Testament, JBL 15 (1896) 118–28

BEGG, C. T., The Chronicler's Non-Mention of Ezekiel in the Deuteronomistic History, the Book of Jeremiah and the Chronicler's History, in: LUST (ED.), Ezekiel, 340–43

— Ben Sirach's Non-Mention of Ezra, BN 42 (1988) 14–18

— The Chronicler's Non-Mention of Elisha, BN 45 (1988) 7–11

— The Classical Prophets in the Chronicler's History, BZ 32 (1988) 100–07

BERGLER, S., Joel als Schriftinterpret (BEAT 16), Frankfurt a. M. / New York: Peter Lang 1988

BERLINERBLAU, J., Preliminary Remarks for the Sociological Study of Israelite "Official Religion," in: CHAZAN, HALLO AND SCHIFFMANN (EDS.), Studies, 153–70

BERTHOLET, A., Deuteronomium (KHC 5), Freiburg i. B: Mohr 1899

BEST, E., Scripture, Traditions and the Canon of the New Testament, BJRL 61 (1978–79) 258–89

BEUKEN, W. A. M., Haggai–Sacharja 1–8. Studien zur Überlieferungsgeschichte der frühnachexilischen Prophetie (SSN 10), Assen: van Gorcum 1967

BEYERLIN, W., Geschichte und heilsgeschichtliche Traditionsbildung im Alten Testament (Richter vi–viii), VT 13 (1963) 1–25

BIRCH, B .C., The Rise of the Israelite Monarchy. The Growth and Development of 1 Samuel 7–15 (SBL.DS 27) Missoula, MT: Scholars Press 1976

BLECH, B., Understanding Judaism. The Basics of Deed and Creed, Northvale, NJ / London: Jason Aronson 1991

BLEEK, M. A., Joshua the Savior, in: KESSLER (ED.), Voices, 145–53

BLENKINSOPP, J., Prophecy and Priesthood in Josephus, JJS 25 (1974) 239–62

— Prophecy and Canon. A Contribution to the Study of Jewish Origins (SJCA 3), Notre Dame, IN: University of Notre Dame Press 1977

— A History of Prophecy in Israel. From Settlement in the Land to the Hellenistic Period, Philadelphia: Westminster 1983

— The Mission of Udjahorresnet and Those of Ezra and Nehemiah, JBL 106 (1987) 409–21

— Ezra–Nehemiah. A Commentary (OTL), Philadelphia: Westminster 1988

— The Pentateuch. An Introduction to the First Five Books of the Bible (AncBRL), New York: Doubleday 1992

BLOOM, H., The Western Canon. The Books and School of the Ages, New York: Harcourt Brace 1994

BLOWERS, P. M., The *Regula Fidei* and the Narrative Character of Early Christian Faith, Pro Ecclesia 6 (1997) 199–228

BLUM, E., C. MACHOLZ AND E. W. STEGEMANN, EDS., Die Hebräische Bibel und ihre zweifache Nachgeschichte (FS R. Rendtorff), Neukirchen–Vluyn: Neukirchener 1990

BOLING, R. G., AND G. E. WRIGHT, Joshua. A New Translation with Notes and Commentary (AncB), Garden City, NY: Doubleday 1982

BOSSHARD, E., Beobachtungen zum Zwölfprophetenbuch, BN 40 (1987) 30–62

BOSSHARD, E., AND R. G. KRATZ, Maleachi im Zwölfprophetenbuch, BN 52 (1990) 27–46

BOSTON, J. R., The Wisdom Influence upon the Song of Moses, JBL 87 (1968) 198–202

BRAATEN, C. E., AND R. W. JENSON, EDS., Reclaiming the Bible for the Church, Grand Rapids / Cambridge: Eerdmans 1995

BRAULIK, G., ED., Studien zum Pentateuch (FS W. Kornfeld), Vienna / Freiburg / Basel: Herder 1977

BRETT, M., Biblical Criticism in Crisis? The Impact of the Canonical Approach on Old Testament Studies, Cambridge: Cambridge University Press 1991

BRETTLER, M. Z., Biblical History and Jewish Biblical Theology, JR 77 (1977) 563–83

BROER, I., ED., Jesus und das jüdische Gesetz, Stuttgart / Berlin / Cologne: Kohlhammer 1992

BRONZNICK, N. M., Qabbalah as a Metonym for the Prophets and Hagiographa, HUCA 38 (1967) 285–95

BROOKE, G. J., The Qumran Scrolls and Old Testament Theology, in: SUN, ET AL. (EDS.), Problems, 59–75

BROOKS, R., AND J. J. COLLINS, EDS., Hebrew Bible or Old Testament? Studying the Bible in Judaism and Christianity (CJAn 5) Notre Dame, IN: University of Notre Dame Press 1990

BRUCE, F. F., The Book of Zechariah and the Passion Narrative, BJRL 43 (1961) 336–53

— ED., Promise and Fulfilment (FS S. H. Hooke), Edinburgh: T & T Clark 1963

— The Canon of Scripture, Downers Grove, IL: Intervarsity 1988.

BRUEGGEMANN, W., Bounded by Obedience and Praise: The Psalms as Canon, JSOT 50 (1991) 63–92

— Old Testament Theology. Essays on Structure, Theme and Text, ed. P. D. Miller, Jr.; Minneapolis: Fortress 1992

— "In the Image of God..." Pluralism, MoTh 11 (1995) 455–69

— Theology of the Old Testament. Testimony, Dispute, Advocacy, Minneapolis: Fortress 1997

BRUEGGEMANN, W., AND H. W. WOLFF, EDS., The Vitality of Old Testament Traditions, Atlanta: John Knox Press ²1982

BRUNS, G., Canon and Power in the Hebrew Scriptures, Critical Inquiry 10 (1983–84) 462–80 = in: VON HALLBERG (ED.), Canons, 65–83 = in: idem, Hermeneutics, 64–82
— Hermeneutics Ancient and Modern, New Haven / London: Yale University Press 1992
BUDDE, K., Canon: Introduction and OT, in: CHEYNE AND BLACK (EDS.), EB(C) I:647–74
— Der Kanon des Alten Testaments, Giessen: Ricker 1900
— Das prophetische Schrifttum (Quellenkunde der israelitischen und jüdischen Religionsgeschichte II.5), Tübingen: Mohr Siebeck 1922
BUHL, F., Kanon und Text des Alten Testaments, Leipzig: Faber 1891
BURKE, P., History and Social Theory, Ithaca, NY: Cornell University Press 1992
BUSS, M. J., Hosea as a Canonical Problem: With Attention to the Song of Songs, in: REID (ED.), Prophets, 79–93
BUTLER, T. C., Joshua (WBC), Waco, TX: Word Books 1983
BUTTRICK, G. A., ED., The Interpreter's Dictionary of the Bible. An Illustrated Encyclopedia (IDB; 4 vols.), Nashville / New York: Abingdon 1962

CALLAWAY, P. R., 4QMMT and Recent Hypotheses on the Origin of the Qumran Community, in: KAPERA (ED.), MOGILANY, 15–29
CAMPENHAUSEN, H. F. VON., The Formation of the Christian Bible, trans. J. A. Baker; Philadelphia: Fortress 1972 = Die Entstehung der christlichen Bibel (BHTh 39), Tübingen: Mohr Siebeck 1968
CARMODY, J., D. L. CARMODY, AND R. L. COHN, Exploring the Hebrew Bible, Englewood Cliffs, NJ: Prentice–Hall 1988
CARR, D. M., Canonization in the Context of Community: An Outline of the Formation of the Tanakh and the Christian Bible, in: WEIS AND CARR (EDS.), Gift, 22–64
CARROLL, R. P., When Prophecy Failed. Cognitive Dissonance in the Prophetic Traditions of the Old Testament, New York: Seabury 1979
CARSON, D. A., AND H. G. M. WILLIAMSON, EDS., It is Written. Scripture Citing Scripture (FS B. Lindars), Cambridge: Cambridge University Press 1988
CHAZAN, R., W. W. HALLO, AND L. H. SCHIFFMANN, EDS., Ki Baruch Hu. Ancient Near Eastern, Biblical, and Judaic Studies (FS B. A. Levine), Winona Lake, IN: Eisenbrauns 1999
CHEYNE, T. K., The Origin and Religious Contents of the Psalter in the Light of Old Testament Criticism and the History of Religions, London: Kegan Paul, Trench, Trubner; New York: Thomas Whittaker 1891
CHEYNE, T. K., AND J. S. BLACK, EDS., Encyclopaedia Biblica. A Critical Dictionary of the Literary, Political and Religious History, the Archaeology, Geography and Natural History of the Bible (EB[C]; 4 vols.), New York: Macmillan 1899–1903
CHILDS, B. S., Memory and Tradition in Israel (SBT 37), London: SCM Press 1962
— Interpretation in Faith: The Theological Responsibility of an Old Testament Commentary, Interp. 18 (1964) 432–49
— Karl Barth as an Interpreter of Scripture, in: DICKERMAN (ED.), Barth, 30–39
— Biblical Theology in Crisis, Philadelphia: Westminster 1970
— Introduction to the Old Testament as Scripture, Philadelphia: Fortress; London: SCM Press 1979
— Response to Reviewers of Introduction to the OT as Scripture, JSOT 16 (1980) 52–60
— The New Testament as Canon. An Introduction, Philadelphia: Fortress; London: SCM Press 1984

— Old Testament Theology in a Canonical Context, Philadelphia: Fortress; London: SCM Press 1985

— Analysis of a Canonical Formula: "It shall be recorded for a future generation," in: BLUM, MACHOLZ AND STEGEMANN (EDS.), Bibel, 357–64

— Biblical Theology of the Old and New Testaments. Theological Reflection on the Christian Bible, Minneapolis: Fortress 1992

— On Reclaiming the Bible for Christian Theology, in: BRAATEN AND JENSON (EDS.), Reclaiming, 1–17

— Retrospective Reading of the Old Testament Prophets, ZAW 108 (1996) 362–77

CHRISTENSEN, D. L., ED., A Song of Power and the Power of Song. Essays on the Book of Deuteronomy (Sources for Biblical and Theological Study 3), Winona Lake, IN: Eisenbrauns 1993

CHURGIN, P., Targum Jonathan to the Prophets (YOS 14), New Haven: Yale University Press 1907

CLEMENTS, R. E., Prophecy and Covenant (SBT 43), Naperville, IL: Alec R. Allenson; London: SCM Press 1965

— God's Chosen People. A Theological Interpretation of the Book of Deuteronomy, London: SCM Press 1968

— Prophecy and Tradition. A Presentation of its Results and Problems (Growing Points in Theology), Atlanta: John Knox 1975

— Patterns in the Prophetic Canon, in: COATS AND LONG (EDS.), Canon, 42–55

— Old Testament Theology. A Fresh Approach (New Foundations Theological Library), Atlanta: John Knox 1978

— Deuteronomy (OTGu), Sheffield: JSOT Press for the Society of Old Testament Study 1989

— ED., The World of Ancient Israel. Sociological, Anthropological and Political Perspectives. Essays by Members of the Society for Old Testament Study, Cambridge / New York: Cambridge University Press 1989

— Jeremiah 1–25 and the Deuteronomistic History, in AULD (ED.), Understanding, 94–113

— Old Testament Prophecy, Louisville: Westminster John Knox 1996

CLINES, D. J. A., Ezra, Nehemiah, Esther (NCB), Grand Rapids: Eerdmans 1984

— Interested Parties. The Ideology of Writers and Readers of the Hebrew Bible (JSOT.S 205; Gender, Culture, Theory 1), Sheffield: Sheffield Academic Press 1995

COATS, G. W., Legendary Motifs in the Moses Death Reports, CBQ 39 (1977) 34–44 = in: CHRISTENSEN (ED.), Song, 181–91

COATS, G. W., AND B. O. LONG, Preface, ix–xiv, in: COATS AND LONG (EDS.), Canon

— EDS., Canon and Authority. Essays in Old Testament Religion and Theology, Philadelphia: Fortress 1977

COGGINS, R. J., Samaritans and Jews. The Origins of Samaritanism Reconsidered, Atlanta: John Knox 1975

— The First and Second Books of Chronicles (CNEB), Cambridge: Cambridge University Press 1976

— Haggai, Zechariah, Malachi (OTGu), Sheffield: JSOT Press for the Society for Old Testament Study 1987

— What Does "Deuteronomistic" Mean? in: J. DAVIES, HARVEY AND WATSON (EDS.), Words, 135–48

COGGINS, R. J., A. PHILLIPS AND M. KNIBB, EDS., Israel's Prophetic Tradition (FS P. R. Ackroyd), Cambridge / New York: Cambridge University Press 1982

COHEN, S. J. D., From the Maccabees to the Mishnah (LEC), Philadelphia: Westminster 1987

COLLINS, J. J., Is a Critical Biblical Theology Still Possible? in: PROPP, HALPERN AND FREEDMAN (EDS.), Bible, 1–17

— Dead Sea Scrolls, in: FREEDMAN (ED.), AncBD II:85–101

— Before the Canon: Scriptures in Second Temple Judaism, in: MAYS, PETERSEN AND RICHARDS (EDS.), Interpretation, 225–41

COLLINS, T., The Mantle of Elijah. The Redaction Criticism of the Prophetical Books (BiSe 20), Sheffield: Sheffield Academic Press 1993

COLSON, F. H., ED., Philo (LCL; 10 vols.), London: Heinemann; Cambridge, MA: Harvard University Press 1962

CONRAD, J., Zur Frage nach der Rolle des Gesetzes bei der Bildung des alttestamentlichen Kanons, ThV 11 (1979) 11–19

COOK, S. L., Prophecy and Apocalypticism. The Postexilic Social Setting, Minneapolis: Augsburg Fortress 1995

CORNILL, C. T., Introduction to the Canonical Books of the Old Testament, trans. G. H. Box; London: Williams & Norgate; New York: Putnam 1907

CORTESE, E., Josua 13–21. Ein priesterlicher Abschnitt im deuteronomistischen Geschichtswerk (OBO 94), Fribourg: Éditions universitaires; Göttingen: Vandenhoeck & Ruprecht 1990

CRAIGIE, P. C., The Book of Deuteronomy (NIC), Grand Rapids: Eerdmans 1976

Twelve Prophets (Daily Study Bible; 2 vols.), Philadelphia: Westminster 1985

The Old Testament. Its Background, Growth, and Content, Nashville: Abingdon 1986

CRENSHAW, J. L., ED., Studies in Ancient Israelite Wisdom (LBS), New York: KTAV 1976

— Old Testament Story and Faith. A Literary and Theological Introduction, Peabody, MA: Hendrickson 1986

CRIM, K., ED., Interpreter's Dictionary of the Bible. Supplement (IDB.S), Nashville: Abingdon 1962

CROSS, F. M., JR., The History of the Biblical Text in Light of Discoveries in the Judaean Desert, HThR 57 (1964) 281–99

— Canaanite Myth and Hebrew Epic. Essays in the History of the Religion of Israel, Cambridge, MA: Harvard University Press 1973

— From Epic to Canon. History and Literature in Ancient Israel, Baltimore, MD / London: Johns Hopkins University Press 1998

CROSS, F. M., W. E. LEMKE AND P. D. MILLER, JR., EDS., Magnalia Dei, the Mighty Acts of God. Essays on the Bible and Archaeology (FS G. E. Wright), Garden City, NY: Doubleday 1976

CROSS, F. M., AND R. J. SALEY, Phoenician Incantations on a Plaque of the Seventh Century from Arslan Tash in Upper Syria, BASOR 197 (1970) 42–49

CROWN, A. D., New Light on the Inter-Relationships of the Samaritan Chronicles, BJRL 54 (1971–72) 282–313; 55 (1972–73) 86–111

CRÜSEMANN, F., Israel in der Perserzeit: eine Skizze in Auseinandersetzung mit Max Weber, in: SCHLUCHTER (ED.), Sicht, 205–32

— Das "portative Vaterland": Struktur und Genese des alttestamentlichen Kanons, in: A. AND J. ASSMANN (EDS.), Kanon II:63–79

— Die Tora. Theologie und Sozialgeschichte des alttestamentlichen Gesetzes, Munich: Chr. Kaiser 1992

DANIELS, D., Is There a "Prophetic Lawsuit" Genre? ZAW 99 (1987) 339–60

DAVIDSON, R., The Old Testament in the Church? in: AULD (ED.), Understanding, 114–26

DAVIES, J., G. HARVEY AND W. G. E. WATSON, EDS., Words Remembered, Texts Renewed (FS J. F. A. Sawyer; JSOT.S 195), Sheffield: Sheffield Academic Press 1995

DAVIES, P. R., Post-exilic Collections and the Formation of the Canon, in: ROGERSON AND P. R. DAVIES (EDS.), OT World, 360–75

— In Search of "Ancient Israel" (JSOT.S 148), Sheffield: JSOT Press 1992

— Scribes and Schools. The Canonization of the Hebrew Scriptures (Library of Ancient Israel), Louisville: Westminster John Knox 1998

DAVIES, P. R., AND R. T. WHITE, EDS., A Tribute to Geza Vermes. Essays on Jewish and Christian Literature and History (FS G. Vermes; JSOT.S 100), Sheffield: Sheffield Academic Press 1990

DEANE, W. J., Joshua. His Life and Times (Men of the Bible), New York / Chicago: Fleming H. Revell 1889

DEISSLER, A., Zwölf Propheten (NEB; 3 vols.), Würzburg: Echter Verlag 1981–88

DEMPSTER, S., An "Extraordinary Fact": *Torah and Temple* and the Contours of the Hebrew Canon, TynB 48 (1997) 23–56; 191–218

DEXINGER, F., AND R. PUMMER, EDS., Die Samaritaner (EdF 604), Darmstadt: Wissenschaftliche Buchgesellschaft 1992

DICKERMAN, D. L., ED., Karl Barth and the Future of Theology. A Memorial Colloquium, New Haven: YDS Association 1969

DIETRICH, W., Prophetie und Geschichte (FRLANT 108) Göttingen: Vandenhoeck & Ruprecht 1972

— David, Saul und die Propheten (BWANT 122), Stuttgart: Kohlhammer 1987

DIMANT, D., The Use and Interpretation of Mikra in the Apocrypha and the Pseudepigrapha, in: MULDER (ED.), CRI 2.1, 379–419

DIMANT, D., AND L. H. SCHIFFMAN, EDS., Time to Prepare the Way in the Wilderness. Papers on the Qumran Scrolls by the Fellows of the Institute for Advanced Studies of the Hebrew University, Jerusalem, 1989–90 (StTDJ 16), Leiden: Brill 1995

DODD, C. H., The Bible and the Greeks, London: Hodder & Stoughton 1935

DOHMEN, C., Der biblische Kanon in der Diskussion, ThRv 6 (1995) 452–60

DOHMEN, C., AND M. OEMING, Biblischer Kanon, Warum und Wozu? Eine Kanontheologie (QD 137), Freiburg: Herder 1992

DONNER, H. H., R. HANHART AND R. SMEND, EDS., Beiträge zur alttestamentlichen Theologie (FS W. Zimmerli), Göttingen: Vandenhoeck & Ruprecht 1977

DRIVER, S. R., An Introduction to the Literature of the Old Testament (International Theological Library), Edinburgh: T & T Clark; New York: Scribner 1891, ⁹1913

— A Critical and Exegetical Commentary on Deuteronomy (ICC), Edinburgh: T & T Clark; New York: Scribner 1895, ³1951

DUHM, B., Die Theologie der Propheten als Grundlage für die innere Entwicklungsgeschichte der Israelitischen Religion, Bonn: Adolph Marcus 1875

— Anmerkungen zu den zwölf Propheten, Giessen: Töpelmann 1911

DULLES, A., The Authority of Scripture: A Catholic Perspective, in: GREENSPAHN (ED.), Scripture, 14–40

DUMBROWSKI, B. W. W., Preliminary Remarks on Ideological and Socio-Structural Developments of the Qumran Association as Suggested by Internal Evidence of the Dead Sea Scrolls, in: KAPERA (ED.), MOGILANY, 31–43

DUNN, J. D. G., The Living Word, Philadelphia: Fortress 1987

EICHRODT, W., Theologie des Alten Testaments (orig. 1933; 2 vols.), Göttingen: Vandenhoeck & Ruprecht; Stuttgart: Klotz ⁴1961) = Theology of the Old Testament (OTL; 2 vols.), trans. J. A. Baker; Philadelphia: Westminster 1961–67

EISSFELDT, O., Einleitung in das Alte Testament. Entstehungsgeschichte des Alten Testaments (NTG), Tübingen: Mohr Siebeck ²1956 = idem, The Old Testament. An Introduction Including the Apocrypha and Pseudepigrapha, and also Works of Similar Type from Qumran, trans. P. R. Ackroyd; New York: Harper & Row 1965

— Das Lied Moses Deuteronomium 32,1–43 und das Lehrgedicht Asaphs Psalm 78 samt einer Analyse der Umgebung des Mose-Liedes (BVSAW.PH 104.5), Berlin: Akademie Verlag 1958

— Sechs Jahrzehnte alttestamentlicher Wissenschaft, in: Volume du Congrès. Genève 1965 (VT.S 15), Leiden: Brill 1966, 1–13

ELIADE, M., ED., Encyclopedia of Religion (EncRel[E]; 16 vols.), New York: Macmillan 1987–88

ELLIGER, K., Das Buch der zwölf Propheten (ATD 25; 2 vols.), Göttingen: Vandenhoeck & Ruprecht 1950

ELLIS, E. E., The Old Testament Canon in the Early Church, in: MULDER (ED.), CRI 2.1, 653–91

— The Old Testament in Early Christianity. Canon and Interpretation in the Light of Modern Research (WUNT 54), Tübingen: Mohr Siebeck 1991; Grand Rapids: Baker 1992.

ESKENAZI, T. C., In An Age of Prose. A Literary Approach to Ezra–Nehemiah (SBL.MS 36), Atlanta: Scholars Press 1988

— Torah as Narrative and Narrative as Torah, in: MAYS, PETERSEN AND RICHARDS (EDS.), Interpretation, 13–30

ESKENAZI, T. C., AND K. H. RICHARDS, EDS., Second Temple Studies 2. Temple and Community in the Persian Period (JSOT.S 175), Sheffield: Sheffield Academic Press 1994

EVANS, C. A., AND S. TALMON, EDS., The Quest for Context and Meaning. Studies in Biblical Intertextuality (FS J. A. Sanders; Biblical Interpretation Series 28) Leiden / New York / Cologne: Brill 1997

EYBERS, I. H., ET AL., EDS., De Fructu Oris Sui (FS A. van Selms; POS 9), Leiden: Brill 1971

FEILCHENFELDT, W., Die Entpersönlichung Moses in der Bibel und ihre Bedeutung, ZAW 64 (1952) 156–78

FELDMAN, L., Prophets in Josephus, JThS 41 (1990) 386–422

FIRMAGE, E. B., B. G. WEISS AND J. W. WELCH, EDS., Religion and Law. Biblical–Judaic and Islamic Perspectives, Winona Lake, IN: Eisenbrauns 1990

FISHBANE, M., Jewish Biblical Exegesis: Presuppositions and Principles, in: GREENSPAHN (ED.), Scripture, 92–110

— Biblical Interpretation in Ancient Israel, Oxford: Clarendon 1985

— The Garments of Torah. Essays in Biblical Hermeneutics (Indiana Studies in Biblical Literature), Bloomington / Indianapolis, IN: Indiana University Press 1989

FISHBANE, M., AND E. TOV, EDS., WITH ASST OF W. W. FIELDS, "Sha'rei Talmon." Studies in the Bible, Qumran, and the Ancient Near East (FS S. Talmon), Winona Lake, IN: Eisenbrauns 1992

FLANAGAN, J. W., AND A. W. ROBINSON, EDS., No Famine in the Land (FS J. L. McKenzie), Missoula, MT: Scholars Press 1975

FLANAGAN, O., Identity and Strong and Weak Evaluation, in: FLANAGAN AND RORTY (EDS.), Identity, 37–65

FLANAGAN, O., AND R. RORTY, EDS., Identity, Character and Morality. Essays in Moral Psychology, Cambridge: Cambridge University Press 1990

FLANDERS, H. J., R. W. CRAPPS, AND D. A. SMITH, People of the Covenant. An Introduction to the Hebrew Bible, Oxford / New York: Oxford University Press [4]1996

FLOSS, J. P., Jahwe dienen — Göttern dienen. Terminologische, literarische und semantische Untersuchung einer theologischen Aussage zum Gottesverhältnis im Alten Testament (BBB 45), Cologne / Bonn: Peter Hanstein 1975

FOLKERT, K. W., The "Canons" of Scripture, in: LEVERING (ED.), Scripture, 170–79

FOWL, S., Texts Don't Have Ideologies, Biblical Interpretation 3 (1995) 15–34

FOX, M. V., ET AL., EDS., Texts, Temples and Traditions (FS M. Haran), Winona Lake, IN: Eisenbrauns 1996

FRANKFURT, H., Freedom of the Will and the Concept of a Person, JPh 67 (1971) 5–20

FRAZER, J. G., Folk-lore in the Old Testament. Studies in Comparative Religion, Legend and Law, London: Macmillan 1918

FREEDMAN, D. N., Canon of the Old Testament, in: CRIM (ED.), IDB.S, 130–36

— The Law and the Prophets, in: Congress Volume. Bonn 1962 (VT.S 9), Leiden: Brill 1962, 250–65 = in: LEIMAN (ED.) Canon, 5–20

— "Son of Man, Can These Bones Live?" Interp. 29 (1975) 171–86

— The Earliest Bible, in: O'CONNOR AND FREEDMAN (ED.), Backgrounds, 29–37

— "Who Is Like Thee Among the Gods?" The Religion of Ancient Israel, in: MILLER, HANSON AND MCBRIDE (EDS.), Religion, 315–35

— The Formation of the Canon of the Old Testament: The Selection and Identification of the Torah as the Supreme Authority of the Postexilic Community, in: FIRMAGE, WEISS AND WELCH (EDS.), Religion, 315–31

— The Unity of the Hebrew Bible, Ann Arbor, MI: University of Michigan Press 1991

— ED., Anchor Bible Dictionary (AncBD; 6 vols.), New York: Doubleday 1992

— The Symmetry of the Hebrew Bible, StTh 46 (1992) 83–108

FREI, H. W., Eclipse of Biblical Narrative. A Study in Eighteenth and Nineteenth Century Hermeneutics, New Haven / London: Yale University Press 1974

FREI, P., Zentralgewalt und Lokalautonomie im Achämenidenreich, in: P. FREI AND KOCH (EDS.), Reichsidee, 7–43

— Die persische Reichsautorisation: ein Überblick, ZAR 1 (1995) 1–35

FREI, P., AND K. KOCH, EDS., Reichsidee und Reichsorganisation im Perserreich (OBO 55), Fribourg: Universitätsverlag; Göttingen: Vandenhoeck & Ruprecht 1984

FRERICHS, E. S., The Torah Canon of Judaism and the Interpretation of Hebrew Scriptures, HBT 9 (1987) 13–25

FRETHEIM, T. E., The Deuteronomistic History (IBT), Nashville: Abingdon 1983

FREY, C., Tora für Protestanten, ZEE 38 (1994) 242–46

FRIEDMAN, R. E., The Exile and Biblical Narrative (HSM 22), Chico, CA: Harper & Row, 1988

FRITZ, V., K.–F. POHLMANN AND H.–C. SCHMITT, EDS., Prophet und Prophetenbuch (FS O. Kaiser; BZAW 185), Berlin / New York: de Gruyter 1989

FRYE, N., The Great Code. The Bible and Literature, San Diego / New York: Harcourt Brace Jovanovich 1982

— Words with Power. Being a Second Study of "The Bible and Literature," San Diego: Harcourt Brace Jovanovich 1990

GALLING, K., ED., Die Religion in Geschichte und Gegenwart. Handwörterbuch für Theologie und Religionswissenschaft (RGG; 7 vols.), Tübingen: Mohr Siebeck ³1962

GAMBERONI, J., Das "Gesetz des Mose" im Buch Tobias, in: BRAULIK (ED.), Studien, 227–42

GARBINI, G., History and Ideology in Ancient Israel, trans. J. Bowden; New York: Crossroad; London: SCM Press 1988

GERBER, C., Die Heiligen Schriften des Judentums nach Flavius Josephus, in: HENGEL AND LÖHR (EDS.), Schriftauslegung, 91–113

GESE, H., Erwägungen zur Einheit der Biblischen Theologie, in: idem, Sinai, 11–30

— Vom Sinai zum Zion. Alttestamentliche Beiträge zur biblischen Theologie (BEvTh 64), Munich: Chr. Kaiser 1974

— The Biblical View of Scripture, in: Essays, 9–33 = Das biblische Schiftverständnis, in: idem, Theologie, 9–30

— Essays on Biblical Theology, trans. K. Crim; Minneapolis: Augsburg 1981 = Zur biblischen Theologie. Alttestamentliche Vorträge (BEvTh 78), Munich: Chr. Kaiser 1977

— Die dreifache Gestaltwerdung des Alten Testaments, in: KLOPFENSTEIN, ET AL. (EDS.), Mitte? 299–328 = in: idem, Studien, 1–28

— Alttestamentliche Studien, Tübingen: Mohr Siebeck 1987–91

GEUSS, R., The Idea of a Critical Theory. Habermas and the Frankfurt School, Cambridge / New York: Cambridge University Press 1981

GINSBURG, C. D., Introduction to the Massoretico–Critical Edition of the Hebrew Bible, London: Trinitarian Bible Society 1897

GLAZIER-MACDONALD, B., Malachi. The Divine Messenger (SBL.DS 98) Atlanta: Scholars Press 1987

GNUSE, R., The Authority of the Bible. Theories of Inspiration, Revelation and the Canon of Scripture, New York: Paulist 1985

GOLDBERG, A., The Rabbinic View of Scripture (trans. A. Samely), in: P. R. DAVIES AND WHITE (EDS.), Tribute, 153–66 = in: FJB 15 (1987) 1–15

GOLDSTEIN, J. A., 2 Maccabees (AncB 41A), New York, NY: Doubleday 1983

GOODENOUGH, E. R., The Jurisprudence of the Jewish Courts of Egypt, New Haven: Yale University Press 1929

GOSHEN-GOTTSTEIN, M. H., Tanakh Theology: The Religion of the Old Testament and the Place of Jewish Biblical Theology, in: MILLER, HANSON AND MCBRIDE (EDS.), Religion, 617–44

GOTTWALD, N. K., All the Kingdoms of the Earth. Israelite Prophecy and International Relations in the Ancient Near East, New York: Harper & Row 1964

— The Tribes of Yahweh. A Sociology of the Religion of Liberated Israel 1250–1050 B. C. E., Maryknoll, NY: Orbis 1979

— The Hebrew Bible — A Socio-Literary Introduction, Philadelphia: Fortress 1985

— Social Matrix and Canonical Shape, ThTo 42 (1985) 307–21

— On Integrating Multiple Truths in Biblical Texts — A Review of Walter Brueggemann, David's Truth in Israel's Imagination, Bib 68 (1987) 408–11 = in: GOTTWALD, World, 201–05

— The Hebrew Bible in Its Social World and in Ours (SBL.SS), Atlanta: Scholars Press 1993

— Ideology and Ideologies in Israelite Prophecy, in: REID (ED.), Prophets, 136–49

GRAHAM, M. P., K. G. HOGLUND AND S. L. MCKENZIE, EDS., The Chronicler as Historian (JSOT.S 238), Sheffield: Sheffield Academic Press 1997

GRAHAM, W. A., Beyond the Written Word. Oral Aspects of Scripture in the History of Religion, Cambridge / New York: Cambridge University Press 1987

GRAY, J., The Legacy of Canaan, Leiden: Brill 1957

— I & II Kings (OTL), Philadelphia: Westminster ²1970

GREEN, W. H., General Introduction to the Old Testament. The Canon, New York: Scribner 1898

GREEN, W. S., The Hebrew Scriptures in Rabbinic Judaism, in: NEUSNER (ED.), Structure, 31–44

GREENBERG, M., On Sharing the Scriptures, in: CROSS, LEMKE AND MILLER (EDS.), Magnalia, 455–63

— On the Political Use of the Bible in Modern Israel: An Engaged Critique, in: D. P. WRIGHT, FREEDMAN, HURVITZ (EDS.), Pomegranates, 461–71 = Der Gebrauch der Bibel im heutigen Israel: eine Sicht, eine Kritik und eine Empfehlung, in: KLOPFENSTEIN, ET AL. (EDS.), Mitte? 343–55

GREENSPAHN, F. E., ED., Scripture in the Jewish and Christian Traditions. Authority, Interpretation, Relevance (University of Denver Center for Judaic Studies), Nashville: Abingdon 1982

— Why Prophecy Ceased, JBL 108 (1989) 37–49

GREENSPOON, L., Max Leopold Margolis. A Scholar's Scholar (BSNA), Atlanta: Scholars Press 1987

GROSS, W., ED., Jeremia und die "deuteronomistische Bewegung" (BBB 98), Weinheim: Beltz Athenäum 1995

GUNKEL, H., Reden und Aufsätze, Göttingen: Vandenhoeck & Ruprecht 1913

GUNN, D., The Story of King David. Genre and Interpretation (JSOT.S 6), Sheffield: JSOT Press 1978

GUNNEWEG, A. H. J., AND O. KAISER, EDS., Textgemäß. Aufsätze und Beiträge zur Hermeneutik des Alten Testaments (FS E. Würthwein), Göttingen: Vandenhoeck & Ruprecht 1979

GUTMANN, J., Synagogue Origins: Theories and Facts, in: idem, Synagogues, 1–6

— ED., Ancient Synagogues. The State of Research (BJSt 22), Chico, CA: Scholars Press 1981

HAASE, W., AND H. TEMPORINI, EDS., Aufstieg und Niedergang der Römischen Welt. Geschichte und Kultur Roms im Spiegel der Neueren Forschung. Judentum. Palästinisches Judentum (ANRW II.19.2), Berlin / New York: de Gruyter 1979

HALLBERG, R. VON, Introduction, in: HALLBERG (ED.), Canons, 2–3

— ED., Canons, Chicago: University of Chicago Press 1984

HALPERN, B., AND J. D. LEVENSON, EDS., Traditions in Transformation, Winona Lake, IN: Eisenbrauns 1981

HANSON, P., The Dawn of Apocalyptic, Philadelphia: Fortress 1975

HARRIS, R. L., Inspiration and Canonicity of the Bible, Grand Rapids: Zondervan 1957

HARRIS, R. L., G. L. ARCHER, JR., AND B. K. WALTKE, EDS., Theological Wordbook of the Old Testament (TWOT; 2 vols.), Chicago: Moody 1980

HECHT, R., Preliminary Issues in the Analysis of Philo's De Specialibus Legibus, StPhilo 5 (1979) 1–56

HENGEL, M., "Schriftauslegung" und "Schriftwerdung" in der Zeit des Zweiten Tempels, in: HENGEL AND LÖHR (EDS.), Schriftauslegung, 1–71. [A shorter version of this essay appears in English as: The Scriptures and Their Interpretation in Second Temple Judaism, in: BEATTIE AND MCNAMARA, Bible, 158–75.]

HENGEL, M., AND H. LÖHR, EDS., Schriftauslegung im antiken Judentum und im Urchristentum (WUNT 73), Tübingen: Mohr Siebeck 1994

HENN, W., One Faith. Biblical and Patristic Contributions Toward Understanding Unity in Faith, New York / Mahwah, NJ: Paulist Press 1995

HERION, G. A., The Impact of Social Science Assumptions on the Reconstruction of Israelite History, JSOT 34 (1986) 3–33

HERRMANN, S., Die konstructive Restauration: das Deuteronomium als Mitte biblischer Theologie, in: WOLFF (ED.), Probleme, 155–70

HERMS, E., Was haben wir an der Bibel? Versuch einer Theologie des christlichen Kanons, JBTh 12 (1997) 99–152

HILL, A. E., Malachi, Book of, in: FREEDMAN (ED.), AncBD IV:478–85

— Malachi. A New Translation with Introduction and Commentary (AncB 25D), New York / London: Doubleday 1998

HÖLSCHER, G., Kanonisch und Apokryph. Ein Kapitel aus der Geschichte des alttestamentlichen Kanons, Naumburg a. S.: Lippert 1905

HOFFMAN, T. A., Inspiration, Normativeness, Canonicity, and the Unique Sacred Character of Scripture, CBQ 44 (1982) 447–69

HOFFMANN, H.-D., Reform und Reformen (AThANT 66), Zürich: Theologischer Verlag 1980

HOGLUND, K. G., Achaemenid Imperial Administration in Syria-Palestine and the Missions of Ezra and Nehemiah (SBL.DS 125), Atlanta: Scholars Press 1992

HOLLADAY, W. L., The Root SUBH in the Old Testament: with Particular Reference to its Usages in Covenantal Contexts, Leiden: Brill 1958

HOLT, E. K., The Chicken or the Egg — Or: Was Jeremiah a Member of the Deuteronomist Party? JSOT 44 (1989) 109–22

HONERICH, T., ED., The Oxford Companion to Philosophy, Oxford / New York: Oxford University Press 1995

HOSSFELD, F. L., AND I. MEYER, Der Prophet vor dem Tribunal: neuer Auslegungsversuch von Jer 26, ZAW 86 (1974) 30–50

HOUSE, P., The Unity of the Twelve (JSOT.S 97) Sheffield: Almond Press 1990

HOUTMAN, C., Der Pentateuch. Die Geschichte seiner Forschung neben einer Auswertung (CBET 9), Kampen: Kok Pharos 1994

HUGHES, J., The Secrets of the Times. Myth and History in Biblical Chronology (JSOT.S 66), Sheffield: JSOT Press 1990

HYATT, J. P., The Deuteronomic Edition of Jeremiah, in: BEATTY, HYATT AND SPEARS (EDS.), VSH 1, 71–95 = in: PERDUE AND KOVACS (EDS.), Prophet, 247–67

JACOB, E., Principe canonique et formation de l'Ancien Testament, in: Congress Volume. Edinburgh 1974 (VT.S 28), Leiden: Brill 1975, 101–22

JACOBS, L., Bible, in: JACOBS (ED.), Companion, 50–52

— ED., The Jewish Religion. A Companion, Oxford: Oxford University Press 1995

JAMESON, F., The Political Unconsciousness. Narrative as a Socially Symbolic Act, Ithaca, NY: Cornell University Press 1981

JANOWSKI, B., Israels Weg zur Tora. Zu Frank Crüsemanns "Theologie und Sozialgeschichte des alttestamentlichen Gesetzes," EvTh 56 (1996) 83–92

JAPHET, S., The Supposed Common Authorship of Chronicles and Ezra–Nehemiah Investigated Anew, VT 18 (1968) 330–71

JENNI, E., WITH C. WESTERMANN, EDS., Theological Lexicon of the Old Testament (TLOT; 3 vols.), trans. M. E. Biddle; Peabody, MA: Hendrickson 1997 = Theologisches

Handwörterbuch zum Alten Testament (THAT; 2 vols.), Munich: Chr. Kaiser; Zurich: Theologischer Verlag 1976

JEPPESEN, K., Is Deuteronomy Hostile Towards Prophets? SJOT 8 (1994) 252–56

JEPSEN, A., Kanon und Text des Alten Testaments, ThLZ 74 (1949) 65–74

— Wissenschaft vom Alten Testament (orig. 1957), in: idem, Herr, 13–38

— Der Herr ist Gott. Aufsätze zur Wissenschaft vom Alten Testament, Berlin: Evangelische Verlagsanstalt 1978

JERICKE, D., Josuas Tod und Josuas Grab: eine redaktionsgeschichtliche Studie, ZAW 108 (1996) 347–61

JEROME, Commentary on Matthew = S. Hieronymi Presbyteri Opera. Pars I:7 (CChr.SL 77), Turnholti: Brepols 1969

JOHNSON, M. D., The Purpose of Biblical Genealogies with Special Reference to the Setting of the Genealogies of Jesus, Cambridge: University of Cambridge Press 1969

JONES, B. A., The Formation of the Book of the Twelve. A Study in Text and Canon (SBL.DS 149), Atlanta: Scholars Press 1995

JOSEPHUS, Against Apion, in: THACKERAY (ED.), Josephus I:162–411

— Antiquities, in: THACKERAY (ED.), Josephus IV–IX

JÜNGEL, E., J. WALLMANN AND W. WERBECK, EDS., Verifikationen (FS G. Ebeling; BEvTh 99), Tübingen: Mohr Siebeck 1982

KAESTLI, J.-D. AND O. WERMELINGER, EDS., Le Canon de l'Ancien Testament. Sa Formation et Son Histoire (MoBi), Geneva: Labor et Fides 1984

KAHLE, P. E., The Cairo Geniza, Oxford: Blackwell ²1959

— Der Hebräische Bibeltext seit Franz Delitzsch, Stuttgart: Kohlhammer 1961

KAISER, O., Introduction to the Old Testament, trans. J. Sturdy; Minneapolis: Augsburg ²1975 = Einleitung in das Alte Testament. Eine Einführung in ihre Ergebnisse und Probleme, Gütersloh: Mohn ⁵1984

— The Law as Center of the Hebrew Bible, in: FISHBANE AND TOV (EDS.), Studies, 93–103

— Die Tora als Mitte der Schrift, in: idem, Theologie I:329–53

— Der Gott des Alten Testaments. Theologie des Alten Testaments (UTB 1747; 2 vols.), Göttingen: Vandenhoeck & Ruprecht 1993

KALIMI, I., The Books of Chronicles. A Classified Bibliography, Jerusalem: Simor 1990

— Was the Chronicler a Historian? in: GRAHAM, HOGLUND AND McKENZIE (EDS.), Chronicler, 73–89

KAPERA, Z. J., ED., MOGILANY 1993. Papers on the Dead Sea Scrolls (FS H. Burgmann; Qumranica Mogilanesia 13), Kraków: Enigma Press 1996

KATZ, P., The Old Testament Canon in Palestine and Alexandria, ZNW 47 (1956) 191–217 and 49 (1958) 223 = in: LEIMAN (ED.) Canon, 72–98

KAUTZSCH, E., AND A. E. COWLEY, EDS., Gesenius' Hebrew Grammar, Oxford: Clarendon ²1910 = KAUTZSCH, E., ED., Wilhelm Gesenius' Hebräische Grammatik, Hildesheim / Zurich / New York: Olms ²⁸1909, repr. ⁴1983

KECK, L. E., Rethinking "New Testament Ethics," JBL 115 (1996) 3–16

KELLERMANN, U., Anmerkungen zum Verständnis der Tora in den chronistischen Schriften, BN 42 (1988) 49–92

KESSLER, M., ED., Voices from Amsterdam. A Modern Tradition of Reading Biblical Narrative (SBL.SS), trans. M. Kessler; Atlanta: Scholars Press 1994

KLEIN, R. W., Ezra and Nehemiah in Recent Studies, in: CROSS, LEMKE AND MILLER (EDS.), Magnalia, 361–76

KLOPFENSTEIN, M. A., ET AL., EDS., Mitte der Schrift? Ein jüdisch-christliches Gespräch. Texte des Berner Symposions vom 6.–12. Januar 1985 (JudChr 11), Bern / Frankfurt a. M. / New York / Paris: Peter Lang 1987

KNIGHT, D. A., ED., Tradition and Theology in the Old Testament, Philadelphia: Fortress 1977

— Deuteronomy and the Deuteronomists, in: MAYS, PETERSEN AND RICHARDS (EDS.), Interpretation, 61–79

KNAPP, D., Deuteronomium 4. Literarische Analyse und theologische Interpretation (GTA 35), Göttingen: Vandenhoeck & Ruprecht 1987

KNOPPERS, G. N., "There Was None Like Him": Incomparability in the Books of Kings, CBQ 54 (1992) 411–31

KNOX, W. L., A Note on Philo's Use of the Old Testament, JThS 41 (1940) 30–34

KOCH, K., Ezra and the Origins of Judaism, JSSt 19 (1974) 173–97

— The Prophets (2 vols.), trans. M. Kohl; Philadelphia: Fortress 1982 = Die Profeten (UB 280-81; 2 vols.), Stuttgart / Berlin / Cologne: Kohlhammer ³1995

KÖNIG, E., Prophetenideal, Judentum und Christentum. Das Hauptproblem der spätisrae-litischen Religionsgeschichte, Leipzig: Hinrich 1906

KOOIJ, A. VAN DER, AND K. VAN DER TOORN, EDS., Canonization and Decanonization. Papers Presented to the International Conference of the Leiden Institute for the Study of Religions (LISOR), Held at Leiden 9-10 January 1997 (SHR 82), Leiden / Boston / Cologne: Brill 1998

KOOPMANS, W. T., Joshua 24 as Poetic Narrative (JSOT.S 93), Sheffield: Sheffield Academic Press 1990

KOOREVAAR, H. J., Die Chronik als intendierter Abschluß des alttestamentlichen Kanons, Jahrbuch für evangelikale Theologie 11 (1997) 42–76

KRAFT, R. A. KRAFT AND G. W. E. NICKELSBURG, EDS., Early Judaism and Its Modern Interpreters, Philadelphia: Fortress; Atlanta: Scholars Press 1986

KRATZ, R. G., Die Redaktion der Prophetenbücher, in: KRATZ AND KRÜGER (EDS.), Rezeption, 9–27

KRATZ, R. G., AND T. KRÜGER, EDS., Rezeption und Auslegung im Alten Testament und in seinem Umfeld (FS O. H. Steck; OBO 153), Freiburg (Switzerland): Universi-tätsverlag; Göttingen: Vandenhoeck & Ruprecht 1997

KRAUS, H.–J., Die prophetische Verkündigung des Rechts in Israel (ThSt[B] 51), Zolli-kon: Evangelischer Verlag 1957

— Geschichte der historich-kritischen Erforschung des Alten Testaments, Neukir-chen–Vluyn: Neukirchener ²1969

— Worship in Israel. A Cultic History of the Old Testament, Richmond: John Knox 1966 = Gottesdienst in Israel. Grundriß einer Geschichte des alttestamentlichen Gottesdienstes, Munich: Chr. Kaiser ²1961

— Die Biblische Theologie. Ihre Geschichte und Problematik, Neukirchen–Vluyn: Neukirchener 1970

— Psalms 60–150. A Commentary, trans. H. C. Oswald; Minneapolis: Augsburg 1989 = Die Psalmen (BK 15; 3 vols.) Neukirchen–Vluyn: Neukirchener ⁶1989

KRAUSE, G., AND G. MÜLLER, EDS., Theologische Realenzyklopädie (TRE), Berlin / New York: de Gruyter, 1980

KRAUTER, S., Brevard S. Childs' Programm einer Biblischen Theologie: eine Untersu-chung seiner systematisch-theologischen und methodologischen Fundamente, ZThK 96 (1999) 22–48

KUGEL, J. L., The Bible in the University, in: PROPP, HALPERN AND FREEDMAN (EDS.), Bi-ble, 143–65

KUGEL, J. L., AND R. A. GREER, Early Biblical Interpretation (LEC), Philadelphia: Westminster 1986

KUTSCH, E., Verheissung und Gesetz. Untersuchung zum sogenannten "Bund" im Alten
Testament (BZAW 131), Berlin / New York: de Gruyter 1973

LABUSCHAGNE, C. J., The Incomparability of Yahweh in the Old Testament (POS 5),
Leiden: Brill 1966

— The Song of Moses: its framework and structure, in: EYBERS, ET AL. (EDS.), De Fructu,
85–98

LASOR, W. S., D. A. HUBBARD, AND F. W. BUSH, Old Testament Survey, Grand Rapids:
Eerdmans 1982

LEBRAM, J. C. H., Aspekte der alttestamentlichen Kanonbildung, VT 18 (1968) 173–89

LEIMAN, S. Z., ED., The Canon and Masorah of the Hebrew Bible. An Introductory
Reader (LBS), New York: KTAV 1974

— The Canonization of Hebrew Scripture. The Talmudic and Midrashic Evidence
(Transactions of the Connecticut Academy of the Arts and Sciences 47), Hamden,
CT: Archon Books 1976

— Inspiration and Canonicity: Reflections on the Formation of the Biblical Canon, in:
E. P. SANDERS, WITH BAUMGARTEN AND MENDELSOHN (EDS.), Self-Definition II:56–63

LE MOYNE, J., Les Sadducéen (EtB), Paris: Gabalda 1972

LEVENSON, J. D., Theology of the Program of Ezekiel 40–48 (HSM 10), Missoula, MT:
Scholars Press 1976

— From Temple to Synagogue: 1 Kings 8, in: HALPERN AND LEVENSON (EDS.), Traditions,
142–66

— The Hebrew Bible, the Old Testament, and Historical Criticism. Jews and Christians in Biblical Studies, Louisville: Westminster John Knox 1993

LEVERING, M., ED., Rethinking Scripture. Essays from a Comparativist Perspective, Al-
bany, NY: State University of New York Press 1989

LEVINE, L. I., The Second Temple Synagogue: The Formative Years, in: idem, Synagogue, 7–31

— ED., The Synagogue in Late Antiquity (Centennial Publication of the Jewish Theological Seminary of America), Philadelphia: American Schools of Oriental Research 1987

— The Nature and Origin of the Palestinian Synagogue Reconsidered, JBL 115 (1996)
425–448

LEWIS, J. P., What Do We Mean By Jabneh? JBR 32 (1964) 125–32 = in: LEIMAN (ED.),
Canon, 254–61

LIEDKE, G., Gestalt und Bezeichnung alttestamentlicher Rechtssätze (WMANT 39),
Neukirchen–Vluyn: Neukirchener 1971

LIGHTSTONE, J. N., The Formation of the Biblical Canon in Late Antique Judaism: Prolegomena to a General Reassessment, SR 8 (1979) 135–42

— Society, the Sacred and Scripture in Ancient Judaism. A Sociology of Knowledge
(SCJ 3), Waterloo, Ont: Wilfrid Laurier University Press 1988)

LINDARS, B., Torah in Deuteronomy, in: ACKROYD AND LINDARS (EDS.), Words, 117–36

LINDBECK, G. A., The Nature of Doctrine. Religion and Theology in a Postliberal Age,
Philadelphia: Westminster 1984

LIWAK, R., AND S. WAGNER, EDS., Prophetie und geschichtliche Wirklichkeit im alten
Israel (FS S. Hermann), Stuttgart: Kohlhammer 1991

LOHFINK, N., Die deuteronomistische Darstellung des Übergangs der Führung Israels von Moses auf Josue, Scholastik 37 (1962) 32–44 = in: idem, Studien I:83–97 = in: idem, Theology, 234–47

— The Distribution of the Functions of Power: The Laws Concerning Public Offices in Deuteronomy 16:18–18:22 (trans. R. Walls), in: CHRISTENSEN (ED.), Song, 336–52 = Die Sicherung der Wirksamkeit des Gotteswortes durch das Prinzip der Schriftlichkeit der Tora and durch das Prinzip der Gewaltenteilung nach den Ämtergesetzen des Buches Deuteronomium (Dt 16,18–18,22), in: WOLTER (ED.), Testimonium, 143–55

— Studien zum Pentateuch (SBAB 4), Stuttgart: Katholisches Bibelwerk 1988

— Studien zum Deuteronomium und zur deuteronomistischen Literatur (SBAB 8, 12, 20; 3 vols.), Stuttgart: Katholisches Bibelwerk 1990

— Theology of the Pentateuch. Themes of the Priestly Narrative and Deuteronomy, trans. L. M. Maloney; Minneapolis: Fortress 1994 [= articles selected and translated from idem, Studien zum Pentateuch; and idem, Studien zum Deuteronomium und zur deuteronomistischen Literatur]

— Gab es eine deuteronomistische Bewegung? in: GROSS (ED.), Jeremia, 313–82 = idem, Studien III:65–142

LONG, B. O., 2 Kings (FOTL 10), Grand Rapids: Eerdmans 1991

LUST, J., ED., Ezekiel and his Book. Textual and Literary Criticism and their Interrelation (BEThL 74), Leuven: Leuven University Press / Peeters 1985

MACDONALD, J., The Theology of the Samaritans (NTL), Philadelphia: Westminster 1964

MACK, B. L., AND R. E. MURPHY, Wisdom Literature, in: KRAFT AND NICKELSBURG (EDS.), Judaism, 371–410

MAIER, G., Der Abschluß des jüdischen Kanons und das Lehrhaus von Jabne, in: MAIER (ED.), Kanon, 1–24

— ED., Der Kanon der Bibel, Gießen / Basel: Brunnen; Wuppertal: Brockhaus 1990

MAIER, J., Jüdische Auseinandersetzung mit den Christentum in der Antike (EdF 177), Darmstadt: Wissenschaftliche Buchgesellschaft 1982

— Early Jewish Biblical Interpretation in the Qumran Literature, in: SÆBØ (ED.), Bible, 108–29

MARGOLIS, M. L., The Hebrew Scriptures in the Making, Philadelphia: Jewish Publication Society of America 1922

MARQUARDT, F.-W., Zur Reintegration der Tora in eine Evangelische Theologie, in: BLUM, MACHOLZ AND STEGEMANN (EDS.), Bibel, 657–76

MARTI, K., Das Dodekapropheton (KHC), Tübingen: Mohr Siebeck 1904

MARTIN, J. D., AND P. R. DAVIES (EDS.), A Word in Season (FS W. McKane; JSOT.S 42), Sheffield: Sheffield Academic Press 1986

MARTIN-ARCHARD, R., Old Testament Theologies and Faith Confessions, ThD 33 (1986) 14–48

MARTÍNEZ, F. G., Deuteronomy 34, the Deuteronomistic History and the Pentateuch, in: MARTÍNEZ, ET AL. (EDS.), Studies, 47–61

MARTÍNEZ, F. G., ET AL., EDS., Studies in Deuteronomy (FS C. J. Labuschagne; VT.S 53), Leiden: Brill 1994

MARTÍNEZ, F. G., AND E. J. C. TIGCHELAAR, The Dead Sea Scrolls Study Edition, Leiden / Boston / Cologne: Brill 1998

MASON, R. A., The Relation of Zechariah 9–14 to Proto-Zechariah, ZAW 88 (1976) 226–39

— The Books of Haggai, Zechariah and Malachi (CNEB), Cambridge / New York: Cambridge University Press 1977
— The Purpose of the Editorial Framework of the Book of Haggai, VT 27 (1977) 413–21
— The Prophets of the Restoration, in: R. J. COGGINS, PHILLIPS AND KNIBB (EDS.), Tradition, 137–54
— Some Echoes of the Preaching in the Second Temple? Traditional Elements in Zechariah 1-8, ZAW 96 (1984) 221–35
— Preaching the Tradition. Homily and Hermeneutics After the Exile, Cambridge / New York: Cambridge University Press 1990
MASON, S., Flavius Josephus on the Pharisees. A Composition-Critical Study (StPB 39), Leiden / New York: Brill 1991
MASON, S., WITH R. A. KRAFT, Josephus on the Canon and the Scriptures, in: S ÆBØ (ED.), Bible, 217–35
MATTHIAS, D., Levitische Predigt und Deuteronismus, ZAW 96 (1984) 23–49
MAYES, A. D. H., Deuteronomy (NCB), London: Oliphants 1979
— The Story of Israel Between Settlement and Exile. A Redactional Study of the Deuteronomistic History, London: SCM Press 1983
— Sociology and the Old Testament, in: CLEMENTS (ED.), World, 39–63
— Deuteronomistic Ideology and the Theology of the Old Testament, JSOT 82 (1999) 57–82
MAYS, J. L., Historical and Canonical: Recent Discussions about the Old Testament and Christian Faith, in: CROSS, LEMKE AND MILLER (EDS.), Magnalia, 510–28
— The Place of the Torah–Psalms in the Psalter, JBL 106 (1987) 3–12
MAYS, J. L., D. L. PETERSEN AND K. H. RICHARDS, EDS., Old Testament Interpretation. Past, Present, and Future (FS G. M. Tucker), Nashville: Abingdon 1995
MCBRIDE, S. D., JR., Polity of the Covenant People: The Book of Deuteronomy, in: CHRISTENSEN (ED.), Song, 62–77 = in: Interp. 41 (1987) 229–44
— Perspective and Context in the Study of Pentateuchal Legislation, in: MAYS, PETERSEN AND RICHARDS (EDS.), Interpretation, 47–59
MCCARTER, P. K., JR., 1 Samuel. A New Translation with Introduction, Notes & Commentary (AncB 8), Garden City, NY: Doubleday 1980
MCCARTHY, D. J., Treaty and Covenant. A Study in Form in the Ancient Oriental Documents and in the Old Testament (AnBib 21A), Rome: Biblical Institute Press ²1981
— Der Gottesbund im Alten Testament, Stuttgart: Katholisches Bibelwerk 1967 = Old Testament Covenant. A Survey of Current Opinions, Atlanta: John Knox 1972, ⁵1978
MCCONVILLE, J. G., Ezra–Nehemiah and the Fulfilment of Prophecy, VT 36 (1986) 205–24
MCDONALD, L. M., The Formation of the Christian Biblical Canon, Peabody, MA: Hendrickson ²1995.
— The Integrity of the Biblical Canon in Light of Its Historical Development, BBR 6 (1996) 95–132.
— The First Testament: Its Origin, Adaptability, and Stability, in: EVANS AND TALMON (EDS.), Quest, 287–326
MCGOWAN, J., Postmodernism and Its Critics, Ithaca, NY / London: Cornell University Press 1991
MCGRATH, A. E., Reclaiming Our Roots and Vision: Scripture and the Stability of the Christian Church, in BRAATEN AND JENSON (EDS.), Reclaiming, 63–88

McKAY, H. A., Ancient Synagogues: The Continuing Dialectic Between Two Major Views, Currents in Research: Biblical Studies (1998) 103–42

McKEATING, H., Ezekiel the "Prophet Like Moses," JSOT 61 (1994) 97–109

McKENZIE, S. L., The Chronicler's Use of the Deuteronomistic History (HSM 33), Atlanta: Scholars Press 1984

McKENZIE, S. L., AND M. P. GRAHAM, EDS., The History of Israel's Traditions. The Heritage of Martin Noth (JSOT.S 182), Sheffield: Sheffield Academic Press 1994

MEIER, S. A., The Messenger in the Ancient Semitic World (HMS 45), Atlanta: Scholars Press 1988

MELUGIN, R. F., Prophetic Books and the Problem of Historical Reconstruction, in: REID (ED.), Prophets, 63–78

MENDENHALL, G. E., Covenant, in: BUTTRICK (ED.), IDB I:714–23

— Law and Covenant in Israel and the Ancient Near East (orig. 1954), Pittsburgh, PA: Biblical Colloquium 1955

— Samuel's "Broken Rib": Deuteronomy 32, in: CHRISTENSEN (ED.), Song, 169–80 = in: FLANAGAN AND ROBINSON (EDS.), Famine, 63–74

MERRILL, A., AND T. W. OVERHOLT, EDS., Scripture in History and Theology (FS J. C Rylaarsdam; PThMS 17), Pittsburgh, PA: Pickwick Press 1977

MEYERS, C. L., AND E. M. MEYERS, Haggai, Zechariah 1–8. A New Translation with Introduction and Commentary (AncB 25B), Garden City, NY: Doubleday 1987

MEYERS, E. M., Priestly Language in the Book of Malachi, HAR 10 (1986) 225–37

MICHEEL, R., Die Seher– und Propheten-Überlieferungen in der Chronik (BET 18) Frankfurt a. M. / Bern: Peter Lang 1983

MICHEL, O., Spätjüdisches Prophetentum, in: Neutestamentliche Studien (FS R. Bultmann; BZNW 21), Berlin: Töpelmann 1954, 60–66

MILLER, J. W., The Origins of the Bible: Rethinking Canon History (Theological Inquiries), New York / Mahwah, NJ: Paulist Press 1994

MILLER, P. D., JR., Faith and Ideology in the Old Testament, in: CROSS, LEMKE AND MILLER (EDS.), Magnalia, 464–79

— Der Kanon in der gegenwärtigen amerikanischen Diskussion, JBTh 3 (1988) 217–39

— "Moses My Servant": The Deuteronomic Portrait, Interp. 41 (1987) 245–55 = in: CHRISTENSEN (ED.), Song, 301–12

— The World and Message of the Prophets: Biblical Prophecy in its Context, in: MAYS, PETERSEN AND RICHARDS (EDS.), Interpretation, 97–112,

MILLER, P. D., JR., P. D. HANSON AND S. D. MCBRIDE, EDS., Ancient Israelite Religion (FS F. M. Cross) Philadelphia: Fortress 1987

MISCHEL, T., ED., The Self, Oxford: Blackwell 1977

MITCHELL, H. G., J. M. P. SMITH AND J. A. BEWER, A Critical and Exegetical Commentary on Haggai, Zechariah, Malachi and Jonah (ICC), New York: Scribner 1912

MOBERLY, R. W. L., The Old Testament of the Old Testament. Patriarchal Narratives and Mosaic Yahwism (OBT), Minneapolis: Fortress 1992

MONTGOMERY, J. A., A Critical and Exegetical Commentary on the Books of Kings (ICC), ed. H. S. Gehman; New York: Scribner; Edinburgh: T & T Clark 1951

MOOR, J. C. DE, ED., Crises and Perspectives. Studies in Ancient Near Eastern Polytheism, Biblical Theology, Palestinian Archaeology, and Intertestamental Literature. Papers Read at the Joint British–Dutch Old Testament Conference at the University of Cambridge, 1985 (OTS 24), Leiden: Brill 1986

MOORE, C. A., Tobit. A New Translation with Introduction and Commentary (AncB 40A), New York / London: Doubleday 1996

MOORE, G. F., The Definition of the Jewish Canon and the Repudiation of the Christian Scriptures, in: Essays in Modern Theology and Related Subjects (FS C. A. Briggs), New York: Scribner 1911, 99–125 = in: LEIMAN (ED.), Canon, 115–41

MORGAN, R., AND J. BARTON, Biblical Interpretation (Oxford Bible Series) Oxford / New York: Oxford University Press 1988

MÜLLER, K., Beobachtungen zum Verhältnis von Tora und Halacha in frühjüdischen Quellen, in: BROER (ED.), Jesus, 105–34

MULDER, M. J., The Transmission of the Biblical Text, in: MULDER (ED.), CRI 2.1, 87–135

— ED., Mikra: Text, Translation, Reading and Interpretation of the Hebrew Bible in Ancient Judaism and Early Christianity (CRI 2.1), Assen / Maastricht: van Gorcum; Philadelphia: Fortress 1988

MURTONEN, A., On the Chronology of the Old Testament, StTh 8 (1954) 133–37

MYERS, J. M., Ezra–Nehemiah (AncB 14), Garden City, NY: Doubleday 1965

NAGEL, T., The Possibility of Altruism, Princeton, NJ: Princeton University Press, 1970

NELSON, R. D., The Double Redaction of the Deuteronomistic History (JSOT.S 18), Sheffield: JSOT Press 1981

— Joshua. A Commentary (OTL), Louisville, Westminster John Knox 1997

NEUSNER, J., Early Rabbinic Judaism. Historical Studies in Religion: Literature and Art. (SJLA 13), Leiden: Brill 1975

— Midrash in Context: Exegesis in Formative Judaism, Philadelphia: Fortress 1983

— Accomodating Mishnah to Scripture in Judaism: The Uneasy Union and Its Offspring, in: O'CONNOR AND FREEDMAN (EDS.), Backgrounds, 39–53

NEUSNER, J., WITH W. S. GREEN, Rabbinic Judaism: Structure and System, Minneapolis: Fortress 1995

NEWSOM, C. A., Bakhtin, the Bible, and Dialogic Truth, JR 76 (1996) 290–306

NICHOLSON, E. W., Preaching to the Exiles. A Study of the Prose Tradition in the Book of Jeremiah, Oxford: Blackwell 1970

— Covenant in a Century of Study since Wellhausen, in: MOOR (ED.), Crises, 54–69

— God and His People. Covenant and Theology in the Old Testament, Oxford: Clarendon 1986 = in: CHRISTENSEN (ED.), Song, 78–93

— Pre–Exilic Israelite Religion, in: MARTIN AND P. R. DAVIES, (EDS.), Word, 3–34

— The Pentateuch in the Twentieth Century. The Legacy of Julius Wellhausen, Oxford: Clarendon 1998

NICKELSBURG, G. W. E., WITH R. A. KRAFT, Introduction: The Modern Study of Early Judaism, in: KRAFT AND NICKELSBURG (EDS.), Judaism, 1–30

NOBLE, P. R., The Canonical Approach. A Critical Reconstruction of the Hermeneutics of Brevard S. Childs (Biblical Interpretation Series 16), Leiden / New York: Brill 1995

NOGALSKI, J., Literary Precursors to the Book of the Twelve (BZAW 127), Berlin / New York: de Gruyter 1993

— Redactional Processes in the Book of the Twelve (BZAW 218), Berlin / New York: de Gruyter 1993

NOORT, E., Das Buch Josua (EdF 292) Darmstadt: Wissenschaftliche Buchgesellschaft 1998

NOTH, M., Die Gesetze im Pentateuch: ihre Voraussetzungen und ihr Sinn (SKG.G 17.2), Halle (Salle): Max Niemeyer 1940 = in: idem, Studien I: 9–141

— The Deuteronomistic History (JSOT.S 15), Sheffield: JSOT Press 1981 = Part I (1–110), in: idem, Überlieferungsgeschichtliche Studien (SKG.G 18.2), Tübingen: Max Niemeyer 1943, ²1957
— A History of Pentateuchal Traditions, trans. B. W. Anderson; repr. Chico, CA: Scholars Press 1972 = idem, Überlieferungsgeschichte des Pentateuch, Stuttgart: Kolhammer 1948
— Das Buch Josua (HAT 7), Tübingen: Mohr Siebeck 1938, ²1953
— Gesammelte Studien zum Alten Testament (TB 6, 39; 2 vols.), Munich: Chr. Kaiser ³1966

O'BRIEN, J. M., Priest and Levite in Malachi (SBL.DS 121), Atlanta: Scholars Press 1990
O'BRIEN, M. A., The Deuteronomistic History Hypothesis: A Reassessment (OBO 92), Freiburg (Switzerland): Universitätsverlag; Göttingen: Vandenhoeck & Ruprecht 1989
O'CONNOR, M. P., AND D. N. FREEDMAN, EDS., Backgrounds for the Bible, Winona Lake, IN: Eisenbrauns 1987
ODEN, R. A., The Bible Without Theology: The Theological Tradition and Alternatives to It, San Francisco: Harper & Row 1987
OEMING, M., Text – Kontext – Kanon: ein neuer Weg alttestamentlicher Theologie? JBTh 3 (1988) 241–51
O'KANE, M., Isaiah: A Prophet in the Footsteps of Moses, JSOT 69 (1996) 29–51
OLSON, D. T., Deuteronomy and the Death of Moses: A Theological Reading (OBT), Minneapolis: Fortress 1994
ÖSTBORN, G., Cult and Canon. A Study in the Canonization of the Old Testament (UUÅ), Uppsala: A. B. Lundequistska Bokhandeln 1950
ORELLI, C. VON, Die zwölf kleinen Propheten (KK 5.2), Munich: Beck ³1908
ORIGEN, Against Celsus = Contra Celsum, trans. and notes H. Chadwick; Cambridge: Cambridge University Press repr. 1965
ORLINSKY, H. M., Some Terms in the Prologue to Ben Sira and the Hebrew Canon, JBL 110 (1991) 483–90
OTTO, R., The Idea of the Holy. An Inquiry into the Non-Rational Factors in the Idea of the Divine and its Relation to the Rational, trans. J. W. Harvey; Oxford / New York: Oxford University Press 1976

PANNENBERG, W., AND T. SCHNEIDER, EDS., Verbindliches Zeugnis I. Kanon – Schrift – Tradition (DiKi 7), Freiburg i. B.: Herder; Göttingen: Vandenhoeck & Ruprecht 1992
PARKER, K. I., Speech, Writing and Power: Deconstructing the Biblical Canon, JSOT 69 (1996) 91–103
PATRICK, D., The Rendering of God in the Old Testament (OBT 10), Philadelphia: Fortress 1981
PATTE, D., Early Jewish Hermeneutic in Palestine (SBL.DS 22), Missoula, MT: Scholars Press 1975
PERDUE, L. G., The Collapse of History. Reconstructing Old Testament Theology (OBT), Minneapolis: Fortress 1994
PERDUE, L. G., AND W. KOVACS, EDS., A Prophet to the Nations. Essays in Jeremiah Studies, Winona Lake, IN: Eisenbrauns 1984

PERLITT, L., Bundestheologie im Alten Testament (WMANT 36), Neukirchen-Vluyn: Neukirchener 1969

— Mose als Prophet, EvTh 31 (1971) 588–608

— Priesterschrift im Deuteronomium? ZAW.S 100 (1988) 65–88

— Deuteronomium (BK 5.1), Neukirchen-Vluyn: Neukirchener 1990

PERROT, C., La Lecture de la Bible. Les Anciennes Lectures Palestiniennes du Shabbat et des Fêtes, Hildesheim: Gerstenberg 1973

— The Reading of the Bible in the Ancient Synagogue, in: MULDER (ED.), CRI 2.1, 137–59

PERSON, R. F., Second Zechariah and the Deuteronomistic School (JSOT.S 167), Sheffield: Sheffield Academic Press 1993

PETERSEN, D. L., Late Israelite Prophecy. Studies in Deutero-Prophetic Literature and in Chronicles (SBL.MS 23), Missoula, MT: Scholars Press for the Society of Biblical Literature 1977

— Zachariah 9-14 and Malachi. A Commentary (OTL), Louisville: Westminster John Knox 1995

PFEIFFER, R. H., Introduction to the Old Testament, New York / London: Harper 1941

— Canon of the OT, in: BUTTRICK (ED.), IDB 1:498–520

PHILO, On the Contemplative Life, in: COLSON (ED.), Philo IX.104–69

PIPPIN, T., Ideology, Ideological Criticism and the Bible, Currents in Research: Biblical Studies (1996) 51–78

PLÖGER, O., Prophetisches Erbe in den Sekten des frühen Judentums, ThLZ 79 (1954) 291–96 = in: idem, Studien, 43–49

— Theocracy and Eschatology, trans. S. Rudman; Oxford: Blackwell 1968

— Aus der Spätzeit des Alten Testaments. Studien, Göttingen: Vandenhoeck & Ruprecht 1971

PORTER, J. R., The Pentateuch and the Triennial Lectionary Cycle: An Examination of a Recent Theory, in: BRUCE (ED.), Promise, 163–74

PORTON, G. G., Midrash: Palestinian Jews and the Hebrew Bible in the Greco-Roman Period, in: HAASE ANDTÉMPORINI (EDS.), ANRW II.19.2, 103–38

— Diversity in Postbiblical Judaism, in: KRAFT AND NICKELSBURG (EDS.), Judaism, 57–80

PREUSS, H. D., Deuteronomium (EdF 164), Darmstadt: Wissenschaftliche Buchgesellschaft 1982

PROPP, W. H., B. HALPERN AND D. N. FREEDMAN, EDS., The Hebrew Bible and Its Interpreters (Biblical and Judaic Studies from the Univ. of California, San Diego 1), Winona Lake, IN: Eisenbrauns 1990

PROVAN, I., Canons to the Left of Him: Brevard Childs, His Critics, and the Future of Old Testament Theology, SJTh 50 (1997) 1–38

PUMMER, R., The Present State of Samaritan Studies, JSSt 21 (1976) 39–61; JSSt 22 (1977) 27–47

— Einführung in den Stand der Samaritaner Forschung (1991), in: DEXINGER AND PUMMER (EDS.), Samaritaner, 1–66

PURVIS, J. D., The Samaritan Pentateuch and the Origin of the Samaritan Sect (HSM 2) Cambridge, MA: Harvard University Press 1968

— The Samaritans and Judaism, in: KRAFT AND NICKELSBURG (EDS.), Judaism, 81–98

PURY, A. DE, ED., Le Pentateuque en Question. Les origines et la composition des cinqs premiers livres de la Bible à la lumière des recherches récentes (MoBi), Geneva: Labor et Fides 1989

QIMRON, E., The Hebrew of the Dead Sea Scrolls (HSS 29), Atlanta: Scholars Press 1986

QIMRON, E., AND J. STRUGNELL, EDS., Qumran Cave 4. Miqsat Ma'ase Ha-Torah (DJD10), Oxford: Clarendon 1994

RABENAU, K. VON, Das wissenschaftliche Werk von Prof. D. Dr. Eißfeldt DD, in: AHRBECK, ET AL. (EDS.), Orient, 7–8

RABINOWITZ, I., 'Az Followed by Imperfect Verb-Form in Preterite Contexts: A Redactional Device in Biblical Hebrew, VT 34 (1984) 53–62

— A Witness Forever. Ancient Israel's Perception of Literature and the Resultant Hebrew Bible, ed. R. Braun and D. I. Owen; Bethesda, MD: CDL Press 1993

RAD, GERHARD VON, Das formgeschichtliche Problem des Hexateuch (BWANT 26), Stuttgart: Kohlhammer 1938 = in: idem, Studien I:9–86 = The Form-Critical Problem of the Hexateuch, in: idem, Essays, 1–78

— The Levitical Sermon in I and II Chronicles, in: idem, Essays, 267–80 = Die levitische Predigt in den Bücher der Chronik (orig. 1934), in: idem, Studien I:248–61

— Studies in Deuteronomy, London: SCM Press 1953 = Deuteronomium–Studien (FRLANT 58), Göttingen: Vandenhoeck & Ruprecht 1947

— Deuteronomy. A Commentary (OTL), trans. D. Barton; Philadelphia: Westminster 1966 = Das fünfte Buch Mose. Deuteronomium (ATD 8), Göttingen: Vandenhoeck & Ruprecht ²1968

— Theologie des Alten Testaments (EETh 1; 2 vols.), Munich: Chr. Kaiser 1957, ⁶1969 = Old Testament Theology (2 vols.), trans. D. G. M. Stalker; New York: Harper & Row 1962–65

— Gesammelte Studien zum Alten Testament (TB 8, 48; 2 vols.), Munich: Chr. Kaiser ⁴1971

— The Problem of the Hexateuch and Other Essays, trans. E. W. T. Dicken; New York: McGraw Hill 1966 [= Gesammelte Studien, I]

RAILTON, P., Ideology, in: HONERICH (ED.), Companion, 392–93

RAINEY, A. F., The Chronicler and His Sources — Historical and Geographical, in: GRAHAM, HOGLUND AND McKENZIE (EDS.), Chronicler, 30–72

READINGS, B., Canon and On: From Concept to Figure, JAAR 57 (1989) 149–72

REID, S. B., ED., Prophets and Paradigms (FS G. M. Tucker; JSOT.S 229) Sheffield: Sheffield Academic Press 1996

RENDTORFF, R., The Problem of the Process of Transmission of the Pentateuch (JSOT.S 89) trans. J. J. Scullion; Sheffield: JSOT Press 1990 = Das Überlieferungsgeschichtliche Problem des Pentateuch (BZAW 147) Berlin / New York: de Gruyter 1977

— The Old Testament. An Introduction, trans. J. Bowden; Philadelphia: Fortress 1986 = Das Alte Testament. Eine Einführung, Neukirchen–Vluyn: Neukirchener 1983

— Esra und das "Gesetz," ZAW 96 (1984) 165–84

— The Image of Postexilic Israel in German Old Testament Scholarship from Wellhausen to von Rad, in: idem, Canon, 66–75 = in: FISHBANE AND TOV (EDS.), Studies, 165–73 = Das Bild des nachexilischen Israel in der deutschen alttestamentlichen Wissenschaft von Wellhausen bis von Rad, in: idem, Kanon, 72–80

— Canon and Theology. Overtures to an Old Testament Theology (OBT), trans. and ed. M. Kohl; Minneapolis: Fortress 1993 = Kanon und Theologie. Vorarbeiten zu einer Theologie des Alten Testaments, Neukirchen–Vluyn: Neukirchener 1991

REVENTLOW, H. G., Problems of Biblical Theology in the Twentieth Century, trans. J. Bowden; London: SCM Press 1986 = Hauptprobleme der Biblischen Theologie im 20. Jahrhundert (EdF 203) Darmstadt: Wissenschaftliche Buchgesellschaft 1983

RHODES, A. B., Israel's Prophets as Intercessors, in: MERRILL AND OVERHOLT (EDS.), Scripture, 107–28

RICHTER, W., Die Bearbeitung des "Retterbuches" in der deuteronomistischen Epoche (BBB 21), Bonn: Peter Hanstein 1964

ROBERTS, B. J., The Old Testament Canon: A Suggestion, BJRL 46 (1963–64) 164–78

ROBERTS, J. J. M., The Hand of Yahweh, VT 21 (1971) 244–51

— The Davidic Origin of the Zion Tradition, JBL 92 (1973) 329–44

ROBINSON, T. H., AND F. HORST, Die zwölf kleinen Propheten (HAT 14) Tübingen: Mohr Siebeck ²1954

ROCHE, M. DE, Yahweh's *rib* Against Israel: A Reassessment of the So-Called "Prophetic Lawsuit" in the Preexilic Prophets, JBL 102 (1983) 563–74

ROFÉ, A., Joshua 20: Historico-Literary Criticism Illustrated, in: TIGAY (ED.), Models, 131–47

ROGERSON, J. W., The Use of Sociology in Old Testament Studies, in: Congress Volume. Salamanca 1983 (VT.S 36), ed. J. A. Emerton; Leiden: Brill 1985, 245–56

— Old Testament Criticism in the Nineteenth Century. England and Germany, London: SPCK; Philadelphia: Fortress 1984

— W. M. L. de Wette, Founder of Modern Biblical Criticism. An Intellectual Biography (JSOT.S 126), Sheffield: JSOT Press 1992

ROGERSON, J. W., AND P. R. DAVIES, EDS., The Old Testament World, Cambridge / New York: Cambridge University Press 1989

ROHLS, J., AND G. WENZ, EDS., Vernunft des Glaubens. Wissenschaftliche Theologie und kirchliche Lehre (FS W. Pannenberg), Göttingen: Vandenhoeck & Ruprecht 1988

ROOY, H. V. VAN, Prophet and Society in the Persian Period according to Chronicles, in: ESKENAZI AND RICHARDS (EDS.), Studies, 163–79

RORTY, R., Philosophy and the Mirror of Nature, Princeton, NJ: Princeton University Press 1979

ROSE, M., Deuteronomist und Jahwist. Untersuchungen zu den Berührungspunkten beider Literaturwerke (AThANT 67), Zürich: Theologischer Verlag 1981

— Empoigner le Pentateuque par sa fin! L'investiture de Josué et la mort de Moïse, in: DE PURY (ED.), Pentateuque, 129–47

ROST, L., Bemerkungen zu dibbär (orig. 1972), in: idem, Studien, 39–60

— Gesetz und Propheten (orig. 1973), in: idem, Studien, 9–38

— Studien zum Alten Testament (BWANT 101), Stuttgart / Berlin / Cologne / Mainz: Kohlhammer 1974

RUDOLF, W., Haggai, Sacharja 1–8, Sacharja 9–14, Maleachi (KAT 13/4), Gütersloh: Mohn 1976

RÜTERSWÖRDEN, U., Es gibt keinen Exegeten in einem gesetzlosen Land (Prov. 29,18 LXX). Erwägungen zum Thema: der Prophet und die Thora, in: LIWAK AND WAGNER (EDS.), Prophetie, 326–47

— Die Persische Reichsautorisation der Tora: fact or fiction? ZAR 1 (1995) 47–61

RYLE, H. E., The Canon of the Old Testament. An Essay on the Gradual Growth and Formation of the Hebrew Canon of Scripture, London / New York: Macmillan 1892

— The Study of the Old Testament with Special Reference to the Element of Compilation in the Structure of the Books, in: idem, Scripture, 72–97

— On Holy Scripture and Criticism. Addresses and Sermons, London / New York: Macmillan 1904

SÆBØ, M., Vom "Zusammen–Denken" zum Kanon: Aspekte der traditionsgeschichtlichen Endstadien des Alten Testaments, in: B ALDERMANN (ED.), JBTh 3, 115–33 = From "Unifying Reflections" to the Canon: Aspects of the Traditio–Historical Final Stages in the Development of the Old Testament, in: idem, Canon, 285–307
— ED., Hebrew Bible / Old Testament. The History of Its Interpretation. Volume I: From the Beginnings to the Middle Ages (Until 1300). Part I: Antiquity, Göttingen: Vandenhoeck & Ruprecht 1996
— On the Way to Canon. Creative Tradition History in the Old Testament (JSOT.S 191), Sheffield: Sheffield Academic Press 1998
SAFRAI, S., Halakha, in: SAFRAI (ED.), CRI 2.3.1, 121–209
SAFRAI, S., ED., The Literature of the Sages. First Part: Oral Tora, Halakha, Mishna, Tosefta, Talmud, External Tractates (CRI 2.3.1), Assen / Maastricht: van Gorcum; Philadelphia: Fortress 1987
SALDARINI, A., Reconstructions of Rabbinic Judaism, in: KRAFT AND NICKELSBURG (EDS.), Judaism, 437–77
SANDERS, E. P., WITH A. I. BAUMGARTEN AND A. MENDELSOHN, EDS., Jewish and Christian Self-Definition II, London: SPCK 1981
SANDERS, J. A., Hermeneutics, in: CRIM (ED.) IDB.S, 402–07
— Torah and Canon, Philadelphia: Fortress 1972
— Adaptable for Life: The Nature and Function of Canon, in: CROSS, LEMKE AND MILLER (EDS.), Magnalia, 531–60 = in: idem, Story, 9–39
— Canon and Community. A Guide to Canonical Criticism (Guides to Biblical Scholarship), Philadelphia: Fortress 1984
— First Testament and Second, BTB 17 (1987) 45–46
— From Sacred Story to Sacred Text. Canon as Paradigm, Philadelphia: Fortress 1987
— Canon, in: FREEDMAN (ED.), AncBD I:837–52
SANDERS, P., The Provenance of Deuteronomy 32 (OTS 37), Leiden: Brill 1996
SAWYER, J. F. A., Combating Prejudices about the Bible and Judaism, Theol 94 (1991) 269–78
— Prophecy and the Biblical Prophets (Oxford Biblical Studies), Oxford: Oxford University Press 1993
SCALISE, C. J., Canonical Hermeneutics: Childs and Barth, SJTh 47 (1994) 61–88
SCHÄFER, P., Die sogenannte Synode von Jamnia, Jud 31 (1975) 54–64
SCHÄFER-LICHTENBERGER, C., "Josua" und "Elischa" — eine biblische Argumentation zur Begründung der Autorität und Legitimität des Nachfolgers, ZAW 101 (1989) 198–222
SCHECHTER, S., Some Aspects of Rabbinic Theology (orig. 1923), repr. Woodstock, UT: Jewish Lights 1993
SCHLUCHTER, W., ED., Max Webers Sicht des Antiken Christentums. Interpretation und Kritik (stw 548), Frankfurt a. M.: Suhrkamp 1985
SCHMID, H., Mose. Überlieferung und Geschichte (BZAW 110), Berlin: Töpelmann 1968
— Die Gestalt des Mose. Probleme alttestamentlicher Forschung unter Berücksichtigung der Pentateuchkrise (EdF 237), Darmstadt: Wissenschaftliche Buchgesellschaft 1986
SCHMID, H. H., Der sogenannte Jahwist. Beobachtungen und Fragen zur Pentateuchforschung, Zürich: Theologischer Verlag 1976
SCHMITT, H.-C., "Priesterliches" und "prophetisches" Geschichtsverständnis in der Meerwundererzählung Ex 13,17–14,31. Beobachtungen zur Endredaktion des Pentateuch, in: GUNNEWEG AND KAISER, Textgemäß, 139–55
— Redaktion des Pentateuch im Geiste der Prophetie, VT 32 (1982) 170–89

— Prophetische Tradition in der Plagenerzählung, in: FRITZ, POHLMANN AND SCHMITT (EDS.), Prophet, 196–216
— Das Spätdeuteronomistische Geschichtswerk Genesis I – 2 Regum XXV und seine theologische Intention, in: Congress Volume. Cambridge 1995 (VT.S 66) ed. J. A. Emerton; Leiden: Brill 1997, 261–79
SCHNABEL, E., Die Entwürfe von B. S. Childs und H. Gese bezüglich des Kanons: ein Beitrag zur aktuellen hermeneutischen Fragestellung, in: G. MAIER (ED.), Kanon, 102–52
— History, theology and the biblical canon: an introduction to basic issues, Themelios 20 (1995) 16–24
SCHNEIDAU, H., Sacred Discontent. The Bible and the Western Tradition (Baton Rouge, LA: Louisiana State University 1976
SCHNIEDEWIND, W. M., The Word of God in Transition. From Prophet to Exegete in the Second Temple Period (JSOT.S 197), Sheffield: Sheffield Academic Press 1995
— Prophets and Prophecy in the Books of Chronicles, in: GRAHAM, HOGLUND AND MCKENZIE(EDS.), Chronicler, 204–24
SCHNUR, N., History of the Karaites (BEAT 29), Frankfurt a. M.: Peter Lang 1992
SCHÜRER, E., The History of the Jewish People in the Age of Jesus Christ (175 B. C. – A. D. 135), ed. G. Vermes and F. Millar; Edinburgh: T & T Clark ²1973–87
SEELIGMAN, I. L., The Septuagint Version of Isaiah (MEOL 9), Leiden: Brill 1948
— Voraussetzungen der Midraschexegese, in: Congress Volume. Copenhagen 1953 (In Memoriam A. Bentzen; VT.S 1), Leiden: Brill 1953, 150–81
— Menschliches Heldentum und Göttliche Hilfe: die doppelte Kausalität im alttestamentlichen Geschichtsdenken, ThZ 19 (1963), 385–411
— Die Auffassung von der Prophetie in der deuteronomistischen und chronistischen Geschichtsschreibung, Congress Volume. Göttingen 1977 (VT.S 29), Leiden: Brill 1978, 254–84
SEGAL, A. F., Torah and *nomos* in Recent Scholarly Discussion, SR 13 (1984) 19–28 = in: idem, Judaisms, 131–45
— The Other Judaisms of Late Antiquity (BJSt 127) Atlanta: Scholars Press, 1987
SEITZ, C. R, The Prophet Moses and the Canonical Shape of Jeremiah, ZAW 101 (1980) 3–27
— Old Testament or Hebrew Bible? Some Theological Considerations, Pro Ecclesia 5 (1996) 292–303
SEITZ, G., Redaktionsgeschichtliche Studien zum Deuteronomium (BWANT 93), Stuttgart: Kohlhammer 1971
SELLIN, E., Einleitung in das Alte Testament (Evangelisch-theologische Bibliothek 2), Leipzig: Quelle & Meyer 1910, ⁶1933
— Das Zwölfprophetenbuch (KAT 12; 2 vols.), Leipzig: Deichert 1930
SHAVER, J. R., Torah and the Chronicler's History Work. An Inquiry into the Chronicler's References to Law, Festivals, and Cultic Institutions in Relationship to Pentateuchal Legislation (BJSt 196), Atlanta: Scholars Press 1989
SHEPPARD, G. T., Wisdom as a Hermeneutical Construct. The Sapientialization of Old Testament Traditions (BZAW 151), Berlin / New York: de Gruyter 1980
— Canonization: Hearing the Voice of the Same God through Historically Dissimilar Traditions, Interp. 36 (1982) 21–33
— Canon, in: ELIADE (ED.), EncRel(E) III:62–69
— The Future of the Bible. Beyond Liberalism and Literalism, United Church of Canada: United Church Publishing 1990
— Canonical Criticism, in: FREEDMAN (ED.), AncBD I:861–66

S ILBERMAN, L. H., Wellhausen and Judaism, Semeia 25 (1982) 76–82

S KEHAN, P., The Structure of the Song of Moses in Deuteronomy (32:1–43), CBQ 13 (1951) 153–63 = in: CHRISTENSEN (ED.), Song, 156–68

SMEND, R., Das Gesetz und die Völker: ein Beitrag zur deuteronomistischen Redaktionsgeschichte, in: WOLFF (ED.), Probleme, 494–509

— Die Entstehung des Alten Testaments (ThW 1), Stuttgart: Kohlhammer ²1981

— Theologie im Alten Testament, in: JÜNGEL, WALLMAN AND WERBECK (EDS.), Verifikationen, 104–17

— Otto Eißfeldt 1887–1973, in: AULD (ED.), Understanding, 318–55

SMITH, G. A., The Book of Deuteronomy, Cambridge: University Press ²1918

SMITH, R. L., Micah – Malachi (WBC), Waco, TX: Word Books 1984

SMITH, W. C., What Is Scripture? A Comparative Approach, Minneapolis: Fortress 1993

SNOEK, J. A. M., Canonization and Decanonization: An Annotated Bibliography, in: KOOIJ AND TOORN (EDS.), Canonization, 435–506

SOGGIN, J. A., שוב, in: JENNI AND WESTERMANN (EDS.), TLOT III:1312–17 = THAT II:884–91

— Joshua. A Commentary (OTL), trans. R. A. Wilson; London: SCM Press 1972

— Introduction to the Old Testament. From Its Origins to the Closing of the Alexandrian Canon (OTL) Philadelphia: Westminster 1976

SOMMER, B. D., Did Prophecy Cease? Evaluating a Reevaluation, JBL 115 (1996) 31–47

SOULEN, R. K., The God of Israel and Christian Theology, Minneapolis: Fortress 1996

STAERK, W., Der Schrift- und Kanonbegriff der jüdischen Bibel, ZSTh 6 (1929) 101–19

STECK, O. H., ED., Zu Tradition und Theologie (BThSt 2), Neukirchen–Vluyn: Neukirchener 1978

— Der Kanon des hebräischen Alten Testaments: historische Materialen für eine ökumenische Perspektive, in: PANNENBERG AND SCHNEIDER (EDS.), Zeugnis, 11–33 = in: ROHLS AND WENZ (EDS.), Vernunft, 231–52

— Der Abschluß der Prophetie im Alten Testament: ein Versuch zur Frage der Vorgeschichte des Kanons (BThSt 17), Neukirchen–Vluyn: Neukirchener 1991

STEGEMANN, W., Tora – Nomos – Gesetz: zur Bedeutung des Judentums für das Christentum, in: STÖHR (ED.), Lernen, 148–68

STEINS, G., Die Chronik als kanonisches Abschlußphänomen. Studien zur Entstehung und Theologie von 1/2 Chronik (BBB 93), Weinheim: Beltz Athenäum 1995

STEMBERGER, G., Jabne und der Kanon, JBTh 3 (1988) 163–74

STENDAHL, K., Biblical Theology, Contemporary, in: BUTTRICK (ED.), IDB I: 418–32 = in: idem, Meanings, 11–44 [see also 1–7].

— The Bible as Document and as Guide, Philadelphia: Fortress 1984

STÖHR, M., ED., Lernen in Jerusalem — Lernen mit Israel: Anstöße zur Erneuerung in Theologie und Kirche (VIKJ 20), Berlin: Institut Kirche und Judentum 1993

STOELLGER, P., Deuteronomium 34 ohne Priesterschrift, ZAW 105 (1993) 26–51

STONEHOUSE, N. B., AND P. WOOLEY, EDS., The Infallible Word. A Symposium by Members of the Faculty of Westminster Theological Seminary, Grand Rapids: Eerdmans 1953

SUN, H. T. C., ET AL., EDS., Problems in Biblical Theology (FS R. Knierim), Grand Rapids / Cambridge: Eerdmans 1997

SUNDBERG, A. C., JR., The Old Testament in the Early Church, HThR 5 (1958) 206–26

— The Old Testament of the Early Church (HThS 20), Cambridge, MA: Harvard University Press 1964

— The Protestant Old Testament Canon: Should it be Re-examined? CBQ 28 (1966) 194–203

— The Old Testament: A Christian Canon, CBQ 30 (1968) 143–55 = in: LEIMAN (ED.), Canon, 99–112

— The Bible Canon and the Christian Doctrine of Inspiration, Interp. 39 (1975) 352–71

SWANSON, T. N., The Closing of the Collection of Holy Scripture. A Study in the History of the Canonization of the Old Testament (Diss., Vanderbilt), Ann Arbor, MI: University Microfilms 1970

SWETE, H. B., Introduction to the Old Testament in Greek, rev. R. R. Ottley; Cambridge: University Press ²1914

TALMON, S., Heiliges Schrifttum und kanonische Bücher aus jüdischer Sicht — Überlegungen zur Ausbildung der Größe "Die Schrift" im Judentum, in: KLOPFENSTEIN, ET AL. (EDS.), Mitte? 45–79

— Tora – Nomos – Gesetz: die Bedeutung des Judentums für die christliche Theologie, in: STÖHR (ED.), Lernen, 130–47

TANNER, K., Respect for Other Religions: A Christian Antidote to Colonialist Discourse, MoTh 9 (1993) 1–18

TAYLOR, C., What is Human Agency? in: MISCHEL (ED.), Self, 103–35 = in: idem, Papers 1:15–44

— Self-interpreting animals, in: idem, Papers 1:45–76

— Human Agency and Language. Philosophical Papers 1, Cambridge: Cambridge University Press 1985

— Philosophy and the Human Sciences. Philosophical Papers 2, Cambridge: Cambridge University Press 1985

— Sources of the Self: the Making of the Modern Identity, Cambridge, MA: Harvard University Press 1989

TENGSTRÖM, S., Moses and the Prophets in the Deuteronomistic History, SJOT 8 (1994) 257–66

THACKERAY, H. ST. J., ED., Josephus (LCL; 9 vols.), trans. H. St. J. Thackeray; London: Heinemann; Cambridge, MA: Harvard University Press 1956

THEN, R., "Gibt es denn keinen mehr unter den Propheten?" Zum Fortgang der alttestamentlichen Prophetie in frühjüdischen Zeit (BEAT 22), Frankfurt a. M. / Bern / New York / Paris: Peter Lang 1990

THEOBALD, C., ED., Le Canon des Écritures. Études historiques, exégétiques et systématiques (LeDiv 140), Paris: Les Éditions du Cerf 1990

THIEL, W., Die deuteronomistische Redaktion von Jeremia 1–25 (WMANT 41), Neukirchen–Vluyn: Neukirchener 1973

— Die deuteronomistische Redaktion von Jeremia 26–45 (WMANT 52), Neukirchen–Vluyn: Neukirchener 1981

THISELTON, A. C., Interpreting God and the Postmodern Self. On Meaning, Manipulation and Promise, Edinburgh: T&T Clark; Grand Rapids: Eerdmans 1995

THOMPSON, T. L., The Historicity of the Patriarchal Narratives. The Quest for the Historical Abraham (BZAW 133), Berlin / New York: de Gruyter 1974

— The Early History of the Israelite People. From the Written and Archaeological Sources (SHANE 4), Leiden / New York: Brill 1992

TIGAY, J. H., ED., Empirical Models for Biblical Criticism, Philadelphia: University of Pennsylvania Press 1985

— The Significance of the End of Deuteronomy (Deuteronomy 34:10–12), in: FOX, ET AL. (EDS.), Texts, 137–43

— Deuteronomy. The Traditional Hebrew Text with the New JPS Translation (JPSTC), Philadelphia / Jerusalem: Jewish Publication Society 5756/1996

TORREY, C. C., The Prophet Malachi, JBL 17 (1898) 1–15

— Ezra Studies, Chicago: University of Chicago Press 1910

TOV, E., ED., Jewish Greek Scriptures, in: KRAFT AND NICKELSBURG (EDS.), Judaism, 223–37

— The Greek Minor Prophets Scroll from Naḥal Ḥever (8ḤevXIIgr) (DJD 8), Oxford: Clarendon 1990

— Textual Criticism of the Hebrew Bible, Minneapolis: Fortress; Assen: van Gorcum 1992

— Groups of Biblical Texts Found at Qumran, in: DIMANT AND SCHIFFMAN (EDS.), Time, 85–102

— The History and Significance of a Standard Text of the Hebrew Bible, in: SÆBØ (ED.), Bible, 49–66

TRACY, D., The Analogical Imagination. Christian Theology and the Culture of Pluralism, New York: Crossroad 1981

TUCKER, G. M., Prophetic Superscriptions and the Growth of a Canon, in: COATS AND LONG (EDS.), Canon, 56–70

TULLY, J., ED., Philosophy in an Age of Pluralism. The Philosophy of Charles Taylor in Question, Cambridge: Cambridge University Press 1994

ULRICH, E., The Canonical Process, Textual Criticism, and Latter Stages in the Composition of the Bible, in: FISHBANE AND TOV (EDS.), Studies, 267–91

URBACH, E. E., The Sages. Their Concepts and Beliefs, trans. I. Abrahams; Jerusalem: Magnes Press 1975

UTZSCHNEIDER, H., Künder oder Schreiber? Eine These zum Problem der "Schriftprophetie" auf Grund von Maleachi 1,6–2,9 (BEAT 19), Frankfurt a. M. / Bern / New York / Paris: Peter Lang 1989

VAN SETERS, J., Prologue to History. The Yahwist as Historian in Genesis, Louisville: Westminster John Knox; Zurich: Theologischer Verlag 1992

VANDERKAM, J. C., Authoritative Literature in the Dead Sea Scrolls, DSD 5 (1998) 382–402

VASHOLZ, R. I., The Old Testament Canon in the Old Testament Church. The Internal Rationale for Old Testament Canonicity (ANETS 7), Lewiston / Queenston / Lampete: Edwin Mellon 1990

VEIJOLA, T., Die ewige Dynastie. David und die Entstehung seiner Dynastie nach der deuteronomistischen Darstellung (AASF.B 193), Helsinki: Suomalainen Tiedeakatemia 1975

— Das Königtum in der Beurteilung der deuteronomistischen Historiographie. Eine redaktionsgeschichtliche Untersuchung (AASF.B 198), Helsinki: Suomalainen Tiedeakatemia 1977

VELTRI, G., Zur traditionsgeschichtlichen Entwicklung des Bewußtseins von einem Kanon: die Yavneh–Frage, JSJ 21 (1990) 210–26

VERHOEF, P. A., The Books of Haggai and Malachi (NIC), Grand Rapids: Eerdmans 1987

VORLÄNDER, H., Die Entstehungszeit des jehowistischen Geschichtswerkes (EHS.T 23.109), Frankfurt a. M. / Bern / Las Vegas: Peter Lang 1978

WALLIS, G., ED., Otto–Eißfeldt–Ehrung 1987. Wissenschaftliche Konferenz der Martin–Luther–Universität, Halle–Wittenberg 30.9–1.10.1987 (Wissenschaftliche Beiträge 1988/36 [A 108]), Halle (Salle): Martin–Luther–Universität Halle–Wittenberg 1988

WALTKE, B. K., AND M. P. O'CONNOR, EDS., An Introduction to Biblical Hebrew Syntax, Winona Lake, IN: Eisenbrauns 1990

WANKE, G., Die Entstehung des Alten Testaments als Kanon, in: KRAUSE AND MÜLLER (EDS.), TRE VI:1–8

WATSON, F., Text, Church and World. Biblical Interpretation in Theological Perspective, Grand Rapids: Eerdmans 1994

WEBER, M., Ancient Judaism, trans. and ed. H. H. Gerth and D. Martindale; New York: Free Press 1952 = Das antike Judentum, in: idem, Aufsätze, III

— Gesammelte Aufsätze zur Religionssoziologie (UTB 1488–90; 3 vols.), ed. Marianne Weber; Tübingen: Mohr Siebeck 1921, ⁸1988

— Wirtschaft und Gesellschaft. Grundriss der verstehenden Soziologie, ed. J. Winckelmann; Tübingen: Mohr Siebeck ⁴1956

— The Theory of Social and Economic Organization, trans. A. M. Henderson and T. Parsons; New York: Free Press 1947 = Soziologische Kategorienlehre, in: idem, Wirtschaft, Part I, I:1–180

— The Sociology of Religion, trans. E. Fischoff; Boston: Beacon Press 1964 = Typen religiöser Vergemeinschaftung (Religionssoziologie), in: idem, Wirtschaft, Part II, Chapter V, I:245–381

WEINFELD, M., Deuteronomy and the Deuteronomistic School, Oxford: Clarendon 1972.

— Judges 1:1–2:5: The Conquest Under the Leadership of the House of Judah, in: AULD (ED.), Understanding, 388–400

WEIPPERT, H., Die Prosareden des Jeremiabuches (BZAW 132), Berlin / New York: de Gruyter 1973

WEIS, R. D. AND D. M. CARR, EDS., A Gift of God in Due Season. Essays on Scripture and Community (FS J. A. Sanders; JSOT.S 225), Sheffield: Sheffield Academic Press 1996

WELLHAUSEN, J., Prolegomena to the History of Ancient Israel, trans. J. S. Black and A. Menzies; repr. Gloucester, MA: Peter Smith 1973. [The first edition of WELLHAUSEN's work appeared as vol. I of his Prolegomena zur Geschichte Israels, Berlin: Reimer 1878, but vol. II never appeared; cf. ²1883.]

— Israel, in: Encyclopaedia Britannica (EBrit), Edinburgh: A. and C. Black ⁹1881, repr. as an appendix in: idem, Prolegomena, 396–431 = Abriss der Geschichte Israels and Juda's, in: idem, Skizzen und Vorarbeiten (5 vols.), Berlin: Reimer 1884, I:5–102

WEST, J. K., Introduction to the Old Testament, New York: Macmillan; London: Collier Macmillan ²1981

WESTERHOLM, S., Torah, nomos, and law: A question of "meaning," SR 15 (1986) 327–36

WESTERMANN, C., Elements of an Old Testament Theology, trans. D. W. Stott; Atlanta: John Knox 1982 = Theologie des Alten Testaments in Grundzügen (GAT 6), Göttingen: Vandenhoeck & Ruprecht 1978, ²1985

WETTE, W. M. L. DE, A Critical and Historical Introduction to the Canonical Scriptures of the Old Testament (2 vols.), trans. and ed. T. Parker; Boston: Little Brown ²1858 = idem, Lehrbuch der historisch-kritischen Einleitung in die Bibel Alten und Neuen Testaments, I: Einleitung in das Alte Testament, Berlin: Reimer 1817, ²1822

WIEBE, J., Form and Setting of the Song of Moses, SBTh 17 (1989) 119–63

WILDBERGER, H., "Glauben": Erwägungen zu האמין, in: Hebräische Wortforschung (FS W. Baumgartner; VT.S 16), Leiden: Brill 1967, 372–86

WILDEBOER, G., Het Ontstaan van den Kanon des Ouden Verbonds, Groningen: Wolters 1889 = idem, Die Entstehung des Alttestamentlichen Kanons, Gotha: Perthes 1891
— Die Sprüche (KHC 15), Freiburg i. B.: Mohr 1897
WILLI, T., Die Chronik als Auslegung: Untersuchungen zur literarischen Gestaltung der historischen Überlieferung Israels (FRLANT 106), Göttingen: Vandenhoeck & Ruprecht 1972
— Thora in den biblischen Chronikbüchern, Jud 36 (1980) 102–25; 48–51
WILLIAMSON, H. G. M., 1 and 2 Chronicles (NCBC), Grand Rapids: Eerdmans 1982
— Ezra and Nehemiah (OTGu), Sheffield: JSOT Press for the Society for Old Testament Study 1987
— History, in: CARSON AND WILLIAMSON (EDS.), Scripture, 25–38
WILSON, R. R., Prophecy and Society in Ancient Israel, Philadelphia: Fortress 1980
— The Former Prophets: Reading the Books of Kings, in: MAYS, PETERSEN AND RICHARDS (EDS.), Interpretation, 83–96
WOLFF, H. W., The Kerygma of the Deuteronomic Historical Work (trans. F. C. Prussner), in: BRUEGGEMANN AND WOLFF (EDS.), Vitality, 83–100 = Das Kerygma des deuteronomistischen Geschichtswerks, ZAW 73 (1961) 171–86 = in: idem, Studien, 308–24
— Gesammelte Studien zum Alten Testament (TB 22), Munich: Chr. Kaiser 1964
— ED., Probleme biblischer Theologie (FS G. von Rad), Munich: Chr. Kaiser 1971
WOLTER, H., ED., Testimonium Veritati (FS W. Kempf), Frankfurt a. M.: Knecht 1971
WOUDE, A. S. VAN DER, Haggai, Maleachi (De prediking van het Oude Testament), Nijkerk: Callenbach 1982
— ED., Prophets, Worship and Theodicy. Studies in Prophetism, Biblical Theology and Structural and Rhetorical Analysis and on the Place of Music in Worship (OTS 23), Leiden: Brill 1984
WRIGHT, D. P., D. N. FREEDMAN AND A. HURVITZ, EDS., Pomegranates and Golden Bells. Studies in Biblical, Jewish, and Near Eastern Ritual, Law, and Literature (FS J. Milgrom), Winona Lake, IN: Eisenbrauns 1995
WRIGHT, G. E., The God Who Acts. Biblical Theology as Recital (SBT 8), London: SCM Press 1952
— The Lawsuit of God: A Form-Critical Study of Deut 32, in: ANDERSON AND HARRELSON (EDS.), Heritage, 26–67
— The Old Testament and Theology, New York: Harper & Row 1969
WÜRTHWEIN, E., Die Bücher der Könige (ATD 11; 2 vols.), Göttingen: Vandenhoeck & Ruprecht 1977, 1984

YOUNG, E. J., My Servants, the Prophets, Grand Rapids: Eerdmans 1952
— The Authority of the Old Testament, in: STONEHOUSE AND WOOLEY (EDS.), Word, 53–87
— An Introduction to the Old Testament, Grand Rapids: Eerdmans 1954
YOUNG, F. M., The Making of Creeds, London: SCM Press; Philadelphia: Trinity 1991

ZEITLIN, S., An Historical Study of the Canonization of the Hebrew Scriptures, PAAJR 3 (1931–32) 121–58 = in: idem, Studies, 1–42 = in: LEIMAN (ED.), Canon, 164–201
— Studies in the Early History of Judaism, New York: KTAV 1974
ZENGER, E., Das Erste Testament. Die jüdische Bibel und die Christen, Düsseldorf: Patmos 1991
— Der Pentateuch als Tora und als Kanon, in: ZENGER (ED.), Tora, 5–34
— ED., Die Tora als Kanon für Juden und Christen (HBS 10), Freiburg: Herder 1996

ZENGER, E., ET AL., Einleitung in das Alte Testament (KStTh 1.1), Stuttgart / Berlin / Cologne: Kohlhammer ³1988

ZIMMERLI, W., Zur Struktur der alttestamentlichen Weisheit, ZAW 51 [N. F. 10] (1933) 177–204 = Concerning the Structure of Old Testament Wisdom (trans. B. W. Kovacs), in: J. L. CRENSHAW (ED.), Studies, 175–99

— Das Wort des göttlichen Selbsterweises (Erweiswort), eine prophetische Gattung (orig. 1957), in: idem, Offenbarung, 120–32 = The Word of Divine Self–Manifestation (Proof–saying): A Prophetic Genre, in: idem, Yahweh, 99–110

— Das Gesetz im Alten Testament, ThLZ 85 (1960) 481–98 = in: idem, Offenbarung, 249–76

— Ort und Grenze der Weisheit im Rahmen der alttestamentlichen Theologie (orig. 1962), in: idem, Offenbarung, 300–15 = The Place and Limit of the Wisdom in the Framework of the Old Testament Theology, SJTh 17 (1964) 146–158 = in: CRENSHAW(ED.), Studies, 314–26

— Wort Gottes, I: Im AT, in: GALLING (ED.), RGG³ VI:1809–12

— Gottes Offenbarung. Gesammelte Aufsätze zum Alten Testament (TB 19), Munich: Chr. Kaiser 1963

— The Law and the Prophets. A Study of the Meaning of the Old Testament, trans. R. E. Clements; Oxford: Blackwell; New York: Harper & Row 1965 = Das Gesetz und die Propheten. Zum Verständnis des Alten Testaments, Göttingen: Vandenhoeck & Ruprecht 1963

— Rezension, Gerhard von Rad, Theologie des Alten Testaments, VT 13 (1963) 100–11

— Alttestamentliche Traditionsgeschichte und Theologie, in: WOLFF (ED.), Probleme, 632–47 = in: idem, Studien II:9–26

— Erwägungen zur Gestalt einer Alttestamentlichen Theologie, ThLZ 98 (1973) 81–98 = in: idem, Studien, II:27–54

— Studien zur alttestamentlichen Theologie und Prophetie. Gesammelte Aufsätze II (TB 51), Munich: Chr. Kaiser 1974

— Der "Prophet" im Pentateuch, in: BRAULIK (ED.), Studien, 197–211

— Die kritische Infragestellung der Tradition durch die Prophetie, in: STECK (ED.), Tradition, 57–86 = Prophetic Proclamation and Reinterpretation (trans. D. A. Knight), in: KNIGHT (ED.), Tradition, 69–100

— The History of Israelite Religion, in: G. W. ANDERSON (ED.), Tradition, 351–84

— I Am Yahweh, trans. D. W. Stott; ed. W. Brueggemann; Atlanta: John Knox 1982 [for a precise publication history of this volume's contents, see Bibliographie Walther Zimmerli: Fortsetzung von 1976 an, comp. J. MOTTE, ThLZ 118 (1993) 1095–98]

ZOBEL, H.–J., Otto Eißfeldt als Theologe. Zum Verhältnis von "Israelitisch-jüdischer Religionsgeschichte" und "Alttestamentlicher Theologie" im Lebenswerk Otto Eißfeldts, in: WALLIS (ED.), Ehrung, 19–44

ZOBEL, K., Prophetie und Deuteronomium. Die Rezeption prophetischer Theologie durch das Deuteronomium (BZAW 199), Berlin / New York: de Gruyter 1992

Additional Bibliography on
Old Testament Canon Formation

2000–2020

ABERNETHY, A. T., ED., Interpreting the Old Testament Theologically: Essays in Honor of Willem A. VanGemeren, Grand Rapids: Zondervan 2018

ACHENBACH, R., The Pentateuch, the Prophets, and the Torah in the Fifth and Fourth Centuries B.C.E., in: LIPSCHITS, KNOPPERS, AND ALBERTZ (EDS.), Judah and the Judeans, 253–85

— "A Prophet like Moses" (Deuteronomy 18:15) — "No Prophet like Moses" (Deuteronomy 34:10): Some Observations on the Relation between the Pentateuch and the Latter Prophets, in: DOZEMAN, SCHMID, AND SWARTZ (EDS.), Pentateuch, 435–58

ACHENBACH, R., M. ARNETH, AND E. OTTO, EDS., Tora in der Hebräischen Bibel: Studien zur Redaktionsgeschichte und synchronen Logik diachroner Transformationen (BZABR 7), Wiesbaden: Harrassowitz 2007

AICHELE, G., The Control of Biblical Meaning: Canon as Semiotic Mechanism, Harrisburg, PA: Trinity 2001

AITKEN, J. K., K. J. DELL, AND B. A. MASTIN, EDS., On Stone and Scroll: Essays in Honour of Graham Ivor Davies (BZAW 420), Berlin: de Gruyter 2010

ALEXANDER, P. S., The Bible in Qumran and Early Judaism, in: MAYES (ED.), Text in Context, 35–62

— The Formation of the Biblical Canon in Rabbinic Judaism, in: ALEXANDER AND KAESTLI (EDS.), Canon of Scripture, 57–80

— Textual Authority and the Problem of the Biblical Canon at Qumran, in: FELDMAN, CIOATĂ, AND HEMPEL (EDS.), Is There a Text, 42–68

ALEXANDER, P. S., AND J.-D. KAESTLI, EDS., The Canon of Scripture in Jewish and Christian Tradition / Le canon des Écritures dans les traditions juive et chrétienne (Publications de l'Institut romand des sciences bibliques 4), Lausanne: Éditions du Zèbre 2007

ALKIER, S., AND R. B. HAYS, EDS., Kanon und Intertextualität (Kleine Schriften des Fachbereichs Evangelische Theologie der Goethe-Universität Frankfurt 1), Frankfurt: Lembeck 2010

ALLERT, C. D., A High View of Scripture? The Authority of the Bible and the Formation of the New Testament Canon, Grand Rapids: Baker Academic 2007

ALTER, R., Canon and Canonicity: Modern Writing and the Authority of Scripture, New Haven: Yale University Press 2000

AMIT, Y., The Role of Prophecy and Prophets in the Book of Chronicles, in: FLOYD AND HAAK (EDS.), Prophets, 80–101

ANDERSON, G. A., R. A. CLEMENTS, AND D. SATRAN, EDS., New Approaches to the Study of Biblical Interpretation in Judaism of the Second Temple Period and in Early Christianity (STDJ 106), Leiden: Brill 2013

ARMSTRONG, K., The Bible: A Biography (Books that Change the World Series), New York: Atlantic Monthly Press 2007

ARNETH, M., Zur "Kanonisierung" der Hebräischen Bibel, VF 60 (2015) 42–51

ASSMANN, J., Five Stages on the Road to Canon: Tradition and Written Culture in Ancient Israel and Early Judaism, in: ASSMANN AND LIVINGSTONE (EDS.), Religion and Cultural Memory, 63–80

— Cultural Memory and Early Civilization: Writing, Remembrance, and Political Imagination, New York: Cambridge University Press 2011

ASSMANN, J., AND R. LIVINGSTONE, EDS., Religion and Cultural Memory: Ten Studies (Cultural Memory in the Present), Stanford: Stanford University Press 2006

AUER, M., AND U. MÜLLER, EDS., Kanon und Text in interkulturellen Perspektiven: "andere Texte anders lesen" (Stuttgarter Arbeiten zur Germanistik 401), Stuttgart: Hans-Dieter Heinz 2001

AUWERS, J.-M., AND H. J. DE JONGE, EDS., The Biblical Canons (BETL 163), Louvain: Peeters 2003

BALENTINE, S. E., ED., The Oxford Encyclopedia of Bible and Theology, Oxford: Oxford University Press 2015

BALL, E., ED., In Search of True Wisdom: Essays in Old Testament Interpretation in Honour of Ronald E. Clements (JSOTSup 300), Sheffield: Sheffield Academic 2000

BALLHORN, E., AND G. STEINS, EDS., Der Bibelkanon in der Bibelauslegung Methodenreflexionen und Beispielexegesen, Stuttgart: Kohlhammer 2007

BARBAGLIA, S., Il testo biblico in tensione tra fissità canonica e mobilità storica: introduzione, RStB 13 (2001) 5–8

BARTHEL, J., Die kanonhermeneutische Debatte seit Gerhard von Rad: Anmerkungen zu neueren Entwürfen, in: JANOWSKI (ED.), Kanonhermeneutik, 1–26

BARTHOLOMEW, C. G., ET AL., EDS., Canon and Biblical Interpretation (SHS 7), Grand Rapids: Zondervan 2006

BARTHOLOMEW, C. G., AND D. J. H. BELDMAN, EDS., Hearing the Old Testament: Listening for God's Address, Grand Rapids: Eerdmans 2012

BARTHOLOMEW, C. G., AND H. A. THOMAS, EDS., A Manifesto for Theological Interpretation, Grand Rapids: Baker Academic 2016

BARTON, J., Reading the Old Testament: Method in Biblical Study, Louisville: Westminster John Knox ²1996

— Canon and Old Testament Interpretation, in: BALL (ED.), True Wisdom, 37–53

— Canons of the Old Testament, in: MAYES (ED.), Text in Context, 200–22

— Canonical Approaches Ancient and Modern, in: AUWERS AND DE JONGE (EDS.), The Biblical Canons, 199–209

— The Old Testament: Canon, Literature and Theology; Collected Essays of John Barton (SOTSMS), Burlington, VT: Ashgate 2007

— Oracles of God: Perceptions of Ancient Prophecy in Israel after the Exile, Oxford: Oxford University Press ²2007

— What Is a Book? Modern Exegesis and the Literary Conventions of Ancient Israel, in: idem, The Old Testament, 137–47

— The Old Testament Canons, in: PAGET AND SCHAPER (EDS.), New Cambridge History of the Bible, I:145–64

BARTON, J., AND M. WOLTER, EDS., Die Einheit der Schrift und die Vielfalt des Kanons / The Unity of Scripture and the Diversity of the Canon (BZNW 118), Berlin: de Gruyter 2003

BAUMGARTEN, A., Sacred Scriptures Defile the Hands, JJS 62 (2016) 46–67

BAUSPIESS, M., C. LANDMESSER, AND F. PORTENHAUSER, EDS., Theologie und Wirklichkeit: Diskussionen der Bultmann-Schule (Theologie Interdisciplinär 12), Neukirchen-Vluyn: Neukirchener 2011

BECKER, E.-M., AND S. SCHOLZ, EDS., Kanon in Konstruktion und Dekonstruction: Kanonisierungsprozesse religiöser Texte von der Antike bis zur Gegenwart; Ein Handbuch, Berlin: de Gruyter 2012

BECKER, M., Grenzziehungen des Kanons im frühen Judentum und die Neuschrift der Bibel nach 4. Buch Ezra, in: BECKER AND FREY (EDS.), Qumran, 195–253

BECKER, M., AND J. FREY, EDS., Qumran und der biblische Kanon (BTS 92), Neukirchen-Vluyn: Neukirchener Verlag 2009

BECKER, U., Die Wiederentdeckung des Prophetenbuches: Tendenzen und Aufgaben der gegenwärtigen Prophetenforschung, BTZ 21 (2004) 30–60

— Abschied von der Geschichte? Bemerkungen zu einem aktuellen Grundproblem der alttestamentlichen Hemeneutik, in: BERLEJUNG AND HECKL (EDS.), Ex Oriente Lux, 592–604

BEHRENS, A., Kanon. Das ganze Alte Testament ist mehr als die Summe seiner Teile, KD 53 (2007) 274–97

BEN ZVI, E., The Prophetic Book: A Key Form of Prophetic Literature, in: BEN ZVI AND SWEENEY (EDS.), Changing Face, 276–97

— Beginning to Address the Question: Why Were the Prophetic Books Produced and "Consumed" in Ancient Israel? in: MÜLLER, THOMPSON, AND LEMCHE (EDS.), Historie og konstruktion, 30–41

— The Concept of Prophetic Books and Its Historical Setting, in: EDLEMAN AND BEN ZVI (EDS.), Production of Prophecy, 102–28

— Toward an Integrative Study of the Production of Authoritative Books in Ancient Israel, in: EDLEMAN AND BEN ZVI (EDS.), Production of Prophecy, 26–43

— Observations on Lines of Thought Concerning the Concepts of Prophecy and Prophets in Yehud, with an Emphasis on Deuteronomy–2 Kings and Chronicles, in: BRENNER AND POLAK (EDS.), Words, 1–19

— Remembering the Prophets through the Reading and Rereading of a Collection of Prophetic Books in Yehud: Methodological Considerations and Explorations, in: BEN ZVI AND LEVIN (EDS.), Remembering and Forgetting, 17–44

— Prophetic Memories in the Deuteronomistic Historical and the Prophetic Collections of Books, in: JACOBS AND PERSON (EDS.), Israelite Prophecy, 75–102

BEN ZVI, E., AND D. V. EDELMAN, EDS., What Was Authoritative for Chronicles? Winona Lake, IN: Eisenbrauns 2011

BEN ZVI, E., AND C. LEVIN, EDS., Remembering and Forgetting in Early Second Temple Judaism (FAT 85), Tübingen: Mohr Siebeck 2012

BEN ZVI, E., AND M. A. SWEENEY, EDS., The Changing Face of Form Criticism for the Twenty-First Century, Grand Rapids: Eerdmans 2003

BERGES, U., Kollektive Autorschaft im Alten Testament, in: MEIER AND WAGNER-EGELHAAF (EDS.), Autorschaft, 29–39

BERLEJUNG, A., AND R. HECKL, EDS., Ex Oriente Lux: Studien zur Theologie des Alten Testaments. (FS R. Lux; ABG 39), Leipzig: Evangelische Verlagsanstalt 2012

BERQUIST, J. L., Postcolonial Imperial Motives for Canonization, in: SUGIRTHARAJAH (ED.), Postcolonial Biblical Reader, 78–95

BERTHELOT, K., 4QMMT et la question du canon de la Bible hébraïque, in: GARCÍA MARTÍNEZ, STUEDEL, AND TIGCHELAAR (EDS.), From 4QMMT to Resurrection, 1–14

BIRD, M. F., AND M. W. PAHL, EDS., The Sacred Text: Excavating the Texts, Exploring the Interpretations, and Engaging the Theologies of the Christian Scriptures (Gorgias Précis Portfolios 7), Piscataway, NJ: Gorgias 2010

BLANCHARD, Y.-M., Le texte dans son corpus. Enjeux herméneutiques du canon scripturaire, in: NIEUVIARTS AND DEBERGÉ (EDS.), Les nouvelles voies, 295–319

BLENKINSOPP, J., Was the Pentateuch the Constitution of the Jewish Ethnos in the Persian Period? in: WATTS (ED.), Persia and Torah, 41–62 = in: idem, Essays on Judaism, 101–18

— Treasures Old and New: Essays in the Theology of the Pentateuch, Grand Rapids: Eerdmans 2004

— ED., Essays on Judaism in the Pre-Hellenistic Period (BZAW 495), Berlin: de Gruyter 2017

BOCCACCINI, G., Is Biblical Literature Still a Useful Term in Scholarship? in: FINSTERBUSCH AND LANGE (EDS.), What Is Bible? 41–52

BOCKMUEHL, M., AND A. J. TORRANCE, EDS., Scripture's Doctrines and Theology's Bible: How the New Testament Shapes Christian Dogmatics, Grand Rapids: Baker Academic 2008

BOGAERT, P.-M., Les frontières du canon de l'Ancien Testament dans l'Occident latin, in: GOUNELLE AND JOOSTEN (EDS.), La Bible, 41–95

BÖHLER, D., Der Kanon als hermeneutische Vorgabe biblischer Theologie. Über aktuelle Methodendiskussionen in der Bibelwissenschaft, TP 77 (2002) 161–78

BOKEDAL, T., The Rule of Faith: Tracing Its Origins, JTI 7 (2013) 233–55

— The Formation and Significance of the Christian Biblical Canon: A Study in Text, Ritual and Interpretation, New York: Bloomsbury 2014

BOMBERGER, J. H. A., AND J. J. HERZOG, EDS., The Protestant Theological and Ecclesiastical Encyclopedia, Philadelphia: Lindsay & Blakiston 1860

BORCHARDT, F., Prologue of Sirach (Ben Sira) and the Question of Canon, in: CHARLESWORTH AND MCDONALD (EDS.), Jewish and Christian Scriptures, 64–71

BOSSHARD-NEPUSTIL, E., Schriftwerdung der Hebräischen Bibel. Thematisierungen der Schriftlichkeit biblischer Texte im Rahmen ihrer Literargeschichte (ATANT 106), Zurich: Theologischer Verlag 2015

BOWLEY, J. E., AND J. C. REEVES, Rethinking the Concept of "Bible": Some Theses and Proposals, Hen 25 (2003) 3–18

BRAKKE, D., Canon Formation and Social Conflict in Fourth-Century Egypt: Athanasius of Alexandria's Thirty-Ninth Festal Letter, HTR 87 (1994) 395–419

BRAKKE, D., A.-C. JACOBSEN, AND J. ULRICH, EDS., Invention, Rewriting, Usurpation: Discursive Fights over Religious Traditions in Antiquity (ECCA 11), Frankfurt: Lang 2012

BRANDT, P., Endgestalten des Kanons: das Arrangement der Schriften Israels in der jüdischen und christlichen Bibel (BBB 131), Berlin: Philo 2001

BREMMER, J., From Holy Books to Holy Bible, in: POPOVIĆ (ED.), Authoritative Scriptures, 327–60

BRENNER, A., AND F. H. POLAK, EDS., Words, Ideas, Worlds: Biblical Essays in Honour of Yairah Amit (HBM 40), Sheffield: Sheffield Phoenix 2012

BRETT, M. G., Canonical Criticism and Old Testament Theology, in: MAYES (ED.), Text in Context, 63–85

BROOKE, G. J., Prophets and Prophecy in the Qumran Scrolls and the New Testament, in: CLEMENTS AND SCHWARTZ (EDS.), Text, Thought and Practice, 31–48

— Between Authority and Canon: The Significance of Reworking the Bible for Understanding the Canonical Process, in: CHAZON, DIMANT, AND CLEMENTS (EDS.), Reworking the Bible, 85–104

— The Qumran Scrolls and the Demise of the Distinction between Higher and Lower Criticism, in: CAMPBELL, LYONS, AND PIETERSEN (EDS.), New Directions, 25–42

— "Canon" in the Light of the Qumran Scrolls, in: Alexander and J.-D. Kaestli (eds.), Canon of Scripture, 81–98

Brooke, G. J., et al., eds., The Scrolls and the Biblical Tradition: Proceedings of the Seventh Meeting of the IOQS in Helsinki (STDJ 103), Leiden: Brill 2012

Brueggeman, W., Canon fire: The Bible as Scripture, ChrCent 118 (2001) 22–26

Bruk, A. A., The Ethopian Orthodox Tewahedo Church Canon of the Scriptures: Neither Open nor Closed, BT 67 (2016) 202–22

Buckley, J. J., F. C. Bauerschmidt, and T. Pomplun, eds., The Blackwell Companion to Catholicism, Malden, MA: Oxford University Press 2007

Buell, D. A., Canons Unbound, in: Fiorenza (ed.), Feminist Biblical Studies, 293–306

Bultmann, C., C.-P. März, and V. N. Makrides, eds., Heilige Schriften: Urprung, Geltung und Gebrauch, Munster: Aschendorff 2005

Buntfuss, M., and M. Fritz, eds., Fremde unter einem Dach? Die theologischen Fächerkulturen in enzyklopädischer Perspektive (Theologische Bibliothek Töpelmann 163), Berlin: de Gruyter 2014

Burnet, R., Le canon des Écritures: vers la fin d'une fausse question? Comm 37 (2012) 5–16

Campbell, J. G., 4QMMT^d and the Tripartite Canon, JJS 51 (2000) 181–90

— Josephus' Twenty-Two Book Canon and the Qumran Scrolls, in: Brooke, et al. (eds.), Scrolls and the Biblical Tradition, 19–46

Campbell, J. G., W. J. Lyons, and L. K. Pietersen, eds., New Directions in Qumran Studies: Proceedings of the Bristol Colloquium on the Dead Sea Scrolls, 8–10 September 2003 (Library of Second Temple Studies 52), New York: T & T Clark 2005

Carr, D. M., Writing on the Tablet of the Heart: Origins of Scripture and Literature, Oxford: Oxford University Press 2009

— The Formation of the Hebrew Bible: A New Reconstruction, New York: Oxford University Press 2011

Carson, D. A., ed., The Enduring Authority of the Christian Scriptures, Grand Rapids: Eerdmans 2016

Caulley, T. S., and H. Lichtenberger, eds., Die Septuaginta und das frühe Christentum (WUNT 277), Tübingen: Mohr Siebeck 2011

Chapman, S. B., "The Law and the Words" as a Canonical Formula within the Old Testament, in: Evans (ed.), Interpretation of Scripture, 26–74

— A Canonical Approach to Old Testament Theology? Deuteronomy 34:10-12 and Malachi 3:22–24 as Programmatic Conclusions, HBT 25 (2003) 121–45

— How the Biblical Canon Began: Working Models and Open Questions, in: Finkelberg and Stroumsa (eds.), Homer, 29–51

— The Old Testament and Its Authority for the Christian Church, ExAud 19 (2003) 125–48

— Reclaiming Inspiration for the Bible, in: Bartholomew, et al. (eds.), Canon and Biblical Interpretation, 167–206

— What Are We Reading? Canonicity and the Old Testament, WW 29 (2009) 334–47

— The Canon Debate: What It Is and Why It Matters, JTI 4 (2010) 273–94

— Canon: Old Testament, in: Coogan (ed.), Oxford Encyclopedia, 1:96–109

— Second Temple Jewish Hermeneutics: How Canon Is Not an Anachronism, in: Brakke, Jacobsen, and Ulrich (eds.), Invention, 281–96

— Brevard Childs as a Historical Critic: Divine Concession and the Unity of the Canon, in: Seitz and Richards (eds.), Bible as Christian Scripture, 63–83

— Modernity's Canonical Crisis: Historiography and Theology in Collision, in: Sæbø (ed.), Hebrew Bible/Old Testament, III/1:651–87

— The Old Testament and the Church after Christendom, JTI 9 (2015) 159–83

— "A Threefold Cord Is Not Quickly Broken": Interpretation by Canonical Division in Early Judaism and Christianity, in: Steinberg and Stone (eds.), The Shape of the Writings, 281–309

— Collections, Canons, and Communities, in: Chapman and Sweeney (eds.), Cambridge Companion, 28–54

— The How as Well as the What: Canonical Formatting and Theological Interpretation. in: Collett, et al. (eds.), Identity of Israel's God

Chapman, S. B., and M. A. Sweeney, eds., The Cambridge Companion to the Hebrew Bible/Old Testament, New York: Cambridge University Press 2016

Charlesworth, J. H., ed., The Bible and the Dead Sea Scrolls, Waco, TX: Baylor University Press 2006

Charlesworth, J. H., and L. M. McDonald, eds., Jewish and Christian Scriptures: The Function of "Canonical" and "Non-Canonical" Religious Texts (Jewish and Christian Texts in Contexts and Related Studies 7), London: T & T Clark 2010

Charlier, R., and G. Lottes, eds., Kanonbildung: Protagonisten und Prozesse der Herstellung kultureller Identität (Aufklärung und Moderne 20), Hannover: Wehrhahn 2009

Chazon, E. G., D. Dimant, and R. A. Clements, eds., Reworking the Bible: Apocryphal and Related Texts at Qumran (STDJ 58), Leiden: Brill 2005

Childs, B. S., Critique of Recent Inter-textual Canonical Interpretation, ZAW 115 (2003) 173–84

— The Canon in Recent Biblical Studies: Reflections on an Era, ProEccl 14 (2005) 26–45 = in: Bartholomew, et al. (eds.), Canon and Biblical Interpretation, 33–57

— Speech-Act Theory and Biblical Interpretation, SJT 58 (2005) 375–92

Choi, J. H., Traditions at Odds: The Reception of the Pentateuch in Biblical and Second Temple Literature (LHBOTS 518), New York: T & T Clark 2010

Clements, R., and D. R. Schwartz, eds., Text, Thought, and Practice in Qumran and Early Christianity: Proceedings of the Ninth International Symposium of the Orion

Center for the Study of the Dead Sea Scrolls and Associated Literature, Jointly Sponsored by the Hebrew University Center for the Study of Christianity, 11–13 January, 2004 (STDJ 84), Leiden: Brill 2009

COHEN, N. G., The Prophetic Books in Alexandria: The Evidence from Philo Judaeus, in: FLOYD AND HAAK (EDS.), Prophets, 166–93

— Philo's Scriptures: Citations from the Prophets and Writings; Evidence for a Haftarah Cycle in Second Temple Judaism (JSJSup 123), Leiden: Brill 2007

COLE, G. A., Why a Book? Why This Book? Why the Particular Order within This Book? Some Theological Reflections on the Canon, in: CARSON (ED.), The Enduring Authority, 456–76

COLLETT, D., M. ELLIOTT, M. GIGNILLIAT, AND E. RADNER, EDS., The Identity of Israel's God in Christian Scripture, Atlanta: SBL Press forthcoming

COLLINS, J. J., The Literature of the Second Temple Period, in: GOODMAN (ED.), Oxford Handbook, 53–78

— Canon, Canonization, in: COLLINS AND HARLOW (EDS.), Eerdmans Dictionary, 460–63

— The Transformation of the Torah in Second Temple Judaism, JSJ 43 (2012) 455–74

— The Penumbra of the Canon: What Do the Deuterocanonical Books Represent? in: XERAVITS, ZSENGELLÉR, AND SZABÓ (EDS.), Canonicity, 1–17

— Uses of Torah in the Second Temple Period, in: LIM, WITH AKIYAMA (EDS.), When Texts are Canonized, 44–62

COLLINS, J. J., AND D. C. HARLOW, EDS., The Eerdmans Dictionary of Early Judaism, Grand Rapids: Eerdmans 2010

COLLINS, N. L., The Library in Alexandria and the Bible in Greek (VTSup 82), Leiden: Brill 2000

CONRAD, E., Reading the Latter Prophets: Towards a New Canonical Criticism (JSOT-Sup 376), London: T & T Clark 2003

COOGAN, M. D., ED., The Oxford Encyclopedia of the Books of the Bible (Volume I), New York: Oxford University Press 2011

COOK, L. S., On the Question of the "Cessation of Prophecy" in Ancient Judaism (TSAJ 145), Tübingen: Mohr Siebeck 2011

CRAWFORD, S. W., Rewriting Scripture in Second Temple Times (SDSSRL), Grand Rapids: Eerdmans 2008

CROSS, F. M., The Biblical Scrolls from Qumran and the Canonical Text, in: CHARLES-WORTH (ED.), The Bible and the Dead Sea Scrolls, 67–75

CUNNINGHAM, V., The Best Stories in the Best Order? Canons, Apocryphas and (Post) Modern Reading, Literature and Theology 14 (2000) 69–80

DARSHAN, G., The Twenty-Four Books of the Hebrew Bible and Alexandrian Scribal Methods, in: NIEHOFF (ED.), Homer and the Bible, 221–44

DAVIAU, P. M. M., J. W. WEVERS, AND M. WEIGL, EDS., The World of the Aramaeans I: Biblical Studies in Honour of Paul-Eugène Dion (JSOTSup 324), Sheffield: Sheffield Academic Press 2001

DÁVID, N., ET AL., EDS., The Hebrew Bible in Light of the Dead Sea Scrolls (FRLANT 239), Göttingen: Vandenhoeck & Ruprecht 2012

DAVIES, P. R., Loose Canons: Reflections on the Formation of the Hebrew Bible, JHebS 1 (1996–7), www.jhsonline.org/Articles/article5.pdf

— Judaism and the Hebrew Scriptures, in: NEUSNER AND AVERY-PECK (EDS.), Blackwell Companion, 37–57

— The Hebrew Canon and the Origins of Judaism, in: DAVIES AND EDELMAN (EDS.), Historian and the Bible, 194–206

— The Dissemination of Written Texts, in: DAVIES AND RÖMER (EDS.), Writing the Bible, 35–46

DAVIES, P. R., AND D. V. EDELMAN, EDS., The Historian and the Bible: Essays in Honour of Lester L. Grabbe (LHBOTS 530), London: T & T Clark 2010

DAVIES, P. R., AND T. RÖMER, EDS., Writing the Bible: Scribes, Scribalism and Script (BibleWorld), Durham (UK): Acumen 2013

DAY, J., Review of John Barton, The Old Testament: Canon, Literature and Theology; Collected Essays of John Barton, JSOT 33 (2009) 4–5

— ED., Prophecy and Prophets in Ancient Israel: Proceedings of the Oxford Old Testament Seminar, New York: T & T Clark 2010

DEINES, R., The Term and Concept of Scripture, in: FINSTERBUSCH AND LANGE (EDS.), What Is Bible? 235–81

DE GROOTE, M., Bemerkungen zum Entstehen des Kanons in der alten Kirche, ZKG 112 (2001) 372–76

DE JONG, M. J., Biblical Prophecy — A Scribal Enterprise? The Old Testament Prophecy of Unconditional Judgement Considered as a Literary Phenomenon, VT 61 (2011) 39–70

DE JONGE, H. J., The Use of the Old Testament in Scripture Readings in Early Christian Assemblies, in: KOET, MOYISE, AND VERHEYDEN (EDS.), Scriptures of Israel, 377–92

DELL, K. J., AND P. M. JOYCE, EDS., Biblical Interpretation and Method: Essays in Honour of John Barton, Oxford: Oxford University Press 2013

DEMPSTER, S. G., From Many Texts to One: The Formation of the Hebrew Bible, in: DAVIAU, WEVERS, AND WEIGL (EDS.), World of the Aramaeans I, 19–56

— Torah, Torah, Torah: The Emergence of the Tripartite Canon, in: EVANS AND TOV (EDS.), Exploring the Origins of the Bible, 87–27

— Canons on the Right and Canons on the Left: Finding a Resolution in the Canon Debate, JETS 52 (2009) 47–77

— Review of Luc Zaman, The Bible and Canon: A Modern Historical Inquiry, JHebS 10 (2010), www.jhsonline.org/reviews/reviews_new/review445.htm

— Canon and Old Testament Interpretation, in: Bartholomew and Beldman (eds.), Hearing the Old Testament, 154–79

— The Canon and Theological Interpretation, in: Bartholomew and Thomas (eds.), Manifesto, 131–48

— The Old Testament Canon, Josephus, and Cognitive Environment, in: Carson (ed.), The Enduring Authority, 321–61

— The Tri-Partite Old Testament Canon and the Theology of the Prophetic Word, in: Abernethy (ed.), Interpreting the Old Testament, 74–94

De Troyer, K., When Did the Pentateuch Come into Existence? An Uncomfortable Perspective, in: Karrer and Kraus (eds.), Die Septuaginta, 269–86

De Troyer, K., and A. Lange, eds., with L. L. Schulte, Prophecy after the Prophets? The Contribution of the Dead Sea Scrolls to the Understanding of Biblical and Extra-Biblical Prophecy (CBET 52), Leuven: Peeters 2009

de Villiers, P. G. R., Perspectives on Canon History and Canonical Criticism in Light of Biblical Spirituality, Scriptura 91 (2006) 117–26

Dickinson, C., The Relationship of Canon and Messiah: The Convergence of Jan Assmann and Walter Benjamin on a Theory of Monotheistic Canon, Bible & Critical Theory 7.1 (2011), https://www.bibleandcriticaltheory.com/issues/vol-7-no-1-2011 -the-relationship-of-canon-and-messiah-the-convergence-of-jan-assmann-and-wal ter-benjamin-on-a-theory-of-monotheistic-canon/

— Between the Canon and the Messiah: The Structure of Faith in Contemporary Continental Thought, London: Bloomsbury 2013

— Canons and Canonicity: Late Modern Reflections on Cultural and Religious Canonical Texts, Annali di storia dell'esegesi 30 (2013) 369–92

— The "Violence" of the Canon: Revisiting Contemporary Notions of Canonical Forms, Hor 40 (2013) 1–27

Dietrich W., et al., eds., Die Entstehung des Alten Testaments (Theologische Wissenschaft), Stuttgart: Kohlhammer 2014

Dimitrov, I. Z., et al., eds., Das Alte Testament als christliche Bibel in orthodoxer und westlicher Sicht: zweite europäische orthodox-westliche Exegetenkonferenz im Rilakloster vom 8.-15. September 2001 (WUNT 174), Tübingen: Mohr Siebeck 2004

Dines, J. M., The Septuagint, London: T & T Clark 2004

DiTommaso, L., and L. Turcescu, eds., The Reception and Interpretation of the Bible in Late Antiquity. Proceedings of the Montréal Colloquium in Honour of Charles Kannengiesser, 11–13 October 2006 (Bible in Ancient Christianity 6), Leiden: Brill 2008

Dohmen, C., Biblische Auslegung: wie alte Texte neue Bedeutungen haben können, in: Hossfeld and Schwienhorst-Schönberger (eds.), Das Manna fällt, 174–91

— Der Kanon des Alten Testaments: eine westliche hermeneutische Perspektive, in: Dimitrov, et al. (eds.), Das Alte Testament, 239–303

— Kanonische Exegese, in: Ortkemper and Schuller (eds.), Berufen, 21–33

Dorival, G., L'apport des Pères de l'Église à la question de la clôture du canon de l'Ancien Testament, in: Auwers and de Jonge (eds.), The Biblical Canons, 81–110

— La formation du canon biblique de l'Ancien Testament. Position actuelle et problems, in: Norelli (ed.), Recueils normatifs, 83–112

— La formation du canon des Écritures juives. Histoire de la recherché et perspectives nouvelles, in: Gounelle and Joosten (eds.), La Bible, 9–40

Doyle, C. C., W. Mieder, and F. R. Shapiro, eds., The Dictionary of Modern Proverbs, New Haven: Yale University Press 2012

Dozeman, T. B., K. Schmid, and B. J. Schwartz, eds., The Pentateuch: International Perspectives on Current Research (FAT 78), Tübingen: Mohr Siebeck 2011

Driver, D. R., Later Childs, PTR 38 (2008) 117–29

— Brevard Childs, Biblical Theologian: For the Church's One Bible, Grand Rapids: Baker Academic rev2012

Du Toit, J. S., Textual Memory: Ancient Archives, Libraries, and the Hebrew Bible (SWBA 2/6), Sheffield: Sheffield Phoenix 2011

Edelman, D. V., and E. Ben Zvi, eds., The Production of Prophecy: Constructing Prophecy and Prophets in Yehud (BibleWorld), London: Equinox 2009

Egger-Wenzel, R., ed., Ben Sira's God: Proceedings of the International Ben Sira Conference, Durham — Ushaw College 2001 (BZAW 321), Berlin: de Gruyter 2002

Egilsson, O., K. Ólason, and S. E. Stefánsson, eds., Shaping Culture: A Festschrift in Honor of Gunnlaugur A. Jónsson on His Sixtieth Birthday, Reykjavik: Hið Íslenska Bókmenntafélag 2012

Ehrlich, L., J. Schildt, and B. Specht, eds., Die Bildung des Kanons: textuelle Faktoren — kulturelle Funktionen — ethische Praxis, Cologne: Böhlau 2007

Eisenbaum, P., The Christian Canon and the Problem of Antisemitism, in: Linafelt (ed.), Shadow of Glory, 3–17

Elgvin, T., Jewish Christian Editing of the Old Testament Pseudepigrapha, in: Skarsaune and Hvalvik (eds.), Jewish Believers in Jesus, 278–304

Evans, C. A., ed., The Interpretation of Scripture in Early Judaism and Christianity (JSPSup 33; SSEJC 7), Sheffield: Sheffield Academic 2000

— The Dead Sea Scrolls and the Canon of Scripture, in: Flint, with Kim (eds.), Bible at Qumran, 67–79

Evans, C. A., and E. Tov, eds., Exploring the Origins of the Bible: Canon Formation in Historical, Literary, and Theological Perspective (Acadia Studies in Bible and Theology), Grand Rapids: Baker Academic 2008

Evans, C. A., and H. D. Zacharias, eds., Early Christian Literature and Intertextuality. Volume I: Thematic Studies (LNTS 391; SSEJC 14), London: T & T Clark 2009

— EDS., Jewish and Christian Scripture as Artifact and Canon: Studies in Scripture in Early Judaism and Christianity (SSEJC 13; Library of Second Temple Studies 70), London: Bloomsbury 2009

EWALD, H., Über die Heiligkeit der Bibel, Jahrbücher der biblischen Wissenschaft 7 (1854–55) 68–100

FABRY, H.-J., Leiden wir an einem Tunnelblick? Überlegungen zu Textentstehung, Textrezeption und Kanonisierung von Text, in: FINSTERBUSCH AND TILLEY (EDS.), Verstehen, 18–33

FALK, D. K., The Parabiblical Texts: Strategies for Extending the Scriptures in the Dead Sea Scrolls (Companion to the Qumran Scrolls 8; Library of Second Temple Studies 63), London: T & T Clark 2007

FANTALKIN, A., AND O. TAL., The Canonization of the Pentateuch: When and Why? (Part I), ZAW 124 (2012) 1–18

— The Canonization of the Pentateuch: When and Why? (Part II), ZAW 124 (2012) 201–12

FELDMAN, A., M. CIOATĂ, AND C. HEMPEL, EDS., Is There a Text in This Cave? Studies in the Textuality of the Dead Sea Scrolls in Honour of George J. Brooke (STDJ 119), Leiden: Brill 2017

FELDMEIER, R., AND H. SPIECKERMANN, EDS., Die Bibel: Entstehung — Botschaft — Wirkung, Göttingen: Vandenhoeck & Ruprecht 2004

FIDDES, P., The Canon as Space and Place, in: BARTON AND WOLTER (EDS.), Die Einheit der Schrift, 127–50

FINKELBERG, M., AND G. G. STROUMSA, EDS., Homer, the Bible, and Beyond: Literary and Religious Canons in the Ancient World (Jerusalem Studies in Religion and Culture 2), Leiden: Brill 2003

FINN, L. G., Reflections on the Rule of Faith, in: SEITZ AND RICHARDS (EDS.), Bible as Christian Scripture, 221–42

FINSTERBUSCH, K., AND A. LANGE, EDS., What Is Bible? (CBET 67), Leuven: Peeters 2012

FINSTERBUSCH, K., AND M. TILLEY, EDS., Verstehen, was man liest? Zur Notwendigkeit historisch-kritischer Bibellektüre, Göttingen: Vandenhoeck & Ruprecht 2010

FIORENZA, E. S., ED., Feminist Biblical Studies in the Twentieth Century: Scholarship and Movement (The Bible and Women: An Encyclopedia of Exegesis and Christianity 1), Atlanta: Society of Biblical Literature 2014

FISHBANE, M., Canonical Text, Covenantal Communities, and the Pattern of Exegetical Culture: Reflections on the Past Century, in: MAYES AND SALTERS (EDS.), Covenant as Context, 135–61

FLINT, P. W., AND T. H. KIM, EDS., The Bible at Qumran: Text, Shape, and Interpretation (SDSSRL), Grand Rapids: Eerdmans 2001

FLINT, P. W., E. TOV, AND J. C. VANDERKAM, EDS., Studies in the Hebrew Bible, Qumran, and the Septuagint Presented to Eugene Ulrich (VTSup 101), Leiden: Brill 2006

FLOYD, M. H., The Production of Prophetic Books in the Early Second Temple Period, in: FLOYD AND HAAK (EDS.), Prophets, 276–97

FLOYD, M. H., AND R. D. HAAK, EDS., Prophets, Prophecy, and Prophetic Texts in Second Temple Judaism (LHBOTS 427), New York: T & T Clark, 2006

FOSTER, R. L., The Christian Canon and the Future of Biblical Theology, HBT 37 (2015) 1–12

FOX, N. S., ET AL., EDS., Mishneh Todah: Studies in Deuteronomy and Its Cultural Environment in Honor of Jeffrey H. Tigay, Winona Lake, IN; Eisenbrauns 2009

FRANKFURTER, D., Sacred Texts and Canonicity: Introduction, in: JOHNSTON (ED.), Religions of the Ancient World, 622–23

FREI, P., Persian Imperial Authorization: A Summary, in: WATTS (ED.), Persia and Torah, 5–40

FREY, J., Die uitbouing van die Bybelse kanon in antieke Judaïsme en die vroeë Christendom, HvTSt 71 (2015), https://hts.org/za/index.php/article/view/2853

GALLAGHER, E. L., Hebrew Scripture in Patristic Biblical Theory: Canon, Language, Text (VCSup 114), Leiden: Brill 2012

— The Blood from Abel to Zechariah in the History of Interpretation, NTS 60 (2014) 121–38

— The End of the Bible? The Position of Chronicles in the Canon, TynBul 65 (2014) 181–99

— The Jerusalem Temple Library and Its Implications for the Canon of Scripture, ResQ 57 (2015) 39–52

— Augustine on the Hebrew Bible, JTS 67 (2016) 97–114

GALLAGHER, E. L., AND J. D. MEADE, EDS., The Biblical Canon Lists from Early Christianity: Texts and Analysis. Oxford: Oxford University Press 2017

GARCÍA MARTÍNEZ, F., Parabiblical Literature from Qumran and the Canonical Process, RevQ 25 (2012) 525–56

GARCÍA MARTÍNEZ, F., A. STEUDEL, AND E. TIGCHELAAR, EDS., From 4QMMT to Resurrection: Mélanges qumraniens en hommage à Émile Puech (STDJ 61), Leiden: Brill 2006

GERNY, H., H. REIN, AND M. WEYERMANN, EDS., Die Wurzel aller Theologie: Sentire cum Ecclesia. Festschrift zum 60. Geburtstag von Urs von Arx, Bern: Stämpfli 2003

GERSTENBERGER, E. S., Prophetie in den Chronikbüchern: Jahwes Wort in zweierlei Gestalt? in: HARTENSTEIN, KRISPENZ, AND SCHART (EDS.), Schriftprophetie, 351–67

— Israel in the Persian Period: The Fifth and Fourth Centuries B.C.E. (BibEnc 8), Atlanta: Society of Biblical Literature 2011

GERTZ, J. C., B. M. LEVINSON, D. ROM-SHILONI, AND K. SCHMID, EDS., The Formation of the Pentateuch: Bridging the Academic Cultures of Europe, Israel, and North America (FAT 111), Tübingen: Mohr Siebeck 2016

GIBERT, P., Comment la Bible fut écrite? Introduction à l'Ancien et au Nouveau Testament, Paris: Bayard ²2011

GIGNILLIAT, M. S., God Speaks Hebrew: The Hebrew Text and Septuagint in the Search for the Christian Bible, ProEccl 25 (2016) 154–72

— Reading Scripture Canonically: Theological Instincts for Old Testament Interpretation, Grand Rapids: Baker Academic 2019

GISZCZAK, M., The Canonical Status of Song of Songs in m. Yadayim 3.5, JSOT 41 (2016) 205–20

GIUNTOLI, F., AND K. SCHMID, EDS., The Post-Priestly Pentateuch: New Perspectives on Its Redactional Development and Theological Profiles (FAT 101), Tübingen: Mohr Siebeck 2015

GOLDINGAY, J., Old Testament Theology and the Canon, TynBul 59 (2008) 1–34

GONZÁLEZ, A. G., AND L. S. NAVARRO, EDS., Canon, Biblia, Iglesia: el canon de la Escritura la exégesis bíblica, Madrid: Publicaciones San Dámaso 2010

GOODMAN, M., Religious Variety and the Temple in the Late Second Temple Period and Its Aftermath, JJS 60 (2009) 202–13

GOSHEN-GOTTSTEIN, A., Ben Sira's Praise of the Fathers: A Canon-Conscious Reading, in: EGGER-WENZEL (ED.), Ben Sira's God, 235–67

GOSWELL, G., The Order of the Books in the Hebrew Bible, JETS 51 (2008) 673–88

— The Order of the Books in the Greek Old Testament, JETS 52 (2009) 449–66

— Having the Last Say: The End of the OT, JETS 58 (2015) 15–30

— Putting the Book of Chronicles in Its Place, JETS 60 (2017) 283–99

— Should the Church Be Committed to a Particular Order of the Old Testament Canon? HBT 40 (2018) 17–40

— The Ordering of the Books of the Canon and the Theological Interpretation of the Old Testament, JTI 13 (2019) 1–20

GOUNELLE, R., AND J. JOOSTEN, EDS., La Bible juive dans l'Antiquité (Histoire du texte biblique 9), Prahins: Éditions du Zèbre 2014

GRABBE, L. L., Poets, Scribes or Preachers? The Reality of Prophecy in the Second Temple Period, in: GRABBE AND HAAK (EDS.), Knowing the End, 192–215

— The Law, the Prophets, and the Rest: The State of the Bible in Pre-Maccabean Times, DSD 13 (2006) 319–38

GRABBE, L. L., AND R. D. HAAK, EDS., Knowing the End from the Beginning: The Prophetic, Apocalyptic, and their Relationship (JSPSup 46), London: T & T Clark 2003

GRÄTZ, S., The Second Temple and the Legal Status of the Torah: The Hermeneutics of the Torah in the Books of Ruth and Ezra, in: KNOPPERS AND LEVINSON (EDS.), Pentateuch as Torah, 273–87

GRAVES, M., The Public Reading of Scripture in Early Judaism, JETS 50 (2007) 467–87

GREENSPAHN, F. E., Does Judaism Have a Bible? in: GREENSPOON AND LE BEAU (EDS.), Sacred Text, 1–12

— Jewish Ambivalence towards the Bible, HS 49 (2007) 7–21

— ED., The Hebrew Bible: New Insights and Scholarship (Jewish Studies in the 21st Century), New York: New York University Press 2008

GREENSPOON, L., By the Letter? Word for Word? Scripture in the Jewish Tradition, in: GREENSPAHN (ED.), The Hebrew Bible, 141–63

GREENSPOON, L. J., AND B. F. LE BEAU, EDS., Sacred Text, Secular Times, Omaha, NE: Creighton University Press 2000

GRISANTI, M. A., Inspiration, Inerrancy, and the OT Canon: The Place of Textual Updating in an Inerrant View of Scripture, JETS 44 (2001) 577–98

GROSS, W., Das Judentum — eine bleibende Herausforderung christlicher Identität, Mainz: Grünewald 2001

— Der doppelte Ausgang der Bibel Israels und die doppelte Leseweise des christlichen Alten Testaments, in: idem, Das Judentum, 9–25

— Prophetie in den Chronikbüchern: Jahwes Wort in zweierlei Gestalt? in: HARTENSTEIN, KRISPENZ, AND SCHART (EDS.), Schriftprophetie, 351–67

GROSSE, S., Theologie des Kanons: der christliche Kanon, seine Hermeneutik und die Historizität seiner Aussagen; Die Lehren der Kirchenväter als Grundlegung der Lehre von der Heiligen Schrift (Studien zu Theologie und Bibel 4), Vienna: LIT 2011

GROSSMAN, M. L., ED., Rediscovering the Dead Sea Scrolls: An Assessment of Old and New Approaches and Methods, Grand Rapids: Eerdmans 2010

GROTTANELLI, C., La scrittura nell'ambiente della Bibbia: Valori culturali e religiosi dello "scritto" nel contesto storico che ha generato l'Antico Testamento, RStB 13 (2001) 11–26

GUILLAUME, P., The Bible in Its Context: An Inquiry into Its Formation, Beirut, Lebanon: Naufal 2005

— New Light on the Nebiim from Alexandria: A Chronography to Replace the Deuteronomistic History, JHebS 5 (2005), www.jhsonline.org/Articles/article_39.pdf

GUSSMAN, O., Flavius Josephus und die Entstehung des Kanons Heiliger Schriften, in: BECKER AND SCHOLZ (EDS.), Kanon in Konstruktion, 345–61

HAGEDORN, A. C., Canons and Curses: Some Observations on the "Canon-Formula" in Deuteronomy and Its Afterlife, in: DELL AND JOYCE (EDS.), Biblical Interpretation, 89–105

HAHN, A., Was meinen wir mit Kanon? Die alttestamentliche Kanonforschung im letzten Jahrhundert zwischen einem funktionalen und einem formalen Kanonbegriff, JET 17 (2003) 45–82

— Canon Hebraeorum — Canon Ecclesiae? Zur deuterokanonischen Frage im Rahmen der Begründung alttestamentlicher Schriftkanonizität in neuerer römisch-katholischer Dogmatik (Studien zu Theologie und Bibel 2), Zurich: LIT 2009

HAHN, F., Das Alte Testament als Heilige Schrift und als Kanon, in: idem, Theologie des Neuen Testaments, 38–63

— Theologie des Neuen Testaments. Volume 2: Die Einheit des Neuen Testaments, Tübingen: Mohr Siebeck ²2005

HALPERN, B., Fallacies Intentional and Canonical: Metalogical Confusion about the Authority of Canonical Texts, in: WOOD, HARVEY, AND LEUCHTER (EDS.), From Babel to Babylon, 3–25

HARTENSTEIN, F., J. KRISPENZ, AND A. SCHART, EDS., Schriftprophetie: Festschrift für Jörg Jeremias zum 65. Geburtstag, Neukirchen-Vluyn: Neukirchener 2004

HARVEY, S. A., AND D. G. HUNTER, EDS., The Oxford Handbook of Early Christian Studies, New York: Oxford University Press 2008

HAYDON, R., A Survey and Analysis of Recent "Canonical" Methods (2000-2015), JTI 10 (2016) 145–55

HAYES, J. H., Historical Criticism of the Old Testament Canon, in: SÆBØ (ED.), Hebrew Bible/Old Testament, II:985–1005

HAYWARD, C. T. R., Scripture in the Jerusalem Temple. in: PAGET AND SCHAPER (EDS.), New Cambridge History of the Bible, I:321–44

HECKL, R., Der biblische Kanon — Glaubenszeugnis der Generationen des Anfangs: Überlegungen zur theologischen Bedeutung der historisch-kritischen Exegese, KD 53 (2007) 145–57

— Das Alte Testament — Grundlage christlicher Identität: von der Entstehung der autoritativen Literatur des Judentums zu einer Hermeneutik des Alten Testament, TLZ 143 (2018) 437–52

HELMER, C., AND C. LANDMESSER, EDS., One Scripture or Many? Canon from Biblical, Theological and Philosophical Perspectives, Oxford: Oxford University Press 2004

HEMPEL, C., The Context of 4QMMT and Comfortable Theories, in: HEMPEL (ED.), The Dead Sea Scrolls, 275–92

— ED., The Dead Sea Scrolls: Text and Contexts (STDJ 90), Leiden: Brill 2010

HENGEL, M., The Septuagint as Christian Scripture: Its Prehistory and the Problem of Its Canon (OTS), trans. M. Biddle; Edinburgh: T & T Clark 2002

HENTSCHEL, G., Ist die jüdische Bibel ein christliches Buch? in: BULTMANN, MÄRZ, AND MAKRIDES (EDS.), Heilige Schriften, 31–54

HENZE, M., ED. Biblical Interpretation at Qumran (SDSSRL), Grand Rapids: Eerdmans 2005

— A Companion to Biblical Interpretation in Early Judaism, Grand Rapids: Eerdmans 2012

HERBERT, E. D., AND E. TOV, EDS., The Bible as Book: The Hebrew Bible and the Judaean Desert Discoveries, London: British Library 2002

HERMS, E., Die Schrift als Kanon, in: idem, Phänomene des Glaubens, 390–407

— Phänomene des Glaubens: Beiträge zur Fundamentaltheologie, Tübingen: Mohr Siebeck 2006

HIEKE, T., ED. Zum Verhältnis von Biblischer Auslegung und historischer Rückfrage, IKaZ 39 (2010) 264–74

— Formen des Kanons: Studien zu Ausprägungen des biblischen Kanons von der Antike bis zum 19. Jahrhundert (SBS 228), Stuttgart: Katholisches Bibelwerk 2013

HIEKE, T., AND T. NICKLAS, "Die Worte der Prophetie dieses Buches": Offenbarung 22,6-21 als Schlussstein der christlichen Bibel Alten und Neuen Testaments gelesen (BTS 62), Neukirchen-Vluyn: Neukirchener 2003

HÖFFKEN, P., Zum Kanonsbewusstsein des Josephus Flavius in Contra Apionem und in den Antiquitates, JSJ 32 (2001) 159–77

HOGAN, M., TRANS., Pontifical Biblical Commission, The Jewish People and Their Sacred Scriptures in the Christian Bible, Vatican City: Libreria Editrice Vaticana 2002

HOLMES, M. W., The Biblical Canon, in: HARVEY AND HUNTER (EDS.), Oxford Handbook, 406–26

HOSSFELD, F.-L., AND L. SCHWIENHORST-SCHÖNBERGER, EDS., Das Manna fällt auch heute noch: Beiträge zur Geschichte und Theologie des Alten, Ersten Testaments. Festschrift für Erich Zenger (HBS 44), Freiburg: Herder 2004

HOVHANESSIAN, V. S., ED., The Canon of the Bible and the Apocrypha in the Churches of the East (Bible in the Christian Orthodox Tradition 2), New York: Lang 2012

ILAN, T., The Torah of the Jews of Rome, JSQ 16 (2009) 363–95

— The Term and Concept of TaNaKh, in: FINSTERBUSCH AND LANGE (EDS.), What Is Bible? 219–34

JACOBS, M. R., AND R. F. PERSON JR., EDS., Israelite Prophecy and the Deuteronomistic History: Portrait, Reality, and the Formation of a History (AIL 14), Atlanta: Society of Biblical Literature 2013

JAFFEE, M. S., Torah in the Mouth: Writings and Oral Tradition in Palestinian Judaism, 200 BCE–400 CE, Oxford: Oxford University Press 2001

JANOWKSI, B., Kanon und Sinnbildung: Perspektiven des Alten Testaments, in: HARTENSTEIN, KRISPENZ, AND SCHART (EDS.), Schriftprophetie, 15–36

— Kanonhermeneutik: eine problemgeschichtliche Skizze, BTZ 22 (2005) 161–80

— ED., Kanonhermeneutik: vom Lesen und Verstehen der christlichen Bibel (Theologie Interdisziplinär 1), Neukirchen-Vluyn: Neukirchener 2007

— The Contrastive Unity of Scripture: On the Hermeneutics of the Biblical Canon (trans. D. R. Driver), in: SEITZ AND RICHARDS (EDS.), Bible as Christian Scripture, 37–62

JANZEN, W., Canon and Canonical Scripture Interpretation, Vision 6 (2005) 22–31

JASSEN, A. P., Mediating the Divine: Prophecy and Revelation in the Dead Sea Scrolls and Second Temple Judaism (STDJ 68), Leiden: Brill 2007

— The Presentation of the Ancient Prophets as Lawgivers at Qumran, JBL 127 (2008) 307–37

JENKINS, P., Which Bible, Whose Canon? ChrCent 128 (2011) 45

JENSON, R. W., Canon and Creed (IntRes), Louisville: Westminster John Knox 2010

JOHNSTON, S. I., ED., Religions of the Ancient World, Cambridge, MA: Belknap/Harvard University Press 2004

JONES, L., ED., Encyclopedia of Religion (Volume III), Detroit: Thomson Gale ²2005

JONKER, L., The Chronicler and the Prophets: Who Were His Authoritative Sources? in: BEN ZVI AND EDELMAN (EDS.), What Was Authoritative? 145–64

JOOSTEN, J., The Origin of the Septuagint Canon, in: KREUZER, MEISER, AND SIGISMUND (EDS.), Die Septuaginta, 688–99

KAESTLI, J.-D., La formation et la structure du canon biblique: que peut apporter l'étude de la Septante? in: ALEXANDER AND KAESTLI (EDS.), Canon of Scripture, 99–113

KALIMI, I., T. NICKLAS, AND G. G. XERAVITS, EDS., WITH H. HÖTZINGER, Scriptural Authority in Early Judaism and Ancient Christianity (DCLS 16), Berlin: De Gruyter 2013

KAMESAR, A., Biblical Interpretation in Philo, in: KAMESAR (ED.), Cambridge Companion to Philo, 65–91

— ED., The Cambridge Companion to Philo, Cambridge: Cambridge University Press 2009

KARRER, M., AND W. KRAUS, EDS., Die Septuaginta: Texte, Kontexte, Lebenswelten (WUNT 219), Tübingen: Mohr Siebeck 2008

KARTVEIT, M. The Origin of the Samaritans (VTSup 128), Leiden: Brill 2009

KATZ, S. T., ED., The Cambridge History of Judaism. Volume IV: The Late Roman-Rabbinic Period, Cambridge: Cambridge University Press 2006

KAYE, B. N., How Can We Speak of "Canonical Scripture" Today? Journal of Anglican Studies 11 (2013) 1–14

KEALY, S. P., Does the Canonical Order of the Bible Matter? TBT 40 (2002) 44–48

KHAN, G., AND D. LIPTON, EDS., Studies on the Text and Versions of the Hebrew Bible in Honour of Robert Gordon (VTSup 149), Leiden: Brill 2012

KLINGHARDT, M., Die Veröffentlichung der christlichen Bibel und der Kanon, ZNT 12 (2003) 52–57

KNOPPERS, G. N., An Achaemenid Imperial Authorization of Torah in Yehud? in: WATTS (ED.), Persia and Torah, 115–34

— Jews and Samaritans: The Origins and History of Their Early Relations, Oxford: Oxford University Press 2013

KNOPPERS, G. N., AND P. B. HARVEY, Omitted and Remaining Matters: On the Names Given to the Books of Chronicles in Antiquity, JBL 121 (2002) 227–43

KNOPPERS, G. N., AND B. M. LEVINSON, EDS., The Pentateuch as Torah: New Models for Understanding Its Promulgation and Acceptance, Winona Lake, IN: Eisenbrauns 2007

KOET, B. J., S. MOYISE, AND J. VERHEYDEN, EDS., The Scriptures of Israel in Jewish and Christian Tradition: Essays in Honour of Maarten J. J. Menken (NTSup 148), Leiden: Brill 2013

KÖHLMOOS, M., Kanon und Methode: zu einer Zwischenbilanz der "kanonischen Auslegung," TRu 74 (2009) 135–46

— Komposition, Redaktion, Tradition: dreißig Jahre Methodenwechsel in der alttestamentlichen Exegese (1984–2014), TRu 79 (2014) 418–35

KÖNIG, E., Die Hauptprobleme der altisraelitischen Religionsgeschichte, gegenüber den Entwicklungstheoretikern beleuchtet, Leipzig: Hinrichs 1884

KOOREVAAR, H. J., The Torah Model as Original Macrostructure of the Hebrew Canon: A Critical Evaluation, ZAW 122 (2010) 64–80

KÖRTNER, U. H. J., Arbeit am Kanon: Der Beitrag Bultmanns und seiner Schüler zur Diskussion über die hermeneutische Bedeutung des biblischen Kanons, in: BAUSPIESS, LANDMESSER, AND PORTENHAUSER (EDS.), Theologie und Wirklichkeit, 27–57

— Arbeit am Kanon: Studien zur Bibelhermeneutik, Leipzig: Evangelische Verlagsanstalt 2015

KRAFT, R. A., Daniel Outside the Traditional Jewish Canon: In the Footsteps of M. R. James, in: FLINT, TOV, AND VANDERKAM (EDS.), Studies in the Hebrew Bible, 121–33

— Para-mania: Beside, Before and Beyond Bible Studies, JBL 126 (2007) 5–27

KRATZ, R. G., "Siehe, ich lege meine Worte in deinen Mund." Die Propheten des Alten Testament, in: FELDMEIER AND SPIECKERMANN (EDS.), Die Bibel, 24–39

— Reflections on the Legal Status of the Pentateuch between Elephantine and Qumran, in: KNOPPERS AND LEVINSON (EDS.), Pentateuch as Torah, 77–104

— The Prophets of Israel (Critical Studies in the Hebrew Bible 2), trans. A. C. Hagedorn and N. MacDonald; Winona Lake, IN: Eisenbrauns 2015

KRAUS, W., AND S. KREUZER, EDS., Die Septuaginta — Text, Wirkung, Rezeption (WUNT 325), Tübingen: Mohr Siebeck 2014

KREUZER, S., M. MEISER, AND M. SIGISMUND, EDS., Die Septuaginta — Orte und Intentionen: 5. Internationale Fachtagung veranstaltet von Septuaginta Deutsch (LXX.D), Wuppertal 24. —27. Juli 2014 (WUNT 325), Tübingen: Mohr Siebeck 2016

KRISTEVA, J., Word, Dialogue, and Novel, in: ROUDIEZ (ED.), Desire in Language, 64–91

KRUGER, M. J., The Definition of the Term "Canon": Exclusive or Multi-dimensional? TynBul 63 (2012) 1–20

— The Question of Canon: Challenging the Status Quo in the New Testament Debate, Downers Grove, IL: InterVarsity 2013

LANDMESSER, C., AND A. KLEIN, EDS., Normative Erinnerung: der biblische Kanon zwischen Tradition und Konstruktion (Veröffentlichungen der Rudolf-Bultmann-Gesellschaft für hermeneutische Theologie), Leipzig: Evangelische Verlagsanstalt 2014

LANGE, A., The Status of the Biblical Texts in the Qumran Corpus and the Canonical Process, in: HERBERT AND TOV (EDS.), The Bible as Book, 21–30

— The Parabiblical Literature of the Qumran Library and the Canonical History of the Hebrew Bible, in: PAUL, ET AL. (EDS.), Emanuel, 305–21

— From Literature to Scripture: The Unity and Plurality of the Hebrew Scriptures in Light of the Qumran Library, in: HELMER AND LANDMESSER (EDS.), One Scripture or Many? 51–107

— Pre-Maccabean Literature from the Qumran Library and the Hebrew Bible, DSD 13 (2006) 277–305

— The Qumran Dead Sea Scrolls — Library or Manuscript Corpus? in: GARCÍA MARTÍNEZ, STEUDEL, AND TIGCHELAAR (EDS.), From 4QMMT to Resurrection, 177–94

— 2 Maccabees 2:13–15: Library or Canon? in: XERAVITS AND ZSENGELLÉR (EDS.), Books of the Maccabees, 155–67

— "The Law, the Prophets, and the Other Books of the Fathers" (Sir, Prologue): Canonical Lists in Ben Sira and Elsewhere? in: XERAVITS AND ZSENGELLÉR (EDS.), Studies in the Book of Ben Sira, 55–80

— The Dead Sea Scrolls and the Date of the Final Stage of the Pentateuch, in: AITKEN, DELL, AND MASTIN (EDS.), On Stone and Scroll, 287–304

— The Canonical History of the Hebrew Bible and the Christian Old Testament in Light of Egyptian Judaism, in: KRAUS AND KREUZER (EDS.), Die Septuaginta, 660–80

LANGE, A., AND E. TOV, EDS., The Hebrew Bible (Textual History of the Bible 1), Leiden: Brill 2016

LANGE, A., AND M. WEIGOLD, Biblical Quotations and Allusions in Second Temple Jewish Literature (JAJSup 5), Göttingen: Vandenhoeck & Ruprecht 2011

LASH, E., The Canon of Scripture in the Orthodox Church, in: ALEXANDER AND KAESTLI (EDS.), Canon of Scripture, 217–32

LAW, T. M., When God Spoke Greek: The Septuagint and the Making of the Christian Bible, Oxford: Oxford Unversity Press 2013

LEE, K.-J., The Authority and Authorization of Torah in the Persian Period (CBET 64), Leuven: Peeters 2011

LeFEBVRE, M., Collections, Codes, and Torah: The Re-characterization of Israel's Written Law (LHBOTS 451), New York: T & T Clark 2006

LEVINSON, B. M., You Must Not Add Anything to What I Command You: Paradoxes of Canon and Authorship in Ancient Israel, Numen 50 (2003) 1–51

— Legal Revision and Religious Renewal in Ancient Israel, Cambridge: Cambridge University Press 2008

LEVY, B. B., Fixing God's Torah: The Accuracy of the Hebrew Bible Text in Jewish Law, New York: Oxford University Press 2001

LEWIS, J. P., Jamnia Revisited, in: MCDONALD AND SANDERS (EDS.), The Canon Debate, 146–62

LIEW, T.-S. B., ED., Present and Future of Biblical Studies: Celebrating 25 Years of Brill's Biblical Interpretation (BIS 161), Leiden: Brill 2018

LIGHTSTONE, J. N., The Rabbis' Bible: The Canon of the Hebrew Bible and the Early Rabbinic Guild, in: MCDONALD AND SANDERS (EDS.), The Canon Debate, 163–84

— The Early Rabbinic Refashioning of Biblical Heilsgeschichte, the Fashioning of the Rabbinic Canon of Scriptures, and the Formation of the Early Rabbinic Movement, in: DITOMMASO AND TURCESCU (EDS.), Reception and Interpretation, 317–55

LIM, T. H., ED., The Dead Sea Scrolls in Their Historical Context, Edinburgh: T & T Clark 2000

— The Alleged Reference to the Tripartite Division of the Hebrew Bible, RdQ 20 (2001) 23–37

— All These He Composed through Prophecy, in: DE TROYER AND LANGE (EDS.), Prophecy after the Prophets? 61–76

— Authoritative Scriptures and the Scrolls, in: LIM AND COLLINS (EDS.), Oxford Handbook, 303–22

— Defilement of the Hands as a Principle Determining the Holiness of Scriptures, JTS 61 (2010) 501–15

— The Formation of the Jewish Canon (AYBRL), New Haven: Yale University Press 2013

— A Theory of the Majority Canon, ExpTim 124 (2013) 365–73

— The Emergence of the Samaritan Pentateuch, in: PERRIN, BAEK, AND FALK (EDS.), Reading the Bible in Ancient Traditions, 89–104

— ED., WITH K. AKIYAMA, When Texts are Canonized (BJS 359), Providence, RI: Brown University 2017

LIM, T. J., AND J. J. COLLINS, EDS., The Oxford Handbook of the Dead Sea Scrolls, New York: Oxford University Press 2010

LINAFELT, T., ED., A Shadow of Glory: Reading the New Testament after the Holocaust, New York: Routledge 2002

LIPS, H. VON, Was bedeutet uns der Kanon? Neuere Diskussion zur Bedeutung des Kanons, VF 51 (2006) 41–56

— Kanondebatten im 20. Jahrhundert, in: BECKER AND SCHOLZ (EDS.), Kanon in Konstruktion, 109–26

LIPSCHITS, O., G. N. KNOPPERS, AND R. ALBERTZ, EDS., Judah and the Judeans in the Fourth Century B.C.E., Winona Lake, IN: Eisenbrauns 2007

LIPSCHITS, O., G. N. KNOPPERS, AND M. OEMING, EDS., Judah and the Judeans in the Achaemenid Period: Negotiating Identity in an International Context, Winona Lake, IN: Eisenbrauns 2011

LISS, H., Kanon und Fiktion: zur literarischen Funktion biblischer Rechtstexte, BN 121 (2004) 7–38

LOADER, J. A., Tenach and Old Testament — the Same Bible? HvTSt 58 (2002), https://hts.org.za/index.php/hts/article/view/720

— The Canon as Text for Biblical Theology, HvTSt 61 (2005), https://hts.org.za/index.php/hts/article/view/494

LOBA-MKOLE, J.-C., Biblical Canons in Church Traditions and Translations, BT 67 (2016) 108–19

LÖFSTEDT, T., The Silence of the Spirit: A Critique of the Cessationist View of the Canon, STK 89 (2013) 126–38

LÖHR, H., Der Kanon in der Bibliothek, ZNT 6 (2003) 18–26

LOMBAARD, C., Dating and Debating: Late Patriarchs and Early Canon, Scriptura 113 (2014) 1–10

LUST, J., Septuagint and Canon, in: AUWERS AND DE JONGE (EDS.), The Biblical Canons, 39–55

LUZ, U., Kanonische Exegese und Hermeneutik der Wirkungsgeschichte, in: GERNY, REIN, AND WEYERMANN (EDS.), Die Wurzel aller Theologie, 40–57

LYONS, W. J., Canon and Exegesis: Canonical Praxis and the Sodom Narrative (JSOTSup 352), Sheffield: Sheffield Academic 2002

MACCHI, J.-D., ET AL., EDS., Les recueils prophétiques de la Bible. Origines, milieux, et contexte proche-oriental (Le Monde de la Bible 64), Geneva: Labor et Fides 2012

MACH, M. F., Der Tenach in der Rezeption des nachbiblischen Judentums, in: DIMITROV, ET AL. (EDS.), Das Alte Testament, 205–35

MAGDALINO, P., AND R. NELSON, EDS., The Old Testament in Byzantium, Washington, D. C.: Dumbarton Oaks 2010

MAIER, C. M., ED., Congress Volume: Munich 2013 (VTSup 163), Leiden: Brill 2014

MAIER, G., Biblical Hermeneutics, trans. R. W. Yarbrough; Wheaton, IL: Crossway 1994

MASON, E. F., ET AL., EDS., A Teacher for All Generations: Essays in Honor of James C. VanderKam (Volume II; JSJSup 153), Leiden: Brill 2012

MASON, S., Josephus and His Twenty-Two Book Canon, in: MCDONALD AND SANDERS (EDS.), The Canon Debate, 110–27

— Josephus, in: COLLINS AND HARLOW (EDS.), Eerdmans Dictionary, 828–32

MAYES, A. D. H., ED., Text in Context: Essays by Members of the Society for Old Testament Study, Oxford: Oxford University Press 2000

MAYES, A. D. H., AND R. B. SALTERS, EDS., Covenant as Context: Essays in Honour of E. W. Nicholson, Oxford: Oxford University Press 2003

MCDONALD, L. M., The Biblical Canon: Its Origin, Transmission, and Authority, Peabody, MA: Hendrickson 2007

— Wherein Lies Authority? A Discussion of Books, Texts, and Translations, in: EVANS AND TOV (EDS.), Exploring the Origins of the Bible, 203–39

— Forgotten Scriptures: The Selection and Rejection of Early Religious Writings, Louisville: Westminster John Knox 2009

— What Do We Mean by Canon? Ancient and Modern Questions, in: CHARLESWORTH AND MCDONALD (EDS.), Jewish and Christian Scriptures, 8–40

— The Origin of the Bible: A Guide for the Perplexed, London: T & T Clark 2011

— Formation of the Bible: The Story of the Church's Canon, Peabody, MA: Hendrickson 2012

— Hellenism and the Biblical Canons: Is There a Connection? in: PORTER AND PITTS (EDS.), Christian Origins and Hellenistic Judaism, 13–49

— The Formation of the Biblical Canon (2 vols), London: Bloomsbury 2017

— The Reception of the Writings and Their Place in the Biblical Canon, in: MORGAN (ED.), Oxford Handbook, 397–413

MCDONALD, L. M., AND S. E. PORTER, EDS., Early Christianity and Its Sacred Literature, Peabody, MA: Hendrickson 2000

MCDONALD, L. M., AND J. A. SANDERS, EDS., The Canon Debate, Peabody, MA: Hendrickson 2002

MCGINNIS, C. M., The Old Testament, in: BUCKLEY, BAUERSCHMIDT, AND POMPLUN (EDS.), Blackwell Companion to Catholicism, 7–21

MEIER C., AND M. WAGNER-EGELHAAF, EDS., Autorschaft: Ikonen — Stile — Institutionen, Berlin: Akademie Verlag 2011

METZGER, B. M., The Bible in Translation: Ancient and English Versions, Grand Rapids: Baker Academic 2001

MILLARD, A., Reading and Writing in the Time of Jesus, New York: New York University Press 2000

MOBERLY, R. W. L., The Canon of the Old Testament: Some Historical and Hermeneutical Reflections from the Western Perspective, in: DIMITROV, ET AL. (EDS.), Das Alte Testament, 239–57

MOENIKES, A., ED., Schätze der Schrift. Festgabe für Hans F. Fuhs zur Vollendung seines 65. Lebensjahres (Paderborner Theologische Studien 47), Paderborn: Schöningh 2007

MORGAN, D. F., ED., The Oxford Handbook to the Writings of the Hebrew Bible, New York: Oxford University Press 2019

— Studying the Writings as Postexilic Literature and Canon, in: MORGAN (ED.), Oxford Handbook, 1–18

MOSIS, R., Die Bücher des "Alten Bundes" bei Melito von Sardes, in: MOENIKES (ED.), Schätze der Schrift, 131–76

MROCZEK, E., The Hegemony of the Biblical in the Study of Second Temple Literature, JAJ 6 (2015) 2–35

— The Literary Imagination in Jewish Antiquity, Oxford: Oxford University Press 2016

— Hidden Scriptures, Then and Now: Rediscovering "Apocrypha," Int 72 (2018) 383–95

MÜHLENBERG, E., Gottes Wort zwischen zwei Buchdeckeln. Wie die frühen Christen zu ihrer Bibel kamen, in: FELDMEIER AND SPIECKERMANN (EDS.), Die Bibel, 71–82

MÜLLER, M., Die Septuaginta als Teil des christlichen Kanons, in: KARRER AND KRAUS (EDS.), Die Septuaginta, 708–27

NAJMAN, H., The Vitality of Scripture Within and Beyond the "Canon," JSJ 43 (2012) 497–518

NEUSNER, J., AND A. J. AVERY-PECK, EDS., The Blackwell Companion to Judaism. Oxford: Blackwell 2000

NEUSNER, J., A. J. AVERY-PECK, AND W. S. GREEN, EDS., The Encyclopedia of Judaism (Volume III), Leiden: Brill ²2005

NICHOLSON, E., Deuteronomy 18:9–22, the Prophets and Scripture, in: DAY (ED.), Prophecy and Prophets, 151–71

NIEHOFF, M. R., ED., Homer and the Bible in the Eyes of Ancient Interpreters (JSRC 16), Leiden: Brill 2012

NIELSEN, K., "From Oracles to Canon" — and the Role of Metaphor, SJOT 17 (2003) 22–33

NIEUVIARTS, J., AND P. DEBERGÉ, EDS., Les nouvelles voies l'exégèse: en lisant le Cantique des cantiques: XIXe congrès de l'Association catholique pour l'étude de la Bible (LD 190), Paris: Cerf 2002

NIGOSIAN, S. A., Formation of Jewish and Christian Scriptures, NETR 24 (2003) 127–40

NIHAN, C., The Emergence of the Pentateuch as "Torah," RC 4 (2010) 353–64

— The "Prophets" as Scriptural Collection and Scriptural Prophecy during the Second Temple Period, in: DAVIES AND RÖMER (EDS.), Writing the Bible, 67–85

NOLL, K. L., The Evolution of Genre in the Hebrew Anthology, in: EVANS AND ZACHARIAS (EDS.), Early Christian Literature, I:10–23

— Did "Scripturalization" Take Place in Second Temple Judaism? SJOT 25 (2011) 201–16

NORELLI, E., ED., Recueils normatifs et canons dans l'antiquité. Perspectives nouvelles sur la formation des canons juif et chrétien dans leur contexte culturel (Publications de l'Institut romand des sciences bibliques 3), Lausanne: Éditions du Zèbre 2004

O'BRIEN, J., ED., The Oxford Encyclopedia of the Bible and Gender Studies (Volume I), Oxford: Oxford University Press 2014

OEHLER, G. F., Canon of the Old Testament, in: BOMBERGER AND HERZOG (EDS.), Protestant Theological and Ecclesiastical Encyclopedia, I:543–50

OEMING, M., Das Alte Testament als Teil des christlichen Kanons? (Studien zu gesamt-biblischen Theologien der Gegenwart), Zurich: Pano-Verlag 2001

— Das Hervorwachsen des Verbindlichen aus der Geschichte des Gottesvolkes: Grund-züge einer prozessual-soziologischen Kanon-Theorie, ZNT 6 (2003) 52–58

— The Way of God: Early Canonicity and the "Nondeviation Formula," in: LIM (ED.), When Texts are Canonized, 25–43

ØKLUND, J., The Power of Canonised Motifs: The Chance for Biblical Studies in a Secular, Canonically Illiterate World? in: LIEW (ED.), Present and Future of Biblical Studies, 216–39

ØKLUND, J., AND T. STORDALEN, Canon/Canonicity/Canonisation, in: O'BRIEN (ED.), Oxford Encyclopedia of the Bible, 17–25

OLSON, D. T., Types of a Recent "Canonical Approach," in: SÆBØ (ED.), Hebrew Bible/Old Testament, III/2:196–218

OORSCHOT, J. VAN, Das Alte Testament im Kreis der theologischen Fächer. Theologische Wahrnehmung altorientalischer und jüdischer Religion innerhalb des christlichen Kanons, in: BUNTFUSS AND FRITZ (EDS.), Fremde unter einem Dach? 23–41

ORTKEMPER, F.-J., AND F. SCHULLER, EDS., Berufen, das Wort Gottes zu verkündigen. Die Botschaft der Bibel im Leben und in der Sendung der Kirche, Stuttgart: Katholisches Bibelwerk 2008

OSSANDÓN WIDOW, J. C., The Origins of the Canon of the Hebrew Bible: An Analysis of Josephus and 4 Ezra (JSJSup 186), Leiden: Brill 2019

OTERO, A. P., AND P. A. T. MORALES, EDS., Textual Criticism and Dead Sea Scrolls Studies in Honour of Julio Trebolle Barrera: Florilegium Complutense (JSJSup 157), Leiden: Brill 2012

PAGET, J. C., AND J. SCHAPER, EDS., The New Cambridge History of the Bible. Volume I: From the Beginnings to 600, Cambridge: Cambridge University Press 2013

PAJUNEN, M. S., Perspectives on the Existence of a Particular Authoritative Book of Psalms in the Late Second Temple Period, JSOT 39 (2014) 139–63

PAJUNEN, M. S., AND H. VON WEISSENBERG, The Book of Malachi, Manuscript 4Q76 (4QXII^a), and the Formation of the "Book of the Twelve," JBL 134 (2015) 731–51

PAKKALA, J. The Quotations and References of the Pentateuchal Laws in Ezra-Nehemiah, in: WEISSENBERG, PAKKALA, AND MARTTILA (EDS.), Changes in Scripture, 193–221

PAPAZIAN, G. E. T., Reading the Old Testament as Christian Scripture: A Critical Assessment of the Canonical Approach of Christopher R. Seitz, Waterloo, ON: Conrad Grebel University College 2007

PAUL, S. M., ET AL, EDS., WITH E. BEN-DAVID, Emanuel: Studies in Hebrew Bible, Septuagint and Dead Sea Scrolls in Honour of Emanuel Tov (VTSup 94), Leiden: Brill 2003

PECKHAM, J. C., Intrinsic Canonicity and the Inadequacy of the Community Approach to Canon-Determination, Them 36 (2011) 203–15

— Canonical Theology: The Biblical Canon, Sola Scripture, and Theological Method, Grand Rapids: Eerdmans 2016

PEELS, H. G. L., The Qumran Biblical Scrolls: The Scriptures of Late Second Temple Judaism, in: LIM (ED.), Dead Sea Scrolls in Their Historical Context, 67–87

— The Blood of Abel to Zechariah (Matthew 23:35; Luke 11:50f.) and the Canon of the Old Testament, ZAW 113 (2001) 583–601

PENTIUC, E. J., The Old Testament in Eastern Orthodox Tradition, New York: Oxford University Press 2014

PERANI, M., Il processo de canonizzazione della Bibbia Ebraica: nuove prospettive metodologiche, RivB 48 (2000) 385–400

PERRIN, A. B., K. S. BAEK, AND D. K. FALK, EDS., Reading the Bible in Ancient Traditions and Modern Editions: Studies in Memory of Peter W. Flint (EJL 47), Atlanta: Society of Biblical Literture 2017

PETERS, F. E., The Voice, the Word, the Books: The Sacred Scripture of the Jews, Christians, and Muslims, Princeton, NJ: Princeton University Press 2007

POFFET, J.-M., ED., L'Autorité de L'Écriture (LD), Paris: Cerf 2002

POIRIER, J. C., The Canonical Approach and the Idea of "Scripture," ExpTim 116 (2005) 365–70

— An Ontological Definition of "Canon"? BBR 24 (2014) 457–66

POKORNÝ, P., AND J. ROSKOVEC, EDS., Philosophical Hermeneutics and Biblical Exegesis (WUNT 153), Tübingen: Mohr Siebeck 2003

POPOVIĆ, M., ED. Authoritative Scriptures in Ancient Judaism (JSJSup 141), Leiden: Brill 2010

PORTER, S. E., AND A. W. PITTS, EDS., Christian Origins and Hellenistic Judaism: Social and Literary Contexts for the New Testament (Early Christianity in Its Hellenistic Context 2), Leiden: Brill 2013

POULSEN, F., Brevard S. Childs: Kanon, metode og teologi: en introduktion, DTT 73 (2010) 213–30

PUECH, É., Quelques observations sur le "canon" des "écrits," in: POPOVIĆ (ED.), Authoritative Scriptures, 117–41

— L'épilogue de 4QMMT revisité, in: MASON, ET AL. (EDS.), A Teacher for All Generations, 309–40

PUMMER, R., The Samaritans and Their Pentateuch, in: KNOPPERS AND LEVINSON (EDS.), Pentateuch as Torah, 237–69

PURY, A. DE., The Ketubim, a Canon within the Biblical Canon, in: ALEXANDER AND KAESTLI (EDS.), Canon of Scripture, 41–57

RAHNER, J., Kanonische und/oder kirchliche Schriftauslegung? Der Kanon und die Suche nach der Einheit, ZKT 123 (2001) 402–22

RAJAK, T., Translation and Survival: The Greek Bible of the Ancient Jewish Diaspora, Oxford: Oxford University Press 2009

REEVES, J. C., Problematizing the Bible... Then and Now, JQR 100 (2010) 139–52

RENDTORFF, R., Der Text in seiner Endgestalt: Schritte auf dem Weg zu einer Theologie des Alten Testaments, Neukirchen-Vluyn: Neukirchener Verlag 2001

— The Canonical Hebrew Bible: A Theology of the Old Testament, Leiden: Deo 2005

RICHELLE, M., Elusive Scrolls: Could Any Hebrew Literature Have Been Written Prior to the Eighth Century BCE? VT 66 (2016) 556–94

RICOEUR, P., The Canon between the Text and the Community, in: POKORNÝ AND ROSK-OVEC (EDS.), Philosophical Hermeneutics, 7–26

RODGERS, Z., Josephus's Biblical Interpretation, in: HENZE (ED.), Companion to Biblical Interpretation, 436–64

ROFÉ, A., The Scribal Concern for the Torah as Evidenced by the Textual Witnesses of the Hebrew Bible, in: FOX, ET AL. (EDS.), Mishneh Todah, 229–42

ROITMAN, A. D., L. H. SCHIFFMAN, AND S. TZOREF, EDS., Dead Sea Scrolls and Contemporary Culture (STDJ 93), Leiden: Brill 2011

ROLLSTON, C. A., Writing and Literacy in the World of Ancient Israel: Epigraphic Evidence from the Iron Age (ABS 11), Atlanta: Society of Biblical Literature 2010

— Inscriptional Evidence for the Writing of the Earliest Texts of the Bible: Intellectual Infrastructure in Tenth- and Ninth-Century Israel, Judah, and the Southern Levant, in: GERTZ, LEVINSON, ROM-SHILONI, AND SCHMID (EDS.), Formation of the Pentateuch, 15–45

RÖMER, T., ED., The Future of the Deuteronomistic History (BETL 147), Leuven: Leuven University Press 2000

— L'école deutéronomiste et al formation de la Bible hébraïque, in: RÖMER (ED.), Future of the Deuteronomistic History, 179–93

— La mort de Moïse (Deut 34) et la naissance de la première partie du canon biblique, in: ALEXANDER AND KAESTLI (EDS.), Canon of Scripture, 27–39

— Moses, Israel's First Prophet, and the Formation of the Deuteronomistic and Prophetic Libraries, in: JACOBS AND PERSON (EDS.), Israelite Prophecy 129–45

RÖMER, T., AND M. Z. BRETTLER, Deuteronomy 34 and the Case for a Persian Hexateuch, JBL 119 (2000) 401–19

RÖMER, T., AND K. SCHMID, EDS., Les dernières rédactions du Pentateuque, de l'Hexateuque et de l'Ennéateuque (BETL 203), Leuven: Leuven University Press 2007

ROUDIEZ, L. S., ED., Desire in Language: A Semiotic Approach to Literature and Art, New York: Columbia University Press 1980

ROWE, C. K., Biblical Pressure and Trinitarian Hermeneutics, ProEccl 11 (2002) 295–312

RÜTERSWÖRDEN, U., ED., Ist die Tora Gesetz? Zum Gesetzesverständnis im Alten Testament, Frühjudentum und Neuen Testament (BTS 167), Göttingen: Vandenhoeck & Ruprecht 2017

SÆBØ, M., From "Unifying Reflections" to the Canon: Aspects of the Traditio-Historical Final Stages in the Development of the Old Testament, in: idem, On the Way to Canon, 285–307.

— On the Way to Canon: Creative Tradition History in the Old Testament (JSOTSup 191), Sheffield: Sheffield Academic 1998

— ED., Hebrew Bible/Old Testament: The History of Its Interpretation. Volume II: From the Renaissance to the Enlightenment, Göttingen: Vandenhoeck & Ruprecht 2008

— ED., Hebrew Bible/Old Testament: The History of Its Interpretation. Volume III/1: The Nineteenth Century, Göttingen: Vandenhoeck & Ruprecht 2013

— ED., Hebrew Bible/Old Testament: The History of Its Interpretation. Volume III/2: The Twentieth Century, Göttingen: Vandenhoeck & Ruprecht 2015

SAKENFELD, K. D., ED., The New Interpreter's Dictionary of the Bible (Volume I), Nashville, TN: Abingdon 2006

SAMELY, A., Rabbinic Interpretation of Scripture in the Mishnah, Oxford: Oxford University Press 2002

SÁNCHEZ CARO, J. M., Configuración del canon bíblico: approximación histórica, in: GONZÁLEZ AND NAVARRO (EDS.), Canon, 19–40

SANDERS, J. A., Torah and Canon, Eugene, OR: Cascade Books 2005

— The Canonical Process, in: KATZ (ED.), Cambridge History of Judaism, IV:230–43

SARNA, N. M., AND S. D. SPERLING, Bible: Canon, in: NEUSNER, AVERY-PECK, AND GREEN (EDS.), Encyclopedia of Judaism, 574–83

SATLOW, M. L., How the Bible Became Holy, New Haven: Yale University Press 2014

SCHAPER, J., The "Publication" of Legal Texts in Ancient Judaism, in: KNOPPERS AND LEVINSON (EDS.), Pentateuch as Torah, 225–36

— ED., Die Textualisierung der Religion (FAT 62), Tübingen: Mohr Siebeck 2009

— Jewish and Christian Scripture as Artifact and Canon, JSOT 34 (2010) 18–22

— Torah and Identity in the Persian Period. in: LIPSCHITS, KNOPPERS, AND OEMING (EDS.), Judah and the Judeans, 27–38

SCHEETZ, J. M., The Concept of Canonical Intertextuality and the Book of Daniel, Cambridge: James Clarke 2011

— Ancient Witnesses, Canonical Theories, and Canonical Intertextuality, in: HIEKE (ED.), Formen des Kanons, 12–39

SCHENKER, A., Die Heilige Schrift subsistiert gleichzeitig in mehreren kanonischen Formen, in: idem, Studien zu Propheten und Religionsgeschichte, 192–200

— ED., The Earliest Text of the Hebrew Bible: The Relationship between the Masoretic Text and the Hebrew Base of the Septuagint Reconsidered (SCS 52), Leiden: Brill 2003

— Urtext, Kanon und antike Bibelausgaben, in: idem, Studien zu Propheten und Religionsgeschichte, 201–10

— Studien zu Propheten und Religionsgeschichte (SBAB 36), Stuttgart: Katholisches Bibelwerk 2003

SCHIFFMAN, L. H., The Judean Desert Scrolls and the History of Judaism and Christianity, in: SCHIFFMAN AND TZOREF (EDS.), Dead Sea Scrolls, 7–26

SCHIFFMAN, L. H., AND S. TZOREF, EDS., Dead Sea Scrolls at 60: Scholarly Contributions of New York University Faculty and Alumni (STDJ 89), Leiden: Brill 2010

SCHLEIERMACHER, F., On Religion: Speeches to Its Cultured Despisers, trans. and ed. R. Crouter; Cambridge: Cambridge University Press 1996

SCHMID, K., The Late Persian Formation of the Torah: Observations on Deuteronomy 34, in: LIPSCHITS, KNOPPERS AND ALBERTZ (EDS.), Judah and the Judeans, 237–51

— The Canon and the Cult: The Emergence of Book Religion in Ancient Israel and the Gradual Sublimation of the Temple Cult, JBL 131 (2012) 289–305

— La formation des "Nebiim." Quelques observations sur la genèse rédactionelle et les profils théologiques de Josué-Malachie, in: MACCHI, ET AL. (EDS.), Les recueils prophétiques, 115–42

— The Old Testament: A Literary History, Minneapolis: Fortress 2012

— Von der Diaskeuase zur nachendredaktionellen Fortschreibung. Die Geschichte der Erforschung der nachpriesterschriftlichen Redaktionsgeschichte des Pentateuch, in: GIUNTOLI AND SCHMID (EDS.), Post-Priestly Pentateuch, 1–18

— The Prophets after the Law or the Law after the Prophets? Terminological, Biblical, and Historical Perspectives, in: GERTZ, LEVINSON, ROM-SHILONI, AND SCHMID (EDS.), Formation of the Pentateuch, 841–50

SCHMID, K., AND J. SCHRÖTER, Die Entstehung der Bibel. Von den ersten Texten zu den heiligen Schriften, Munich: C. H. Beck 2019

SCHNEIDER, T., AND W. PANNENBERG, Binding Testimony: Holy Scripture and Tradition, trans. M. M. Matesich; Frankfurt: Lang 2014

SCHNIEDEWIND, W. M., How the Bible Became a Book: The Textualization of Ancient Israel, Cambridge: Cambridge University Press 2004

— Writing and Book Production in the Ancient Near East, in: PAGET AND SCHAPER (EDS.), New Cambridge History of the Bible, I:46–62

SCHORCH, S., The Libraries in 2 Macc 2:13–15, and the Torah as a Public Document in Second Century BC Judaism, in: XERAVITS AND ZSENGELLÉR (EDS.), Books of the Maccabees, 169–80

— Communio lectorum. Die Rolle des Lesens für die Textualisierung der israelitischen Religion, in: SCHAPER (ED.), Die Textualisierung der Religion, 167–84

— What Kind of Authority? The Authority of the Torah during the Hellenistic and Roman Periods, in: KALIMI, NICKLAS, AND XERAVITS (EDS.), Scriptural Authority, 1–15

SCHRÖDER-FIELD, C., Der Kanonbegriff in Biblischer Theologie und evangelischer Dogmatik, in: BARTON AND WOLTER (EDS.), Die Einheit der Schrift, 195–238

SCHÜLE, A., Kanonisierung als Systembildung: Überlegungen zum Zusammenhang von Tora, Prophetie und Weisheit aus systemtheoretischer Perspective, in: THOMAS AND SCHÜLE (EDS.), Luhmann und die Theologie, 211–28

— Das Alte Testament und der verstehende Glaube. Holzwege und Wegmarken in der Debatte um den christlichen Kanon, KD 62 (2016) 191–211

SCHULLER, E., The Dead Sea Scrolls and Canon and Canonization, in: BECKER AND SCHOLZ (EDS.), Kanon in Konstruktion, 293–314

SCHUTTE, P. J. W., The Ongoing Canon Debate, HvTSt 60 (2004), https//hts.org.za /index.php/hts/article/view/629

SCHWARTZ, B. J., Bible, in: WERBLOWSKY AND WIGODER (EDS.), Oxford Dictionary, 121–22

SCHWIENHORST-SCHÖNBERGER, L., Einheit statt Eindeutigkeit: Paradigmenwechsel in der Bibelwissenschaft? HK 57 (2003) 412–17

SCORALICK, R., Kanonische Schriftauslegung: eine Skizze, BK 38 (2009) 645–47

SCOTT, I. W., A Jewish Canon before 100 BCE: Israel's Law in the Book of Aristeas, in: EVANS AND ZACHARIAS (EDS.), Early Christian Literature, I:42–53

SECKLER, M., Über die Problematik des biblischen Kanons und die Bedeutung seiner Wiederentdeckung, TQ 180 (2000) 30–53

SEITZ, C. R., Figured Out: Typology and Providence in Christian Scripture, Louisville: Westminster John Knox 2001

— The Canonical Approach and Theological Interpretation, in: BARTHOLOMEW, ET AL. (EDS.), Canon and Biblical Interpretation, 58–110

— Prophecy and Hermeneutics: Toward a New Introduction to the Prophets (STI), Grand Rapids: Baker Academic 2007

— Canon, Narrative and the Old Testament's Literal Sense: A Response to John Goldingay's "Canon and Old Testament Theology," TynBul 59 (2008) 27–34

— The Goodly Fellowship of the Prophets: The Achievement of Association in Canon Formation (Acadia Studies in Bible and Theology), Grand Rapids: Baker Academic 2009

— The Character of Christian Scripture: The Significance of a Two-Testament Bible (STI), Grand Rapids: Baker Academic 2011

— Scriptural Author and Canonical Prophet: The Theological Implications of Literary Association in the Canon, in: DELL AND JOYCE (EDS.), Biblical Interpretation, 176–88

— The Elder Testament: Canon, Theology, Trinity, Waco, TX: Baylor University Press 2018

SEITZ, C. R., AND K. H. RICHARDS, EDS., The Bible as Christian Scripture: The Work of Brevard S. Childs (BSNA 25), Atlanta: Society of Biblical Literature 2013

SESBOÜÉ, B., La canonisation des Écritures et la reconnaissance de leur inspiration: une approche historico-théologique, RSR 92 (2004) 13–44

SHEMESH, A., Halakhah in the Making: The Development of Jewish Law from Qumran to the Rabbis, Berkeley: University of California 2009

SHEPPARD, G. T., Canon, in: JONES (ED.), Encyclopedia of Religion, 1405–11

SKA, J.-L., Introduction to Reading the Pentateuch, trans. P. Dominique; Winona Lake, IN: Eisenbrauns 2006

SKARSAUNE, O., AND R. HVALVIK, EDS., Jewish Believers in Jesus: The Early Centuries, Peabody, MA: Hendrickson 2007

SMEND, R., Das Alte Testament, in: DIETRICH, ET AL. (EDS.), Die Entstehung des Alten Testaments, 17–52

SMIT, P.-B., Wegweiser zu einer kontextuellen Exegese? Eine Miszelle zu einem Nebeneffekt der kanonischen Hermeneutik von Brevard S. Childs, TZ 62 (2006) 17–24

— From Canonical Criticism to Ecumenical Exegesis? A Study in Biblical Hermeneutics (Studies in Reformed Theology 30), Leiden: Brill 2015

SMITH, M. S., What Is a Scriptural Text in the Second Temple Period? Texts between Their Biblical Past, Their Inner-Biblical Interpretation, Their Reception in Second Temple Literature, and Their Textual Witnesses, in: SCHIFFMANN AND TZOREF (EDS.), Dead Sea Scrolls, 271–98

— Textual Interpretation in 7th–6th Century Israel: Between Competition, Textualisation and Tradition, in: OTERO AND MORALES (EDS.), Textual Criticism, 317–23

SÖDING, T., Der Kanon des Alten und Neuen Testaments zur Frage nach seinem theologischen Anspruch, in: AUWERS AND DE JONGE (EDS.), The Biblical Canons, 47–88

— Einheit der Heiligen Schrift? Zur Theologie des biblischen Kanons (QD 211), Freiburg: Herder 2005

— Der biblische Kanon: Geschichte und Theologie, ZKT 128 (2006) 407–30

SOMMER, B. D., Unity and Plurality in Jewish Canons: The Case of the Oral and Written Torahs, in: HELMER AND LANDMESSER (EDS.), One Scripture or Many? 108–50

— Revelation and Authority: Sinai in Jewish Scripture and Tradition, New Haven: Yale University Press 2015

— ED., Jewish Concepts of Scripture: A Comparative Introduction, New York: New York University Press 2012

SPELLMAN, C., Toward a Canon-Conscious Reading of the Bible: Exploring the History and Hermeneutics of Canon, Sheffield: Sheffield Phoenix 2014

STEINBERG, J., Die Ketuvim: ihr Aufbau und ihre Botschaft (BBB 152), Hamburg: Philo 2006

STEINBERG, J., AND T. J. STONE, The Historical Formation of the Writings in Antiquity, in: STEINBERG AND STONE (EDS.), The Shape of the Writings, 1–58

— EDS., WITH R. STONE, The Shape of the Writings (Siphrut 16), Winona Lake, IN: Eisenbrauns 2015

STEINS, G., Der Bibelkanon als Text und Denkmal. Zu einigen methodologischen Problemen kanonischer Schriftauslegung, in: AUWERS AND DE JONGE (EDS.), The Biblical Canons, 177–98

— Der Bibelkanon — Schlüssel zur Bibelauslegung: ein Paradigmenwechsel, PT 95 (2006) 329–34

— Kanonisch lesen, in: UTZSCHNEIDER AND BLUM (EDS.), Lesarten der Bibel, 45–64

— Der Kanon ist der erste Kontext. Oder: Zurück an den Anfang! BK 62 (2007) 116–21

— Mose, dazu die Propheten und David: Tora, Torauslegung und Kanonstruktur im Lichte der Chronikbücher, in: STEINS AND TASCHNER (EDS.), Kanonisierung, 107–31

— Zwei Konzepte — ein Kanon: neue Theorien zur Entstehung und Eigenart der Hebräischen Bible, in: STEINS AND TASCHNER (EDS.), Kanonisierung, 8–45

STEINS, G., AND J. TASCHNER, EDS., Kanonisierung: die hebräische Bibel im Werden (Biblisch-Theologische Studien 110), Neukirchen-Vluyn: Neukirchener Verlag 2010

STEMBERGER, G., La formation et la conception du canon dans la penseé rabbinique, in: NORELLI (ED.), Recueils normatifs, 113–31

— Judaica Minora. Volume I: Biblische Traditionen im rabbinischen Judentum (TSAJ 133), Tübingen: Mohr Siebeck 2010

— Entstehung und Auffassung des Kanons im rabbinischen Denken, in: idem, Judaica Minora, I:69–87

STENSTRUP, K. G., Scripture and Interpretive Method: Why Read Scripture as Canon? BTB 33 (2003) 158–67

STERLING, G. E., The Interpreter of Moses: Philo of Alexandria and the Biblical Text, in: HENZE (ED.), Companion to Biblical Interpretation, 415–35

STERN, D., The First Jewish Books and the Early History of Jewish Reading, JQR 98 (2008) 163–202

STONE, M. E., Some Considerations on the Categories "Bible" and "Apocrypha," in: ANDERSON, CLEMENTS, AND SATRAN (EDS.), New Approaches, 1–18

STONE, T. J., The Biblical Canon according to Lee McDonald: An Evaluation, EuroJTh 18 (2009) 55–64

— The Compilational History of the Megilloth: Canon, Contoured Intertextuality and Meaning in the Writings (FAT 2/59), Tübingen: Mohr Siebeck 2013

— The Canonical Shape and Function of the Writings, in: MORGAN (ED.), Oxford Handbook, 414–29

STORDALEN, T., Law or Prophecy? On the Order of the Canonical Books, TTKi 71 (2001) 131–50

— The Canonization of Ancient Hebrew and Confucian Literature, JSOT 32 (2007) 3–22

— What Is a Canon of Scripture? in: EGILSSON, ÓLASON, AND STEFÁNSSON (EDS.), Shaping Culture, 15–33

STROUMSA, G. G., The Scriptural Universe of Ancient Christianity Cambridge, MA: Harvard University Press 2016

STUCKENBRUCK, L., Apocrypha and the Septuagint: Exploring the Christian Canon, in: CAULLEY AND LICHTENBERGER (EDS.), Die Septuaginta, 177–201

SUGIRTHARAJAH, R. S., ED., The Postcolonial Biblical Reader, Malden, MA: Blackwell 2006

SUMPTER, P., The Trinity and the Canonical Process, ThTo 72 (2016) 379–97

TALMON, S., The Crystallization of the "Canon of Hebrew Scriptures" in the Light of Biblical Scrolls from Qumran, in: HERBERT AND TOV (EDS.), The Bible as Book, 5–20

— Text and Canon of the Hebrew Bible, Winona Lake, IN: Eisenbrauns 2010

TALSHIR, Z., Several Canon-Related Concepts Originating in Chronicles, ZAW 113 (2001) 386–403

TASCHNER, J., Kanonische Bibelauslegung — Spiel ohne Grenzen? in: STEINS AND BALLHORN (EDS.), Der Bibelkanon, 31–44

THOMAS, G., AND A. SCHÜLE, EDS., Luhmann und die Theologie, Darmstadt: Wissenschaftliche Buchgesellschaft 2006

THOMASSEN, E., ED., Canon and Canonicity: The Formation and Use of Scripture, Copenhagen: Museum Tusculanum 2010

— Some Notes on the Development of Christian Ideas about a Canon, in: THOMASSEN (ED.), Canon and Canonicity, 9–28

TOV, E., Textual Criticism of the Hebrew Bible, Minneapolis: Fortress ³2012

— Textual Criticism of the Hebrew Bible, Qumran, Septuagint: Collected Essays, Leiden: Brill 2015

TREBOLLE BARRERA, J., A "Canon within a Canon": Two Series of Old Testament Books Differently Transmitted, Interpreted and Authorized, RevQ 19 (2000) 383–99

— Origins of a Tripartite Old Testament Canon, in: MCDONALD AND SANDERS (EDS.), The Canon Debate, 128–45

— Canon of the Old Testament, in: SAKENFELD (ED.), New Interpreter's Dictionary, I:548–63

TUCKER, G. M., The Law in Eighth-Century Prophets, in: TUCKER, PETERSEN, AND WILSON (EDS.), Canon, 201–16.

TUCKER, G. M., D. L. PETERSEN, AND R. R. WILSON, EDS., Canon, Theology, and Old Testament Interpretation: Essays in Honor of Brevard S. Childs, Philadelphia: Fortress 1988

ULRICH, E. C., The Dead Sea Scrolls and the Origins of the Bible (SDSSRL), Grand Rapids: Eerdmans 1999

— The Absence of "Sectarian Variants" in the Jewish Scriptural Scrolls Found at Qumran, in: HERBERT AND TOV (EDS.), The Bible as Book, 179–95

— The Notion and Definition of Canon, in: MCDONALD AND SANDERS (EDS.), The Canon Debate, 21–35

— From Literature to Scripture: Reflections on the Growth of a Text's Authoritativeness, DSD 10 (2003) 3–25

— The Non-attestation of a Tripartite Canon in 4QMMT, CBQ 65 (2003) 202–14

— Qumran and the Canon of the Old Testament, in: AUWERS AND DE JONGE (EDS.), The Biblical Canons, 57–80

— The Jewish Scriptures: Texts, Versions, Canons, in: COLLINS AND HARLOW (EDS.), Eerdmans Dictionary, 97–119

— Methodological Reflections on Determining Scriptural Status in First Century Judaism, in: GROSSMAN (ED.), Rediscovering the Dead Sea Scrolls, 145–61

— Clearer Insight into the Development of the Bible: A Gift of the Scrolls, in: ROITMAN, SCHIFFMAN, AND TZOREF (EDS.), Dead Sea Scrolls, 119–37

— The Dead Sea Scrolls and the Developmental Composition of the Bible (VTSup 169), Leiden: Brill 2015

UTZSCHNEIDER, H., AND E. BLUM, EDS., Lesarten der Bibel: Untersuchungen zu einer Theorie der Exegese des Alten Testaments, Stuttgart: Kohlhammer 2006

VAN AARDE, A. G., The Use and Origin of the (Old and) New Testament as Christianity's Canon, HvTSt 68 (2012), https://hts.org.za/index.php/hts/article/view/1262/2523

VANDERKAM, J. C., From Revelation to Canon: Studies in the Hebrew Bible and Second Temple Literature (JSJSup 62), Leiden: Brill 2000

— Revealed Literature in the Second Temple Period, in: idem, From Revelation to Canon, 1–30

— Questions of Canon Viewed through the Dead Sea Scrolls, BBR 11 (2001) 269–92

— The Dead Sea Scrolls and the Bible, Grand Rapids: Eerdmans 2012

VANDERKAM, J., AND P. FLINT, The Meaning of the Dead Sea Scrolls: Their Significance for Understanding the Bible, Judaism, Jesus, and Christianity, San Francisco: HarperSanFrancisco 2002

VAN DER KOOI, C., Kirche als Lesegemeinschaft: Schrifthermeneutik und Kanon, VF 51 (2006) 63–72

VAN DER KOOIJ, A., De canonvorming van de Hebreeuwse bijbel, het Oude Testament. Een overzicht van recente literatuur, NedTT 49 (1995) 42–65

— Canonization of Ancient Books Kept in the Temple of Jerusalem, in VAN DER KOOIJ AND VAN DER TOORN (EDS.), Canonization and Decanonization, 17–40

— Canonization of Ancient Hebrew Books and Hasmonaean Politics, in: AUWERS AND DE JONGE (EDS.), The Biblical Canons, 27–38

— Preservation and Promulgation: The Dead Sea Scrolls and the Textual History of the Hebrew Bible, in: DÁVID, ET AL. (EDS.), Hebrew Bible, 29–40

VAN DER KOOIJ, A., AND K. VAN DER TOORN, EDS., Canonization and Decanonization: Papers Presented to the International Conference of the Leiden Institute for the Study of Religions (LISOR), held at Leiden 9–10 January 1997 (SHR 82), Leiden: Brill 1998

VAN DER TOORN, K., From Catalogue to Canon? An Assessment of the Library Hypothesis as a Contribution to the Debate about the Biblical Canon, BO 63 (2006) 5–15

— Scribal Culture and the Making of the Hebrew Bible, Cambridge, MA: Harvard University Press 2007

VANHOOZER, K. J., The Drama of Doctrine: A Canonical-Linguistic Approach to Christian Theology, Louisville: Westminster John Knox 2005

VANONI, G., Der biblische Kanon: institutionalisierte Erinnerung, TPQ 151 (2003) 29–36

VAN SETERS, J., The Origins of the Hebrew Bible: Some New Answers to Old Questions. Part One, JANER 7 (2007) 87–108.

— The Origins of the Hebrew Bible: Some New Answers to Old Questions. Part Two, JANER 7 (2007) 219–37

VASSILIADIS, P., The Canon of the Bible: Or the Authority of Scripture from an Orthodox Perspective, in: POFFET (ED.), L'Autorité de L'Écriture, 113–35

VELTRI, G., Libraries, Translations, and "Canonic" Texts: The Septuagint, Aquila and Ben Sira in the Jewish and Christian Traditions (JSJSup 109), Leiden: Brill 2006

VENTER, P. M., Kanon in die kanon, HvTSt 57 (2001), https://hts.org.za/index.php/hts/article/view/1876/0

— Kanon: Eenheid en diversiteit, HvTSt 62 (2006), https://hts.org.za/index.php/hts/article/view/394

VERHEYDEN, J., K. ZAMFIR, AND T. NICKLAS, EDS., Prophets and Prophecy in Jewish and Early Christian Literature (WUNT 2/286), Tübingen: Mohr Siebeck 2010

VERMEYLEN, J., L'école deutéronomiste aurait-elle imaginé un premier canon des Écritures? in: RÖMER (ED.), Future of the Deuteronomistic History, 223–40

— Une étape majeure dans la formation du canon des Écritures: l'oeuvre deutéronomiste, in: AUWERS AND DE JONGE (EDS.), The Biblical Canons, 213–26

— Les écrivains deutéronomistes travaillaient-ils en Babylonie ou en Palestine? in: MAIER (ED.), Congress Volume, 154–81

VIEZEL, E., The Formation of Some Biblical Books according to Rashi, JTS 61 (2010) 16–42

VOITILA, A., AND J. JOKIRANTA, EDS., Scripture in Transition: Essays on Septuagint, Hebrew Bible and Dead Sea Scrolls in Honour of Raija Sollamo (JSJSup 126), Leiden: Brill 2008

VROOM, J., The Authority of Law in the Hebrew Bible and Early Judaism: Tracing the Origins of Legal Obligation from Ezra to Qumran (JSJSup 187), Leiden: Brill 2018

WAGNER, J. R., The Septuagint and the "Search for the Christian Bible," in: BOCKMUEHL AND TORRANCE (EDS.), Scripture's Doctrines, 17–28

WALL, R., Canon, in: BALENTINE (ED.), Oxford Encyclopedia of Bible, 111–21

WALLRAFF, M., Kodex und Kanon: das Buch im frühen Christentum (Hans-Lietzmann-Vorlesungen 12), Berlin: de Gruyter 2013

WANKE, G., Kanon und biblische Theologie. Hermeneutische Überlegungen zum alttestamentlichen Kanon, in: WITTE (ED.), Gott und Mensch, 1053–61

WARHURST, A. K., The Chronicler's Use of the Prophets, in: BEN ZVI AND EDELMAN (EDS.), What Was Authoritative? 165–81

WASSERSTEIN, A., AND D. J. WASSERSTEIN, The Legend of the Septuagint: From Classical Antiquity to Today, Cambridge: Cambridge University Press 2006

WATSON, D. F., AND A. J. HAUSER, EDS., The Ancient Period (A History of Biblical Interpretation 1), Grand Rapids: Eerdmans 2003

WATTS, J. W., ED., Persia and Torah: The Theory of Imperial Authorization of the Pentateuch (SBLSS 17), Atlanta: Society of Biblical Literature 2001

WEBSTER, J., The Dogmatic Location of the Canon, Neue Zeitschrift für systematische Theologie und Religionsphilosophie 43 (2001) 17–43

— A Great and Meritorious Act of the Church? The Dogmatic Location of the Canon, in: BARTON AND WOLTER (EDS.), Die Einheit der Schrift, 95–126

WEISSENBERG, H. VON, "Canon" and Identity at Qumran: An Overview and Challenges for Future Research, in: VOITILA AND JOKIRANTA (EDS.), Scripture in Transition, 629–40

— 4QMMT: Reevaluating the Text, the Function, and the Meaning of the Epilogue (STDJ 82), Leiden: Brill 2009

WEISSENBERG, H. VON, J. PAKKALA, AND M. MARTTILA, EDS., Changes in Scripture: Rewriting and Interpreting Authoritative Traditions in the Second Temple Period (BZAW 419), Berlin: de Gruyter 2011

WEISSENBERG, H. VON, AND E. UUSIMÄKI, Are There Sacred Texts in Qumran? The Concept of Sacred Text in Light of the Qumran Collection, in: FELDMAN, CIOATĂ, AND HEMPEL (EDS.), Is There a Text, 21–41

WERBLOWSKY, R. J. Z., AND G. WIGODER, EDS., The Oxford Dictionary of the Jewish Religion, New York: Oxford University Press 1997

WILLIAMS, M. H., The Monk and the Book: Jerome and the Making of Christian Scholarship, Chicago: University of Chicago Press 2006

WILLIAMS, P. J., The Bible, the Septuagint, and the Apocrypha: A Consideration of Their Singularity, in: KHAN AND LIPTON (EDS.), Studies on the Text, 169–80

WILLIAMSON, H. G. M., The Vindication of Redaction Criticism, in: DELL AND JOYCE (EDS.), Biblical Interpretation, 26–36

WITTE, M., ED., Gott und Mensch im Dialog: Festschrift für Otto Kaiser zum 80. Geburtstag (BZAW 345), Berlin: de Gruyter 2004

— Der "Kanon" heiliger Schriften des antiken Judentums im Spiegel des Buches Ben Sira/Jesus Sirach, in: BECKER AND SCHOLZ (EDS.), Kanon in Konstruktion, 229–55

WOOD, J. R., J. E. HARVEY, AND M. LEUCHTER, EDS., From Babel to Babylon: Essays on Biblical History and Literature in Honour of Brian Peckham (LHBOTS 455), New York: T & T Clark 2006

WRIGHT, B. G., Why a Prologue? Ben Sira's Grandson and His Greek Translation, in: PAUL, ET AL. (EDS.), Emanuel, 633–44

— The Use and Interpretation of Biblical Traditions in Ben Sira's Praise of the Ancestors, in: XERAVITS AND ZSENGELLÉR (EDS.), Studies in the Book of Ben Sira, 183–207

— Biblical Interpretation in the Book of Ben Sira, in: HENZE (ED.), Companion to Biblical Interpretation, 363–88

WYRICK, J., The Ascension of Authorship: Attribution and Canon Formation in Jewish, Hellenistic, and Christian Traditions, Cambridge, MA: Harvard University Press 2004

XERAVITS, G. G., AND J. ZSENGELLÉR, EDS., The Books of the Maccabees: History, Theology, Ideology (JSJSup 118), Leiden: Brill 2007

— EDS., Studies in the Book of Ben Sira: Papers of the Third International Conference on the Deuterocanonical Books (JSJSup 127), Leiden: Brill 2008

XERAVITS, G. G., J. ZSENGELLÉR, AND X. SZABÓ, EDS., Canonicity, Setting, Wisdom in the Deuterocanonicals: Papers of the Jubilee Meeting of the International Conference on the Deuterocanonical Books (DCLS 22), Berlin: de Gruyter 2014

XUN, C., Theological Exegesis in the Canonical Context: Brevard Springs Childs's Methodology of Biblical Theology (Studies in Biblical Literature 137), New York: Peter Lang 2010

ZAGORIN, P., History, the Referent, and Narrative: Reflections on the Postmodern Now, History and Theory 38 (1999) 1–24

ZAHN, M. M., "Editing" and the Composition of Scripture: The Significance of the Qumran Evidence, HeBAI 3 (2014) 298–316

ZAMAN, L., Bible and Canon: A Modern Historical Inquiry (SSN 50), Leiden: Brill 2010

ZENGER, E., Der Psalter im Horizont vor Tora und Prophetie: Kanongeschichtliche und kanonhermeneutische Perspektiven, in: AUWERS AND DE JONGE (EDS.), The Biblical Canons, 111–34

ZEVIT, Z., The Second-Third Century Canonization of the Hebrew Bible and Its Influence on Christian Canonizing, in: VAN DER KOOIJ AND VAN DER TOORN (EDS.), Canonization and Decanonization, 133–60

— From Judaism to Biblical Religion and Back Again, in: GREENSPAHN (ED.), The Hebrew Bible, 164–90

Author Index

Source Index

Biblical Literature

Old Testament

Septuagint (LXX)

New Testament

Apocrypha

Ancient Sources

Dead Sea Scrolls

Rabbinic Literature

Classical Authors

Subject Index